MW00769212

Revelation

THE LECTIO CONTINUA
EXPOSITORY COMMENTARY ON THE NEW TESTAMENT

Series Editors

Joel R. Beeke | Jon D. Payne

Other available books in this series:
First Corinthians — Kim Riddlebarger
Galatians — J. V. Fesko
Hebrews — David B. McWilliams

Revelation

Joel R. Beeke

REFORMATION HERITAGE BOOKS
Grand Rapids, Michigan

Revelation
© 2016 by Joel R. Beeke

All rights reserved. No part of this book may be used or reproduced in any manner whatsoever without written permission except in the case of brief quotations embodied in critical articles and reviews. Direct your requests to the publisher at the following addresses:

Reformation Heritage Books
2965 Leonard St. NE
Grand Rapids, MI 49525
616-977-0889
orders@heritagebooks.org
www.heritagebooks.org

Printed in the United States of America
20 21 22 23 24/10 9 8 7 6 5 4 3 2

Library of Congress Cataloging-in-Publication Data

Names: Beeke, Joel R., 1952- author.
Title: Revelation / Joel R. Beeke.
Description: Grand Rapids, Michigan : Reformation Heritage Books, 2016. | Series: The Lectio Continua expository commentary on the New Testament | Includes bibliographical references.
Identifiers: LCCN 2016040758 (print) | LCCN 2016042063 (ebook) | ISBN 9781601784575 (hardcover : alk. paper) | ISBN 9781601784582 (epub)
Subjects: LCSH: Bible. Revelation—Commentaries.
Classification: LCC BS2825.53 .B44 2016 (print) | LCC BS2825.53 (ebook) | DDC 228.07—dc23
LC record available at https://lccn.loc.gov/2016040758

For additional Reformed literature, request a free book list from Reformation Heritage Books at the above regular or e-mail address.

With heartfelt appreciation for

David Van Brugge
and
Maarten Kuivenhoven

Christ-loving brothers of integrity:
formerly, two of my finest theological students;
now, my two colleagues in pastoral ministry,
with whom I am privileged to serve
in unity and love,
thankful for how they feed my soul
through their preaching and friendship.

Contents

Series Introduction

The greatest need of the church today is the recovery of sound biblical preaching. We need preaching that faithfully explains and applies the text, courageously confronts sin, and boldly trumpets forth the sovereign majesty, law, and gospel promises of God. This type of powerful proclamation has vanished in many quarters of the evangelical church only to be replaced by that which is anemic and man-centered. Instead of doctrinally rich exposition which strengthens faith and fosters Christian maturity, the standard fare has become informal, chatty, anecdote-laden massages, devoid of instruction in the truths of the Christian faith. This approach leaves unbelievers confused, and keeps believers in a state of chronic spiritual adolescence.[1]

There is indeed a dire need for the recovery of solid biblical preaching. Not only does reformation of this sort lead Christ's sheep back to the verdant pastures of His soul-nourishing Word, it also provides a good example for present and future generations

---

1. A stinging, yet constructive critique of modern-day preaching is found in T. David Gordon's *Why Johnny Can't Preach: The Media Have Shaped the Messengers* (Phillipsburg, NJ: P&R, 2009). "I have come to recognize that many, many individuals today have never been under a steady diet of competent preaching.... As starving children in Manila sift through the landfill for food, Christians in many churches today have never experienced genuine soul-nourishing preaching, and so they just pick away at what is available to them, trying to find a morsel of spiritual sustenance or helpful counsel here or there" (Gordon, *Why Johnny Can't Preach,* 17). Elements of this introduction are adapted from Jon D. Payne, "The Roaring of Christ through *Lectio Continua* Preaching," *Modern Reformation* 19, no. 6 (Nov.–Dec. 2010): 23–24, and are used by permission of the publisher.

of ministers. For this reason, we are pleased to introduce *The* Lectio Continua *Expository Commentary on the New Testament,* a new series of expository commentaries authored by an array of seasoned pastor-scholars from various Reformed denominations on both sides of the Atlantic.

What is the *lectio continua* method of preaching?[2] It is simply the uninterrupted, systematic, expository proclamation of God's Word—verse by verse, chapter by chapter, book by book—that endeavors to deliver the whole counsel of God (Acts 20:26–27). Christian discipleship is impoverished when large portions of Scripture are ignored. Carried out faithfully, the *lectio continua* method ensures that every passage is mined for its riches (even those verses which are obscure, controversial, or hard to swallow). Paul states that "all scripture is given by inspiration of God, and is profitable for doctrine, for reproof, for correction, for instruction in righteousness: that the man of God may be perfect, thoroughly furnished unto all good works" (2 Tim. 3:16–17).

Lectio continua preaching has a splendid heritage. It finds its roots in the early church and patristic eras. Its use, however, was revived and greatly expanded during the sixteenth-century Protestant Reformation. When Huldrych Zwingli (d. 1531) arrived at the Zurich Grossmunster in 1519, it was his desire to dispense with the standard lectionary[3] and introduce *lectio continua* preaching to his congregation by moving systematically through the Gospel of Matthew. At first, some members of his church council were suspicious. They were uncomfortable replacing the lectionary with this

---

2. In Christianity, *lectio continua* (Latin for continuous reading) originally referred to the practice of reading Scripture sequentially in public worship, as was the practice of the ancient church. This practice is recommended by the Westminster divines in the Directory for Public Worship, which in turn, served as an impetus for *lectio continua* preaching. Sadly, Scripture reading in this manner has been neglected in Reformed and Presbyterian churches for many generations, perhaps as far back as the eighteenth century, when public worship was reduced to sermon-hearing sessions.

3. A lectionary is a plan or table of Scripture passages to be read in the services of church for each day or week of the year.

seemingly new approach. But Zwingli explained that the *lectio continua* method of preaching was not new at all. On the contrary, important figures such as Augustine (d. 430), Chrysostom (d. 407) and Bernard of Clairvaux (d. 1153) all employed this homiletical approach. Zwingli is quoted by his successor, Heinrich Bullinger (d. 1575), as saying that "no friend of evangelical truth could have any reason to complain" about such a method.[4]

Zwingli rightly believed that the quickest way to restore biblical Christianity to the church was to preach the whole counsel of God verse by verse, chapter by chapter, book by book, Lord's Day after Lord's Day, year after year. Other Reformers agreed and followed his pattern. In the city of Strasbourg, just ninety miles north of Zurich, preachers such as Martin Bucer (d. 1551), Wolfgang Capito (d. 1570), and Kaspar Hedio (d. 1552) practiced *lectio continua* preaching. Johannes Oecolampadius (d. 1531) boldly preached the *lectio continua* in Basel. And let us not forget John Calvin (d. 1564); between 1549 and 1564, the Genevan Reformer preached sequentially through no fewer than twenty-five books of the Bible (over 2,000 sermons), which he was able to do because he also preached regularly for weekday services.[5]

The example of these Reformers has been emulated by preachers throughout the centuries, from the Post-Reformation age down to the present. In the last half of the twentieth century, Donald Grey Barnhouse (1895–1960), Martyn Lloyd-Jones (d. 1981), William Still (d. 1997), James Montgomery Boice (d. 2000), and John MacArthur all boldly preached straight through books of the Bible from their pulpits. But why? Surely we have acquired better, more

---

4. It is interesting to note that the year before Zwingli began preaching sequentially through books of the Bible, he had received a new edition of Chrysostom's *lectio continua* sermons on Matthew's Gospel. See Hughes Oliphant Old, *The Patristic Roots of Reformed Worship* (Black Mountain, N.C.: Worship Press, 2004), 195. Cf. Hughes Oliphant Old, *The Reading and Preaching of the Scriptures in the Worship of the Christian Church*, vol. 4: *The Age of the Reformation* (Grand Rapids: Eerdmans, 2002), and Timothy George, *Reading Scripture with the Reformers* (Downers Grove, Ill.: IVP Academic, 2011), 228–53.

5. T. H. L. Parker, *Calvin's Preaching* (Edinburgh: T&T Clark, 1992), 159.

contemporary methods of preaching? Is the *lectio continua* relevant in our twenty-first century context? In a day when biblical preaching is being increasingly undermined and marginalized by media/story/therapy/personality-driven sermons, even among the avowedly Reformed, these are important questions to consider.

Shortly before the Apostle Paul was martyred in Rome by Emperor Nero, he penned Second Timothy. In what proved to be some of his final words to his young disciple, he wrote, "I charge thee therefore before God, and the Lord Jesus Christ...*preach the word;* be instant in season, out of season; reprove, rebuke, exhort with all longsuffering and doctrine" (2 Tim. 4:1–2). This directive was not meant only for Timothy. It is the duty of every Christian minister (and church) to heed these timeless words; according to God's divine blueprint for ministry, it is chiefly through the faithful proclamation of the Word that Christ saves, sanctifies, and comforts the beloved church for which He died.[6] In other words, the preaching of the gospel and the right administration of the sacraments are the divinely sanctioned and efficacious means by which Christ and all His benefits of redemption are communicated to the elect. For this reason alone the *lectio continua* method of preaching is a helpful practice in our churches, providing a steady diet of law and gospel from the entirety of God's Word.

Some may ask, "Why another expository commentary series?" First, because in every generation it is highly valuable to provide fresh and reliable expositions of God's Word. Every age possesses its own set of theological, ecclesiastical, and cultural challenges. Thus, it is beneficial for both current and rising ministers in every generation to have trustworthy contemporary models of biblical preaching. Second, these volumes uniquely feature the expositions of an array of pastors from a variety of Reformed and confessional traditions. Consequently, this series brings a wealth of exegetical, confessional,

---

6. See Matthew 28:18–20; Romans 10:14–17; 1 Corinthians 1:18–21; 1 Peter 1:22–25; Westminster Shorter Catechism, Q. 89.

experiential, and practical insight, and furnishes the reader with an instructive and stimulating selection of *lectio continua* sermons.

This series is not meant to be an academic or highly technical commentary. There are many helpful exegetical commentaries written for that purpose. Rather, the aim is to provide *lectio continua* sermons, originally delivered to Reformed congregations, which clearly and faithfully communicate the context, meaning, gravity, and application of God's inerrant Word. Each volume of expositions aspires to be redemptive-historical, covenantal, Reformed and confessional, Trinitarian, Christ-centered, and teeming with spiritual and practical application. Therefore, we pray that the series will be a profound blessing to every Christian believer who longs to "grow in the grace and knowledge of our Lord and Savior Jesus Christ" (2 Pet. 3:18).

We are pleased to announce that this series of commentaries is now being published by Reformation Heritage Books, who have graciously agreed to take over this large task from *Tolle Lege Press*. We thank *Tolle Lege* for printing the first three volumes (*First Corinthians* by Kim Riddlebarger, *Galatians* by John Fesko, and *Hebrews* by David McWilliams). We, Jon Payne and Joel Beeke, look forward to co-editing the remainder of the series for Reformation Heritage Books. The goal is to publish two volumes per year in the King James or New King James Version, according to the choice of each author.

In addition to thanking Reformation Heritage Books and its faithful team for producing their first book in this series, we wish to thank our churches, Christ Church Presbyterian, Charleston, South Carolina, and the Heritage Reformed Congregation, Grand Rapids, Michigan, for warmly encouraging us as ministers to work on projects such as this one that impact the wider church. Furthermore, we thank our dear wives, Marla Payne and Mary Beeke, and our precious children, for their heartwarming support which makes editing a series like this one possible. We both feel that God has greatly blessed us with God-fearing wives and children who mean more to us than words can express.

Finally, and most importantly, thanks and praise must be given to our blessed triune God, the eternal Fountain of all grace and truth. By His sovereign love and mercy, and through faith in the crucified, resurrected, and ascended Christ, we have been "born again, not of corruptible seed, but of incorruptible, by the word of God, which liveth and abideth for ever. For all flesh is as grass, and all the glory of man as the flower of grass. The grass withereth, and the flower thereof falleth away: but the word of the Lord endureth for ever. And this is the word which by the gospel is preached unto you" (1 Peter 1:23–25).

—Jon D. Payne and Joel R. Beeke, Series Editors

Preface

When Jon Payne asked me to provide a volume of sermons on the Book of Revelation for *The* Lectio Continua *Expository Commentary on the New Testament,* I tried hard to decline due to other commitments and the length of time it would take to preach through the book for my congregation, which I regarded as an obvious prerequisite. When Jon continued to press me, eventually I relented. Though I had often desired to preach through Revelation in the first thirty-five years of my ministry, I had never dared to do so. It seemed too overwhelming. I had always excused myself when church members requested me to do so by saying, "Well, if Calvin never wrote a commentary on this complex and challenging book, who am I to preach on it?"

By 2011, however, the internal desire and sense of calling to preach through Revelation was burning within me. That desire was increased by reading some of the great commentaries that had been published on Revelation since I first entered the ministry in the 1970s. Then too I had listened with great joy to the sermons of Eric Alexander, Sinclair Ferguson, and others who had preached through Revelation in a gripping way. With much prayer, fear, and trepidation, I took the plunge at the beginning of 2012 and preached through this beautiful book of comfort for God's persecuted children, completing it in June 2014. I must confess that preaching through Revelation was one of the greatest joys and comforts of my ministry, with the possible exception of preaching through Genesis.

If you are looking for something novel in these sermons, I fear you will look in vain. My goal was to preach through Revelation in a thoroughly biblical, doctrinal, experiential, and practical way intended to comfort and mature God's people, warn the unsaved to flee to Christ for salvation, and exalt Christ as the King of kings and only Head of His church. I wish to make clear that though I am deeply indebted to the commentaries I have read and the sermons I have heard, any erroneous exegesis or application still remaining in these sermons is my own fault. I should also make clear that since I regard myself as an "optimistic amillennialist" in eschatology, my approach in preaching has not been to try to find some literal or historical meaning in every detail of every verse. For more insight, please read the first chapter, which explains the various approaches to the Book of Revelation.

You will also notice throughout these sermons there are scores of references to the Old Testament. This is because the secret to a sound interpretation of many portions in Revelation lies in researching the roots of this book in the Old Testament. Once that rootage is properly understood, the basic meaning of a chapter will often become readily apparent.

My heartfelt thanks first of all to the Heritage Reformed Congregation of Grand Rapids, Michigan, who eagerly listened to these thirty-six sermons and gave me more encouragement than I deserve. I love this flock so much, and am humbled and grateful to be in my thirtieth year of serving them. What a joy they have been for nearly half of my life! Special thanks as well to Greg Bailey, Gary den Hollander, Ray Lanning, Paul Smalley, and Phyllis TenElshof for their valuable editorial assistance on this volume. I also thank Linda den Hollander for her expert typesetting work. As usual, I owe my greatest debt, under God, to my dear wife, Mary, who means far more to me than language can ever express. Except for saving union with Christ, her love for me, her commitment to be as involved in my ministry as I am, and her unceasing kindness mean more to me than anything else in this world.

I also thank Jon Payne not only for persuading me to write this volume and approving it, but also for proposing that our publishing house, Reformation Heritage Books, take over the publishing of this series, *The* Lectio Continua *Expository Commentary on the New Testament,* in light of the fact that the previous publisher, Tolle Lege, was not able to see it through to completion. Jon also asked me to serve as co-editor of the remaining volumes with him, which I gratefully agreed to do: who wouldn't want the privilege of reading and editing volumes of sermons that expound the entire New Testament?

Finally, I wish to acknowledge God's grace in that today, as I write these words, it has been forty years since I first preached as a theological student with the sanction of the church. I preached in the morning from Matthew 5:3, and in the evening from Psalm 40:2, in Waupun, Wisconsin. It was an unforgettable day for me, as I felt greatly helped. In the forty years that have followed, I have been privileged by God's amazing grace to bring His Word in sermons, conference addresses, and lectures 15,000 times, in about forty countries, and on every continent of the globe—all despite my unworthiness. I can't speak well enough of my Sender, Commissioner, and Employer for the mercy He has shown to me in those four decades that now seem more like one or two at most. Countless times I have experienced God's strength in the midst of weakness. "Great is Thy faithfulness!" "Ebenezer, hitherto hath the Lord helped us." Oh for grace to persevere to the end, "looking unto Jesus, the author and finisher of our faith" (Heb. 12:1–2)!

May God richly bless this series of sermons to many thousands of preachers and other readers to His own glory and the well-being of His precious bride, the church, against which the gates of hell will never prevail.

—Joel R. Beeke

June 2016
Grand Rapids, Michigan

1

Introducing the Book of Revelation

REVELATION 1:1–3

The Revelation of Jesus Christ, which God gave unto him, to shew unto his servants things which must shortly come to pass; and he sent and signified it by his angel unto his servant John: who bare record of the word of God, and of the testimony of Jesus Christ, and of all things that he saw. Blessed is he that readeth, and they that hear the words of this prophecy, and keep those things which are written therein: for the time is at hand.

The Revelation of Saint John the Divine, the last book of the Bible, is sometimes referred to by its Greek name, The Apocalypse. The word *apocalypse* repeatedly appears in various forms of social media today. Many people describe the times in which we live as *apocalyptic*, saying these days are the end times. People inside and outside the church are talking about eschatology, the doctrine of the last things. Scientists, politicians, and world leaders are quite at home talking about Armageddon and the end times. Politicians frequently discuss the likelihood of a nuclear holocaust from a world war or an attack by rogue nations, which could cause the final breakdown of society—indeed, of the world. Even unbelievers are using language and imagery from the Bible, specifically from the book of Revelation, and talking—albeit flippantly—about the end of the world.

What will happen to the United States and, by extension, to the world? Will our children and grandchildren continue to enjoy the freedoms and pleasures of peace that we know today? Some young people wonder whether they will live long enough to marry and have children before Christ returns. To address such concerns, we can turn to no better source than the Bible, specifically to Revelation.

However, I must confess that I approached this series of studies on Revelation with considerable trepidation. I had wanted to take on this task for more that three decades, but did not dare to do so because of the difficulty of correctly interpreting several chapters in the book. Yet the importance of this book and a growing internal urge to attempt this study with God's help brought me to a point where I could no longer hold back.

I hope that you will approach this book with a sense of awe and wonder, as I attempted to do. I pray that God will use this book to help you explore Revelation biblically, doctrinally, experientially, and practically in an accurate and edifying way, so that you may be blessed by the Holy Spirit and bring God the glory due to His name.

We will begin by considering the first three verses of Revelation 1. These verses are the title page and foreword for Revelation. They contain all you would expect to find at the beginning of a book. The *title* is The Revelation of Jesus Christ. The *contents* of the book are everything that John saw and attested of this revelation, including things that would shortly come to pass. The *author* of the book is the apostle John. John does not identify himself as an apostle, but he assumes that everyone will know who he is. There must have been hundreds of people named John in the churches of that time, but referring to himself as a servant of Christ was sufficient to identify him as the beloved disciple and apostle who wrote the Gospel of John and the three epistles of John found in the New Testament today.

These verses also give us a foreword to the book, offering details about the agencies and forces that helped John write it. As revelation, this book is a prophecy that came from God through Christ. It was given to John by an angel and then delivered to the churches. Furthermore, the apostle commends the reading of this book, promising a blessing to those who read it, and he exhorts those who hear it read to observe and safeguard what they hear.

To summarize, these verses offer us (1) the title and contents of Revelation; (2) the manner in which the contents of this book were communicated; and (3) words of commendation from John to those who read and hear it. Let us use these divisions to help us look at the opening verses of the Bible's last book.

The Title and Contents of Revelation

Christians are often divided about the book of Revelation. Many ignore the book altogether, except for some well-known texts found in the letters to the seven churches of Asia (chaps. 2–3) and some texts here and there that are often preached at funerals. Some Christians ignore Revelation because of its unfamiliar context and its extraordinary imagery: a sea of glass; a lake of fire; six-winged beasts full of eyes before and behind; dragons, scorpions, and serpents; vials of wrath; stars falling to earth; and a bottomless pit—such things are the stuff of myths and legends. The symbolism is foreign to most of us and difficult to interpret. Many people think Revelation is so dreamlike and confusing that it cannot really be understood.

At the other extreme are Christians who are obsessed with the book and read it more than any other part of Scripture. They say the book holds the answers to all our questions and concerns regarding the distant past, the upheavals of our times, and the shape of future events.

Happily, there is a way to understand Revelation that falls between these two extremes, and it is hinted at in the title of the book. The contents of the book are summarized as The Revelation of Jesus Christ. The word for *revelation* in Greek is *apokalupsis*, from which we derive our word *apocalypse*, and it literally means an uncovering or unveiling of something that was previously hidden or kept secret. Thus, this book is an unveiling or uncovering of Jesus Christ.

Revelation was never meant to be an obscure or closed book. It was not meant to be enigmatic. It was written to be read and understood. You may have read this book in times past without attempting to understand it. You were confused by the book's imagery and symbolism, and put off by the many conflicting interpretations people have given to that imagery. You became so frustrated that you gave up trying to understand the book. That is a pity, because this book was meant to be understood. The very title suggests that we can and should try to understand what is written in this book.

We admit there are many strange things in the book of Revelation. So perhaps we should begin our study by imagining ourselves as missionaries who are about to go out to a strange land.

One of the first things we do to prepare for that mission is to go to orientation school. There we learn *how the language works* in this new country. People who have never learned a second language are often astonished to be told that not every language works the same way or in the same order as the English language. We need to approach the language of the book of Revelation as a new language that must be mastered.

Second, we must learn *the culture* of this new country. We need to understand that what we do may convey a different meaning to people in a foreign culture. Only when we know a culture can we begin to grasp what dress, habits, gestures, and other forms of body language mean in that setting. In some cultures, you may present a gift with one hand, but in other cultures, you must use both hands or you will insult the receiver. You might say, "I am not insulting you," but your actions will speak louder than your words. Some of us give up and say: "I'm not going to change my ways to suit those people. I want to do things my way." If we do that, we will never understand a new culture or be comfortable living with the people who belong to it.

In that light, how can we begin to understand the language and culture of Revelation? Above all, we must view the content of this book as The Revelation of *Jesus Christ*, not merely as The Revelation of *St. John the Divine*, as the title in our English Bible (KJV) puts it. This title simply implies that John was the human instrument who recorded the prophecy and that he was also instrumental in delivering it to the churches. John himself recognizes that his book is the revelation of Jesus Christ given to him as Christ's servant.

This vision is about Jesus Christ, not the pope, Adolf Hitler, Napoleon Bonaparte, Saddam Hussein, or any other person in world history. It has much to say about world history and tells us much about the motives and methods of world leaders, but it is primarily focused on Jesus Christ and His further revelation of Himself to His church. Because Revelation is not primarily about world events or world personalities, we must take care not to read them into the book; rather, we are to look at them in the light of the book. We may then understand what goes on in our world according to principles we find in the book of Revelation, as it discloses who Jesus Christ is and what He is doing in the world, and what He will do to bring all things to an end. So the book of Revelation is first of all a book about Christ.

Let me put it this way: *The Bible was not written to satisfy the hunger of the human mind for knowledge of future events.* Many Christians use the book of Revelation as a kind of horoscope to predict the future. They might as well read the stars. The Bible is not a horoscope; it is a revelation of Jesus Christ. It is to be understood rationally, spiritually, and practically—not superstitiously or speculatively. Indeed, reading Revelation as a horoscope is not only useless but downright sinful because all such efforts are forbidden in Scripture (Deut. 18:9–14). The technical term for this abuse of Scripture is *bibliomancy*, or using the Bible as a literary divining rod or Ouija board.

Jesus said, "It is not for you to know the times or the seasons, which the Father hath put in his own power" (Acts 1:7). Instead, walking by faith, we live one day at a time, knowing that Jesus is Lord, committing the keeping of our souls to a faithful Creator, and casting all our cares upon Him. We must not attempt to pry into the future, for God alone holds the key to it. If He were to hand over that key to us, we would be sorry. So we are not to interpret Revelation speculatively or superstitiously. We must understand the book in terms of our Lord Jesus Christ, because it is a revelation of Him.

Revelation tells us that Jesus Christ, as the Lamb of God, is seated on the throne of heaven. He is the theme of this book, as the

One revealed. But He is also the Revealer, the author of the book. Verse 1 says this book is "the revelation of Jesus Christ, which God gave unto him, to shew unto his servants things which must shortly come to pass." "Things which must shortly come to pass" can also be translated as "things which must soon begin to happen." This phrase is the key to understanding the book of Revelation: Jesus Christ wants to show us things that must shortly come to pass.

Some interpreters say these words refer to the immediate historical context of the apostle John, who lived in the first century after Christ. They say Revelation refers to events of that time, such as the persecution of Christians under Domitian, who ruled as emperor of Rome from AD 81 to 96. At that time, it was a capital offense for a person to be a Christian. Following this view, "things which must shortly come to pass" should thus be understood in that specific historical context. Others view these words differently. They say that "things which must shortly come to pass" refers to events and people that extend long into the future. They think that many of these events will occur during the Millennium, or the thousand-year period prior to the second coming of the Lord. Still others believe "things which must shortly come to pass" refers to what will happen in all of church history—from the first advent of Christ to His second coming.

We will be studying this book extensively, so from the beginning we must lay a solid foundation that will help us know exactly what we are doing, where we are going, and how we should best interpret this book. I am taking the risk of being technical, but with a book like Revelation, we must be technical.

In church history, five predominant ways of interpreting Revelation emerged. While these approaches have substantial overlap at points, they represent five distinct views of the message and themes of Revelation. Let us summarize those approaches.[1]

First is the *preterist* approach. This view sees Revelation wholly in terms of the circumstances that transpired in John's day prior to the destruction of the temple in Jerusalem in AD 70, without any reference to future events. The word *preterism* is derived from the Latin word *praeteritum*, meaning "that which is past." Preterists believe that any interpretation of Revelation must be confined to the historic past rather than projected into the future. This view interprets Revelation's opening words, "things which must shortly come to pass," as events that happened in John's own time. Preterists argue that, just as the seven churches of Asia were real first-century churches to which letters were addressed, so the entire book of Revelation contains only things that came to pass in John's day or shortly thereafter, with the exception of chapters 21–22, which clearly refer to the time of the new heaven and new earth. The strength of this approach is that it strongly affirms the operative framework of the book as "things which must shortly come to pass." Its weakness is that Revelation then has little to say to the church today in the midst of her struggles.

Second is the *historicist* approach. This view, which was held by most of the sixteenth-century Reformers, sees the book of Revelation as a symbolic representation of the panorama of church history, from the first coming of Christ to His second advent at the end of the world. A historicist might say that the seven churches mentioned in Revelation 2–3 do not refer to seven particular churches in Asia Minor, but to seven ages of church history. They would then conclude that today we live in the age of Laodicea, or the era of the lukewarm church. They thus view Revelation as a chart of church history, offering a series of historical pictures moving from Christ's first coming to the end of the present age. In Revelation 13, the beast rising from the sea could be the rise of Islam in the seventh century, while Revelation 17, several centuries further along, may refer to the Roman Catholic Church and the rise of the papacy. The strength of this approach is that it embraces all of church history; its weakness is that it too easily assumes that Revelation prophesies a linear movement through church history, with no recapitulation of events seen from different points of view.

Third is the *futurist* approach. This was the most popular view of evangelicals at the beginning of the twentieth century, especially premillennial dispensationalists, but it has lost ground in recent decades. The futurist believes that the visions of Revelation 4–22 refer to events that are still future, but that they will transpire immediately prior to and along with Christ's second coming at the end of history, ushering in the millennial age. Most futurists are premillennial; that is, they believe that Christ's return will precede the millennial age. The problem with this view is that it reads the book as almost entirely without reference to the needs and struggles of the churches to which John first sent this book. It also affords little consolation for the suffering church at any other point in church history, including today, because it is exclusively focused on events surrounding Christ's second coming. The strength of this view is that it emphasizes the ultimate victory of Christ and His elect over the world at His second coming.

Fourth is the *idealist* approach, sometimes called the *poetic* or *inspirational* approach. This position is sometimes called *iterism*, from the Latin verb *itero*, meaning "to repeat," because idealist interpreters hold that the events described in Revelation are repeated from time to time in the experience of the church from age to age. This approach teaches that Revelation is relevant for everyone, since it deals with principles and symbols that are always valid in our personal history and experience. The idealist scarcely wrestles with the problem of chronology in Revelation, preferring to see this book and its symbolism as a tract written for persecuted Christians of any period. The symbolism is interpreted loosely, in a very general way, to give comfort and encouragement to persecuted Christians. The strength of this approach is its applicability to the church of all ages; its weakness is that it is difficult to affirm this view exegetically, based on the description "things which must shortly come to pass" (1:1).

Fifth is the *eclectic* approach. It embraces the apparent strengths and rejects the apparent weaknesses of the other four approaches. This approach acknowledges that there are elements of truth in all of these approaches. Personally, I believe this is the best and safest approach to take. Though there are serious problems with each of these approaches, we can also glean something from each. Cornel Venema explains this approach well:

> Preterism rightly insists that the visions of Revelation reflect events and circumstances contemporaneous with its writing or the period immediately thereafter. But preterism fails to adequately account for the way Revelation also reveals events and circumstances that characterize the struggles of the church throughout the entire inter-advental age. Futurism partially solves the problem of preterism by emphasizing the way the visions of Revelation portray events that will take place shortly before the end of history. But in doing so, futurism exaggerates the future orientation of the book. As for historicism, although the events portrayed in the vision of Revelation have occurred in the past or may reoccur at various points in history, these events are not limited to a particular time in the past, present, or even future.
>
> The obvious strength of eclecticism is its ability to incorporate the primary emphasis of the other approaches without the one-sidedness that often characterizes alternative views. The weakness of the approach may be its tendency to ascribe different meanings to the same vision.[2]

In accord with many Reformed theologians, I propose an eclectic approach that accents the idealist or iterist approach. This approach has also been called the *parallel* or *cyclical* view of Revelation. Imagine a man with a video camera who is recording a church congregation. He pans over the people, starting on one side of the church and going all around. Then he goes up into the gallery and does the same thing. Then he goes to the back, comes from behind, and pans over everyone again. That is what we see in Revelation. The book offers us views of the entire history of the church, but seen from different vantage points.

I believe there are seven parallel sections in Revelation. Each section offers a different view of the church in history, as we will

---

2. Venema, "Interpreting Revelation," 13.

see as we make our way through the book. With this parallel or cyclical view of the book, we will see how each section spans the entire dispensation of the gospel, from the first coming of Christ two thousand years ago down to His coming again at the last day.

The great theme of Revelation is the victory of Christ and His church over the old serpent, his helpers, and all the kingdoms of this world. We will track that theme through each of the seven sections and see how this book accomplishes its purpose: to inspire, comfort, and encourage God's people in the church in every era to press on in the face of persecution and amidst all our struggles, knowing we are on the winning side in this anti-Christian world. I believe this is the right way to interpret Revelation. It puts Christian warfare into proper perspective. God pulls back the curtains to offer us a glimpse behind the events we read and hear about in the news media or learn about in history, so we can see what unseen but powerful forces are shaping reality in the world around us. Such insights from Revelation help us fight the good fight of faith and endure to the end. I hope this revelation of Jesus Christ will strengthen our faith and afford us greater hope and comfort.

Here are the seven sections of the book of Revelation, each dealing with the entire present age or dispensation, from the first to the second coming of Christ:

1. The Son of Man and the Seven Churches (1:1–3:22)
2. The Lamb and the Seven Seals of God's Scroll (4:1–8:1)
3. The Seven Trumpets (8:2–11:19)
4. The War with the Dragon (12:1–14:20)
5. The Seven Bowls of Wrath (15:1–16:21)
6. The Fall of Babylon the Whore (17:1–19:21)
7. The Victory of Jerusalem the Bride (20:1–22:21)[3]

---

3. This outline is derived from *The Reformation Heritage KJV Study Bible*, ed. Joel R. Beeke, Michael P. V. Barrett, Gerald M. Bilkes, Paul M. Smalley (Grand Rapids: Reformation Heritage Books, 2014), 1866.

In summary, the book of Revelation is about Jesus Christ and His victory over the powers of evil. It was written to offer hope to Christians in times of difficulty and darkness, and to warn others of judgment to come because of their persistent unbelief and impenitence. You might say the personal themes of Revelation are (1) Christ's revelations of His glorious victory over evil, (2) hope for believers in the midst of persecution, and (3) warnings to unbelievers who are fast approaching judgment day. Remember that each of these themes applies to you personally, but do not approach Revelation as if you were solving a difficult puzzle. Do what John did: fall at the feet of the Lord Jesus Christ (Rev. 1:17). If studying Revelation doesn't make you bow before the Lord Jesus Christ in wonder, adoration, and joy, then you have missed the point of the whole book.

The Communication of Revelation

Revelation has been communicated to us in four ways that we must keep in mind to properly understand this book:

First, it comes to us *from God through our Lord Jesus Christ*. It was delivered by an angel to the apostle John so that we all might benefit from it. It comes to us as an apostolic epistle (1:4), handed from one person to another, from church to church and from age to age. When you want to send a valuable item through the mail, you don't just stuff it in a mail slot and hope for the best. You send it by registered mail to ensure that the item is received and signed for by the person to whom it is addressed. Revelation has come to us as a letter registered by God for believers in the church throughout history.

The last verse of the book is much like the ending of many other epistles in the New Testament: "The grace of our Lord Jesus Christ be with you all. Amen" (Rev. 22:21). This benediction implies that, although this epistle was sent to the churches in Asia Minor in the first century, it has profound implications for all Christians and for the church everywhere and in all times—even in our present century.

Second, this book comes to us *as an apocalypse*. It therefore must not be read literally throughout. As a specimen of apocalyptic literature, it is filled with imagery, symbolism, and other kinds of

figurative language. To read it all literally is a basic error in interpretation, a failure to do justice to the literary character of the
book. These verses at the opening of Revelation root this book in
the prophecy of Daniel, itself full of divine revelations of things
to come (Dan. 2:28–30, 45–47).[4] Daniel contains symbolic dreams
and visions, and we must interpret Revelation in a similar way.

Most of us understand this when we read a book. Fiction has
different rules than non-fiction: one allows for imaginary people,
places, and things, while the other is based on reality. Allegorical
literature must be read allegorically; you cannot read John Bunyan's
Pilgrim's Progress as you would read John Calvin's *Institutes of the
Christian Religion.* Thus, it is crucial to understand that the book of
Revelation cannot be interpreted as mere factual data. Most books
in Scripture can be accepted at face value, but Revelation was not
meant to be read that way. If you read it that way, you end up with
things that are simply impossible. You must view it as a book that
uses imaginative symbolism to help you see more clearly the glory
of the Lord Jesus Christ. So, for example, numbers in this book
are symbolic rather than mathematical. Colors are symbolic. So are
animals, many of which we have never seen. So are patterns that
keep repeating.

Revelation draws us into a world which is full of symbols that
leave us with profound impressions. As we examine these symbols
and see what they mean, we will begin to understand the message
of this book. Revelation is a kind of picture book of the glory of
Jesus Christ. It is, as John says, the revelation of Jesus Christ. What
you and I are meant to see in this book is not a book of puzzles but
a catalog of paintings depicting the glory of our Lord and Savior.

Third, this book is communicated *as a divine vision.* Ordinarily
Scripture speaks of words and hearing. But Revelation uses the language of seeing and perceiving. In this revelation, Christ is not just
speaking to His servants but *showing* them things that must soon

---

4. G. K. Beale with David H. Campbell, *Revelation: A Shorter Commentary*
(Grand Rapids: Eerdmans, 2015), 35–36.

take place. Indeed, as you read through Revelation, you will find the recurring expression, "I saw." In most of the Bible, the recurring expression is, "Hear the Word of God." But Revelation invites us to *see* the Word of God. John is offering us these views of the Lord Jesus Christ, saying, "I saw this" and "I saw that." As he presents one image after another, the scenario builds in scope and depth until, at the very end of the book, what we see finally becomes patently clear.

Fourth, this book is communicated *as prophecy*. John says in verse 3, "Blessed is he that readeth, and they that hear the words of this prophecy." We usually understand a prophecy as something that foretells the future. But in the Bible, most prophecy does not speak about the future as much as it applies the Word of God to the present situation. There may be indications about the future, but by and large prophecy is given so that we may know how to live for God's glory in the present.

Revelation 1:1 says God gave this revelation to Christ "to shew unto his servants things which must shortly come to pass." At the end of verse 3, God says these servants should "keep those things which are written therein: for the time is at hand." So the book reveals things that must "shortly come to pass...for the time is at hand." We have things that will happen *soon* and events that are *near*, but that is not so much for us as it is for John and his companions. The language here echoes Daniel 2, in which Daniel interprets an astonishing vision of God's kingdom that is to be fulfilled "in the latter days" (v. 28), or at the beginning of the *last days*. Now John has been shown that those promises have come to fruition because of the work of Jesus Christ, and the time is short. As the Lord Jesus often declared, "The kingdom of God is at hand" (Mark 1:15). So this revelation of Jesus Christ is a revelation for Christians living in the last days.

When people ask me if I think we're living in the last days, I answer, "Of course we are living in the last days, but we have been living in the last days from the Bible's point of view for the last two thousand years." The New Testament says the onset of the last days was marked by Christ's pouring out His Spirit on the church on the Day of Pentecost (Acts 2:17). That is when Christ inaugurated His kingdom, which is now spreading to the ends of the earth. The last days include the days in which we are living. Thus, John is being told, "You stand at the beginning of the days when the kingdom of Jesus Christ will extend to the ends of the earth." That is what Revelation is all about. It is communicated to us as a letter from God, an apostolic epistle; as an apocalypse; as a divine vision; and as a prophecy.

The Commendation of Revelation

In verse 3, the apostle John commends the book of Revelation to all who read it or hear it read. He says, "Blessed is he that readeth, and they that hear the words of this prophecy, and keep those things which are written therein: for the time is at hand." We must remember that this book was sent out in times of controversy. Not everyone acknowledged the authority of John; thus, he could by no means be sure that everyone would receive this epistle with the due measure of faith, reverence, and submission.

We must also remember that in those days, many in the church could not read. One of the duties of the minister of the Word was to "give attendance to reading" (1 Tim. 4:13), that is, the reading and exposition of Holy Scripture, so that those who could not read could at least hear it read and expounded for their edification. John promises a blessing to both faithful ministers who read and expound this book, and also to those who hear it with faith and do what it teaches and commands. We may therefore conclude that we shall be blessed by doing the following things:

- *Reading and studying this book with faith, reverence, and godly fear, as the Word of God and the Word of Christ.* Repent of any past neglect of this part of Scripture. Embrace Revelation as a book God wants you to read and understand. Read it "with an high and reverent esteem...with a firm persuasion that [it is] the very word of God...with desire to know, believe, and obey the will of God revealed in [it];

with diligence, and attention to the matter and scope of [it]; with meditation, application, self-denial, and prayer" (Westminster Larger Catechism, Q. 157).[5]

• *Being obedient to Christ.* John says in verse 3 that people are blessed who hear what Revelation says and "keep those things which are written therein." Notice that God's blessing is not pronounced upon those who own a copy of this precious book, nor upon those who only read it or have it read to them, nor upon those who specialize in debating the meaning of this prophecy. The blessing is pronounced upon those who "keep those things" written in it. We *keep* the words of this prophecy by cherishing them as the Word of God and by applying them to ourselves and to our lives in such a way that, as followers of Jesus Christ, our Lord and Savior, we look forward to his coming. We want to live as He would have us live until He comes. Knowing that this world will pass away, we look forward to a city with a foundation whose builder and maker is God (Heb. 11:10; 2 Peter 3:10–15), and we live as strangers and pilgrims in the earth.

So Revelation calls us to be faithful, willing, obedient subjects of the King of kings and the Lord of lords. The book of Revelation is primarily about Christ the King. Like Psalm 2, it calls on us and all mankind to "kiss the Son" in sweet submission, "lest he be angry, and ye perish from the way, when his wrath is kindled but a little" (v. 12). But Christ also speaks in Revelation as Prophet and intercedes as High Priest while He reigns as King. The book of Revelation calls us to bow before Christ as Prophet, Priest, and King, and then to go out and be

---

5. James T. Dennison Jr., comp., *Reformed Confessions of the Sixteenth and Seventeenth Centuries in English Translation: 1523–1693* (Grand Rapids: Reformation Heritage Books, 2008–2014), 4:340.

prophets, priests, and kings standing under His banner and ministering to a perishing world.

- *Being prepared for Christ's coming.* Verse 3 concludes: "for the time is at hand." The lesson embedded in these words for every person in every age of the Christian church is *be prepared to meet your King in righteousness and peace at all times.* We ignore or resist Christ's lordship to our peril. You may bend the knee to culture, gurus, Pharisees, libertines, false prophets and prophetesses, or idols of the times, but know that the sure judgment of King Jesus will soon fall upon you and all others who live carelessly or walk disorderly, and on every church that does not submit to Christ as Lord.

- *Overcoming through Christ.* The implication of verse 3 is that Christ has power to bless His people even in the midst of severe persecution, and they will be blessed in overcoming the world by faith in Him. Christ promises in Revelation 2:7, "To him that overcometh will I give to eat of the tree of life, which is in the midst of the paradise of God." God's overcoming grace and your overcoming faith will be a blessing to you, enabling you by faith to overcome the powers of evil at work in a wicked world. This blessing is sure because, as Peter declared at Pentecost, "God hath made that same Jesus...both Lord and Christ" (Acts 2:36).

The counterpart to this promise of blessing is a curse upon those who do not keep the things written in Revelation (cf. Rev. 22:18–19). Believers who read these words are promised blessings, but unbelievers are warned against the danger of despising and disregarding God's warnings, for the end is near. "Behold, the judge standeth before the door" (James 5:9). Here, John specifically invokes the wrath of God, in the form of a deadly curse, upon those who deal lightly or deceitfully with these words, imposing on it ideas and words of their own choosing, or else discarding anything they disagree with or don't understand.

Dear friend, examine yourself. Are you saved by grace through faith in Christ, the blessed Lamb of God who as our representative perfectly satisfied the holy requirements of God's law, bore God's wrath on the tree, and rose victoriously from the grave? Are you abiding by faith in the One who accomplished our redemption? Are you being obedient to Christ, preparing to meet Christ, and overcoming sin through Christ?

If you have not found blessing in Christ, you are ignoring Christ at your peril. You will be cursed forever if you do not repent of your sins and take refuge in the mercy of the Lord of glory. But if you seek for blessing in the reading, hearing, and keeping of the words of this revelation of Jesus Christ, then you will be blessed indeed.

2

A Salutation from the
Throne of Heaven

REVELATION 1:4–8

John to the seven churches which are in Asia: Grace be unto you, and peace, from him which is, and which was, and which is to come; and from the seven Spirits which are before his throne: and from Jesus Christ, who is the faithful witness, and the first begotten of the dead, and the prince of the kings of the earth. Unto him that loved us, and washed us from our sins in his own blood, and hath made us kings and priests unto God and his Father; to him be glory and dominion for ever and ever. Amen. Behold, he cometh with clouds; and every eye shall see him, and they also which pierced him: and all kindreds of the earth shall wail because of him. Even so, Amen. I am Alpha and Omega, the beginning and the ending, saith the Lord, which is, and which was, and which is to come, the Almighty.

When people greet you, who they are and how they greet you is important. There is nothing in this world that can be compared to being warmly and distinctly greeted by each of the three persons of the Trinity. To know God the Father and to have fellowship with Him through the Son and by the Spirit is a foretaste of heaven on earth. Do you know experientially for yourself, at least to some degree, the Father, the Son, and the Holy Spirit? Do you treasure their warm words and greetings conveyed to you through the Word of God by the Spirit?

The Book of Revelation presents us with what I believe is the most beautiful and profound greeting from the triune God to His people contained in all of the Bible. This rich greeting ought to stir within us a sense of excitement and anticipation as we begin to expound this comforting Bible book for you, with God's help, in a series of sermons.

Revelation is a book that, by the grace of Christ and His Spirit, should be opened, read, and understood by all believers. Revelation 5:5 says, "And one of the elders saith unto me, Weep not: behold, the Lion of the tribe of Judah, the Root of David, hath prevailed to open the book, and to loose the seven seals thereof." This book is a revelation from God to Jesus Christ for us. Our Lord Jesus, the Lion of the tribe of Judah, is our Savior, who shed His blood for us. As Head of the church, Christ sent the book of Revelation via an angel to His servant, the apostle John, so that he could write it down for believers in all ages.

In the previous chapter, we looked at the theological setting of Revelation. Now let us consider the rich salutation, doxology, and promise that preface this book (Rev. 1:4–8). Sometimes when we begin a book, we are able to skip over the introduction quite easily, but with Revelation, if we are to understand things properly, we must begin at the beginning, where God explains to us what this book is all about and what its purpose is.

Revelation's Historical Setting

The salutation reminds us that we are reading an epistle or letter. In verse 4, John identifies himself as the writer and addresses the letter "to the seven churches which are in Asia." In verse 9, John relates the circumstances in which this letter was written: "I John, who also am your brother, and companion in tribulation, and in the kingdom and patience of Jesus Christ, was in the isle that is called Patmos, for the word of God, and for the testimony of Jesus Christ."

In verse 11, we are reminded that John is told to write what he sees in a book and send it to a circuit of seven local churches in the Roman province of Asia, the land known today as Turkey: Ephesus, Smyrna, Pergamos (or Pergamum), Thyatira, Sardis, Philadelphia, and Laodicea. During the time of the apostles, letters were addressed so they could be read and passed along to churches along the main Roman road in the province. These churches do not exist any longer, but they certainly did when John wrote Revelation. Church tradition locates John in Ephesus in the later years of his life and ministry, so these churches were familiar with him. They knew him, trusted him, and had read his earlier writings.

These seven churches were experiencing sore persecution. According to Irenaeus, John wrote Revelation "towards the end of Domitian's reign," about AD 95.[1] Secular writers of the Roman Empire described Emperor Domitian as a savage monster who conducted a "reign of terror." He abused distinguished citizens in front of crowds. He hated Christians and despised the church of Christ. He reigned in darkness, loving the pains and lamentations of people he tortured. He was a beast of a man. He commanded everyone in the empire to call him "Lord and God." When Christians refused to do so, he persecuted and killed them.

But Domitian was not the only one who might fit this description of the "beast" of Revelation 13:11–18. Revelation says there will be many false prophets and antichrists. Many have and will fit this description. But to understand Revelation, you must realize that it first saw the light of day in the reign of Domitian. The persecutions he initiated were some of the "things which must shortly come to pass." Revelation is not only about future events, but also about what was already happening in Asia Minor and these seven local churches under Domitian's reign of terror.

But our understanding of Revelation cannot be confined to the first century. There were many churches in Asia Minor, but John draws our attention to just seven. As a number, seven is often used in Scripture to signify completeness. These seven churches represent the entire church of Christ in every age to the end of the world. In the same way, verse 4b of our text speaks of "the seven Spirits which are before his throne." Only one Spirit of God stands before God's throne, not seven, but this Spirit is described as sevenfold in the

---

1. Irenaeus, *Against Heresies*, 5.30.3, in *Ante-Nicene Fathers*, ed. Alexander Roberts, James Donaldson, and A. Cleveland Coxe (Buffalo, N.Y.: Christian Literature Company, 1885), 1:559. Cf. William Hendriksen, *More Than Conquerors: An Interpretation of the Book of Revelation* (Grand Rapids: Baker, 1982), 14.

sense of being complete and perfect. Likewise, the church of Christ exists as many churches, in many lands, with great diversity, but, as the Belgic Confession says, "This holy church is not confined, bound, or limited to a certain place or to certain persons, but is spread and dispersed over the whole world; and yet is joined and united with heart and will, by the power of faith, in one and the same Spirit" (Art. 27).[2]

Applying Revelation to the church today should not surprise us any more than viewing Paul's letters as written to us. We don't say that the epistles of Paul to the Romans, the Corinthians, or the Ephesians apply only to those specific churches. Rather, we say, "Paul is also writing to today's church and to me as a member of the church." Thus, we are to receive Revelation as addressed to the church in every age. This is important to remember, because some modern interpreters say Revelation has nothing to do with today's church. Others believe that what follows after Revelation 3 has to do only with ethnic Israel and the church of the future in the days just before the world's end. They lose sight of the church universal. But we believe that the entire book of Revelation is addressed to the whole church of Jesus Christ in every age under all circumstances.

When John wrote Revelation, he may have been already in his nineties. The youngest of the disciples, John was the last living apostle. Now, as verse 9 says, he is in exile on Patmos, an island ten miles long that is "volcanic, rocky, and mostly treeless," one of several places where exiles were sent.[3] One source in the early church said that John had to work in the marble quarries. It is little wonder then that in verse 9 he calls himself a "companion in tribulation" with the persecuted believers of Asia.

John says in verse 9 that he is suffering "for the word of God, and for the testimony of Jesus Christ." This statement can be read two ways. John was exiled as a martyr, or witness, suffering

---

2. *The Three Forms of Unity* (Birmingham, Ala.: Solid Ground Christian Books, 2010), 47.

3. I. A. Sparks, "Patmos," ed. Geoffrey W. Bromiley, *The International Standard Bible Encyclopedia, Revised* (Grand Rapids: Eerdmans, 1979–1988), 690.

for Christ's sake. But he was also there, in the providence of God, to receive the Word of God and the testimony of Jesus, which he faithfully transmitted to the seven churches in Asia, and, through them, to the whole church of Christ.

The historical circumstances for the writing of the book of Revelation offer many practical lessons for us today. Let us look at three:

First, *we are immortal until our work is done.* John lived many years for a purpose. Some people who live to the age of one hundred are asked, "What helped you live so long?" Their answers typically include factors such as diet, exercise, and other aspects of lifestyle. But what helped John the apostle live so long? Christ still had work for him to do. God ordained that he should furnish the church with the written record of this Revelation of Jesus Christ to complete and close the canon of inspired, inerrant, and infallible Holy Scripture. Aged Christians today, Christ is keeping you here because the work He has for you to do is not done. Our time is in His hands (Ps. 31:15). We will be kept alive, safe, and immortal until our work on earth is done.

Second, *living according to the purpose of God is the best and safest place to be.* On the island of Patmos, John's outward circumstances could scarcely have been more bleak. Yet there is no trace of resentment or despair in John. He is living by faith, bearing his cross, following Christ to the end. So in verses 9 and 10, the apostle says, "I John…your brother, and companion in tribulation…was in the isle that is called Patmos…. I was in the Spirit on the Lord's day."

On Patmos, John found his way to the altar of the living God! He lifted up his voice to praise his Savior, saying, "Unto him that loved us, and washed us from our sins in his own blood…to him be glory and dominion for ever and ever" (vv. 5–6). John loved the Lord Jesus Christ so much that the very mention of His name made him burst into praise. If you love Christ, you can understand something of John's passion. He begins to record the prophecy given to him for the churches, and, in greeting his readers, he invokes the name of Jesus Christ. That is enough to make him lay down his pen and worship the Lord.

So do not pity this old man. Marvel at the grace of God in him. Too often, you and I have to drag ourselves to church to worship or to a prayer meeting as a matter of duty. But this old man has to restrain himself from praising God because he has other important work to do. He must remind himself: "I'm not in heaven yet, so I must keep going! I still have work to do on earth." Examine your heart, dear believer, then look at John's, which explodes with love for Christ.

Living on a remote island is difficult, however, in terms of loneliness. When we're alone, we have to come face to face with ourselves. That is probably the biggest challenge for John. He is content only because he has Christ. He worships his Savior, yet he still feels the pain of being cut off from fellow believers. He is confined to a lonely island with nothing but the sound of the sea; so he reminds himself: "I am a prisoner, but Christ has freed me from my sins with His blood. Man has put chains on me, but Christ has released me from eternal condemnation!" Working in a stone quarry is excruciating work for an old man, but John says: "Christ has made me a prophet, priest, and king. Praise Him!" In the midst of the most difficult circumstances, the old disciple worships God with all his mind and soul.

Life often brings us experiences that crush us physically and emotionally. What do we do when that happens? Should we withdraw from others and feel sorry for ourselves? No. We must realize that God is at work. He is preparing other brothers and sisters to help us through times of tribulation, and He is preparing us to help others when they are crushed by life. John knows he is alone for his spiritual welfare as well as that of other believers. He writes to the seven churches and to us, saying, "I am on this island for your sake." God is preparing John in his suffering to offer others the comfort with which he himself is being comforted.

God is still emptying this aged believer of self. God has already reshaped John from the rashness he displayed when, as a young disciple, he wanted to call down fire from heaven to consume those who opposed Jesus (Luke 9:54). He also wanted the honor of being seated at Christ's right hand in glory (Matt. 20:20–24). God has transformed John from this ruthless, insensitive, and ambitious young disciple into the apostle of love. But God is still working in John; He put John on Patmos to be alone so that He might comfort him in his loneliness, and so that John might be even more able to comfort others, as Paul did (2 Cor. 1:4).

Third, *God is sovereign over all things, but He is not the author of sin.* This present life is but a "valley of tears," in which evil of many kinds touches us.[4] Every hardship that John experiences is meant to strengthen him. God permits Satan to distress and harm the people of God, but He is not the author of such evil; Satan is. Revelation teaches us that there are worldly and spiritual principalities and powers that are always at war with the church.

John is confined to this rocky island because of persecution that originates from sinful men and Satan, the father of murder and lies. But God can make the wrath of men and the hostility of Satan into a song of God-glorifying praise (cf. Ps. 76:10). Out of the barren island of Patmos comes the beautiful book of Revelation.

Many of the epistles of the New Testament were written from prison. Besides the Bible, I don't suppose there is another book that has had so much influence against the kingdom of Satan as John Bunyan's *The Pilgrim's Progress.* The book was written from the Bedford County Jail, where Bunyan suffered for many years. Time after time in history, the devil tries to destroy the faith of believers and thwart the will of God, but God makes all these things work together for good to them that love Him, accomplishing His holy purpose for their lives (Rom. 8:28).

The greatest proof is Calvary. Crucifying God's Son was surely the greatest evil that humans ever did. When soldiers came to arrest Jesus, He said, "This is your hour, and the power of darkness" (Luke 22:53). The blackest moment in history was Christ's death on Calvary, but out of that sacrifice God brought the highest possible good—our salvation. On the cross, the Messiah crushed the head of

---

4. Heidelberg Catechism, LD 9, Q. 26, in *Three Forms of Unity*, 76.

the old serpent, Satan. He washed us in His blood and freed us from
the bondage of sin. And He makes us kings and priests unto God:

> *He maketh the rebel a priest and a king,*
> *He hath bought us and taught us this new song to sing:*
> *Unto Him who hath loved us and washed us from sin,*
> *Unto Him be the glory forever. Amen.*[5]

Revelation's Trinitarian Foundation

Having surveyed the historical setting of Revelation, let us now
look at the salutation itself and the way it bases the whole book
squarely on the church's confession of faith in the triune God. On
the one hand, the salutation is announced in the name of each person of the Godhead, that is, each member of the Trinity. On the
other, special prominence is given to the third person of the Trinity,
God the Holy Spirit. Let us note its trinitarian structure. Verses 4b
and 5a say, "Grace be unto you, and peace, from him which is, and
which was, and which is to come; and from the seven Spirits which
are before his throne; and from Jesus Christ." These words convey
the triune God's greeting to the church of all ages.

This trinitarian salutation begins with *grace* and *peace*. I suppose
many people think of Revelation as a book of gloom and doom,
couched in terms of wrath, conflict, and judgment. They think of
fire and brimstone, thunder and lightning, cursing, tribulation, and
wrath—anything but grace and peace! But these dark elements are
features of a much larger picture: the grace of God in Christ and the
peace of God that passes understanding. These are seen against the
backdrop of wrath and tribulation.

"Grace and peace" is the common apostolic greeting. The words
grace and *peace*, in that order, summarize the means and the end of
the salvation of God. Grace is God's undeserved love, or, putting it
even more strongly, God's de-merited salvation. Peace flows out of

---

5. Stanza 3 and refrain from the gospel hymn of Arthur T. Pierson, "The New
Song" (1874).

that grace, for peace is the reflection of God's smile. In our natural condition of sin, God must frown upon us. We are sons of disobedience, and our father is the devil. But through the blood of Jesus, by God's grace, all that changes. God now deals with us not as we deserve but according to the merit of His Son, Jesus Christ. He extends His grace to us as hell-deserving sinners. When God smiles upon us, we have peace with God through our Lord Jesus Christ in our hearts and minds.

This greeting is brought from each person of the Trinity. We read, first, *the greeting of the eternal Father*: "Grace be unto you, and peace, from him which is, and which was, and which is to come." That is a description of God the Father, the everlasting and unchanging Jehovah. The ancient name of God announced to Moses from the burning bush was, "I AM THAT I AM" (Ex. 3:14). As the eternal Son, Jesus Christ is also "the Lord, which is, and which was, and which is to come, the Almighty" (Rev. 1:8).

Sometimes we need to be reminded that God *is*, because we live so much of the time as though God *is not*. John wants all believers to understand that the dark clouds of tribulation are about to come upon them, yet they will not be destroyed, because God is the great I AM who was, is, and ever shall be.

Nothing is more basic to our faith than to believe that God is. We are told that if any man will come to Christ, he must first of all believe that God is (Heb. 11:6). Jesus says, "Let not your heart be troubled: ye believe in God, believe also in me" (John 14:1). Dear child of God, God not only is, but He is committed to you through the blood of His Son. The God who is "from everlasting to everlasting" (Ps. 90:2), the Lord who does not change (Mal. 3:6), has pledged Himself to you by the blood of the covenant. There could be no greater grace and no more lasting peace.

Second, we read *the greeting of the sevenfold Spirit*. John also writes in the salutation, "Grace be unto you, and peace…from the seven Spirits [that is, the Holy Spirit] which are before his throne." Some people question whether this verse refers to God the Holy Spirit, since we are told there are seven Spirits before the throne, not just one. The verse simply must refer to the Holy Spirit, since nowhere does Scripture say that grace and peace come to us from any being other than God. Nor can these "seven" Spirits be viewed as seven angels or seven seraphim.[6] Rather, as we have seen already, they refer to God the Holy Spirit in all His fullness, as symbolized by the number seven.

This idea is confirmed in other places in the Bible, such as Isaiah 11:2, a prophecy that Christ, as the "Branch of Jesse," will be anointed with a sevenfold fullness of the Spirit. Then, too, in Zechariah, God asks the prophet what the seven lamps of the candlestick signify. God then explains, saying, "Not by might, nor by power, but by my spirit, says the LORD of hosts" (4:2–6). In other words, the church of God shines in the darkness of this world with a sevenfold fullness of light, sustained by a sevenfold supply of the Spirit of God.

In Revelation 3:1, Christ describes Himself as "he that hath the seven Spirits of God," a reminder that the Father gave the Spirit to the incarnate Son at the time of His exaltation and enthronement (Acts 2:33), and, as John the Baptist declared, "God giveth not the Spirit by measure unto him" (John 3:34). Theologians call this the economic subordination of the Spirit to the Son. Christ has the Spirit completely at His disposal to do His work and will in the church and in the lives of believers.

Finally, Revelation 4:5 offers another reference to the Holy Spirit: "And out of the throne proceeded lightnings and thunderings and voices: and there were seven lamps of fire burning before the throne, which are the seven Spirits of God." The light of the Spirit shines with sevenfold, or *perfect*, brightness. At the same time,

---

6. According to the common understanding of Isaiah 6:2–3, there are only two seraphim attending on God's throne, just as there were only two golden cherubim standing on the cover of the ark of the covenant in the most holy place (Ex. 25:22). John Calvin, *Commentary on the Book of the Prophet Isaiah*, trans. William Pringle (Grand Rapids: Eerdmans, 1953), 1:203.

John consistently affirms, in references found throughout Revelation, that the Holy Spirit is one.[7]

John says this sevenfold Spirit is *before* the throne. This, too, is a symbolic way of speaking of the Holy Ghost. As the third person in the Godhead, within the Trinity, the Spirit is not *before* the throne; He is *on* the throne. However, here in this passage, He is *before* the throne. That is because John is talking here about the Spirit as given to Christ and the church. As the Spirit of Christ, the Spirit reveals and applies all the work of Christ, including His death on the cross and His resurrection, to us. The Holy Spirit is thus before the throne in His sevenfold fullness, ready to go out and reveal Jesus Christ to His church.

If we are believers, God has given Himself to us in Christ and put His Spirit within us. God's grace and peace come to us through the sevenfold Spirit who is before the throne. This picture is parallel to the one in Revelation 22:1: "And he shewed me a pure river of water of life, clear as crystal, proceeding out of the throne of God and of the Lamb." John sees the Spirit as the river of life that flows from under the throne of God to heal the nations (cf. Ps. 46:4). This is another reference to the work of the sevenfold Spirit of God. The Spirit of God comes to the church and to the heart of the believer as a mighty thundering river from the throne of God. The glory of being a Christian is that you have a mighty river of life that flows through you and carries you along as it sweeps away the sins of your past.

Third, we read *the greeting of the mediatorial Son*: Jesus Christ, who is the faithful witness, and the first begotten of the dead, and the prince of the kings of the earth. Christ is *the faithful witness.* The term for "witness" in the New Testament is the same word from which we get our English word *martyr*. Christians who are experiencing persecution and martyrdom are treading the way that Jesus Christ has already taken. God is thus saying to His people, "You

---

7. Rev. 1:10; 2:7, 11, 17, 29; 3:6, 13, 22; 4:2; 11:11; 14:13; 17:3; 19:10; 21:10; 22:17.

are to follow the example of the Lord Jesus, who would not be deflected from obeying His Father's will." The great temptation for people who are experiencing hostility, opposition, persecution, pain, and possible death is to become so discouraged that they cease to be faithful. History tells us that this was precisely what happened to the Christians of John's day. So here God says that Jesus was a faithful witness who did not turn aside, even from the shameful death of the cross.

He is *the first-begotten of the dead.* Jesus Christ is also the first-born of His Father. As such, He has supreme and absolute authority over all things. He demonstrated that authority in His resurrection by conquering death. He has authority even over death itself. A firstborn son ordinarily has younger siblings who follow him. So John is saying here that Christ, as the firstborn, has brothers and sisters whom He is taking to glory. They too will experience glorious victory over death and all other enemies because Christ has risen from the dead.

He is *prince of the kings of the earth.* No matter what world leader struts the stage of human history, imagining himself to be all-powerful and using that power to exhibit his cruelty, the apostle John says that Jesus Christ is sovereign over all. Every king, ruler, president, or dictator who seeks to bear authority is subject to Jesus Christ. John thus issues the warning, "Let all tyrants tremble because Jesus Christ is King, the Prince of the kings of the earth, and they shall have to answer to Him for all their crimes."

This salutation is a comfort for John, the seven churches of Asia, the church of all ages, and every believer. The triune God puts His blessing upon all of us. Each person of the Trinity labors for the salvation of believers whom God has chosen from eternity past to inherit life eternal. Samuel Rutherford thus says he didn't know which divine person he needed most, but he loved each of them and needed them all.

God the Father provides salvation for us; God the Spirit dispenses salvation to us; and God the Son merits salvation for us. That order is unique. Usually, when you read about the triune God in

Scripture, it is in the order of Father, Son, and Spirit, but here the reference is to Father, Spirit, and Son. The reason for that is the imagery of Revelation, which includes candlesticks, bowls, altars, incense, and fire. These furnishings remind us of the tabernacle or temple of God. Revelation not only presents God to us in the nakedness of His being, but also as He dwells within His heavenly tabernacle or temple. John saw God the same way Isaiah did, "sitting upon a throne, high and lifted up, and his train filled the temple" (Isa. 6:1).

God is thus presented here as the God of salvation. He is seated on His throne in the Holy of Holies. Just outside the throne room is the seven-branched candlestick, which represents the Holy Spirit. Just beyond that is the altar of burnt offerings, symbolizing the atoning death of our Savior. So grace and peace come to us from God, who is, was, and is to come; from the sevenfold Spirit; and from Jesus Christ, "who is the faithful witness, and the first begotten of the dead, and the prince of the kings of the earth." God is presented to us not simply as God, but as the God of salvation, the God of the covenant, and the God who is totally committed in all three persons of the Godhead to the salvation of sinners.

One of the joys of marriage is making a vow of commitment to another and hearing that person make a similar vow of commitment to you. It is even more wonderful to view God's trinitarian commitment to us against the black background of Revelation. As believers, we are trinitarian not only in our beliefs but also in our experience of God and salvation. We are Christians because we have come to the Father through Jesus the Son by the Holy Spirit. We are baptized into the name of the Father, Son, and Holy Spirit. We are blessed in the name of the Father, Son, and Holy Spirit. Oh, that people would speak more of the triune God, and exalt Him more as Father, Son, and Holy Spirit!

A biblical experience of salvation is a trinitarian experience. Our Lord Jesus Christ came to this earth to bear witness to His Father in heaven. Peter says Jesus died, "the just for the unjust, that he might bring us to God" (1 Peter 3:18), and our experience should reflect that. That is what salvation is all about. It is not to make us

Jesus's people but to make us *God's* people. We should know and enjoy all three Persons of the blessed Trinity.

Throughout this salutation, John is saying that there is no trial in your life that the triune God is not fully equipped to deal with. He was, He is, and He is to come. He is the sevenfold Holy Spirit. He is Jesus Christ, who has faithfully borne witness of God. We may ask how we sinful, broken, fragile sinners can be brought through this sin-sick world to everlasting glory, but John's salutation provides us with the answer: God the Father, the Son, and the Spirit have said with one accord, "Let Us give all Our resources to every single one of Our children to bring them safely through whatever befalls them to Our everlasting glory."

Revelation's Christ-Centered Doxology

As important as the Trinity is, Jesus Christ is central in John's vision. Having delivered the trinitarian salutation, John now breaks out in a doxology that centers upon Christ as our Savior: "Unto him that loved us, and washed us from our sins in his own blood, and hath made us kings and priests unto God and His Father; to him be glory and dominion for ever and ever. Amen. Behold, he cometh with clouds; and every eye shall see him, and they also which pierced him: and all kindreds of the earth shall wail because of him. Even so, Amen" (vv. 5–7). John is bursting out into praise to the One who brings blessing to us. He does this for the following reasons:

First, *He has suffered and died for our salvation.* John acknowledges that believers will suffer persecution even unto death, but what matters above all else is that Christ has set His love upon them. He has demonstrated that love supremely by washing them from their sins in His blood. All of us live with consciences that accuse us of guilt and shame. However, just as the blood of the old covenant sacrifice cleansed the Israelite so that he was no longer unclean in a physical sense, much more the blood of Christ washes the conscience of the believer spiritually clean so that he can worship God with freedom (Heb. 9:13–14). John says we may face even death with peace and grace because God loves us, and nothing in heaven, earth, or hell can change that. Jesus Christ has freed us from our sins by His blood. We are more free in prison bonds than our captors are in their apparent freedom.

Second, *He has made us kings and priests unto God.* Christ has given us the highest and noblest work—that of serving God as our Father in heaven. The ultimate aim of Jesus Christ is not to relieve us of unhappiness, although He frequently does that by His redeeming grace. His ultimate aim is not even to forgive us of sin. His ultimate aim is to produce an order of royal priests whose work is to serve, worship, honor, and praise the God and Father of our Lord Jesus Christ. This was God's calling upon ancient Israel (Ex. 19:6), and it is the privilege of the church of Jesus Christ (1 Peter 2:9).

Third, *He will come again in glory.* The words, "He cometh with clouds," allude to the promise of Daniel 7:13–14, "Behold, one like the Son of man came with the clouds of heaven, and came to the Ancient of days, and they brought him near before him. And there was given him dominion, and glory, and a kingdom." John is assuring believers that Jesus is coming; He is on His way. Mantled in clouds of divine glory, Christ will return to earth to judge every person who lives or has ever lived.

With His coming, we will experience a day of perfect salvation from Satan, this evil world, our old nature, and sin. There will be no more tears, pain, sorrow, temptation, night, or death. We will have perfect fellowship with Christ, and we will worship Him, serve Him, exercise authority with Him, and reign with Him. We will enjoy communion with our precious Bridegroom greater than what the angels, who have been in His presence for thousands of years, have ever known. We will know Christ, see Him, love Him, praise Him, and glorify Him forever.

When Christ returns to earth, every eye will see Him, even those who have pierced Him with sinful deeds, hard-hearted unbelief, and blatant rejection—just as the prophet Zechariah foretold (Zech. 12:10). Those who are not ready to meet Christ will be filled with fear at His coming. That fear will be justified, for the Lamb's wrath will burst forth on their heads. Too late they will discover the error of their ways. Then, as verse 7 says, "all kindreds of the earth shall wail because of him." What tragic words those are! All around the globe, millions of people reject the Lamb of God. Those unhappy people will weep and wail when Christ returns.

The concluding words of verse 7 underscore this truth. "Even so, Amen" declares the solemn truth of what John declares. A great, collective cry of grief will go up from unbelievers when Jesus summons them to His throne to be judged by Him! Will you also wail when you remember how you have slighted Christ, despised Him, rebelled against Him, rejected His salvation, and refused to live for Him? James Ramsey writes, "Christ rejected, an offered salvation neglected, a day of grace wasted, this is the thing that will give the lost sinner his keenest anguish, and wring from him at the last a bitterer wail than devils ever uttered."[8]

Unless you receive the testimony and authority of our Lord Jesus Christ, you cannot be saved. He is the great prophet of our God. He has come to instruct us. He is the Faithful Witness, the First Begotten of the Dead, and Prince of the Kings of the Earth. He is at the Father's right hand in glory, exercising dominion over all things in heaven and on earth. God has highly exalted Christ Jesus and given Him a name above every name. He is on the throne of the universe and will be there until all His enemies are made His footstool. He says, "All authority in heaven and earth is given to me."

All the resources of that government are committed to our salvation. Everyone whom the Father has given to Christ will be presented faultless before the Father's throne. Christ is committed to that. He rules the world. He controls everything in government, economics, politics, and society so that He might exercise His glory and dominion for the salvation of believers. But now John warns believers that something awful will happen to them. Domitian, the Roman emperor, will torture and kill Christians. It will look as though the end is coming. But all the while, Jesus will still be in

---

8. James R. Ramsey, *Revelation* (1873; reprint, Edinburgh: Banner of Truth Trust, 1977), 56.

control. While it lasts, Domitian's reign of terror will be turned to the profit of every Christian, and in the end, Christ will arise and deliver His people from it. "To him be glory and dominion forever and ever" (v. 6b).

Revelation's Promise of Eternal Security

In verse 8 of our text, we read, "I am Alpha and Omega, the beginning and the ending, saith the Lord which is, and which was, and which is to come, the Almighty." With these words, Christ Jesus stakes His claim upon history. He puts history in its place, setting it in the context of God's eternal purpose and showing how it is accomplished in Him. At every point, from start to finish, Christ is Lord of history. He was present at the beginning and is at work through all time in the lives of men, the affairs of nations, the rise and fall of civilizations, and the cycles of nature. And when time has run its course, He will write the final chapter and give final disposition to all things. He makes three claims:

First, *Christ is Alpha and Omega*. In the Greek alphabet, the first letter is *alpha* and the last is *omega*. These two letters take on a meaning of their own. In Revelation 1:8, they are used to define "the beginning and the ending," and in Revelation 1:11, "the first and the last." *Alpha*, then, has come to mean "the beginning, the origin, or the first cause." When Christ says He is Alpha, he is saying that wherever there is a beginning, He is there, creating a world, calling a people, gathering a church, and founding a kingdom.

But Christ is also the Omega of history. *Omega* has come to mean "the goal at which all things must arrive." It is last in terms of finality, fullness, and consummation. As the Omega of salvation, Christ Jesus will save us to the uttermost. He will finish the work He has begun in us. He who gives you grace to live will give you grace to die, for He is your end as well as your beginning. He will accomplish all of His purposes for you, fulfill all His promises of love made to you, and carry out all His counsels of infinite wisdom for you.

He [Christ] will complete what He begins
To save from sorrows and from sins;
The work that Jehovah undertakes
Jehovah-Jesus ne'er forsakes.[9]

Second, *Christ is the everlasting Lord.* John goes on to say that Christ "is, and…was, and…is to come." The Lord Jesus has the same eternal divine nature as God the Father (v. 4). John thereby links Christ to time and history at every point, as does Hebrews 13:8: "Jesus Christ the same yesterday, and to day, and for ever." This gives us three great comforts:

1. *Christ's divine powers and Person never change.* The wisdom He displayed in creation, His power and faithfulness in upholding all things, His grace and mercy in redemption—all are eternal and unchangeable aspects of His being.

2. *Christ's special qualities as our Savior never change.* These include His love for God, His faithfulness to us, His obedience, His compassion for the fallen, and His willingness to receive sinners and die for their salvation. He will ever be our merciful High Priest. If we truly believe this, we can embrace all our yesterdays, with their afflictions, through Christ by faith. We can yield all our todays, with their formidable obstacles, to Christ with love. And we can face all our tomorrows, with fears of the unknown, looking to Christ in hope.

3. *The comfort that we have in Christ never changes.* People change from year to year, even from day to day. That is not true of Christ, who was, who is, and who is to come! He is constantly devoted to His Father, steadfast and abundant in His labors, true to His Word, and faithful to His people. Praise God that the Lord of history was and is the same Lord who will come on the clouds as the Almighty!

If Christ is unchangeable as the Son of God, we may submit our lives to Him (Job 23:13–14), set our hopes on His promises (Ps. 33:11), and commit our plans to Him (Prov. 19:21), while expecting

---

9. *The Gospel Advocate, for Promoting Spiritual Unity,* ed. Andrew Joseph Baxter, 16, no. 169 (January 1884):76.

eternal blessings from Him (Heb. 6:17–18) and believing that He will always work for our good (James 1:16–18). How futile, then, it is to challenge Him, His Word, His people, or Christianity itself (1 Sam. 15:29; Num. 23:19; Heb. 1:10–12; 2:1) when we may live by the immutability of the Lord who is, was, and is to come.

Third, *Christ is almighty and omnipotent over history.* In our English Bible, Christ describes Himself as "the Almighty" by using the Greek word *Pantokrator*, meaning "ruler of all," and in the Old Testament by using *El Shaddai*, or "God Almighty." As *El Shaddai* and *Pantokrator*, Christ wields the very might of God to bring all things into subjection to Himself as God's anointed King and "governor among the nations" (Ps. 22:28).

Christ is Lord and Master of history, never its slave or pawn. Whatever powers oppose Him, Christ will prevail. This claim is central to Revelation. Though the power of Christ is contested, He masters all the powers of creation, puts His enemies to flight, conquers the world, establishes His kingdom, condemns the wicked, and brings His loved ones safely home to God.

This is good news for the poor and needy, the oppressed and the downtrodden, and the helpless and the weak. It assures believers who, by grace, trust that the gates of hell shall not prevail against the church, for her Head is the Almighty, the *Pantokrator*, who wields supreme power. The Lord of history is Lord over every detail of your life. He has numbered every hair of your head. Christ loves you too much to let you go your own way. He meets your every need every day. Sometimes this is hard for you to believe. You look at the confusion in the world, in the church, and in your soul, and nothing makes sense. It seems as if Satan is lord of all rather than Christ. But that is not true. Christ, as *El Shaddai* and *Pantokrator*, is still building His church. Sinners are still being saved and saints are still growing in grace.

Though the battle rages between our *Pantokrator* and His archenemy, Satan, Christ is mightier than Satan, for He is God. In the holy warfare that transpires every day in the world, in the church, and in our souls, we should not expect a life of ease. Even though the church often looks like a messy building site that includes piles of bricks and boards, ugly trenches, waste, rubble, and scattered tools, Christ is still building the church. He promises, "I will build my church; and the gates of hell shall not prevail against it" (Matt. 16:18).

Before complaining about the messiness of the church, we should consider the growth process of every believer. Every one of us is under construction. Some of us are not very impressive; we have a long way to go. Our faith may be true, but it is not strong. Even after being a Christian more than forty years, I am ashamed at how easily I can stumble into sin. But my hope is that my Savior, who came in the fullness of time to suffer and die for me, rose from the dead to justify me, ascended into heaven to intercede for me, sent His Spirit to work salvation in my soul, and even now preserves me day by day, is *the Almighty*. He is Lord of all history, but He is also the Lord of my personal history. So as surely as He will bring this world to perfection in the Great Day, so He will bring me to perfection as a believer. He who has begun a good work in me will finish it. When He comes again, I will be His finished product.

We may have things in our lives that have deeply broken us. We carry many burdens and wounds. People forget that we have these wounds, but we are still struggling. How can we find the strength to live for Jesus Christ in a world where sins seem to multiply? The answer is that Christ is *El Shaddai* and *Pantokrator*, the Almighty, who can sustain us both in this life and that to come. He is our eternal security.

In closing, let me ask you if you have received the Lord Jesus Christ as the faithful witness. No one can be saved apart from His testimony. You cannot be saved without believing and appropriating what Jesus said about Himself, about God, and about you. Hear what He has to say about the way of salvation and consider how He sealed His words with the shedding of His blood. Pray for grace to believe in Him, and be saved by Him, so that you too can say, "To him be glory and dominion for ever and ever. Amen" (v. 6b).

3

First Vision: Christ among the Seven Candlesticks

REVELATION 1:9–20

I John, who also am your brother, and companion in tribulation, and in the kingdom and patience of Jesus Christ, was in the isle that is called Patmos, for the word of God, and for the testimony of Jesus Christ. I was in the Spirit on the Lord's day, and heard behind me a great voice, as of a trumpet, saying, I am Alpha and Omega, the first and the last: and, What thou seest, write in a book, and send it unto the seven churches which are in Asia; unto Ephesus, and unto Smyrna, and unto Pergamos, and unto Thyatira, and unto Sardis, and unto Philadelphia, and unto Laodicea. And I turned to see the voice that spake with me. And being turned, I saw seven golden candlesticks; and in the midst of the seven candlesticks one like unto the Son of man, clothed with a garment down to the foot, and girt about the paps with a golden girdle. His head and his hairs were white like wool, as white as snow; and his eyes were as a flame of fire....

The first great vision in Revelation is one of many, but the drama of this first vision surfaces repeatedly throughout the book. We find this vision in Revelation 1:9–20. John tells us in verses 9 and 10 that on one occasion during his exile on the island of Patmos,[1] he "was in the Spirit on the Lord's Day." This is the first reference in Scripture to the Christian Sabbath as the *Lord's Day* (cf. Mark 2:28). Note that it is the *Lord's Day*, not the *Day of the Lord*. Some

---

1. For Revelation's historical setting with John on Patmos, see the beginning of chapter 2.

scholars wrongly say John is being carried forward in a vision to the day of judgment. Not so—John is relating what he sees on a particular Lord's Day, the first day of the week.

These verses give us more than a description of John's spiritual state of mind on this Lord's Day. In exile on Patmos, John's thoughts turn to his brothers and sisters in Christ to whom he had ministered on the mainland. As John prays about these people, something remarkable happens to him. He is taken up in the Spirit, lifted out of the realm of time and space, so that he may see heavenly things.

Let me illustrate this. Nearly all of us have been in airplanes. We fly over large cities, seeing people below who move like tiny ants and cars that scurry about like ladybugs. How small everything looks from the heights above!

This is similar to what John experienced. On earth, in time and space, we do not know what the future will bring. But John says God lifted him up to see a heavenly vision of the church, represented as candlesticks or lampstands. In that vision, God showed John the whole sweep of church history, from beginning to end. God doesn't have to wonder what lies around the next corner; He already knows. He sees everything at a glance. "Known unto God are all his works from the beginning of the world" (Acts 15:18). This is what John experiences while "in the Spirit on the Lord's day." He is given an unforgettable view of the church, the world, and reality. The book of Revelation is exciting because it lets us see this same view. John sees things as God sees them, and we see them through John.

In the first vision, John says, "I was in the Spirit on the Lord's day, and heard behind me a great voice, as of a trumpet, saying, I am Alpha and Omega, the first and the last…what thou seest, write in a book, and send it unto the seven churches which are in Asia…. And I turned to see the voice that spake with me" (Rev. 1:10–12a). John had often heard the voice of the Lord Jesus when Christ was among the twelve on earth. But this voice is so very different. It is a great voice, much like a trumpet. It is a strange voice, yet there is something recognizable about it. When John turns around to see who is speaking, he says, "Being turned, I saw seven golden candlesticks; and in the midst of the seven candlesticks was one like unto the Son of man" (vv. 12b–13a). There then follows a fantastic description of this man (vv. 13b–16).

John offers us a word picture here, not an artist's impression. Some people have tried to paint this description of Christ, and the results have been absurd. You cannot and should not try to produce a picture of Christ in any way.[2]

God was wise to send His Son in human flesh before the age of the camera, videotape, and the Internet. He came before it was possible for us to make a permanent record of His physical appearance. We are not meant to have such information. Whatever else you do, do not think about Christ's physical appearance. John wants to tell us *who* Jesus is, not *what* He looks like. So this vision is not to be understood literally. How can you paint a man whose head is white like wool or as snow and whose eyes are as flames of fire? How can you paint a face shining like the noonday sun? Feet that burn as brass in a furnace? A hand great enough to hold seven stars? A mouth out of which goes a two-edged sword? We are meant to understand this vision scripturally and spiritually so that we may know who and what our Lord Jesus Christ is.

So let us examine this word picture of Christ, looking at it in three ways: (1) the identity of Christ in verses 12–16; (2) the impact Christ has on John in verses 17–18; and (3) the interpretation of this vision in verses 19–20.

Christ's Identity Established

John's vision includes a description of Christ's clothing, head, hair, eyes, feet, voice, right hand, mouth, and face. But again, we should resist the temptation of probing these features in detail, for if we did so, we would lose the overall effect of this vision. We need first to regard it as a whole to see just whom it is that John beholds. Bearing this in mind, here is what John sees:

---

2. See Heidelberg Catechism, LD 35, Q. 96–98, in *Three Forms of Unity*, 94.

First, he sees *Christ as the Son of man*. John says that he saw "one like unto the Son of man" (v. 13). "Son of man" was one of our Lord's favorite titles for Himself. The New Testament refers eighty-one times to the Son of man, and in all but a few places, our Lord is speaking about Himself. Liberals have misunderstood Jesus's use of the term, saying He was trying to impress on people that He was only human. Indeed, some evangelicals also make that mistake. They say "Son of God" refers to Christ's deity, while "Son of man" refers exclusively to His humanity; but this is not the true meaning of "Son of man." When our Lord uses this title, it is loaded with Messianic connotations from the Old Testament, where the title is introduced in Daniel 7:13–14.

At His crucifixion trial, when Christ identifies Himself as the Son of man, the reaction of the high priest is stunning. Scripture says that after tearing his clothes, the priest asks: "What need we any further witnesses? Ye have heard the blasphemy: what think ye?" (Mark 14:63–64a). Everyone present then condemns Jesus to death (v. 64b). The high priest understands that by calling Himself the Son of man, Jesus is declaring Himself to be the Son of God. He is saying: "Yes, I am the Christ; I am the Son of the blessed God. And I tell you something else: I am the Son of man prophesied by Daniel. I am the Son of man who will come in the clouds of God's divine and heavenly glory."

Notice that John says, "I saw...one *like* unto the Son of man." John knew the Lord intimately here on earth. John was called the disciple whom Jesus loved, implying a special relationship between John the man and Jesus the man. They were close friends. John was part of the inner circle of disciples. But when John says, as he gazes into heaven, that he saw "one *like* unto the Son of man," he is saying, in effect: "There is something both familiar and yet different about the One I see. He has changed beyond all recognition, yet I recognize Him." That is what John means when he says the person he sees is "like unto the Son of man." He says, "I see Jesus, but oh, He is so exalted, so magnificent, so glorious, that I can scarcely believe my eyes."

If we are believers, we too will be changed in glory. We will have new bodies like Christ's glorified body. We will have souls made perfect in holiness. We will see Jesus as He is, and we will be like Him! We will be gloriously changed, yet we will still be ourselves, and those who are with us in heaven will recognize us.

Second, John sees *Christ as the Great High Priest.* When John turns to see who is speaking to him, he sees one like the Son of man standing in the midst of seven candlesticks, which are symbols of His churches (Rev. 1:20). That is hinted at in Matthew 5:15, where Jesus says, "Neither do men light a candle, and put it under a bushel, but on a candlestick; and it giveth light unto all that are in the house." (The Greek word translated "candlestick" in these texts literally refers to the stand for an oil lamp.) Christ has kindled these lights and placed them on the lampstands, and He continues to tend the lamps, trimming their wicks and refueling them with the oil of the Spirit so they continue to burn brightly. The image is of the priest in the temple, tending the golden lampstands so that their light burns continually (Ex. 25:31; Lev. 24:1–4). What John sees is the exalted and heavenly Christ in relationship to His church on earth, caring for her and upholding her so that her light continues to shine in the darkness of this world.

How wonderful it is to know that our exalted, glorious, majestic Savior is also our Great High Priest "that is passed into the heavens, Jesus the Son of God" (Heb. 4:14). As the propitiation for our sins, He presents His crucified body to the Father as a perpetual memorial that He has fully satisfied for all our sins with His precious blood. As our Advocate with the Father, He ever lives to make intercession for us, pleading the merits of His shed blood.

As He walks among the churches, Christ's head and hair are white with holiness and purity (cf. Dan. 7:9). His holiness is the perfect holiness of the living God: "Holy, holy, holy, is the LORD of hosts: the whole earth is full of his glory" (Isa. 6:3). By contrast, we read about fallen man's lack of holiness in Isaiah 1:18: "Come now, and let us reason together, saith the LORD: though your sins be as scarlet, they shall be as white as snow; though they be red like crimson, they shall be as wool."

Note the two extremes. Man's depravity and sin is one extreme, staining him with guilt that is red like crimson. Sin is not just a stain on the surface of our lives; it has penetrated the very fabric of our nature. We cannot eradicate it because it is part of our being as the offspring of fallen Adam. Yet Scripture promises us that though our sin is red as crimson, we can be washed in the blood of Christ and become as white as snow. Total depravity gives way to perfect holiness. Our sins are covered by the perfect righteousness and holiness of Christ, and in God's eyes, we are accounted as He is, without spot or blemish.

What a wonder that is! Recently, I was visiting a family when a young lady tipped over a glass containing a red beverage onto a white carpet. The women of the home sprang into action, using various cleansing solutions and a ton of energy to rub out the stains. Despite their best efforts, they could not make the carpet white again. When it comes to the scarlet stain of sin, only Jesus Christ, the Great High Priest, can make us white as snow.

Third, John sees *Christ as the Heavenly Messenger.* The Lord appears as One "clothed with a garment down to the foot, and girt about the paps [chest] with a golden girdle." In the prophecy of Daniel, an angelic messenger appeared to Daniel clothed in gold and with "eyes as lamps of fire" and "feet like in colour to polished brass" (Dan. 10:5–6). By using similar imagery, Christ declared Himself to be the messenger of heaven, the Revealer of God's glory come to grant knowledge to the beloved of the Lord.

Fourth, John sees *Christ as Almighty God.* As John looks at Christ, he perceives that He is God. He says, "His head and his hairs were white like wool, as white as snow." Very similar words appear in Daniel 7:9: "I beheld till the thrones were cast down, and the Ancient of days did sit, whose garment was white as snow, and the hair of his head like the pure wool: his throne was like the fiery flame, and his wheels as burning fire." Daniel sees the Ancient of days and the Son of man as distinct persons: "I saw in the night visions, and, behold, one like the Son of man came with the clouds of heaven, and came to the Ancient of days, and they brought him near before him. And there was given him dominion, and glory, and a kingdom" (vv. 13–14a). Daniel says, in effect: "I saw the Ancient of days, and His head and His hair were white like wool. I saw the Son of man, who came to the Ancient of days." We would identify them as the Father and the Son. But John doesn't see the Ancient of days and the Son of man as separate; he sees that the Son of man *is* the Ancient of days. This teaches us that the Father and the Son are one God.

Fifth, John sees *Christ as the righteous Judge.* Verses 14b–16 say of Christ, "His eyes were as a flame of fire; and his feet like unto fine brass, as if they burned in a furnace; and his voice as the sound of many waters. And he had in his right hand seven stars: and out of his mouth went a sharp twoedged sword: and his countenance was as the sun shineth in his strength." All of these word pictures point to Christ as the coming Judge:

1. John says, "his eyes were as a flame of fire" (v. 14b). Christ's eyes are like laser beams penetrating the heart of His church and its people. John here is telling us that the light of Christ's omniscient gaze allows nothing to be hidden from Him. He is the eternal God, dazzling in holiness and purity, and He sees everything. The psalmist cries out, "If thou, LORD, shouldest mark iniquities, O Lord, who shall stand?" (Ps. 130:3). The prophet Malachi asks: "Who may abide the day of his coming? And who shall stand when he appeareth?" (Mal. 3:2).

A radio commentator once asked a guest, "Do you believe in God?" The man answered: "I don't know whether there is a God and I don't really care, but if there is a God and if there is a day of judgment, I'll have a thing or two to say to Him. When I look at everything that has gone wrong in this world, I'll stand before God, and ask Him my questions, looking Him in the eye." Oh, my friend, who could stand and look into those burning eyes? Who would dare to so much as lift up his head in the presence of such a righteous Judge?

2. John looks at Jesus's feet, saying they were "like unto fine brass, as if they burned in a furnace" (v. 15a). Brass must be purified in a furnace and then thoroughly burnished to shine with its customary luster. Here, too, is an image of purity and perfection. Perfect in holiness from head to foot, with white-as-wool hair, laser-like eyes, and burnished feet, Jesus, the Son of man, is coming to judge the world in righteousness.

3. John says Christ's voice is "as the sound of many waters" (v. 15b). It is like the crashing of the surf against the rocks of Patmos. His voice is the ultimate, definitive, authoritative voice of judgment day. We will be speechless as He pronounces His verdict, for His voice will be "as the sound of many waters." "The voice of the LORD is powerful; the voice of the LORD is full of majesty" (Ps. 29:4).

4. John says, Christ has in His right hand seven stars (v. 16a). These stars are His messengers or servants (Rev. 1:20; 2:1), for whose immediate benefit these things are being written in a book (Rev. 1:1). We must realize that whenever we hear a faithful preacher of God's Word, we are hearing the servant of Christ, and will be judged according to our response. Christ gave warning of this very thing in Mark 4:23–25: "If any man have ears to hear, let him hear…. Take heed what ye hear: with what measure ye mete, it shall be measured to you: and unto you that hear shall more be given. For he that hath, to him shall be given: and he that hath not, from him shall be taken even that which he hath." The key to this warning is the biblical requirement to hear the Word with faith. To hear the Word without faith is only to add to your guilt and condemnation when you appear before the righteous Judge.

5. John says that out of Christ's mouth comes a "sharp twoedged sword" (v. 16b). The sword is a symbol of Christ's Word, full of life and power (Heb. 4:12; Isa. 49:2). Philip Hughes says: "The sword which is the Lord's word has two edges [so] it never fails to cut. If it does not cut with the edge of salvation, it cuts with the edge

of condemnation; for the word of redemption to all who believe is at the same time the word of destruction to those who refuse to believe."[3]

6. John says, the Son of man's face is as bright as the sun in full splendor (v. 16c). According to Charles Spurgeon, John sees an "inexpressible, indescribable, infinite splendour" on Christ's face, an "overpowering pre-eminence" that is "justly terrible" to the ungodly and "intensely joyful" for the godly.[4]

Who can stand before this righteous Judge? He is coming to judge the living and the dead. And He is none other than God's only begotten Son, Jesus Christ, the Son of man in His glorious and exalted state as the Great High Priest of His people, the Almighty God, and the Judge of all the earth.

Christ's Impact on John

It is almost impossible to convey all that John sees, but we can see something of the impact. John tells us in verse 17, "When I saw him, I fell at his feet as dead." When he sees his Master in the full glory of His exaltation, John is overwhelmed. We would expect John to be overjoyed to see his Savior again, but, no, he falls into a dead faint at the awesome glory of Christ. James, the half-brother of Christ, reflects a similar awe and esteem for his Lord. He refers to Jesus not as his brother, but as "the Lord of glory" (James 2:1).

We grieve the Holy Spirit when we take the name of Jesus lightly upon our lips. No New Testament writer would have done that. Certainly they wrote in their narratives that "Jesus did this or that." But when they approached Him in worship or prayer, they addressed Him as "the Lord Jesus Christ." As believers, we too know Jesus in a very personal way. However, we must never address Him or speak of Him in a way that detracts from His glory. He is

---

3. Philip Edgcumbe Hughes, *The Book of Revelation, A Commentary* (Grand Rapids: Eerdmans, 1990), 27.

4. Charles H. Spurgeon, *Metropolitan Tabernacle Pulpit* (Pasadena, Tex.: Pilgrim, 1969), 43:9.

infinitely more than a personal friend of ours; He is the Lord and Master of the universe.

John was a cherished friend of Jesus while He was on this earth, but John is not yet prepared to look upon Christ as the glorified Son of man. Paul says in 1 Corinthians 15:50 that flesh and blood cannot inherit the kingdom of heaven. This means that we cannot enter the kingdom of God or look upon God in His glory as earthly creatures. To do that, we must have souls made perfect in holiness and resurrected bodies like Christ's. God told Moses no man can see God's face and live (Ex. 33:20). After we die and go to heaven, we will understand why even John, though a holy man, was yet unable to look upon the glorified Christ without falling down "as dead" (v. 17a). John was a dear child of God, but he was still a sinner. We look up to New Testament saints such as John, Peter, and Paul, yet we must remember that they too were men like us. They still battled sin and corruption. So John could not look upon this revelation of the risen and exalted Christ without fear.

We see similar reactions throughout the Old Testament when God appears to people such as Abraham, Moses, Elijah, Job, and Isaiah. In Isaiah 6, the glory of God is revealed to Isaiah in the temple. The prophet cries out, "Woe is me! for I am undone; because I am a man of unclean lips, and I dwell in the midst of a people of unclean lips" (v. 5). Likewise, when God appears to Elijah on Mount Horeb, the prophet covers his face with a mantle (1 Kings 19:13).

Daniel had a vision of Christ similar to that of John. He says: "Therefore I was left alone, and saw this great vision, and there remained no strength in me: for my comeliness was turned in me into corruption, and I retained no strength. Yet heard I the voice of his words: and when I heard the voice of his words, then was I in a deep sleep on my face, and my face toward the ground" (Dan. 10:8–9). In describing the physical impact of this vision, Daniel is saying: "I became like a corpse. I was white as a sheet, and all my strength drained out of me. I fell to the ground like a dead man."

On the road to Damascus, Saul had the same experience. He encounters Christ, and "suddenly there shined round about him a light from heaven" (Acts 9:3). He sees "the glory of God in the face of Jesus Christ" (2 Cor. 4:6). The proud, self-righteous Pharisee responds to the sight of Christ by falling to the ground. Divine glory overwhelms earthly humanity; heavenly light is too much for earthly eyes. Saul is struck blind and must be led by the hand into the city of Damascus. Like all others who have truly seen the glory of Christ, Paul is humbled to the dust.

You are not a Christian unless you have experienced a sense of humiliation before the glory of the Lord. God's Word tells us we have not come into the presence of Christ until we have fallen on our faces before Him. You can clap your hands and sing at the top of your voice, but if you have never felt your unworthiness and sin in the presence of Christ, you have never seen Him at all.

Two wonderful truths are taught here. First, though John is overwhelmed by the glorified Christ, his response is different from that of an unbeliever. In Gethsemane, the enemies of Jesus fell backward in terror when Jesus declared His glory as "I am" (John 18:6). By contrast, John falls toward his Lord. He falls down at His feet. Enemies fall *away* from Christ, but His people fall *toward* Him.

Second, Christ does not leave believers to lie in the dust. Christ lays His right hand on His beloved disciple and says, "Fear not; I am the first and the last" (v. 17b). While He was on earth, Jesus laid His hands upon many people, healing them of sickness, disability, and sin. He could have just spoken a word and healed them, but He usually accompanied those words with the touch of His hand. With that touch, He conveyed that He loved those poor, wounded sinners.

When Jesus Christ touched sinners during His three-year ministry, He was in the state of humiliation. As the Man of Sorrows, He was one of us, bone of our bone. His Godhead was hidden. But even in His state of exaltation, He touches John as the Son of man. Though exalted as the King and Head of His church, Christ remembers what it was like to move among sinners and rub shoulders with them. So He reaches for John as if to say, "I understand your fear; I sympathize with your human weakness and your inability to take in this great revelation."

"Fear not!"—how often John heard Christ say those words. He heard them during the storm on the Sea of Galilee, on the Mount of Transfiguration, and when Christ first appeared to His disciples after His resurrection. Now, years later, John hears these same reassuring words from Christ as exalted King, "Fear not."

Those words are not only for John. They are also spoken to those who humble themselves before the Lord, those who suffer for the sake of Christ, those who endure hardships because of the gospel, and those who are distressed and discouraged. If your sins bring you to fall down at the feet of Jesus Christ, He will also say to you, "Fear not!" We must approach the holy and majestic God in fear and trembling. But the Lord then reveals Himself to us in mercy and says, "Fear not, I am the Savior."

He speaks about Himself for our comfort and that of the living church of all ages. He says, "I am the first and the last" (v. 17b), just as He said earlier, "I am Alpha and Omega, the beginning and the ending…the first and the last" (vv. 8, 11). John already understands part of this "I am" statement because he had already written in the first chapter of his Gospel, "In the beginning was the Word, and the Word was with God, and the Word was God" (John 1:1). So John already knows that Jesus was from the beginning. But he now realizes that Jesus is also the end of all things. Christ stands at the beginning of history as the Creator who made all things; but He will also appear as the Judge when everything comes to an end. In between, everything that happens is under His control. The grand theme of Revelation is that Christ is the King of kings who controls all things visible and invisible, all forces of nature, all affairs of men and nations, and every aspect of our lives.

Christ is the Alpha and the Omega of your salvation, too. He was the Alpha when He began His saving work in you, when He revealed Himself to you in His holiness and majesty, when He showed you your sins and misery, but also when He first brought you to faith and repentance. He began that good work in you. But He is also your Omega, meaning He will bring what He has started in you all the way to perfection (Phil. 1:6). All the while in between, from beginning to end, Christ provides for and protects His people, individually and as a body, in the church. He is the first and the last. Fear not.

Christ goes on to say, "I am he that liveth, and was dead; and, behold, I am alive for evermore, Amen" (Rev. 1:18a). He is reminding John of His death and resurrection in order to assure John that the Master whom John knew and loved on earth is the same exalted One who stands before him now. Christ endured death because God required it. But when Christ died, He overcame death. He rose from the dead so that now He can say, "I am alive forevermore." So now He assures John: "Behold, I am alive. You know I did not stay in that grave because you saw Me after My resurrection, but now I repeat this again for your comfort: *I am alive forevermore. Amen.*" The word *Amen* here is a resounding affirmation of the truth of Jesus's statement. Jesus says He is alive forevermore, so no one need ever lose the hope of eternal life.

Then He says, "[I] have the keys of hell and of death." Hell in this place is used to translate the Greek word Hades, understood as the grave, the state of the dead, and the power of death. In Greek, the place of eternal punishment is Gehenna, an entirely different word. When Christ says, "I have the keys of Hades," He reminds us that the wages of sin is death. Death is a prison where sinners must endure confinement under the power of death, with no hope of escape. But now Jesus says: "The devil tells people that he wields the power of death, and has taken everyone captive to it, but that is not true. I have the keys of Hades and of death." A key both locks and unlocks a door. Jesus says: "I lock the door when My people go into the grave at my command, but I will also unlock that door so they may come out. My people will not abide under the power of death, but will come out of their graves to be with Me, to live with Me forever."

Now Jesus tells John to write down the things "which thou hast seen, and the things which are, and the things which shall be hereafter" (v. 19), so that the church may receive instruction and comfort. To have this comfort we must be like John, who trembles before the resurrected and glorified Christ. Do we have personal knowledge of Christ? Have you experienced the bond of love to the Savior? Are you His? If the Lord Jesus Christ is going to *reconstruct* our lives and make us like Himself, He must first *deconstruct* us. He must break us in pieces, then transform us into glorious creatures remade in His image. Are you a child of God? Do you live for Him and suffer for His name?

Today few people tremble before God. Few are willing to endure suffering for His name's sake. My friend, if you have never trembled before God, you will tremble very soon when the Lord takes you. Then you will be brought face to face with the One whom John saw in His glorious revelation, but then it will be too late. God will say: "Depart from Me, ye cursed. If you have never learned to tremble here, never learned to seek Me and give your life to Me and say farewell to the world for My sake, then you will tremble forever."

Christ's Interpretation of This Vision

The vision given to John is not meant to terrify believers, but to encourage us. Look at the last two verses in our text: "Write the things which thou hast seen, and the things which are, and the things which shall be hereafter; the mystery of the seven stars which thou sawest in my right hand, and the seven golden candlesticks. The seven stars are the angels of the seven churches: and the seven candlesticks which thou sawest are the seven churches" (vv. 19–20). Jesus is saying to John: "You have seen this vision and felt its impact. Now I will explain what it is all about."

The vision is about the church. The seven stars are the seven "angels" or "messengers" of the church. People differ over how to interpret this, but I don't see how it can refer to anyone other than a minister of the gospel. John is instructed to write down the visions he sees and give them to the messengers sent to the churches. The word translated as "angels" in the King James Version is sometimes used in Scripture to refer to supernatural beings, that is, angels sent from heaven. But it also is used to refer to human messengers, such as prophets or preachers of the Word.[5]

Jesus Christ is saying that ministers have been given a heavenly work to do in bringing the Word of God to His people. Our forefathers, particularly the Puritans, made much of this. James Janeway writes, "His ministers are sent to do the work of inferior angels, to preach glad tidings of great joy."[6] Cotton Mather says that if you bring the gospel to those in the shadow of death, your ministry "will do the work, and give you the welcome, of a good angel unto them."[7] In this he echoed the apostle Paul's statement that the Galatians once welcomed him "as an angel of God, even as Christ Jesus" (Gal. 4:14).

These writers were referring to the basic meaning of the Hebrew and Greek words, which link angels and ministers ultimately to Christ as the Angel of the Covenant (Mal. 3:1).[8] The Hebrew word *malak* and the Greek word *angelos* are usually translated as *angel* in the English Bible, and both mean "messenger." Thus, the Old Testament priest who taught God's Word was "the messenger [literally, 'angel'] of the LORD of hosts" (Mal. 2:7).[9] The name of the prophet Malachi means "My Angel" or "My Messenger."

The Puritans also found evidence of the angelic nature of a pastor's calling in Revelation 2, where each of the seven letters is addressed to the "angel" of the church (Rev. 2:1, 8, etc.).[10] William Fenner reasons that these angels could not be the angels in heaven because they are sometimes rebuked for faults. They could not be fallen angels, either, because they are sometimes commended. He

---

5. Mal. 2:7; 3:1; Matt. 11:10; Mark 1:2; Luke 7:24; 9:52; James 2:25.

6. James Janeway, *The Saints' Encouragement* (Pittsburgh: Soli Deo Gloria, 1994), 43.

7. Cotton Mather, *Bonifacius: An Essay upon the Good* (Cambridge: Harvard University Press, 1966), 74.

8. *The Complete Works of Thomas Manton* (London: James Nisbet, 1871), 10:468.

9. James Durham, *Commentary upon the Book of the Revelation* (Willow Street, Pa.: Old Paths, 2000), 63.

10. Matthew Poole, *A Commentary on the Whole Bible* (Peabody, Mass.: Hendrickson, n.d.), 3:952.

says, "It remains then, that a metaphorical angel is here understood as the minister of the church."[11]

Other Puritans confirm this interpretation by citing Revelation 14:6, in which an angel in heaven preaches the everlasting gospel to every nation. James Durham comments: "The angels are ministering spirits, sent forth to minister to the heirs of salvation (Heb. 1:14), but they do not have the everlasting gospel to preach. This treasure is put in earthen vessels so that the excellence of its power may be of God (2 Cor. 4:7)." Likewise, "ministers are called angels because they are God's messengers, entrusted with a high and heavenly employment."[12] Matthew Poole (1624–1679) writes, "This angel seems to me to represent faithful ministers' speed and diligence to preach the gospel in all parts of the world."[13]

Puritan writers identified the following points of likeness between angels and ministers:

First, *they both study God's mysteries.* Benjamin Keach writes, "Angels desire to pry into the mysteries of grace and mercy in Jesus Christ (1 Peter 1:12). Christ's true ministers also make it their business to dig into the hidden mysteries."[14]

---

11. William Fenner, *Christs Alarm to Drowsie Saints* (London: for John Rothwell, 1650), 6. Fenner realized that at least some of these churches had more than one elder (Acts 20:17). He interpreted the singular "angel" to refer to the ministers collectively, implying that they should stand together in unity (p. 19). So also Durham, "By *angels* we understand all the bishops and presbyters that were over those churches.... Therefore take we the style *angel*, to be collective...*ministers* of such a church" (*Commentary upon the Book of the Revelation*, 63–64).

12. Durham, *Commentary upon the Book of the Revelation*, 736. In Durham's historicist interpretation, the angels of Revelation 14 represent the preaching of the gospel and shaking of the kingdom of the Roman Babylon, that is, the Roman Catholic Church, by the Reformers like Luther. See also Goodwin, "An Exposition of Revelation," in *The Works of Thomas Goodwin* (Grand Rapids: Reformation Heritage Books, 2006), 3:86–88.

13. Poole, *Commentary on the Whole Bible*, 987. See also Arthur Dent, *The Ruine of Rome, or, An Exposition vpon the whole Revelation* (London: by N. O. for Simon Waterson, 1633), 271.

14. Benjamin Keach, *Preaching from the Types and Metaphors of the Bible* (Grand Rapids: Kregel, 1972), 828.

Second, *they are both God's servants*. Angels do not come to men unless God sends them, Fenner says. Likewise, ministers may not serve unless they are sent by God (John 1:6; Rom. 10:15).[15] As angels fly to do God's will (Isa. 6:6), ministers also must heed the command to bring in the harvest (John 4:38).[16] Keach writes, "Angels are very obedient to God, they do his commands, and wait for his word. The faithful preachers of the gospel are very ready to obey God's commands; though they are thereby exposed to great danger, if God bids them go, they go (Rom. 1:15)."[17]

Third, *they both serve the church*. God sends angels to minister to the heirs of salvation (Heb. 1:14). Likewise, Fenner says, ministers exist for the good of the church of Jesus Christ (1 Cor. 3:22).[18] They work mainly for God's elect.[19]

Fourth, *they both comfort the downcast*. Keach writes: "Angels are often sent to comfort the saints when cast down, as they ministered to Christ in his agony. So are gospel preachers sent to comfort the feeble-minded[20] [those given to doubt and indecision], and support the weak; they know how to comfort others with the same comfort whereby they themselves are comforted of God (2 Cor. 1:4)."[21]

So our Lord is saying to John that the seven stars in his vision are seven gospel preachers, and the seven candlesticks are the seven churches they serve. Though these churches face a hostile environment that threatens their very existence, Christ is in their midst. He commends their graces, comforts them in their sufferings, rebukes their faults, calls their members to repentance, warns them of judgment to come, commands them to cast out the unrepentant who live in sin, exhorts them to persevere in the grace He supplies, and

---

15. Fenner, *Christs Alarm to Drowsie Saints*, 9.

16. Fenner, *Christs Alarm to Drowsie Saints*, 12–13.

17. Keach, *Types and Metaphors*, 828.

18. Fenner, *Christs Alarm to Drowsie Saints*, 9.

19. Fenner, *Christs Alarm to Drowsie Saints*, 16.

20. See 1 Thessalonians 5:14; W.E. Vine prefers the translation, "fainthearted." See *An Expository Dictionary of New Testament Words* (Old Tappan, N.J.: Fleming H. Revell, 1940), 70.

21. Keach, *Types and Metaphors*, 829.

holds forth the promise of great reward. The church will always shine in the midst of all the darkness of this world, for Christ is ever with her.

A Fourfold Comfort

Let us conclude this chapter with four comforts that we find in John's first vision:

First, *Christ comforts His church.* The true church has no reason to fear the present or the future, for all is safe in our Lord's hands. Our divine, glorious, exalted Prophet, Priest, and King is with His church to the very end of time itself. He has every situation under control. He will ever be the defender of His people. He promises, "Lo, I am with you alway, even unto the end of the world" (Matt. 28:20).

Second, *Christ enables His church to shine in the world.* In the Old Testament sanctuary, the lamps on the candlestick burned continuously. Likewise, Jesus says to us, "Ye are the light of the world" (Matt. 5:14). The church may not merge into the background of this dark world. We are told to stand out, shine forth, and be different because we are new creatures in Christ. If there is no difference between believers and unbelievers, why should people take notice of the gospel? Christ's presence will not allow that, for He makes the church shine. He stands in the midst of the lampstands. He fills them with the oil of the Holy Spirit (Zech. 4:1–7). Even when He rebukes the faults of His church, He also tells her members to ask Him for whatever they need. He says, "I counsel thee to buy of me gold tried in the fire, that thou mayest be rich; and white raiment, that thou mayest be clothed, and that the shame of thy nakedness do not appear; and anoint thine eyes with eyesalve, that thou mayest see" (Rev. 3:18). In her lowest state, the church is not beyond the power of Christ to raise her up and restore her to health and strength, that she might shine once more in the darkness of this world.

Third, *Christ is jealous for His church, for she professes His name.* He will not indulge her in any error, weakness, sin, or folly. Often in Israel's history, God's wrath broke out against ungodliness in Israel, the professing church of God, to show the whole world that the name of God and His holy things must not be trifled with.

Fourth, *Christ maintains His church*. Sometimes the church is expanding, sometimes diminishing. Christ will keep His church forever, even if only a remnant remains to serve Him (Ps. 22:30–31). The Belgic Confession says, "This Church hath been from the beginning of the world and will be unto the end thereof.... And this church is preserved or supported by God against the rage of the whole world; though she sometimes (for a while) appears very small, and in the eyes of men, as to be reduced to nothing."[22]

Christ's first vision to John teaches us that He is Almighty. He can save anyone; there are no hopeless cases with him. Spurgeon graphically portrayed this truth in a gripping story:

> I have read of a woman who prayed long for her husband. She used to attend a certain meeting-house in the north of England, but her husband never went with her. He was a drinking, swearing man, and she had much anguish of heart about him. She never ceased to pray, and yet she never saw any result. She went to the meeting-house quite alone, with this exception, that a dog always went with her, and this faithful animal would curl himself up under the seat and lie quiet during the service.
>
> When she was dead, her husband was still unsaved, but doggie went to the meeting-house. His master wondered whatever the faithful animal did at the service. Curiosity made him follow the good creature. The dog led him down the aisle to his dear old mistress's seat. The man sat on that seat, and the dog curled himself up as usual. God guided the minister that day; the word came with power, and that man wept till he found the Savior.
>
> Never give up your husbands, good women, for the Lord may even use a dog to bring them to Christ when you are dead and gone! Never give up praying, hoping and expecting. Fear not! Believe.[23]

---

22. The Belgic Confession, Art. 27, in *Three Forms of Unity*, 47.
23. Spurgeon, *Metropolitan Tabernacle Pulpit*, 26:234.

Today, there is little for tourists to see on the island of Patmos. But when the apostle John was there, he saw everything necessary for believers to continue to hope to the end, until Jesus Christ comes again. Let us thus turn with John to see who speaks to us, then worship the glorious, exalted Son of man, who says to those who trust in Him alone for salvation, "Fear not, I am the first and the last."

4

Christ's Message to a Church Whose Love Has Faded

REVELATION 2:1–7

Unto the angel of the church of Ephesus write; these things saith he that holdeth the seven stars in his right hand, who walketh in the midst of the seven golden candlesticks; I know thy works, and thy labour, and thy patience, and how thou canst not bear them which are evil: and thou hast tried them which say they are apostles, and are not, and hast found them liars: and hast borne, and hast patience, and for my name's sake hast laboured, and hast not fainted. Nevertheless I have somewhat against thee, because thou hast left thy first love. Remember therefore from whence thou art fallen, and repent, and do the first works; or else I will come unto thee quickly, and will remove thy candlestick out of his place, except thou repent. But this thou hast, that thou hatest the deeds of the Nicolaitans, which I also hate. He that hath an ear, let him hear what the Spirit saith unto the churches; to him that overcometh will I give to eat of the tree of life, which is in the midst of the paradise of God.

Wouldn't it be amazing if Jesus Himself would write a personal letter to you and your church evaluating your spiritual progress, telling you, in His great love, both your strengths and weaknesses, and then call you to some specific action? Wouldn't you be fascinated to hear such a letter read to your church?

Well, that is exactly what we have before us in Revelation 2 and 3—in fact, Jesus here presents us with seven such letters to various churches in Asia, each of which applies particularly to our own lives and the life of our churches today. Each of these fascinating letters, therefore, are extremely important for each of us. Let us listen carefully to Jesus, take His letters to heart, and by His grace, make some very important and necessary changes in our lives.

The seven churches of Asia named in the book of Revelation were real churches in real places. Those churches are named in Revelation chapters 2 and 3 in geographic order according to the circuitous route followed by a traveler. If you were a mailman delivering letters to those churches, you would pick a route that began at Ephesus. You would go to Smyrna next, then on to the other churches in the order given, ending up at Laodicea. These seven churches were also centers from which the letters could be further distributed to other churches of Asia in those days. The seven letters in Revelation addressed real-life situations and conditions in these churches, and were written to encourage the persecuted Christians of John's day.

The seven churches also represent Christ's universal church of all ages. The conditions described in these churches are found in churches everywhere and in all times. The New Testament itself is addressed to Christians of all ages. When we read Romans, we don't say, "This has nothing to do with me, but only the church in Rome of two thousand years ago." Yes, Romans was written to the church at Rome, but it also applies to believers today. That is true of all Scripture, including all the letters to the seven churches in Revelation. Thus, everything in these letters is for all of us, for all time.

Let us examine the first letter, the letter to the church in Ephesus, looking specifically at what our Lord *perceives* about this church, what He *prescribes* for this church, and how He *encourages* this church to receive His prescription.

Christ's Perception of the Church at Ephesus

Ephesus was a prominent city of two-hundred-thousand people. It was situated on a major trade route about fifty miles from Patmos, so it was the closest of the seven churches to where John wrote his letters. Ephesus was the center of the worship of Artemis (the Roman Diana, cf. Acts 19:24–35), twin sister of Apollo, and in Asia her identity had merged with the Phoenician goddess of fertility, Ashtoreth, mentioned in the Old Testament (1 Kings 11:5, 33;

2 Kings 23:13). The magnificent temple of Artemis at Ephesus was one of the seven wonders of the ancient world. Ephesus was known in the world for its wealth, power, fame, superstition, and idolatry.

But one of the most important Christian churches of the day had been planted in the midst of that city. God sent many great men to lead that church, including the apostle Paul, who served there three times, once for more than three years. Priscilla, Aquila, and Apollos also labored there. So did Tychicus, Timothy, and the apostle John, author of our text. According to Jerome, when John was very old, he returned to Ephesus. He was carried into the church, where he admonished the congregation, saying, "Little children, love one another."[1]

Probably no New Testament church outside of Jerusalem had as many eminent ministers as Ephesus. The fruits of their many labors were evident. Revelation 2:2–3 records three wonderful truths about the church of Ephesus:

First, the Lord Jesus praises the church for *diligence*. Christ says in verse 2, "I know thy works, and thy labour, and thy patience." He mentions the church's labors again in verse 3. Ephesus worked hard for the Lord. By grace the people strove to be a church that could say, "We are his workmanship, created in Christ Jesus unto good works, which God hath before ordained that we should walk in them" (Eph. 2:10).

Second, the Lord Jesus praises the church for *discernment*: "Thou canst not bear them which are evil: and thou hast tried them which say they are apostles, and are not, and hast found them liars" (Rev. 2:2). And: "This thou hast, that thou hatest the deeds of the Nicolaitans, which I also hate" (v. 6). The Ephesian church could discern the difference between true and false prophets and between truth and error. She would not tolerate heretics and was firm in exercising Christian discipline against them.

---

1. Jerome, *Commentary on Galations,* cited in Period I, 3b, of Joseph Cullen Ayer, Jr., *A Source Book for Ancient Church History* (N.p., 1924).

Like her Lord, the Ephesian church was intolerant of evil. Without engaging in perpetual witch hunts or endless polemics, the elders at Ephesus acted firmly and decisively when the truth was at stake. Unlike too many of today's churches, which tolerate nearly everything, the Ephesian church would not allow beliefs or morals to be corrupted by heretical teaching or immoral behavior. She refused to compromise the biblical convictions that our Lord had delivered to her through the Word as expounded by the apostles.

Third, the Lord Jesus praises the church for *determination.* This church patiently endured persecution for her convictions; she persevered with determination. Verse 3 says she "hast borne, and hast patience, and for my name's sake hast laboured, and hast not fainted." The Ephesian church went on doing Christ's work for Christ's sake despite difficulties and persecutions. So the Lord Jesus commends the church at Ephesus for her diligence, discernment, and determination.

Likewise, Christ knows what is going on today in your church from Sunday to Sunday. He knows what is going on in your heart, in your mind, and in your life. He loves each church and is concerned about her.

Sometimes we get the wrong idea about Christ. We think of our Lord walking among the candlesticks of the churches as a kind of policeman, whose flashing lights signal you to pull over to the side of the road. As the officer walks around your car, he is not impressed that you polished it that morning or have installed new headlights. He is looking for faults, for infractions of the law. That is his job.

Our Lord is not like that policeman. He is a gardener who walks around the flower beds He has planted to appreciate their rich color, texture, and growth. If you are a gardener, it is wonderful to enjoy the fruits of your labors. But occasionally you spot something—mildew, insects, or shriveling leaves—that indicates a problem that must be dealt with. That is how we should think of Christ amid His churches. He walks among them, not as a policeman or fault-finder, but as a gardener rejoicing in the fruits of His labors. He comes as the Savior who laid down His life for His bride. He walks among the churches to admire, appreciate, and enjoy what He has accomplished by the shedding of His blood and by His Word and Spirit. And He seemingly says in chapter 2: "I know your strong points and I appreciate your labors of love, patience, perseverance, soundness, church discipline, purity, and activities. I rejoice in those things. But my heart aches because in the midst of all that lovely foliage and color, I see a blight that will destroy you if it is not dealt with." The blight He sees at Ephesus is that the church had left her first love (v. 4).

We can learn something here about how we should relate to one another in the church. Christ sees something wrong in the church at Ephesus, but He doesn't just lower His spade to dig it up and throw it away in a violent or destructive way. He first takes time to assess and affirm the church's positive attributes, and then proceeds to deal with what is wrong. Likewise, we should not plunge a knife of criticism or rebuke into someone without first taking time to appreciate his or her many positive attributes.

Some people say, "If I can't say something good, I'll not say anything." There is some wisdom in that. But if you can't see any of God's grace in another person, you may have the wrong attitude. We must learn to appreciate one another in the Lord. In that context, we might say: "I love you as a brother in Christ. I can see the grace of God in your life. I was so blessed the other day when you did this or said that, but I am concerned about something that I would like to talk with you about." In that spirit, Christ comes to the church at Ephesus. Even later, when He offers a more severe warning to the church, He joins it with a final word of commendation. He says: "I will come unto thee quickly, and will remove thy candlestick out of his place, except thou repent. But this thou hast, that thou hatest the deeds of the Nicolaitans, which I also hate" (vv. 5b–6). We should remember this example of Christ when we interact with others in the church.

But the big lesson here is that, for all her external zeal, the Ephesian church had lost her first love, that is, the love she had for

Jesus Christ when she first heard the word of the Lord Jesus proclaimed by the apostle Paul (Acts 19). She was no longer captivated and motivated by Christ's love to surrender herself to Him and to magnify His name. Long since, she had slipped into the bad spiritual habit of going through the motions of church life, doing all the right things, but not for the right reasons.

A "first love" is what we most long for to capture our hearts and set the goals of our lives. Jeremiah called it "the love of thine espousals" (Jer. 2:2), that is, the love of a wife who has eyes for none but her newly wedded husband. In our text, "first love" refers to the love when our souls are first captivated by the beauty, fullness, and loveliness of the Lord Jesus Christ and therefore rest upon Him for salvation. First love springs up when we lay all our sins at the foot of Calvary's cross and embrace Christ's righteousness by faith, through the Spirit. First love wins my heart for the Lord Jesus Christ. He becomes so lovely that I want to be united forever to Him. By His grace, I am then bound to Him by saving faith. By His grace, I will endure all things in order to reach Him in glory. As Samuel Rutherford says, believers in this condition have such a love for Christ that, "If you saw Him who is standing on the shore, holding out His arms to welcome you on land, you would not only wade through a sea of wrongs, but through hell itself to be at Him."[2]

The entire Bible speaks to us of this first love regarding Jesus Christ and the way of salvation. First love moves us to say, "I am my beloved's, and my beloved is mine!" (Song 6:3). With this kind of love, we cannot keep silent, but are compelled to speak to others about their need for Christ and how precious He is. With this love, it is easy to pray. In the time of first love, we cannot wait to get into a secret place where we may talk with God as a beloved friend. Our hearts are filled with Jesus Christ. We say with assurance, "Lord, thou knowest all things; thou knowest that I love thee" (John 21:17).

---

2. *Letters of Samuel Rutherford* (1891; repr., Edinburgh: Banner of Truth, 2006), 128.

But our Lord tells the church at Ephesus, "I have this against you, Ephesus, that you have left your first love." This complaint is serious for four reasons:

First, this complaint is serious because *Christ is the one who complains.* The One who is worthy above all others to be loved is saying, "I am your loving Bridegroom, I have poured out My life for you, drawn you to My side, saved you from sin, lifted you from the mire, and given you everything—and you have left your first love." I pray that we men who are married truly love our wives. How sad it would be if our wives came to us and said, "I sense that your love for me has faded away." Nothing they could say would get our attention as much as that! Yet we seem to accept as a matter of course that our love for God will turn cold. So Jesus says to us: "I have something against you. Don't I deserve your love? Do you see anything unlovable in Me? Have I been unfaithful to you in any way? I bought you with My blood, but I have this against you—you have left your first love."

Second, this complaint is serious because *your fading love can't be hidden from Christ.* You may not be aware of it, and others may not see it in you. Force of habit can keep you going through the motions of church life for a long time without your first love. But the Lord Jesus knows the very day and hour when your love began to fade. That makes the problem especially tragic. You have been grieving your Lord for so long, and you didn't even know it.

Third, this complaint is serious because *the relationship of the church to Jesus Christ is at stake.* The bride's loss of love for Christ is a destructive sin. Though Christ is the faithful Bridegroom who will never cease loving His people, our relationship with Him is seriously and negatively affected if we leave our first love. A fading love may not keep us out of heaven, but we can keep heaven out of our hearts if we fail in our love for Christ here on earth.

Fourth, this complaint is serious because *it is love's complaint.* We are sinning against the greatest love we shall ever know. Love constrained the One who walks among the candlesticks of the churches to give His life for them. He says, "If this first love is not rekindled, I will remove your candlestick from its place, and you will be a church no more." How serious is the problem of leaving one's first love!

What specifically does the Lord see in the church at Ephesus? This church is a beehive of activity, sustained across many years. This church is scrupulous about who fills her pulpit. She despises evildoers and exposes false teachers. She has persevered despite trials, discouragements, and severe persecution. She has kept her doors open, continued to meet, and been active in evangelism. She is a large, active church, sound in doctrine and successful in her many efforts to promote Christianity in her community. Christ commends her for all that.

She has even stood firm against the Nicolaitans, who compromised with the world by teaching that superior light gave them liberty to practice idolatry and immorality without sin. Jesus commends the Ephesian church once again for seeing through this heresy. In effect, He says: "You hate their deeds as I hate their deeds. You have not allowed the world to invade your church. You are sound, active, and uncompromised." In short, they hate what they should hate.

However, they no longer love the One they should love best of all. Sadly, the church has left its first love. That is very serious. Their love for the Lord Jesus has faded, meaning the heart has gone out of their religion. That blight is going to ruin them, and something must be done at once!

Losing one's first love is serious in any marriage. You can commend any wife or husband who perform their spousal duties, but it is sad when their service becomes *mere* duty. The love has gone out of the marriage.

That is how it is at Ephesus. The church's relationship with Christ is still intact, but what she does for Him has just become merely a matter of duty. Her heart is no longer in it. So Jesus says, "You have left your first love." But notice here that the church has *left* its first love, not *lost* it. John Owen, a great Puritan writer, says that some leave their first love for Christ because they would think that abiding in Christ is "a plant that needs neither watering, manuring, nor pruning, but that which will thrive alone of itself."[3] Christians too often leave their first love today because they do not understand that love for Christ needs continual nurture and replenishment.

A potted plant may be beautiful when we first receive it. But if we put it on a table and forget to tend and water it, the leaves on that plant will fade from green to yellow, then die and drop off. Eventually, the plant itself will die. Likewise, some Christians think their relationship with Christ doesn't need any maintenance. That is a dangerous mistake. Your love for Christ must be nurtured and protected, for it is the most precious thing you have. It is more precious than your orthodoxy, your churchgoing, your Christian activities, your evangelism, or any other aspect of your life as a Christian. Without nurturing, your relationship with Christ will wither. That is what our Lord says has happened to the church at Ephesus.

We lose our first love gradually. The loss begins inside, when our prayer life cools. When that happens, we lose our heart for God, our concern for our souls, and our love for the souls of others. Like a plague, this coolness then spreads to how we listen to sermons, how we read our Bibles, what other books we read, and the conversations we have with people. We no longer have the freedom to speak openly to believers because the shadow of a faded love has darkened our souls and undercut our boldness.

We go through the motions of religion out of force of habit or of fear over what others may think if we don't, but corruption festers and multiplies within. We talk more *about* God than *to* God, more about church than about Christ, more about "religion" or "spirituality" than true Christianity. We still confess our sins and make solemn vows, but both are poses more than true piety. Such confessions don't result in repentance or forsaking of sin, and such vows don't bind us when we are called upon to honor them. Self-examination becomes less frequent and more shallow, and carnal presumption sets in. We think we are strong enough in ourselves to

---

3. John Owen, *Exposition of the Epistle to the Hebrews*, ed. W. H. Goold (1854; repr., Edinburgh: Banner of Truth, 1991), 4:159.

withstand trials, temptations, and weaknesses. However, the more we rely on our own strength rather than God's, the less we realize how close we are to falling away altogether. We continue to presume we are believers in spite of our want of love and God's silence. As love fades, faith weakens, godliness declines, and worldliness gains ground. Worldly people make more sense to us. We think more like they think, speak more like they speak, and act more like they act. We set our affections on things below rather than on things above. We are more concerned about worldly possessions than we are about laying up treasure in heaven. Gradually, we become strangers to those who long for heaven and friends with those who are happy on earth. The devices of Satan are no longer so apparent to us, for, when love fades, so does our vigilance and perception. As a result, we no longer miss God or desire to be in His presence, which is the great place of safety for the believer.

The letter to the Ephesian church is the first in a series of seven letters. That is because the sin of Ephesus is the first step on the way to the sins of Laodicea. You may think Ephesus is a long way from Laodicea, but if you allow your love for Christ to fade away, you are already on the way to becoming so indifferent or "lukewarm" that the Lord threatens to spit you out of His mouth (Rev. 3:16). This fading away of love begins so subtly that nobody sees it, not even "the angel of the church." But Jesus says: "I see it, and that is why I am writing to you now. You have left your first love."

He also says to one of the most impressive New Testament churches: "You can go on the way you have been going for years, but it will come to nothing in the end. All the work you are doing is no longer being powered by the love that should constrain, compel, and sustain you to the end." What our Lord says to the church also applies to us as individual believers. A church leaves its first love bit by bit as individual members, such as you and I, neglect our relationship with the Lord and the things that keep our love for Him on fire.

Christ's Prescription for the Church at Ephesus

In verse 5, the Lord offers this church a prescription for recovering her first love. He says: "Remember therefore from whence thou art fallen, and repent, and do the first works." Simply put, the way to rekindle your first love is *remember*, *repent*, and *repeat*.

First, *remember your first love*. In the preface to his autobiography, *Grace Abounding to the Chief of Sinners*, John Bunyan says, "It is profitable for Christians to be often calling to mind the very beginnings of grace within their souls."[4] He describes young David, for whom the sword of Goliath was a constant reminder of what God has done for him (1 Sam. 21:9). Likewise, we need constant reminders of what the Lord Jesus Christ has done for us. Each time someone is baptized, we remember that Christ washed us from our sins with His precious blood. Why? Because He loved us! Each time we partake of the Lord's Supper, we remember that Christ's body and blood were sacrificed for our salvation—because He loved us! At a funeral, we remember that Christ saved us from death and woe, and one day will raise us from the grave to serve Him in eternal glory, because He still loves us! We need such reminders of the basic facts of the gospel as the great revelation of the love of Christ for His own. In the presence of such reminders, love is reborn. "We love him, because he first loved us" (1 John 4:19). Likewise, in the presence of such reminders, we can measure how much our love for Him has faded over time.

Perhaps you have a picture of your daughter when she was only a week old. Periodically, you look at the photograph, perhaps to see whom she most resembles. Does she look more like her mother now or her father? Do you see Grandma in her? Her aunt? You hadn't noted a resemblance to a family member before because you saw her every day. Yet when you look at the picture of her as an infant, you see how much she has changed.

---

4. John Bunyan, preface to *Grace Abounding to the Chief of Sinners*, in *The Works of John Bunyan* (1854; repr., Edinburgh: Banner of Truth, 1991), 1:4–5.

That is how it is with us spiritually. We see ourselves so regularly that we cannot be objective about our looks. We can't get away from ourselves. To notice spiritual changes in ourselves, we must go back to the time when we first knew the Lord. We need to recall the vows we made, the prayers we prayed, and the closeness we felt. "Remember," says Jesus, "from whence thou art fallen." A Christian's falling does not have to be so blatant as to involve murder or adultery. It can be the kind of inward falling that no one but Christ notices. So think about how you were before you fell, before your love began to fade. Then think about how a stone gathers momentum after it begins falling. Who will check your fall before you drop off a cliff? You have left your first love. You are still a believer, but you are falling. With God's help, only you can stop it, but first you have to realize that something has gone wrong, something has been lost, and you are headed in the wrong direction.

If you are truly a Christian, you cannot lose your salvation. You will still be saved, but only as a brand plucked from the burning (Zech. 3:2; 1 Cor. 3:15). Yet there is a thin line between backsliding and apostasy. Unless you are careful, you might discover too late that you have deceived yourself and have never been a true believer. The worst advice a backslider can receive from fellow Christians is, "Don't worry; God will restore you." The glib, modern idea of "eternal security" has deceived many. That is not what you need to hear when you have left your first love. You need to know and feel that you are falling away from your Lord! Get alone with God, open your memory bank, and examine where you were and what it was like when you were first converted. Remember the sweetness and joy of your first love for Christ.

Please do not misunderstand. Love does mature. The first flush of love you felt when you were regenerated will probably not return to you, at least not in the same way. Your love will deepen as it matures and will be mingled with wisdom as to how best to express it. New Christians make much of words of love; mature Christians know we must love in deed and in truth, and not in word only. Your relationship with the Beloved will likewise deepen and grow.

It is as if Jesus is saying: "Remember how it was in those early days between you and Me. Remember the height from which you have fallen, and repent."

Second, *repent*. Remember what Christ has done and repent of neglecting your love for Him and allowing it to fade. Then go back and start anew to love Christ as you should. True repentance—what we might call evangelical repentance as opposed to legal repentance—involves four things:

1. Evangelical repentance *grieves over and hates sin*. I sorrow over my sin against God. I grieve over my response to the most holy God and loving Father, the suffering Savior and interceding Mediator, and the indwelling Spirit. I hate the evil that I have done in neglecting the things that should matter most.

2. Evangelical repentance *confesses specific sins*. In Psalm 51, David owns his transgressions against God by saying, "I have sinned." He confesses the sin of murder ("blood-guiltiness") in verse 14 and the impurity of his heart that led to adultery in verses 6–7. Further, in verse 10, he pleads for a clean heart (cf. Matt. 5:8). True repentance identifies our particular sins down to their roots, then lays them out in order before God.

3. Evangelical repentance *forsakes sin*. Repentance turns us away from sin not only with the heart but also with the will. Evangelical repentance is far more than emotion; it is an act of the will. Repentance turns from sin with holy resolve and self-denial. True repentance gets serious about forsaking *all* sin.

4. Evangelical repentance *cries for mercy*. In Psalm 51:1, 9, and 17, David casts himself upon God's mercy. He knows that, as a wretched sinner, his condemnation is just and he doesn't deserve mercy, so he turns, pleads for mercy, and trusts in the gospel promise of the forgiveness of sins. The gospel promises that for the sake of His Son, Jesus Christ, God will not forsake us, but will forgive and restore us if we cast ourselves upon Him in true repentance, confessing our sins and crying out for mercy.

Third, to rekindle your first love, you must *repeat the works of your first love*. You can't summon up the feelings and emotions you had when you first came to know the Lord. But you can repeat what you did when you first came to true repentance, and if you do, the feelings will follow. By the Spirit's grace, you can renew your covenant with God. You can recall how much the Lord loves you and all that He has done to show that love. You can love Him anew, because once more you see and know how much He has loved you and how much He loves you still. In love, you can forsake sin and seek the Lord's face once more. In love, you can call upon His name. With love and delight, you can once more begin to live not according to some, but all, of His commandments. Love is not just feeling; it is doing. The great thing about the New Testament concept of love is that it is practical. It is something that you do, which in turn reflects who you are. Jesus says, "Remember, return, repeat the first works; come as you came the first time in repentance and faith to Me." Repeat the first works, confessing that you are a sinner. Don't wait for change to happen; come as you are in repentance and faith. "Seek, and ye shall find" (Matt. 7:7).

Christ's Encouragement for the Church of Ephesus

Finally, Jesus adds an encouragement for the church at Ephesus to follow this prescription. He does so first by warning or admonishing her. He says in verse 5, "Repent, and do the first works; or else I will come unto thee quickly, and will remove thy candlestick out of his place."

Our Lord says to the church at Ephesus: "You have been orthodox and sound, but I will take away your candlestick unless you repent of leaving your first love and recover that love as the chief treasure of your life as a church." That was no idle threat. Over and over, the Lord has removed the candlestick—that is, withdrawn His care and support—from churches that have lost their love for Him. Such churches fade and die. From our point of view, all may be well with our church, but the Lord Jesus knows better, for He sees the fatal flaw of sin that one day will bring us down.

If so, our Lord loves us enough to warn us about our condition. He persuades us through His threats, but also by giving us

His promises. He says in verse 7: "To him that overcometh will I give to eat of the tree of life, which is in the midst of the paradise of God." He encourages us, saying, "If you overcome, if you endure to the end, if you don't make shipwreck of your faith, you will eat of the tree of life in paradise with God." Eating of the tree of life is symbolic of communion with God in eternal life (Gen. 2:8–9; 3:22). "Paradise" is a garden, here picturing heaven as a new garden of Eden (Luke 23:43; Rev. 22:2). What Christ holds before us to encourage us in our Christian lives is the hope of once more walking with God in the garden in the cool of the day. Everything that we have forfeited by sin has been recovered by the blood of Christ and will be restored to us in the end. With such promises of great reward, nothing should keep us from using all possible means to recover our first love, that we may overcome by faith and obtain the promised blessing.

So ask the Holy Spirit to help you remember your first love, repent of allowing it to fade away, and repeat the things you did at the beginning, when love first burst into flame. On the one hand, to go on as you are will only end badly. On the other, there is the hope of heaven and communion with God in everlasting life, promised to all who love the Lord Jesus with an incorruptible love (Eph. 6:24).

We can't eat of the tree of life unless we repent. So let us turn to the Lord our God and seek His face afresh. Let us appeal to the One who is exalted at the right hand of God to bring us to repentance, to work it irresistibly in our hearts, and to bring us back to the living God. Let us ask for His mercy, that we may know Him afresh, embrace Him, and say: "My first love has been revived. To Him be the glory forevermore!"

5

Christ's Message for a Suffering Church

REVELATION 2:8–11

And unto the angel of the church in Smyrna write; These things saith the first and the last, which was dead, and is alive; I know thy works, and tribulation, and poverty, (but thou art rich) and I know the blasphemy of them which say they are Jews, and are not, but are the synagogue of Satan. Fear none of those things which thou shalt suffer: behold, the devil shall cast some of you into prison, that ye may be tried; and ye shall have tribulation ten days: be thou faithful unto death, and I will give thee a crown of life. He that hath an ear, let him hear what the Spirit saith unto the churches; He that overcometh shall not be hurt of the second death.

Suffering is no fun. Are you suffering right now from one or more heavy crosses in your life? Your suffering might be physical, emotional, relational, or spiritual—or perhaps a combination of these. Perhaps you cannot see how any good can come out of your pain.

I have good news for you: God is bigger than your pain. Your suffering is not in vain. If you are an unbeliever, He can use your suffering to bring you to Himself. If you are a believer, He can use your suffering to grow you in dependency upon Himself (Heb. 12:11). It is, in fact, His normal way to work gain through pain. That's why Christ's message to the suffering church of Smyrna is so important for all of us to hear—even if we are not suffering much at the moment, for our non-suffering times are great times to prepare for suffering.

The church of Smyrna is the second of seven churches to receive letters from the apostle John conveying messages from Jesus Christ.

The letter to Smyrna is the briefest of the seven. The city of Smyrna, known today as Izmir, Turkey, is thirty-five miles north of Ephesus in Asia Minor. In biblical times, it was known as "the pride of Asia" because it had a natural harbor and a flourishing export trade. It was not as large as Ephesus, but it was a significant town. Smyrna is reputed to have been the birthplace of Homer, the greatest of all Greek poets, author of the *Iliad* and the *Odyssey*, chronicling the war of the Greeks against Troy (Illium) and the subsequent adventures of the Greek hero Odysseus on his homeward journey. Smyrna had the largest theater in Asia. It also had magnificent public architecture, including scores of temples dedicated to the pagan gods and goddesses. The city was refined in culture and decidedly pagan in its religion and philosophy. No religion that challenged Greek culture was popular in Smyrna.

Smyrna also had strong ties with the Roman Empire. Legally, the emperor of Rome had to be worshiped as a god. This demand clashed with the Christian gospel, as well as with the faith of the large community of Jews who had helped Smyrna to flourish.

The small Christian church in the city was probably established by Paul on his way to Ephesus during his third missionary journey. When John was on the island of Patmos, the church in Smyrna was struggling. The only people who were excused from worshiping Caesar were the Jews. For a time, the church in Smyrna enjoyed the same immunity. But by the end of the first century, the Jews had disowned any association with Christians, which exposed the latter to the Romans as people who denied the existence of Roman gods and refused to worship Roman emperors. Christians refused to offer incense on the altar before the emperor's image. Confessing that "Jesus is the Lord" (1 Cor. 12:3), they refused to call Caesar "Lord," an act of defiance that was viewed as treasonous, even blasphemous, in Smyrna. The persecution that ensued against the Christians was encouraged and exacerbated by local Jews. History books are filled with acts of Jewish hostility against the early church in Smyrna.

Christ sent this suffering church a threefold message. He countenanced the church and acknowledged that she was suffering and warned her that there were more severe trials to come. He counseled the Christians there to remain faithful, even if it cost them their lives. Finally, He offered the comfort that none of her sufferings were escaping His notice, and, if she remained "faithful unto death," He would one day give her a crown of life.

Christ Countenances Smyrna in Persecution

Jesus speaks no words of admonition to the church at Smyrna. Rather, He commends her, like her sister church at Philadelphia (Rev. 3:7–13), without qualification. Both of those churches were suffering persecution. This is a reminder that the more we seek to please Christ and gain His approval, the more we will antagonize and infuriate the world around us. We cannot expect to be patted on the back for our testimony. If we are powerful and generous but worldly, the world will give us all sorts of honors. But the more we become like Christ, the more we can expect persecution. The world can admire goodness, but it cannot stand godliness.

In this letter, Jesus describes four aspects of Smyrna's persecution. As He does so, He is offering the church His support. The word countenance derives from the Latin word for "aspect" or "face," the part of our body that reflects our moods, emotions, and character. In biblical times, to turn or "lift up" one's countenance upon another meant offering support and approval. So in the Aaronic benediction, the Lord is said to "lift up his countenance" upon His people (Num. 6:24–26). Here, Jesus lifts up His countenance upon the church at Smyrna with regard to four aspects of the persecution she is suffering:

First, *the Smyrnian church is suffering poverty.* Jesus says, "I know thy works, and tribulation, and poverty" (Rev. 2:9a). Smyrna was one of the wealthiest cities in the world, but the Christians there were poor. They were poor because of the hostility of the world around them. Many Christians were losing their jobs because they refused to bow to the emperor. They suffered in business because their pagan and Jewish neighbors took their trade elsewhere. Yet Christ says the Smyrna church is rich because she has remained true to her confession. She is willing to pay the price of economic impoverishment to be loyal to Jesus, her crucified King and risen Lord. Poor in this world's goods, she is laying up treasure in heaven (Matt. 6:20; 19:21).

America's Christians live in an age of affluence. We may not suffer as the Smyrnian believers did, but we too face temptations and persecutions that make us spiritually needy. Following Jesus Christ can be both risky and costly. Paul says that "all that will live godly in Christ Jesus shall suffer persecution" (2 Tim. 3:12).

Second, *the Smyrnian church is suffering blasphemy.* Jesus says, "I know the blasphemy of them which say they are Jews, and are not" (Rev. 2:9b). Blasphemy, or "evil speaking," here means that "men shall revile you...and shall say all manner of evil against you falsely" for Christ's sake (Matt. 5:11). The deadly evil of an untamed tongue poisoned the minds of many against the beliefs of Christians in Smyrna. Christ calls these tongue-lashing persecutors "the synagogue of Satan" (Rev. 2:9b). Jews were persecuting Christians by saying false things about them. These blasphemers followed their master, Satan, who is the accuser, slanderer, liar, and father of lies.

Because the Christians in Smyrna refused to bow before Caesar's image, believing it was a false idol, their Jewish and pagan neighbors accused them of disloyalty to the emperor. No doubt they also spread malicious rumors about the beliefs and practices of the Christians. This second form of persecution may be harder to bear than poverty. Proverbs 26:22 says, "The words of a talebearer are as wounds, and they go down into the innermost parts of the belly."

When the church of Smyrna was reviled, she did not revile others in return, but, by grace, responded to blasphemy with Christlike meekness. Jesus says to these suffering ones, "Do not be frightened. Do not panic." He advises them to understand what is going on and who is behind it. The people who are persecuting them are not true Jews, but people who are being used by Satan to accomplish his purposes. At the same time, Christ comforts the church by saying that though the world views these believers as poor, persecuted, and despised, they are truly rich toward God (Rev. 2:9a). They have "treasures in heaven, where neither moth nor rust doth corrupt, and where thieves do not break through nor steal" (Matt. 6:20).

Viewed in this way, Smyrna appears to have been the most blessed church in Asia Minor. Whereas Ephesus was less than what she appeared to be, Smyrna was much more than she appeared to be. Though small in numbers and oppressed by poverty and persecution, this church abounded in spiritual life. The more she was tried, the more she was blessed.

When things go wrong and we can't understand why, we should consider how Christ views us. Smyrna was a church that Christ delighted in and smiled upon. Likewise, when Lazarus became ill and was near death, his friends sent a message to Christ, saying, "Behold, he whom thou lovest is sick" (John 11:3). Never think that because you are sick or suffering that Christ has forgotten you or has something against you. The Bible says, "Whom the Lord loveth he chasteneth, and scourgeth every son whom he receiveth" (Heb. 12:6; Prov. 3:12). He disciplines those sons whom He is bringing to glory. If you are experiencing great suffering, you should praise God that He loves you enough to take you to task and that He counts you worthy to suffer for His sake.

Third, *the Smyrnian church is suffering imprisonment*. Christ says in Rev. 2:10a, "Fear none of those things which thou shalt suffer: behold, the devil shall cast some of you into prison, that ye may be tried; and ye shall have tribulation ten days." By telling the Smyrnian Christians not to fear this trial, Christ is saying that He will be with them even in prison. He was the fourth one who walked in the fiery furnace with Shadrach, Meshach, and Abednego (Dan. 3:23–25). Eternity itself will reveal how many prison cells in church history were sanctified by the prayers, praises, and tears of faithful believers who were poor in this world's goods but rich in Christ. If cast into prison, Smyrnian believers are assured that their Master will go with them and suffer alongside them, for He is "a brother… born for adversity" (Prov. 17:17).

Jesus also informs these Christians that they will suffer imprisonment because of the devil. Likewise, when things go wrong in our faith walk, we should remember that God is not the author of sin, nor does He tempt us with sin. Even so, the devil, though the author of sin, tribulations, and suffering, is not the boss in the matter. Jesus said, "The devil shall cast some of you into prison, that ye may be tried." The devil's intent is not to try us but to destroy us. But he is not in control! Our Lord tells us: "Although the devil is going to attack you, I am in control, so he may do only that which serves My purpose. And My purpose is that you may be purged, purified, and increased in holiness." That is one of the main reasons why God allows His people to suffer.

Fourth, *the Smyrnian church is suffering death.* Jesus says in verse 10, "Be thou faithful unto death." As a tried and tested church, Smyrna is willing to die for Christ's sake. It is as if Jesus is saying: "Smyrna, the opposition against the pure gospel of grace will become so severe in your city that martyrdom will become a reality for many of you. But fear not. Be faithful even unto death, for My favor abides on you."

When Christ's countenance is lifted up toward us, no suffering is too great, for His favor or "lovingkindness" is "better than life" (Ps. 63:3). Have you experienced the comfort of God's countenance lifted up toward you in Christ when you have suffered affliction or persecution? Is there anything more comforting or sustaining? It is so great that you would rather die with Christ's countenance shining upon you than live without it. It is no wonder, then, that when he was in great trouble, David prayed, "Lord, lift thou up the light of thy countenance upon us" (Ps. 4:6).

Christ Counsels Smyrna to Be Faithful

Christ counsels the Smyrnian believers to persevere in faith to the end. History tells us that He also gave them the grace to do so. For the gospel's sake, many Smyrnians faced death by sword or by the rigors of prolonged imprisonment. Polycarp, one of the best-known ancient Christian martyrs, was a member of the Smyrnian church. According to the ancient church fathers Tertullian and Irenaeus, Polycarp became the senior minister of the church after he was ordained by the apostle John. No doubt this letter from Christ via John to Smyrna was a great encouragement to Polycarp.

Polycarp was in his twenties when this letter came to the church of Smyrna, and he died when he was eighty-six. On February 22, AD 156, this venerable bishop, who had fled from Smyrna at the urging of his local church, was tracked down in a hiding place twenty miles from Smyrna. He made no attempt to flee but instead offered food and drink to his captors. When they asked him if he had any special requests before being martyred, he asked for two hours for prayer. The officers granted his request, then bound him and brought him back to Smyrna for trial.

Two weeks later, Polycarp was led into the amphitheater, where he would be put to death before thousands of people. The proconsul[1] said: "Polycarp, I will have respect for your old age. Swear just once by the genius of Caesar,[2] and I will immediately release you." Polycarp replied: "Eighty-six years have I served Christ, and He has done me no wrong. How then can I blaspheme my King and my Savior?" The proconsul persisted, saying: "The wild beasts are ready. If you refuse to swear by Caesar, you will be thrown to them." Polycarp answered, "Bid them be brought." Infuriated, the proconsul responded: "As you despise beasts, I give you one last opportunity to change your mind. Else I shall destroy you by fire." But Polycarp refused to recant.

Polycarp was brought to the stake. Before he was fastened with cords, he said, "I have one request; leave me unfastened, for I will die voluntarily for my Master's sake." The captors left him unfastened as they kindled the fire. Wind drove the flames away, prolonging Polycarp's agony, but also giving him more time to confess Christ. Over the flames and wind, Polycarp cried out, "O Lord, Almighty God, the Father of Thy beloved Son, Jesus Christ, through whom we have received knowledge of Thee, I thank Thee that Thou hast thought

---

1. The proconsul was the chief magistrate or governor of the province, or his deputy.

2. That is, to invoke the name of Caesar as a god and a witness, as part of a solemn oath.

me worthy this day, this hour to share the cup of Thy Christ among the number of Thy witnesses." That so angered one soldier that he took his sword and pierced the old man who refused to run from the flames of death.

Polycarp is one example of a man who followed Jesus' counsel to the Smyrnian church, "Be thou faithful unto death." Polycarp portrays the profound truth that it may cost the true believer everything to be a faithful disciple of the Lord Jesus Christ. That is still true today in many parts of the world. In more countries than at any other time in history, thousands of Christians are languishing in prisons or being killed for no other reason than that they confess the name of Christ. In other countries, they are denied work or must risk their lives to obtain one page of Holy Scripture. The church in the United States is an exception to this rule. Not long ago, a Christian from Kenya said, "Christianity is the easiest religion in the world as it is exemplified in America. You have money; you go to church a few times a week; and the rest of the week many may compromise their beliefs with the spirit of the world."

Do you know what Paul means when he says, "All that will live godly in Christ Jesus shall suffer persecution" (2 Tim. 3:12)? Does your faith cause trouble with your peers or those with whom you work? Can they see and hear that you think, speak, and act differently from the world? Do you know what it means to be tried from within and without, sometimes by the world and sometimes even by other professing Christians? Martin Luther once said that his trials from those in the household of faith were greater than from the Roman Catholics. "Ye shall have tribulation," said Jesus (John 16:33).

The ugly truth of our nature is that by compromising and sacrificing the truth, many of us seek to avoid suffering. We want to be respectable, conventional, and inoffensive. But the Smyrnian church drew a line for the truth for Christ's sake. She obeyed Christ's counsel not to compromise with the world. The cost of that obedience was great. So it is today, for when we walk the straight and narrow paths of inspired Scripture, many people regard us as puritanical, old-fashioned, rigid, or impractical. They ridicule and despise us—and, at times, even seek to do us grievous harm (1 John 3:12–13).

But when we hear the truth of God's Word with faith and seek to live according to it, we become rich in Christ Jesus. Smyrna was a church in the wilderness, but she rejoiced in God her Savior. She enjoyed the fellowship of God in the midst of suffering. What a blessing it is to receive the Lord's approval when we suffer and to sense His presence in the midst of it!

Smyrna received grace to obey the counsel of Christ, which was, "Be thou faithful." What beautiful, tender, firm counsel that was. Jesus did not tell the church to be faithful only in times of popularity and prosperity, but to be faithful in times of persecution and death, in times when faith falters, and in times when we cannot see the Master or understand His way with us.

Believers cannot be faithful in their own strength. They need God's grace even to pray to be faithful. Ultimately, such faithfulness is possible only because Christ was faithful in all His trials and sufferings. Because Jesus Christ was faithful unto death, we can be faithful unto death. Because He died for us and now lives at the Father's right hand, ever interceding for us, we should seek grace from Him to die daily to ourselves so that we can live to His praise.

Each of us must pray: "Lord, in all my weakness and faltering faith, grant to me the grace to be faithful. In times of tribulation and persecution, grant me not to be weakened in my principles or to compromise the truth. Whether it be darkness or light, drought or showers, storm or sunshine, grant me, Lord, to be faithful, to place my confidence in Thee by grace, and to live out what we sing: 'What time I am afraid, I put my trust in Thee.'[3] O God, give me grace to be faithful, and I shall be faithful."

Christ has every right to expect faithfulness from His church. When you see what He has done for her, what He continues to do for her, and what He shall do for her when He returns to earth on

---

3. *The Psalter, With Doctrinal Standards, Liturgy, Church Order, and Added Chorale Sections*, rev. ed. (Grand Rapids: Eerdmans, 1965), #151:2; #152:1 (Ps. 56:3).

the clouds of glory, how fitting is the mandate He has given to His church, "Be thou faithful."

By nature, we are prone to be faithful to Satan, to sin, and to our self-ruination. But Christ says, "Be faithful to me." Dear children of God, how unfaithful we tend to be in times of prosperity, when it is so easy to forget God! How unfaithful and rebellious we are prone to be in times of adversity, when we tend to resent and resist what God is doing! How long we can leave Christ out of our thoughts or forget the Lord, even for days without number. How unfaithful and inconsistent we so often are, even on the battlefields of spiritual life. Therefore, we must pray, "Lord, Thou hast righteously commanded us, but give us what Thou commandest, and we will be faithful unto death. Forgive my faithless heart and give me of Thy faithfulness that I may, in turn, be faithful unto Thee."

The child of God is faithful when the grace of God is operating in his heart; when he confesses his sin; when he acknowledges his guilt; when he wets Jesus' feet with his tears; when he wears the ropes of self-condemnation about his neck; when he flees to Christ with all his needs; when he seeks grace to live life to God's glory; and when he loves the triune God above all and his neighbor as himself. He is faithful when he renounces his own will, receives the grace to surrender to his Master, and no longer belongs to himself or lives to himself.

May Christ's counsel be more deeply impressed upon your heart, dear child of God. Christ has a right to command your faithfulness. May your weakness and inconsistency also drive you to be faithful in times of trial and tribulation. Jesus, who countenanced Smyrna's sufferings, will also comfort us in the midst of ours.

Christ Comforts Smyrna with Himself

Christ comforts the Smyrnian believers with truths about Himself. Here are some of the beautiful truths contained in the letter to this church:

First, *Jesus Christ is eternal and unchangeable.* Verse 8 says, "And unto the angel of the church in Smyrna write; These things saith the first and the last." Christ was before all worlds, and what He is today, He will be to the very end of time. What a great comfort it must have been to the church of Smyrna to be assured that Jesus is eternal and unchangeable. He who is "the first and the last" can assure His persecuted believers with these words: "You may think there is no end to your tribulation, but remember, with Me, there is no beginning of days nor end of life. I am the same yesterday, today, and forever. With Me, you are secure for all eternity. O church in Smyrna, the seas of life may ebb and flow; they may be deep or shallow, calm or rough, or even overflowing; but I stand immoveable as your Rock. I am the first and the last. I do not become weary nor grow old. I was the *Alpha* before you were born, and I will be the *Omega* after you have passed into eternity. I will be your God for ever and ever, and your guide even unto death."

Dear believer, what greater comfort can there be in the midst of tribulation than to know that your Master is the first and the last? Your tribulations will come to an end because Christ will outlast all of them. Your Savior will abide with you forever because He is Jehovah, the eternal, ever-living One.

Second, *Jesus Christ is victorious.* Verse 8 also assures us, saying: "These things saith the first and the last, which was dead, and is alive." Christ is victorious even over death. The empty tomb of Joseph of Arimathea is the grand dividing line between Christianity and all the religions of the world. Christianity is true and real because Christ conquered death, hell, and the grave, and arose to say, "I am he that liveth, and was dead; and, behold, I am alive for evermore, Amen; and have the keys of hell and of death" (Rev. 1:18).

Jesus, in essence, says to Smyrna: "The very worst that can possibly happen to anyone has happened to Me. I did not just happen to die, but went to death deliberately and voluntarily on behalf of My people. My death was not just a physical death but also a spiritual descent into hell. In My death, I endured the wrath of God against sin on behalf of My people. And behold, I am alive forevermore."

"Christians of Smyrna, you shall live because I was obedient unto death. When you go into the flames of death, you will be faithful unto death because I have walked that road before you. For thirty-six hours, I was held in the very grip and agony of death. But I gave My life as a victor, for I died, was buried, and rose again. I was obedient unto death, even the shameful and accursed death of the cross, so that when you die, death cannot harm you, but only be the abolition of sin for you and your entrance into eternal life. So be encouraged. No matter how dark things look for you, no matter how dismal your prison cells may be, no matter how hot the flames are around you, no matter how impossible it seems for you to endure, remember that I was dead but now I am alive! The victory is Mine, and so the victory is yours as well, My dear bride, for I am married to My church."

Be comforted, for He who was the first and is the last once was dead but is now alive forevermore. He is interceding for you this very moment, dear believer!

Third, *Jesus Christ is all-knowing.* Jesus says, "I know thy works, and tribulation, and poverty, (but thou art rich) and I know the blasphemy of them which say they are Jews, and are not, but are the synagogue of Satan" (Rev. 2:9).

Sometimes when people are in trouble, you go up to them and put your arm around them and say, "I know." But do you really know what it means to suffer as they do? Christ does. He comes to the suffering church in Smyrna, puts His arm around her shoulders, and says: "I know all these things; I know your poverty, your riches, your tribulation, the blasphemy of your enemies—everything. I know your every need."

What sweet comfort it is to come to the Lord with all our sins, fears, and tribulations and say, "Lord, Thou knowest all things; Thou knowest that I love Thee; Thou knowest that I am not what I desire to be, yet I am not what I once was. O Lord, Thou art all-knowing. Thou art my comfort in the midst of tribulation."

What a blessing it is to know that Christ walks among the candlesticks of His churches and knows all there is to know about them. He comes to them as the resurrected Lord of glory, but also as One who stoops to meet them on their level. He comes with

His Godhead, majesty, grace, and Holy Spirit to enter fully into the sufferings of His people. "I know everything about you," He says. "I know all your sorrows, all your temptations, and all your trials. Turn to Me, dear Smyrnian church, and be comforted, because I know everything about you, including all your sins—and I love you still!"

Fourth, *Jesus Christ is compensatory*. He compensates us for every loss that we sustain for His sake. Verse 9 says, "I know thy...poverty, (but thou art rich)." Christ promises in Mark 10:29–30 that "there is no man that hath left house, or brethren, or sisters, or father, or mother, or wife, or children, or lands, for my sake, and the gospel's, but he shall receive an hundredfold now in this time, houses, and brethren, and sisters, and mothers, and children, and lands, with persecutions; and in the world to come eternal life." The One who allowed the Smyrnian church to sink into poverty compensates them with His exceeding riches in grace. The Lord typically acts that way toward us, dear believers. He balances our afflictions with His tailor-made comforts. He causes joy to follow the most bitter times and provides a measure of joy even in the midst of our bitterness. "Weeping may endure for a night, but joy cometh in the morning," says Psalm 30:5. Jesus says, as it were: "Be comforted, Smyrnians, because I will repay you for every loss. I know what you need better than you know yourself."

Fifth, *Jesus Christ is sovereign*. Jesus says in verse 10 that Smyrna will suffer tribulation ten days. The Lord knows exactly how long we must suffer. Though ten is a symbolic number here, its specificity indicates to the Smyrnian church that her suffering is limited. Satan is on a leash and is allowed to attack the church only so far or so long as it pleases God. Thus, Jesus comforts believers by saying, in effect, "Whether it be imprisonment, burning at the stake, or any other kind of persecution, I will give you sufficient strength to bear every trial. I am sovereign, and My sovereignty is your comfort."

By nature, we are not fond of sovereignty. "We will not have this man to reign over us" (Luke 19:14). But when the Lord works in our hearts an impression of what we deserve, then His sovereignty may well become our favorite divine attribute, for God's sovereignty gives the lost sinner hope. God's sovereignty gives the hell-worthy an expectation outside of themselves. God can do for us what we cannot do for ourselves. Thank God that He is in control as the almighty One.

The book of Revelation is written in symbols. Our Lord wants His people to understand that they may have to go through the affliction, but they need not fear because it will last only "ten days." *Ten* is a number that indicates completion and fullness. Thus, this tribulation will last for a definite period of time. As Proverbs 23:18 says, "For surely there is an end; and thine expectation shall not be cut off." In His faithfulness, God will not suffer us to be tempted more than we can bear (1 Cor. 10:13). He will not give us too much or too little. He will give us as much as will be for our profit, and no less. He gives us our "ten days," and no more.

Sixth, *Jesus Christ is purposeful.* Jesus says to His believers: "I give you tribulation that you may profit thereby. I have a goal in mind. I will sift you as wheat when it is winnowed [see Luke 22:31] to blow away the chaff. Satan tempts you to destroy you, but I try you to refine you and purify you. Be comforted, because all that you suffer has a purpose. You may not understand the reason for your tribulations, but I assure you that My purpose is to use such trials to refine and purify you. Take comfort in My wise and loving purposes for you" (cf. Jer. 29:11).

Christ's purposefulness in our sufferings ought to assure us that we need exactly what we must endure. Let me illustrate this by saying it is not by chance that the letter to Smyrna follows the one to Ephesus. Very often, when a church or an individual has left his first love, Christ comes to them through the preaching of the Word and by other means to confront, warn, and even threaten them. If those means are ignored, He may come with the rod of suffering. If we would only heed His warnings, we would be spared a lot of pain. If we would sit up and take notice when Christ frowns at us, we would not have to endure as much suffering as we do.

Often, when we begin to slide away from Christ and our relationship with Him becomes cold and distant, He will send something grievous into our lives to bring us back to Him. This can be the case in an individual life, in a church, in a nation, or even in the world at large. When you have left your first love, Christ uses the rod of discipline to chastise you in order to draw you back to where you belong.

A.W. Pink writes: "When you observe that the fire in your room is going down you don't just put on more coals. You need the poker to stir the fire. God often uses the black poker of adversity in order that the flame of devotion may bring more blessing."[4] That is a good way of putting it. When we find that our first love is in decline, what do we do? Before we pile on more coal, we must sift ourselves and examine our ways. God's ways, which are not our ways, often include using the black poker of adversity. He gives our lives a good stir through suffering, but He does so for a wise and good purpose: to rekindle our faith and love toward the Lord Jesus Christ and to prepare us for glory. Thank Christ for His purposefulness in suffering.

Seventh, *Jesus Christ is our promise giver and promise fulfiller.* Christ concludes His letter to Smyrna with two precious promises. First, He promises a "crown of life" (v. 10b). This is not the crown of a king or queen; it is the laurel wreath that is placed on the head of a victor in a contest. Jesus is saying, "Be faithful and keep running the race set before you, and I will give you the crown [Greek, *stephanos*] of life." Christians in Smyrna knew about Stephen or Stephanos, the first martyr, who was honored by a vision of the exalted Lord Jesus Christ in the hour of his death (Acts 7:55–56). Now Jesus is saying: "That crown was not just for Stephen, but is for all of My people who are faithful. I will give to them the crown of life, the victor's wreath."

This crown is a reward not of merit but of grace, as God's crowning His work in us, for only Christ can enable a believer to be faithful unto death. In effect, our Savior says: "You may lose your life, but you will not lose the crown of life. I am the first and the last. I stand at

4. A. W. Pink, *An Exposition of Hebrews* (1954; repr., Grand Rapids: Baker, 1979), 969.

the beginning of your race; I run beside you in the race; and I will stand with you at the end of the race. Therefore, look to Me by faith and run with patience the race that is set before you, looking unto Me as the Author and Finisher of your faith" (see Heb. 12:1–2).

The awarding of this final crown will be part of the eternal celebration in heaven. Every trial that we go through in this present life is designed to prepare us for that eternal celebration, when we shall, by God's grace, appear without terror before the judgment seat of Christ.

Remember when you were little and you wanted to go to a friend's birthday party? Your mother made sure you were clean, properly dressed, and presentable. She saw to it that your face was scrubbed and your hair combed. You didn't always appreciate that preparation, but it was necessary to make sure you were presentable. What our Lord says to us here is that all the suffering we endure in this life is necessary to prepare us for the biggest and best celebration imaginable. The Lord is preparing us for our entrance into glory. He is bathing and dressing us so that we can sit down at the wedding supper of the Lamb with Abraham and all the other saints. He is not going to give us little paper hats to wear, but the victor's crown of life. He is going to present us faultless, blameless, and without spot or wrinkle before His Father in heaven.

There is great glory waiting for us, and the afflictions we suffer in this life are only momentary and light compared to that. God is saying: "Hold still; the longer you struggle against it, the longer it is going to take. Suffering will be for only a little while, then you can go off to the celebration and enjoy life in the presence of My Son and the glories of heaven." As Paul says to the Corinthians: "Our light affliction, which is but for a moment, worketh for us a far more exceeding and eternal weight of glory" (2 Cor. 4:17).

When we get to heaven, we will be able to sing and bless the divine hand that guided us, and we will see that glory dwells in Immanuel's land. For as Jesus says, "Fear none of those things which thou shalt suffer…be thou faithful unto death, and I will give thee a crown of life" (v. 10).

The second promise of Christ is, according to verse 11, "He that overcometh shall not be hurt of the second death." What does this mysterious phrase, "the second death," mean? Of course, the first death refers to physical death, but that is not as deadly as the second death. God warned Adam and Eve not to eat from the tree of the knowledge of good and evil, saying, "In the day that thou eatest thereof thou shalt surely die" (Gen. 2:17). Their eventual physical death was only the seal and consequence of the spiritual death they died that day when they ate the fruit of the tree and were banished from the presence of God. The second death, then, is eternal death in hell—the dreadful state of total separation from God and subjection to His wrath forever (Rev. 21:8). No wonder Jesus said, "Fear not them which kill the body, but are not able to kill the soul: but rather fear him which is able to destroy both soul and body in hell" (Matt. 10:28). The everlasting destruction of soul and body in hell is the second death.

The only way to avoid the second death is by being born again, or by the *second birth*. Those who have been born of the Spirit of God need not fear the second death, for Christ says to the church in Smyrna, "He that overcometh shall not be hurt of the second death." Through Jesus Christ, believers have victory over death, hell, and all the kingdoms of Satan.

So Jesus is saying that the Christians in Smyrna will die only in order to enter into eternal life and be in the presence of their Lord forever. No matter if death comes by the stake, the sword, wild animals, or any other form of persecution, it can be only "an abolishing of sin, and a passage into eternal life."[5] Jesus is saying, "Remember this promise when the crisis comes, for when you are under pressure and in the grip of fear, you may cave in. So think about this: the second death cannot touch you. The first death, the physical death of the body, is simply the gateway to eternal life."

---

5. Heidelberg Catechism, LD 16, Q. 42, in *Three Forms of Unity*, 81.

Conclusion

Now do you understand why the Lord Jesus says that the church at Smyrna is rich? The believers there were rich in Christ because Christ is eternal, victorious, all-knowing, all-compensating, sovereign, almighty, purposeful, exceedingly generous in His promises, and ever faithful to keep them. They were rich in Him who is the storehouse of the glorious riches of God (Phil. 4:19). Therefore, in Christ, they were rich in grace, rich in patience and endurance, rich even in the furnace of affliction, rich in faith, rich in faithfulness, rich in comfort, and rich in hope and expectation.

The true believer remains poor in himself, but in Christ he is very rich. "For ye know the grace of our Lord Jesus Christ, that, though he was rich, yet for your sakes he became poor, that ye through his poverty might be rich" (2 Cor. 8:9). Do you know what it means to say experientially, "I am poor yet rich. I am a poor sinner in myself but possess the greatest riches in Christ"? Are you by grace, and grace alone, a true Smyrnian Christian, who puts all your hope in your rich Savior? Then you are rich indeed.

6

Christ's Message
to a Worldly Church

REVELATION 2:12–17

And to the angel of the church in Pergamos write; these things saith he which hath the sharp sword with two edges; I know thy works, and where thou dwellest, even where Satan's seat is: and thou holdest fast my name, and hast not denied my faith, even in those days wherein Antipas was my faithful martyr, who was slain among you, where Satan dwelleth. But I have a few things against thee, because thou hast there them that hold the doctrine of Balaam, who taught Balac to cast a stumblingblock before the children of Israel, to eat things sacrificed unto idols, and to commit fornication. So hast thou also them that hold the doctrine of the Nicolaitans, which thing I hate. Repent; or else I will come unto thee quickly, and will fight against them with the sword of my mouth. He that hath an ear, let him hear what the Spirit saith unto the churches; to him that overcometh will I give to eat of the hidden manna, and will give him a white stone, and in the stone a new name written, which no man knoweth saving he that receiveth it.

How are you doing spiritually? When you take spiritual inventory of yourself, do you have to confess that personal godliness is on the wane and personal compromise with the world is growing? Are you living more for this world than for the next? Are you more forward-looking than upward-looking?

If so, may I lovingly warn you that you are entering dangerous waters. You urgently need to hear Christ's message to the church at Pergamos and take it to heart. I pray God that you will do so.

The third of Christ's seven messages to the churches of Asia
Minor is addressed to the church in Pergamos,[1] which had endured
much as a true church of Christ, at least in the past. However, at the
time John wrote Revelation, this church was guilty of compromising
with the world by failing to hate sin and its corrupting influences.
Christians in Pergamos were too eager to listen to the overtures
of the world. This church had been faithful under the assaults
of the world's violence, but it was yielding to the allures of the
world's friendship.

In Ephesus, the church had rooted out heretics, even though
her love for Christ was waning. But in Pergamos, heretics were tolerated in the name of love. Thus, the church in Pergamos reversed
the problem that faced the Ephesian church; Pergamos had a record
of loving zeal for the cause of Christ, even to the point of suffering
martyrdom, but her doctrinal purity and spirituality were on the
decline. Her moral power was broken as she gave in to the worldly
spirit of compromise.

The letter to Smyrna reveals the church in the world, whereas the
letter to Pergamos reveals the world in the church. It is remarkable
how often in church history a church like Pergamos has followed
one like Smyrna. The classic example is what happened to the
church throughout the Roman Empire after Emperor Constantine
(272–337). Prior to Constantine, the church had endured centuries
of persecution. Under Constantine, who claimed to be a Christian,
the empire supposedly became Christianized. Constantine made
Christianity respectable. Suddenly it was quite fashionable to be
a Christian. The result was that, in a very short time, the newly
established religion of the Roman Empire in many ways ceased to
be genuine biblical Christianity.

That is what happened with the church in the transition from
the situation at Smyrna to the situation at Pergamos, and this problem has continued down to our time. There is no historical sequence

---

1. In some translations of the New Testament, the form of the name is "Pergamum." Both forms of the name were used by the ancient church.

here, but rather a spiritual one. Often a church that endures a period of persecution then goes through a subsequent period of compromising with the world by allowing worldliness to enter its doors. This is a dangerous transition.

A ship at sea is where it was designed to be—in the water. But once water starts to get into the ship, if no action is taken, it is only a matter of time before the ship sinks. Although the ship is meant to be in the water, the water is not meant to be in the ship. As Christians, we are meant to be in the world, but the world must not be in us. The church in Pergamos had sailed through troubled waters and withstood many storms, but through lack of diligence, her hull had been perforated and she was beginning to take on water.

Verses 12–13 tell us the church at Pergamos had gone through turbulent times. The waves of persecution had crashed over this church with deadly force. Our Lord initially commends the church for staying afloat and keeping on her course under such adverse conditions. But then He warns her that He has found a leak in her sides, and the spirit of the world is seeping in. That is what the references to "the doctrine of Balaam" and "the doctrine of the Nicolaitans" are all about. Heretical groups or parties in the church (vv. 14–15) are not only promoting compromise with the world, but seeking to bring the world into the church. Our Lord is warning the church about this danger and urging her leaders to take strong measures to avert it.

Worldliness in the church is a problem today. Many of us live in cities very much like Pergamos, which was an old and prominent city in the Roman province of Asia. It had long been the seat of royal and imperial governments. It was a city of wealth and culture. It was also a center of pagan worship. Nearly all the pagan religions had shrines in Pergamos; there was even one for the emperor. That is why our Lord called Pergamos the home of "Satan's seat...where Satan dwelleth" (v. 13).

Though Satan operates everywhere, I believe that in the prominent cities of this world, such as Pergamos, Satan is even more active. There he influences world governments, world affairs, world culture, and world religions. Because you and I must live in the same world where Satan works, these verses are very relevant to us. We dwell where Satan is seated in power. In order to keep satanic worldliness out of the church, we must know our dangers and submit to our Savior's dealings.

Know Your Dangers

We Christians need to know the dangers of worldliness. We must first be aware of our surroundings and the godless and negative spiritual influences that are at work in them. What made Pergamos an ideal place for Satan to dwell and to use as a center and base for his operations?

Pergamos was fifty-five miles north of Smyrna. It had a population of 120,000 people at the time when John was composing the book of Revelation. Pergamos was famous for her architecture, but, sadly, all of her splendid buildings were dedicated to various pagan gods and goddesses. A magnificent altar, 120 feet long and sixty feet high, was dedicated to Zeus. Less than a quarter of a mile away stood an elegant temple dedicated to Athena. Another quarter of a mile away was a beautiful structure dedicated to Dionysus. Yet another temple had been built by the Romans to honor the "divine" Caesar Augustus. But Pergamos was especially a center of worship for Asclepius, the god of medicine and healing, whose symbol was a serpent entwined about a staff. That symbol, the *asklepian* or "Rod of Asclepius," is still used in medicine today.

In New Testament times, Pergamos was tolerant of many forms of religion, but it was devoted especially to the worship of Caesar. In 29 BC, Caesar granted permission for Pergamos to dedicate a temple to him. Thus, people in Pergamos were devoted to the oft-repeated pagan creed or confession, "Caesar is Lord."

Pergamos was also famous for its worldly art and literature. It had one of the most famous libraries in the world, which housed more than two hundred thousand volumes. Parchment was discovered and used for the first time in Pergamos, where it was called *pergamene.* It was also a place famous for medicine. Galen, one of the greatest names in the history of medicine, was born there.

Within this world-renowned city, infested with heathen temples, shrines, and other worldly influences, Christ established a small church. He introduces Himself to Pergamos in Revelation 2 as the One "which hath the sharp sword with two edges" (v. 12). This sword that cuts two ways is a fitting symbol of the mixed message Christ sends to the church in Pergamos concerning things yet to come.

No doubt the faithful believers in Pergamos were delighted to receive a message from Him "who walketh in the midst of the seven golden candlesticks" (Rev. 2:1), "the messenger of the covenant" (Mal. 3:1), and "the King of kings" (Rev. 17:14). What a wonderful thing it must have been, in the midst of all the heathen idolatry surrounding them, to receive a personal letter from the Lord Jesus, the King and Head of the church. And how encouraging it must have been to read the opening words of that letter: "I know thy works, and where thou dwellest" (Rev. 2:13).

In effect, Jesus is saying: "Pergamos, I know your temptations. I know you are surrounded by the powers of darkness. I know you are in the midst of heathendom and superstition. And I know, too, that when you refuse to say 'Caesar is Lord,' you will suffer persecution. I know that your city is the seat of the authority and power of Satan himself, the old serpent."

The Lord of life knows where every one of us lives. He knows all that we think, say, or do. He knows all the circumstances of our lives. But think also of His encouraging words, as He says to us: "I know your battles. I know your sincere resolution for obedience. I know the temptations that confront you. I know the sins that plague you."

A true child of God may experience such joy in taking refuge in the omniscience of Christ that it is hard to put into words. When Satan buffets him on all sides, what a blessing it is to be able to say, "Lord, Thou knowest where I dwell." Under Satan's relentless accusations, the Christian can only say: "Satan, much of what you are saying is true. I do have the evil heart you accuse me of. I am inconsistent in trusting God. But one thing I have that you don't reckon with is that Christ, my Master, knows where I dwell."

Have there been times in your life when you had no answer for Satan except to say, "My Lord knows where I dwell"? This statement does not have only a literal or geographical meaning; it also has a spiritual meaning: "Thou knowest the state of my soul; Thou knowest the struggles of my soul; Thou knowest everything about me."

The hope of every believer is that God knows that we dwell in His dear Son, who said, "Abide in me" (John 15:4). God sees us as we are in Christ, not as we are in ourselves. Think of the apostle Peter, who had denied his Lord three times. Confronted by the risen Christ, he had nothing left to say but, "O Lord, my love for Thee is but a small beginning at best, and a beginning which seems to grow ever smaller as I probe my heart, but Lord, I have only one refuge to which I may go. Thou knowest all things; Thou knowest that I love Thee."

But now Jesus says something rather ominous to the believers at Pergamos. He does this deliberately to awaken them to the danger that surrounds them. He says, "I know...where thou dwellest, *even where Satan's seat is.*" I can imagine the shock of the pastor of that congregation as he read these words. Perhaps he was rather proud of his role as the minister of Pergamos. How could his famous and beautiful city be described as the seat of Satan?

As a minister of the Church of England, John Newton lived in London for a time and served a church there. He wrote just over two hundred years ago: "London appears to me like a sea wherein most are tossed by storms and many suffer shipwreck." He then stressed the need of "having London grace in order to live in London." He explained, "By *London grace* I mean grace in a very advanced degree."[2]

How relevant is this "London grace" for believers today in all cities, including our own! Many of you have lived in cities all your

---

2. *The Works of the Rev. John Newton*, 2 vols. (Philadelphia: Uriah Hunt, 1839), 1:357.

lives. Are you aware that to live in a city you must have "city grace"? According to Newton, you need an advanced degree of help from God if you are to survive and flourish in such an environment. Do you plead with God at His throne to give you that kind of help?

When you are immersed in a situation, you often become immune to its dangers. It is like taking a bath. You get into water that is comfortably warm, but soon you begin to add more hot water. That can become dangerous if you add too much. This is how it can be in a city: when you are living there, evil increases so gradually that you don't notice the dangers around you until it's too late. Ask yourself, "Are there things that I tolerate in my life today that I would not have tolerated three or four years ago? Do I settle for things more easily now than I did a few years back? Do I allow things in my home now that I would never have allowed a few years ago?"

Evil has a way of creeping up on us. That's why our Lord, in speaking to the church in Pergamos, also warns us when He says, "You must live in the place where I have put you, but remember where you are. You are living in the place where Satan has his seat and dwelling place, and where he is powerfully at work."

That doesn't mean that we should all move out of the city and relocate to the country. On the contrary, our Lord commends believers who stay in the city and persevere as His faithful servants. In verse 13, Jesus says, "I know thy works…even where Satan's seat is: and thou holdest fast my name, and hast not denied my faith." He does not disapprove of where these believers are living. He doesn't advise them to flee to the country. He says: "I know where you live. I know the peculiar dangers and temptations you face, and I am pleased that in the midst of powerful temptation you have not denied the faith but have held fast to My name." He commends them for such perseverance.

Some of you may have wrestled with the dilemma of where to live. You may have argued, "It would be better for the children if we got out of the city where the schools are not so bad. The neighborhood is getting less safe. It would be easier if we moved out." But Christ says, "No, I am pleased that you are staying where Satan has his seat. You are just where I want you to be. I approve of My people living in the city, but you must be aware of the dangers that you face."

In Revelation 2, our Lord urges His people to remain where they are, even if it is the seat of Satan. But as they live in such a place, they must be aware of the dangers there. They must have "city grace" to survive and flourish spiritually in such a place. That grace is evident in the promise of Jesus that He is coming to believers in Pergamos with a sharp two-edged sword, which includes both power to deliver and protect them and judgment to confront and punish their wrongdoing.

He begins with encouragement, saying, "Thou holdest fast my name, and hast not denied my faith." The church in Pergamos was a confessing church, faithfully proclaiming Jesus as Lord and the truths that every Christian must believe. What a blessing it was that the Lord could say this of the church in Pergamos! The church had maintained the truth of God in its confession, its proclamation, and its experience. She had stood firm against the temptation to trim her sails, that is, to modify her message to suit the times. She had not indulged in idolatry. She had persisted in confessing that "Jesus is the Lord" (1 Cor. 12:3), not Caesar. These were no small things, for the church in Pergamos was bombarded with temptations to give in at just these points.

Then Jesus cites a particular example of faithfulness. In the midst of this wicked environment, the Lord says that a certain believer named Antipas was a glowing example of faithfulness even to the point of suffering death as a martyr or witness to Christ. Antipas was put to death ("slain among you") for his faith in the Lord Jesus. That happened before the time this letter to Pergamos was written. It seems now that intense persecution has eased off. Christ goes on to say that although active persecution has ceased, the church must still remember that she is in the place "where Satan dwelleth."

This is a reminder to us that the devil has more than one way of attacking God's people. Sometimes he appears as "a roaring lion" who "walketh about, seeking whom he may devour" (1 Peter

5:8)—as he did during the persecution of believers in Pergamos. But at other times, he appears as an "angel of light" (2 Cor. 11:14), that is, as a false prophet or false teacher with beguiling powers of communication. That is how Satan was now at work in Pergamos.

We too must be aware that the devil has many disguises. We live in an age of sensationalism, and that is also true of Christian things. The only thing that seems to awaken Christians is the spectacular and the sensational—even when it comes to the devil. When you talk to Christians about the devil's devices, many think only in terms of occult practices and demon possession. Those are serious things, indeed, but the devil normally works in much less sensational ways.

In an old Puritan book titled *Precious Remedies Against Satan's Devices*, Thomas Brooks lists scores of ways in which the devil attacks God's people, most of which are very subtle. He also describes ways to safeguard ourselves against these attacks. In becoming aware of the weapons Satan uses against believers, we should remember that the devil is most effective in attacking God's people in the realm of the mental, moral, and practical, rather than the supernatural. We must be aware of that in the church as well as in our personal lives. We must learn how the devil insinuates himself among us and how he operates. We are not to be ignorant of his devices (2 Cor. 2:11).

Look at how he found a way into the church in Pergamos. Having failed to conquer the church by direct assault, Satan planted a kind of "fifth column," or subversive organization, in the church. Jesus says, "I have a few things against thee, because thou hast there them that hold the doctrine of Balaam, who taught Balac to cast a stumblingblock before the children of Israel, to eat things sacrificed unto idols, and to commit fornication. So hast thou also them that hold the doctrine of the Nicolaitans, which thing I hate" (vv. 14–15).

It is clear from what is recorded in these verses that two groups within the ranks of the church were promoting serious doctrinal and moral errors. No one seems to know exactly who the Nicolaitans were, but we do know the devil planted those people within the church to attack her from within. Also, we know that the Balaamites mentioned in verse 14 and the Nicolaitans in verse 15 appear to be similar types of people, for the Lord says, "so hast thou also them which hold the doctrine of the Nicolaitans, which thing I hate." Whatever that doctrine was, it must have been seriously erroneous, and even deadly, for the Lord to hate it so.

Balaam was a false prophet in Old Testament times. He was involved with the occult and witchcraft, but he was occasionally used by God to prophesy truth. One lesson here is that we must not confuse gifts with grace. A man may have special or extraordinary gifts and yet be unsaved. He may be like Balaam, who had the gift of prophecy but was unsaved, if we are to judge by the fruits of his ministry. Jesus speaks of the judgment day in the Sermon on the Mount and predicts: "Many will say to me in that day, Lord, Lord, have we not prophesied in thy name? And in thy name have cast out devils? And in thy name done many wonderful works? And then will I profess unto them, I never knew you: depart from me, ye that work iniquity" (Matt. 7:22–23).

So God can sovereignly give all kinds of gifts to people, but such gifts by themselves are not saving grace. The old Presbyterians held that "Truth is in order to goodness." As Paul says, "Though I speak with the tongues of men and of angels, and have not charity, I am become as sounding brass, or a tinkling cymbal…I am nothing" (1 Cor. 13:1–2).

Balaam, who had the gift of prophecy, was hired by Balak, king of Moab, to curse the Israelites, who were traveling through Moab on their way to Canaan. Balaam accepted the assignment, but a strange thing happened. Every time he opened his mouth to curse Israel, he pronounced a blessing instead. After several failed attempts, he finally told Balak, "Behold, I have received commandment to bless: and he hath blessed; and I cannot reverse it…. Surely there is no enchantment against Jacob, neither is there any divination against Israel: according to this time it shall be said of Jacob and of Israel, What hath God wrought!" (Num. 23:20–23). But this was not all that Balaam told Balak; he explained that there was a way to induce the children of Israel to bring down God's wrath upon their own heads: let them commit whoredom with the daughters of Moab!

"And they called the people unto the sacrifices of their gods: and the people did eat, and bowed down to their gods. And Israel joined himself unto Baal-peor: and the anger of the LORD was kindled against Israel" (Num. 25:1–3).

Satan often defeats God's people in ways that are far subtler than mere military conquest. As Israel was corrupted from within through sexual immorality and religious unfaithfulness, so the church in Pergamos was in danger from forces already at work in her ranks. Thus, Jesus warns the church: "Be alert to what is happening among you. You are in Satan's domain, and the devil is at work. You resisted him when he attacked the front door through persecution, and that is good. But now he has entered by the back door, and he is working through the Balaamites and Nicolaitans. He is trying to destroy your distinctiveness as the people of God. He is trying to bring the world into the church. He is trying to bring you into an alliance with the world, and that will prove to be your downfall."

Every night before we go to bed, we check to make sure that all the doors of our homes are locked. Locking the front door is not enough; a burglar could find another way to come in. In the same way, we must be sure that all the doors and windows of the church are locked against false doctrine, while welcoming all who are willing to hear and follow the truth. Jesus is warning Pergamos that Satan has crept into the church. The front door is locked and bolted, and that is good, but the devil is getting in through the back door with the help of people in the church who are willing to compromise with worldliness. These Balaamites and Nicolaitans are trying to get the church to mix with the world, adopt its customs, and live like unbelievers while professing to be followers of Jesus Christ.

Believers today need to heed this danger, for the conservative, biblical principles of our Reformation and post-Reformation fathers dictate to us that there should be a clear line of demarcation between the church and the world. The doctrine of these Balaamites and Nicolaitans perverted the grace of God into a justification for licentiousness and wickedness in the form of idolatry and fornication. It was no less than a denial that Jesus Christ is Master and Lord (Jude 4). Such an insidious doctrine might not overtly condone immorality, but it will encourage us to think and act as the world does to the point that we ultimately lose the distinctive spiritual identity that Christ calls us to maintain in the midst of a wicked and perverse generation.

Think, for example, of our passion for sports and other forms of entertainment. We waste valuable time indulging in things that do not profit us as Christians. They encourage an unwise use of the Sabbath Day, as well as advocate for self-indulgence, self-assertion, and self-exaltation. They revive the doctrines of the Balaamites and the Nicolaitans by bringing worldly thinking, worldly values, and worldly pursuits into our churches. This worldliness is evident in our outward way of life, our dress, our behavior, and our daily conversation.

Each one of us needs to be reminded of this danger, for we live in the midst of a world, in the midst of a city, and in the midst of various kinds of churches, even nominally Reformed churches, where the spirit of worldliness has crept in and now predominates. We are told in some Reformed churches that as Christians we must do what we can to "redeem" television and movies, theater, dance, sports, and most everything else in the world so that the world may be reclaimed for Christ, His covenant, and His kingdom.

There is something seriously wrong with that kind of thinking. Indeed, everything good and true in this world must be reclaimed by believers for Christ. But we must not attempt to reclaim what is sinful for Christ. We cannot sanctify that which tends to promote sinful thinking and immoral behavior. We must avoid the very appearance of evil. We must flee from temptations to sin, whether blatant or subtle. We need grace to abhor the false doctrines and immoral practices of today's Balaamites and Nicolaitans. Of course, we must not estrange ourselves from our neighbors but befriend them so that we may bring them the gospel. But we need to walk in a way that is clearly free from worldly influences, temptations, and fashions. We must live in godly simplicity, embodying sobriety and faithfulness in the midst of our peers, our families, and our society.

Often we define worldliness in negative terms and try to avoid it by observing various prohibitions and regulations, staying away from certain kinds of establishments, or giving up certain activities or pursuits. But worldliness is much more serious than that. It is an attitude of the mind and heart. James asks, "Ye adulterers and adulteresses, know ye not that the friendship of the world is enmity with God?" (James 4:4a). Worldliness is spiritual adultery, says James. It isn't just breaking a few house rules; it is whoring after the world and gross infidelity to Christ, who loves you and has shed His very blood to save you.

James continues: "Whosoever therefore will be a friend of the world is the enemy of God" (James 4:4b). Spiritual adultery results in enmity with God, and that is a very serious thing. To have God as your enemy is to put yourself in the gravest possible danger. James is not talking about a momentary lapse into worldliness, which we all struggle with. Rather, James is speaking here about a deliberate, conscious act on our part and a sin that grieves the Holy Spirit. In verse 5, he asks, "Do ye think that the scripture saith in vain, The spirit that dwelleth in us lusteth to envy?" In other words, James says: "Don't you realize that this Spirit that lives in you is the Spirit of a possessively loving and jealous God? He will not tolerate rivals. He wants the best for you. The Holy Spirit cannot idly stand by while you whore after the world. He is jealous for your highest good. He longs that you might have the best. And He will not let you get away with forming liaisons with the world."

In the same way, the Lord comes to the church in Pergamos as the One "which hath the sharp sword with two edges." In verse 16, He says, "Repent; or else I will come unto thee quickly, and will fight against them with the sword of my mouth." He presents Himself as a man of war whose love has been compromised. He will not tolerate such infidelity in His bride, the church. He says, "I will come and visit you, and I will fight against those who seek to draw you aside into the way of the world." He will come to win back His bride from the attentions of the world.

Submit to Your Savior's Dealings

Not only do we need to be aware of the spiritual danger that surrounds us, but we must submit ourselves to the Lord's dealings with us to purify us. The Lord deals with worldliness, whether in a church or in an individual Christian, in two ways:

First, *He calls us to repent of our worldliness.* The Lord says, "Repent; or else I will come unto thee quickly, and fight against them with the sword of my mouth" (Rev. 2:16). To repent, we must search our hearts, identify our sin, grieve over it, confess it, flee from it, and bow under the just punishment of it. I wonder if you truly know what it means to come before the Lord stripped of your righteousness and confessing: "Lord, not only am I no better than those of Pergamos, but worse, I am full of pollution. I cannot repent as I should, I cannot do anything that I should or as I should, but, Lord, I accept my punishment. I deserve to perish."

To such persons, Jesus promises, "To him that overcometh will I give to eat of the hidden manna, and will give him a white stone, and in the stone a new name written, which no man knoweth saving he that receiveth it" (Rev. 2:17b). Christ says that sinners who are brought to the end of themselves will be overcomers. To do so, they will have to repent of their sins and surrender to Him as their Lord and Master. "Him that overcometh" is the one who is wounded over sin, gives up the battle against God, and engages to fight in the Lord's army against worldliness. It is to him that Christ offers overcoming grace.

Christ also says, "To him...will I give to eat of the hidden manna," that is, the ability to feed by faith upon Christ as the manna or "bread which came down from heaven" (John 6:41), being refreshed and renewed unto life eternal. Christ is manna *par excellence* for His people, "the true meat and drink of life eternal."[3] Just as God provided the manna as food for the children of Israel to sustain them in the wilderness, so Christ promises to sustain His people in their pilgrimage through this world, if only they are faithful to Him.

---

3. "Form for the Administration of the Lord's Supper," *The Psalter*, 138.

He calls it "the hidden manna," as a reference to the manna hidden in the ark of the covenant, because this promise is made "to such as keep his covenant, and to those that remember his commandments to keep them" (Ps. 103:18).

Second, *He fights against our worldliness.* In Revelation 2:16, Christ says, "Repent; or else I will come…quickly, and will fight against them." It is encouraging that Jesus promises to come to us and fight against our enemy of worldliness. He will visit this church and fight against evil. He will also fight against evildoers in the church, such as the Balaamites and the Nicolaitans.

Christ does not always fight people to destroy them but to save them. A classic example of this is Jacob at Peniel (Gen. 32:24–30). We are told that Jacob wrestled with "a man" until "the breaking of the day." That was not just some exercise on God's part; it was an expression of saving grace, for Jacob was never the same after that.

Christ comes to us through His Word and in the circumstances of our lives. He fights against us, not vindictively or punitively, but to stop us from fighting against Him and to compel us to cling to Him. The strengths in which we take pride are crushed until we have nothing left in this world to cling to but Christ.

If you are a follower of Christ who is flirting with the world today, you will have to contend with your Savior. He will not let you get away with it. He may have to do something painful and even disabling to you to draw you back to Himself, but draw you back He will, because His love is an everlasting love that will not let you go.

Then Christ adds a further promise. To those who have not been contaminated by the false teaching of the Balaamites and the Nicolaitans, He says in verse Revelation 2:17: "To him that overcometh will I give…a white stone, and in the stone a new name written, which no man knoweth saving he that receiveth it."

Commentators have written at length about the meaning of the white stone. Some suggest it refers to the stones that the high priest wore in his breastplate, which were inscribed with the names of the tribes of Israel. Others say the stone is a reference to Greek games, in which the winner of an event was given a white stone with a special name on it. Others say it has to do with the judicial courts. When a verdict was announced, the judge would take one of two stones, either black or white, and put it in a jar. If the stone was black, the person was declared guilty; if white, the person was declared innocent. Though all of these explanations may contain some truth, I believe the white stone indicates four things:

1. *Justification.* The verdict of forgiveness is the most valid explanation, for this says the white stone refers to God the Father as Judge, who hands a believer the stone of acquittal because of the atoning blood of His only begotten Son. The stone is a symbol of the work of the Holy Spirit in sealing what the Father declares: "This sinner is freed from sin on the basis of the work and merit of the Lord Jesus Christ." That is what God does for unworthy sinners who put their trust in His incarnate Son as the only Savior.

2. *Sanctifying grace.* The stone refers to the work of the Holy Spirit in "applying unto us that which we have in Christ, namely, the washing away of our sins and the daily renewing of our lives."[4] In this sense, the white stone is a token of sweet fellowship with the Lord. My friend, think of the white stone as a token or memento of every time the Lord gives you an answer to prayer, every time He applies His truth with divine unction and savor to your soul, every time He grants you a refreshing season for your soul, and every time He gives a sweet manifestation of the beauty of Christ in your heart. How sweet it is when God gives His people such white stones!

3. *Victory and honor.* During the time when Revelation was written, people voted for candidates for office. The person who won was awarded a white stone. A white stone was a symbol of victory.

Today, the Lord may give us a foretaste of the day on which He will give all His people the white stone of victory. On the day of judgment, He will give each of His dear children a white stone as a kind of pass or token admitting them to the wedding feast of the Lamb and His bride (Rev. 19:6–9). One day He will say, "Friend,

4. "Form for the Administration of Baptism," *The Psalter*, 126.

come up higher; enjoy this everlasting feast at My right hand, where there are pleasures for evermore" (see Luke 14:10; Ps. 16:11).

Oh, for Christ's sake—to whom we have awarded the black stone of suffering, of all our sins and iniquities, and of our guilt and punishment, and who has borne it all in the black shadows of the darkness of Golgotha's cross—God will now give you a white stone of everlasting testimony that He is your God and Father, and that you are His child and a member of His household forever.

4. *Personal communion or fellowship with Christ.* Jesus knows His sheep and calls them each by name (John 10:3). Jesus has a private name for every believer who will enter heaven. Scripture says the day is coming when believers will be received into glory and have intimate fellowship with the triune God. But there shall always remain, even in everlasting bliss, a special flavor of personal intimate acquaintance that Jesus reflects by giving each believer a white stone upon which his new name is written, a name known only to him and his Lord. This indicates even now the unique relationship that every believer has with Christ.

With this white stone, Christ shows the very personal nature of His work in the lives of His people. We receive the gift of life and salvation personally and privately from the hand of God. We must know fellowship with the Lord. We must know what it means to have contact with the Lord, to touch the hem of His garment by faith, and to receive the crumbs that fall from the Master's table.

When my father was serving as an elder in a church in Kalamazoo, Michigan, I preached in that church fairly often. Before I would go to the pulpit, each of the four elders would shake my hand, wish me God's blessing, and append my name. One said, "Blessing, Doctor"; another, "Blessing, Reverend"; and yet another, "Blessing, Pastor." My dad would say, "Blessing, Son." I don't have to tell you which one of these names was the most personal.

That is what our Lord is saying here about the significance of the hidden manna and the new name that no one else knows. He is saying, "If you remain faithful, I will bring you into such a rich and satisfying relationship with Me that you will never again hunger for the world."

Are you one of Jesus' loved ones, or has your love grown cold? Has it been supplanted and usurped by the love of this world, with all its sights and sounds? Do you know what it is to go through life with "hidden manna" to feed upon? Let me urge you to turn your eyes once more upon Jesus, the living manna in the wilderness, and to look full in His wonderful face. When you do so, you will know in your heart that, having Him, there is nothing on earth that you can yet desire.

Finally, there is a word for you in all seven of these letters. The Lord says in verse 17, "He that hath an ear, let him hear what the Spirit saith unto the churches." He is addressing the churches, but He is also addressing the individual members of those churches. He begins by saying, "He that hath an ear, let him hear." You have been considering this sermon, but have you been *hearing what the Spirit is saying*? It is time for you to reckon with what the Spirit of Christ has said and continues to say to you, as well as to the church to which you belong.

7

Christ's Message to an Overly Tolerant Church

REVELATION 2:18-29

And unto the angel of the church in Thyatira write; these things saith the Son of God, who hath his eyes like unto a flame of fire, and his feet are like fine brass; I know thy works, and charity, and service, and faith, and thy patience, and thy works; and the last to be more than the first. Notwithstanding I have a few things against thee, because thou sufferest that woman Jezebel, which calleth herself a prophetess, to teach and to seduce my servants to commit fornication, and to eat things sacrificed unto idols. And I gave her space to repent of her fornication; and she repented not. Behold, I will cast her into a bed, and them that commit adultery with her into great tribulation, except they repent of their deeds. And I will kill her children with death; and all the churches shall know that I am he which searcheth the reins and hearts: and I will give unto every one of you according to your works. But unto you I say, and unto the rest in Thyatira, as many as have not this doctrine, and which have not known the depths of Satan, as they speak; I will put upon you none other burden. But that which ye have already hold fast till I come. And he that overcometh, and keepeth my works unto the end, to him will I give power over the nations: and he shall rule them with a rod of iron; as the vessels of a potter shall they be broken to shivers: even as I received of my Father. And I will give him the morning star. He that hath an ear, let him hear what the Spirit saith unto the churches.

Tolerance is a burning issue in our day. We live in a tolerant age that calls for ever-increasing tolerance—in theology, in religion, in relationships, in sexuality, yes, in nearly every area of life. And yet, those who call the loudest for tolerance of their views and lifestyles are often the most intolerant of those who don't tolerate sin. This has led D. A. Carson to write his well-known book, *The Intolerance of Tolerance.*[1]

So what do you think about tolerance? Should you be more tolerant? Should the church be more tolerant? If so, in what areas and how? If not, in what areas and how not? Jesus' message to the tolerant church of Thyatira, therefore, ought to be of great interest to all of us. How did Jesus handle their tolerance? And what message does he have for you and me and your church in this letter?

Christ's fourth letter in Revelation is addressed to the church in Thyatira. This is the longest of the letters to the seven churches of Asia, even though the church was in the least important of the seven cities. Situated forty miles southeast of Pergamos, Thyatira numbered no more than twenty-five thousand in population. Though not politically or culturally important, Thyatira did have significance commercially. This small city was a prosperous trading center. Inscriptions found by archaeologists bring to light the fact that Thyatira boasted of numerous so-called "trade guilds." These guilds, the forerunners of modern labor unions, were developed and organized according to occupations, such as bakers, bronze workers, cobblers, weavers, tanners, dyers, and potters. In Thyatira, it was almost compulsory for a tradesman to belong to one of these guilds. Without guild membership, a business could hardly prosper.

On the surface, these organizations seemed to be important but innocent associations. But to join and participate in meetings, members had to celebrate pagan festivals. At these festivals, participants ate food that had been offered and dedicated to the gods and goddesses claimed as patrons by the particular trades involved. If a person wished to join a trade guild, he was compelled to worship the guild's patron deity by joining in the sacrificial feasts and eating food dedicated to that god. Besides that, after the celebrations had

---

1. D. A. Carson, *The Intolerance of Tolerance* (Grand Rapids: Eerdmans, 2012).

gone on for several hours, participants often indulged in immoral practices and other forms of idol worship.

In the midst of this primarily heathen city noted for its trade guilds, it pleased God to establish a small Christian church. We don't know who planted the church in Thyatira. The only other time the Bible mentions this city is in Acts 16, where we read of Lydia, who was converted under Paul's ministry by a river in Philippi. She was "a seller of purple," either purple dye or purple cloth, and a devout Gentile "which worshipped God" even before she was converted. Lydia hailed from Thyatira (Acts 16:14–15). Historians have often speculated that Lydia's influence may have encouraged a church plant in this city, but so far we have discovered nothing to confirm that view.

The heart of this letter is a mixture of commendation and concern. Let us consider Christ's approach to the church of Thyatira, His assessment of the church, His admonition for the church, and, finally, His reward for the church.

Christ's Approach to Thyatira

Christ approaches the church in Thyatira in a moving way. Revelation 2:18 says, "Unto the angel of the church in Thyatira write; these things saith the Son of God, who hath his eyes like unto a flame of fire, and his feet are like fine brass." Note particularly the description of Christ's eyes repeated from Revelation 1:14. The Lord Jesus has eyes that can burn through every conceivable façade and defense that we can devise to hide our true selves from others, eyes that penetrate right into our hearts. When his eyes are upon you, He sees right through you. He knows all things; nothing in my life is shielded from His gaze, even those things that I hide from myself. *Nothing* is hidden from Him.

There is a prayer long in use in the Church of England known as The Collect for Purity, which reads as follows: "Almighty God, unto whom all hearts be open, all desires known, and from whom no secrets are hid: cleanse the thoughts of our hearts by the inspiration of thy Holy Spirit, that we may perfectly love thee, and worthily magnify thy holy name; through Christ our Lord. Amen."[2] It is true of God in general, and therefore true of the incarnate Son of God, that all hearts are open and all desires known to him; therefore, no secret may be hidden from Him.

Later, in Revelation 2:23, Christ adds that He "searcheth the reins and hearts" (cf. Ps. 7:9), literally, the kidneys and the viscera or internal organs. The kidneys were thought to be the seat of the emotions, and thus the equivalent of the heart or mind. Our Lord says to this church, with its prophetess (v. 20) and its tendency, as we shall see, to tolerate unbiblical mysticism (v. 24): "I am the One who knows the difference between what is merely emotional and what is truly spiritual. I am the One who sees to the heart of the matter. There is a great cover-up in Thyatira, and a great scandal there, but I am not at all deceived or taken in by it."

Jesus Christ approaches each of the seven churches in a different way. That is not to say that He is all things to all men. Indeed, quite the reverse. Rather, by virtue of the divine fullness that is uniquely His (Col. 1:19; 2:9), our Lord is the complete answer to any situation that can arise in any church. That is true of our churches today as well. He is the answer to His church's needs.

Christ approaches the Thyatiran church in a rather unsettling way. This picture of Christ coming with eyes of flaming fire holds nothing comfortable for the minister of the church in Thyatira or anyone else who may be trying to keep the scandal undercover. But while it may not have been what he or the church liked, it was what they needed. Christ does not consult our likes and preferences. He always knows what is going on, what to say, and how best to approach a church. That can be very comforting to those who cling to Him in faithfulness, but at the same time very disturbing for those who do not.

Christ's description of Himself to the Thyatiran church is full of authority. In the previous letters, Christ's self-descriptions were

---

2. *The Book of Common Prayer: The Texts of 1549, 1559, and 1662*, ed. Brian Cummings (Oxford: Oxford University Press, 2011), 20.

beautiful pictures of Himself. He is the One who holds the seven stars (Rev. 2:1); He is the One who is the first and the last (v. 8); He is the One who has the sharp two-edged sword (v. 12). But here He describes Himself in terms of His absolute authority as "the Son of God" (v. 18). So these are the words of the very Son of God—that is, of Almighty God.

These words, like the rest of this passage, reflect Psalm 2, which notes how the nations rage against the Lord and His Anointed; how God has set His Son to reign as King upon His holy hill of Zion; and how He has given to that Son power and authority over all things and over all peoples. Here in Revelation 2, Jesus invokes that absolute power and authority (cf. v. 26). These are words that come from the very throne of God.

Jesus' self-description here is repeated from chapter 1, from that great vision of Christ walking in the midst of the seven golden candlesticks. But in writing to Thyatira, He identifies Himself particularly as the Son of God (v. 18). One reason is that He wants to remind the Thyatirans that they have to deal with the living God. They are not just playing church or building a spiritual empire for themselves. The scandal He is about to expose in the church touches His name and His honor. We need to remind ourselves, as we come to God's house each week and when we celebrate the Lord's Supper, that how we conduct ourselves has everything to do with the Son of God and His reputation. The church is the manifestation of the body of Christ, and what we do and what we are touch His name and His reputation in the world. This is clear as Christ comes to the church of Thyatira as the Son of God who is jealous for the honor of His name.

Christ's Assessment of Thyatira

How does our Lord assess the condition of the church in Thyatira? He sees two things that seem to be contradictory. On the one hand, He sees a record of faithfulness past and present, but on the other, he sees evidence of decline and deterioration.

The situation in Thyatira was almost exactly the opposite of that in Ephesus. In Ephesus, there was great concern about biblical standards, soundness in the pulpit, purity in the church, and the faithful exercise of church discipline—and yet, the church had lost her first love. Her relationship with the Lord was deteriorating. Of Thyatira, however, Christ says, "I know thy works, and charity, and service, and faith, and thy patience, and thy works; and the last to be more than the first" (Rev. 2:19). Christ commends the church in Thyatira for her steadfastness in works and service, her growth and progress in love and faith, and her "patience" or endurance under trial. He sums up this record by saying that the "last" or latest works are "more" or greater than the first (cf. v. 5). There was great love and zeal for good works in the church at Thyatira.

But the Thyatirans were weak precisely where the Ephesians were strong. In their warmth and fervency and in their emphasis on Christian experience, the believers of Thyatira had lost their doctrinal moorings. They had drifted away from concern for soundness in faith and holiness in life. This church did not "try the spirits" by Scripture (1 John 4:1). Her charity, her devotion, and her experience had become divorced from the Word of God. In tolerating "that woman Jezebel" (Rev. 2:20), this church had become more interested in what Christ calls the "depths of Satan" (v. 24), literally, "deep things" or "deep secrets." The church in Thyatira had fallen into an unhealthy and unbiblical mysticism.

In Thyatira, proper instruction in "head knowledge" was being neglected for the belief that experience and love were all that counted. This church was doing the opposite of some of the other churches, and thus she was trying to place a cloak of love over all her shortcomings. In Thyatira, the only important thing was that the love of God be shed abroad in the heart (Rom. 5:5). So, gradually, a false mysticism that separated justification from sanctification had begun to captivate the Thyatiran church. The net effect was that the church had started to cease disciplining her members. She spoke only of love; she did not bring a word of admonition, a warning against immorality, or a teaching against worldliness and sin. Gradually, her Sunday talk in the house of prayer and her Monday-through-Saturday walk in society had begun to part ways.

There is great need for you and me to have experiences of God that are scripturally grounded and verifiable. The cold, arid intellectualism of Ephesus is a detriment to true Christianity. But so too is the unbiblical, though very warm and fervent, mysticism of Thyatira. Experience outside the framework of Scripture is dangerous. We need to have a right balance in our lives between God's objective truth and our subjective experience of that truth. If the devil doesn't draw us in one direction, he will draw us in another. If he can't get us in doctrine and practice, he will get us in our personal relationship with the Lord. He will loosen our devotion and experience from its biblical moorings, and before we know it, we will be adrift in a dangerous sea of unbiblical mysticism. Soundness in doctrine is not everything; neither is Christian experience everything. We need both.

This error crept into the church of Thyatira especially through a woman who called herself a prophetess, to whom Christ gives the name of "Jezebel." This evil woman, who nearly destroyed the Thyatiran church, is so called because her character and her devious, influential teachings reflected the sins of King Ahab's pagan queen, Jezebel (1 Kings 16–22; 2 Kings 1–9). The Old Testament Jezebel promoted Baal worship in the midst of God's covenant nation. The latter-day Jezebel in Thyatira tried to corrupt the church with the devilish doctrine of the toleration of evil. Being the spokeswoman, history tells us, of the sect of the Nicolaitans, she taught that the gospel sets us absolutely free—even from all obligation to keep the law. Her list of *adiaphora*, things indifferent or non-essential, was very long. You could freely transgress moral boundaries and could eat and drink things sacrificed to idols. She argued, as many others have done, that since we are saved by grace, we may live as we desire. So she flatly rejected the admonition of the Jerusalem Council, which stated that as "necessary things," Christians should "abstain from meats offered to idols... and from fornication" (Acts 15:28–29).

Jezebel may have been the Thyatiran pastor's wife, as an alternative reading in the margins of some Bibles says "that woman Jezebel" can also be translated as "thy wife Jezebel." If this is true, it certainly helps explain how this woman got into the position of influence that she held, why she was tolerated, and how she was able to get away with her unbiblical and ungodly teaching.

Despite the fact that Jezebel's teachings were not based on God's Word but on her own notions and feelings, she began to influence many in the Thyatiran church. She said, as it were: "The trade guilds are not so bad. You may join in their feasts and in their fornication, and you may know in your heart all the while that you serve the living God." In other words, "Unlike Daniel in Babylon, you need not stand apart or alone; you may live as the Babylonians and still keep your Christianity." Jezebel promoted what we today call antinomianism—the teaching that once you are saved, you are free from the law and may live as you desire.

What a grave danger this is! There is excessive legalism, on one side, that squelches the life of vital orthodoxy, reducing Christianity to a matter of keeping rules and regulations. But on the other hand, a religion that knows nothing of the fear of God and has no sense of what is holy and becoming in His people produces a congregation without a backbone, without discipline—a loving congregation, even zealous for good works, but inwardly void of true experience, that is, experience that can stand up to close examination in the light of God's Word. What need there is for true, godly balance!

Likewise, what need there is for the Lord Jesus Christ to admonish us not to indulge in an antinomian style of living.[3] Christ comes and says: "O church in Thyatira, I know what you are doing. My eyes are like unto a flame of fire, My feet are like fine brass" (see v. 18). Again in verse 23 we read, "I am he which searcheth the reins and hearts." Jesus is saying, "I know, Thyatira, that at its core your religion is turning into a self-centered mystical adventure

---

3. Antinomianism refers to Christians feeling no need to live according to God's law as a rule of life. For excellent sources on this error, see Mark Jones, *Antinomianism: Reformed Theology's Unwelcome Guest* (Phillipsburg, N.J.: P&R, 2013); Sinclair B. Ferguson, *The Whole Christ: Legaliism, Antinomianism, and Gospel Assurance* (Wheaton, Ill.: Crossway, 2016).

rather than a religion rooted in Scripture and aiming at the glory of My name."

So, my friends, the great question for us is this: Does our religion serve only or primarily ourselves, our qualms of conscience, and our earthly ambitions and desires, or do we have that true religion, which makes us yearn, from the bottoms of our hearts, for the honor and glory of God's name? What is our goal? And where is our balance? These are the questions that the situation in Thyatira especially poses for us. Thyatira warns us to seek that true mysticism that is grounded in God's Word, that is, true experience and communion with Him that is confirmed by divine authority—"Thus saith the Lord"—to the heart of a poor and needy sinner. It also admonishes us to flee from a false mysticism that covers shortcomings and sins with a cloak of shallow charity and that teaches that we may live as we will. Thyatira is a flashing yellow light, warning us to walk in the ways of God with fear and trembling, seeking His honor and His glory.

Whether she was the pastor's wife or not, Jezebel had great power in the Thyatiran church. She was so dangerous because she really was, like the Jezebel of the Old Testament, a hater of God and His people. So she became a symbol for worldliness, or what we might term the spirit of "Jezebelism." Jezebelism is only a more blatant form of Balaamism. Balaam and Jezebel are similar characters in Scripture, and they were after the same thing. They wanted to overthrow the distinctive testimony of the people of God. Balaam did it because he wanted to collect a handsome fee for his services. He had been hired by the king of Moab to do it. He was simply doing a job. But Jezebel is a different story. If you read the story in 1 Kings, you get the impression that she simply hated the God of Israel, His servants the prophets, and the people of God. Jezebel and Balaam were both aiming at the same thing; Jezebel was just one step further down the road than Balaam.

We need to warn each other of this problem of the spiritual "slippery slope." Once you begin to neglect the secret place of prayer and begin to get into an Ephesus situation, losing your first love, you are on the slippery slope that leads on to Thyatira and finally to Laodicea. Many of us may already be somewhere along that road, and we need to understand the seriousness of the extent of our spiritual drift and decline. It is a road that, apart from the keeping grace of God, ends in total apostasy. That is what Balaam and Jezebel were all about. That is what the devil is aiming at in your life and in mine. He wants that to happen to your church and in the life of every member of it. He wants to see you apostatize. Unless we are aware of Satan's devices, we will go on down that slippery slope and soon find ourselves tolerating the Jezebels and Balaams, along with all their evil ways. It is a very sorry state that they were in at Thyatira—a very sad picture of decline.

It is not surprising, therefore, that a grave problem arose in the church at Thyatira. Must a businessman or tradesman reject membership in a trade guild if he had joined the Christian church? Certainly he would suffer a serious loss of income and lose a great deal of his position and reputation in society were he to do so. Possibly he would be reduced to poverty, and certainly he would be exposed to persecution. But could he belong to one of the guilds and not partake of its feasts and sacrifices, not believing in its gods and goddesses? Would he, merely by belonging to a guild, deny the name and lordship of Jesus Christ? Or was it possible to combine membership in a guild with an inward, living Christianity? Could he somehow enjoy the benefits that a guild provided and reject the evil they espoused? This was the question and dilemma.

We face a similar dilemma today in the midst of a worldly, entertainment-focused society. We must endure persecution at work and in society when we refuse to embrace systems and modes of thinking, as well as activities and behaviors, that are militant against the living power of authentic Christianity. The whole system today in government, in public education, and in society at large espouses a mindless toleration, mixing *Christianity*, which is God-centered thinking, with *humanism*, or man-centered thinking. Just as Satan subtly worked in Thyatira, so he works today to persuade us that the true Christian and the unbeliever can really work and live together harmoniously with similar goals and with a similar end in view—man's fulfillment.

The result in our society, as in Thyatira, is that there is no exclusive or distinctive Christian goal. Christ is no longer at the center of our thoughts, our lives, or our churches. We are co-opted by the world. We merge the goals of the Christian and the unbeliever so that we say that Christianity differs from the world around her only in degree and not in kind. This was the temptation in Thyatira. This has been a temptation for Christians throughout all the ages—the temptation to dress up humanistic thinking in the outward cloak of Christianity, to reinterpret Christianity as a means of human self-fulfillment, and to forget that true Christianity teaches an altogether different way of living than the world knows.

It is not surprising that the Thyatiran church was split on this issue. Some took a firm stand that guild membership was absolutely forbidden. Though it brought social isolation and economic hardship, they felt there was no other way to follow in order to remain loyal to Christ and His cause. Jesus affirms that decision: "I know thy works, and charity, and service, and faith, and thy patience, and thy works; and the last to be more than the first" (Rev. 2:19).

Others in Thyatira were not so sure. They thought that the whole business of guild membership could be relegated to the *adiaphora*: things that are indifferent or non-essential; things that neither harm nor profit; things about which the Word of God does not give an explicit command; and things that fall under the domain of Romans 14:5: "One man esteemeth one day above another: another esteemeth every day alike. Let every man be fully persuaded in his own mind." This second group, spearheaded by Jezebel, argued that it was quite acceptable to eat things sacrificed to idols and even to participate in guild-sponsored acts of fornication. The second group believed that to refuse membership in the guilds was an excessive form of legalism. Instead of seeing it as Christ saw it, they argued for mixing Christianity with Jezebelian man-centered thinking.

The lessons we can learn from this letter today are many. Let me mention just three. First, we must recognize that the spirit of these more liberal Thyatiran Christians involved trying to creep as close as possible to sin or at least to worldly ways of thinking. Call it spiritual brinkmanship. They hoped to avoid paying the price of persecution—to avoid the reality of the dictum laid down by Paul: "All that will live godly in Christ Jesus shall suffer persecution" (2 Tim. 3:12). In the same way, we do wrong today when we come as close to sin as we dare and when we flirt with the evils of our time, perhaps not indulging aggressively in those evils but developing a willingness to accommodate them. When we indulge in worldly entertainments, worldly fashions, worldly materialism, and a worldly way of thinking, we are following the Thyatiran inclination to go beyond the borders of God's Word and what conscience, based on that Word, allows. The net effect is that we no longer regard sin as sin. Then worldly influences permeate a church and, in the end, usurp the place of authentic piety and godliness.

A second lesson we can learn from this letter concerns the faulty thinking in Thyatira that lay behind their cozying up to worldly ways. The fault was that concern for God's glory had been supplanted by the quest for personal happiness. This is precisely what divides true Christendom from false Christendom; what divides authentic Christianity from worldly patterns and lifestyles. To whom do we live? Whose will must be done? Whose name must be honored? Do we target our lives on self-satisfaction or do we focus upon the will, the Word, and the glory of God? If God is our center, then we will not desire to do those things that are contrary to His Word and His will. We will long to live holy lives despite our weaknesses and stumbling.

True happiness is to be found only in being God-centered. After all, isn't that how God created us—made in His image, to focus on Him as the source and the epitome of all true joy? But by nature, through our deep fall in Adam, we have become man-centered and self-centered. We try to fill our eternal, triangular souls with a round and empty world. We try to fill the call to God's service with the shallow pleasures of self-service. The net effect is that we reap unhappiness, sorrow, disappointment, and disillusionment, like the prodigal son in the far country, before he came to himself and saw the misery he had brought upon himself.

A third lesson is that the real problem in Thyatira was not that everyone was supporting Jezebel and lining up behind her, but that they were tolerating her and the godless teachings she was promoting. Christ's complaint in Revelation 2:20 is that "thou sufferest that woman Jezebel"; in other words, "You are tolerating or putting up with this false teaching." The interesting thing is that the risen Christ is criticizing not the teaching primarily but the toleration of the teaching. And the Thyatirans tolerated it because they were not testing it by the Word of God. That is a principle of immense importance. What is the test of all teachings? The test, of course, is apostolic teaching, as recorded in God's Word. But the Thyatirans had never done that. They just said, "Oh well, these Jezebelians have their own views and their own ways of thinking." Thus, they tolerated them.

History makes clear that toleration of error of this kind eats away at the heart of the church of Christ and ultimately, like worms in a great oak tree, brings it crashing down! That is why there is a need for discipline in the church. This is why the Reformers said, as did the apostles, that discipline is one of the great essential marks of the true church. Where the Word is faithfully preached and the sacraments are administered as Christ instituted them, discipline is exercised in the church. That discipline is necessary to *preserve the church's life* so that the people know what false teaching is and reject it forthrightly. So the commandment Christ gives to the church in Thyatira, and to us, is not only to repent of false teaching, but to repent of toleration of such teaching.

But there is another side to the picture, a brighter side. In the days of Jezebel in the Old Testament, there was a remnant of those who had refused to bow the knee to Baal. In Thyatira, there was a remnant also. In Revelation 2:24, Christ speaks to "the rest in Thyatira, as many as have not this doctrine, and which have not known the depths of Satan." There were those who had refused to bow to Jezebel and refused to come under her influence, and Christ points out their progress. Go back to verse 19, where He refers to the remnant, saying: "I know thy works, and charity, and service, and faith, and thy patience, and thy works; *and the last to be more than the first.*" I wonder, if the Lord were to assess your life, would He be able to say that your works in these last few months were more and of a better spirit than your first works?

How much are we even concerned about progress in the Christian life? Do you know what I find when I look around the conservative Reformed church? I find Christians with a watertight theology and system of beliefs. But even here, I see that we are slow to learn from God's Word. We accept what we already believe. But we have not arrived in our knowledge or understanding of the truth. God has fresh light to bring to us from His Word. We still have much to learn. We need to beware of a closed mind.

That is true not only in the realm of doctrine but also in the realm of sanctification. Friends, we are just looking at one another and comparing ourselves, and we are content with so little. We are not straining forward; we are not striving after holiness. Remember Hebrews 12:14: "Follow peace with all men, and holiness, without which no man shall see the Lord." He uses a strong word for *follow*— the word for "persecute." Paul knew what it was to be persecuted, and he knew what it was to be a persecutor. Remember how he hated the Christians in Damascus, "breathing out threatenings and slaughter" (Acts 9:1). He was bearing down upon that little church before the Lord stopped him in his tracks. Now he says, "Strive after holiness like that; track it down like that; bring into play every faculty you possess, and strain after it." Are you and I doing that?

The same is true in the realm of experience. God is a great God, and we are only treading water in the shallows as far as our experience of Him is concerned. We grow content with this. If we are moved by a sermon somewhat or by a favorite psalm selection, we are grateful and just carry on. But God can be known intimately. God can reveal Himself to us in ways that we have scarcely begun to understand.

In Thyatira, there was progress at least, and our Lord commends them for it. Look at the way He describes this progress: "I know thy works, and charity, and service, and faith, and thy patience, and thy works; and the last to be more than the first." Notice that He speaks about their works before their love, and their service before their faith. There is a reason for that. It is the law of progress in the Christian life. Let me illustrate what I mean.

When a tree grows, the taller and wider it grows, the deeper into the ground its roots grow. Otherwise, it just topples over. If a tree is planted in shallow soil, it grows for a time and seems to be all right, but then the roots begin to come up out of the ground because they have nowhere to go. The tree ends up toppling over at strange angles. That is what happens with the church sometimes. Are you today more deeply rooted in Christ than you were three months ago? As you grow up and out, as you get more teaching into your mind, and as you become more active in the work of the Lord, are you clinging even more deeply and tenaciously to your Savior with your love and faith? How much of our Christianity is underground? You see, unless we are growing in love for and faith in the person and redemptive work of Christ, our works and our service will come to an end. We will just come toppling down.

Robert Murray M'Cheyne uses the illustration of a shipwrecked sailor clinging to a rock in the middle of the ocean. He says that the more the waves sweep down upon this man, the more tightly he clings to the rock. The waters rise and try to suck him away from the rock, but he clings for dear life; if not, he will be swept away and drown.

That is how it is with a Christian. We say we have been saved. What does that mean? We are saved out of this world and are holding on by faith and love to Christ. He is the Rock that is higher than we are (Ps. 61:2). You are not a Christian at all unless you know this. You are not a Christian just because you come to church, do certain things, and read certain books. A true Christian has love and faith for Christ, and he is clinging to Him for dear life, for eternal life. Then the world batters us with wave after wave of worldliness. The waves of this world try to drag us away from our Savior, so we cling to Him more tightly. Is that how it is with you? If we are to endure to the end in love and faith, we must cling to Christ tenaciously every moment of our existence.

That is what our Lord exhorts the remnant to do in Revelation 2:24–25, saying, "Hold fast till I come." The waves are bearing down and things are getting tough even in the church. Things are happening that we don't approve of, bringing dishonor to the name of Christ. But Jesus says, "Hold fast; don't be disillusioned by it; don't give up but cling more tenaciously to Me with love and faith."

Christ's Admonition for Thyatira

Next, Christ delivers a twofold admonition to the church in Thyatira in Revelation 2:22–25. First, He warns Jezebel and her partisans of what He will do to them if they don't repent: "Behold, I will cast her into a bed, and them that commit adultery with her into great tribulation…. And I will kill her children with death…and I will give unto every one of you according to your works" (vv. 22–23).

Second, Jesus also admonishes the remnant in Thyatira who are walking faithfully before Him and rejecting Jezebel's influence. He provides a loving admonition that counterbalances and counteracts Jezebelism. Jesus says in verses 24–25: "But unto you I say, and unto the rest in Thyatira, as many as have not this doctrine, and which have not known the depths of Satan, as they speak; I will put upon you none other burden. But that which ye have already hold fast till I come." So Jesus says, "Hold fast; I know the situation you are in; I will not ask you to do more than you are doing now."

In these last words, there is a distinct allusion to the decisions of the Jerusalem Council, as reported in Acts 15: "For it seemed good to the Holy Ghost, and to us, to lay upon you no greater burden than these necessary things; that ye abstain from meats offered to idols, and from blood, and from things strangled, and from fornication: from which if ye keep yourselves, ye shall do well. Fare ye well" (vv. 28–29).

Our Lord is saying to the members of the church in Thyatira that they are being influenced by the teaching of Jezebel. She is influencing them to conform to the world and to taste the "deep things" of Satan. But now the Lord admonishes the faithful remnant of believers in Thyatira, saying: "Don't go to the opposite extreme. Don't overreact against this Jezebelism, this lawlessness. Don't retreat into Pharisaism and legalism."

That is what we are prone to do. We try to balance the extreme behavior of others by going to the opposite extreme. Jesus is saying here: "Don't do that. All I ask you to do is to carry on as you have been taught. I put no other burden on you. Abstain from meats offered to idols, yes, and from fornication, but do not go overboard in the opposite direction and enact man-made rules and regulations, tightening things up in the church because of this lawlessness. You are not under the law; you are under grace. I put no other burden upon you."

This is another reminder of our great need for balance in the Christian church. We all tend to overreact, one against the other. We must be careful not to do that; it is not scriptural. We are not to be extreme, but we are to be scriptural.

Christ's Reward for Thyatira

Finally, as He does for nearly all of the seven churches, our Lord leaves the Thyatirans with a word of promise and encouragement— a promised reward, if they remain faithful to the end. He says: "And he that overcometh, and keepeth my works unto the end, to him will I give power over the nations: and he shall rule them with a rod of iron; as the vessels of a potter shall they be broken to shivers: even as I received of my Father. And I will give him the morning star" (vv. 26–28). Jesus says to the church in Thyatira: "If you hold fast and overcome, the day is coming when the tables will be turned and you will share in My victory over the nations. Remember Psalm 2. Don't surrender; don't imagine that things will be like this forever. You are going to share in My mediatorial victory when I come. And in the meantime, I will give you the morning star."

What is this morning star? It is Christ Himself, offered here in rich symbolism (Rev. 22:16; cf. Num. 24:17). The morning star is the rising sun that dispels all the darkness of night. This metaphor is used to describe Christ's coming into the world (Luke 1:78–79); His illumination of the heart by His Word and Spirit (2 Peter 1:19); and His coming again, in glory, at the last day (Mal. 4:2). Christ is promising to these overcomers, to the remnant at Thyatira: "If you hold fast and cling to me, even though it is difficult, and if you remain untainted by Jezebelism, I will give you Myself. I will always be in your sight. There will never be a cloud between us. You will be in the light, though darkness be all around you."

That is a beautiful thing. Our most miserable and vulnerable moments as Christians are the times when we lose sight of Christ. A cloud comes between us or we lose our bearings spiritually, and thus we don't know quite where to look for Him. That is when we are in the most danger and when we are the unhappiest. Our Lord promises: "If you cling to Me, I put no other burden on you. All I ask is that you continue in the way you are going, holding fast, progressing in the Christian life by looking to Me and My grace, and I will be your morning star. I will guide you, and I will be in your sight whenever you look for Me. Hold fast until I come."

8

Christ's Message to a Dying Church

REVELATION 3:1–6

And unto the angel of the church in Sardis write; these things saith he that hath the seven Spirits of God, and the seven stars; I know thy works, that thou hast a name that thou livest, and art dead. Be watchful, and strengthen the things which remain, that are ready to die: for I have not found thy works perfect before God. Remember therefore how thou hast received and heard, and hold fast, and repent. If therefore thou shalt not watch, I will come on thee as a thief, and thou shalt not know what hour I will come upon thee. Thou hast a few names even in Sardis which have not defiled their garments; and they shall walk with me in white: for they are worthy. He that overcometh, the same shall be clothed in white raiment; and I will not blot out his name out of the book of life, but I will confess his name before my Father, and before his angels. He that hath an ear, let him hear what the Spirit saith unto the churches.

How is your church doing? Is it abiding faithful to the truth? Is it spiritually alive? Is it a repenting, gospel-embracing church, that is striving to walk in the King's highway of holiness?

What should you do if you feel like you have good evidence that your church is slipping back from God—His truth and His ways—and even dying? Should you abandon the church right away or should you seek to be a force for good in the church, aiming for her reformation and revival? And if you stay and do so, how can God use your own faithfulness for the church's welfare? Christ gives us good practical advice for such questions in his letter to the church of Sardis, teaching us how to walk in the midst of the church and the world without soiling our garments.

As we turn again to one of the seven letters to the churches in Revelation 2 and 3, let us remember that these letters are not history or geography lessons. They are messages of the risen Christ to His church in every age, and thus they should be understood spiritually. The number *seven* represents completeness, so these letters are the complete message of Christ to His complete church in every age, place, and generation. However, the history and geography behind the letters are not irrelevant. Because the letters were written to seven churches in seven places, the history and geography impact how we understand the messages.

The fifth church addressed by Christ in Revelation 2–3 is that church of Sardis. Sardis was thirty miles southeast of Thyatira. Before the time of Christ, trade and traffic converged in Sardis. The city reached the peak of its glory in the sixth century BC under Croesus, king of the state of Lydia. At that time, it was called "the queen of Asia" or "the impregnable city." Because Sardis was surrounded by cliffs, it was considered unassailable. However, the city was conquered twice, both times by surprise: once by Cyrus in 546 BC and once by Antiochus III in 214 BC. Both conquests were due to the Sardians' lack of vigilance. In AD 17, Sardis was partly destroyed by an earthquake. However, it had been rebuilt with the assistance of the Emperor and once again experienced a measure of prosperity.[1]

The complacent spirit of Sardis affected people in the Christian church there. There is something unspeakably tragic about a dying church that professes to serve a living Savior. The ancient church of Sardis was such a church. Churches today urgently need to hear Christ's message to this ancient church, because all too many of them are dying just as the Sardis church was.

Let us consider three points under the theme of Christ's message to the dying church of Sardis: the rebuke Christ administers

---

1. Grant R. Osbourne, *Revelation*, Baker Exegetical Commentary on the New Testament (Grand Rapids: Baker Academic, 2002), 171–72.

to this church, the remedy He proposes for her, and the reward He promises her.

The Rebuke Christ Administers to Sardis

The Lord Jesus said to the church in Sardis, "I know thy works, that thou hast a name that thou livest, and art dead" (Rev. 3:1). The Sardian church thought it had developed a reputation ("name") that surpassed that of the other six churches of Revelation. No false doctrine was preached in Sardis—Christ doesn't warn the church of Balaam's doctrine, the doctrine of the Nicolaitans, or of the fornications of the woman Jezebel—and Sardis was proud of that. For this reason, Christ says in Revelation 3:1 that Sardis had the reputation in Asia Minor of being a church that was alive.

But in reality, the church was dying, and in large measure already dead. This letter describes a church that was about to be extinguished altogether because its members had become lethargic and complacent. Jesus says: "Be watchful.... If therefore thou shalt not watch, I will come on thee as a thief" (vv. 2–3).

The city of Sardis had been destroyed centuries earlier when a soldier of Cyrus had climbed up the rock face that was so sheer that the Sardians did not feel it was necessary to guard it. Likewise, Jesus warns the church: "Unless you put a sentry on guard and are vigilant, I will come and take away your candlestick; and you will cease to be a church. And it will happen in the night when you least expect it." The trouble with this church was that her members rested in their reputation as strong Christians. They had become complacent. There was no one to guard them from slipping into unbelief, even their minister.

All of the seven letters are addressed to the ministers of the churches. No doubt the minister at Sardis had a reputation for being a preacher of the gospel. He was a good preacher, and his sermons were memorable. Like his church, he had the reputation of being alive. But as far as Christ was concerned, he was dead, and his ministry, for lack of vigilance, had become a ministry of death.

No doubt visitors to the Sardian church were impressed. They were warmly welcomed. They heard the doctrine taught with joy and came away convinced that this church maintained the truth. Of such a church today, many would say, "What a fine evangelical church you have." Yet we are told that this church was dying, if it was not already spiritually dead. Though it appeared to be alive to the eyes of men, Jesus saw through it to the wasted skeleton.

Jesus rebukes the church, saying, "I have not found thy works perfect before God" (v. 2). In the original Greek, the statement is stronger: "Nothing you do pleases me," Jesus says. "In everything you turn your hand to, something is lacking." The Greek word translated here as *perfect* literally means "filled" or "fulfilled." Christ is saying: "I have not found your works fulfilling. Your works do not satisfy Me." Christ is saying: "Your works are as an empty shell. There is no substance to what you are doing, Sardis. I look for the fruits that accompany justifying faith, but I look in vain" (cf. Isa. 5:1–7).

This was, indeed, a serious rebuke. We might have a name with other people, but it means nothing when the Lord is not satisfied with us. Man looks on the outward appearance, but the Lord looks upon the heart. He can see if our professions about what we believe and the values by which we live have substance.

The great problem was that Sardis was living for people, not *coram Deo* ("before the face of God"), as the Reformers used to say. Those who live for men will perish with men. Their lives are empty shells. They may have the form of religion, go to church regularly, use the means of grace in their homes, and pray. But something is missing. They ignore the living, breathing substance of spiritual life—union with God through His dear Son.

We are all prone to be Sardians, for it is natural to backslide. In Hosea 11:7, the Lord says, "My people are bent to backsliding from me." How easy it is to slip from substance to shell in our prayers, our conversation, and our daily walk. So this rebuke comes also to us: "I have not found thy works perfect before God."

The Sardians were too much concerned about the praise and blame of men, and they had begun to take everything for granted.

Worse, they had begun to compromise with the world. They had soiled their garments, Christ says in verse 4. That is, they defiled their lives with sin (Zech. 3:4; Jude 23). Their fellow church members may have failed to notice, but the holy eyes of Christ did not miss this sin. So the admonition to Sardis is, "Love not the world, neither the things that are in the world" (1 John 2:15).

Sardis closely resembles many churches around the world today. Let us pray that we may be saved from becoming nothing but an outward shell, nothing but nominal Christians who are living a lie in the way that Sardis was living a lie. She had a reputation for being alive, but she was dead. It is a terrible and solemn thing to be physically alive and at the same time spiritually dead.

A church may be orthodox. We may have a name for upholding the orthodox doctrines of our Reformed ancestors. But, oh, how we need to be a living church! We need to demonstrate in our personal lives the truth that makes men strive for holiness unto God in the service of His dear Son. How we need to demonstrate the authenticity of our Christianity in our lifestyles, in being separate from the world, and in being dedicated unto the Lord God. We need spiritual substance in our orthodoxy. We need to watch and pray, lest the Lord say to us: "This people draw near to me with their mouth, and with their lips do honour me, but have removed their heart far from me" (Isa. 29:13; cf. Matt. 15:8).

Lord, save us from hypocrisy and from make-believe orthodoxy. Give us substance in our hearts. Let us feel the reality of the truths of Christianity, and let these truths motivate our lives. Give us drive and zeal. We need the mind of Christ: "The zeal of thine house hath eaten me up" (Ps. 69:9).

The Remedy Christ Proposes for Sardis

The remedy for this dying church had to begin with the godly remnant left in Sardis. Christ says in Revelation 3:4, "Thou hast a few names even in Sardis which have not defiled their garments." He will work with these few people to change the church.

That has always been the case in the world. Noah and his family found favor in God's sight and were spared from the flood, but they were a small remnant (Genesis 6–9). Lot was a lonely man in Sodom (Genesis 19). Elijah thought he was the only prophet left in Israel when Jezebel sought to kill him, but the Lord told him there were still seven thousand servants of the Lord (1 Kings 19). All throughout church history, we read, "Except the LORD…had left unto us a very small remnant, we should have been as Sodom, and…Gomorrah" (Isa. 1:9) and, "For though thy people Israel be as the sand of the sea, yet a remnant of them shall return" (Isa. 10:22). The nation of Israel might be consumed, but the holy seed would remain to grow again. Jesus said, "Fear not, little flock; for it is your Father's good pleasure to give you the kingdom" (Luke 12:32). He also asked, "When the Son of man cometh, shall he find faith on the earth?" (Luke 18:8).

In Revelation 3:3, the Lord says to Sardis, "Remember therefore how thou hast received and heard, and hold fast, and repent." Much like Ephesus, Sardis had to begin again at the beginning, recalling how they had received the Word of God with faith and joy. They needed to hold fast to the promises of the gospel and the commands of Christ, and not let them slip away through carelessness or compromise. They had to repent of their folly, their fear of men, their love of the praise of men, and their love of the world. They needed to renew their covenant with God and begin once more to watch and pray. "Blessed are those servants, whom the lord when he cometh shall find watching" (Luke 12:37).

The faithful in Sardis had not yet defiled their garments, but they were beginning to walk carelessly. They were slipping away from His call to holiness. So Christ warns them that He will come like a thief. This was a special warning to Sardis, which, as we have seen, had been invaded twice in surprise attacks during the night. Christ says: "If you are so careless for your safety, then beware. If you do not care for the things that remain and are not watchful, then I will come like a thief; and you will not know what hour I will come upon you. Remember therefore what you have received."

The Sardians had received the gift of the Holy Spirit from Christ's hand. Revelation 3:1 says, "These things saith he that hath the seven Spirits of God, and the seven stars." The seven stars are the seven churches, or the seven candlesticks among which Christ walks. The "seven Spirits," as we have seen, is a description of the sevenfold ministry of the Holy Spirit.

So Christ says to the church of Sardis: "I have the seven Spirits; that is, the Holy Spirit in all His fullness of life and power. As *seven* is the number of fullness, I have this Spirit without measure. And I also have the churches in my hand. You, Sardis, have received this Spirit, but pray again, Sardis; pray that I might pour out His saving work."

The whole counsel of God had been proclaimed and received by the believers in Sardis. But Jesus says the gift of the Holy Spirit had also been given to them. Many of them had known the gift of Pentecost and received the Spirit of God. They knew that the indwelling Spirit is the great Comforter that Christ sends to His children. This Spirit fills the believer with conviction of sin, causing him to flee to Christ for forgiveness, then to live a life of joy and humility in God's holy sight. The greatest gift that we can receive is for this Spirit to enter the sanctuary of the soul and remake it from within.

So the true believer is the temple of the Holy Ghost. Prior to Christ's coming, God had a special temple. It was a physical building that was so sacred that no one could enter it but priests. But now God comes to make His abode within the believer's soul and to fulfill what Paul says: "Know ye not that your body is the temple of the Holy Ghost?" (1 Cor. 6:19).

The children of God must walk worthy of the vocation to which they are called, for they have received the Holy Spirit and been taught by Him. So Jesus comes to the church of Sardis and reminds her that she had received the gospel and the gift of the Holy Spirit, and now she must remember that, repent, and turn back to Him, lest what remained in them die away.

Embedded in Christ's admonition is the solution: the Word and the Spirit are the answer to the church's need, whatever she lacks.

Who but the Spirit could bring Sardis to remember the Word of truth that she had lost? Only the Holy Spirit can enlighten the true believer. Only the Spirit can help him remember the days of initial conviction and tenderness when he walked in the fear of God. The Holy Spirit can bring him to true repentance and cause him once more to take firm hold on what he has received and heard. Therefore, the great need of the church at Sardis was that the Holy Spirit might be poured out with fresh vigor in her midst.

Note that the Lord comes to this church as the One who has the authority to send revival. The biblical definition of revival is "the renewal of the church by the Word of God preached in the power of the Spirit." It is the sevenfold Spirit of God and the seven stars brought together. All this is in the hands of Christ. No church can stage a revival. Revival belongs to the sovereign prerogative of Christ; it is in His hands. That is how He presents Himself to this dead church. He is her only hope. He says, "I am the One who has the answer to your spiritual death and your spiritual need. I am the One who has in the one hand all My servants, and in the other, the Spirit in all His fullness."

Sardis was grieving the Holy Spirit with a lifestyle not conducive to holiness. She walked with indifference and not "circumspectly" (Eph. 5:15). She exhibited a subtle form of carelessness, perhaps clothed in the language of grace. Yet she was walking toward destruction. She was resisting the leading of the Holy Spirit. She was overlooking her need for daily repentance in the sight of God. So she is told, "Return and repent." And her greatest need was for the Holy Spirit to bring individual and corporate revival at the hand of Christ. We have the same need today.

Only the Holy Spirit can bring true revival. He does that in the following ways:

First, *He shows us our backsliding.* He brings sin to our remembrance, as Jesus says. He opens our eyes to our iniquity.

Second, *He moves us to grieve over our sin.* How undeserving is God of our backsliding against Him? He says to us, "What could have been done more to my vineyard, that I have not done in it?"

(Isa. 5:4). He also says in Micah 6:3, "O my people, what have I done unto thee? and wherein have I wearied thee? Testify against me." The Spirit shows us our sin and our backsliding. Then we grieve because we realize we have sinned against our God. We have been cold or lukewarm toward the Lord whom we are called to love with all our heart, soul, mind, and strength. We feel deep within our hearts that the Lord deserves better.

Third, *He prompts us to confess our sins.* Where there is true sorrow for sin, there will be true confession. The believer pours out his heart in confession before God and learns to bemoan himself. And when there is true confession, there are times when the child of God has such a holy abhorrence of himself that he cries: "Oh Lord, I yearn to cast out this evil wicked heart. Oh, that I could be delivered from myself for a few moments! I long for Thy Holy Spirit to dwell in me in all His fullness—that He might be poured out in me in His sevenfold abundance. I thirst to taste the Holy Spirit's indwelling and fulfilling so that my cup may run over with Spirit-wrought grace, that sin might be far from me."

Fourth, *He rouses us to flee from sin.* Whoever confesses and forsakes his sin will find mercy (Prov. 28:13). A holy aura of fresh morning dew, as it were, rests with the Spirit's fresh anointing on a believer's life. And when the Spirit speaks to the heart of His people, there is fresh vigor. Scripture and the means of grace become alive again. The minister who preaches seems to be more relevant than before. The believer experiences once again the promise of the Lord: "Behold, I make all things new" (Rev. 21:5).

When things become dead and dry inside, we often look for causes outside of ourselves. But when we truly repent of sin, we find that the reason for deadness is inside us. We then flee from sin, bow before the Lord, and say, "Have mercy on us, O Lord, thou Son of David" (Matt. 20:30).

Fifth, *He humbles us to bow under sin's punishment.* The just punishment for sin is death. The true believer acknowledges that he deserves to perish forever. He fears he has spoiled all his sanctification, and he confesses that it is a wonder that the Lord will continue to save and sanctify him. He repents and bows under God's justice and says, "Lord, Thou art righteous to cast me away." But how amazing God's grace is! To those who, by grace, truly repent, Christ says, "They shall walk with me in white: for they are worthy" (Rev. 3:4).

The Reward Christ Promises to Sardis

Even in a church that was "dead" and what good things that remained were "ready to die" (Rev. 3:1), there were still "a few" who were godly. The Lord promises four things to the faithful who remain in Sardis:

First, Christ says, "They shall walk with me in white" (Rev. 3:4a). "White," said Richard Trench rather quaintly, "is everywhere the colour and livery of heaven."[2] This is especially true in the book of Revelation, where we read of a white stone, a white cloud, and a great white throne. White also stands for festivity and victory. And white is the color of purity (Ps. 51:7, Isa. 1:18).

So those who walk with Jesus are dressed in the white of heavenly purity and glorious victory. He declares: "Those who remember and return shall walk in white. They shall be made pure and holy by the power of My Spirit. They shall be made holy after My holiness and be made conformable to My image. They shall receive sanctifying grace." What an encouragement it is to believers to walk worthy of Christ, not only because He is worthy, but also because He has promised that they shall walk with Him in white.

Second, Christ says, "For they are worthy" (Rev. 3:4b). They are not worthy in themselves, surely, but only insofar as they are in Christ, that is, joined to Him by a true faith. God gives His gifts in Christ to His people and calls those gifts theirs. Jesus once said to blind Bartimaeus, "Thy faith hath made thee whole" (Mark 10:52). We know it was Christ's faith that healed the blind man, but Christ *gave* that faith to Bartimaeus. All that belongs to Christ is conferred on the believer. Thus, God can say, "By the worthiness of Christ,

---

2. Richard C. Trench, *Commentary on the Epistles to the Seven Churches in Asia: Revelation II, III* (London: Parker, Son, and Bourn, 1861), 119.

I give worthiness to all My people." That does not mean that the believer can do one worthy act or pray one worthy prayer in his own merit or power. But it means that in Christ, he can do all things. In Christ, he is worthy.

Believers, then, are worthy as comprehended in Christ and as living out of Christ, so that others may see Christ in them as the salt of the earth and a light on a hill. Some of the members of Sardis, by walking in Christ's strength, retained their spiritual integrity.

Third, Christ says, He will not blot their names out of the book of life (Rev. 3:5). The book of life is God's eternal record of those whom He will save by giving them persevering faith and repentance.[3] The image here is of a city's register of its citizens. Even if Christians lose their citizenship, rights, and privileges here on earth, they can never lose their citizenship in heaven. Those who persevere in faith, pursue holiness, and work out their salvation with fear and trembling need never fear condemnation. The good work God has begun in them will be brought to full and glorious completion in the day of Christ (Phil. 1:6; Ps. 138:8).

Fourth, He says He will confess the names of these believers before His Father and before His angels (Rev. 3:5). The third statement is negative, while this fourth one is positive. It is hard to separate these blessings that Jesus promises. They are joined together as the guarantee of the victory and assurance of the living church. But if we had to choose one of them, then we would choose this promise as the greatest of all blessings: "I will confess your name before My Father." The intercession of Christ on our behalf is cause for great joy. In all our unworthiness, Jesus Christ continues to keep us worthy. He does this by continuing to show His Father His work. He spreads before His Father His people's names and makes continual intercession for them. And He will publicly testify for us on judgment day that we are His (Matt. 10:32).

These are pure gifts of free sovereign grace. But the Sardians also needed to walk worthy of their profession. The fruits of their lives

3. Dan. 12:1; Rev. 13:8; 17:8; 20:12, 15; 21:27.

would tell what they most treasured. If their treasure was in heaven where Christ is, then they would be counted worthy in Christ.

We must examine ourselves. Are we dying spiritually like the great part of the Sardians, or are we among the few who are counted worthy for Christ's sake? Some people think they know what orthodoxy is and think they practice it, but they ignore its living dimension. How dreadful it is to have a name for maintaining orthodoxy, yet to lack the living, vibrant, life-changing power of it. Is there an emptier way to live? Is there a more tragic way to die?

Are you alive unto God through Jesus Christ? Is the Spirit working in you in the fullness of His life and power? Or is your Christianity only an empty shell, a name with no substance behind it? Pray that you might receive an ear to hear what the Spirit says to the churches and that the Savior might confess your name before His Father and before His angels for His name's sake. May God reward us, not with what we have done, but with what He has done. And may we have no rest until we can profess, speak, and live truly for Christ's sake and to God's glory.

9

Christ's Message to a Favored Church

REVELATION 3:7–13

And to the angel of the church in Philadelphia write; These things saith he that is holy, he that is true, he that hath the key of David, he that openeth, and no man shutteth; and shutteth, and no man openeth; I know thy works: behold, I have set before thee an open door, and no man can shut it: for thou hast a little strength, and hast kept my word, and hast not denied my name. Behold, I will make them of the synagogue of Satan, which say they are Jews, and are not, but do lie; behold, I will make them to come and worship before thy feet, and to know that I have loved thee. Because thou hast kept the word of my patience, I also will keep thee from the hour of temptation, which shall come upon all the world, to try them that dwell upon the earth. Behold, I come quickly: hold that fast which thou hast, that no man take thy crown. Him that overcometh will I make a pillar in the temple of my God, and he shall go no more out: and I will write upon him the name of my God, and the name of the city of my God, which is new Jerusalem, which cometh down out of heaven from my God: and I will write upon him my new name. He that hath an ear, let him hear what the Spirit saith unto the churches.

There is nothing so important in life as God's favor. God's favor is bigger and better than life itself. David said, "Thy favor is more than life" (Ps. 63:3). My dad used to say to me, "If something is in God's favor, you should do it; if it isn't, you shouldn't do it."

How important is God's favor to you? Do you proceed to do things at times even when your conscience speaks that they are not in God's favor? That is a very dangerous road to travel, my friend.

If you're a believer who isn't backsliding, you do yearn for God's favor in Christ Jesus. You want to know what motivates Christ's favor. You want to know the fruits that accompany that favor and the promises that He attaches to that favor. All of that and more Christ explains to us in the fascinating letter He wrote to the church of Philadelphia.

The sixth of Christ's messages to the seven churches in Asia Minor is to the church of Philadelphia, which we might call "the favored church." Philadelphia was thirty miles southeast of Sardis. It lay in a valley and served as an important center for trade. Founded in 189 BC, the city was almost demolished in AD 17 by an earthquake, but had been rebuilt by means of tax relief from the Roman Emperor. The word *philadelphia* literally means "brotherly love" or "love of the brethren" (Heb. 13:1). The name was bestowed on the city by its founder, King Eumenes II (d. 159 BC) of Pergamos, in honor of his brother, Attalus II (220–138 BC). Attalus had shown such steadfast loyalty to his brother that he received the epithet *philadelphus*—"the one who loves his brother."

In the midst of Philadelphia was a small Christian church that displayed much love. The church's members loved one another in the Lord Jesus Christ. They loved the work of God's grace in one another and considered one another higher than themselves. They consistently showed the spirit of love in their walk of life.

As with Smyrna, Jesus has no reproof for the church in Philadelphia. He is more pleased with her than any other church. The persecuted church at Smyrna gets Christ's sympathy. But the church at Philadelphia gets unqualified praise and encouragement from Him.

Philadelphia was not perfect, for there is no perfect church on earth. "The purest churches under heaven are subject both to mixture and error" (Westminster Confession, 25.5).[1] Hypocrites mix with true believers in every church, and any church can stray from the truth in doctrine or practice. As long as we are in the flesh, we are all imperfect. Yet with her imperfections, weaknesses, and failures, the church of Philadelphia pleases Christ. He commends and praises the church without reservation or qualification. He smiles upon her.

Philadelphia was the only one of the seven cities of Revelation where Christianity lasted. Robert Murray M'Cheyne said that in the nineteenth century, Philadelphia, with a population of two thousand people, still had eight hundred professing Christians in its five churches.[2] Today those numbers have dwindled substantially, especially in the mass exodus of Greeks from the area in the early 1920s. There is little if any Christianity left in modern-day Philadelphia, now known as Alashehir.

We will examine Christ's letter under three points: causes motivating Christ's favor; fruits accompanying that favor; and promises following that favor.

Causes Motivating the Favor of Christ

Philadelphia is a prominent example of what a church ought to be. The fruits of grace abounded in this church as Christ worked in her by His Word and Holy Spirit. In commending this church, Christ is placing a crown upon the work He has done in her midst. As John Owen says of the Holy Spirit, "He is the Spirit of love; he is love. All his actings towards us and in us are fruits of love, and they all leave an impression of love upon our souls."[3] Philadelphia showed that love.

---

1. *Reformed Confessions of the Sixteenth and Seventeenth Centuries*, 4:264.
2. Robert Murray M'Cheyne, *The Seven Churches of Asia* (Ross-shire, Scotland: Christian Focus, 2001), 69.
3. John Owen, *Pneumatologia*, in *The Works of John Owen* (1850–1853; repr., Edinburgh: Banner of Truth, 1965–1968), 4:414.

All the reasons for that love and for Christ's favor, however, are due to the Lord Jesus Christ Himself. All causes for Christ's favor lie ultimately in Christ Himself. When Christ introduces His message to Philadelphia, He lists three of those causes. In Revelation 3:7, He says, "These things saith he that is *holy*, he that is *true*, he that hath the *key of David*." Let us examine those qualities one by one.

First, *the holiness of Christ*. Jesus Christ opens His letter to Philadelphia by saying, "These things saith he that is holy." "The Holy One" is one of the names of God and one of the titles of His Anointed (Ps. 89:18). In His holiness, Christ gathers His church and sanctifies her, to make her holy and without blemish in the sight of His holy Father. The church of Philadelphia and of all ages can know the favor of God only through the righteousness and holiness of Christ.

Second, *the truthfulness of Christ*. Philadelphia was a favored church because Christ was true to His Father's eternal purpose to work within her His glorious salvation, in fulfillment of His covenant promise. He kept truth and covenant as He worked in her from generation to generation. He was true to His promise that He would love His brethren in the Philadelphia church to the end. He was true to His love and loyalty to her as the Friend "that sticketh closer than a brother" (Prov. 18:24). Christ's love and His promise cannot fail, for His name is true. All God's promises to Philadelphia are yea and amen in Jesus Christ (2 Cor. 1:20).

Third, *the power of Christ*. Revelation 3:7 says Christ is "he that hath the key of David, he that openeth, and no man shutteth; and shutteth, and no man openeth." These words are taken from Isaiah 22:20–25, which speaks of a man named Eliakim, one of three delegates sent to negotiate for the kingdom of Judah with an Assyrian ruler (2 Kings 18:18). Eliakim was chosen because of the honorable place that he occupied as head over King Hezekiah's household. God presents Eliakim to Isaiah as a type of Christ, to whom God will commit the government of His people, saying, "The key of the house of David will I lay upon his shoulder; so he shall open, and none shall shut; and he shall shut, and none shall open" (Isa. 22:22).

Isaiah's words affirm Christ as the chosen Messiah, the Son of David, who has absolute power over entry into the kingdom of heaven. He says that when He opens, no one can shut, and when He shuts, no one can open. Christ has the key to salvation and controls the door of the kingdom of God. Likewise, Christ presents Himself as the Holy One, the true and faithful One, in contrast to the elders of the local synagogue, who abused their authority when they cast out anyone who confessed that Jesus was the Christ (Rev. 3:9).

The church at Philadelphia needed to know that the key that opens the kingdom of God is not man-made. This key is not human wisdom; it is not majority rule; it is not the power of the state. It is the power that is vested in the Lord Jesus Christ and in Him alone. He is the Head and Steward of God's household, which is the church of the living God and Christ's household (Heb. 3:6). He is the One who is faithful over God's house. To Him is given all power in heaven and earth. He has the keys of hell and death, the keys of grace and salvation. He is invested with divine and royal authority, dignity, honor, and glory. He can convert the hardest of hearts; He can bring back every backslider from His corrupt ways. He preserves His saints to the end. "This is why, Philadelphia, your church was so favored," we can say two thousand years later. "It is because of the holiness, truthfulness, and power of Christ, who conquers hearts, subdues sinners, and preserves them in His saving grace."

Why does God's favor rest on you? Can you say, "Lord, it is only for the sake of Thy Son, only because Christ is holy, true, and almighty, that there is hope for me"? Have you learned that you are so unholy apart from Christ that your only hope rests in His blood and righteousness? Have you learned that you are so weak and powerless in yourself that your only hope lies in Christ Jesus, who has the key of David? In His sovereign mercy and justice, God sent His only begotten Son to redeem believers in Philadelphia and us today. May we learn to find all our hope of God's favor in the life, death, and resurrection of Jesus Christ, who holds the key of David in His hand.

Fruits Accompanying the Favor of Christ

Christ's grace and favor will inevitably produce fruits, as is apparent in the next verse of our text, Revelation 3:8. Let's look at these three fruits:

The first of the fruits produced by the favor of Christ is *an open door*. Verse 8 says, "I know thy works: behold, I have set before thee an open door, and no man can shut it." Some biblical scholars say this door refers to Christ Himself as the portal of salvation. In the Gospels, Jesus does speak of Himself in that way: "I am the door: by me if any man enter in, he shall be saved, and shall go in and out, and find pasture" (John 10:9). Other commentators view this door as one of escape or deliverance. In Revelation 3:10, Christ mentions the hour of temptation that will come upon the world. People who believe in the rapture see this door as the emergency exit for believers to escape from approaching tribulation. Since this position is not scriptural, it cannot possibly be what this door represents.

The open door might also remind us of regeneration. Think of such texts as Luke 13:24: "Strive to enter in at the strait gate." Indeed, God sets before His elect an open door and then brings them through it. And what a beautiful door of salvation Christ has opened by the shedding of His invaluable blood. Yet that is not the meaning of these words, either.

This is a door of usefulness, service, and effective witness for the gospel. This open door is promised to those who, by grace, already have been brought through the door of regeneration. To them the Lord says: "I now set before you an open door of opportunity to bring My gospel tidings to your families, neighbors, and all whom providence allows you to interact with. I set before you an open door." When we learn to know the gospel experientially, we also come to love the souls of others and yearn to share the gospel with them. We long for an open door of opportunity to invite them, inform them, admonish them, and teach them that there is only one way of salvation: Jesus Christ.

The symbol of an open door is used frequently in the New Testament, each time in the context of evangelism. When Paul and

Barnabas, for example, returned from their missionary journey and reported to the church, they rejoiced because God "had opened the door of faith unto the Gentiles" (Acts 14:27). In this context, Christ used the faithful preaching and sacrificial service of the apostles to "open the door of faith" so that the Gentiles might enter into the kingdom of God thereby.

In 1 Corinthians 16:9, the apostle writes, "For a great door and effectual is opened unto me, and there are many adversaries." Whenever there is an open door, Satan will oppose it and try with all his might to close it. In this context, Paul is saying: "There is a great deal of opposition in Ephesus. I haven't seen much going on until now, but at last God has opened a great and effectual door. I can't think of leaving Ephesus now because God has opened the door of effective testimony to the gospel."

In 2 Corinthians 2, Paul refers to the vision he had in Troas of a man urging him to come to Macedonia to preach the gospel (Acts 16:9). Paul says of this call: "When I came to Troas to preach Christ's gospel, a door was opened unto me of the Lord...I went from thence into Macedonia" (2 Cor. 2:12–13). It was a door of opportunity for usefulness and effective service.

In Colossians 4:2–3, the apostle enjoins the Colossians to "continue in prayer...; withal praying also for us, that God would open unto us a door of utterance, to speak the mystery of Christ, for which I am also in bonds." Whenever they thought of Paul at church, at home, or in a prayer meeting, he wanted them to ask "that a great door of utterance might be opened to speak the mystery of Christ."

So the door at Philadelphia is a door of usefulness and faithful service in witnessing. Revelation 3:9 tells us that even the sworn enemies of the church will be converted and brought into the church through this open door. Jesus says, "Behold, I will make them of the synagogue of Satan, which say they are Jews, and are not, but do lie; behold, I will make them to come and worship before thy feet, and to know that I have loved thee." In other words, Christ says: "Those relatives and friends who have ostracized you for years because of your Christianity will soon be coming to your worship services. And

I will convert them. They will fall at your feet and say, 'What must we do to be saved?' I am going to open a door that no one can shut—a door for the gospel, an effectual door, a door of salvation."

All of us wish that a door would open for us and others, such as friends, relatives, and work associates. We have been evangelizing some of them for years. But the door doesn't open automatically. Even if you have the right methods, the right approach, the right time, and the right manpower, gifts, talents, and personality, salvation doesn't come automatically. People can be saved only if Christ opens the door.

So Philadelphia was greatly blessed. Christ set an open door before her, and she responded. The Lord gave her opportunities to proclaim the gospel, and she used those opportunities zealously. The Philadelphian believers were mission-minded. They declared this by their "works"—that is, in speaking about and living out the gospel. They testified to their loved ones, neighbors, work associates, and community that the way to full and free salvation for sinners is through the Lord Jesus Christ. And Christ blessed these efforts.

The second of the fruits produced by the favor of Christ is *a little strength*. Philadelphia did not have great strength, but what she did have had great value in the eyes of her Lord. So Christ says, "Thou hast a little strength" (Rev. 3:8), meaning there was an open door before them, and the Lord had given them strength to go through it, that is, to make good use of the opportunity it presented. He had given them strength for the day and strength for their calling, both individually and collectively as a church. They had enough strength to pursue the open door.

Today the church has many forms of outreach, but she must realize her dependence upon the Lord. She has to use the means of grace diligently and prayerfully. She must use the strength the Lord gives her to pursue evangelism in the way of His Word.

Philadelphia received "a little strength" to walk in God's ways. Some members had a bit more courage than others to reach out to the world. But each one received the strength that was needed. So the Lord Jesus Christ is saying to this church: "My strength is made perfect in your weakness. And through your weakness, your brokenness, and your infirmities, I will give you strength to testify to others through that open door that there is a way also for them to be saved in My blood."

The true child of God does not have great strength in himself. He is strong at times in Christ, but in himself he remains broken, weak, and dissatisfied with what he is and how little he makes use of God's open doors. But in all the believer's brokenness and weakness, Christ Jesus says, "I will give you a little strength, enough for the day, enough for the hour, enough to testify of My name and to show the way for lost sinners in Me, the strong and almighty King of kings."

As long as you flaunt your gifts as a Christian, as long as you trust in your organization, your manpower, your numbers, or whatever, you will never be of any use to Christ. You must learn to say with Paul that it is when you are weak that you are strong. In 2 Corinthians 12, Paul says he was given "a thorn in the flesh" (v. 7). We don't know what that was, but it made him miserable. In verse 9, Paul tells us that God told him, "My grace is sufficient for thee: for my strength is made perfect in weakness." Paul's response is in verse 10: "Therefore I take pleasure in infirmities, in reproaches, in necessities, in persecutions, in distresses for Christ's sake: for when I am weak, then am I strong."

Paul came to Corinth and accomplished a mighty work. Corinth may have been one of the most difficult cities in the world in which to preach. No one ever would have expected to see a Christian church in Corinth. And Paul felt his weakness in the face of that daunting challenge. He says: "I came in fear and trembling. I came with my knees knocking. I came terribly conscious that in myself I was not equal to the task" (cf. 1 Cor. 1:3). The only thing he knew to do was to preach the Word of Christ in the Spirit's power. People were saved, and a church was established.

The people at Philadelphia were conscious of their weakness, but they also knew where their strength lay. Christ says, "I have set before thee an open door" (Rev. 3:8a). In this Christ is saying:

"I am giving you an opportunity to witness about Me. You have a little strength." He says He is giving the believers this opportunity because they are weak. He adds, "Thou…hast kept my word, and hast not denied my name" (v. 8b). Christ says: "I am giving you this opportunity because you are conscious of your weakness and have turned to Me and to My Word for strength. You have clung to My Word despite all the temptations to trust in something else. You have kept My Word and have not denied My name."

What an encouragement this is for office-bearers in the church. When you are working late at night in your ministry, you cry out: "Lord, give me a little strength for one more night, one more visit, one more task. Oh, let me pursue the open door Thou hast called me to. Let me follow that calling; let me follow Thy ways. Lord, give me a little strength."

Martin Luther said that every true believer is called to be a priest to others. Luther and the other Reformers said we must be gospel witnesses to others both in our talk and our walk. As the Lord enables us, we are called to use divinely provided open doors to testify of God's grace in Christ Jesus.

You can excuse yourself from using those open doors by saying: "I don't know how to explain true Christianity very well. I feel so weak." You might have only a little strength, but are you using that little strength, or are you burying the one talent the Lord has given you? When the Lord asks you to proclaim His name at home, at work, or in society, are you making use of the open doors He provides with the strength and wisdom you have been praying for?

The third of the fruits produced by the favor of Christ is *perseverance in obedience*. Revelation 3:8 goes on to say that the Philadelphian church had kept God's Word; that is, they had persevered in obeying Christ's commandments. Philadelphia remained true to her calling. They knew experientially the truth stated in 1 Peter 1:5 that believers are "kept by the power of God through faith unto salvation." The church persevered by the grace of God.

The members of this church persevered in looking to Christ, striving against sin, pursuing holiness, and living according to all of

God's commandments. They stayed in the race, they kept fighting the good fight, and they never wearied in well-doing. Even in times of persecution, Philadelphia persevered in keeping Christ's Word and upholding His name. She continued to proclaim Christ's Word in words and works, and to confess His name as Lord and Savior.

Furthermore, Philadelphia glorified Christ's name in times of rejection, when the door was shut and it was tough to persevere. The Jews around Philadelphia opposed her religion. Society in general mixed law and gospel. But the Lord says of Philadelphia, "She has not denied My name." This church maintained the pure doctrine of free grace that glorifies God to the highest. Christ's favor causes us to not deny His name, no matter what happens.

Do you manifest the fruits of Christ's favor? Can you say, "My earnest prayer in life is, 'Lord, do not let me deny Thy name'"? Oh, how tempted we often are to deny God's name. How much easier it would be to slink away from the open door and go our own way rather than live for Christ. Then our enemies would rejoice because the gospel would no longer be pronounced with its glorious invitations and admonitions. The open door would shut.

No matter what the price, Christ will give strength to those who refuse to deny His name. That is the fruit of Christ's favor. There are surely times when our trust in that promise will be tried. There are times when the child of God will say, "Oh, Lord, it is enough. All these things are against me. Lord, it is no longer any use to pursue the open door." But the Lord says: "As long as I have set it before you, you are called to pursue it. Do not deny My name."

When we are in a right relationship with God, we would rather die than deny the name of Christ. We would rather die than deny His calling to testify about Him. We say with John Calvin, "My heart, O Lord, I offer to Thee promptly and sincerely."[4] Then we

---

4. These words come from Calvin's seal, which pictures a heart held in an open hand, with the words "promptè et sincerè." E. Doumergue, *Iconographie Calvienne* (Lausanne: Georges Bridel, 1909), 67, plate XV. Calvin wrote from Strasbourg to Farel in August 1541 that though he did not desire to return to Geneva, "When I remember that I am not my own, I offer up my heart, presented as a sacrifice to the

give everything into Christ's hands and follow Him. But woe be to us if we try to shut what He has opened. Then God's disfavor will rest upon us, and that is a burden that a true believer cannot bear. As David says of the Lord, "In his favour is life" (Ps. 30:5). If that is so, then surely there is nothing in His disfavor but spiritual and eternal death.

Promises Following the Favor of Christ

For those who exercise the fruits of Christ's favor, He provides remarkable promises. The promises fit the trials we experience the way a glove fits a hand. The God who grants us afflictions also grants us exactly the comfort we need in those trials. Likewise, the God who tries us through open doors will grant us the promises we need to persevere.

Christ makes four promises to the church of Philadelphia:

First, *the promise of victory.* Revelation 3:9 says, "Behold, I will make them of the synagogue of Satan, which say they are Jews, and are not, but do lie; behold, I will make them to come and worship before thy feet, and to know that I have loved thee." Christ is saying to the church, "Though there will be challenges, trials, and persecutions, in the end, I will show your persecutors that I love you and that you are My favored people." There is no better victory than that, because when God shows us His favor, even those who oppose the gospel will respect us and the gospel we proclaim.

That is true even in little ways. No long ago, I was coming through customs when a fellow passenger asked me, "What is your occupation?" When I said I was a preacher, teacher, and author, he asked what I wrote about. "Christianity," I said. "I write Christian books." When I asked the man if he was a Christian, he said: "Well, not really. I'm too much of a free spirit." Then he said, "I like to write, too, but I wish I could write what I knew was true." I replied, "That is the joy of writing *Christian* books—you know what you

---

Lord." *Letters of John Calvin,* ed. Jules Bonnet (Philadelphia: Presbyterian Board of Publication, 1858), 1:280–81.

write is true and can truly help people." We must pray for people like this to bow under Christ's gospel and come to know the love of God. They need to see that the world's "free spirit" drives them along the road to unhappiness, but Christ's Spirit leads to true joy.

Christ says that those who are of the synagogue of Satan will come and worship at the feet of the Philadelphian believers. The word *worship* here does not mean divine worship, but rather a kind of respect. These people will cease persecuting believers and will come to honor and respect them because they see the love of God for them. This is the promise that the Lord gave to Israel among the nations (Isa. 45:14; 49:23; 60:14). Ironically, it is applied here to Christians with respect to unbelieving Jews. Those who persevere in faith toward Jesus Christ are the true, spiritual Israel, and will receive the honor God promised to His ancient people.

In response to Christ's love for His own, they love Him in return. Every true Christian longs to love the Lord and to show it by his lifestyle. He shows that by pursuing open doors of Christian service, finding his strength in the Lord, persevering in doing His will, and openly confessing Christ as Lord and Savior. Others see it, and glorify our Father in heaven, and many are won to Christ. God longs for the salvation of sinners. He longs for the doors to open for lost ones and for the name of Christ to be glorified in many hearts, young and old.

But there is more here. When Christ says those who are of the synagogue of Satan will come and worship, He is also saying: "I will give you the best possible victory over your enemies. I will bring them into the church where you are. I will cause them to cry out, 'Men and brethren, what must we do to be saved?' I will open the eyes of these proud, self-righteous, arrogant, scornful Jews, who have been looking down their noses at you as the despised Nazarene sect. I will show them that I love you. I will bring them into your gatherings; I will bring them to the truth. I will convert them."

That is a wonderful promise. Do you want your difficult relatives, who have been holding out for years, to be converted? Do you want your work associates, who have been making your life a misery for months because you are a Christian, to be saved? Do you want those whom you have been witnessing to without success to come to Christ? Do you want these people to be brought into God's kingdom? Jesus says, "I promise to save some of them if, conscious of your weakness, you hold fast to My Word and keep it."

Second, *the promise of Christ's continual presence.* Christ also promises to be present with His church in times of trial. Revelation 3:10–11 says, "Because thou hast kept the word of my patience, I also will keep thee from the hour of temptation, which shall come upon all the world, to try [that is, to tempt] them that dwell upon the earth. Behold, I come quickly: hold that fast which thou hast, that no man take thy crown." Jesus promises to be with His people who continue to bear God-glorifying fruits. He will be with them in trial. He will give them strength for each day's challenges. He will carry them through, even when they sigh and say, "Lord, canst Thou really do it again?" And the Lord will say: "Yes, because you have kept the word of My patience. I shall be with you. I shall not leave you or forsake you." That doesn't make the trial go away, but it does give us strength to bear it, go forward in the trial, rejoice in a prison cell, sing psalms of joy at midnight, and to say in the midst of the fiery furnace, "There is a fourth one who walks in the midst and loosens my bands." The Lord says, "I will be with you."

The Lord will grant you strength to bear anything, even martyrdom, if need be. He gives strength for each hour of trial. At times, you beg for relief, saying, "Lord, let me escape—let this cup pass from me," but He says: "Go forward, My child; I will be with you all the way through your trial. Though you cannot understand or believe it now, and though the trial may become even darker before light dawns, be still and know that I am God. The God of Jacob is with you." Philadelphia was favored because to her, the presence and favor of God were more than life.

Third, *the promise of being a pillar in the church.* Revelation 3:12a says, "Him that overcometh will I make a pillar in the temple of my God." In yourself, you are unstable as water. Everything that is of real value and strength comes to you through Christ. In the

Song of Songs, the bride says of Christ, "His legs are as pillars of marble" (5:15). He is the strong One, but in His strength, you too may become a pillar.

M'Cheyne says: "There are some of you that would be glad to be stones in the temple; but Christ says of some, that He will make them a *pillar*. There are some of you that would be glad if you just *got in*; but Christ says, you *shall go no more out*."[5] If, conscious of your weakness, you turn to Him and cling to Him and His Word, He promises not just an anonymous little place in a stone wall. He promises to make you a pillar in His temple. He promises to build you into His house in such a way that you become structurally significant. You will become an adornment to that place.

Fourth, *the promise of a new name*. Revelation 3:12b says, "I will write upon him the name of my God, and the name of the city of my God, which is new Jerusalem…and I will write upon him my new name." How does Christ write the name of His God upon His children? By sanctifying them through His Word and Spirit, that is, by bringing them into conformity to Himself. The "name" is the likeness between the Head and the members of His body, between the children of God and their Father in heaven. We have begun to be conformed to that image of holiness and truth, and in heaven, we shall possess this likeness in perfection and fullness. As citizens of New Jerusalem, we will always reflect the name, the beauty, and the glory of almighty God (Isa. 62:2–4).

Sometimes here on earth, you sigh, "Lord Jesus, if only I were more conformed to Thy image!" But when you get to heaven, the Lord will write the name of God upon you. You will be like God in holiness, in purity, and in singleness of eye. Then you will walk with Christ in the heavenly garden in the cool of the eternal day. Then you will know intimate friendship with your best Friend, the King of kings.

You will also have written on you the name of the city of God, Christ says. That means all believers shall be one in glory. They will

---

5. M'Cheyne, *Seven Churches of Asia*, 79.

be one family, with no division, no difference of opinion, and no hard feelings. They will all be one city, one family, and one people. And they all will have the name of the same city written on them.

Then Christ says, "I will write upon him my new name." That is the name of eternal victory. It is also the name of eternal office-bearing with Christ. We shall all be priests, prophets, and kings unto God. We will rule and reign with Christ. We will be followers of Christ, named with Christ's name in perfection.

The church of Philadelphia was highly favored. But today the door is still open, and Christ still has the master key to all the doors we have shut by nature. There is still room for poor sinners on earth to be transformed into pillars in heaven. Pray that you too may become, by God's grace, a pillar in the temple of God.

Christ's Message to a Lukewarm Church

REVELATION 3:14–22

And unto the angel of the church of the Laodiceans write; These things saith the Amen, the faithful and true witness, the beginning of the creation of God; I know thy works, that thou art neither cold nor hot: I would thou wert cold or hot. So then because thou art lukewarm, and neither cold nor hot, I will spue thee out of my mouth. Because thou sayest, I am rich, and increased with goods, and have need of nothing; and knowest not that thou art wretched, and miserable, and poor, and blind, and naked: I counsel thee to buy of me gold tried in the fire, that thou mayest be rich; and white raiment, that thou mayest be clothed, and that the shame of thy nakedness do not appear; and anoint thine eyes with eyesalve, that thou mayest see. As many as I love, I rebuke and chasten: be zealous therefore, and repent. Behold, I stand at the door, and knock: if any man hear my voice, and open the door, I will come in to him, and will sup with him, and he with me. To him that overcometh will I grant to sit with me in my throne, even as I also overcame, and am set down with my Father in his throne. He that hath an ear, let him hear what the Spirit saith unto the churches.

Jesus Christ is either worth everything or He is worth nothing. If He is the true Savior and Lord—the way, truth, and life—as He claims to be, He is worth everything. He is worthy to be served with our entire soul, entire mind, and entire strength. If He is not what He claims to be, then, God forbid, He is an imposter, a sham, a fake—and He is worth nothing. It is impossible that Jesus is only worth something. He either deserves your whole heart or none of your heart. It makes no sense at all to give him only half your heart. The Bible tells us repeatedly that He despises half-hearted religion; He is disgusted with lukewarmness. That is what He tells us again in His message to the church of Laodicea.

The final letter in Christ's messages to the seven churches of Asia Minor is directed to the church of Laodicea, which was a lukewarm church. Laodicea, some forty miles southeast of Philadelphia, was the chief city in the southern region of Phrygia. It was known for its school of medicine, which specialized in diseases of the eye, and for its soft black wool, which was woven into luxurious garments. Many of the people in the city and perhaps in the church of Laodicea were upper class. And as a center of banking and finance, Laodicea was a city of immense wealth. It was so rich, in fact, that when much of the city was destroyed by an earthquake in AD 60 and the Roman government offered emergency assistance, the Laodiceans declined to accept it. At the same time, the city had no natural water supply, and had to bring in water via an aqueduct from a town six miles to the south.[1]

Laodicea was proud of its self-sufficiency. The people believed they didn't need help from the government or anyone else; they could do things on their own. That self-reliance was both Laodicea's passion and its downfall. Jesus alludes to this spirit of self-sufficiency when He says to the church at Laodicea, "Thou sayest, I am rich, and increased with goods, and have need of nothing" (Rev. 3:17a).

We do not know whom God used to plant a Christian church in Laodicea, though Epaphras, who had first evangelized Colosse, also preached in Laodicea (Col. 1:7; 4:12–13). By the time John wrote Revelation, the congregation there had become self-satisfied, self-righteous, and spiritually lukewarm. Christ has no praise for her. In the letters to the six other churches, our Lord always finds something favorable to say. But Christ says nothing good about the church at Laodicea. Rather, He says she is lukewarm, neither hot nor cold.

---

1. Osborne, *Revelation*, 201–202.

We will consider Christ's message to this church under two headings: Christ's serious disgust and Christ's remarkable remedy.

Christ's Serious Disgust

Christ comes to wake up the Laodicean church. That is implied in His titles in verse 14: "These things saith the Amen, the faithful and true witness, the beginning of the creation of God."

First, Jesus calls Himself "the Amen." The word amen is a synonym for what is certain or true. Jesus uses the word frequently. When He says, "Verily, verily I say unto you," He is using the word amen in the original. He is saying, "Amen, amen," or "Truly, truly." Jesus is the Amen because He is ultimate truth. His words are absolutely reliable. All the promises of God are yea and amen in Christ Jesus (2 Cor. 1:20), because He is the One in whom is ultimate truth and authority.

Amen served as a seal of truth and trustworthiness in a society that depended much upon the spoken word, as distinct from written communication. *Amen* is a verbal seal, and Jesus is the great Amen of God. So what He is saying is utterly true, utterly authoritative, and utterly trustworthy.

Second, He calls Himself "the faithful and true witness." This goes beyond the significance of His title as the Amen. This tells us that what Christ says is without error, deception, or exaggeration; He gives us "the truth, the whole truth, and nothing but the truth," as we say today. Every word our Lord Jesus says is faithful and true. These titles take us back to Revelation 1:5, where Christ is described as "the faithful witness."

Third, Christ describes Himself as "the beginning of the creation of God." In the opening sentence of John's gospel, we read of Christ, "In the beginning was the Word" (John 1:1). Now Jesus is called the beginning of the creation of God. The word *beginning* can be used temporally, as the starting point of some work or process, but Christ is not simply the starting point of creation. The word can also mean the "first cause," that is, the One by whom all things were made, the One through whom all things were made, and the One for whom all things were made. In other words, behind everything that exists we find Jesus Christ. All things begin with Him, exist through Him, and have their end in Him (Col. 1:16–17). There is no higher power, no more exalted being, and no one more to be feared or honored than Christ.

When Jesus speaks to the church in Laodicea, He is brutally honest. He says she is "lukewarm, and neither cold nor hot" (Rev. 3:16). Hot and cold are temperature extremes; the words used here refer to boiling hot and refreshingly cold (Matt. 10:42). "Lukewarm" is neither the one nor the other. The picture arises from local circumstances. The nearby town of Colosse enjoyed deliciously cool water. Another town a few miles away, Hierapolis, boasted hot springs believed to have medicinal properties. However, the Laodiceans had only the tepid flow that passed through miles of aqueducts to drink. Christ speaks with exquisite irony: the Laodicean church is no better than its water. Rather than bringing healing (hot) or refreshment (cold), the church was useless and disgusting.[2] Consequently, Christ says, "I will spue thee out of my mouth." Their spirituality made Christ nauseous, as if the Son of God would vomit them out.

What was it about this church that Christ found so repulsive? The metaphor of lukewarm water has often been taken to suggest Christians who make a virtue out of mediocrity, content to go through the motions of worship and service with no real zeal or commitment. Think of Paul's description of those "having a form of godliness, but denying the power thereof" (2 Tim. 3:5). If so, then Laodicean lukewarmness was the opposite of Paul's attitude in Philippians 3:8, where the apostle says that he has looked at everything that he once valued as a Pharisee and has concluded, "I...do count them but dung, that I may win Christ." This out-and-out commitment to Christ and the gospel was missing in Laodicea.

Perhaps people in Laodicea feared that being on fire for Christ might cause others to think their faith was just emotionalism. Maybe they were concerned lest others call them fanatics. If fanaticism

---

2. Beale, *Revelation: A Shorter Commentary*, 91.

means wholehearted devotion to Christ, every Christian should be a fanatic. But fanaticism is not wholeheartedness. Fanaticism is a mindless form of carnal zeal. The heart runs away with the head. The kind of zeal that God urges upon us never promotes such mindlessness. In Romans 12:1–2, Paul urges us to present our bodies "a living sacrifice, holy, acceptable unto God, which is your reasonable service. And...be ye transformed by the renewing of your mind." True Christianity involves the mind as much as any other part of our human nature. Zeal for the Lord of hosts does not arise from mindlessness. It ponders the depths and the glory of the gospel of Jesus Christ. It penetrates the truth of Holy Scripture as we daily yield ourselves to Him with the kind of zeal that will burn until the day when we see Him face to face. Zeal is the heat that should accompany the light of God's truth as it shines in our hearts.[3]

However, as valuable as the call to zealous Christian living is, this is not the main point of verses 15–16. Certainly, we should not read this text as if Christ would commend spiritual coldness, or prefer it to spiritual mediocrity. After all, a complete lack of love for the Lord brings down God's curse upon sinners (1 Cor. 16:22). Spiritual coldness is a condition of grave danger, and when found in the church is a sign of apostasy (Matt. 24:12).

Though the Laodiceans did need to renew their zeal (Rev. 3:19), Christ focused His rebuke upon their pride and self-sufficiency: "Because thou sayest, I am rich, and increased with goods, and have need of nothing; and knowest not that thou art wretched, and miserable, and poor, and blind, and naked" (v. 17). Here is the foul taste that disgusted the Savior: rather than being poor in spirit (Matt. 5:3), this church was quite impressed with herself! The bitter root of lukewarmness is being satisfied with where you are spiritually.

Self-righteousness is offensive to our Savior, who says, "Without me ye can do nothing" (John 15:5). The Laodicean church members were so worldly, wealthy, and self-sufficient that they could not see

---

3. See Joel R. Beeke and James A. La Belle, *Living Zealously*, Deepen Your Christian Life (Grand Rapids: Reformation Heritage Books, 2012).

they were spiritually wretched, miserable, poor, blind, and naked. Such complacency is an insult to Christ, who spent His life suffering and dying for His church to provide for them the spiritual riches that we utterly lack (2 Cor. 8:9).

What a contrast there is between what Laodicea thinks of herself and what the Lord thinks of her! Christ says: "I know your works. You are poor because you have nothing with which to purchase forgiveness or entry into God's kingdom. You are naked because you have no clothing of righteousness in which to stand before God. You are blind because you have no awareness of your spiritual poverty. You are miserable, but you are blind to your misery."

The Lord is more displeased with the Laodicean church than any other. That is because the Lord hates sham, pretense, and hypocrisy—and that is what He sees in Laodicea. Laodicea has a "Let's pretend" religion. We, too, can easily pretend that we're all right. We do that when we think we're not quite as bad as our neighbors or not quite as bad as the Word of God says we are.

Such arrogance is a grave insult to the Savior, for if we are rich in ourselves and our good works, then Christ died for nothing (Gal. 2:21). Just think of how much trouble Christ has taken to save us. Think of how, before the creation of the world, He, the Father, and the Holy Spirit drew up the plan of salvation and entered into a solemn agreement to save the likes of you and me. Think of how Christ entered this world, became a man, and lived among sinners. Think of how He sweat blood and shed tears in Gethsemane, endured a trial of cruel mockings and scourgings, permitted Himself to be nailed to a cross, and poured out His soul unto death, shedding His blood to save sinners. When Christ went to such lengths to save us, how can we possibly think that we "have need of nothing"?

Nothing dishonors Christ more in the eyes of the world than a self-satisfied church. Such a congregation preaches the gospel of grace to needy sinners, but lives as if it has no spiritual needs. It tells people that they are guilty sinners, but acts as if it had no guilt of its own for Christ's blood to cover. It calls people to pray for salvation, but cannot rouse itself to come to a prayer meeting to cry out for divine mercies. A self-satisfied church is a living contradiction to the gospel of Christ.

The Lord says, "I warn you, Laodicea, if you go on in this way, I will spue you out of My mouth." In Greek, the word translated as *spue* implies an imminent action—it is what the Lord is about to do. "I am just about ready to spue you out of My mouth, Laodicea. I won't take much more of your lukewarmness, Laodicea. Continue this way, and I will surely spue you out of My mouth very soon."

Christ's patience is nearly at an end. He is ready to spit out the Laodicean church. But He is reluctant to do so. He still yearns to be gracious. You sense that in the remainder of this letter, which is more tender toward believers. This is just like the Lord Jesus. He is longsuffering to us, not willing for anyone to perish, but that all should come to repentance (2 Peter 3:9).

Christ's Remarkable Remedy
In His grace and mercy, Christ holds out hope for Laodicea. There is a way for her backslidings to be healed. The remedy for self-sufficiency is presented in Revelation 3:17b–22. Christ directs the Laodiceans to do three things:

First, the Laodiceans should *buy Christ's riches*. Christ says to them, "I counsel thee to buy of me gold tried in the fire, that thou mayest be rich; and white raiment, that thou mayest be clothed, and that the shame of thy nakedness do not appear; and anoint thine eyes with eyesalve, that thou mayest see" (v. 18). Laodicea was a city of commerce that had many marketplaces. The Lord is saying, as it were: "Laodicea, I am standing in your market. Come and buy of Me."

Of course, the gospel calls us to buy these riches without money or price (Isa. 55:1; Rev. 22:17). The only cost to ourselves is the loss of our sin and pride. So the Lord tells the church at Laodicea: "Exchange the artificial riches you possess for My riches. Exchange your self-righteousness for My true righteousness. Exchange your sins for My holiness." Christ is the *great exchange*. Here is the very principle of the gospel. Christ says, as it were: "I have true riches.

Laodicea, you think you are rich, but I will teach you that you are poor. If you would be rich, you must buy of Me gold tried in the fire. You might have fancy clothes, but you must cast off those garments and buy white raiment from Me. You have medicine for diseased eyes, but you need to buy from Me eye salve that will help you truly see."

Christ is giving Laodicea a final warning. He is saying: "Laodicea, you think your hope is in yourself, but you are going the wrong way. Your only hope is in Me. Buy of *Me.*" The Laodiceans had to learn that salvation is all of the Lord. They thought they were building their Christian church themselves, but they had to understand, "From Thee, O Lord, is our fruit found."

So Christ says: "Despite My holy disgust with your self-sufficiency, I tell you that though you are poor, I have gold. Though you are naked, I have clothing. Though you are blind, I have eye salve. Oh, Laodicea, trust no more in your banks, in your clothing factories, or in your medical science; trust in Me."

Christ specifically offers three things to the Laodiceans, things that are symbolic of what every sinner needs spiritually—eye salve, clothing, and gold tried in the fire.

1. *Eye salve.* Laodicea was famous for the production of medicinal lotions for eye problems, compounded out of Phrygian powder.[4] Christ turned their pride on its head by saying that He must heal their spiritual vision. Eye salve here is a symbol of spiritual illumination. Christ works through the preaching of the word to open the eyes of the blind (Acts 26:18; 2 Cor. 4:4–6). When the Lord gives us eyes to see, the first thing we see is how blind we were. We begin to see our foolishness. We begin to see our sins, realizing that we break all the commandments of God. Like the man born blind but healed by Christ, every true Christian can say, "One thing I know, that, whereas I was blind, now I see" (John 9:25). Even after He saves us, we continually need the influence of the Holy Spirit to enable us to see more of His grace and glory (Ps. 119:18; Eph. 1:17).

---

4. Osborne, *Revelation*, 201.

2. *White raiment.* Again, Christ uses language that confronts the Laodiceans right at the point of their pride. The city was famous for its textile products, but Christ tells them that the only way to cover their spiritual shame was with the garments He supplies. Jesus is the righteousness of His people. He met all the demands of God's justice by obeying the law and by paying for the punishment of sin through His suffering and death. He took the unrighteousness of His people upon Himself and sewed together, without seam, a perfect white robe of righteousness. To those who are lost and needy, He comes with His white raiment so that they may see that there is salvation in His blood and righteousness for poor, miserable, blind, and wretched sinners (Isa. 61:10; Zech. 3:3–4). Like the hymn writer, they may sing:

> Jesus, Thy blood and righteousness
> My beauty are, my glorious dress;
> 'Midst flaming worlds, in these arrayed,
> With joy shall I lift up mine head.
> Bold shall I stand in that great day,
> For who aught to my charge shall lay;
> Fully absolved through these I am
> From sin's tremendous curse and shame.[5]

Christ offers believers the shining raiment of righteousness, which far surpasses the clothing produced by Laodicea's factories. Christ's clothing allows us to stand in the sight of a holy God.

3. *Gold tried in the fire.* Despite all the wealth of the Laodicean church, Christ alone can give them genuine, pure gold. Gold was heavily used in the tabernacle and temple as a sign of God's holiness (Exodus 39). Gold refined by fire represents the covenant faithfulness of God's people when they have been purified by sanctifying grace and providential trials (Zech. 13:9; Mal. 3:3). Therefore, Christ offers them the true wealth: holiness produced by God's Spirit.

---

5. Nikolaus von Zinzendorf, "Jesus, Thy Blood and Righteousness," trans. John Wesley (1739).

Christ Himself became our golden holiness when His obedience was tried in the fire of Gethsemane, the fire of Gabbatha, and the fire of Golgotha. The Spirit brings that gold into the souls of those who trust in Christ, refining them and forming Christ in us. No two children of God are alike on this earth, yet every child of God becomes golden through the golden Christ.

We see the great irony of Christ's words when we compare them to what He said to the church of Smyrna. Christ rebuked the Laodiceans for thinking that they were rich, and told them they were poor and needed "to buy of me gold tried in the fire, that thou mayest be rich" (Rev. 3:17–18). However, Christ said to the Smyrnans, "I know thy works, and tribulation, and poverty, (but thou art rich)" (Rev. 2:9). In other words, the wealthy Laodiceans would be better off being like the persecuted Smyrnans, for their gold was the currency of heaven.

So Christ says to Laodicea: "You think you have everything, but you have nothing. But here is illumination with eye salve; here is justification with white raiment; here is sanctification with gold tried by fire. Here are My wares—will you take them from Me?"

Second, the Laodiceans should respond to Christ's knocking. In Revelation 3:20a, Christ says, "Behold, I stand at the door, and knock." This can be applied in three ways.

1. Christ is knocking at the door of the church of Laodicea. Christ is outside that church, and the church does not even realize it. Christ should be in the midst of His church. He should be in the pulpit and at the table. Christ should be in the midst of the life of every congregation. But at Laodicea, He has withdrawn from her life and work, and now stands outside, knocking on the door.

When Christ withdraws from a church, it is always for a purpose. However, He has not yet entirely abandoned the church at Laodicea. He stands outside to confront the church with its woeful condition. Jesus stands at the door, but He is knocking to be let back in. He stands there knocking and calling to those who are inside.

The Lord likely alludes here to the words of the Song of Songs.[6] In that poetic description of His relationship to His people, we find a sleepy bride who hears her Beloved knocking at the door and calling, "Open to me," but she is too lazy to get up and finds that He has withdrawn His presence (Song. 5:2–6). The church in Laodicea has grown spiritually sleepy and lethargic, and Christ calls her to awake, get up, and enjoy His presence again.

2. Jesus is knocking at the door of the hearts of individual believers—lukewarm though they be—in the Laodicean church. Although Jesus might leave a church, He will never leave His own. He will never abandon His elect who truly love Him and desire fellowship and communion with Him. It is to these that our Lord says, "If any man hear my voice, and open the door, I will come in to him, and will sup with him, and he with me" (v. 20b). Notice the focus on the individual, literally: "if anyone hear." Each individual person in the church must hear and respond in order to enjoy fellowship with Christ.

For the believer, Christ's knocking is an internal knocking on the very door of the heart. When Christ knocks on the doors of the hearts of those He loves, He shakes those hearts with His knocking. He gains entrance, for He is the Amen who knocks. He knocks with the hard knocks of love, and He calls His people to come out of the world and says to them, as He said to Adam, "Where art thou?" (Gen. 3:9).

When Bartimaeus was told, "Rise; he calleth thee," he stood, cast away his cloak, and came to Jesus (Mark 10:49–50). Jesus says, "I stand at the door, and knock." Blessed are they who know what this means and can no longer hold back, but must throw open the door. When the Lord applies His grace to His people, they can then rise and give entrance to their Beloved. Everything goes open to the Lord—especially the heart. When Christ opens Himself up to His people, His people open themselves up to Him.

---

6. Beale, *Revelation: A Shorter Commentary*, 93.

In a close interpersonal relationship, two people open up to each other bit by bit. This kind of mutual self-disclosure proceeds in steps over time. So it is between the Lord and His people. The Lord inclines His people to open their hearts unto Him until they learn to trust Him. As this mutual, mystical ebbing and flowing of the openings of God's grace and the returning of that grace in the believer proceed, there is a yielding and surrendering by grace to Jesus Christ, who woos and wins the heart of His bride.

In John 14:23, Christ says, "If a man love me, he will keep my words: and my Father will love him, and we will come unto him, and make our abode with him." When Christ comes, He brings a feast. And when the door is open, He eats with His friends. Oh, what a tender picture Jesus is painting here in His appeal to the Laodiceans.

Jesus is saying, just as the man says in Song of Songs 5:1, "I am come into my garden, my sister, my spouse: I have gathered my myrrh with my spice; I have eaten my honeycomb with my honey; I have drunk my wine with my milk: eat, O friends; drink, yea, drink abundantly, O beloved." In Revelation 3:20, He says, "I…will sup with him, and he with me." There is a mutual exchange. Jesus is saying, "This is the fruit of buying from Me, of this exchange with Me." The Lord says, "We will come and take up Our abode with you."

When the Lord sups with His people, their hearts burn within them. They begin to feel like the men of Emmaus, saying, "Did not our heart burn within us, while he talked with us by the way, and while he opened to us the scriptures?" (Luke 24:32). There is something here that defies description. I can only say that supping with Jesus means that Christ enters into the joys, needs, and concerns of the sinner, but the sinner also enters into the joys of Christ. To sup with Christ is to enter into His joy in relation to the Father's will. Christ says, "I have meat to eat that ye know not of" (John 4:32), but then explains, "My meat is to do the will of him that sent me, and to finish his work" (v. 34).

Now His people who sup with Christ may say the same thing. They enter into His joy and say, "My meat, my joy, is to do the will of the Father in heaven." The highest form of supping with Christ is to know and do the will of Christ, and through Him, to know and do the will of God the Father.

3. Christ is knocking by way of gospel overtures to lost sinners. Given that Christ speaks no commendation to this church, and describes its condition is such dire terms, we must conclude that at least some, perhaps many, among them were not converted. When people are lost, Christ comes knocking with tender mercies. When the Lord comes to a lost sinner who has already heard the knockings of the law and conviction, He comes also with the knockings of His gospel grace. He inclines a sinner, like a bride, to rise and answer the knock of her bridegroom. The sinner opens to Christ in the faith that Christ Himself grants to that sinner. The soul goes out to Christ with the sweet longings and incense of prayer. When the Lord knocks irresistibly, how shall we not come to the door and let Him in?

Revelation 3:20 is often interpreted to mean that Christ is doomed to go on knocking until we decide to let Him in, for it is up to us to open the door. To adopt such a view is, on the one hand, to set a limit on the sovereign power of God, and on the other, to attribute a power and freedom to sinners that they simply do not possess. Christ's standing at the door and knocking is proof of His mercy and grace toward us, not any sign of weakness or helplessness on His part. On the contrary, Christ saves His people by sovereign grace, and is never defeated by Satan or men, "for he is Lord of Lords, and King of kings: and they that are with him are called, and chosen, and faithful" (Rev. 17:14).

When we encounter a text like Revelation 3:20, we can err in two different directions. On the one hand, some people are so afraid of saying they can do anything that they underplay the reality that God really knocks and really invites. But the Lord does sincerely knock. He commands all who hear the gospel to repent (Acts 17:30). As the Canons of Dort say, "As many as are called by the gospel are unfeignedly called. For God hath most earnestly and truly declared in His Word what will be acceptable to Him;

namely, that all who are called, should comply with the invitation. He, moreover, seriously promises eternal life and rest to as many as shall come to Him and believe on Him."[7]

On the other hand, we can err by thinking that a man can come to God in his own strength. By nature, we cannot open the door, because by nature we have no desire to open the door (John 6:44). We are dead in our sins and trespasses (Eph. 2:1). We are miserable, polluted, blind, and naked. We don't hear, don't desire, and don't see (Isa. 6:10). We can't arise; we have no legs to run and no arms to embrace. We chose that route in Paradise, and we by nature we choose that route every day. That is why we need our Savior's healing eye salve, His spotless white raiment, and His pure gold.

Our greatest sin is rejecting God's sincere invitation. Our greatest transgression is to push away the grace that is proffered to us and say, "I have no desire for Thee to be King over me." That is why the depths of hell are reserved for those who have heard the gospel and have not obeyed it.

We reject Christ's invitation because we are Laodiceans at heart; we are self-sufficient, or at least we think we are. We pretend that we need nothing, not knowing that we are in desperate need of what Christ offers.

How can we bring Christ back to the church if, as in Laodicea, He is not in the preaching, not in our prayer meetings, and not with us when we read our Bibles and pray? Here are some suggestions:

1. *Face up to your condition.* The Laodiceans did not see eye to eye with Christ concerning their condition. "I know your works" (vv. 15, 17), says Jesus, the Amen, the truth of God, the faithful and true witness. "I know your works, but you don't. You think you are rich and have need of nothing, and you don't realize your true condition. You don't know what I know about you. You are wretched, pitiable, poor, blind, and naked." Christ will come back into a congregation that has driven Him away only if they come to see things as He sees them. That is what confession of sin is all

7. Canons of Dort, Head 3/4, Art. 8, in *Three Forms of Unity*, 143.

about. Literally, to confess is "say together with." When you confess your sins, you say together with Christ what you have done. You come without excuse and say: "Yes, I am wretched. I am miserable. I am poor, blind, and naked." You acknowledge your true condition, confess your sins, and agree with Christ on these things.

In the book of Hosea, the Lord asks, "How shall I give thee up, Ephraim?" (Hos. 11:8). Yet He also says in Hosea 5:15, "I will go and return to my place, till they acknowledge their offence, and seek my face: in their affliction they will seek me early." So the first thing we must do is to say before Christ: "We are wretched, miserable, poor, blind, and naked. We are not what we thought we were; we are not what others think we are. But Thou knowest, Lord what we truly are and what we truly need."

2. *Return to the fundamentals of the gospel.* In Revelation 3:18, Christ tells the Laodicean church, "I counsel thee to buy of me gold tried in the fire, that thou mayest be rich; and white raiment, that thou mayest be clothed, and that the shame of thy nakedness do not appear; and anoint thine eyes with eyesalve, that thou mayest see."

My friend, if Christ has withdrawn Himself from your life and is outside the door, confess the sin that drove Him there and remember who He is. Remember that He is your Prophet, your Priest, and your King. He is the One who can give you eye salve for your blindness, clothe you in your nakedness, and make you rich in your poverty. Remind yourself of who He is and what He means to you, and you will find that suddenly He is there alongside you again.

3. *Submit to His discipline.* Jesus says, "As many as I love, I rebuke and chasten" (v. 19a). Some view discipline as a threat. They think this verse means that unless we return to Christ, He will punish us. But I see this as less a threat than an explanation. Jesus is saying: "I want you to understand why I am outside the door. I haven't gone off in a huff; I have been standing here for some time, and I am still knocking and speaking to you. I want you to understand that My withdrawal from your midst is disciplinary."

There are times when Christ withdraws His presence so that we might seek after Him more. Sometimes we don't miss someone until we lose him or her. The trouble with us as Christians is that though we love Christ, many other things crowd in on that relationship, and we find ourselves trusting in those things. Christ then has to withdraw Himself from us until we realize our need for Him.

4. *Be zealous for Christ.* Finally, we are told to be zealous and repent (v. 19b). Literally, we are to become "boiling hot." Zeal is not something we can work up. That is why Christ does not ask it of us until after we have faced up to our sinful condition, returned to the fundamentals of the gospel, and submitted to His discipline. Rekindled zeal is the fruit of doing all that Christ recommends to the lukewarm Laodicean church.

What saved the church in the eighteenth century was not the writing of people such as Bishop Joseph Butler and John W. Haley, with their demonstrations and proofs about the existence of God. No; it was John Wesley and George Whitefield, who were on fire with God's Spirit. Today we need that same fire from heaven. We need an outpouring of the Holy Spirit. We don't need to make Christianity more palatable to the unbeliever. We need the Holy Spirit to raise the spiritual temperature of His church.

"Be zealous therefore" (v. 19b), Christ says. This is something that God in His sovereignty can do, but it is also something for which you and I are responsible. We lose our zeal by our folly and wrongdoing. Repentance will rekindle it. There is no better way than to heed Christ's warning and avail ourselves of the remedy He prescribes. "If any man hears what I have to say from outside the church," He says, "I will come in to him and will sup with him, and he with Me, for My name's sake."

5. *Cling to the promise of Christ.* Christ promises the church at Laodicea, "To him that overcometh will I grant to sit with me in my throne, even as I also overcame, and am set down with my Father in his throne" (v. 21). That Christ should come and sit and sup with His people is honor enough, but He also promises to lead them to glory, to crown them, and to espouse them to Himself. He promises to change them from paupers into princes, to allow them to rule with Him, to seat them with Him in His throne.

Christ said to Peter and the other disciples, "Ye which have followed me, in the regeneration when the Son of man shall sit in the throne of his glory, ye also shall sit upon twelve thrones, judging the twelve tribes of Israel" (Matt. 19:28).

Christ now reiterates that promise, saying: "As I have overcome and have sat down on My throne in glory, so I shall cause you, My people, also to overcome by grace only and by faith only. I shall bring you where I am and seat you with Me on My throne, where you also shall rule in glory. As I share the Father's throne, true believer, so you shall share My throne. And I speak this with authority, for My name is the Amen. My word is true; I am the faithful and true witness."

The Lord is rich, and we are poor. The Lord has clothing, and we are naked. The Lord has eye salve, and we are blind. But by His grace, we can learn that life without Christ is nothing but vanity, while life with Him is life abounding. As Augustus Toplady wrote,

> Lord, it is not life to live,
> If thy presence thou deny;
> Lord, if thou thy presence give,
> Then it is not death to die.[8]

The Laodiceans tried to avoid dying to this world in order to live with Christ. God's true people learn that there is no life to live without Him.

6. *Listen to the Spirit of Christ.* If you have ears to hear, listen to the Spirit's warning against lukewarmness. One day, you will stand before the judgment seat of Christ. Will He claim you as His own or will He spew you out of His mouth, saying you were neither hot nor cold but only lukewarm toward Him? Will you then wish you had been more zealous for Him?

Laodicea soon ceased to be a church. Only the Lord knows what happened to those who read the letter warning them about their lack of zeal. Some may be seated in glory around Christ's throne this very day, while many others have been cast into the lake of fire.

---

8. Augustus Toplady, "Lord, It Is Not Life to Live" (1774).

Christ knocks on the doors of His church and the hearts of sinners. He knocks with invitations, with love, and with sincerity. He knocks with judgments, with afflictions, and with death. He knocks every day of our lives. He knocks in the small things of His daily goodness. How will you respond to His knockings?

11

The Throne of God

REVELATION 4:1–11

After this I looked, and, behold, a door was opened in heaven: and the first voice which I heard was as it were of a trumpet talking with me; which said, Come up hither, and I will shew thee things which must be hereafter. And immediately I was in the spirit: and, behold, a throne was set in heaven, and one sat on the throne. And he that sat was to look upon like a jasper and a sardine stone: and there was a rainbow round about the throne, in sight like unto an emerald. And round about the throne were four and twenty seats: and upon the seats I saw four and twenty elders sitting, clothed in white raiment; and they had on their heads crowns of gold. And out of the throne proceeded lightnings and thunderings and voices: and there were seven lamps of fire burning before the throne, which are the seven Spirits of God. And before the throne there was a sea of glass like unto crystal: and in the midst of the throne, and round about the throne, were four beasts full of eyes before and behind. And the first beast was like a lion, and the second beast like a calf, and the third beast had a face as a man, and the fourth beast was like a flying eagle. And the four beasts had each of them six wings about him; and they were full of eyes within: and they rest not day and night, saying, Holy, holy, holy, Lord God Almighty, which was, and is, and is to come. And when those beasts give glory and honour and thanks to him that sat on the throne, who liveth for ever and ever, the four and twenty elders fall down before him that sat on the throne, and worship him that liveth for ever and ever, and cast their crowns before the throne, saying, Thou art worthy, O Lord, to receive glory and honour and power: for thou hast created all things, and for thy pleasure they are and were created.

We have reached the point of no return in our study of the book of Revelation. Many preachers end their series of sermons on Revelation when they complete chapter 3. This is probably because the first three chapters are comparatively easy to understand and interpret. From chapter 4 on, the book of Revelation can be very challenging.

It is helpful to remember two principles for interpreting this book. First, we must interpret Revelation cyclically rather than linearly. With the first words of chapter 4, John opens his account of the second of seven parallel cycles of visions he was given. Each cycle applies to the church of all ages. The first of the seven is the vision of Christ in the midst of the golden candlesticks, with His messages to the churches of Asia (chs. 1–3). Chapters 4 through 7 record the second cycle of visions John saw on the island of Patmos.

Earlier, we said that Revelation can be viewed in terms of a video. It begins at one vantage point and then goes on to present six additional points. Collectively, they provide a panoramic view of the entire gospel age, from the first coming of Christ to His second advent. It is important to understand the book of Revelation this way rather than as a continuous, unbroken line of history.

Second, we must remember that Revelation is written symbolically. It is impressionistic—almost surrealistic in places. This material is more the genre of the artist, the poet, or the composer than that of the historian or scientist. Please don't misunderstand me—I am not suggesting there is anything in Revelation or the Bible that is historically or scientifically inaccurate. But there are different ways of conveying truth. The scientist conveys truth through concrete reports of his experiments and discoveries, and the historian does so by means of historical research. But the poet, artist, and musician convey truth in a symbolic, impressionistic way rather than literally. Many of the prophets of Scripture were poets, singers, and musicians. We must grasp that before we plunge into this chapter if we are to understand what yet lies ahead.

In Revelation 4, John sees a throne surrounded by a rainbow, a sea of glass, seven lamps of fire, and four living creatures covered with eyes. Each of these creatures has six wings. They each resemble, in turn, a lion, a calf or ox, a man, and an eagle. John also sees twenty-four elders seated on thrones around this rainbow throne.

What does all this symbolism mean? In order to answer this question, we need to look carefully at the overall picture. We must search for the central truth rather than press for details. We should not pick out a symbol here and a symbol there, then attempt to explain in detail what each symbol means in some spiritual sense. Rather, we should look for the overall central truth and interpret this vision from that vantage point. Such an approach is crucial for rightly understanding the book of Revelation.

What is the central thought or picture in Revelation 4? Verse 2 offers the explanation. John says, "And immediately I was in the spirit; and, behold, a throne was set in heaven, and one sat on the throne." The occupied throne is the focus of this second cycle of visions. Seventeen times in Revelation 4 and 5, John speaks about this throne. All other symbols, such as colors, numbers, and pictures, should be understood in relation to this throne. Let's survey this throne under three headings: its sovereignty, its symbolism, and its significance.

The Sovereignty of the Throne

Nicolaus Copernicus was the first modern astronomer to deny that the earth is the center of the universe. He taught that the earth actually revolves around the sun. This view was very controversial, because almost everyone at that time believed that the earth was the center of everything. The sun, moon, stars, and planets all appeared to revolve around the earth.

Today we know that Copernicus was right: the earth is not the center of the universe. The universe contains much more than just our solar system or even our galaxy. In fact, scientists consider our galaxy, the Milky Way, to be actually rather small in comparison to others. There are many solar systems and galaxies beyond our own.

However, though the universe may not have a physical center, it does have a governmental and spiritual center. John says in Revelation 4 that at the center of all the universe there sits a throne. The universe is not earth-centered or sun-centered, but God-centered.

Christ takes John, in the Spirit, into heaven's throne room. John sees a door opened in heaven, and a trumpet-like voice says to him, "Come up hither, and I will shew thee things which must be here-after" (Rev. 4:1). John is then carried to the doorway of the throne room of heaven, and on that throne John sees One robed in dazzling light. And His throne is the center of all things that surround it.

God's throne is the primary picture in Revelation. The word throne occurs in the New Testament sixty-two times, and forty-seven of these are in Revelation. The book is dominated by the idea that there is a throne in heaven at the center of all things and that there is a glorious One who sits upon that throne.

The centrality of God's throne signifies His sovereignty. It pre-sents His royalty, authority, and control of the universe. From His throne, God summons sinners to judgment and dispenses grace to saints. The sight of His throne is glorious, majestic, and overwhelm-ing. John is so overcome by what he sees that he can scarcely take it in, much less describe it. The One who sits on the throne is too glorious to describe.

This causes John to relate the sight of God's sovereign throne with fantastic imagery. He first compares the enthroned Sovereign to a jasper stone, a gemstone that is found in a variety of colors. John then looks again and says that this One is like a sardine stone, that is, an opaque red stone that reflects light in all hues of red. Both these stones were among the precious gems on the high priest's breastplate (Ex. 28:17, 20). They are also among the foundation stones of New Jerusalem (Rev. 21:19–20). Then John sees a shimmering rainbow encircling the throne with the many hues of an emerald (Rev. 4:3). And before this throne is a sea of glass "like unto crystal" (v. 6a). Glass was scarce in New Testament times, and crystal-clear glass was almost impossible to find. This sea of glass reflects the magnificence and holiness of the sovereign One on the throne.

John hears "lightnings and thunderings and voices" proceeding from the throne (v. 5). He sees seven lamps or torches symbolizing "the seven Spirits of God" (v. 5; cf. 1:4). This is a description of the Holy Spirit in terms of His "sevenfold gift" (Isa. 11:2). Long before

John, the prophet Zechariah recorded his vision of the candlestick of gold with seven lamps (Zech. 4:2–6). This symbolized the one Spirit of God and the many facets of His work.

All around the great throne are twenty-four lesser thrones, each occupied by an elder dressed in white and wearing a golden crown or victor's wreath on his head (Rev. 4:4). John also sees four creatures with six wings that surround the throne (vv. 6b, 8). They are "full of eyes before and behind" (v. 6b), and they cry continually, "Holy, holy, holy, Lord God Almighty, which was, and is, and is to come" (v. 8; cf. Isa. 6:2, 3).

All of these living creatures—the four beasts and the twenty-four elders—are continually worshiping the sovereign One on the throne. The elders proclaim, "Thou art worthy, O Lord, to receive glory and honour and power: for thou hast created all things, and for thy pleasure they are and were created" (Rev. 4:11).

What a worship service this is, and how it speaks of the sovereignty of God! The inhabitants of heaven are worshiping the Lord who made heaven and earth (Ps. 124:8). He alone is worthy of such worship, for He is the Creator of all that is. All creation exists to please and serve Him. His creatures declare His glory, honor Him with their heartfelt submission, and rely on His power alone to sustain and bless them. "Honour and majesty are before him; strength and beauty are in his sanctuary" (Ps. 96:6). Such is the joy in heaven on the part of all around God's throne. They are filled with the satisfaction, joy, and pleasure of wholehearted worship of the Lord of salvation.

These worshipers experience such satisfaction, joy, and pleasure because their eyes are fixed upon the One who is seated on the throne. You can experience the true joy of worship only when your worship is centered upon the triune God and when the presence of the Lord evokes in you the joy of the amazing privilege of knowing Him and being known by Him.

Focus for a moment on the centrality of the throne. This is significant doctrinally rather than pictorially. The throne's centrality declares that everyone and everything should acknowledge the triune God of the universe in the person of Jesus Christ as the Lord God. All derive their very existence from His will alone, and they were made to serve His pleasure. The throne is the center of everything.

The sovereignty of God explains everything in the realm of grace and in the realm of nature. That is the significance of the twenty-four elders and the four living creatures. The elders represent the church of God under both the Old and the New Testaments—the twelve patriarchs of the Old Testament and the twelve apostles of the New Testament.

The four living creatures, which have the faces of a lion, a calf, a man, and an eagle (Rev. 4:7), are somewhat difficult to understand. Some say the four beasts are the cherubim, the highest order of angels. Just as the Holy Spirit is viewed symbolically in the seven lamps, so the appearance of the four living creatures represents the holy attributes of God. The beast like a lion is a symbol of God's power. The beast like a calf or ox speaks of God's faithfulness. The beast with the face of a man denotes God's intelligence. And the beast like a flying eagle expresses God's sovereignty. These beasts, like the cherubim, proclaim God's holy attributes, fill heaven with their worship, and guard God's throne. They do this continually; they are in constant motion. With six wings and eyes all around, they can fly in any direction and see from every quarter (v. 8a). They form the closest circle around the throne, and they cry out continually, "Holy, holy, holy, Lord God Almighty, which was, and is, and is to come" (v. 8b).

Still others say the activity of these beasts ultimately represents God's sovereignty over all of His creation and all powers within His creation. Herman Hoeksema writes, "Four is the number that is symbolic of creation in all its fullness. Think of the four winds of heaven, and the four corners of the earth. In their number they therefore represent the entire creation…. What the lion is among the beasts of the field, the ox is among the cattle, man among the intelligent creatures, and the eagle among the birds."[1] Much like Ezekiel's similar vision of "four living creatures" (Ezek. 1:5–10), John's vision indicates that God is sovereign in all created realms. He is always on the throne. He is the focal point of worship for all the assembled powers of the universe. He is sovereign over all.

Because He is sovereign, God must be worshiped by everyone in heaven and earth. Thus, ultimately, the point of Revelation 4 is that all things in heaven and earth should praise and honor God because He is the Creator and Sustainer of all. The four living creatures proclaim His infinite, eternal, and unchanging holiness as the sovereign God, and the twenty-four elders worship Him as their Creator and Judge. The elders take off their victor's crowns and cast them at the feet of the sovereign God on the throne (Rev. 4:10), declaring that He alone is worthy "to receive glory and honour and power" (v. 11). Revelation 4 declares that God is sovereign in grace and in nature, in church and in creation, and in gospel and in science.

This is a message that we badly need to hear today, especially in the realm of science, nature, and creation. With respect to science, too often He is seen as only the God of the gaps—that is, He just fills in our pockets of ignorance. The trouble with that view of God is that our gaps are perceived to be getting smaller and fewer as the years go by, as man seems to amass more understanding of the world in which he lives.

The Bible does not teach a God of the gaps. The sovereign God cannot be invoked only when we need Him to explain something that we don't understand. He is the God who is in all and behind all. He is sovereign in the realm of humanity, creation, science, and nature. He decrees all, preserves all, and governs all. The God of the universe is on the throne, ruling over all creatures and all things, both great and small!

God is also the Head of the church and the God of one-sided, gracious salvation. We need to hear this today because so

---

1. Herman Hoeksema, *Behold He Cometh: An Exposition of the Book of Revelation* (Grand Rapids: Reformed Free Publishing Association, 1969), 160–61.

many evangelical Christians have the idea that God is only waiting in the wings for us to claim His promises or ask for His Spirit.
He has done everything for us, they say. Now it is all up to us to
claim salvation as ours. Even when it comes to the focal point of
the gospel—the atonement, the death of the Son of God upon the
cross—we are told: "Jesus has shed His blood upon the cross to
make salvation possible. It is up to you now to repent and believe. If
you do that, He didn't die in vain." That is what people believe, but
it is a travesty to the truth! The truth is that in the church, in the
realm of grace, and in the gospel, God is sovereign. He is working
out His sovereign purposes. He is doing these things not according
to our whims but according to His good pleasure. He is sovereign;
He is seated upon the throne. Because this throne is very important,
let us delve more deeply into its symbolism.

The Symbolism of the Throne

Scripture says that God is Spirit; He does not have a body like our
bodies. He inhabits eternity. He does not literally or physically sit
upon a throne; indeed, He has no need of a literal throne. Rather,
this throne is a symbol, not a physical reality. It symbolizes the *eternal glory of the ever-living God.*

John sees a heavenly throne, upon which is seated One who is
glorious beyond description. John doesn't attempt to describe this
One; all he can do is give us his impression. He says: "I looked,
and this is what I saw. I saw bright glowing light in hues of many
colors." To try to determine precisely what the jasper stone and the
sardine stone mean would not be helpful; rather, it would detract
from the impression we receive from the unity of the entire scene.
The best John can do is to compare this light to the luster of polished gemstones to show us the glory of the living God.

The apostle Paul describes this same throne. He portrays the
glorious Being who sits upon it as "the blessed and only Potentate,
the King of kings, and Lord of lords; who only hath immortality,
dwelling in the light which no man can approach unto; whom no

man hath seen, nor can see: to whom be honour and power everlasting. Amen" (1 Tim. 6:15–16).

Revelation 4:5 adds sound to John's vision: "And out of the throne proceeded lightnings and thunderings and voices." This reminds us of God's descent to Mount Sinai when Moses was given the Ten Commandments (Exodus 19). That mountain also shook with lightning, thunder, and voices. "And so terrible was the sight, that Moses said, I exceedingly fear and quake" (Heb. 12:21). The lightning, thunder, and voices signify that the throne of glory is also a throne of judgment. God is a God of unapproachable, indescribable majesty and glory. At the same time, He is a God of absolute justice and perfect holiness. That is the significance of Revelation 4:5. There is something fearful and ominous about this throne, for this throne of glory is also a throne of judgment.

But something about this throne is also wonderful and beautiful. Verse 3 says: "And there was *a rainbow round about the throne*, in sight like unto an emerald." A rainbow is always a glorious sight, especially if you can see 180 degrees of it. But the rainbow around the great throne of heaven is even more glorious, for it can be seen in 360 degrees; that is, it completely surrounds the throne. Beginning with Noah, the rainbow has been a symbol of God's grace toward erring humanity (Gen. 9:12–17). It is the sign of His covenant and His goodness and longsuffering. It is the pledge that He writes in the skies for all generations to read. It says that He is a God of mercy who has no pleasure in the death of the wicked (Ezek. 33:11).

As a symbol, the rainbow tells God's children in every age that the storm is past and the judgment over, for God's wrath has expended itself by falling on Christ. As the prophet Isaiah declares, "All we like sheep have gone astray; we have turned every one to his own way; and the LORD hath laid on him the iniquity of us all" (Isa. 53:6). On the basis of Christ's finished work, God's covenant of grace is as firm and dependable as His oath to Noah that the flood would never come again (Isa. 54:9–10). Just as storm clouds and sunshine are needed for a rainbow to appear, so the storm of God's anger and the smile of His love have met at Calvary so that sinners might be saved. "Mercy and truth are met together; righteousness and peace have kissed each other" (Ps. 85:10). That is the significance of the rainbow that encircles the great throne.

So the center of this universe is not the earth, the sun, or the stars; it is the throne of God. The holiness and justice of this throne threaten judgment on all sin. But a rainbow encircles this throne as a sign of God's promised grace and mercy to sinners.

Sometimes we view the sovereignty of God as something harsh, arbitrary, or iron-like. We must remember that God's throne is encircled by a rainbow, indicating that in Christ Jesus our God also offers grace and mercy. God is the monarch of all He surveys; He is absolutely sovereign over all things in creation. God can do whatever He wants to do. But this chapter also tells us that God wants to save sinners. He has committed Himself to do so in an everlasting covenant that cannot be broken.

The Significance of the Throne for Us

What, then, is the significance of this vision of the throne of God for us today? We have discussed the sovereignty and symbolism of the throne. Let us now explain its significance for us under three headings: its explanation, comfort, and salvation.

Explanation

Revelation 4 offers us an explanation of God's purpose for His church. This is why it is crucial to understand how we are to interpret this book. The idea that God somehow whisks or raptures His church away after the "Laodicean Age" (Revelation 3) and that the rest of Revelation has nothing to say to the church today is nonsense. As we saw earlier, John tells us in Revelation 1 that the purpose of this book is to give comfort to the church in the midst of what will happen in the future. Revelation prepares God's people in all ages for the tribulations and sufferings they must endure.

The message for the church of John's day is the same for us today: Life is not purposeless or meaningless. Nothing comes to us by mere chance. The One who is seated on the throne of heaven has His hand in everything that happens, from great international events to the minute matters of your spiritual world, your emotional world, your domestic and interpersonal world, your work world, and your physical world. Nothing that happens to you or in the world around you is purposeless or meaningless. God is on His throne.

Notice that the Lord says to John, "Come up hither, and I will shew thee things which must be hereafter" (4:1). The things John sees are things that must come to pass. Yes, these are things that sometimes hurt and bewilder us. We cannot understand why many things happen, for they seem so hard and so cruel. Yet God has decreed these things because He is working out His purposes of grace, and all things serve those purposes. He is sovereign, yes, but His throne is bounded by His grace, as evidenced by the encircling rainbow. "I am the LORD, and there is none else. I form the light, and create darkness: I make peace, and create evil: I the LORD do all these things" (Isa. 45:6, 7). He can even turn the wrath of men into praise (Ps. 76:10). He alone can bring good out of evil.

The psalmist says it well, as we sing in the Psalter:

> Thy word and works unmoved remain,
> Thy every purpose to fulfill;
> All things are Thine and Thee obey,
> And all as servants wait Thy will.
>
> I should have perished in my woe
> Had not I loved Thy law divine;
> That law I never can forget;
> O save me, Lord, for I am Thine.[2]

We believers make so many mistakes that we wonder how the Lord can use us. If God can bring good out of evil, it is a very small thing for Him to put your mistakes right and get you back on course again. He is sovereign; He rules over all. As is often said, only God

---

2. *The Psalter*, #332:2, 3 (Ps. 119:91–94).

can draw straight lines with crooked sticks. We are to submit to Him, not with Islamic fatalism, but with childlike trust and confidence. So the wonder of living in the midst of a bewildering world is that we have an ultimate explanation for all that befalls us, namely, the will of our Father exercised from His throne in heaven.

Because our Father is on His throne, we must live always *coram Deo*, that is, before the face or the presence of God. We must view our Father as the primary cause of all things. People and circumstances are only secondary causes; God is the primary cause. And the more you learn to look past the secondary causes to gaze upon Him as the primary cause, the more peaceful your life will be. Isaiah 26:3 puts it this way: "Thou wilt keep him in perfect peace, whose mind is stayed on thee: because he trusteth in thee."

Comfort

We should take comfort from the truth that our Father's throne is the center of the universe. We also can take comfort in knowing that we do not belong to ourselves, but to Jesus Christ, who, as the Heidelberg Catechism says in Question 1, "so preserves me that without the will of my heavenly Father, not a hair can fall from my head; yea, that all things must be subservient to my salvation."[3]

Not a hair can fall without our Father's will—what a comfort this is! God's sovereignty is at the service of a Father's tender love. His sovereignty is neither capricious nor despotic. He aims at your highest good. He has committed Himself, His throne, and all the resources of His government to save you and keep you saved. He cannot fail. That is comforting indeed.

David expresses this comfort in terms we can all understand:

> The tender love a father has
> For all his children dear,
> Such love the Lord bestows on them
> Who worship Him in fear.

---

3. *Three Forms of Unity*, 68.

Unchanging is the love of God
From age to age the same,
Displayed to all who do His will
And reverence His name.[4]

Just before the Lord shows John the vials of wrath and tribulation that depict the terrible suffering that will come to God's
people, Christ shows him a throne encircled by a rainbow. He will
not whisk us up and rapture us away from tribulation. Rather, Jesus
says, "In the world ye shall have tribulation: but be of good cheer; I
have overcome the world" (John 16:33). You can endure tribulation
because God's throne of justice and power is now a throne of grace
for you in Christ Jesus. In Christ, divine power and fatherly love
unite to help you. Hebrews 4:16 says, "Let us therefore come boldly
unto the throne of grace, that we may obtain mercy, and find grace
to help in time of need." Let us boldly come to this throne and to
the One who sits upon it. Let us not be afraid of Him. Your Father
in His throne room is committed to your highest good.

Knowing what the throne of God signifies and the character
of the One who sits upon it has helped comfort the saints of God
in every age. In Psalm 18, David testifies to the help he found in
a time of distress, when "the sorrows of death compassed me, and
the floods of ungodly men made me afraid" (v. 4). He found himself
surrounded by people bent on doing him harm and was looking
death in the face. What did he do? "In my distress I called upon the
LORD, and cried unto my God: he heard my voice out of his temple,
and my cry came before him, even into his ears" (v. 6). Remember,
there was no temple on earth in David's lifetime; he refers here to
God's temple and throne room in heaven. God heard and answered
David's cry for help by coming to his aid and delivering him from
the hand of all his enemies.

God has promised to do the same for all who are in Christ
Jesus. Those who believe, as David believed, in the power and love of

---

4. *The Psalter*, #278:2, 4 (Ps. 103:13, 17).

the One who sits upon the rainbow throne of justice and mercy can say with the Heidelberg Catechism, Question 52, "In all my sorrows and persecutions, with uplifted head I look for the very same person, who before offered Himself for my sake,...to come as judge from heaven: who shall cast all his and my enemies into everlasting condemnation, but shall translate me with all his chosen ones to himself, into heavenly joys and glory."[5] Our God reigns! Lift up your heads, look to the Lord, and call on His name!

Salvation

How marvelous it is to know that the throne of God is the center of the universe today. If you espouse the view that divides the first three chapters of Revelation from what follows, you are cutting yourself off from the saving gospel that this book so richly offers. There is a throne in heaven and that it is a throne of grace to which you and I can go. David expressed this truth in song:

> Thou, O Lord, art God alone;
> Everlasting is Thy throne;
> Through the ages men shall sing
> Praise to heaven's eternal King.
> Thou enthroned above the skies,
> Wilt for Zion's help arise
> Let thy grace to her appear,
> For the promised time is near.
>
> As one lays a garment by,
> Thou wilt change the starry sky
> Like a vesture worn and old,
> But Thy years shall ne'er be told.
> Thou wilt make Thy servant's race
> Ever live before Thy face,

---

5. *Three Forms of Unity*, 84.

And forever at Thy side
Children's children shall abide.[6]

We too have this assurance because we have a Savior who has washed away our sins. We have a Savior who has taken the wrath of God upon Himself and borne it away. Praise be to our Savior, who put Himself under the dark wrath of God's justice so that the sunshine of God's fatherly love might fall on us. Praise be now and forever to Him who sits upon the throne of heaven!

On the surface, there seems to be no mention of Christ here. But look again—isn't Christ the essence of the rainbow? Without Him, the rainbow that symbolizes God's covenant mercies would be only an empty sign, a promise that could not be kept. His death and resurrection are the seal of God upon that promise, certifying that it has been fulfilled and that salvation is offered to all who come to the Father by the Son (John 14:6).

Then, too, His is the voice that says, "Come up hither." John describes this voice "as it were of a trumpet talking with me" (Rev. 4:1), exactly as he describes it in Revelation 1:10. With the clarity and authority with which He always taught His disciples, Christ invites His beloved disciple once more to come to Him and be taught by Him. A door is opened in the Father's house, and Christ bids us come in. There we join with all the company of heaven to offer praise to the triune God—Father, Son, and Holy Spirit, our Creator, Redeemer, and life-giving Sanctifier. Paul puts it this way in Ephesians 2:18: "For through him we both have access by one Spirit unto the Father." It is by the blood of Christ and the fellowship of the Spirit that we have access to the Father. As Jesus takes John by the hand and says, "Come up hither," so too He extends that invitation through John to every one of God's children. "Come unto me," He says. "Look unto me, and be ye saved, all the ends of the earth" (Isa. 45:22).

---

6. *The Psalter*, #275:1, 4 (Ps. 102:12–13, 26–28).

12

A Scroll, a Savior,
and a Song

REVELATION 5:1–14

And I saw in the right hand of him that sat on the throne a book written within and on the backside, sealed with seven seals. And I saw a strong angel proclaiming with a loud voice, Who is worthy to open the book, and to loose the seals thereof? And no man in heaven, nor in earth, neither under the earth, was able to open the book, neither to look thereon. And I wept much, because no man was found worthy to open and to read the book, neither to look thereon. And one of the elders saith unto me, Weep not: behold, the Lion of the tribe of Juda, the Root of David, hath prevailed to open the book, and to loose the seven seals thereof. And I beheld, and, lo, in the midst of the throne and of the four beasts, and in the midst of the elders, stood a Lamb as it had been slain, having seven horns and seven eyes, which are the seven Spirits of God sent forth into all the earth.... And they sung a new song, saying, Thou art worthy to take the book, and to open the seals thereof: for thou wast slain, and hast redeemed us to God by thy blood out of every kindred, and tongue, and people, and nation; and hast made us unto our God kings and priests: and we shall reign on the earth.... And every creature which is in heaven, and on the earth, and under the earth, and such as are in the sea, and all that are in them, heard I saying, Blessing, and honour, and glory, and power, be unto him that sitteth upon the throne, and unto the Lamb for ever and ever. And the four beasts said, Amen. And the four and twenty elders fell down and worshipped him that liveth for ever and ever.

Would you like to know what heaven is like? Would you like to speak with someone who has been to heaven? Today you can often find imaginative books in Christian bookstores written by people who claim to have been at least briefly in heaven and are now writing to tell you about it. All such books are fluff at best and blasphemy at worst.

But in Revelation 5 the apostle John figuratively does go to heaven and by the Spirit's inspiration wants to tell us about it so that we can be educated about this grand and glorious place, which, if we are true believers, is our future home. By God's grace, let's join John now and let him instruct us on this important subject.

We have already covered the first of the seven cycles of visions in Revelation, which draws our attention to the condition of the church and her relationship with Christ. Much of what we have seen has remarkable parallels with what we observe at the present time as we experience the Christian life and church life around us and within us. We are now dealing with the second cycle, which encompasses chapters 4–7. In this second cycle, John is taken up into heaven. Christ says to John, "Come up higher, and I will shew thee things which must be hereafter" (4:1). In other words, "I will show you things from My perspective." Christ shows John things that were yet in the future in his day, but not to us, for we experience the book of Revelation day by day. Christ says to John, "I will show you for the sake of all suffering and persecuted Christians how I see things from My heavenly viewpoint."

Let us continue examining this second cycle of visions by focusing on the portion found in Revelation 5. The first verse of this chapter says: "And I saw in the right hand of him that sat on the throne a book written within and on the backside, sealed with seven seals." With God's help, we will look at this section under three main headings: a sealed scroll, a strong Savior, and a spontaneous song.

The Sealed Scroll: God's Eternal Plan

We saw from Revelation 4 that there is a throne at the center of the universe. God is seated on that throne, and around His throne is a rainbow depicting God's sovereign grace, faithful promises, and abiding covenant. But in Revelation 5, John sets this heavenly scene before us in a different way. Now we see something more: a book. In the right hand of the One who sits upon the throne, there is, literally, a scroll, "written within and on the backside, sealed with seven seals."

Remember that John is speaking figuratively. God does not physically or literally sit upon a throne; nor does He literally have a right hand; nor does He literally hold a book. God is Spirit, and He does not have a body like ours. In addition, even the heaven of heavens cannot contain Him (1 Kings 8:27), for He inhabits eternity (Isa. 57:15). So what does this figurative language mean?

It helps to think in terms of hieroglyphics or pictographs, the symbols or figures used to reduce some languages to writing. Instead of letters put together to spell out a word such as *horse*, a small picture of a horse is used to represent the word. To understand the book of Revelation, we need to interpret the hieroglyphics. We must understand the symbolism of these pictures.

John describes for us a scroll, that is, a roll of parchment, paper, or other material suitable for writing upon. This was the ancient form in which books were produced. Notice where this book is. It is in the right hand of the One who sits upon the throne. The right hand of God always symbolizes His authority, power, and sovereignty. That is consistently the case right through the Scriptures. This book that God holds, as we are told in verse 1, is full of writing, "within and on the backside." That is significant because normally a scroll would have writing only on the inside. This scroll, however, is written on both the inside and the outside. It is full of writing, with no omissions and no need of additions. And it is sealed with seven seals.

Scrolls, as attested by medieval Jews like Maimonides, could be over a hundred feet long when unrolled. The longest of the Dead Sea Scrolls may have approached 30 feet in length. If they were too long, it was difficult for a reader to handle them or find his place in them. When rolled up, the writing was hidden inside, and the scroll was sealed to keep it from being opened. The seals were either wax or clay, which was put on soft or wet, imprinted with a signet ring, and then left to harden or dry. Thus secured, the scroll could not be opened accidentally. Its contents were such that only a particular kind of person was considered worthy to open it. The fact that the scroll in God's hand is sealed with seven seals means that the contents are matters of great importance, and the scroll can be opened and read only by someone authorized or qualified to do so.

We need not be in doubt as to what this scroll represents. From what follows (Revelation 6–8), we know that it contains the eternal decrees of God, namely, "his eternal purpose, according to the counsel of his will, whereby for his own glory, he hath foreordained whatsoever comes to pass."[1] The scroll of Revelation 5 symbolizes for us God's plan. It is His purpose for the entire universe and all creatures in all ages and unto all eternity. It is His plan of sweet salvation and bitter judgment (Ezek. 2:9–3:3).

That is the significance of the writing on both sides. There is no space for additional writing. There are no omissions waiting to be filled in or corrections needed. There is completeness here. The book is full. The scroll is God's comprehensive, detailed, unchangeable plan for His creation. From the falling of a hair from your head, dear believer, to the latest world-shaking events reported in today's news, everything is on that scroll. The destinies of every atom in the earth, as well as the mighty galaxies of the cosmos, are all there.

Nothing is left to chance, for God's purpose embraces all His creatures and all their actions. Everything is in this book, including all of our human decisions; they, too, are part of God's plan. There are no indications that God is ever surprised or nonplussed by what comes to pass in heaven or on earth. "Known unto God are all his works from the beginning of the world" (Acts 15:18). Nothing is missing. Nothing can be changed. Nothing can be added. Nothing is left to chance.

---

1. Westminster Shorter Catechism, Q. 7, *Reformed Confessions of the Sixteenth and Seventeenth Centuries*, 4:354.

Note, too, that John cannot read what is written on the scroll. Some people think they can infer predictions about the future from current events or insights into human behavior. But our knowledge is too limited for that. We certainly cannot know when Christ is coming again. What is written on the scroll is comprehensive, but it is also hidden, kept secret until the time God has appointed for the execution of particular decrees. What is in the scroll is the secret will of God.

This second cycle of visions fits in beautifully with Revelation's overarching theme of comfort. Remember, Revelation is essentially a book of comfort; it is a pastoral book. John says to his brothers and sisters in Christ: "I want you to lay hold of this great truth— that God is on the throne. He is sovereign over all things. He is in control." This is John's intent from the first chapter. He is in exile on Patmos, thinking of his persecuted brethren on the mainland. The storm clouds are gathering, and it is going to get a lot worse. John knows this perhaps from his own reading of things, but he also knows it by revelation. Christ has told him that there soon will be more persecution, and it will be a very difficult time for the church. So Christ gives John this revelation to comfort and encourage God's people through persecution, tribulation, and trials of many kinds.

Through all these things, God has a plan in His hand. God is not a capricious tyrant who does things on a whim. He is a God who is absolutely sovereign, the Monarch of all He surveys. He works according to plan. That plan is fully thought out; it is fixed and unchangeable. It is sealed completely with seven seals.

Many people are confused about this doctrine of divine decrees. They are prepared to admit that God foresees and foreknows every-thing that will happen. They accept that He knows who will and who will not believe. But then they say that because God knows all this, He gathers in all the facts, makes His estimations, and then draws up His plans. Because He foresees and foreknows everything, He can make His plans accordingly.

The Bible completely reverses that order. Ephesians 1:11 says, "In [Christ] also we have obtained an inheritance, being predestinated according to the purpose of him who worketh all things after the counsel of his own will." This text does not say that God draws up a plan *after* He has gathered all the pertinent information and formed estimates of human behavior. Rather, He determines His plan according to the counsel of His will. He foresees all things because He has foreordained all things. He knows what will happen because He has decreed that it should come to pass. These sovereign, determined divine decrees are symbolized by the scroll in the right hand of the One who sits upon the throne in John's vision.

What is more comforting than to know that God's decrees for this world are not mere contingency plans but real determinations of all that comes to pass? Those who know this God as their Father in heaven can live in the confidence that no matter what happens, He will provide them with all things necessary for soul and body. He will make whatever He sends upon them in this valley of tears turn out for their salvation and advantage.

The Strong Savior: The Lion-Lamb

But how are these plans to be carried out? How is God's plan to be executed? That is the second line of inquiry we want to follow. As John sees it, there is a problem with regard to the scroll and its sealed contents: "I saw a strong angel proclaiming with a loud voice, Who is worthy to open the book, and to loose the seals thereof?" (Rev. 5:2). Breaking the seals and opening the scroll will initiate the realization of God's kingdom, that is, its coming into time and space. Who, then, will break the seals and open the scroll? Who is equal to the task of executing God's plan, realizing His decrees, and carrying out His purposes for the universe? If it were up to us, there would be no kingdom of God, no salvation for mankind, no reconciliation to God, and no way to escape from His righteous judgment. No one, not even the most brilliant or the holiest of men from human history, is worthy to open the scroll to read the purposes and promises of God, to vindicate His name, to bring forth righteousness, and to save His people and bring them to heaven. Sin has made it impossible.

John is reduced to tears by the realization that there is no man among the saints in glory or on earth who is truly worthy to open the book or even "to look thereon" (vv. 3–4). So vivid is this vision and so much is John a part of it that he is taken up into it. He is not merely a spectator, watching from a safe distance with no stake in the proceedings, but he has taken the challenge to heart. Who indeed is worthy to open the scroll? John's heart is broken by the realization that not one of Adam's fallen, sinful race is worthy of such an honor or equal to such a task.

John's weeping underlines one of the chief differences between apostolic Christianity and contemporary Western Christianity. He weeps! He weeps because he knows that there will be no salvation for God's people, no coming of God's kingdom, and no hope for the human race unless someone can accomplish the purposes of God and fulfill His promises.

Every time you find an apostle weeping in the New Testament, it is because he is burdened with his need for forgiveness or the need of the world for forgiveness. Peter weeps because of his sin (Matt. 26:75). Paul weeps because his fellow Jews lie in wait to assail him (Acts 20:19) and because his fellow Christians are preyed upon by false teachers (Acts 20:31). He also weeps over a church that has fallen into disorder (2 Cor. 2:4) and because many walk as enemies of the cross of Christ (Phil. 3:18). Here in Revelation, John weeps because nobody can open the scroll.

Dear friends, what do you weep about? Do you weep about your need for forgiveness of your sins? Do you weep for a perishing world? Do you weep for the disorder and corruption of the visible church today? Do you weep for those who walk as enemies of the cross of Christ? Many Christians seem complacent or indifferent; some are angry; and others are fearful. But who is weeping today, and why?

Let us pause to take in this very important truth. Have you fully appreciated that apart from the Lord Jesus Christ, there is simply no hope at all for you and the world you live in? That is what made John weep. No human being before Christ's earthly ministry or since has been capable of saving the created universe. Have we ever fully appreciated the sheer depth of the human predicament? We are hopelessly lost. Even if the whole human race could put off the enmity that lives in our hearts and work together at the task, we don't have what it takes.

And what a critical task it is, for as we read through this chapter and the rest of the book of Revelation, it becomes increasingly plain that the future purposes of God depend on what is written in that scroll and on its seals being broken. So all that the Lord has said in the earlier chapters—the way in which He will purify His people, the way in which He will bring vindication to His great name, and the way in which He will enable His children to overcome and to be more than conquerors through Him—depends on someone being able to open those seals and fulfill the purposes of God.

At this moment, an elder steps forward to comfort John with good news: "Behold, the Lion of the tribe of Juda, the Root of David, hath prevailed to open the book" (Rev. 5:5). These Messianic titles are taken from Genesis 49:9–10 and Isaiah 11:10. John's eyes are redirected from the scroll in the hand of God Almighty to the lion-like King who stands in the midst of the throne, the beasts, and the elders. He has conquered! The elder says, "Look! The Messiah, the Lion of the tribe of Judah, has conquered." He is affirming that "there is none other name under heaven given among men, whereby we must be saved" but the name of Jesus Christ of Nazareth (Acts 4:12). Only Jesus Christ is up to the task.

Jesus is the Lion, the King. He has immense power, majesty, and strength. He is the Christ of mighty works and uncompromising holiness. This Christ needs to be so powerful because of the task before Him. To lead the church through history and advance the kingdom of God, He must triumph over every one of the enemies of His people: Satan, the world, the false prophet, death, and the grave. Christ, of course, met them all throughout His life and overcame them all.

John looks more closely. To his utter surprise, he sees a *Lamb*, bearing all the marks of having been slain. What would you have expected to see? Perhaps you might have expected a knight clad in shining armor, robed in purple, riding on a prancing steed, followed by the captives he has taken and wagonloads of spoil from the wars he has fought and won. But that is not the nature of this King. "And I beheld, and, lo, in the midst of the throne and of the four beasts, and in the midst of the elders, stood a Lamb as it had been slain" (Rev. 5:6). "Lo!" John says. This is a shock to him. It is something marvelous and totally unexpected.

John's favorite title for Christ in Revelation is "Lamb." He uses it twenty-eight times in Revelation to refer to Jesus. John first heard the title from John the Baptist, who directed his attention to Jesus of Nazareth, saying, "Behold the Lamb of God!" (John 1:29, 36).[2] Such language communicates the gentleness and purity of Christ as God's appointed sacrifice.

The paradox of a Lamb doing the work of a fierce lion fulfills David's prophecy: "Out of the mouth of babes and sucklings hast thou ordained strength because of thine enemies, that thou mightest still the enemy and the avenger" (Ps. 8:2). This Lamb indeed is granted all power and prepared fully for His work. He is the One anointed by God "with the Holy Ghost and with power" (Acts 10:38). This is the meaning of the "seven horns and seven eyes" of this conquering Lamb (Rev. 5:6). The horns signify His God-given power, while the eyes are emblems of the fullness of the Spirit's power and operations.

Versed as he was in Scripture, John could not help but think back to Abraham, who assured Isaac that "God will provide himself a lamb for a burnt offering" (Gen. 22:8). John thought of the first Passover, when the blood of the lambs slain for each family delivered the Israelites when the plague of death passed through the land of Egypt (Exodus 12). Surely John saw here Isaiah's Suffering Servant, on whom God laid the sins of His people. He was the One to be led "as a lamb to the slaughter" (Isa. 53:7). Israel would go on

---

2. To be exact, John 1:29 uses the word *amnos* for lamb (cf. John 1:36; Acts 8:32; 1 Peter 1:19), whereas Revelation uses *arnion* (cf. John 21:15).

to perform the sacrifice of the Passover every year until the Messiah came—until the day when John the Baptist pointed to the Lord Jesus and said, "Behold the Lamb of God."

John sees that the Lamb is standing in the center of the throne (Rev. 5:6). He stands for a reason. It is not only because He is victorious, but also because the salvation of His people is not complete until all of them are glorified with Him in heaven. Christ stands ever busy. He is sending forth His Spirit. He is building His church. He is ruling and active in the government of His kingdom. He ever lives to make intercession for those who come to God by Him, and He saves them to the uttermost. Furthermore, John sees that the Lamb has been slain, but He is now alive again (v. 6).

Even as John looks on, the Lamb shows Himself worthy to take the scroll from the right hand of God (v. 7). And when He has taken it, the four beasts and twenty-four elders fall down before the Lamb, saying, "Thou art worthy to take the book, and to open the seals thereof" (v. 9).

The challenge of verse 2 has been met. Who is worthy? The Lamb is worthy. The One who is worthy to take the book and break its seals is "a lamb without blemish and without spot" (1 Peter 1:19). Perfectly righteous, He has made satisfaction for the sins of fallen humanity. By the power of His Godhead, He has sustained in His person the burden of God's wrath, obtaining righteousness and life for all who belong to Him. Delivered to death for our offenses, He has been raised again for our justification (Rom. 4:25). Yes, this Lamb alone is worthy to take the scroll and open its seals.

John brings our attention to Christ as both Lion and Lamb. He says, "I was told to look and see a Lion, and I looked and saw a Lamb standing in the midst of the throne." The Lord Jesus Christ, the eternal Son of God, carries out God's plan of salvation for the world in His dual capacity as Lion and Lamb. It is in this twin role of conquering King and suffering Lamb that He breaks the seals and opens the book. As the Lion of the tribe of Judah and "the Lamb slain from the foundation of the world" (Rev. 13:8), He stands now in heaven to save sinners and, ultimately, this universe.

What is this Lion and Lamb telling us? He is saying that the way of God's gospel is to achieve *victory through sacrifice.*

Have you understood that about the Lord Jesus Christ? Have you seen in this crucified, risen Savior the power of God and the wisdom of God? Have you seen in that slaughtered Lamb the majesty and strength of the Lion? Lion-like, He prevails. He has conquered, but He has done so by allowing Himself to be led as a lamb to the slaughter. That is the gospel. Nobody could have thought that up; no one could have come up with that as the answer to the problems of the universe. But this is God's answer.

No wonder, then, that the Lion-Lamb is in the midst of the throne. From His place "on the right hand of the Majesty on high" (Heb. 1:3), He can see every worshiper. In Him, they all meet as one. This Lion-Lamb is not only *at* the center of heaven; He *is* the center of heaven. All of heaven is focused on Him. All the worshipers surround Him and look to Him, beginning with the Father, whose deepest delight is in His Son. (And delighting in the Son, the Father delights in you, dear child of God.) John sees a Christocentric universe. Everything in our lives revolves around Him. Everything in the church revolves around him. Everything in the whole universe revolves around him. No wonder, then, that all the hosts of heaven break out into spontaneous song.

The Spontaneous Song: "Thou Art Worthy"
The Lamb takes the scroll from the hand of Him who sits on the throne (Rev. 5:7). He is worthy; He can take the scroll; He can break the seals. He knows what's written in the scroll. He can execute everything that God has planned. All power in heaven and on earth is given to the Lamb.

The Lamb's taking the scroll is a sign that all that is written therein shall be executed, accomplished, and fulfilled. The mere fact that the scroll is now in His possession is a guarantee of the final victory of the kingdom of God over the kingdoms of this world. Christ could look up to His Father in heaven and say, "I have finished the work thou gavest me to do" (John 17:4). He can now execute everything that God has planned.

The response of everyone in heaven is to fall down before Him as an act of worship and total submission. "When he had taken the book, the four beasts and four and twenty elders fell down before the Lamb, having every one of them harps, and golden vials full of odours, which are the prayers of the saints" (Rev. 5:8). The prostrations, the playing of the harps, and the bowls of incense recall the day of the dedication of Solomon's temple, when fire came down from heaven and the glory of the Lord filled the house. "When all the children of Israel saw how the fire came down, and the glory of the LORD upon the house, they bowed themselves with their faces to the ground upon the pavement, and worshipped, and praised the LORD saying, For he is good; and his mercy endureth for ever" (2 Chron. 7:3).

Then those who have prostrated themselves before the Lamb begin to sing a new song: "Thou art worthy to take the book, and to open the seals thereof: for thou wast slain, and hast redeemed us to God by thy blood out of every kindred, and tongue, and people, and nation" (Rev. 5:9). It is significant that this song is sung by the church of God, represented by the twenty-four elders. They stand in front of the angels, proclaiming the worthiness of the Lamb to take the book and open its seals. They account for that worthiness by extolling the Lamb as their propitiatory sacrifice, their Redeemer, and their King, in whose exaltation they themselves are exalted. For this reason, their "new song" can be called the song of redemption (Rev. 14:3–4). This song of praise ascends from heaven's majestic choir, made up of saints of "every kindred, and tongue, and people, and nation" (Rev. 5:9c), together with all the heavenly host. But note that all of these saints are experientially acquainted with the fruits of that redemption; thus, they sing: "[Thou] hast made us unto our God kings and priests" (v. 10a). They look forward to the future, when, as they sing, "we shall reign on the earth" (v. 10b).

Those who are closest to the throne are not the angels; they are you and me, represented by the twenty-four elders, which symbolize the entire church of the Old Testament and the New. These are the ones who are seated around the throne of God and of the Lamb. And they have more to say than anyone else. The song of the redeemed is fuller, deeper, and more profound than the songs of the angels and the song of creation, for we who are saved by the blood of Jesus Christ can praise Him in a way that angels cannot. We can claim a more intimate interest in the Son of God than angels can.

All this is in line with the rest of the teaching of the New Testament. Angels, we are told, are spectators and subordinates in the drama of salvation. They are deeply interested in the salvation of sinners because they deeply love God. The Bible tells us that there is rejoicing in the presence of the angels in heaven over one sinner who repents (Luke 15:10). When you were saved, tens of thousands burst into song. They were happy—perhaps happier than you were, because you hadn't fully understood at that point all that had happened to you. They rejoiced!

That is what we see here in Revelation 5:11. John adds, "I beheld, and I heard the voice of many angels round about the throne and the beasts and the elders: and the number of them was ten thousand times ten thousand, and thousands of thousands." The song of the church stirs the hearts of all the angels in heaven and rouses them to praise. They unite with the church in proclaiming the worthiness of the Lamb to receive all the treasures of the glory of God Himself. "Worthy is the Lamb that was slain to receive power, and riches, and wisdom, and strength, and honour, and glory, and blessing" (v. 12).

Peter tells us in his epistle that the angels desire earnestly to look into the things that concern or belong to our salvation (1 Peter 1:12). Paul tells us in Ephesians 3:10 that the angels see the manifold grace of God expressed in His dealings with the church. They can see God's power, wisdom, and holiness elsewhere in the creation of the world, but it is only in the church and only in the salvation of sinners that they perceive His mercy and love. In the church, the angels see the manifold grace of God, and they worship Him all the more. That is why they give place to the church in heaven.

Meantime, as Paul says, creation itself "groaneth and travaileth in pain" (Rom. 8:22). You might say it is standing on its toes and craning its neck as it waits for an event of tremendous importance. It is waiting for the redemption of the body. The very sticks, stones, and hills, and the fish, birds, and animals, all groan with anticipation as they await the completion of history.

What a wonderful picture of heaven we have here in Revelation 5! And you and I, if we are Christians, are at the center of it. We are in the middle of it all. We are as near as we possibly can be to the Lamb, our Savior. There behind us, with great admiration and wonder, are thousands and thousands upon thousands of angels; and, along with them, the whole creation is declaring the glory of God, singing His praises.

Will you be there in this marvelous heavenly choir? How tragic if you miss out on this! You can't presume you will be there. Notice how careful the apostle is to describe those who are there singing the song of the redeemed. He provides us with three important marks of grace about them.

First, they *trust in Christ's blood alone for salvation.* In Revelation 5:9, the twenty-four elders sing, "Thou art worthy to take the book, and to open the seals thereof: for thou wast slain, and hast redeemed us to God by thy blood out of every kindred, and tongue, and people, and nation."

Jesus died to redeem sinners, but not sinners in general. He died to redeem particular individuals. There is nothing narrow or elitist about this. The redemption of the Lord Jesus Christ is universal in the sense that it is worldwide in scope. It embraces all sorts of men: all kinship; all ethnic, linguistic, political, and social groups; every kindred, tongue, people, and nation. There is no favoritism or partiality, for God is no respecter of persons. He draws His elect from every group of people and every type of person. There is no snobbery, no class distinction, and no racial preferences or bias.

Second, they *live by praying to Christ and live to praise Christ.* They are a praying, praising people. Verse 8 says that "every one of them [have] harps, and golden vials full of odours, which are the prayers of the saints." Our prayers rise to God like sweet-smelling incense. The bowls in the hands of the elders are a sign that we do not call on God in vain. Prayer is the chief part of the thankfulness God requires of us. The harps in their hands remind us that prayer is always to be joined with praise. As David played on his harp while he sang the psalms given to him by inspiration of the Spirit, so we today sing these psalms with grace in the heart, "singing and making melody in [our] heart to the Lord" (Eph. 5:19).

Spurgeon borrowed an illustration from Ambrose to compare Christ's work as sanctifier of His people's prayers to the work of a mother. Her little child returns from the woods with a bouquet of flowers that he plans to give to his father. The mother sees that all kinds of weeds are mixed with the flowers, so she quickly takes out the weeds and adds more flowers. Then the mother and child present the bouquet to the father. Likewise, Christ takes the weeds out of our prayers. He sanctifies our prayers by cleansing them with His blood and adding His own superior petitions. Then He presents this offering to the Father. Spurgeon writes: "If we could see one of our prayers after Christ Jesus has amended it, we should scarce know it again. He has such skill that even our good flowers grow fairer in his hand; we clumsily tie them into a bundle, but he arranges them into a [beautiful] bouquet."[3]

What about you? Do you know something of a life of prayer and praise? Are you ever calling on His name and continually offering "the sacrifice of praise to God...the fruit of [your] lips giving thanks to his name" (Heb. 13:15)? Do you depend on your praying High Priest to make your prayers acceptable to God?

Third, they *delight in Christ as the center of their lives*. In heaven, the delight of the saints is Christ. That delight in heaven begins, however, by delighting in Christ on earth.

An old Puritan writer said, "Heaven must be in you before you can ever be in heaven." Is heaven in you? The Lamb is all the glory in Immanuel's land. That is how it is in heaven. Is that how it is in

---

3. Spurgeon, *Metropolitan Tabernacle Pulpit*, 18:279.

your life? Is the Lamb all the glory? Is He at the center? If you do not know and delight in the Lord Jesus Christ here, you would be out of place there.

If you possess something of these marks of grace, lift up your hearts and sing the praises of the Lion-Lamb. If you don't know these marks of grace, I urge you to go with all your sins to this Lion-Lamb for your salvation. He is the One whom God has sent into the world for us and for our salvation. He can save you and wash you in His blood. Cast your sins upon Him. There is no other way to be saved. In Christ, you will be saved for all eternity; outside of Him, you will be lost forever.

Two emotions are very evident in this chapter: weeping and singing. When John first looked around heaven, he could not see his Savior. No one in creation was qualified to take up the task of saving this world. John wept and wept. But then John looked again and saw the Lamb. His weeping was turned into song.

How is it with you? When you die, will you be in a place that resounds with weeping, wailing, and the gnashing of teeth? Or will you join the great choir in heaven to sing and rejoice with the angels over the triumph of the Lion-Lamb?

13

Seals, Four Horses, Four Riders

REVELATION 6:1–8

And I saw when the Lamb opened one of the seals, and I heard, as it were the noise of thunder, one of the four beasts saying, Come and see. And I saw, and behold a white horse: and he that sat on him had a bow; and a crown was given unto him: and he went forth conquering, and to conquer. And when he had opened the second seal, I heard the second beast say, Come and see. And there went out another horse that was red: and power was given to him that sat thereon to take peace from the earth, and that they should kill one another: and there was given unto him a great sword. And when he had opened the third seal, I heard the third beast say, Come and see. And I beheld, and lo a black horse; and he that sat on him had a pair of balances in his hand. And I heard a voice in the midst of the four beasts say, A measure of wheat for a penny, and three measures of barley for a penny; and see thou hurt not the oil and the wine. And when he had opened the fourth seal, I heard the voice of the fourth beast say, Come and see. And I looked, and behold a pale horse: and his name that sat on him was Death, and Hell followed with him. And power was given unto them over the fourth part of the earth, to kill with sword, and with hunger, and with death, and with the beasts of the earth.

In our gospel age, we are often amazed that the church and the world seem to be decaying as much as they are. As an American, I am alarmed at how quickly our nation is sinking into the quicksand of sin and spinning out of control. The future seems so insecure. It all seems so puzzling at times that the question can arise in our hearts almost before we have a chance to squelch it: is God really in control? Can I really trust Him in all things? Is my future secure with God even when everything in this world seems so tenuous? In the first half of Revelation 6, John provides us with powerful answers to questions like these.

John's second cycle of visions on the island of Patmos, recorded in chapters 4–7, offers a picture of the gospel age from God's perspective. The first cycle of visions, in chapters 1–3, gives a picture of the gospel age from our earthly church perspective. It gives us a surface view of the church and its relationship to Jesus Christ. But the second cycle of visions opens with John being told to come up to God's throne to view this age from God's perspective.

As we have begun unpacking this second cycle of visions, we have been shown two things: first, the throne of God (chapter 4), and second, the book of God (chapter 5). John goes on in Revelation 6 to show us the opening of that book so that we may know what to expect as Christians in this world between the two comings of Christ. Jesus Christ is the Lamb with seven horns and seven eyes (5:6), who alone is able to expedite what is written in God's book. He can break the seals, open the book, and unfold the plan of God for His church.

I am so glad that chapters 4 and 5 come before chapters 6 and 7. It is comforting to see the throne and to see who holds the book before seeing the tribulation, suffering, and persecution that are to come. It is good to know that behind this sin-sick world of ours is the sovereign God, who works according to His plan and His timetable. He does all things after the counsel of His will (Eph. 1:11). God wants us to see our entire lives, yes, everything that exists, from that perspective. That is why He shows us the throne and the book before He reveals what is in store for us, namely, tribulation. We already have tribulation in the world today; there is no escaping it. Jesus says to His disciples in John 16:33: "These things I have spoken unto you, that in me ye might have peace. In the world ye shall have tribulation: but be of good cheer; I have overcome the world."

There is no hint in Revelation of the rapture that many American preachers speak about. They think that during the tribulation in the end times, God will "rapture" the saints—that is, move them out of this world—to spare them from tribulation. But this doctrine is not scriptural. There is no hint in John 16:33 of such escape, is there? Christ simply says, "In the world ye shall have tribulation." Jesus does not promise to whisk His disciples away when trouble comes; on the contrary, He promises to bring us through it. Notice that He says, "But be of good cheer; I have overcome the world." The implication is that if you are with Christ and in Christ, you will overcome the world. You will be made more than conquerors through Jesus Christ (Rom. 8:37). That is the message of Revelation, particularly in the chapters we are now considering. In Christ, we are more than conquerors, come what may.

Let us now look at the next stage in the second cycle of visions, which tells us what God has in store for His people in this world. Chapters 6 and 7 are a vivid dramatization of all the principles that work together in human history for the consummation of Christ's kingdom.

First, let us look at the opening of the first four seals (Rev. 6:1–8). Because they are grouped together, we will look at them as a whole. One of the four living creatures says in a voice like thunder, "Come and see" (v. 1). Then, as the Lamb opens each seal, four extraordinary horsemen, commonly known as "the four horsemen of the apocalypse," gallop across the scene of human history. They are the rider on a white horse (v. 2); the rider on a red horse (v. 4); the rider on a black horse (v. 5); and, finally, the rider on a pale horse (v. 8).

These horses and horsemen are a powerful representation of what is happening today. Sometimes it seems as if what is going on in the world is happening fairly slowly, and that things don't change too much from one day to the next. But when we view things from God's perspective, we realize the truth of what Peter says in his epistle: "One day is with the Lord as a thousand years, and a thousand years as one day" (2 Peter 3:8). Revelation 6 gives us a picture of human history galloping to its consummation. From an eternal perspective, things are happening very quickly in this world. Christ and His squadron are galloping through the centuries to carry out God's eternal decrees. And a thousand years are like a day's ride for Christ.

There are four horses and four riders because each team rides to one of the four corners of the earth: north, south, east, and west. The number *four* in Scripture is the universal number. Just as *seven* is the number of completeness, *four* is the number for the world in its universal aspects. The point of four horses is that there is no area of the earth that they do not cover. There is no boundary they cannot cross, and no ground they do not ride over.

Notice that these four horses and their riders belong together. Each horse and its rider are combined as one symbol. The horses don't run at random; each is directed and controlled by a rider. However frightening these horses are, we must remember that they are not riderless. They are saddled and bridled by the Lamb, the Lion of the tribe of Judah. Jesus Christ holds their reins. How comforting it is to know that the powers and principles that gallop through human history are not wild horses, but that they are directed by the Savior! As John's allusion to the parallel vision in Zechariah, these horsemen are the forces of the Lord at work in the whole world (Zech. 6:1–8).

Life can be frightening. Sometimes we are bewildered by what is going on around us. Great forces and powers bear down upon us, and we have no control. We feel like a cork in the ocean, tossed about by economic forces, spiritual forces, social forces, and psychological forces. When we feel paralyzed by worldly forces, we must remind ourselves that the powerful horses that are unleashed in human history are saddled and bridled by Christ.

Let us look at each of these four horses and their riders, then at how they work together.

The White Horse

The identity of the rider of the first horse is obvious from John's description. In Revelation 6:2, John says, "I saw, and behold a white horse: and he that sat on him had a bow; and a crown was given unto him: and he went forth conquering, and to conquer."

Some commentators say the rider on the white horse is the antichrist. A few think he is some obscure Roman emperor or modern-day Hitler. Others think he is the devil or the devil's henchman. Those are just a few of many interpretations, most of which make little sense when they are considered within the greater context of Scripture.

Revelation is best understood by what our forefathers called "the analogy of Scripture," that is, by comparing Scripture with Scripture. Revelation 19:11 makes clear the identity of the rider of the white horse: "And I saw heaven opened, and behold a white horse; and he that sat upon him was called Faithful and True, and in righteousness he doth judge and make war." Whatever else the devil is, he is *not* faithful and true. This description, rather, is of our Lord Jesus Christ advancing the cause of His gospel. That is in line with the rest of the book of Revelation and its overall message. Remember, Revelation is not a series of visions about what might happen in the future; it is the revelation of Jesus Christ today, who, in the power of His gospel, rides forth to conquer all the forces of evil.

This interpretation is also in harmony with the rest of Scripture. Many commentators go astray in interpreting this passage because they do not compare Scripture with Scripture. Specifically, they do not go to the Old Testament to find background for the imagery of Revelation. Take Psalm 45, for example, which is a well-known Messianic psalm. This psalm offers a parallel description of the first rider. It says: "Gird thy sword upon thy thigh, O most mighty, with thy glory and thy majesty. And in thy majesty ride prosperously because of truth and meekness and righteousness; and thy right hand shall teach thee terrible things. Thine arrows are sharp in the heart of the king's enemies; whereby the people fall under thee" (vv. 3–5). This is a picture of Christ in His reign as Messiah (cf. Heb. 1:8–9). Likewise, Revelation 6 says the rider of the white horse has a crown on his head.

Hebrews 1:8 provides further confirmation that the psalmist has Jesus Christ and the advancement of His gospel in mind. This passage quotes from Psalm 45:6–7 and says, "But unto the Son he saith, Thy throne, O God, is for ever and ever: a sceptre of righteousness is the sceptre of thy kingdom." It is perfectly clear when you compare Scripture with Scripture who this rider is.

Zechariah offers another parallel picture of this rider as a background for Revelation 6. Zechariah 6:1–3 says: "And I turned, and lifted up mine eyes, and looked, and, behold, there came four chariots out from between two mountains; and the mountains were mountains of brass. In the first chariot were red horses; and in the second chariot black horses; and in the third chariot white horses; and in the fourth chariot grisled and bay horses." There are slight differences between Zechariah 6 and Revelation 6, but the overall picture is the same: a powerful squadron of horses leads four chariots. In this context, the horseman at the front of this squadron is none other than Jehovah Himself, the Lord of hosts who rides on behalf of His people.

In Revelation 6, the first rider is Jesus Christ going forth to conquer. He is followed by His cohorts. This first rider is not the devil's henchman, some modern-day Hitler, or a Roman emperor. It is Christ in the power of His gospel who is galloping across the plain of world history. Let us be comforted by knowing that the greatest force—the leading power in this world—is Christ and His gospel. This horse and its rider first advanced into Jerusalem, then into Judea and Samaria, and then to the uttermost parts of the earth. This horse and its rider have advanced throughout history through the preaching of the apostles, the early church fathers, the Reformers, the Puritans, and missionaries in China, Africa, and around the world. Nothing can prevent the white horse and its rider from advancing throughout the world.

Christ and His gospel lead the battalions of history. Every other power, force, or influence is subservient to Christ and His gospel. No army, no world power, no economic force, no war, and no powers of evil are more powerful than that. History is Christ's story. It is the story of the gospel of our Lord Jesus Christ. By the power of the cross, Jesus Christ has defeated all the forces of this world and brought them under His hand. Economics, politics, social forces, psychological forces, and all other forces may bear down upon us like a herd of horses, but Christ has rounded them up and brought them into subservience to His purposes. Christ, the Captain of our salvation, rides forth to conquer. The other horses and their riders are simply His outriders, which Christ has gathered behind Himself to support Him.

First, the white horse gallops across history. Then, close behind Christ are the other horses and their riders, following as a group. When you compare Scripture with Scripture, you soon realize that these riders are with Christ for the good of God's people. Wherever this squadron appears in Scripture, they ride for the good, comfort, and welfare of God's people.

The entire book of Zechariah confirms that. Zechariah 1:11 says: "We have walked to and fro through the earth, and, behold, all the earth sitteth still, and is at rest." The context of this verse is that God's people are troubled while the whole earth is at rest. Likewise, in John's day, the world is at peace under the Roman Empire while God's people are troubled by ongoing persecution.

In Zechariah 1:13, the prophet says, "The LORD answered the angel that talked with me with good words and comfortable words." The purpose of the horses and their chariots is to comfort Zion. Led by Jehovah God, the other riders lead their horse-drawn chariots to show God's people that the forces that are with them are far greater than any forces that could be mustered against them. The Lord rides forth on His powerful steed to assure and comfort His church. As frightening as the horses and riders of Revelation 6 appear on the surface, they gallop forth for our comfort.

The Red Horse

Revelation 6:4 says, "And there went out another horse that was red: and power was given to him that sat thereon to take peace from the earth, and that they should kill one another: and there was given unto him a great sword." This second horse and its rider are given power to remove peace from the earth and to make men slay each other. The rider is given a large sword with which to do this.

The red horse and his rider are symbols of persecution, as well as of the killing and bloodshed of war. In the two thousand years since Christ's earthly ministry, there has been a major war every century except for two. Thirty million people were killed in World War I and considerably more in World War II. Pol Pot slaughtered more than 1,500,000 Cambodians in less than two years. In 1994, more than half a million Rwandans were massacred in a hundred days. The twenty-first century has by no means been immune to war, as multiple conflicts in the Middle East attest. War is an ongoing menace in this world.

But the red horse also refers to persecution, specifically the persecution of the church. Christ's words here seem to allude to Matthew 10:34–36, "Think not that I am come to send peace on earth: I came not to send peace, but a sword. For I am come to set a man at variance against his father, and the daughter against her mother, and the daughter in law against her mother in law. And a man's foes shall be they of his own household."

Throughout history, the red horse of bloody persecution has followed the white horse of the conquering Christ. Wherever the gospel is preached and believed, persecution follows. As Paul says, "All that will live godly in Christ Jesus shall suffer persecution" (2 Tim. 3:12).

As Christians in this world, we too suffer persecution. It may be a subtler form of persecution than what Christians in Muslim or Communist countries endure, but our time for more overt suffering for our faith in Christ Jesus may yet come. Meantime, not a day passes without news of bloodshed, killing, rioting, and warfare somewhere. Nations rise against nations, and kingdoms rise up against Christians in other parts of the world. In his vision, John recognizes that all over the world and throughout history, we will see persecution.

With the red horse and its rider, Jesus is saying that believers should expect persecution. It has always been with us and will continue throughout human history. Only the return of our Lord Jesus Christ to earth will put an end to violence, strife, wars, and persecution.

You may argue that all this is the result of sin in the world. That is true. We do not live in the world as God created it, but as sin spoiled it. Yet even the red horse and its rider are under the Lord Christ's control. So, though we may pray for an end to specific outbreaks of severe persecution, we should not pray for an end to persecution as much as perseverance in persecution.

The Black Horse

The black horse and its rider in Revelation 6 are symbols of extreme poverty, represented through the price of food. Verses 5 and 6 say: "I heard the third beast say, Come and see. And I beheld, and lo a black horse; and he that sat on him had a pair of balances [scales] in his hand. And I heard a voice in the midst of the four beasts say, A measure of wheat for a penny, and three measures of barley for a penny; and see thou hurt not the oil and the wine."

The rider of the black horse holds scales. These are not the scales of judgment, but scales of measurement. Thus, the black horse represents the economic forces that propagate poverty. We see extreme poverty today in many countries around the world. The black horse and its rider show what life is often like in this world because of the selfishness and greed of men.

In the language of the Bible, a "penny" is a day's wages. In John's vision, as a result of the black horse and his rider, a penny can buy a quart of wheat. Barley is a rougher form of food and therefore cheaper; a penny can buy three quarts. This is not a picture of starvation but of inflation, for these prices are many times higher than normal.

In this vision, a laborer can barely make enough to feed himself and his family. As for other necessities of life, such as oil and wine, they are outside of his reach. They are considered luxuries rather than necessities. So Christ is saying to His church: "Do not expect riches or luxuries, but poverty. Expect to lose your job because you are a Christian. Expect to be overlooked for a promotion because you are a Christian. Expect injustice and unfairness in this world, because that is the kind of world you live in. All of this is what sin has done."

The black horse and its rider are galloping through many parts of the world today. Will they come to our land during our lifetime? Will we lose jobs and suffer poverty because we believe in Christ? Will the United States, which is in debt far beyond its ability to repay what it has borrowed, reach the breaking point and collapse economically? Will America then descend into poverty? Will there be another Great Depression? Will Christians be hardest hit because they are the most hated?

Perhaps. Yet this horse and its rider are also under Christ's sovereign control.

The Pale Horse

The idea of paleness doesn't quite convey the horror of the next horse and its rider. Literally, the horse is not pale, but the greenish, sickly color of a decaying corpse. Revelation 6:8a clearly tells us what this horse and rider represent: "And I looked, and behold a pale horse: and his name that sat on him was Death, and Hell followed with him." The word *Hell* (Greek *Hades*) here should be understood as the state of death, whether of the saved or the damned. The picture here is of death riding indiscriminately through the world, with Hell, or Hades, following after. Death does not discriminate. It comes through disease, pestilence, and disasters, riding through the world to gather up corpses. None of us can escape this horse and its rider.

The four ways in which the fourth rider brings death are basically quoted from Ezekiel 14:21, which says death comes by the sword, famine, evil beasts, and pestilence. Similarly, Revelation 6:8b says, "And power was given unto them over the fourth part of the earth, to kill with sword, and with hunger, and with death, and with the beasts of the earth." Regardless of how it comes, death will ride across the earth until our Lord Jesus Christ returns. That is part of the reality that we face as professing Christians in a fallen world.

As there are four horses, there are also four ways in which the earth is denuded of its manhood. Death is due to man's inhumanity to man. This is by the sword; by famine (resulting in the injustice revealed in the breaking of the third seal); by plague; and by wild beasts (i.e. natural disasters).

Yet, thanks be to God, even death is under Christ's control. For the believer, death will lead to eternal healing and life.

Trust In God

The opening of the first seal prepares us for warfare, as well as for the tribulation and affliction that are peculiar to the believer. That is what is written in the little book in God's right hand. The breaking of the seals unfolds God's eternal decrees. Jesus says in Matthew 24: "Ye shall hear of wars and rumours of wars.... Nation shall rise against nation, and kingdom against kingdom: and there shall be famines, and pestilences, and earthquakes, in divers places. All these are the beginning of sorrows" (vv. 6–8). The four horsemen of the apocalypse are symbols of the bloodshed, warfare, famine, pestilence, disease, and death that will accompany the preaching of the gospel.

But Jesus goes on to say, "And this gospel of the kingdom shall be preached in all the world for a witness unto all nations; and then shall the end come" (v. 14). What will bring this world to an end? Will it be economic forces, famine, pestilence, or earthquakes? No, this world will continue to exist until Christ is finished riding with His gospel through the nations. That is the picture we have here.

I cannot guarantee peace and prosperity for those who believe in Christ. That is simply unbiblical. If you are a Christian, the four horses of the apocalypse will be more evident to you than to non-believers. Furthermore, persecution, poverty, economic hardship, difficulty in making ends meet, and rejection for the best jobs may become our portion as professing Christians in the not-so-distant future. Neither can I promise you immunity from disease and disaster. I cannot say that if you become a Christian you will never have another illness. It is just not true.

Revelation 6 presses us to be realistic about the world and its history. Secular thinking today swings like a pendulum from humanistic pessimism to humanistic optimism. Humanistic pessimism includes an awful sense of despair. The literary figures of the past fifty years have been prone to this kind of pessimism, as are the intellectuals of our time. Meantime, others are obsessed with man's ability to do anything that he wants. The power he wields, the wisdom he manifests, and the discoveries he makes are fueled by this humanistic optimism.

The biblical position is God-centered realism. We understand what Scripture tells us about history and the world. We will experience wars and rumors of wars, battles, violence, and famine because such things happen in a fallen world. In the midst of all that, however, the Lord Jesus is building His church. And when the church is complete, Christ will bring down the curtain on human history. In the meantime, we must keep our eyes not on what man does but what God is doing. The right perspective on the world and on society is to see them from God's throne, where reality begins. God in His grace will enable us to do that.

If you know the Lord Jesus Christ, you will be able to cope with whatever shakes our confidence, because Christ has everything under control. I know that war, famine, persecution, and death are frightening, destructive, and powerful, but when they are seen in association with Christ and His gospel, they shrink in importance. As Paul says, all things work together for the good of those who love God and are the called according to His purpose (Rom. 8:28).

We live under the threat of a nuclear Iran. Pakistan reportedly possesses over a hundred nuclear warheads, and India about the same. Wars, rumors of wars, the possibility of economic slump or collapse, poverty, disease, and even death, the king of terrors itself— the Bible tells us that all these things work together for good for subjects of King Jesus. All things come in behind Christ and ride with Him for your salvation, dear believer.

The message is simple: none of these terrors, not even the worst of them, happen outside the sovereignty of the triune God. Many unbelievers complain that the God of the Christian gospel wants to interfere in their lives. Yet they also complain when things go wrong for them: "Why doesn't God do something about this?" The church needs to know that nothing happens outside of the will of God. We can rest our hearts in the knowledge that no matter what disaster strikes the world, everything is under His absolute sovereignty. We may hide ourselves in the Rock and say:

> When all around my soul gives way;
> He then is all my hope and stay.[1]

There are times when we are bent low and think we cannot carry our trials one day longer. Then we must listen to Christ, who says, "Even this is set within the framework of My gracious providences for your life." We do not now understand, but afterwards God will show us the whole tapestry of His good and wise plan.

In Romans 8, Paul asks: "Who shall separate us from the love of Christ? shall tribulation, or distress, or persecution, or famine, or nakedness, or peril, or sword?…Nay, in all these things we are more than conquerors through him that loved us" (vv. 35, 37). Is that how you look at the frightening, sin-sick, love-starved, God-hating world in which we live? Christ in the power of His gospel has rounded up all the wild horses of history. They now serve His purposes for your salvation and the salvation of sinners all over the globe.

---

1. Edward Mote, "My Hope Is Built On Nothing Less" (1836).

14

Seals Five and Six:
The Persecuted Church

REVELATION 6:9–17

And when he had opened the fifth seal, I saw under the altar the souls of them that were slain for the word of God, and for the testimony which they held: and they cried with a loud voice, saying, How long, O Lord, holy and true, dost thou not judge and avenge our blood on them that dwell on the earth? And white robes were given unto every one of them; and it was said unto them, that they should rest yet for a little season, until their fellowservants also and their brethren, that should be killed as they were, should be fulfilled. And I beheld when he had opened the sixth seal, and, lo, there was a great earthquake; and the sun became black as sackcloth of hair, and the moon became as blood; and the stars of heaven fell unto the earth, even as a fig tree casteth her untimely figs, when she is shaken of a mighty wind. And the heaven departed as a scroll when it is rolled together; and every mountain and island were moved out of their places. And the kings of the earth, and the great men, and the rich men, and the chief captains, and the mighty men, and every bondman, and every free man, hid themselves in the dens and in the rocks of the mountains; and said to the mountains and rocks, Fall on us, and hide us from the face of him that sitteth on the throne, and from the wrath of the Lamb: for the great day of his wrath is come; and who shall be able to stand?

No one likes to be persecuted. Yet Scripture tells us that is part of the territory that we inherit if we are godly Christians, for all who live godly in Christ Jesus shall suffer persecution (2 Tim. 3:12).

How do you handle persecution? How should you handle persecution? How should you support Christians who are persecuted around the world today much more severely than you have ever faced?

And what about future persecution? As society becomes increasingly intolerant to Christianity even as it boasts of its tolerance, would you be prepared to go to jail for Christ's sake? We can find help in addressing these questions and many more from the second part of Revelation 6.

The message of the second cycle of visions of Revelation (chapters 4–7) so far is that behind this world and everything in it, there is a sovereign God who works not according to whim or caprice, but according to His purpose. He carries out that plan in every detail through the crucified and risen Savior, Jesus Christ, the Lamb that was slain.

In the first cycle of visions in the book of Revelation (chapters 1–3), the Lord gives John a vision of the church in the world and Christ's relationship to it. We see things on the surface, as it were. From chapter 4 onward, John is shown what is going on behind those scenes. He sees things from God's perspective. He sees a throne, a book, and the One who alone is able to open the book and carry out the plan that is written inside it.

Revelation 6 and 7 detail the things that typically happen to us in this world before the Lord's return and what it means to be a Christian. The opening of the seven seals of the book reveals God's purposes for Christians in this world. These seven seals are not to be regarded as seven successive phases of history, but as the complete picture of what God has in store for Christians in this world.

In the previous chapter, we examined the opening of the first four of the seven seals, which launched the four horsemen of the apocalypse, bringing war, famine, and plague. The red horse, black horse, and pale horse come to our doors as well. We live under the same kind of pressures as the Christians of John's day. But the message of the first four seals is that if we are in Christ, we shall be victorious over these difficulties. All the terrible forces and influences that bear down on us like a stampede of horses will not conquer us, but will be conquered by us in the power of Christ.

The opening of the fifth and sixth seals also brings destruction. Wherever Christ comes in the power of His gospel, the sword is bound to follow. There is antagonism, opposition, hostility, and persecution.

Let us continue our study of the second cycle of visions in Revelation under the following headings: the outrage of persecution (Rev. 6:9); the outcry of the persecuted (v. 10); and the outcome of persecution (vv. 11–17).

The Outrage of Persecution

When the fifth seal is opened (v. 9), John sees the souls of believers who were slain (butchered) for the Word of God and their testimony. This seal describes something that has happened throughout the ages to God's people, wherever they have been.

Genesis 3 records the first preaching of the gospel in the Garden of Eden by God Himself. He came looking for Adam, who was hiding because he had disobeyed God by eating the forbidden fruit. God asked, "Where art thou?" (v. 9). Then God preached the gospel to Adam and Eve, saying to the serpent, "I will put enmity between thee and the woman, and between thy seed and her seed; it shall bruise thy head, and thou shalt bruise his heel" (v. 15). That is the gospel. This promise foreshadowed what would happen on Calvary. Christ, as the seed of the woman, goes forth "conquering, and to conquer" (Rev. 6:2) the serpent.

But the sword is also involved. For God said, "I will put enmity between thee and the woman, and between thy seed and her seed." Hostility, hatred, antagonism, persecution, and murder follow in the wake of this enmity. Genesis 4 tells us that Cain killed his brother Abel, and Abel's blood cried out to God for vengeance. Likewise, being a Christian in this world means confronting the sword of this world and its anti-Christian agenda.

Jesus says in Matthew 10:34–39: "Think not that I am come to send peace on earth: I came not to send peace, but a sword. For I am come to set a man at variance against his father, and the daughter against her mother, and the daughter in law against her mother in law. And a man's foes shall be they of his own household. He that loveth father or mother more than me is not worthy of me: and he that loveth son or daughter more than me is not worthy of me. And he that taketh not his cross, and followeth after me, is not worthy of me. He that findeth his life shall lose it: and he that loseth his life for my sake shall find it."

Jesus is saying that true Christians will suffer persecution. All Christians must take up their crosses. They must lose their lives for Christ's sake. That may be literally true, as in physical martyrdom in some countries, but it is also true metaphorically and spiritually. To be a Christian in this world means to lose one's life for Christ's sake. It might happen in the context of an Islamic or North Korean prison, but it might also happen in a believer's own home. Mother will rise against daughter; brother against brother. This is part of what it means to be a Christian. It means suffering for Christ's sake.

Daniel certainly suffered for his faith. Though he knew he might be thrown to the lions if he didn't stop praying to his God in Babylon, Daniel did not shrink from doing his duty. He trusted in God even in the lions' den. And God preserved him. According to Daniel 6:23, "Daniel was taken up out of the den, and no manner of hurt was found upon him, because he believed in his God."

The apostle Paul viewed persecution as a constant reminder of his weakness and utter dependence on God (2 Cor. 12:9–10). The heroes of faith in Hebrews 11 learned through persecution that their focus must be on the eternal rather than the temporal (vv. 1–3). They were to trust the Lord in the midst of suffering, and they were to desire a "better country" (v. 16).

Many Christians have been martyred for their faith throughout church history. Consider the believers who were tortured to death under Roman emperors. Remember the Reformers who were driven from place to place, whipped, and then burned alive or beheaded. Today, more than fifty thousand churches in 115 countries hold a special service each year commemorating the worldwide persecution of Christians. We should not ignore the plight of persecuted Christians around the world.

Millions who profess the name of Christ around the world meet secretly for worship in their homes, because they are oppressed by hostile governments. If their allegiance to Christ is discovered, their homes are attacked and burned. The women and children are sold into slavery. Husbands and wives, parents and children, have their throats slit in front of each other for no other reason than refusing to deny the name of Christ. Hundreds of thousands are brutally tortured and brainwashed in an effort to force them to recant their faith. They spend years in solitary prison cells and hard labor camps. They fear daily for their lives.

Tens of thousands of believers are martyred each year for their faith. More Christians have been martyred for their faith in the past century than in the previous nineteen centuries combined.[1] Millions more face discrimination in their daily lives. Their access to education is restricted. They are forced to take the most menial jobs. They are excluded from the political and judicial processes of their societies. They are ridiculed and despised.

This is still relatively hard to imagine here in the United States. We do face increasing opposition for our Christian beliefs, but not the intense persecution that millions of others suffer for the faith. The law of our land still allows us the freedom to worship. It is hard to imagine living in constant fear that your wife, husband, or neighbor might betray you. It is hard to imagine having no legal recourse, no hope for justice, and nowhere to hide. But that is precisely what millions of Christians face in other parts of the world.

When the fifth seal is opened, John sees the souls of these martyrs under the altar. This refers to the altar of burnt offerings, as described in Leviticus. When an animal was sacrificed on the altar of burnt offerings, the blood would be caught in a basin under the altar. In his vision, John doesn't see the blood of animals under the

---

1. "Report: Christian Dies for Beliefs Every 5 *Minutes*" (http://www.wnd. com/2011/06/311393/#!—accessed June 21, 2016).

altar, but rather the souls of men, women, and children who have lost their lives for Christ's sake. He sees those who did not count their lives dear for Christ's sake.

In John's vision, these saints are not being slain, but have already passed through persecution and are now in heaven, waiting for their full glory. One purpose of this seal is to show that the martyrdom of the saints is controlled by Christ, for only when Christ opens the seal do the believers who were slain cry out for vengeance.

Being a Christian means laying down your life for Christ. It requires total commitment and consecration. It means you live your life as under the altar for Christ's sake. The Christian life is marked by consecration and sacrifice.

Paul describes this life in Romans 12: "I beseech you therefore, brethren, by the mercies of God, that ye present your bodies a living sacrifice, holy, acceptable unto God, which is your reasonable service" (v. 1). He is saying: "Think of what Christ has done for you. He has poured out His soul unto death for you. Now the only reasonable thing you can do is to pour out your life as a thank offering to Him."

In 2 Corinthians 5:14–15, Paul explains what he means by reasonable service. He says, "The love of Christ constraineth us; because we thus judge, that if one died for all, then were all dead: and that he died for all, that they which live should not henceforth live unto themselves, but unto him which died for them, and rose again." When he says, "The love of Christ constrains us," he is not talking about some sentimental feeling, but rather the love of Christ as demonstrated on the cross. Paul is saying, as it were: "When I consider Calvary, I think that if He did that for me, I can no longer live for myself. My life is not my own, but I have to put it under His altar. I have to give it up to Him and live for Him. That is the reasonable thing to do."

How much of your life is under the altar? How much have you sacrificed for your faith? Do you offer the Lord only leftovers or things you no longer want? A man was once given two calves. He said, "I will give one of them to the Lord." One of the calves grew sick and died, so the farmer declared, "The Lord's calf has died." How easy it must have been, under the old covenant, to come to the Lord's house with a diseased, weak, or dying animal from the flock. But that was sacrilege. God's people were to bring Him the best of the flock and the firstfruits of their fields.

Likewise, we are to give God our best. If Christ died upon the cross, bearing God's wrath for our sin, then it is sacrilege for us to hold anything back from Him. And the scandal is that people who are living not for themselves but for Christ—those whose lives are a fragrant offering to God—are the very people hounded, persecuted, and butchered by the world.

The Outcry of the Persecuted

In Revelation 6:10, we read, "And they cried out with a loud voice, saying, How long, O Lord, holy and true, dost thou not judge and avenge our blood on them that dwell on the earth?" To understand this verse, we must remember that it is part of a vision, not a literal picture of heaven. There is no literal altar in heaven, just as there is no literal throne. Also, there is no unhappiness, frustration, impatience, suffering, or thirst for revenge in heaven. No matter how we understand this outcry from beneath the altar, we are not to understand it as a thirst for revenge. It is clear from verse 11 that the glorified saints here are at rest and perfectly happy. The white robes they wear signify sinlessness, happiness, and acceptance with God.

So they do not cry out for revenge; rather, they pray for the vindication of God's holy name as "Judge of the earth" (Ps. 94:2). This outcry of the martyrs is similar to the prayers in the imprecatory psalms, the "cursing psalms," in the Old Testament.

The wrong that was done to these slaughtered saints cries out to be put right. It reminds us of Abel's blood in the ground crying out to God (Gen. 4:10). We are not to understand that literally, because blood is not able to cry out. Neither are we to understand it in a sinister sort of way. The slain Abel did not become some kind of malignant force, seeking to take revenge on Cain. No, Abel is in heaven with the spirits of just men made perfect, and he is perfectly happy. He did not ask for revenge. But what happened to Abel did not go unnoticed. It was dealt with; it was put right.

The same outcome is in view in this outcry of the souls under the altar. These glorified saints are not thirsting for mere personal revenge. They are yearning for God's name to be vindicated and for His righteousness to be upheld.

Do you yearn for the vindication of God's holy name? Can you say with the psalmist in Psalm 119:127–128: "Therefore I love thy commandments above gold; yea, above fine gold. Therefore I esteem all thy precepts concerning all things to be right; and I hate every false way"? Stephen, the first Christian martyr, died praying, "Lord, lay not this sin to their charge" (Acts 7:60). There was no personal vindictiveness or thirst for revenge in those words. Yet what happened to Stephen and millions like him cannot go unpunished. If God is God, these crimes must be punished.

So we cry out: "LORD, how long shall the wicked, how long shall the wicked triumph? How long shall they utter and speak hard things? and all the workers of iniquity boast themselves?" (Ps. 94:3–4).

Christians are persecuted for various reasons. One is because we say there is only one way to salvation, and that is through Jesus Christ, God's Son. This exclusive claim does not fit the New Age movement. Neither does it accommodate radical Islam.

Christians are also persecuted because Satan wants to destroy the people of God. Peter thus advises believers, "Be sober, be vigilant; because your adversary the devil, as a roaring lion, walketh about, seeking whom he may devour" (1 Peter 5:8). Satan aims to swallow or destroy all believers.

Christians are persecuted so that they might be strengthened in faith. James 1:3–4 says: "The trying of your faith worketh patience. But let patience have her perfect work, that ye may be perfect and entire, wanting nothing." God tests the faith of His people to develop spiritual endurance in their walk with Him.

Persecution is also the pathway to God's gracious reward. Paul says to Timothy near the end of his life, "I have fought a good fight,

I have finished my course, I have kept the faith: Henceforth there is laid up for me a crown of righteousness, which the Lord, the righteous judge, shall give me at that day: and not to me only, but unto all them also that love his appearing" (2 Tim. 4:7–8).

But most of all, persecution is the way to God's kingdom of glory. The day of judgment, which follows a time of intense persecution, will make clear to the church and the entire world that Christ is holy and true, and that He represents God in His perfect justice.

The saints under the altar do not cry in vain. Everything is done to comfort them and to reassure them that the day on which God will judge the world in righteousness is not far off.

First, "white robes were given unto every one of them" (Rev. 6:11a). Christians who suffer persecution will one day be adorned in white robes as they praise the triune God. White is a symbol of eternal justification by Christ's blood and acquittal by the Father. It is also a symbol of sanctification, for in heaven the saints are perfectly holy before God in Christ. And it is a symbol of their victory. Just as the rider on the white horse symbolizes Christ's victory, so the white robes given to souls under the altar symbolize that they are more than conquerors in the battle of faith. In short, white is the symbol of their perfected, glorified nature (Heb. 12:23).

Second, "it was said unto them, that they should rest yet for a little season, until their fellow-servants also and their brethren, that should be killed as they were, should be fulfilled" (Rev. 6:11b). This promise is meant to reassure these souls that they have not cried out in vain. They must rest until the gathering in of all the elect, and especially the offering up of all the martyrs of God, has been accomplished. God knows all who are His, and He knows the exact number of people who will die for the faith. His timetable is also absolutely perfect. He is never one step out of sync with His glorious purposes to gather, preserve, defend and glorify His Son's church.

But we are inclined to ask: "When is Christ coming? Why does He tarry?" Peter tells us we are mistaken if we think that Christ is tarrying or delaying; rather, He is ever at work, gathering and building His church: "The Lord is not slack concerning his promise…

but is longsuffering to us-ward, not willing that any should perish, but that all should come to repentance." He urges us therefore to "account that the longsuffering of our Lord is salvation," that is, salvation for all those who are ordained to eternal life through Christ (2 Peter 3:9, 15).

We have a significant responsibility to alleviate the suffering of Christians who are being persecuted for their faith. God will keep them, but we must do what lies in our power to do here on earth. Here are some ways to help persecuted Christians today:

First, *be informed.* Write to religious liberty advocacy groups, requesting updated information on worldwide persecution.

Second, *empathize with those who are suffering for Christ.* As 1 Corinthians 12:26 says, "And whether one member suffer, all the members suffer with it; or one member be honoured, all the members rejoice with it."

Third, *pray for them.* When Peter was imprisoned, the church gathered to pray without ceasing for his release (Acts 12:5). We, too, must pray for those who are languishing in horrible conditions. We should pray also for Christians in specific countries.

For example, Afghanistan has 48,000 mosques and not one church building. It has seventy unreached people groups who have never heard the gospel. Of the fifty languages spoken, the New Testament has been translated into only two, while none of the fifty has a complete Bible.

Likewise, Sudanese Christians are often forced to flee *jihad* or holy war into the snake-infested bush. Thousands struggle to survive by eating leaves off trees. Thousands more are killed by government-backed militias.

Fourth, *support them.* Speak of their faithfulness in the church. As 2 Thessalonians 1:4 says, "So that we ourselves glory in you in the churches of God for your patience and faith in all your persecutions and tribulations that ye endure." Speak of their plight to your friends. Write letters to the media. Write to your leaders in Congress and urge them to act on behalf of persecuted Christians around the world. Tell them a double crime is being committed:

the crime of persecution by Communist and Islamic governments against Christians, and the crime of free nations like ours that ignore such wrongdoing out of self-interest or political cowardice.

Fifth, *go to them.* If we can't visit suffering Christians, we can find ways to contact them. Follow the example of Peter, who wrote to brethren scattered far and wide in his day (1 Peter 1:1). At the very least, contribute to mission groups that work among persecuted people.

When the lives of her people were in jeopardy, Esther was tempted to avoid the plight of her fellow Jews until Mordecai, her guardian, said to her: "Think not with thyself that thou shalt escape in the king's house, more than all the Jews. For if thou altogether holdest thy peace at this time, then shall there enlargement and deliverance arise to the Jews from another place; but thou and thy father's house shall be destroyed: and who knoweth whether thou art come to the kingdom for such a time as this?" (Esth. 4:13–14).

Today, we are citizens of the most powerful nation in the world. Like Esther, we feel safe in the United States, secure in the possession of freedom of speech, religion, and assembly. But like Esther, we must speak out against the extermination of our brethren in other countries, even if it costs us something to do that. If we don't speak out, no one is safe. We may be next in line for intense persecution.

We must heed the words of Hebrews 13:3: "Remember them that are in bonds, as bound with them; and them which suffer adversity, as being yourselves also in the body."

The Outcome of Persecution

If evil triumphs, the world gets worse, and the wicked prosper, what is the point of being a Christian? The opening of the sixth seal (Rev. 6:12–17) answers that question. It tells us that the day of judgment is coming, when God in His almighty power will right every wrong with the world. He will shake the world and everyone in it. He will move mountains and islands, darken the sun, turn the moon into blood, and cause the stars to fall from heaven. It will be a terrifying day for those who are not right with God.

The symbols of this passage, including falling stars, the cries of the wicked, the quaking earth, and the rolling up of the sky as a scroll are all descriptive of the tremendous and terrifying upheaval that is coming on that day that God has appointed to judge the world. The opening of the sixth seal tells us about the complete overthrow of all earthly powers, rulers, movements, and systems. Every power and authority in earth and in hell will be confounded. No words could more powerfully express the total hopelessness, ruin, and despair of all earthly powers and interest.

The key figure in all of this is the Lamb. Verses 15–17 describe a dislocated universe and a terrified human race. People of all classes— kings of the earth, great and rich men, mighty men, and bondmen and free men—hide themselves in the dens and caves of the mountains and cry out, "Fall on us, and hide us from the face of him that sitteth on the throne, and from the wrath of the Lamb: for the great day of his wrath is come; and who shall be able to stand?"

These hardened men have been slaughtering Christians without a pang of guilt, yet now they cannot look into the face of the Lamb. They call upon the rocks to fall upon them and cover them. They call to the mountains to collapse upon them. They would rather perish in a nuclear holocaust than look into the face of Jesus Christ.

The wrath of the Lamb is indeed terrifying to those who have rejected Him and scorned His love. There is nothing more frightening than the face of perfect love turned against you. That is what the day of judgment is all about. When God judges the world, He will judge through the Man He has appointed, His Son, Jesus Christ. The very Jesus who went to the cross to die for sinners will be in charge on the day of judgment.

Unbelievers will plead to be delivered from the wrath of the Lamb. How horrible it will be to be damned by Him who came to save sinners! This reminds us of Psalm 130, which asks, "If thou, LORD, shouldest mark iniquities, O Lord, who shall stand?" (v. 3). But the psalm also offers this comfort: "But there is forgiveness with thee, that thou mayest be feared" (v. 4).

For many, it will be too late to repent. Before, they felt no need to repent of sin and cling to a Savior to deliver them from the wrath to come, because they thought they could get through it on their own. Now they are calling for the mountains to fall upon them. Is the Lord pleading with you even now to come to the Lamb who died to save sinners? If He is, it is comforting to know He is still speaking to you. The next time you hear His voice, it may be too late. Then you will have to bear the wrath of the Lamb.

Ultimately, the only thing that matters is that we are on the right side of Jesus. The only thing that matters is that you and I are able to look Him in the face on the day of judgment, clothed in His white robes of righteousness. Ultimately, it does not matter what kind of a nest we have made for ourselves in the short time we are here on earth. The only thing that matters is how we are related to Him. Philip Doddridge puts it like this:

> Ye sinners seek His grace
> Whose wrath ye cannot bear;
> Fly to the shelter of His cross
> And find salvation there.[2]

Christ is the Lamb of God who takes away the sin of the world. God has sent forth Jesus in this day of grace to be the covering, the propitiation for sin, to hide you from His anger and righteous judgment. Let me urge you, by the grace of the Holy Spirit, to flee to Jesus as the only Savior. Hide yourself in Him today.

---

2. Phillip Doddridge, "And Will the Judge Descend" (1755).

15

Visions of the Church

And after these things I saw four angels standing on the four corners of the earth, holding the four winds of the earth, that the wind should not blow on the earth, nor on the sea, nor on any tree. And I saw another angel ascending from the east, having the seal of the living God: and he cried with a loud voice to the four angels, to whom it was given to hurt the earth and the sea, saying, Hurt not the earth, neither the sea, nor the trees, till we have sealed the servants of our God in their foreheads. And I heard the number of them which were sealed: and there were sealed an hundred and forty and four thousand of all the tribes of the children of Israel.... After this I beheld, and, lo, a great multitude, which no man could number, of all nations, and kindreds, and people, and tongues, stood before the throne, and before the Lamb, clothed with white robes, and palms in their hands; and cried with a loud voice, saying, Salvation to our God which sitteth upon the throne, and unto the Lamb. And all the angels stood round about the throne, and about the elders and the four beasts, and fell before the throne on their faces, and worshipped God, saying, Amen: Blessing, and glory, and wisdom, and thanksgiving, and honour, and power, and might, be unto our God for ever and ever. Amen.... These are they which came out of great tribulation, and have washed their robes, and made them white in the blood of the Lamb. Therefore are they before the throne of God, and serve him day and night in his temple: and he that sitteth on the throne shall dwell among them. They shall hunger no more, neither thirst any more; neither shall the sun light on them, nor any heat. For the Lamb which is in the midst of the throne shall feed them, and shall lead them unto living

*fountains of waters: and God shall wipe away all tears from their
eyes. And when he had opened the seventh seal, there was silence in
heaven about the space of half an hour.*

The book of Revelation is a bit like a Russian nesting doll. You
take it apart, only to find a smaller one inside. You open that, and
there is still another doll inside—and so on. As we have worked our
way through the second of the seven cycles of visions in Revelation
(chapters 4–7), we have seen Christ open six seals on the scroll,
telling what He has in store for us. When Christ opens the seventh
seal (chapter 8), we find seven trumpets. With the blowing of the
seven trumpets comes the outpouring of the seven vials of wrath.
The book of Revelation is constantly unfolding itself.

But chapter 7 offers a welcome interlude between the opening of the first six seals and the seventh seal. After the sixth seal is
opened at the end of chapter 6, we read in 7:1a, "And after these
things I saw…." Those words indicate that something new is about
to happen. Christ puts John's vision of the opening of the seals on
pause, and says, as it were: "Before we get to the seventh seal, I
want to give you a break, John, because what I am showing you is
too much for you to take in. There are certain things that I need to
explain before opening the seventh seal."

This is a welcome and relevant interlude because it answers a
very pertinent question that is raised at the end of chapter 6: "The
great day of his wrath is come; and who shall be able to stand?"
(v. 17). The same question was posed long before by the prophet
Malachi: "Who may abide the day of his coming? And who shall
stand when he appeareth?" (Mal. 3:2). Certainly not the impenitent
unbelievers of this world: "the ungodly shall not stand in the judgment, nor sinners in the congregation of the righteous" (Ps. 1:5).
But what about the people of God? What will happen to those who
belong to Jesus Christ as God's wrath is poured out on our world?

Revelation 7 is divided into two sections. Verses 1–8 describe a
vision of the *church militant*, in the midst of tribulation, in the thick
of the things John has seen coming upon this world. Verses 9–17

describe the *church triumphant*, the church that has come out of tribulation and is out of harm's way. Then Revelation 8:1 describes the *church silent*, for the day of the Lord has come. Christ gives these visions to John to encourage him, to show him first the church on earth in the midst of tribulation and then the church in heaven beyond tribulation.

The Sealed Church Militant

In the opening verses of Revelation 7, Christ assures John that He will have a sealed and militant church on earth. There are three important things to notice in these verses.

The Sealed

Verse 4 says, "And I heard the number of them which were sealed: and there were sealed an hundred and forty and four thousand of all the tribes of the children of Israel." This number is not to be taken literally, for if we view this and other numbers in Revelation literally, we will soon be confronted with all kinds of exegetical and historical problems. If you take 144,000 as a literal number, then you also have to take literally the six wings of the four angels, and everything else. Given the genre of Revelation, its numbers are not to be understood mathematically but spiritually.

At times, numbers are not to be taken literally even in non-apocalyptic books. When Peter asks the Lord Jesus: "Lord, how oft shall my brother sin against me, and I forgive him? Till seven times?" Jesus replies, "I say not unto thee, Until seven times: but, Until seventy times seven" (Matt. 18:21–22). Peter and the Lord are speaking numerically, but the meaning is clearly spiritual. Jesus is telling Peter that we are not to forgive a brother precisely 490 times, but continuously, completely, and forever. It is quite all right in Scripture to use numbers spiritually, and that is how we are to understand the 144,000 and other numbers in the book of Revelation.

Revelation 7:5–8 lists twelve groups of twelve thousand. Each group bears the name of one of the twelve tribes of Israel. Some dispensationalists say that means the church has been raptured at this point and is no longer on earth. All that is left on earth is the nation of Israel. God does a great work among these people and 144,000 are saved.

But that does not harmonize with the rest of Scripture. It doesn't even fit in with Revelation 7. These verses are not a description of the nation of Israel. For one thing, two tribes are missing. Then, too, the order of the tribes here is very different from the customary order in which the tribes are listed in the Old Testament. Judah is listed first here, but he wasn't the oldest of Jacob's sons, so he is not first in any list of the tribes in the Old Testament. He is listed first here because the Lord Jesus Christ came from the tribe of Judah. The order of the tribes has been changed in the light of the gospel and the way in which the promises of the Old Testament have been fulfilled in Christ. So what we have here is not a picture of literal Israel, but a picture of the true Israel of God. One of the most repeated symbols in the Bible is the symbol of Israel as the people of God, and that symbol reappears here.

This chapter is in line with what we are taught in other parts of the New Testament. For example, in Romans 9–11, Paul tries to help Gentile Christians understand that they are not second-class Christians because they are not Jewish. He wants them to know that the covenants and promises given to Israel are for Gentile Christians as well, for in Christ, the Gentiles now belong to the commonwealth of Israel. He says that being a true Israelite is not a matter of nationality but of faith. It is not a question of whether one is born a Jew, but whether one is born again and in a right relationship with the Messiah, the Lord Jesus Christ. "They are not all Israel, which are of Israel" (Rom. 9:6). Not everyone who calls himself a Jew is a true Israelite. True Israelites are those who believe in Christ.

Paul also argues this point in Ephesians, reminding the Ephesian Christians of what they once were as Gentiles—cut off from the commonwealth of Israel, without hope and without God in the world (Eph. 2:12). Paul says that everything has changed: "But now in Christ Jesus ye who sometimes were far off are made nigh by the blood of Christ.... Now therefore ye are no more strangers and foreigners, but fellow-citizens with the saints, and of the household of God" (vv. 13, 19).

This is an important biblical doctrine. The church is the spiritual embodiment of the nation of Israel and therefore is the heir to all the covenants and all the promises made to the Old Testament saints. That means that all the promises in the Old Testament relating to the land and everything else belong to the true spiritual Israel, that is, to true believers.[1] When the prophet Isaiah promises that the wilderness will blossom like a rose, that is true for spiritual Israel. As a general rule, the great promises that are made to Israel in the Old Testament belong, dear child of God, to you. That is a great comfort in this world of tribulation.

So what we have here is a symbolic description of the church militant, the true spiritual Israel of God, God's servant people. They are numbered as 12 x 12 x 10 x 10 x 10, symbolizing the fullness of God's covenant people. Revelation 7:3 describes these 144,000 as "the servants of our God." They are not citizens of national Israel but of spiritual Israel. They are born-again Christians. Yet, comparing 144,000 to the numbering of ancient Israel, which consisted of over 600,000 men *plus* women and children, we see that many people are not saved.

The Sealing

Verses 2 and 3 tell us how the saints are sealed: "I saw another angel ascending from the east, having the seal of the living God: and he cried with a loud voice to the four angels, to whom it was given to hurt the earth and the sea, saying, Hurt not the earth, neither the sea, nor the trees, till we have sealed the servants of our God in their foreheads."

---

1. See O. Palmer Robertson, *The Israel of God: Yesterday, Today, and Tomorrow* (Phillipsburg: N.J.: P&R, 2000).

The New Testament speaks about sealing in a number of ways. In the ancient world, a seal was made with a signet ring or some other device that was pressed onto clay or wax to leave its mark, indicating security, identification, and confirmation. God is saying, "When I seal My own, they are not to be tampered with, for I protect and secure them."

For example, the tomb in which Jesus was buried was sealed with a stone and guards. Matthew 27:65–66 says: "Pilate said unto them, Ye have a watch: go your way, make it as sure as ye can. So they went, and made the sepulchre sure, sealing the stone, and setting a watch." Pilate didn't want Jesus' body to be stolen. So he put some of his soldiers at the disposal of the Jewish leaders, to whom he said, "Go and make the tomb as secure as you know how." Pilate had strong feelings about this.

Security is of crucial importance in the sealing of the 144,000. They are in the world, and the world is a dangerous place. As Christians, we are subject to the same pressures, influences, and forces as nonbelievers. We are not immune to sorrow, sickness, and anxiety. We struggle to make ends meet. Death comes to our doors and claims our loved ones. All the terrible trials that emanate from the opening of the first six seals are ours to bear. God is saying to John and his readers that He protects His people so that the pressures and influences of this world will not destroy them. God grants His people the security in Christ that the world cannot experience.

Sometimes we are frightened and wonder how we will be able to be true to God until the end. We look at our hearts, and we know how weak we are. We fear that one day we will make shipwreck of our faith and be swept away. But God assures us: "I have sealed you and made you secure; I will protect you from all interference and danger. Nothing shall separate you, dear believer, from My love in Christ Jesus" (see Rom. 8:39).

At the beginning of Revelation 7, four angels hold back the four winds. They are given power over everything upon land and sea to the four corners of the earth. They are given power to harm everything—except for God's people. They are held back from injuring believers. The four winds have the potential to hurt us, but they can't do so because God will not tolerate that. If we are sealed by God, then when God unleashes the four winds, we won't be swept away.

Paul says in 1 Corinthians 10:13, "There hath no temptation taken you but such as is common to man: but God is faithful, who will not suffer you to be tempted above that ye are able; but will with the temptation also make a way to escape, that ye may be able to bear it." That is what this vision says. No trial can happen to us that is not common to all people. However, when we suffer tribulations that threaten to overwhelm us, God provides a way out of our difficulties. Literally, He provides "a way to escape." Therefore, the church of Jesus Christ is indestructible. The King-Lamb on the throne confirms, "I will build my church; and the gates of hell shall not prevail against it" (Matt. 16:18).

Identification is another function of sealing. A seal is a mark of ownership. God says of His sealed child, "He is Mine." In 2 Corinthians 1:22, Paul speaks about how Christ has established us, anointed us, and "hath also sealed us, and given the earnest of the Spirit in our hearts." He is saying that God has set His seal of ownership upon us.

Identification is also part of the process of sealing in Revelation. The 144,000 are sealed on their foreheads. They are not given a secret tattoo that is hidden by their robes, but a clear mark on their foreheads. God marks His people to publicly claim them as His. In the midst of the trials and temptations of life, when the winds blow from the four corners of the earth, God not only protects His people, but also owns them as His. He puts His mark on us so everyone knows who we are. When you are on your deathbed, those who ridiculed you for your faith during your lifetime can hear you testify of Christ and say, "Yes, there is something real in this."

In John 6:27, Jesus tells us, "Labour not for the meat which perisheth, but for that meat which endureth unto everlasting life, which the Son of man shall give unto you: for him hath God the Father sealed." The Son of God can give us this meat because the Father has sealed Him. He publicly owned Jesus as His Son. On two occasions, God said from heaven, "This is my beloved Son, in whom I am well pleased" (Matt. 3:17; 17:5). God owned His Son publicly so that people could believe in Him and trust in Him. Likewise, the resurrection was a seal. When God raised Jesus from the dead, He was saying: "This is My beloved Son. I own Him; I delight in Him; I am well pleased with Him; you can trust Him."

If you are truly sealed, you can face anything in life. You can cast off doubts and fears about your salvation, for Christ has sealed you as His own. You can say as the bride says to her husband: "My beloved is mine and I am his" (Song 2:16). If you are a sealed Christian, you know in the midst of trials and persecutions that God is your God. You belong to Him. When you know something of that, you are in a position of power.

Don't misunderstand; the Christian life is not easy. If you are owned and sealed by God, you will be persecuted. You are a marked person as far as the world is concerned. Your sealing means that you are called to live a godly and faithful life, to endure hardship, and to suffer shame for the sake of His name.

Authenticity is another benefit of sealing. When God seals us, He is saying: "This child is genuinely Mine. He or she has been adopted into My family, and My act of adoption is sealed by My Spirit."

Finally, a seal is a *confirmation* of a promised inheritance. The seal is an earnest or down payment on what is yet to come. It is a foretaste of heaven. Paul uses this word in Ephesians 1:13–14, where he notes that "after that ye heard the word of truth, the gospel of your salvation: in whom also after that ye believed, ye were sealed with that holy Spirit of promise, which is the earnest of our inheritance until the redemption of the purchased possession, unto the praise of his glory." The Holy Spirit is God's down payment or deposit on our inheritance. Having the Holy Spirit in you and being consciously aware of His presence is a foretaste of glory. It is the first installment of your life in heaven.

John tells us in Revelation 14:1 that the church militant has God's seal on their foreheads: "I looked, and, lo, a Lamb stood on the mount Sion, and with him an hundred forty and four thousand, having his Father's name written in their foreheads." Believers are sealed by the Father, Son, and Holy Spirit for the fourfold purpose of security, ownership, identification, and confirmation.

Here, of course, note that all 144,000 are sealed. Not some or many, but all of these believers are sealed. That is what the Bible says. From God's perspective, all Christians are sealed, even if not all Christians are conscious of having been sealed.

After describing the Spirit as God's seal, Paul goes on in Ephesians 4:30 to warn them not to grieve or offend Him. "Grieve not the holy Spirit of God, whereby ye are sealed unto the day of redemption." It is possible to grieve the Holy Spirit in such a way that you lose the sense and comfort of His sealing work. Those who grieve the Spirit by sins of anger or malice should not be surprised if they feel bereft of Him or forsaken by Him.

The Sealer

Notice the description we have of the One who seals in these verses: "I saw another angel ascending from the east, having the seal of the living God: and he cried with a loud voice to the four angels, to whom it was given to hurt the earth and the sea, saying, Hurt not the earth, neither the sea, nor the trees, till we have sealed the servants of our God in their foreheads" (Rev. 7:2–3).

The angel who gives this command can be no one but the Lord Jesus Christ. John says he saw an angel, but that can mean various things. In Revelation's opening chapters, the word *angel* refers to a minister. John addresses his letters to the "angels" of the seven churches, that is, to the ministers of those churches. An angel can also be a supernatural being who serves God as a flame of fire. But specific angels, such as "the angel of the covenant" (Mal. 3:1) and "the angel of the Lord" (Ex. 3:1–6) as well as the angel with the loud voice here in Revelation 7, must be understood to be Christ. Who else has all authority in heaven and on earth? Who else could cry out with a loud voice, "Hurt not the earth, neither the sea, nor the trees, till we have sealed the servants of our God in their foreheads"?

There is something very beautiful about the way Christ the Mediator holds back the four winds and desists from opening the seventh seal and sending His judgment upon the earth until all His elect are gathered in. He holds everything back until everyone whom the Father has given to Him is saved and has the mark of the Lamb. He holds everything back until all that is signed and sealed in the everlasting covenant of grace has been delivered in full.

This sealing is also mentioned in Revelation 14, where the 144,000 are described as the company of the redeemed—those who follow the Lamb wherever He goes. They, too, have a mark upon their foreheads, the mark of the Father and the Lamb.

The idea of sealing is an integral part of the Passover. When God's judgment was being poured out in plagues on Egypt, specifically the killing of the first-born sons in every home, God spared only those families who put the mark of the blood of the Passover lamb on their doors. Is the blood mark of the Lamb upon you? Is the name of the Lamb upon your forehead? Is the mark of His atoning blood in your heart? Do you belong to the church militant?

When the world asks, "Who makes you to differ from another?" the answer is: God does. Why are some saved while others perish? When the day of judgment comes, when the seventh seal is opened and all the wrath and fury of God is unleashed upon the earth, why will some be able to stand while others fall? Being delivered from that terrible day has nothing to do with your nationality, upbringing, or spirituality. It all depends on the blood mark of the Lamb. The 144,000 will stand and endure to the end, for they are the true Israel of God. They have the mark of the Lamb upon them. They are sealed unto God for eternity.

The Numberless Church Triumphant

In the first part of Revelation 7, John sees a group of 144,000 people. In verse 9 he looks again and sees a great crowd that no man can number. It is the same group he is seeing, only from a different viewpoint. In the first half of the chapter, he sees the true Israel of God passing through the wilderness of this world through great tribulation. The 144,000 represent the true church of God in any place at any given time in this world. But in verse 9, John sees a numberless throng that represents the sum of all believers of every generation, place, and time gathered together in glory. It represents the total ingathering of God's elect, the church triumphant.

Let us consider four things about this numberless throng: who they are; where they are; how they got there; and what their occupation is.

Their Identity: Who Are They?

Dispensationalists view this throng as "tribulation saints." They say the great tribulation referred to in verse 14 is going to happen in the future. Some scholars say it will last about three and a half years; others say it will continue about seven years. This unparalleled time of suffering and persecution will happen after the church has been removed from the world in the rapture. The Holy Spirit will be withdrawn so that Satan can be given freedom to stalk through the earth and wreak all kinds of havoc. During this period, the numberless throng will be converted.

Such teaching makes little sense and brings little comfort. The apostles spent decades preaching the gospel in the power of the Spirit, and multitudes were converted as a result; yet we are supposed to expect that in some future time, without the witness of the church and without the power of the Spirit, there will be so many converts that no one can number them? That would make the efforts of the apostolic era insignificant. It would also render the witness of the church and the work of the Holy Spirit unnecessary in the saving of sinners.

What John is describing is what was promised to Abraham in the covenant of grace: descendants as many as the grains of sand on the seashore or the stars in the sky, too numerous to count (Gen. 22:17). John is using the same language that God used when He revealed the gospel to Abraham. We are to understand this numberless throng in terms of the heirs and beneficiaries of the covenant of grace. These people are the spiritual seed of Abraham. They are the sum total of believers. This is the culmination of all that was promised in the eternal covenant of grace, sealed by the blood of the Lamb.

John tells us in verse 9 that this multitude cannot be numbered. That does not mean that this crowd of saints is infinite in number; rather, it is a great multitude that *no man* can number. But God can number them. According to 2 Timothy 2:19, God does number His saints: "Nevertheless the foundation of God standeth sure, having this seal, The Lord knoweth them that are his." The Lord knows every single saint by name. They are innumerable as far as you and I are concerned, but God knows every one of them.

Verse 9 also says that John sees a multitude "of all nations, and kindreds, and people, and tongues...before the throne." He sees people with all kinds of national and ethnic differences, yet they are praising the Lamb with one voice. Jesus says in Matthew 24:14 that the gospel must be preached to every nation before the end comes. He wants heaven to be full of color and variety. That is part of the biblical picture of heaven.

Their Surroundings: Where Are They?

The numberless company of the redeemed is in glory. That is evident from the white robes they wear, the palm branches they wave, and their surroundings. The palm branches are also an allusion to the feast of tabernacles in the Old Testament (Lev. 23:39–43), that reminded the children of Israel of the forty years they wandered in the wilderness. The feast was a celebration of their deliverance from Egypt and anticipated arrival in the Promised Land. Likewise, the glorified saints have come through the great tribulation (v. 14) in victory and are now in the kingdom of God (Zech. 14:16).

This great tribulation is not three and a half years of intense persecution yet to come. It refers to the entire journey of God's people between the Red Sea and the Jordan. In other words, the great tribulation represents our "wilderness wanderings." It is life from that moment when God intervenes to rescue you from the slavery of sin and Satan and set you on the path of life until the day your earthly life ends. It is life in this world as a Christian. We are told in Revelation that the numberless throng, having passed through tribulation, is now out of harm's way, beyond pain and suffering.

Verses 15–17 say: "Therefore are they before the throne of God, and serve him day and night in his temple: and he that sitteth on the throne shall dwell among them. They shall hunger no more, neither thirst any more; neither shall the sun light on them, nor any heat. For the Lamb which is in the midst of the throne shall feed them, and shall lead them unto living fountains of waters: and God shall wipe away all tears from their eyes." There will be no more tears in heaven, for God offers more than comfort. He gives us bliss and joy.

The Lamb who took upon Himself our human nature, lived in the wilderness of the world, and suffered for us, will meet us when we get to heaven. He will supply all our wants and needs. That is what heaven is; that is what glory is all about—living in the presence of the Lord.

God's presence will overshadow us. It will be like living in the Garden of Eden, only much better. God's presence will be everywhere, and we will be more alive than we have ever been. Heaven pulsates with life. Those who are there already are far more alive than we are today, and we will one day join those saints before the throne of God and of the Lamb.

We live in a world of people who are frustrated, dissatisfied, and unfulfilled. These feelings are evident even in the children of God, because we have a sense of incompleteness. Something within us argues that we were made and redeemed for something more than what we have now. Though some joys of this present life are sweet, we find that they do not satisfy something deep within us. We see something of eternity "as through a glass, darkly" (1 Cor. 13:12), and we long for more. That something is what the saints of glory experience, John says. They no longer hunger or thirst, for Christ has led them to springs of living water.

Notice that Revelation 6 and 7 both conclude with a statement about the Lamb. In chapter 6, unbelievers who have hidden from the face of God all their lives call on the mountains to fall upon them and save them from the wrath of the Lamb (vv. 16–17). In chapter 7, we see the redeemed in glory, where they no longer hunger, thirst, or shrink from the heat of the sun: "For the lamb which is in the midst of the throne shall feed them, and shall lead them unto living fountains of waters.... And God shall wipe away all tears from their eyes" (vv. 16–17).

Their Origin: How Did They Get There?

One of the elders says to John in verse 13: "What are these which are arrayed in white robes? and whence came they?" The elder is not asking John for information. Rather, he is drawing attention to the all-important question of how the great multitude of the saved in heaven got there. John says, "Sir, thou knowest" (v. 14a). He is saying, "Tell me." So the elder tells him these are the ones who came out of great tribulation and have washed their robes and made them white in the blood of the Lamb (v. 14b).

These people are not in glory *because* they went through tribulation. They are not there because they had difficult times in this life and God owed them some sort of compensation. They are there because they washed their robes in the blood of the Lamb. They washed their robes not in their own tribulations or sufferings, but in the blood of Christ. They got through the tribulation by trusting in Him and by washing themselves in the blood of atonement.

Notice that *they* had to wash their garments. Salvation is from God alone. We cannot save ourselves, but we do have to come to Him with our dirty lives. We have to come with our filthy robes, so they can be washed. That is the way to heaven. You and I as sinners come to Christ, conscious of our filthiness. We think we are rather good people until the Spirit opens our eyes to what we really are. Then we come in the filthiness of our sin to the Savior and cry out, "Wash me, Savior, or I die!" That is the only way to get to heaven. That is how these people got there, says the elder to John. They came by grace, trusting in the blood of Christ.

Their Occupation: What Are They Doing There?

In verse 15, the elder says, "Therefore are they before the throne of God, and serve him day and night in his temple." The saints in heaven are constantly worshiping God, ascribing salvation to God and to the Lamb. You might think that when they got to heaven, they didn't need to think about salvation anymore. But that is not the case. We will need an eternity to appreciate what God has done for us in Jesus Christ. The saints sing: "Salvation to our God which sitteth upon the throne, and unto the Lamb" (v. 10).

Doxologies and praises intensify as we go through the book of Revelation. They get more and more profound. Likewise, salvation consists of an infinite journey into our appreciation of what God has done for us in Jesus Christ.

Paul says, "For to me to live is Christ, and to die is gain" (Phil. 1:21). If you live for Christ, dying will be your gain. But if you do not live for Christ, you are in grave danger of confronting eternity without Christ. "The great day of His wrath is come; and who shall be able to stand?" (Rev. 6:7).

The Adoring Church Silent

Revelation 8:1 says that when the Lamb opened the seventh seal, "there was silence in heaven about the space of half an hour." Though interpretations of this verse vary, G. K. Beale rightly states that "the key to the significance of the 'silence' must lie in the connotation that it has in the OT and in Jewish writings."[2] Beale goes on to say that most commonly the Old Testament "associates silence with divine judgment" (Ps. 31:17). For example, Habakkuk 2:20 says, "But the LORD is in his holy temple: let all the earth keep silence before him." Zechariah writes about the coming judgment and says, "Be silent, O all flesh, before the LORD: for he is raised up out of his holy habitation" (Zech. 2:13). The opening of the seventh seal is a

---

2. G. K. Beale, *The Book of Revelation*, New International Greek Testament Commentary (Grand Rapids: Eerdmans, 1999), 445.

revelation of God's holy majesty that results in a profound silence.[3] This silence is like the quietness after a storm, for God's dreadful judgments have been poured out. Even the angels are awestruck at God's judgment, which involves the dissolution of all things.

Thus the seven seals climax in a thunderous silence. The cries of the martyrs for divine justice, the roaring earthquake in the dissolution of the world, and the screams of the wicked as Christ's wrath falls upon them (Rev. 6:9–17) give way to an awe-filled silence as every mouth is quiet, and even the saints and angels stand amazed at the glory of the Lord.

There are times in this life when the only appropriate response is silence. Certainly grief and bereavement call for periods when our ordinary chatter is replaced by quietness. Silence may also intrude into our lives when we come suddenly upon a view of some majestic mountain, broad ocean, or deep canyon, and find ourselves with eyes wide, mouth open, and nothing to say.

How much more do we need to cultivate times of silence in worship before God! Ecclesiastes reminds us that when we go to the house of God, "Be not rash with thy mouth, and let not thine heart be hasty to utter any thing before God: for God is in heaven, and thou upon earth: therefore let thy words be few" (Eccl. 5:2). Rather than multiply babbling words in prayer (Matt. 6:7–8), let us learn to wait in silence upon the Lord (Ps. 62:1, KJV margin).

Could it be there is a connection between our society's continual immersion of itself in music, talking, and noise and its utter lack of reverence for God? May the Lord give us hearts to hear Him say, "Be still, and know that I am God: I will be exalted among the heathen, I will be exalted in the earth" (Ps. 46:10). Amen.

---

3. Beale, *The Book of Revelation*, 446–48.

16

Angels, Prayers, and Trumpets

REVELATION 8:2–13

And I saw the seven angels which stood before God; and to them were given seven trumpets.... The first angel sounded, and there followed hail and fire mingled with blood, and they were cast upon the earth: and the third part of trees was burnt up, and all green grass was burnt up. And the second angel sounded, and as it were a great mountain burning with fire was cast into the sea: and the third part of the sea became blood; and the third part of the creatures which were in the sea, and had life, died; and the third part of the ships were destroyed. And the third angel sounded, and there fell a great star from heaven, burning as it were a lamp, and it fell upon the third part of the rivers, and upon the fountains of waters; and the name of the star is called Wormwood: and the third part of the waters became wormwood; and many men died of the waters, because they were made bitter. And the fourth angel sounded, and the third part of the sun was smitten, and the third part of the moon, and the third part of the stars; so as the third part of them was darkened, and the day shone not for a third part of it, and the night likewise. And I beheld, and heard an angel flying through the midst of heaven, saying with a loud voice, Woe, woe, woe, to the inhabiters of the earth by reason of the other voices of the trumpet of the three angels, which are yet to sound!

When I was a boy, my dad once said to me, "Son, do you know what a child of God always possesses that the unconverted person doesn't have?" After telling me that he wished he could write the answer to this question with an iron pen on my heart (and he did because I

never forgot it!), he said, "A child of God always has a place to go."
He then proceeded to tell me that there is nothing so valuable in all
the earth as an open throne of grace, that prayer was more valuable
than all the money in the world, and that to neglect prayer was to
neglect one of the greatest privileges we have on earth.

What is your prayer life like? Do you truly believe in prayer?
Could you go a week without praying? Do you agree with John
Bunyan that prayer ought always to come first in our life—that we
can do more than pray after we have prayed, but we cannot do more
than pray until we have prayed?[1]

Prayer is the thermometer of our spiritual life, the breath of our
soul. Through it, we commune with God, who communes with us
through His Word.

I want to show you how Revelation 8 wonderfully opens up the
value of prayer for us.

The opening of the seventh seal in Revelation 8:1 concludes the
second cycle of visions and introduces a new cycle. Having brought
the reader to the awesome, mysterious silence of judgment day, the
visions of Revelation now backtrack to consider the last days from
another perspective.

Just as Christ brings in the kingdom of God by opening the
seven seals, so also He sends judgment upon the wicked through
the sounding of the seven trumpets. However, before the trumpets
sound, Christ reveals how these events are rooted in one of the
most amazing privileges possessed by Christians: Spirit-empowered
prayer to their God and Father through the mediation of Christ.

In this way, the third cycle of visions mingles themes already
seen by John in the ascent of the prayers of God's suffering people
(Rev. 6:9–11) and the descent of God's answering judgments upon
the earth (Rev. 6:12–17). Mercy and judgment join hands as God
glorifies His great name through His Son.

In this chapter, we will consider how the saints' prayers ascend
(vv. 2–5) and how the first four angels sound their trumpets (vv. 6–13).

---

1. John Bunyan, *Prayer* (Edinburgh: Banner of Truth, 1965), 13.

The Saints' Prayers Ascend to God

Though the heavenly silence of Revelation 8:1 is a sign of judgment, it also opens the way for the church's prayers to reach the throne of grace. God stills heaven, as it were, to hear the prayers of His children.[2] Revelation 8:2–6 is a prologue to the vision of the seven trumpets. We are told twice in verse 3 and again in verse 4 that these opening verses picture what happens to the prayers of the saints. This is a beautiful section that teaches us about prayer. Let us examine prayer under five headings.

The Point of Prayer

Revelation 8:2–5 must be understood within the context of what Christ has already revealed. Consider the significance of the scroll with seven seals in the right hand of Him who sits upon the throne. When the Lamb takes the book and opens its seals, He is fulfilling the eternal decrees of the sovereign God. The scroll contains all that God, as absolute Sovereign, has purposed and decreed—down to the most minute details.

What, then, is the point of praying? Why pray about things that trouble you when you believe in the absolute sovereignty of God? God answers these questions in this little paragraph. He says that we are to view our prayers as included in the eternal decrees of God. God has not only decreed from all eternity what will happen, but has also decreed that our prayers should be a means by which these things happen. He has ordained the end, but also the means to the end. And prayer is a very important means.[3]

That is also true of other means of grace, such as evangelism and the preaching of the gospel. God chose His elect before the foundations of the world were laid. He chose them not because of any goodness or worth in them, but because of His love and goodness. God chose a vast number that no man can count to be saved,

---

2. Beale, *The Book of Revelation*, 451.
3. Douglas F. Kelly, *If God Already Knows, Why Pray?* (Brentwood, Tenn.: Wolgemuth & Hyatt, 1989).

and God knows every one of them. So why bother to preach the gospel or witness to unbelievers when the Bible clearly teaches that God has already chosen those who will be saved?

The answer is that God has not only decreed who are to be saved, but has also decreed how they are to be saved. Again, He has decreed the means as well as the end. It pleases God to work through the preaching of the gospel and the testimony of believers to save unbelievers.

We might ask the same question about sanctification. If we are God's elect, and if God knows His own and chooses whom He will save, then why bother to live holy lives? Because God has decreed that a certain number of people will be saved, we might assume that, if we belong to that number, we will be saved no matter how we live. But that is not what the Bible teaches. The Bible says that God not only chooses us, but He also saves us by grace through faith and causes us to persevere in holiness. God decrees not only the end but the means to the end.

We should think of prayer the same way. In ways that we don't fully understand, God uses the prayers of His saints to carry out His eternal decrees. That is the message of Revelation 8:3–5. This teaching about prayer is not an appendix to the visions of God's mighty acts in history. It is an integral part of God's fulfilling His decree. Notice how verse 2 tells us the seven angels are given trumpets, but in the vision their sounding of the trumpets is delayed until after we see our prayers rising to heaven. Our prayers are intimately bound up with what is going on in the world today. They are a part of the execution of God's eternal decrees.

Prayer does not twist God's arm to induce Him to change His mind. The old cliché that prayer changes things is only partly true. Prayer does not change *God's* mind, for His mind is already made up. However, prayer changes *our* minds. It brings us in line with the will of God.

Let me illustrate. When a man in a boat wants to come back to land, he guides his boat into a harbor and then throws out a line to the shore. When the rope is secured on the shore, the man pulls on the rope as though he were pulling the shore to him. But really he is pulling himself to shore. Likewise, when we pray, we think we are pulling God to us, but really we are pulling ourselves to God. That is what it means to lay hold of God. You cannot bring God in line with your plans. Rather, when you pray, you bring yourself in line with God's eternal purposes and decrees. To lay hold upon God is to align yourself with His will and purposes.

Richard Trench writes that we must not "conceive of prayer as an overcoming of God's reluctance, when it is, in fact, a laying hold of his highest willingness."[4] Yet many of us think of prayer as persuading a reluctant God. We have a horrible view of God as a distant deity who is reluctant to have anything to do with us. We do not pray to overcome God's *reluctance*, but to lay hold of His *willingness*. It is the unchangeableness of God and His decrees that gives meaning and significance to prayer, for as we pray, the Holy Spirit leads us to pray according to the will of God (Rom. 8:26–27). If God acted like a chameleon, changing His will from one day to the next depending on the prayers sent His way, then what would be the point of praying? But our God is not like that. He is immutable in His eternal decrees. In Him there is no variableness or shadow of turning. So when you pray to Him, you may be assured that what you say really matters, for God is aligning your desires and requests with what He intends to accomplish.

Prayer is not just a way to beautify your spiritual life or a self-help therapy to make you feel good. Prayer is a powerful means that God uses to carry out His eternal decrees. And, as verse 3 says, He uses the prayers of *all* the saints. The devil tries to tell you that prayer doesn't count, but he is a liar and has been so from the beginning. God always listens to the prayers of His saints, for they are a part of His plan.

---

4. Richard C. Trench, *Notes on the Parables of the Lord*, 10th ed. rev. (London: Macmillan and Co., 1866), 330.

The People Who Pray

In verses 3 and 4, John says "the prayers of all saints" are brought to
God. So who is a saint? Look through the New Testament Epistles
and see how Christians in places such as Rome, Corinth, Philippi,
and Ephesus are addressed. All believers in those places are called
saints. The Bible applies the word *saint* to any person who genuinely
trusts Jesus Christ as Savior and Lord. The word *saint* is synonymous with the word *Christian*.

    Saint literally means "set-apart one" or "sanctified one." When
we turn from sin to Christ, God sets us apart from the world around
us, seals us with His Holy Spirit, and calls us to pursue holiness of
life. We now belong to Christ as members of His body, and we
belong to God as His children and heirs. And God listens to the
prayers of all His saints. This passage tells us that.

    Scripture does not guarantee that God will hear the prayers of
people who are not believers. Nor does it say that God is deaf to
them. Old writers used to call God's answers to unbelievers' prayers
uncovenanted blessings. By that, they meant that it sometimes pleases
God to answer the prayers of those who are not in covenant with
Him. Many unconverted people believe in the power of prayer. They
do not know Christ as their Savior and Lord, but they still can say,
"There have been many times when God has answered my prayers
and helped me." God, for His own glory, might hear the prayers of
unbelievers, but He is not bound to do so. He has not covenanted to
do so. But this passage and the rest of the Bible teach us that God
has promised to hear the prayers of all His saints.

    Where do our prayers reside? According to verse 3, the prayers
of the saints are "upon the golden altar which was before the throne."
Some people use this passage to justify erroneous doctrine. They
teach that God has a storehouse of the saints' meritorious prayers
that have not yet been used. Roman Catholicism teaches that God
enables saints in heaven to hear our prayers. Because they can join
their prayers to ours, we must ask them for help in our prayers.

    None of this is to be found in the Scriptures, however. There
is no merit laid up for us in heaven in the prayers of the greatest

saints. The image of the golden altar points to the priestly work of Christ to make blood atonement and intercession for His people (Ex. 30:10). The prayers of all the saints, however holy and good, rest upon the altar of God, Jesus Christ. All the merit is in Christ's bloody atonement placed upon the altar. You and I have no right to be heard in heaven because of who we are. Our prayers are accepted only through the merits of Christ.

We need to remind ourselves often of this truth. At times, even a believer may say: "I pray to God and I believe according to His will, but He has not answered my prayers. I can't understand it. I have been a Christian for years and been faithful to the church. Why won't God hear my prayers?" Perhaps the problem is that your prayers have not been offered on the altar of Christ's bloody atonement, but upon what you think you have done for the Lord. God hears our prayers only when they rest on the altar of sacrifice and are based on the merits of our Lord Jesus Christ.

The Presentation of Our Prayers to God

Also in verses 3 and 4, John records how the prayers of all saints are presented to God: "And another angel came and stood at the altar, having a golden censer; and there was given unto him much incense, that he should offer it with the prayers of all saints upon the golden altar which was before the throne. And the smoke of the incense, which came with the prayers of the saints, ascended up before God out of the angel's hand."

This special angel is either Christ or someone who represents Him. He has been given "much incense" to mingle with the prayers of the saints. Charles H. Spurgeon says of this image: "Our great High Priest is here represented as standing at the golden altar which is before the throne of God, having in his hand a golden censer full of incense, the fragrance of which would give acceptance to the prayers of the saints for his sake."[5] As Spurgeon notes, the addition of this incense makes the prayers of the saints acceptable to God. It

---

5. Spurgeon, *Metropolitan Tabernacle Pulpit*, 57:613.

completely absorbs what is earthly, fleshly, sinful, and selfish in their prayer, and infuses their prayer with the sweet savor that is pleasing to the nostrils of God.

The incense that is mingled with our tainted prayers so they become acceptable to God is *the intercession of Christ*. It is encouraging to know that Jesus ever lives to make intercession for us (Heb. 7:25). He is our Great High Priest, who has more than enough incense to absorb all the faults of our prayers. Christ mingles His intercession with our intercession to cover the taint, selfishness, and earthiness of our prayers, and then He transforms them into that which is acceptable to His Father and presents our poor prayers to Him, washed in His own blood-purchased merits. He makes something big out of something small; something beautiful out of something homely.

Just as Christ intercedes for us in heaven, so also the Holy Spirit helps us in our weakness on earth. There are times when I find it difficult to pray in words; all I can do is groan or sigh. I want to pray, but I don't have the words to say. As Paul says, "We know not what we should pray for as we ought." As the gift of Christ, the Spirit dwells in us and assists us in prayer: "The Spirit also maketh intercession for us with groanings which cannot be uttered" (Rom. 8:26). So we have not one but two divine supports in prayer: the intercession of Christ and the intercession of the Spirit. This two-fold support means that however flawed, incoherent, or feeble our prayers may be, they have substance and value in the sight of God. Such is the plentiful incense that is added to our prayers as they are presented to God.[6]

God wanted the Christians whom John addresses to understand this, for some would be thrown into prison; some would be tortured; and some would be martyred. In their suffering and pain, when all they could do was groan and sigh, those sounds would become powerful prayers because of the intercessory work of Christ in heaven and the Holy Spirit in their hearts.

---

6. See KJV marginal note on Revelation 8:3.

It is also encouraging to know that there is *much* incense, because our prayers are so poor. James tells us we often ask amiss, if we ask at all (James 4:2–3). Also, as we saw above, we don't know what we should ask of God. But when we come in the name of Christ, trusting in His merits and convinced that He is our Great High Priest in heaven, and when we rely on the help of the Spirit, then our feeblest attempts at prayer go to heaven, where they rest on the altar of God. Our prayers are not lost in space. They go further than the ceiling of the church, the bedroom, or the dining room. They are mingled with the intercessions of Christ and the Spirit, and they are presented before the throne of God.

The Potential of Our Prayers
After the prayers of the saints have been presented to the Father through the intercessions of Christ, we read, "And the seven angels which had the seven trumpets prepared themselves to sound" (Rev. 8:6). Seven angels are in attendance upon your prayers. They are waiting around the throne of grace for your prayers to be accepted by the Father.

We are unsure about the precise meaning of many images in Revelation. For example, should we think of the angels in verse 6 as "presence angels"—angels who stand in the immediate presence of God? There is some support for the idea of a hierarchy of angels in the Bible. Gabriel refers to himself as the angel "that stand[s] in the presence of God" (Luke 1:19). But in some sense, that could be said of all the angels. Within the context of Revelation 8, it is perhaps better to understand these seven angels the way we interpret the number seven throughout this book. It is a number of completeness. We should then think of these angels as representative of the multitude of angels who are in the presence of God. The comfort for us here is that God has a multitude of angels standing by to carry out His answers to our prayers. This interpretation is in line with the teaching of the rest of Scripture. Hebrews 1:14 describes angels as God's "ministering spirits, sent forth to minister for them who shall be heirs of salvation." They are far greater than we are in many respects, yet they wait on us as servants.

Think of a young prince who, as an infant, is waited upon by lords and ladies. He is inferior to them in attainments, but he is superior to them in status. That is the picture we have here. As believers, we are designed by God to be kings and priests. We have the royal blood of heaven in us. Thus, God's angels exist to stand around heaven and wait for our prayers to ascend so that they might carry out our wishes.

The parable of the rich man and Lazarus beautifully illustrates this. Luke 16:22 describes what happened after the two men died: "And it came to pass, that the beggar died, and was carried by the angels into Abraham's bosom: the rich man also died, and was buried." There is a stark contrast. The rich man's body was buried, and his soul sank into hell. But when Lazarus died, God sent His angels to carry him into the glory of heaven.

That is a wonderful truth, not just a parable. God has given His angels charge over us to keep us in all our ways, lest we should dash our foot against a stone (Ps. 91:11–12). What a comfort that was for John on Patmos, where he lived in exile near the end of his life. What a comfort that was to the saints on the mainland, who were about to be brutally persecuted by Roman authorities. What a comfort it is for us to know that God has a battalion of angels ready to lift us up, lest we fall and hurt ourselves. As the hymn writer says,

> Come, make your wants, your burdens known,
> He will present them at the throne;
> And angel bands are waiting there
> His messages of love to bear.[7]

That is the message of Revelation 8. We may come with all our needs and burdens to the throne, where Jesus Christ, our Great High Priest, stands at the right hand of God the Father. He is ready and willing to accept our prayers. He improves them, corrects them,

---

7. Josiah Conder, "The Lord Is King! Life Up Thy Voice" (1824).

and presents them to His Father. Bands of angels constantly wait around the prayer desk of God. No cold, distant answering service takes messages for later processing. Instead, multitudes of angels attend the throne of grace, eager to carry out God's will.

The Power of Prayer
When God's saints pray in the name of Jesus, great things happen. Revelation 8:5–6 says: "And the angel took the censer, and filled it with fire of the altar, and cast it into the earth: and there were voices, and thunderings, and lightnings, and an earthquake. And the seven angels which had the seven trumpets prepared themselves to sound."

Prayer is powerful and effective in this world because God takes more notice of the prayers of His saints than He does of the dictates or decrees of governments. When the prayers of the saints ascended to God in heaven, John writes that the earth was shaken with thunder, rumblings, flashes of lightning, and an earthquake as seven angels prepared to sound seven trumpets. God wants to impress upon us the effectiveness of prayer. That is what this symbolism of thunder, lightning, and an earthquake means—as if God were coming to earth again as He did on Mt. Sinai (Ex. 19:16). God is saying this: "By your prayers, I will overthrow governments. I will confound human plans; I will turn the world upside down, casting the wicked to the ground and delivering My ransomed people."

Consider the early church and its saints, who were being persecuted by the Romans. They were a despised minority within an empire that ruled most of the known world. Yet within a few centuries, Rome had fallen. In Acts, Christians were charged with turning the world upside down (Acts 17:6). The same was true of the Christians John writes to; eventually they would turn the world on its head, not by fighting or waging war, but by preaching the gospel and by praying. Preaching and prayer are so powerful that they shake the world like earthquakes, thunder, and lightning.

Derek Thomas writes, "Our prayers may make little impact to those who hear them in this world, but when they reach heaven, they are sent back (in George Herbert's phrase) as 'reversed thunder.' The power of prayer is truly immense!"[8]

Preaching and prayer are linked throughout history. For example, think of how the Protestant Reformation shook the Roman Catholic Church as if by thunder and lightning. Through the prayers of God's saints—Martin Luther, John Knox, and his son-in-law, John Welsh, as well as ordinary believers—church and state were turned upside down.[9]

Consider as well the Great Awakening in our country. For years, people had been praying for revival in the church, including, perhaps, some old men and women who had been praying quietly for years for the salvation of their children. God responded by moving the hearts of tens of thousands of people to repent of their sin and cleave to Christ. So the thunder, lightning, and voices of Revelation 8:5 represent the immense effectiveness of prayer.

That precedes the sounding of the seven trumpets, beginning in verse 6 and continuing all the way to Revelation 11:15. Notice what happens when the last trumpet is blown. Revelation 11:15 says, "And the seventh angel sounded; and there were great voices in heaven, saying, The kingdoms of this world are become the kingdoms of our Lord, and of his Christ; and he shall reign for ever and ever." That is what the sounding of the seven trumpets leads up to: the earth quakes; powers are shaken; governments are overthrown; and suffering saints are delivered by the return of Jesus Christ, who will establish His kingdom on the earth.

Joshua 6 makes a similar point. When the Israelites were confronted with the mighty fortress of Jericho, God told them to march around the city for seven days. On the seventh, they were to march around seven times. On the last trip around, seven priests blew their trumpets. The people shouted, and the walls of Jericho

---

8. Derek Thomas, *Let's Study Revelation* (Edinburgh: Banner of Truth, 2003), 69.

9. See Joel R. Beeke and Brian G. Najapfour, ed., *Taking Hold of God: Reformed and Puritan Perspectives on Prayer* (Grand Rapids: Reformation Heritage Books, 2011).

collapsed. That is what God is going to do in the world. At present, God is encircling the stronghold of the enemy. When the last trump sounds, however, earth will crumble, and the kingdoms of this earth will become the kingdoms of God and His Christ. Revelation 8:5 says God will do that by hurling fire on the earth.

That reminds us of Luke 12:49, where Jesus says to His disciples, "I am come to send fire on the earth." He tells them about His coming to earth, including His birth, life, death, and resurrection, as if to say: "This is the effect of My coming into the world. I have come to spread fire upon the earth." Through the prayers of the saints and the faithful preaching of the crucified Savior, God's eternal purposes will be carried out.

We too need the fiery preaching of the cross. We need fire from the altar to be hurled upon the earth. We need a live coal from the altar to touch our lips. We need the great truth of the gospel to be burned into us. And when fire from the altar comes upon sinners, there will be thunder, lightning, and voices. It is through the gospel that God saves His people, and it is through the gospel that God judges the world.

The Angels' Trumpets Sound

When John moves from the seven seals to the seven trumpets, we can't help but notice a pattern. Just as the first four seals belong together, the sounding of the first four trumpets also seem to belong together. After the four seals are opened, we are given a glorious picture of the saints in heaven. But then we move from the blessed security of the redeemed in glory to the terrible state of those who do not know the Lord Jesus Christ. Likewise, after the first four trumpets blow, there is a kind of pause, during which John hears an angel cry, "Woe, woe, woe" (Rev. 8:13), as if to say, "The worst is yet to come."

Each of the seven angels is given a trumpet. Trumpets, especially in apocalyptic writing in the Bible, are often associated with the end times. For example, in Matthew 24:31, which closely parallels what happens in Revelation 5 and 6, Jesus speaks about the sounding of a trumpet. In 1 Corinthians 15:52, Paul speaks about the day when the trumpet shall sound and when the dead in Christ shall rise. But these angelic trumpets do not immediately herald the return of Christ. They warn us of disasters in the world. Three things happen when the first four trumpets blow in Revelation 8:7–13.

Worldly Security Ends

The unraveling of worldly security is the first message of the trumpets. That echoes how God used Moses to bring plagues upon Egypt to teach the Egyptians that they could not depend on their own strength or resources. Archaeology tells us that Egypt at the time of Moses had amazing, almost limitless riches. The pharaohs of Egypt had built great monuments, such as temples, sphinxes, and pyramids that are still among the greatest wonders of the world. Egypt was rich, strong, and self-sufficient. But then, under the hand of God, one eighty-year-old man who walked out of the desert brought this proud country to its knees to teach its people that their power was not in riches, prestige, or man-made gods. None of those refuges are secure in this life.

The theme of unraveling security is everywhere in Revelation. It is apparent as the first angel blows a trumpet, and a third of the earth is burned up, along with a third of the trees and all the green grass (v. 7). It is apparent in the sounding of the second trumpet, when "a great mountain burning with fire" falls into the sea, turning a third of the water into blood, killing a third of the sea creatures, and destroying a third of the ships (vv. 8–9). With the third trumpet comes the fall of a great star that blazes like a torch before landing in a third of the rivers and springs of water on earth, turning them bitter (vv. 10–11). With the fourth trumpet, a third of the light from the sun, moon, and stars is extinguished, resulting in thick darkness a third of the day and a third of the night (v. 12). Because all life depends on the energy of the sun, this sign is a powerful warning for people not to feel secure even in the sources of light and physical life. The Lord is warning us, too, not to trust in our own strength, attainments, or riches.

Yet these verses are also comforting for believers. Believers stand in awe when God shakes their communities, nations, or the whole world order. They learn once more that they have no resources in themselves. But when the praise of man, earthly glory, and our temples and towers fall to the dust, the believer has an unshakable hope, for God is our refuge (Psalm 46). John, who is marginalized on the island of Patmos, writes to the marginalized Christians on the mainland to tell them that the great empires of the world will be destroyed. Though they are ruled by cruel and wicked men who despise the gospel, all will be overthrown because everything they trust for security is utterly unreliable. Kingdoms rise and fall; men and women build little castles on the sand, that are then washed over by the sea. Nothing of this world or in it lasts forever.

Some people today are feeling the pain of unraveling security in the loss of jobs, spouses, homes, or friends. Though this process is painful, it may be an answer to some of the prayers of God's people. Such insecurity might be necessary to bring people to their knees before God. Conversion does not always happen in sweetness and light. Saul of Tarsus was thrown to the ground and struck blind before he acknowledged that Jesus Christ is Lord (Acts 9). He had to come to the end of himself to be transformed by God, who offers eternal security only through the blood of His Son.

Judgment Is Imminent

In the Old Testament, a trumpet was used to sound an alarm. Likewise, the trumpets of Revelation 8 warn us of what is to come. They do not refer to the final judgment, but to God's judgments in history that warn us of the final judgment. "He is the LORD our God: his judgments are in all the earth" (Ps. 105:7). They are much like God's judgments in the form of the plagues on Egypt. For example, Revelation 8:7 says, "The first angel sounded, and there followed hail and fire mingled with blood, and they were cast upon the earth: and the third part of trees was burnt up, and all green grass was burnt up." Compare that with what Exodus 9:23–26 says: "And Moses stretched forth his rod toward heaven: and the LORD sent thunder and hail, and the fire ran along upon the ground; and the LORD rained hail upon the land of Egypt. So there was hail, and fire mingled with the hail, very grievous, such as there was none like it in all the land of Egypt since it became a nation. And the hail smote throughout all the land of Egypt all that was in the field, both man and beast; and the hail smote every herb of the field, and brake every tree of the field. Only in the land of Goshen, where the children of Israel were, was there no hail." In both passages, terrible things happen to unbelievers, but the people of God are secure. Likewise, both passages do not refer to the final judgment, but to the series of judgments upon the powers of this world, who harden their hearts to the word of God.

Note also Revelation 8:8–9a: "And the second angel sounded, and as it were a great mountain burning with fire was cast into the sea: and the third part of the sea became blood; and the third part of the creatures which were in the sea, and had life, died." The creatures of the sea died because God turned the water into stinking blood. Similarly, many fish died when God used Moses to turn the Nile into blood as a warning to Pharaoh (Ex. 7:20–21).

Revelation 8:10–11 describes the sounding of the third trumpet, which provokes the fall of "a great star from heaven, burning as it were a lamp, and it fell upon the third part of the rivers, and upon the fountains of waters; and the name of the star is called Wormwood: and the…waters…were made bitter." That echoes Exodus 7:21-25, which says that the Egyptians could not drink the water of the Nile because it had been turned into blood.

Then the next trumpet sounds. According to Revelation 8:12a, "The fourth angel sounded, and the third part of the sun was smitten, and the third part of the moon, and the third part of the stars." That judgment of darkness is very much like that of Exodus 10:21–23, when thick darkness covered Egypt. Surpassing this judgment of darkness upon Egypt, however, is the judgment of darkness upon all the earth when our Lord Jesus Christ was crucified on Calvary (Matt. 27:45).

These judgments include economic, ecological, industrial, and physical disasters upon the earth. The apostle John teaches us that we are to listen to the voice of God in history, particularly to His judgments against sin. Furthermore, we must respond to them by repenting of our sins, unlike Pharaoh, whose heart clamped shut against God. Sadly, this failure to listen to God and repent is often recounted by the prophets of the Old Testament. For example, Amos quotes God saying to the people, "I have smitten you with blasting and mildew...yet have ye not returned unto me" (Amos 4:9).

The extreme and terrifying images of disaster need not be taken to refer to the end of the world. Rather, they echo symbolism used through the Old Testament for temporal, national judgments. As Reformed exegetes have noted:

> Storm images can symbolize historical judgments against nations (Ps. 18:11–14; Isa. 28:1–3; 30:30–31). The fall of a *mountain* into the sea is a symbol of national calamity (Ps. 46:2). Blowing trumpets, casting down mountains, and throwing a rock into the sea are images of the overthrow of Babylon ([Rev.] 18:21; Jer. 51:25–29, 63–64). Forcing people to drink bitterness (*wormwood*) signifies bitter experiences like invasion, defeat, and exile (Jer. 8:14–16; 9:15–16; 23:15; Lam. 3:15, 19). Sun and moon struck (*smitten*) with darkness can be a sign of conquest by a foreign power (Ezek. 32:2, 7–8, 11). Therefore, these trumpets symbolize natural and political disasters throughout this age that display God's sovereignty over creation, supremacy over man's idols, and wrath against sin.[10]

This judgment does not happen only on a national or international level. God also chastens us personally. When we live in disobedience to Him, He chastens us. At the same time, He is patiently working with us to turn us back to Him. Despite warnings, many people will not repent. Revelation 9:20–21 says: "The rest of the men...yet repented not of the works of their hands, that

---

10. *Reformation Heritage KJV Study Bible*, 1877.

they should not worship devils, and idols of gold, and silver, and brass, and stone, and of wood: which neither can see, nor hear, nor walk. Neither repented they of their murders...their sorceries... their fornication, nor of their thefts." C. S. Lewis says, "God whispers to us in our pleasures, speaks to us in our conscience, but shouts to us in our pains."[11]

Characteristically, when a seal is opened, damage is done to a quarter of things on earth. But when the trumpets sound, damage increases to a third. And when the seven vials are poured out, the damage is done to everything. There is a sense that things are moving toward the climax of what God is going to do.

God Is Patient

The world has not yet been destroyed, even though it has been nearly two thousand years since the time of John's vision. That tells us our God is patient. As Paul asks, "Despisest thou the riches of his goodness and forbearance and longsuffering; not knowing that the goodness of God leadeth thee to repentance?" (Rom. 2:4). In the course of history, God has granted such periods of remission as space for repentance. There were times when it has seemed as if the world was moving toward some extraordinary disaster. Yet in His infinite mercy and patience, God held back the tide of judgment.

God is patient not because He is slack about fulfilling and carrying out His judgments. Peter warns us that some people may have that misunderstanding, and that it could lead to their everlasting peril: "There shall come in the last days scoffers, walking after their own lusts, and saying, Where is the promise of his coming? for since the fathers fell asleep, all things continue as they were from the beginning of the creation. For this they willingly are ignorant of, that by the word of God the heavens were of old, and the earth standing out of the water and in the water" (2 Peter 3:3b–5). Peter then describes the judgment of God upon the world in the days of Noah. Verses 7–10a say: "But the heavens and the earth, which are

---

11. C. S. Lewis, *The Problem of Pain* (New York: Macmillan, 1948), 81.

now, by the same word are kept in store, reserved unto fire against the day of judgment and perdition of ungodly men. But, beloved, be not ignorant of this one thing, that one day is with the Lord as a thousand years, and a thousand years as one day. The Lord is not slack concerning his promise, as some men count slackness; but is longsuffering to us-ward, not willing that any should perish, but that all should come to repentance. But the day of the Lord will come as a thief in the night."

God's patience is amazing, but it is also a mystery to us. When an earthquake levels a city or a tsunami kills thousands of people, we tend to ask, "Why did God allow this disaster to happen?" The real question is why God allows us to go on unscathed. Why does He allow the world to continue despite its outrageous sinfulness against Him? Why doesn't He destroy it now, just as He once destroyed Sodom and Gomorrah? Are we less sinful than the people of those cities?

God allows us to go on because of His amazing patience. The heart of God longs for people to come to repentance. That is the mystery that lies at the heart of the universe. Very few people are perplexed by that. They are much too occupied with why God allows disasters to happen. They should heed the tragic words of Revelation 9:20: "And the rest of the men which were not killed by these plagues yet repented not of the works of their hands, that they should not worship devils, and idols of gold, and silver, and brass, and stone, and of wood: which neither can see, nor hear, nor walk." The real tragedy is the iniquity that persists despite God's warnings.

As the fourth angel blows his trumpet, John hears an eagle cry, "Woe, woe, woe" (Rev. 8:13). When a speaker or writer in the Bible wants to emphasize a word, he repeats it. For example, when Jesus says "Verily, verily" or "Amen, amen," He is stressing the importance of His words. But rarely do you hear the same word said three times in a row.

John teaches that as long as you are in the world, you must be a witness to it, even if you are persecuted or killed for your testimony. You can do that trusting that you are sealed and secure in

Christ Jesus, for He is the same yesterday, today, and forever. If you are without Christ, however, heed the warning of Revelation 8:13: "Woe, woe, woe, to the inhabiters of the earth by reason of the other voices of the trumpet of the three angels, which are yet to sound!" In other words, *repent, repent, repent*—before God sounds the final trump, and the gospel door of opportunity is forever shut.

17

The Woes of Demon-Commissioned Judgment

REVELATION 9:1–21

And the fifth angel sounded, and I saw a star fall from heaven unto the earth: and to him was given the key of the bottomless pit. And he opened the bottomless pit; and there arose a smoke out of the pit, as the smoke of a great furnace; and the sun and the air were darkened by reason of the smoke of the pit. And there came out of the smoke locusts upon the earth: and unto them was given power, as the scorpions of the earth have power. And it was commanded them that they should not hurt the grass of the earth, neither any green thing, neither any tree; but only those men which have not the seal of God in their foreheads.... And the sixth angel sounded, and I heard a voice from the four horns of the golden altar which is before God, saying to the sixth angel which had the trumpet, Loose the four angels which are bound in the great river Euphrates. And the four angels were loosed, which were prepared for an hour, and a day, and a month, and a year, for to slay the third part of men. And the number of the army of the horsemen were two hundred thousand thousand: and I heard the number of them. And thus I saw the horses in the vision, and them that sat on them, having breastplates of fire, and of jacinth, and brimstone: and the heads of the horses were as the heads of lions; and out of their mouths issued fire and smoke and brimstone. By these three was the third part of men killed, by the fire, and by the smoke, and by the brimstone, which issued out of their mouths.... And the rest of the men which were not killed by these plagues yet repented not of the works of their hands, that they should not worship devils, and idols of gold, and silver, and brass, and stone, and of wood: which neither can see, nor hear, nor walk: Neither repented they of their murders, nor of their sorceries, nor of their fornication, nor of their thefts.

The book of Job and other passages in the Bible teach us that Satan's judgments are ruled by God, who actually commissions them. True believers who repent before God, are sealed by His grace, and take refuge in Christ by faith will be protected from God's ultimate judgment. But those who do not repent and do not believe the gospel will perish forever. God controls Satan so that he cannot ultimately harm believers, but is an instrument for the destruction of the wicked—that is the theme of Revelation 9.

The book of Revelation comforts God's suffering saints and warns hardened unbelievers. When we deal with the woes, the plagues, and the descriptions and symbols in this book, we should understand them spiritually. Revelation is a spiritual book meant for the whole church of Christ.

In the previous chapter, we began studying John's account of the seven trumpets. As we will see, seven vials of wrath follow the seven trumpets. The trumpets warn, whereas the vials pour out. The account of the seven trumpets is God's warning to us of judgment to come. They are not trumpets of doom but of warning.

We learned in the previous chapter that the first four trumpets speak about judgments on creation and are grouped together much like the first four of the seven seals. The first four seals are grouped into one picture of the four horsemen (6:1–8). Likewise, the first four trumpets are separated from the other three by a kind of intermission in Revelation 8:13, which pronounces a triple "woe" in regard to the three trumpets to come. During the intermission, John prepares himself emotionally and spiritually for the massive woes to follow. God is sensitive to the emotions of the apostle, for John is about to see things even more terrifying than what has already been revealed.

Let us look at these great woes under three headings: the fifth trumpet and the first woe (Rev. 9:1–12); the sixth trumpet and the second woe (vv. 13–19); and finally, the greatest woe (vv. 20–21).

The Fifth Trumpet and the First Woe

Revelation 9:1 says, "And the fifth angel sounded, and I saw a star fall from heaven unto the earth: and to him was given the key of the bottomless pit." Next John sees clouds of smoke billowing out of this abyss, along with an awful plague of locusts (vv. 2–3). The only way to understand the symbolism of this vision is in terms of the devil and his angels. We cannot understand the plague of locusts in terms of nature because these locusts cannot be found in any book of natural history. Locusts don't wear crowns, nor do they have teeth like lions or hair like that of women (vv. 7–8). We do not have here a literal account of a plague of locusts.

Neither do we find the significance of this vision in human history. We should not identify this plague of locusts with Muslims, Communists, Nazis, Roman Catholics, or any human army. Though many people have tended to do this in the past, we cannot see this vision as a particular movement of human history.

We must find the proper understanding of this imagery in the supernatural realm. John describes the unseen principalities and powers that operate behind the affairs of this world. Infernal forces and powers are seeking to destroy mankind. Satan and his demons want to destroy every human being. Thus, the warning of the fifth trumpet is simply this: the only alternative to salvation is destruction.

The locusts are given power to harm all people except those who have the seal of God on their foreheads (v. 4). The sealed ones have been freed from their sins by Christ's blood through faith in Him (Rev. 7:1–3, 14). They now serve as priests and kings in God's kingdom. Blessed are those who are forever sealed by the Holy Spirit as citizens of God's kingdom! Are you one of them? Have you been freed from your sins by the blood of Christ?

This trumpet warns that those who are not sealed or owned by Christ do not belong to Him. If that is the case for you, you are wide open to demonic forces and influences. The teaching of the Bible is clear: if you do not belong to Christ today, then you must belong to Satan and his demons.

Paul sounds a similar warning in 1 Corinthians 5. He tells the church to "deliver such an one unto Satan" (v. 5), treating him as an unbeliever and excommunicating him from the church. To be excommunicated is to be pushed out of the church and into the devil's realm. That is how the Bible sees it. Not to be Christ's is to be the devil's. If you are an unbeliever; if you do not have the seal of God upon your forehead; if you are not owned by Christ, then your life is vulnerable to infernal forces and powers that will destroy you forever. This fifth trumpet warns you to ask whether your future is with Christ or with the devil.

John tells us in verse 1 that when the fifth trumpet sounded, he saw a star fall to the earth. The Greek tells us that John saw a star that had already fallen. This star is given the key to the bottomless pit—the abyss. Since the star uses the key (v. 2), it symbolizes a person. John is not describing the cosmic catastrophe of a falling star; he is not talking in terms of astronomy. This star has personality. Therefore, John is talking about a person.

Revelation 9 offers us a symbolic description of Satan and his power in this world. This description is confirmed in other places in Scripture. In Isaiah 14, the prophet, who is speaking about the king of Babylon and his influence in the world, suddenly moves beyond history. You might say he goes backstage to describe what lies behind the forces of history: "How art thou fallen from heaven, O Lucifer, son of the morning! how art thou cut down to the ground, which didst weaken the nations! For thou hast said in thine heart, I will ascend into heaven, I will exalt my throne above the stars of God: I will sit also upon the mount of the congregation, in the sides of the north: I will ascend above the heights of the clouds; I will be like the most High. Yet thou shalt be brought down to hell, to the sides of the pit" (vv. 12–15). Lucifer, or Satan, is the star that has fallen from heaven. He is the leader of the fallen angels (Jude 6) whom God has cast out of heaven.

Similarly, in Ezekiel 28, the prophet sees Satan and all the forces of hell represented by the king of Tyre: "Thou hast been in Eden the garden of God…. Thou wast perfect in thy ways from the day that thou wast created, till iniquity was found in thee…. Thou hast sinned: therefore I will cast thee as profane out of the mountain of God" (vv. 13–16). This is a prophetic account of what lies behind human history. It is a hint, not a full explanation, about the origin of evil in this world. Beyond creation and human history, and beyond even the fall of man in the Garden of Eden, stands this fallen angel. He is the destroyer, this angel of the pit who has been cast out of heaven. His name is Lucifer.

This is later confirmed in Revelation 9:11: "They had a king over them, which is the angel of the bottomless pit, whose name in the Hebrew tongue is Abaddon, but in the Greek tongue hath his name Apollyon." *Abbadon* (Hebrew) and *Apollyon* (Greek) both mean "destroyer." Satan is the evil one who seeks to torment and destroy. John looks behind the curtain of history, as it were, to see what stands behind the Roman Empire and its persecuting forces. He sees the destroyer and his hordes of hell, the principalities and powers of evil, the spiritual hosts of wickedness that are set against us. That is the meaning of "the pit" or "the abyss," which in Scripture is a description of hell before the judgment.

What a frightening picture of the powers of hell! The smoke billows out of the pit, blocks the light of the sun, and darkens the atmosphere (v. 2). Satan always works under the cover of darkness. The devil blinds the eyes of those who are lost, lest they should believe and be saved. He works through delusion and deceit. He works in the dark and keeps his victims in the dark.

Then, out of the pit of delusion comes a plague of locusts (v. 3). What a picture of devastation! These locusts, unlike any that we know of, are not allowed to harm the grass, green things, and trees on the earth (v. 4). Yet what awful destruction these locusts wreak on human beings! William Hendriksen writes:

> We should take the picture as a whole. The locusts like horses prepared for battle; those crowns of pseudo-gold foreboding

victory; those faces like human beings who are bent only
on destruction; that hair as of furies; those teeth as of lions;
those breastplates of iron portending invincibility; that sound
of wings like the noise of countless prancing horses and jolt-
ing chariots on the field of battle; and last but not least, that
exceedingly painful and burning, yet not fatal, scorpion-sting,
striking terror into the hearts of men and filling their souls
with the worst conceivable dread and utter hopelessness, so
that they seek death but cannot find it—can you conceive of
a more frightful and horrible *and true* picture of darkness in
the souls of the wicked during this present age? Here are the
demons, robbing men of all light, that is, righteousness and
holiness, joy and peace, wisdom and understanding.[1]

Borrowing imagery from the prophet Joel, John compares these
locusts to a mighty invading army of demons let loose by their leader,
Satan. They devour everything in their path, including the work of
Christ on the earth. The locusts appear to have human faces, showing that demonic powers are intelligent and discerning. John speaks
of them as having women's hair and teeth like lions to show how
they can be both seductive and ferocious. The sting of this plague
of locusts is described in verses 4–5 as the torment of the scorpion,
which is so painful its victims want to die: "And in those days shall
men seek death, and shall not find it; and shall desire to die, and
death shall flee from them" (v. 6). What a description of life without
God! People will beg to die. Yet death will flee from them.

Have you ever felt that your life was meaningless and futile?
Have you wanted to give up on family, friends, and work? Have you
so lost heart that you longed for death? When you shut God out,
the sun is obscured by clouds from hell, the smoke from the pit,
the -*isms* of the world, the lies and errors of Satan, and repeated,
unrepented sin. When you push God behind a smoke screen, life
becomes nothing but vanity: "Vanity of vanities; all is vanity," as
Ecclesiastes 1:2 says. You go from one day to the next and see no

1. Hendrickson, *More Than Conquerors*, 121–22.

purpose in it. Life becomes a burden. In one sense, you may want to die, yet you are afraid to die.

John offers us an accurate picture of life under the power of the evil one. This trumpet blast is a powerful warning about the work of the devil and his angels. John shows us what lies behind what you and I can see and touch, the spiritual realm of the hosts of wickedness.

Someone might object that if the whole world is under the power of the evil one, how does the real world fit with the gospel message of a sovereign God and a saved people? If Satan and his hordes of demons roam this world and hold sway in the hearts of men and women, where is the sovereignty of God? Ultimately, how can we have any hope?

The answer appears in Revelation 9:1. The devil is given the key to the pit. The fact that the key must be given to him reminds us that Satan has limited access to this world, for he and his servants are already under divine judgment. Within the sovereignty of God, however, the devil with his hordes of hell are granted a measure of freedom. The devil is thus under the control of God and Christ. There are not two opposing lords and forces in this world—God and the devil. There is only one Sovereign, the risen and ascended Christ. The Father has given all power into Christ's hands. He reigns supreme, and He has the devil under His control.

Furthermore, the devil's use of the key is limited: "And there came out of the smoke locusts upon the earth: and unto them was given power, as the scorpions of the earth have power. And it was commanded them that they should not hurt the grass of the earth, neither any green thing, neither any tree; but only those men which have not the seal of God in their foreheads. And to them it was given that they should not kill them, but that they should be tormented five months: and their torment was as the torment of a scorpion, when he striketh a man" (vv. 3–5). Verse 10 adds, "They had tails like unto scorpions, and there were stings in their tails: and their power was to hurt men five months." The power of the devil and his minions is not absolute power; it is given to them by God, and it is limited and used only under God's direction and command.

In some ways, this makes the problem worse. Someone might object, saying: "If the Bible says that behind the fall of man and everything that happens in this world are the devil and his angels, and if the devil can work only with God's permission, doesn't that make God ultimately responsible for evil? If God has the key and gives it to the devil, isn't God responsible? If God reigns over the devil, then why is he still loose in this world? Doesn't that mean God ultimately can be blamed for the problem of evil and suffering?"

The question of the origin of evil has plagued theologians and philosophers for many centuries. But there is an answer to it. I don't want you to misunderstand what I am saying, but there is a sense in which God *is* responsible for evil. I am not for one moment saying that God is the author of sin and that He is responsible for what has gone wrong in this world. But in a sense, He is responsible, because He permits or allows evil to happen. He has the power to stop evil, but He doesn't. So in that sense, He is responsible—yet without being guilty.

Let me illustrate this. If a criminal is brought before a judge who sentences him to prison, then the judge is responsible for sending the man to prison. But the judge is not in any way guilty for doing so. And if the imprisoned man does not change his evil ways but plots new schemes of wickedness that he passes on to other prisoners and visitors, the judge is in no way morally responsible for these new crimes. He is somewhat responsible, because his act of judgment put the man in prison, but he is not guilty of doing so. Thus, responsibility is not necessarily a statement about morality.

God could have stamped out evil at the beginning. He could have destroyed the devil and his angels. He could have made man so that he would always be perfect and do no wrong. But such a man would have been a puppet rather than a being capable of choosing whether to obey and honor God or to disobey and dishonor Him.

But the Bible teaches us that Satan is not only a fall*en* creature, but a fall*ing* creature. God's rule over Satan was not limited to his banishment; it continues to overcome him all the time. In comparison to the spread of the gospel, Satan's power is in free fall. Satan is cast out every time the gospel is preached and sinners are sealed, saved, and brought to Christ. The gospel is God's way of dealing with the destructive power of the devil and his hosts of hell. John says that Jesus came to earth to destroy the works of the devil (1 John 3:8). He came into the world to take on Satan and to break his hold upon the human race. He did that by dying on the cross. We often think about the cross purely in terms of sin and salvation, but there is another dimension of Calvary. There, Jesus defied and defeated Satan. The Son of God took upon Himself a human nature of flesh and blood when He entered the world, the very stronghold of Satan. By His death on the cross, Jesus destroyed the power of death (Col. 2:15; Heb. 2:14).

Revelation describes Satan as an insect with a terrible sting in its tail. Some insects can sting only once, and then they must die. Jesus came into this world to subject Himself to the sting of death. He did that to extract all the venom, poison, and pain of a sinner's death. He absorbed it into His body on the tree. In subjecting Himself to the sting of death, Jesus Christ destroyed the devil's power in death. There is no destructive sting left in Satan's tail for you and for me if we trust in Christ alone for salvation. Paul says: "The sting of death is sin; and the strength of sin is the law. But thanks be to God, which giveth us the victory through our Lord Jesus Christ!" (1 Cor. 15:56–57). There is no sting in death for the Christian because the devil has been defeated and his power vanquished.

So if you are in Christ, you have nothing to fear. But if you do not belong to Christ and are still clinging to sin and the world, then you are under the power of the devil and his angels. The only way to stand against the hordes of locusts from hell is to be sealed by Christ. When the judgments of God fall upon the world, you must have Christ's seal on your forehead. Confess your sins now to God and ask for grace to believe in Christ alone for your salvation. Put on the whole armor of God and be sealed by His Spirit. If you are Christ's, you are safe. If you are not, you are prey for the awful demonic influences that fill this world. You are prey to every lust of the flesh and every vain deceit that fills this world. You are prey to all the destructive powers that come from the pit. Ultimately, you are prey to the everlasting abyss of damnation.

The Sixth Trumpet and the Second Woe

The sounding of the sixth trumpet continues the theme of demon-commissioned judgments. Revelation 9:13 introduces the second woe: "And the sixth angel sounded, and I heard a voice from the four horns of the golden altar which is before God." This voice comes from the altar before God, proving once more that these judgments are ultimately from Him.

When the sixth trumpet sounds, four demonic angels are released to kill a third of humanity by fire, smoke, and brimstone, or sulfur. This trumpet warns us of human calamities and man-made disasters that are designed to bring us to repentance. It hones in on war particularly as the classic example of human destruction. These verses do not describe any particular war but all war at every time and at every period of history. War, like poverty, is always with us. Not a single generation in human history has escaped war and its devastation. Jesus warns us in Matthew 24:6, saying, "Ye shall hear of wars and rumors of wars."

Revelation 9:14 seems to imply the universality of war. It says, "Loose the four angels which are bound in the great river Euphrates." In Revelation, the number four often refers to the four points of the compass, which sum up the entire world. So the description of war in verses 14 and following does not refer to Armageddon or a nuclear holocaust, but to military conflicts that will rage all over the world. The number four symbolizes that no part of the globe or point of the compass will escape the ravages of war.

How then are we to understand verse 16, which speaks of two hundred million horses and riders? There is no place on earth where a literal army of two hundred million horsemen could gather. Thus, we should not understand this figure literally, but as a representation of the monstrousness, ugliness, and awfulness of war. War has been called the ultimate obscenity. That is what Revelation 9 tells us in its portrayal of lions' heads and serpents' tails, as well as smoke, fire, and brimstone. God is warning us about the monstrousness of what we are capable of when He removes His restraining hand.

Think about the millions of people who have been killed in wars. According to some estimates, between 1480 and 1941, Britain engaged in seventy-eight wars; France, in seventy-one wars; Spain, in sixty-four wars; Russia, in sixty-one wars; Austria, in fifty-two wars; Germany, in twenty-three wars; the United States, in thirteen wars; China, in eleven wars; and Japan, in nine wars.[2] And still the war drums keep sounding. Many countries are at war right now. Think of how much bloodshed there has been and how many people have been exterminated during times of war. A third of mankind will perish under the awful calamity of war, says verse 15. War is the single most monstrous act of man's rebellion. It is the single most awful illustration of man's depravity and what he is capable of.

Recently, my wife, Mary, met a sixty-three-year-old woman from Vietnam who has been in the United States for twenty-two years. When the woman was a teenager, Communist soldiers came to her village. They told every family to stay in their houses if they did not want to get shot. Then the soldiers burned every house to the ground. People who ran outside to escape the fires were gunned down.

The woman told Mary that she ran from the flames as bullets exploded around her. She was hit in the neck and leg. She fell to the ground, where she decided to play dead so the soldiers would leave her alone. She knew that if they could see her breathing, they'd put another bullet in her. When she heard soldiers approach, she held her breath. They assumed she was dead and let her be.

She married sometime later, and her husband decided to sell everything they had to pay for a boat trip to Indonesia to escape the ravages of war. He gave the money to those who were organizing

---

2. Quincy Wright, *A Study of War*, 2nd ed. (Chicago: University of Chicago Press, 1965), 649–50, cited in David O. Wilkinson, *Deadly Quarrels: Lewis F. Richardson and the Statistical Study of War* (Berkeley, Ca.: University of California Press, 1980), 123.

the voyage, who took his money and that of others, then took them out to sea, drowning nearly all of them. For years, the wife cried every day.

God says in the message of the sixth trumpet: "Look what happens when I remove the restraints and you take over the reins." Modern man likes to imagine he is the master of his destiny, the captain of his fate. God says: "All right, I'll give you the helm. Then look what a mess you make of things."

Martyn Lloyd-Jones said God allowed two world wars in the twentieth century because man thought he had things under his control, so God had to show him what an animal he was and what inhumanity he was capable of. Who would have thought that during the Second World War, six million Jews would be exterminated? And think about what is happening today in Syria and elsewhere. Then consider the murder of unborn children in the wombs of mothers. In the United States alone, we have killed fifty to sixty million babies in the past forty years under sanction of law. With the sixth trumpet, God is warning us: "This is what you are like, men and women; this is what you are capable of. When I remove My restraints, this is what happens."

It is the same warning Paul sounds in Romans 1, where he says that the wrath of God is being revealed from heaven "against all ungodliness and unrighteousness" (v. 18). God gave up unbelievers to themselves, Paul says, because they did not want to retain the knowledge of God and chose instead to serve the creature rather than the Creator. He gave them over to their sinful lusts and desires. He removed His restraints. The sixth trumpet warns that God will deal with us in the same way if we ignore Him. He will show us what life is like when He withdraws from us.

Let us conclude this point with some specific lessons from this chapter:

Lesson 1: Rejoice in the Sovereignty of God

God's sovereignty is clearly evident in Revelation 9. In verses 14 and 15, the sixth angel is told: "Loose the four angels which are bound in the great river Euphrates. And the four angels were loosed, which were prepared for an hour, and a day, and a month, and a year, for to slay the third part of men." These four angels are not the same four angels described in Revelation 7:1, who stand on the four corners of the earth, holding back its four winds. Those are good angels of the Lord, while the angels in Revelation 9:14–15 serve the devil. The four angels in chapter 7 restrain, while the four angels in chapter 9 are restrained. They are bound and held in check. They relish the thought of mankind plunging into war, but they are held back from interfering—until God allows them to do so. That clearly reveals the sovereignty of God.

God is in no way the author of evil, but He does control it, right down to the hour. The Greek text of verse 15 literally says "the hour" rather than "an hour." God knows the specific hour of the specific day, month, and year when war will break out because everything is under His control. Nothing can happen without His approval. Nothing can happen until His moment arrives. It is comforting to know that the future of this world does not depend upon a leader who picks up a phone. The future of this world is not in the White House, the Kremlin, in China, or in the Middle East. It is in the hands of our sovereign God.

President John F. Kennedy said in 1961 at the United Nations: "Every man, woman, and child lives under a nuclear sword of Damocles, hanging by the slenderest of threads, capable of being cut at any moment by accident or miscalculation or by madness."[3] His view is still that of many people today, who say there are enough weapons in the arsenals of the countries of this world to wipe out the population of the earth. If the future hangs only upon chance, upon the calculations of fallible human politicians, or upon the sanity or insanity of a particular leader, then this is a frightful world in which to live.

3. David B. Frost, comp., *John F. Kennedy in Quotations: A Topical Dictionary, with Sources* (Jefferson, N.C.: McFarland and Co., 2013), 160.

But Revelation calms such fears. It spoke to first-century Christians under the iron fist of Rome. And it speaks to us today as we face the threat of nuclear holocaust. The message is that God holds the key to everything that happens and to all that is yet to come, for which we can be grateful. If other hands held the key, we would be in deep trouble. But we know that God reigns. He manages these things according to His plan and His timetable, right down to the very hour, day, month, and year. In His meticulous sovereignty, He sends His judgments upon men through Satan. The fifth and sixth trumpets are demon-commissioned judgments of our sovereign God.

But there is also something precious here about God's sovereignty. In verse 14, we are told that the four angels are bound in "the great river Euphrates." That is not a geographic hint about where Armageddon will take place. We should understand the symbolism of Revelation in terms of the Old Testament, not in terms of someone's fevered imagination or in terms of current events. We should interpret Scripture by Scripture. What, then, does John mean when he tells us these four angels are bound at the Euphrates River?

One of the key passages of Scripture, Genesis 15:18, tells about the covenant God made with Abraham: "In the same day the LORD made a covenant with Abram, saying, Unto thy seed have I given this land, from the river of Egypt unto the great river, the river Euphrates." Deuteronomy 1:7–8 tells about the fulfillment of that promise. God tells Moses: "Turn you, and take your journey, and go to the mount of the Amorites, and unto all the places nigh thereunto, in the plain, in the hills, and in the vale, and in the south, and by the sea side, to the land of the Canaanites, and unto Lebanon, unto the great river, the river Euphrates. Behold, I have set the land before you: go in and possess the land which the LORD sware unto your fathers, Abraham, Isaac, and Jacob, to give unto them and to their seed after them." Joshua 1:4, as well as many other verses of the Bible, also refers to the Euphrates River. This river is a frontier or boundary. Actually it is a double frontier. It is a geographic boundary of the land God promised to the Israelites, and it is a spiritual boundary between God's kingdom and the kingdom of the prince of this world.

Symbolically and prophetically, the Euphrates River is the boundary between the kingdom of light and the kingdom of darkness. God protects His people. His sovereignty is not capricious but covenantal. He reigns for the sake of His elect. Whatever evil He permits people to do in this world, He will not permit them to destroy His church. What a comfort that must have been for the Christians to whom John wrote, who were steeped in the Old Testament history of the covenant that God had made with Abraham. What a comfort it was to know that the destructive forces of Rome would yet be bound at the Euphrates. Whatever natural disaster, calamity, or inhumanity came their way, it couldn't touch their inheritance. It might hurt them in this life, but it couldn't rob them of what was theirs in Christ.

That is likewise true of what is yours in Christ, for God says to the demonic forces that would attack us, "Thus far and no further." These forces are bound at the great River Euphrates. Satan, war, and all the forces of evil cannot move an inch beyond what our faithful, covenant-keeping, sovereign God allows.

So if you are a true believer, rest in God's sovereign plan. His seal is on your forehead, so you will be protected from His wrath. Believe that He has a plan that will be accomplished for your good.

Lesson 2: Recognize the Depravity of Man
What happens to those who survive this terrible destruction? Revelation 9:20–21 tell us: "And the rest of the men which were not killed by these plagues yet repented not of the works of their hands, that they should not worship devils, and idols of gold, and silver, and brass, and stone, and of wood: which neither can see, nor hear, nor walk: neither repented they of their murders, nor of their sorceries, nor of their fornication, nor of their thefts." Despite the dreadful carnage of war, the masses of people remain impenitent, fearing neither God nor man. They are totally depraved.

People are inveterate sinners. Their nature is radically wrong. They're not just unreasonable; they are rebels. You and I are totally depraved by nature. When truth stares us in the face, we often ignore it. We despise the goodness of God and shrug off His warnings against sin. The unbeliever says, "I don't believe in God," then blames Him for bad things that happen. James 4:1–3 explains: "From whence come wars and fightings among you? Come they not hence, even of your lusts that war in your members? Ye lust, and have not: ye kill, and desire to have, and cannot obtain: ye fight and war, yet ye have not, because ye ask not. Ye ask, and receive not, because ye ask amiss, that ye may consume it upon your lusts." James says war is the result of our sinful hearts. God is not morally responsible for war; we are. If we were not self-centered, proud, greedy sinners, there would be no war. The world is made up of nations, which are made up of communities, which are made up of families, which are made up of individuals. It all comes down to the individual. Sadly, both within and outside the church, people are sinners—twisted, self-centered, and depraved. The fiercest, bloodiest, costliest wars on this earth began with one man's dark heart. That is the warning sounded in Revelation 9:20–21.

Lesson 3: Repent and Take Refuge in Jesus Christ
What should sinners do in response to the dreadful warnings of the fifth and sixth trumpets? Verse 13 says, "The sixth angel sounded, and I heard a voice from the four horns of the golden altar which is before God." This verse reminds us that all the woes sounded by the trumpets are done in connection with the altar of God, particularly its horns, which are the four corners of the altar.

In the Old Testament, the altar was the place of atoning blood and priestly intercession. It was the place of forgiveness and cleansing from the defilement of sin. Standing just outside the veil of the Most Holy Place, where the ark of the covenant was, the golden altar was positioned by God for the propitiation of His holy wrath so that sinners would be reconciled to Him. All of this was fulfilled in Jesus Christ when He, the perfect Lamb of God, laid down His life on the cross as a ransom for many (John 1:29; Matt. 20:28). There at the heavenly altar, by faith in Jesus Christ we find the only safe place to be: at peace with God.

This is an illustration of what God is saying to us in Revelation 9. Why does God allow war to happen when killing goes against His loving purposes? He allows wars and rumors of wars because He wants us to know that we are not safe apart from Christ. When you hear of man's inhumanity and atrocities around the globe, understand that God has sounded His trumpet to warn us to flee from the wrath that is to come upon the earth. We are to flee to the only place where we can be safe—Golgotha, where Christ suffered and died for us. We must hold on to Him for dear life. An old hymn says it this way:

> A refuge for sinners
> The gospel makes known;
> 'Tis found in the merits
> Of Jesus alone.
>
> The weary, the tempted
> And burdened by sin
> Were never exempted
> From entering therein.
>
> Here's refuge for sinners
> Whose guilt should appear
> As black as the confines
> Of endless despair.
>
> Who stripped of all merit
> Whereon to rely
> Are taught by the Spirit
> To Jesus to fly.[4]

---

4. John Kent, "A Refuge for Sinners" (1803).

Conclusion: The Greatest Woe

As the trumpets sound their warnings, John reminds us that Jesus Christ rules all things in accordance with the scroll of God's eternal decrees. Between His first coming in Bethlehem and His second coming on the clouds, Christ will repeatedly "punish the persecutors of the church by inflicting upon them disasters in every sphere of life, both physical and spiritual," writes Hendriksen. He continues:

> The blood of the martyrs is precious in the sight of the Lord. The prayers of all the saints are heard. God sees their tears and their suffering. Yet, in spite of all these warning voices, mankind in general does not repent. Foolish and stubborn men continue to transgress both the first (v. 20), and the second table of the law (v. 21). The persecuting world becomes the impenitent world. It is impenitence that brings about not only the outpouring of the bowls of final wrath (chapters 15, 16), but also the culmination of this wrath in the final judgment.[5]

The concluding verses of Revelation 9 present us with the greatest woe of all—the woe of ultimate impenitence: "And the rest of the men which were not killed by these plagues yet repented not of the works of their hands, that they should not worship devils, and idols of gold, and silver, and brass, and stone, and of wood: which neither can see, nor hear, nor walk: neither repented they of their murders, nor of their sorceries, nor of their fornication, nor of their thefts" (vv. 20–21).

Are you penitent and believing or impenitent and unbelieving? Every assault of Satan and every war in the world is a warning for you. The destructive forces and massive armies of sin prepare to destroy you. With this, as well as the countless sins that you are accumulating in your life, will you still refuse to repent before God? Let the fifth and sixth trumpets so frighten you that you flee to God and cry out for mercy. God's judgments will be terrible upon those who refuse to believe; only those whom He seals will escape

---

5. Hendrickson, *More than Conquerors*, 123.

His judgment. It will be dreadful if God must say of us at the end of our lives that despite all His plagues we did not repent of our idols or acts of hatred, sexual immorality, and greed.

Though they are warned about this agony and destruction, unbelievers still refuse to repent of their wickedness before God. This is the tragedy of Revelation 9. If you do not worship God and obey Him, you are choosing "death rather than life, darkness rather than light, bondage rather than freedom, guilt rather than peace, shame rather than honor, and Hell rather than Heaven."[6] The greatest of all woes is God's judgment upon the spiritually impenitent, the spiritually dead: they will be cast into the darkness of the abyss forever.

---

6. James M. Hamilton, Jr., *Revelation: The Spirit Speaks to the Churches*, Preaching the Word (Wheaton, Ill.: Crossway, 2012), 217.

18

The Angel with
the Little Scroll

REVELATION 10:1–11

And I saw another mighty angel come down from heaven, clothed with a cloud: and a rainbow was upon his head, and his face was as it were the sun, and his feet as pillars of fire: And he had in his hand a little book open: and he set his right foot upon the sea, and his left foot on the earth, and cried with a loud voice, as when a lion roareth: and when he had cried, seven thunders uttered their voices. And when the seven thunders had uttered their voices, I was about to write: and I heard a voice from heaven saying unto me, Seal up those things which the seven thunders uttered, and write them not. And the angel which I saw stand upon the sea and upon the earth lifted up his hand to heaven, and sware by him that liveth for ever and ever, who created heaven, and the things that therein are, and the earth, and the things that therein are, and the sea, and the things which are therein, that there should be time no longer: but in the days of the voice of the seventh angel, when he shall begin to sound, the mystery of God should be finished, as he hath declared to his servants the prophets. And the voice which I heard from heaven spake unto me again, and said, Go and take the little book which is open in the hand of the angel which standeth upon the sea and upon the earth. And I went unto the angel, and said unto him, Give me the little book. And he said unto me, Take it, and eat it up; and it shall make thy belly bitter, but it shall be in thy mouth sweet as honey. And I took the little book out of the angel's hand, and ate it up; and it was in my mouth sweet as honey: and as soon as I had eaten it, my belly was bitter. And he said unto me, Thou must prophesy again before many peoples, and nations, and tongues, and kings.

The Bible is a precious book like no other. We are called to feed upon it. Jeremiah speaks of eating the words of God (Jer. 15:16). What does it mean to you to feed on Scripture? How can you feed on the living Word, Jesus Christ, by eating the written Word, the Holy Bible? And how can you then pass the word of God on to others? Questions like these are answered in the rather challenging tenth chapter of Revelation.

Just as Revelation 7 presented an interlude between the opening of the sixth and seventh seals, so Revelation 10 is an interlude between the sixth and seventh trumpets. The delay heightens the tension and suspense as we wait for the final installment of each visionary sequence. It also helps us to step back and put these events in proper perspective. For the seals, the interlude reminded us that in the midst of the troubles that Christ has ordained for this world, culminating in the final judgment, God is saving a people for Himself by the blood of the Lamb. With respect to the trumpets, the interlude is a sweet relief from the horrible visions of demonic armies in chapter 9. It reminds us that though Satan rages, Christ reigns, and His kingdom will come according to God's decreed plan.

The vision of Revelation 10 centers upon the descent of a glorious figure from heaven, bringing with Him a little scroll that, surprisingly, John is commanded to eat. The meaning of these two symbols is the focus of this chapter.

Gazing upon the Angel

John says in Revelation 10:1, "I saw another mighty angel come down from heaven." When the pre-incarnate Christ appears in human form in the Old Testament, He is often called the angel of the Lord.[1] The prophecy of Malachi 3:1 calls Him "the messenger [angel] of the covenant" (Mal. 3:1). The word *angel* simply means "messenger," as we saw in the opening chapters of Revelation. In John's vision of the seven churches in Asia, God's message to each church is addressed to the "angel" or "messenger" of that church. So

---

1. Cf. Gen. 16:7–13; 22:1–2, 11–18; Ex. 3:2, 6; 13:21.

it is legitimate to identify the mighty angel of Revelation 10:1 as Jesus Christ. This identification is confirmed by how John describes the appearance of this mighty angel.

The Description of the Angel

John reports that this angel comes "down from heaven, clothed with a cloud: and a rainbow was upon his head, and his face was as it were the sun, and his feet as pillars of fire" (v. 1). All the insignia of deity are evident with this angel: a cloud, a rainbow, a shining face, and fiery feet.

According to Psalm 97:2, the clouds and darkness that surround this angel are symbols of God's righteousness and justice, which are the fixed place or foundation of His throne. The rainbow is the sign of God's covenant with Noah, to whom God promised that He would never again destroy the world with a flood. The face like the sun in all its strength and the feet that look like pillars of fire remind us of Revelation 1:14–16. There, the One who stands in the midst of the candlesticks also has a face like the sun shining in full strength and feet like burnished brass. Both of these passages are magnificent descriptions of the glorified Lord Jesus Christ.

Have you ever climbed a mountain until you were above the clouds? When you see the cloud bank below you, you realize that a beautifully clear and shining day exists above the clouds. That is the kind of picture we have here of the Lord Jesus Christ, whose face shines like the sun and who is clothed in clouds. In this life, you and I are sinners who live below the cloud line in our relationship with the Lord Jesus Christ. We live in a world under judgment. The message of the seven trumpets is that the wrath of God is revealed from day to day against all the unrighteousness and ungodliness of man. But the glorious truth is that by grace through faith, you and I can break through the cloud line and rise into heavenly places in Christ Jesus. We can be warmed by the sunshine of His smile.

In Ephesians 2, the apostle Paul explains what it means to be saved. First, he reminds believers of what they were before they trusted Christ: "We…were by nature the children of wrath, even as others. But God, who is rich in mercy, for his great love wherewith he loved us, even when we were dead in sins, hath quickened us together with Christ, (by grace ye are saved;) and hath raised us up together, and made us sit together in heavenly places in Christ Jesus: that in the ages to come he might shew the exceeding riches of his grace in his kindness toward us through Christ Jesus" (vv. 3–7). Like everybody else in the world, we are sinners who deserve the wrath of the holy God against sin. We are beneath the cloud line. But in His mercy and great love, God raises us above the clouds of His judgment to heavenly places in Christ Jesus. In effect, Paul says, "God took you from under condemnation and brought you into a relationship with the Lord Jesus Christ so that you can see His face and live above the clouds beyond condemnation."

Christ's face is like the shining sun, yet He is clothed with clouds. Those are ideal conditions for a rainbow, the beautiful colors of which remind us that it is not just a meteorological phenomenon but the token of God's covenant of grace. When you see a rainbow in the sky, you know the storm has broken and the sun is about to shine.

The storm clouds of God's anger against sin gathered around Jesus' head as He suffered and died for sinners. That is why He sweated great drops of blood in Gethsemane. He was not afraid to die. Other people have died without sweating blood. Others have suffered even more horrific deaths than crucifixion. Some of the great martyrs of the church were roasted alive, yet they did not sweat drops of blood. They didn't pray to God that their cups might be removed. They marched triumphantly to their deaths. Yet in the garden, the incarnate Son of God bowed to the ground, sweating blood, groaning in His spirit, and pleading with His Father that, if possible, He might remove the cup. The only explanation for this agony is that the storm clouds of God's anger against sin were gathering around Christ's head.

At Calvary, that storm broke, and all the concentrated anger of God against all the sins of His people fell upon Jesus Christ. On the cross, the Son bore that judgment in His body. He took upon Himself what our sin deserved so that the sunshine of God's face might shine upon us. The rainbow signifies that in Christ the clouds of judgment and the sunshine of mercy meet. The storm of God's wrath passes for all who receive Him as Savior.

Malachi 3:1–2 tells us, "And the Lord, whom ye seek, shall suddenly come to his temple, even the messenger of the covenant, whom ye delight in: behold, he shall come, saith the LORD of hosts. But who may abide the day of his coming? And who shall stand when he appeareth?" That warns us to ask how we stand in relation to this mighty angel. Are you living below the cloud line or above it in heavenly places? Are you under the cloud of God's wrath, or have you been saved from that wrath through faith in Christ? If you have sincerely repented of your sins and learned by grace to trust in Jesus Christ as your Savior, then the storm has passed by, and the sunshine and mercy of the heavenly places await you. Then you can confess with Charles Wesley:

> No condemnation now I dread;
> Jesus, and all in Him, is mine!
> Alive in Him, my living Head,
> And clothed in righteousness divine,
> Bold I approach the eternal throne
> And claim the crown, through Christ my own.[2]

The Posture of the Angel

Verses 2–3 describe the posture of this angel: "And he had in his hand a little book open: and he set his right foot upon the sea, and his left foot on the earth, and cried with a loud voice, as when a lion roareth." Despite the plagues, the famines, the cruelty of war, and the demonic powers that besiege the world, Christ stands above it all. What a magnificent picture this is of Jesus' lordship over heaven, the earth, the sea, and everything in them. He can declare, "All power is given unto me in heaven and in earth" (Matt. 28:18). He

---

2. Charles Wesley, "And Can It Be that I Should Gain?" (1738), stanza 6.

claims the kingdoms of this world for Himself, for He represents the glory of God.

Placing a foot upon something is an act of conquest and possession. In Joshua 10, Joshua and his army defeat five kings, who then hide in a cave. Joshua tells his officers to seal up the cave with huge rocks until the end of the battle between the soldiers of the kings and Israel. Later, Joshua sends for the men in the cave. We read, "And it came to pass, when they brought out those kings unto Joshua, that Joshua called for all the men of Israel, and said unto the captains of the men of war which went with him, Come near, put your feet upon the necks of these kings. And they came near, and put their feet upon the necks of them. And Joshua said unto them, Fear not, nor be dismayed, be strong and of good courage: for thus shall the LORD do to all your enemies against whom ye fight" (Josh. 10:24–25).

Like Joshua, God proclaims the conquest of His enemies by putting His foot on them. He puts His foot upon all who defy Him to show their subjection to Him. Likewise, the Lord Jesus towers above this rebel world, planting one foot upon the land and the other upon the sea to show that all the nations of the earth are subject to Him. All the tumultuous movements and powers of human history are as dust under His feet.

When we hear about terrible things that are happening in the world, such as kidnappings, civil unrest, earthquakes, and fires, we must remember that Christ towers over everything. All is under His control. We are witnessing the fulfillment of the great prophecy that Christ will have the victory, repeated again and again, particularly in the Psalms, such as, "Sit thou at my right hand, until I make thine enemies thy footstool" (Ps. 110:1).

In Greek mythology, a giant named Atlas is ordered to hold up the heavens. The giant bends and bows under the weight of the celestial sphere. He is not like our Lord Jesus, who holds and upholds everything by the word of His power. He is neither bent nor bowed under the weight of managing this world. Like a mighty colossus, He grasps the universe, dwarfing everything that exists and all that happens. He governs and presides over the comings, goings, and doings of angels, men, and devils. Such is the sovereignty of Christ.

In Ephesians 1, Paul recalls what happened to Christ after His death and resurrection. God raised His Son from the dead and set Him at His right hand in the heavenly places, far above all principalities and powers. Everyone who has ever lived or will live is placed under the authority of Christ. He is Head over all things, particularly the church, which is His body here on earth. He reigns over all principalities and powers. He stands above every name that is named, and He is far above the gods of this world. Christ is at the right hand of the Father, who has put all things under His feet. That should be a tremendous comfort to us, as it was to the Christians of John's day, who were persecuted for their faith under Rome. The feet that were once nailed to a cross now straddle the universe. As David prophesied:

> The just shall flourish in His day,
> And evermore shall peace extend;
> From sea to sea shall be His sway,
> And to the earth's remotest end.

> The desert lands to Him shall bow,
> And all the islands of the sea.
> And kings with gifts shall pay their vow,
> His enemies shall bend the knee.[3]

The Angel's Little Book and Oath

Revelation 10:2 says the angel is holding something: "He had in his hand a little book open." This is some version of the book of God's eternal decrees that we read about earlier. Verses 5–7 go on to say that He "lifted up his hand to heaven, and sware by him that liveth for ever and ever…that there should be time no longer: but in the days of the voice of the seventh angel, when he shall begin to sound,

---

3. *The Psalter*, #198:5, 6 (Ps. 72:7–10).

the mystery of God should be finished, as he hath declared to his servants the prophets."

John sees Christ as the great and all-sufficient Savior. Christ is the mighty Sovereign of the universe, who has everything under His control. With the little book in His left hand, the angel raises His right to swear by Almighty God that He will tell nothing but the truth. This is similar to the oath taken by a witness in a courtroom.

Some commentators question whether the angel is really Christ. They say, "God cannot swear by God." But that is precisely what God does. When God established His covenant with Abraham, He did so by swearing by Himself. Hebrews 6:16–18 says: "For men verily swear by the greater: and an oath for confirmation is to them an end of all strife. Wherein God, willing more abundantly to shew unto the heirs of promise the immutability of his counsel, confirmed it by an oath: that by two immutable things, in which it was impossible for God to lie, we might have a strong consolation, who have fled for refuge to lay hold upon the hope set before us." God wants believers who have fled for refuge to the Savior to be convinced that He is with them in the midst of judgment, persecution, heartache, and suffering.

Christ swears by Almighty God that the things foretold by the prophets of old will soon be accomplished. Revelation 10:6 says "that there should be time no longer," which means, "there shall be no more delay." In effect, the mighty angel is saying, "I swear to you, by God Himself, the Creator of the ends of the earth, that there shall be no more delay in the accomplishment of God's eternal decrees." When the seventh trumpet sounds, God's kingdom will come immediately, and His purposes of grace and justice will be fulfilled.

Almost two thousand years have passed since Revelation was written, but that does not mean God has had second thoughts about judging sin. The angel says: "I swear by the God who made the heavens and the earth. There will be no delay, and everything that is in this little book will be accomplished. The final trumpet will sound." As incredible as it sounds, especially to unbelievers, the Son of God will return visibly. Every eye shall see Him. History will end, judgment day will dawn, and eternity will be upon us. So we can take comfort in these words of 2 Peter 3:9: "The Lord is not slack concerning his promise, as some men count slackness; but is longsuffering to us-ward, not willing that any should perish, but that all should come to repentance."

The Sound of the Angel's Voice

Next, John tells us about the sound of the angel's voice: He "cried with a loud voice, as when a lion roareth: and when he had cried, seven thunders uttered their voices. And when the seven thunders had uttered their voices, I was about to write: and I heard a voice from heaven saying unto me, Seal up those things which the seven thunders uttered, and write them not" (vv. 3–4). John hears not just seven thunders, but *the* seven thunders. It seems that these thunders are in the same category as the seven seals or the seven vials. These thunders answer the cry of the angel and reveal something to John, speaking to him as so many voices. He is about to write down what he has heard, but God forbids him to do so.

It is hard to understand the meaning of the seven thunders and God's order not to write about what they say. Commentators have suggested several helps for interpreting these verses. Derek Thomas asks the following thought-provoking questions:

- Does the order for John not to write down what he has heard mean that some things in the future are not to be revealed so that we might live more in dependence on God?
- Is this an example of the principle of Deuteronomy 29:29, which says the secret things belong to God and we are to be content with what He has disclosed to us in His revealed will?
- Was the message so extraordinary that, like the vision Paul relates in 2 Corinthians 12, the church on earth has no business knowing it?

- Is this an example of God delaying His work of judgment
  so that more people may be encouraged to repent of their
  sin and be rescued from the certain effects of sin?[4]

All of these questions help us to understand why God might choose
not to reveal the information that John sees or hears in the seven
thunders. The point is that only God has the complete picture of
what is and will transpire in this world. There are certain things that
God has not revealed to us.

Verse 4 tells us that the seven thunders echo the voice of the
angel, who roars like a lion. In the Word of God, thunder is always
a symbol of God's wrath and judgment. So also is the roar of the
lion. Proverbs 19:12 says, "The king's wrath is as the roaring of
a lion." And the book of Amos describes the roar of the lion within
the context of God's judgment upon the nations (Amos 3:4, 8). Joel
3:16 also describes the wrath of God: "The LORD also shall roar out
of Zion, and utter his voice from Jerusalem; and the heavens and the
earth shall shake: but the LORD will be the hope of his people, and
the strength of the children of Israel." The context of this prophecy
is the day of the Lord, when the harvest will come to fruition and
multitudes will hover in the valley of decision as the sun and moon
lose their light and the stars stop shining. In that context, Joel tells
us, the Lord will roar out of Zion. In other words, the significance
of this voice is judgment.

How near the mark are you in the way that you think of the
Lord Jesus Christ? Do you see Him as a roaring lion? Or do you see
Him as only a meek lamb? We need the biblical perspective on this.
The Lamb that was slain for the sins of hell-worthy sinners is also
the Lion of the tribe of Judah. The Savior who was led as a Lamb
to the slaughter and died in humility, who was obedient unto death,
even the death of the cross—this Lamb is also the Lion who is
coming again to judge the living and the dead. An old hymn speaks
of the only security we will have during that time:

---

4. Thomas, *Let's Study Revelation*, 84–85.

Should storms of sevenfold thunder roll
And shake the globe from pole to pole;
No flaming bolt could daunt my face,
For Jesus is my hiding place.

On Him almighty vengeance fell,
That must have sunk a world to hell;
He bore it for the chosen race
And thus became their hiding place.[5]

Is Jesus Christ your hiding place? Is He someone you want to hide *from* or someone to hide *in*? You cannot hide from Him. Soon, the last trump will sound; the archangel will roar; and sevenfold thunders will roll across this globe. God's day of wrath will be here. Will you be secure in Christ, or will you be crying for the rocks and the mountains to fall on you to hide you from the wrath of the Lamb?

The Apostle's Eating the Little Book

Books are meant to be read, not eaten! Thus, the little book in the angel's hand, as well as its contents, should be seen as symbolic. To understand this symbolism correctly, we must answer two questions: First, what does the book represent? Second, why does John have to swallow it?

What the Book Represents

The word for book or scroll in Greek is *biblos*, from which we get our word *Bible*. Revelation often uses a form of this word (*biblion*) for various books.[6] Here in chapter 10, a diminutive form (*biblaridion*) is used, which implies that what Christ holds open for John to take is an abridged version of the book with the seven seals. It appears to be a compendium of the book in Revelation 5 that only Christ can open, that is, the book that contains the eternal decrees of God. This

---

5. Jehoiada Brewer, "Hail Sovereign Love that Formed the Plan" (1776).
6. Rev. 5:1–9; 6:14; 17:8; 20:12; 21:27; 22:7, 9, 10, 18, 19.

vision tells us that there are many things in God's eternal decrees that we don't know and are not meant to know.

Deuteronomy 29:29 says this beautifully: "The secret things belong unto the LORD our God: but those things which are revealed belong unto us and to our children for ever, that we may do all the words of this law." The small book in the hand of this angel contains the things that we are meant to know about. There are other things in the book of God's covenant that only Christ knows about, but we are not to concern ourselves with that content. Rather, we are to do our best to understand what is in this small book. What we *need* to know is all here. The little book explains how we can know God, how we can be saved from sin, and how we can progress toward glory. But it does not tell us everything because we would not be able to grasp it. So John Calvin says, "The best limit of sobriety for us will be not only to follow God's lead always in learning but, when he sets an end to teaching, to stop trying to be wise."[7]

It is important to remember that God does not reveal everything to us, especially in Revelation. Many people search Revelation for timetables, dates, personifications of evil, and predictions of the end times. But the Bible only reveals what we need to know. Some things God has ordered to be sealed until the last day.

Some believers do not expect to be surprised in glory. They think they have already learned so much that there is nothing more to know. Yet on the day when the King comes in glory, we shall all exclaim: "Ah, now I understand. Now I see."

In verse 7, we are also told that this little book is a mystery book. We are told that it is about "the mystery of God," which John is to prophesy to God's servants. The word *mystery* is used often in the Bible; Paul uses this word twenty-one times in his epistles. This word might conjure up certain images in our minds, such as a spy novel with dark plots and complicated secrets. We think of a mystery as something nebulous or vague that we can't grasp or

---

7. John Calvin, *Institutes of the Christian Religion*, trans. Ford Lewis Battles, ed. John T. McNeill (Philadelphia: Westminster, 1960), 3.21.3.

understand. Some people look at the gospel as something that is too difficult to understand. They say religion is better caught than taught. There is some truth in that, but it is not entirely true. The whole emphasis of the New Testament is that Christianity can be told, taught, and explained. When the Bible speaks about Christianity and the gospel as a mystery, it does not mean it is something beyond our comprehension.

In the New Testament, *mystery* refers to God's revelation of the gospel (Rev. 16:25; Eph. 3:4–5). It is the revelation of the secret of ages past, namely, how a holy God can save sinners. It is not a closely guarded body of special knowledge for only a few select people. It is something that God has made known. It is something we never would have dreamed of without the Bible. Who could have imagined that God would save sinners through the death of His only Son? Who could have thought that God would save sinners by sending Jesus into the world to bear the penalty of sin for all the church? But God has made this mystery known; He has revealed it.

Paul says in 1 Timothy 3:16a, "And without controversy great is the mystery of godliness." He is not saying, "Without any doubt Christianity is a very mysterious affair." Rather, Paul declares the greatness of the things God has done in Christ: "God was manifest in the flesh, justified in the Spirit, seen of angels, preached unto the Gentiles, believed on in the world, received up into glory" (v. 16b). What was once only a matter of prophecy has come to great and glorious fulfillment.

Let me explain what the gospel mystery is. You and I are sinners. We have broken God's law, and we keep on breaking it. Because of that, we deserve the wrath and judgment of God against sin. We deserve hell. But because God loves sinners, He sent His only Son, Jesus, to the world to live how we should live and to die for us to pay for our sin. Whoever believes in Christ Jesus will have everlasting life. That is the mystery.

As Christians, we have an obligation to tell people around us about this secret. The world desperately needs to know that the six trumpets of judgment have already sounded and soon the seventh will blow. The day of grace will come to an end and the day of judgment will dawn. These are urgent times in which we must testify to others about the gospel. The mystery has been revealed to us, and we are in this world to make that secret known.

What We Should Do with This Book
Notice what John is told to do with the little book. Revelation 10:8–10a says: "And the voice which I heard from heaven spake unto me again, and said, Go and take the little book which is open in the hand of the angel which standeth upon the sea and upon the earth. And I went unto the angel, and said unto him, Give me the little book. And he said unto me, Take it, and eat it up; and it shall make thy belly bitter, but it shall be in thy mouth sweet as honey. And I took the little book out of the angel's hand, and ate it up."

This action of taking and eating this little book offers us two important lessons—one for ourselves and the other for the evangelization of others. The first lesson is that it is not sufficient to have the Word of God in hand. We must digest it, meaning we must take it into our innermost being. We must say, like the prophet Jeremiah, "Thy words were found, and I did eat them; and thy word was unto me the joy and rejoicing of mine heart" (Jer. 15:16). In other words, we must take the gospel to heart. We must take it into our inmost being so that it can give strength to our lives and transform us, just as food nourishes and strengthens our bodies.

The result of feeding on the Word of God is not only a schooled theological intellect, but also a Christ-like character. The purpose of such feeding is to change our being so that Jesus Christ in all His beauty and glory begins to shine forth in our character and lives.

The second lesson of eating the scroll is that we must witness to others, particularly while the trumpets are sounding. We must first go to Christ, who holds the book in His hand. The book is open for us but closed to unbelievers. We know that from experience. Before we came to know the Lord Jesus, the Bible was so difficult for us to understand that it might as well have been written in a foreign language. But when we came to Christ, the book was opened to us.

John is told to take the book from the angel of the covenant, but not just to copy it and pass it on to the church. He, like us, is to read it, yes, but he is specifically told to eat it, swallow it, digest it, and appropriate it into his life. This is how we can witness most effectively to relatives and friends. We will not persuade them to come to Christ by hurling texts at them. Scripture tells us the most effective way to testify about the gospel of the grace of God is to *carry it in our hearts and live it out.* The Word must become an integral part of our daily lives.

That is true both individually and corporately, for Paul says in Ephesians that it is through the church that the mystery of God is made known. For example, Ephesians 3:8–11 says: "Unto me, who am less than the least of all saints, is this grace given, that I should preach among the Gentiles the unsearchable riches of Christ; and to make all men see what is the fellowship of the mystery, which from the beginning of the world hath been hid in God, who created all things by Jesus Christ: to the intent that now unto the principalities and powers in heavenly places might be known by the church the manifold wisdom of God, according to the eternal purpose which he purposed in Christ Jesus our Lord."

By *church*, Paul doesn't mean the church building or its programs. He means the people, for we are the church. We exist not just for times of worship or meeting, but to testify seven days a week and twenty-four hours a day. As the content of the gospel is incorporated into our lives and our relationships with others, the mystery of God's grace in Jesus Christ is made known; that is, the secret is shared. As valuable as it is to distribute tracts, booklets, and other literature, it is usually only when an unbeliever *sees the gospel in us* that the secret is shared. John is told to eat and digest the book so that its great truths become part of him.

When we bear witness to Christ, we become gospel people. As such, we go to the world humbly and lovingly to share the gospel secret with others, for it is God's desire that men and women from every class, ethnic group, race, tribe, and nation be told this secret (Rev. 10:11). God wants us to go into the world, as Jesus says, and preach the gospel to all men. All people need to hear and know the secret. Everyone in this world needs to be saved by God's grace.

Conclusion: What Will It Mean?

Eating the little book is not all sweetness and light. John says in verse 10: "I took the little book...and ate it up; and it was in my mouth sweet as honey: and as soon as I had eaten it, my belly was bitter." It is a bittersweet experience.

The prophet Ezekiel had a similar experience. He was given a little book to eat. He says: "Then did I eat it; and it was in my mouth as honey for sweetness" (Ezek. 3:3). Afterward, however, when the prophet tried to bring those words of lament, warning, and woe to the people of Israel, the people hardened their hearts against him and his message. Ezekiel was so discouraged that God said to him: "These people have hard faces against My Word, but I will make your face hard too. I will enable you to withstand" (see vv. 6–9).

The apostle Paul also notes this struggle in his ministry. He says in 2 Corinthians 4:10 that he is "always bearing about in the body the dying of the Lord Jesus, that the life also of Jesus might be made manifest in our body." While death is at work in us when we testify about the gospel, life is at work in those who receive it.

Even Jesus Christ felt the bittersweet taste of passing the gospel to people who refused to accept it. Jesus loved the gospel and rejoiced over its triumphs, but He also wept deeply about the stubbornness of the city of Jerusalem, where the people refused to recognize Him as Messiah.

In Revelation 10, John echoes the thoughts of Ezekiel, Paul, Jesus, and many others who attempt to warn unbelievers to repent of sin. He is saying that as we digest the gospel and it becomes part of us, our lives become different from those around us. We then share the message of the gospel with them, but we can suffer a kind of acid reflux when our testimony is rejected. So, believer, do not forget the sweetness of the gospel when life has a bitter taste.

John is also being told here to prophesy again, for the little book contains God's revealed will that He wants John to share with others. The way that Jesus Christ calls John to receive His word is surely no different from the way He calls us to receive the Bible today. He says to us: "Now, My child, take the scroll and eat it. Yes, there may be hard and difficult and even bitter experiences to go through, but you will taste the sweetness."

When you digest the gospel and its great truths begin to work in your day-to-day living, you too might find it a bittersweet experience. In the home, some of your children or your spouse may never have tasted the sweetness of the gospel. It is difficult to be a Christian in that setting, for just by being a believer, you drive a wedge between yourself and those you love. It is utterly impossible to be faithful to Christ without incurring some of the world's displeasure and contempt. Some people might choose to give up at this point and say: "If that's the way things are going to be, there is nothing we can do about it. People will not be saved in the last days, anyway." That thought is totally unbiblical.

The six trumpets have sounded in heaven, heralding God's wrath and warning of its approach. Now the seventh trumpet will sound without delay—and very soon. Eternity will dawn, and you and I will stand before God in judgment. But in the meantime, as people of Christ's church, we are to bear witness to Him, crying with all the saints, here and in heaven, "Behold the Lamb!" We are told to bear witness to Christ up to the last moment before the trumpet sounds and Christ returns. We are to go into all the earth and preach the gospel to every living creature. There are peoples, nations, and kings yet to be converted (v. 11). God's message to us is to keep on bearing witness until the last trumpet sounds.

19

The Church's Witness to Jesus Christ

REVELATION 11:1–13

And there was given me a reed like unto a rod: and the angel stood, saying, Rise, and measure the temple of God, and the altar, and them that worship therein. But the court which is without the temple leave out, and measure it not; for it is given unto the Gentiles: and the holy city shall they tread under foot forty and two months. And I will give power unto my two witnesses, and they shall prophesy a thousand two hundred and threescore days, clothed in sackcloth. . . . And when they shall have finished their testimony, the beast that ascendeth out of the bottomless pit shall make war against them, and shall overcome them, and kill them. . . . And they that dwell upon the earth shall rejoice over them, and make merry, and shall send gifts one to another; because these two prophets tormented them that dwelt on the earth. And after three days and an half the Spirit of life from God entered into them, and they stood upon their feet; and great fear fell upon them which saw them. And they heard a great voice from heaven saying unto them, Come up hither. And they ascended up to heaven in a cloud; and their enemies beheld them. And the same hour was there a great earthquake, and the tenth part of the city fell, and in the earthquake were slain of men seven thousand: and the remnant were affrighted, and gave glory to the God of heaven.

Everyone wants comfort and needs comfort, but most people look for comfort in all the wrong places. What about you? Where do you turn for real comfort? If you are a Christian, you find true comfort in God's Word, God's Son, and God's truth. Such comfort is extra special when you feel persecuted and challenged. Revelation 11 is another one of those rather challenging chapters in the Book of Revelation that is designed by God to comfort you. I pray that you may be strengthened under its exposition.

The purpose of the book of Revelation is to comfort God's persecuted saints. The book is full of spiritual and practical help. It is an important part of the sacred canon of Scripture, which God has given for our instruction, reproof, and correction, so that we might be thoroughly equipped unto all good works. This book belongs to all of God's people. We are studying this book to hear what God has to say to His church today.

Chapters 10 and 11 tell us that the key to world history and to current events is Jesus Christ and His church. God has exalted His Son, setting Him at His right hand in heaven, and putting all things under His feet. Christ rules as Head over the church, which is His body. Christ, the angel of the covenant, stands astride the globe as the Governor of the nations (Ps. 22:28). He orders all the affairs of men—even raising up and pulling down governments, kingdoms, and rulers—for the good of His church.

Meanwhile, the trumpets are sounding, revealing the wrath of God against all ungodliness and unrighteousness. People are being warned in many different ways about the judgment that is to come, and the church is in the midst of them, bearing witness to the truth. So the theme of chapters 10 and 11 is the church's witness to the Lord Jesus Christ, which will last throughout history.

The church of God has outlived empires and civilizations through the ages. Many times the world has celebrated the demise of the church, only to find that it springs back to life again. The early church father Tertullian said, "The blood of the martyrs is the seed of the church,"[1] and the message of chapter 11 is that he was right. Revelation reveals here not just an episode in the future, but a picture of the church across the ages bearing witness to the Lord Jesus Christ. The book was written to comfort the church in the

---

1. Tertullian, *Apology*, ch. 50, in *Ante-Nicene Fathers*, 3:55.

days of imperial Rome, but it was also written for those in the pre-Reformation days of John Wycliffe and the Lollards, the Hussites, and the Waldensians. Revelation was for the church of the Reformers and the Puritans. And it is for the church today in Ethiopia, China, and Brazil. The church keeps coming back to life, despite being pronounced dead by unbelievers, because it is the church of the Lord Jesus, who says, "I will build my church; and the gates of hell shall not prevail against it" (Matt. 16:18).

"Gates of hell" is a picturesque way of describing the council chamber of hell. Ancient leaders used to meet at the gates of a city, which was the equivalent of a town hall. So Jesus is saying that He is building His church, and all the councils of the devil and his minions will not prevail against what He is doing. The gates of hell may be in Moscow, Beijing, Washington, D.C., or wherever the devil persuades humans to oppose the church. But such efforts are doomed to failure, for Revelation 11 says Christ's church can never be written off.

Let us look closer at the church's witness to Jesus Christ, specifically under four points about the church: the true identity of the church (Rev. 11:1-2); the twofold testimony of the church (vv. 3-6); the terrible ordeal of the church (vv. 7-10); and the final triumph of the church (vv. 11-13).

The True Identity of the Church

In Revelation 11, Christ gives John a measuring rod, saying: "Rise, and measure the temple of God, and the altar, and them that worship therein. But the court which is without the temple leave out, and measure it not; for it is given unto the Gentiles: and the holy city shall they tread under foot forty and two months" (vv. 1-2). It is critical that we interpret these verses rightly, for our interpretation will influence our understanding of the entire book of Revelation. In chapter 1, I introduced five major views on the interpretation of Revelation. It will be helpful to consider how two of the most popular of these views—the futurist and preterist approaches—interpret Revelation 11, and then to consider a more measured symbolic view.

Futurist View

Our passage describes the temple, the altar, and the outer court. The futurist view of Revelation—the prevailing view of many evangelicals today—says that this passage describes a literal building that will be constructed in the future. This approach is associated with dispensationalism, which teaches that God's plans for Israel and the church are fundamentally different. Dispensationalists say that when the Bible talks about Israel, it is not referring to the church, and when it talks about the church, it does not mean Israel. The two are separate bodies, and God is doing different things for each.

One problem with this view is that if the book of Revelation is seen primarily as God's future plans for ethnic Israel (except for its opening chapters), then it has no direct message for the Christian church of John's day or ours. Such a view is hardly credible, especially since the church of John's day was experiencing severe persecution under the Roman Empire.

Dispensationalists say that the temple that John measures in chapter 11 is a literal building that a reconstituted Israelite state will build on Mount Zion in the future. Today that mountain is occupied by two prominent Islamic holy sites—the Dome of the Rock and the Al-Aqsa Mosque. If dispensationalism is correct, these structures would have to be demolished and replaced by a Jewish temple prior to Christ's return. When the Jewish state of Israel was established in 1948, and when Jerusalem was captured by Israel in the Six-Day War of 1967, dispensationalists viewed these events as signs of the imminent return of Jesus Christ. This is one reason why the futurist view became popular among many evangelicals in the twentieth century.

There are significant problems with this approach. For one, when Jesus foretold the destruction of the temple in Matthew, He said nothing about a rebuilt temple. That should not be surprising, since there was no valid purpose for the temple and its priesthood once Christ had died. The temple was a place for sacrificing animals to atone for sin, but Christ's death put an end to all those sacrifices. When Jesus died on the cross, the veil of the temple was torn from top to bottom (Matt. 27:51). This signified that God was putting an end to the symbol because its reality had come.

Second, in AD 70, God destroyed the temple precisely because the Jews rejected Jesus' atonement. A rebuilt temple would merely reinforce that rejection. So even though we may believe, in accord with Romans 11, that God may revive His ancient people Israel in the last days, resulting in the conversion of many Jews to Christ, the dispensational idea of God restoring Israel to the very temple that He destroyed is simply unbiblical. If such a temple were built by the Jews, it would stand as a monument to their rejection of the cross of Jesus Christ. The idea of rebuilding the temple and reinstituting its sacrifices denies the sufficiency of Christ's atoning death.

Third, Revelation 11:1–2 is not about rebuilding a literal temple because under the gospel, true worship is spiritual and is not confined to any building. In John 4:21, Jesus tells the Samaritan woman that true worship is no longer tied to a particular place. The center of worship is no longer a mountain, a city, or a building. The Father now seeks men and women who worship Him in Spirit and in truth (v. 23). Christ's coming into this world abrogated the ceremonial law, putting an end to buildings, altars, priests, vestments, sacrifices, incense, and other symbolic elements of Old Testament worship. Now the true temple is the church of Jesus Christ. That is the teaching of the entire New Testament.

As believers, we are living stones of a new temple in which God dwells. That is what Revelation 11 is about—not a reconstructed Jewish temple in Jerusalem, but the church of the Lord Jesus Christ. As Paul says in Ephesians 2:19–22, "Now therefore ye are no more strangers and foreigners, but fellow-citizens with the saints, and of the household of God; and are built upon the foundation of the apostles and prophets, Jesus Christ himself being the chief corner stone; in whom all the building fitly framed together groweth unto an holy temple in the Lord: in whom ye also are builded together for an habitation of God through the Spirit." This temple is far more impressive than any structure built with human hands. Revelation 11 is not about politics, geography, buildings, places, or world events. It is about the church of Jesus Christ, the true temple of the living God.

Preterist View

A second approach to Revelation is the *preterist* view. This view says the prophecies of Revelation were fulfilled in the past, in the destruction of Jerusalem and the temple in AD 70. Some preterists view the temple of Revelation 11 as a symbol of the church, with the outer court containing unbelieving Jews, while the holy city of verse 2—Jerusalem—is trod under foot for forty-two months.

There are two problems with this approach. One is that it requires belief that Revelation was written prior to the fall of the temple in AD 70 and that the persecution it refers to is the suffering of believers under the Emperor Nero, who reigned from AD 54 to 68. However, the early church uniformly says Revelation was written much later, in the mid 90s.

The other problem with this view is its inconsistent use of literal and symbolic interpretation. The preterist view says the temple is symbolic and the court is symbolic, but the holy city is literal. That is because the literal temple was destroyed in AD 70, but in our passage, the temple is not destroyed. So the preterist view cannot be the correct interpretation of Revelation 11.

Symbolic View

A third approach consistently interprets the images as symbols. Dispensationalists say that a symbolic reading denies the literal meaning of Scripture, but that is not true if Scripture is using symbols as symbols. Symbolism is Revelation's common method of communicating historical reality.

This view neither foretells future events, with a literal temple being rebuilt, nor describes events that happened prior to John's writing of Revelation. The apostle describes what believers have experienced and will experience in all ages of church history, including our own, until Christ comes again.

The vision of Revelation 11:1–2 centers on the temple. Throughout the New Testament, the temple is used to describe the Christian church. All through their writings, the apostles stress that believers are the temple. In the New Testament, the true temple of God is the church. As Peter says in 1 Peter 2:5, "Ye also, as lively stones, are built up a spiritual house, an holy priesthood, to offer up spiritual sacrifices, acceptable to God by Jesus Christ." In the New Testament context, the word *temple* refers not to a building like the one that was replaced by Christ in His church, but, as Beale says, "The focus is now on the whole covenant community forming a spiritual temple in which God's presence dwells."[2]

According to this symbolic understanding, then, we see that John is told in Revelation 11:1–2 to measure the temple, just as a surveyor is sent out to determine the precise boundaries of a parcel of land that is being purchased. John is determining the boundaries of the true church that God is committed to preserve through all the tribulations of every age. This vision is thus analogous to the vision of the sealing of the saints in Revelation 7, which says that in the midst of God's judgments, the angel puts a mark on true believers so they will be saved throughout the great tribulation and make it safely into heaven. As Paul says, "the foundation of God standeth sure, having this seal, The Lord knoweth them that are his" (2 Tim. 2:19).

At the same time, John is told in verse 2 that he is not to measure the court outside the temple. That court is a symbol of nominal Christians—people who are associated with the church but are not true members of the body of Christ. They have not genuinely been saved through living faith in the Lord Jesus. In times of persecution, many of these nominal Christians fall away. As John says in 1 John 2:19, "They went out from us, but they were not of us; for if they had been of us, they would no doubt have continued with us."

As we saw earlier, a concern about false faith and false teaching dominates Christ's letters to the seven churches of Asia in Revelation 2 and 3. Over and over Jesus says: "Don't be lukewarm, or I

---

2. Beale, *Revelation: A Shorter Commentary*, 217.

will spew you out of My mouth. Don't tolerate false teaching. Don't be merely outwardly associated with the Bible and with Me, but be an actual living member, a true believer." That is the concern again here in Revelation 11, for the outer court of the nominal believers is not protected.

In verse 2, John is given a measuring stick to distinguish between the sanctuary and the outer courts. He is told to measure the sanctuary, the altar, and the people who worship at the altar in the sanctuary. He is told to count these people, but not those who are on the periphery in the outer courts. The idea is that those in the inner court, in the sanctuary, who worship God are safe and are counted. But those in the outer courts on the circumference are not counted and are liable to be trampled on by the world. The Gentiles, pagans, and other nonbelievers are not in the sanctuary and do not dwell in the secret place of the Most High. They have not come to worship the living God through the blood of Christ, but merely to attend church. They are Christians in name only, so there is no safety for them

Are we inside or outside of God's sanctuary? Are we worshiping God at the altar or merely going through the motions of being Christians? Do we know what it is to dwell in the secret place of the Most High under the shadow of His wings? Have we entered the holiest of holies by the blood of Jesus?

The thick veil of the temple separated the Holy of Holies, where God Himself dwelt, from the Holy Place and the rest of the temple. It shut out everybody except the high priest, who could enter the Holy of Holies only once a year on the Day of Atonement. When Jesus died, that veil was torn in two from top to bottom. The very moment when he cried from the cross, "It is finished," the way into the Holy of Holies opened for sinners.

Have you entered through that torn curtain of Christ's flesh to the blood that He shed upon the cross? Have you entered into the Holy of Holies? Do you know God? Have you been reconciled to Him? Do you live in His presence? Or does your Christianity just consist of attending Sunday services? The Bible says that not everyone who calls himself an Israelite is a true Israelite. Likewise, not everyone who calls himself a Christian is a true Christian. As far as God is concerned, only those who worship through the blood of Jesus are counted. The others are wide open to the influences of the world.

Revelation 11 describes the true church as those who have entered by the blood of Jesus into the Holy of Holies. They are those who worship at the altar in the inner sanctuary and who dwell in the secret place of the Most High. They are saved out of this world and sheltered in the inner court of the living God.

The Twofold Testimony of the Church

The next four verses are the heart of this passage. Verse 3 says, "And I will give power unto my two witnesses, and they shall prophesy a thousand two hundred and threescore days, clothed in sackcloth."

Numbers in Revelation are sometimes difficult to understand. But if we compare verses 2 and 3, we realize that the 42 months of verse 2 are the same as the 1,260 days of verse 3. So John is told that the holy city will be trampled by the nations for a specific duration, variously described as 42 months or 1,260 days—three and a half years.

Again, there are differing approaches to understanding those numbers. The *literal* approach of the dispensationalists, which is undoubtedly the prevailing interpretation of many evangelical churches today, says that during a literal three-and-a-half-year period, tribulation will prevail upon a literal Jerusalem with its temple. The tribulation will follow the secret rapture of the Christian church. The *preterist* approach says that the numbers describe the siege of Jerusalem in AD 70, which lasted forty-two months. The *symbolic* approach sees the numbers as expressing not so much a quantity of time as a quality of time. Forty-two months represent an intense period of persecution for a designated period that is limited by God's will.

As noted above, this period of persecution is numbered in months in verse 2 and in days in verse 3. It is difficult to say with

certainty why that is so. Still, when Scripture describes a siege of
a city, the duration is often expressed in months. Revelation 11:2
describes the church as besieged by the world. The church is like
a city set upon a hill that is surrounded and under attack. Those
who are true believers are safe, but nominal Christians are vulnerable to the world's power and persecution. That is also a picture
of the church. The world comes into the church through nominal
confessions of faith and takes over the outer circle of the church.
The church is a city besieged by the world throughout the New
Testament age.

By contrast, verse 3 describes the church as going out into the
world as a powerful witness of the gospel of Jesus Christ. Perhaps
the reason for numbering the time in days in this verse is to remind
us that witnessing is an everyday requirement. Every day that we are
in this world we are to testify about the Lord Jesus Christ.

Notice in verse 3 that the two witnesses are clothed in sackcloth.
People often talk about evangelism that is positive rather than negative and that stresses salvation rather than a call to repentance, but
that is a profound mistake. The message that you and I must proclaim to a world under the judgment of God is repentance toward
Him and faith in the Lord Jesus Christ. That is what the sackcloth
is all about: it is a frequent Old Testament symbol of repentance. To
ignore God's call to repentance is to mishandle the Word of God.

God speaks to us through the foolishness of preaching. There
is plenty of room for celebration in our worship, but the missing
note in so much evangelism today is its lack of urgency concerning repentance. The message of Revelation is that the trumpets of
God are sounding. The wrath of God is being revealed from heaven
against the ungodliness and unrighteousness of men. This world is
under judgment. You and I are here as God's mouthpieces to warn
the world of the wrath that is to come.

To fully appreciate this mission of the church, we must read
verses 4–6 as a compendium of evangelism: "These are the two
olive trees, and the two candlesticks standing before the God of
the earth. And if any man will hurt them, fire proceedeth out of

their mouth, and devoureth their enemies: and if any man will hurt them, he must in this manner be killed. These have power to shut heaven, that it rain not in the days of their prophecy: and have power over waters to turn them to blood, and to smite the earth with all plagues, as often as they will."

The first part of verse 6 recalls the prophet Elijah, who proclaimed God's Word to a nation beset by drought. The second part of the verse reminds us of Moses, who, like these witnesses, had "power over waters to turn them to blood, and to smite the earth with all plagues, as often as [he would]." And verse 5 warns, "If any man will hurt them, fire proceedeth out of their mouth, and devoureth their enemies: and if any man will hurt them, he must in this manner be killed." This is like what God said to the prophet Jeremiah, "I will make my words in thy mouth fire, and this people wood, and it shall devour them" (Jer. 5:14). Of course, Jeremiah did not literally turn into a human flamethrower; however, the word of God in His mouth was powerful to convict sinners and ultimately condemn them if they rejected his testimony.

These accounts of witnessing in the Old Testament do not imply that Moses, Elijah, and Jeremiah will physically reappear in Jerusalem someday. These men are not presented as apocalyptic figures who will reappear on the world stage, but as men who were willing to witness to a world under the judgment of God.

Moses, Elijah, and Jeremiah suffered greatly for their testimony. Moses proclaimed plagues on Egypt while living in that country. Elijah preached the Word of God during the reign of Ahab and Jezebel, who made him run for his life. Jeremiah wept as his people were carried off into exile. In the same way, we may expect to suffer as we witness to a world under judgment. Yet Revelation 11 also offers a beautiful picture of how God equips His people to witness.

In verse 4, the candlesticks or lampstands are the church, which is called to shine a light into the dark world. But since the world is so dark and we believers are so weak, how do we know that our light will not go out? We need oil if our light is to continue to shine. Zechariah 4:6 tells us that God provides us with a reservoir of oil, as well as the olive trees that produce the oil. The verse says, "Not by might, nor by power, but by my spirit, saith the LORD of hosts." The church will prevail against the opposition of this world, not by its words, might, or organizational power, but by the Holy Spirit, who fuels and empowers the light of the gospel through the witness of the church.

Do you pray that by your walk and your talk you will be an effective witness for Jesus Christ as Savior and King? Do you ask God to open doors so that you might evangelize others; and, when He does so, do you walk through those doors? Do you make a consistent effort to bring the whole counsel of God to unsaved sinners?

The Terrible Ordeal of the Church

Being a prophet was difficult for Moses, Elijah, Jeremiah, and others. Revelation 11 puts the suffering, persecution, and opposition that they endured into proper perspective. Verses 7–10 offer a description of the terrible ordeal that the church of Christ will go through when it bears witness to a world under judgment: "And when they shall have finished their testimony, the beast that ascendeth out of the bottomless pit shall make war against them, and shall overcome them, and kill them. And their dead bodies shall lie in the street of the great city, which spiritually is called Sodom and Egypt, where also our Lord was crucified. And they of the people and kindreds and tongues and nations shall see their dead bodies three days and an half, and shall not suffer their dead bodies to be put in graves. And they that dwell upon the earth shall rejoice over them, and make merry, and shall send gifts one to another; because these two prophets tormented them that dwelt on the earth."

Some view these verses as events that will happen in the future, but we can see them as a constant aspect of church history. Jerusalem is not to be seen as a literal city, but as a symbol of the place where Christ was crucified. That city is constantly reappearing in history. It appears under different names, such as Sodom, Egypt, Babylon, Rome, New York, Paris, and London. The city is a symbol of any place where men and women, egged on by the beast from the pit, shout against Christ, "Crucify Him; crucify Him!" This opposition appears wherever men and women, motivated by the devil, set themselves up against Christ and His people.

The leaders of the Soviet Union once predicted that they would stamp out Christianity. Mao Zedong tried to do the same thing in China. There have been other times in history when the church has been left for dead in the streets of this world. Over two hundred years ago, the French Deist Voltaire scoffed at the Bible and hoped that he was living in the twilight of Christianity, but a century later, the very house where Voltaire once lived in Geneva was the home of the Evangelical Society of Geneva and being used as a storage site for Bibles.[3] The world may write off the church, but God is constantly turning the tables upon this world.

Yet the world's opposition to the church is fierce. Revelation 11 says the two witnesses are slain, and their bodies are left lying in the street. The world doesn't even give them a proper burial. Instead, the world begins to celebrate the death of the two witnesses because it thinks it will no longer be troubled by the voice of the church. This happens not just in one city at a future time. It is happening in the world around us all the time as people reject the gospel.

The Final Triumph of the Church

Verses 11–13 speak of the triumph of the church in spite of opposition: "And after three days and an half the Spirit of life from God entered into them, and they stood upon their feet; and great fear fell upon them which saw them. And they heard a great voice from heaven saying unto them, Come up hither. And they ascended up to heaven in a cloud; and their enemies beheld them. And the same hour was there a great earthquake, and the tenth part of the city

---

3. The Evangelical Society of Geneva was organized as a result of the nineteenth-century *Réveil* movement among Swiss and French Reformed churches. On this account, see W. Acworth, "Bible Notices in Switzerland and Italy," *Missionary Register* 24 (August 1836): 352, https://books.google.com.au/books?id=IH0oAAAAYAAJ&pg=PA352#v=onepage&q&f=false, accessed June 9, 2016.

fell, and in the earthquake were slain of men seven thousand: and the remnant were affrighted, and gave glory to the God of heaven."

This passage certainly applies to the future because it describes what will happen when the last trumpet sounds and Jesus returns to earth. But verse 12 does not mention a secret rapture; rather, it vindicates an open one, for when Jesus Christ comes back to earth, the church will be caught up to heaven in full sight of the enemy. The last trumpet will announce God's final vindication of the gospel. God will have the final word. That is what John is saying to persecuted Christians.

The kingdoms of this world try to crush believers, but John is assuring them that God will not let that happen. At times, it seems that the church is finished, but it is never so.

That was true in Old Testament times. For example, King Nebuchadnezzar, whom Daniel called "king of kings," fell prostrate on the ground when he heard what would happen in the future. He gave glory to God, saying, "Of a truth it is, that your God is a God of gods, and a Lord of kings" (Dan. 2:47). Likewise, the day will come when unsaved men and women will give glory to God, for Scripture says, "Every knee should bow…and…every tongue should confess that Jesus Christ is Lord" (Phil. 2:10–11).

God also had the final word during the Great Awakening. Prior to that time of evangelical fervor, the church appeared to be dying, if not dead, in England. There was little spiritual life left in people who professed to be believers. But then God raised up George Whitefield, Howell Harris, Daniel Rowland, and other evangelists throughout England and Wales. Through them, God breathed life back into the church, and that valley of dead bones began to stand on its feet. If asked, "Son of man, can these bones live?" (Ezek. 37:3), you might have answered, "No way; the church is dead." But God has the final word. He revives and restores His church to give glory to His name.

At the beginning of the sixteenth century, the church in the West was in dire condition. The Renaissance Popes of the fifteenth and early sixteenth centuries devoted themselves to the secular concerns of political and military expansion, personal gratification (often in an immoral fashion), and pursuit of the arts—all while the body of Christ cried out for truth and justice.[4] The Lollards had been suppressed and the Hussites silenced through the Inquisition. It seemed that gospel truth was nearly extinguished. But in 1517, Martin Luther nailed his 95 Theses to the cathedral door in Wittenberg, stating the main elements of the gospel. That fueled the greatest revival the church has ever known: the Protestant Reformation. The church had appeared to be sunk down in corruption, decay, and spiritual death. But God visited His people and raised them to new life by the power of His Word and Spirit.

Today, the institutional church and its leaders are often co-opted by the world. The Church of Rome has gone the way of worldly institutions, but so have many Protestant denominations. They question the truth of the Bible and no longer require their members to have a living faith in Jesus Christ. They object to proclaiming God's judgment against sin and a salvation that is possible only through faith in Jesus. They are lukewarm about Christ's kingdom and the gospel. Without true love for Christ, they become servants of Satan who persecute the church. In the developing world, true Christians are persecuted in part by nominal Christians and their officers. However, God will preserve His church. Remember that Jesus has promised to build His church, so the gates of hell will not prevail against it.

Revelation 11 is a great comfort to true believers. It shows that the witnessing church shares in Christ's death, resurrection, and exaltation to glory (vv. 8–12). Christians will eventually triumph over suffering, even though, in the meantime, they experience much tribulation, for those who profess to believe in Christ will follow Him through His entire career. But if they share in His suffering, then they will also share in His glory, for His name's sake.

---

4. Williston Walker, *A History of the Christian Church*, ed. Cyril C. Richardson, Wilhelm Pauck, Robert T. Handy (New York: Charles Scribner's Sons, 1959), 283–84.

John also has a message for people who attend church but do not belong to the spiritual body of Christ's true followers. He says that they are like the Gentiles who were restricted to the outer court of the temple. Non-Jews could enter the outer court, but could not enter the temple itself. They were outsiders. So John is saying in Revelation 11, "If you are a nominal member of the church, you are not saved." God's banner does not fly over you. His omnipotence does not protect you. You go through the motions of being a church member, but you have never come as a lost sinner before a holy God to beg forgiveness of Him. You have never said, "I need to be saved by Jesus Christ, who died on the cross for sinners like me."

So do not think you will be saved by merely associating with the church or attending its services when they are convenient for you. You must come to God by grace through faith in Jesus Christ. When Christian in *Pilgrim's Progress* learned that he lived in the City of Destruction, Evangelist directed him to take the narrow road where he would find the cross of Jesus Christ. Likewise, you must go to Christ and the cross. Pray that you will meet Jesus, repent of your sin, be saved, and become a part of the true, living church of Jesus Christ.

20

The Seventh Trumpet Sounds

REVELATION 11:14–19

The second woe is past; and, behold, the third woe cometh quickly. And the seventh angel sounded; and there were great voices in heaven, saying, The kingdoms of this world are become the kingdoms of our Lord, and of his Christ; and he shall reign for ever and ever. And the four and twenty elders, which sat before God on their seats, fell upon their faces, and worshipped God, saying, We give thee thanks, O Lord God Almighty, which art, and wast, and art to come; because thou hast taken to thee thy great power, and hast reigned. And the nations were angry, and thy wrath is come, and the time of the dead, that they should be judged, and that thou shouldest give reward unto thy servants the prophets, and to the saints, and them that fear thy name, small and great; and shouldest destroy them which destroy the earth. And the temple of God was opened in heaven, and there was seen in his temple the ark of his testament: and there were lightnings, and voices, and thunderings, and an earthquake, and great hail.

When you are expecting visitors, you are not exactly sure when they will arrive, but you know they are coming. You get the house ready; you get the vacuum cleaner going; you put the kids' toys out of sight; and you take food out of the freezer. You get ready for your guests. Likewise, we are to prepare for the Lord's coming, which is not timed to satisfy our human wishes for horoscope-like predictions. We are to be ready all the time, for His return is always imminent.

When Jesus returns, everyone will know it (Matt. 24:30). If the trumpet sounds after you've been in the grave for two thousand years, you will stand on your feet and rise to meet Christ. Next, those who are still alive will ascend to meet Christ in the air. As Paul says in 1 Thessalonians 4:16–17: "For the Lord himself shall descend from heaven with a shout, with the voice of the archangel, and with the trump of God: and the dead in Christ shall rise first: then we which are alive and remain shall be caught up together with them in the clouds, to meet the Lord in the air: and so shall we ever be with the Lord." No one will miss out on the second coming. When the trumpet sounds, we will all hear it.

As we have seen, Revelation contains a series of visionary cycles. Each cycle begins with the advent of the Lord Jesus and continues up to His second coming. In the third cycle, consisting of the seven trumpets, we encountered an interlude between the sixth and seventh trumpets (Rom. 10:1–11:13). There we saw the vision of the mighty angel with the little scroll, and the vision of the two witnesses in God's holy city.

Now we return to the sequence of the seven trumpets, specifically to the final scene, in which the seventh and final trumpet sounds. Verse 14 says this will happen soon: "The second woe is past; and, behold, the third woe cometh quickly." Revelation 10:6–7 also says that the sounding of the seventh trumpet will not be delayed. Those words were written almost two thousand years ago, so we in the twenty-first century may think there has been a considerable delay in their fulfillment. Yet we must remember that the seventh trumpet is always about to sound. That has been the message of Revelation to generations of Christians, from the first century on. Whenever a preacher, teacher, or writer claims that all the events of Revelation belong to a particular generation, you should be suspicious. People have been making such claims throughout the history of the church. However, Revelation says the last trumpet can sound anytime, heralding the return of Jesus Christ.

The apostle John is echoing in Revelation what the Lord Jesus often teaches in the Gospels, namely, that He will return soon and that the end of the world is imminent. He can return at any time. Jesus says His second coming will be as a thief in the night

(Matt. 24:42–44; cf. 1 Thess. 5:2). A thief doesn't send a calling card or announce in the local newspaper when he will enter your house. He comes suddenly and unexpectedly. That is how it will be when the last trumpet sounds, when Christ returns and the world comes to an end. It could happen before we go to bed tonight. Then again, it might not happen for another hundred or even a thousand years. The message of Revelation and the Bible as a whole is that we are to live as authentic Christians until Jesus Christ returns, whenever that is.

The passage in Revelation describing what will happen after the blowing of the last trumpet is *proleptic* or anticipatory. John is so certain of the fulfillment of what he prophesies that he speaks of it in the past tense, as though it were already an accomplished fact. These events are certain because of the eternal covenant of God's redemption. Because He has determined all things, they can be spoken of as though they have already happened. We find that comforting proleptic use often in Paul's epistles as well. For example, Romans 8:30 speaks of our glorification in this way: "them he also glorified." Paul is saying that in one sense, our glorification has already happened, for it is already in the mind and will of God; hence, it is absolutely sure to transpire in its fullness in the future. Similarly, the sounding of the seventh trumpet is presented as an accomplished fact, for it is sure in the eternal mind of God and it will therefore certainly take place in the future. Beyond a shadow of a doubt, John is saying, when the seventh trumpet does sound, we will all be ushered into eternity; we will no longer be creatures of time. Then we will experience what the rest of Revelation describes as our destiny in Christ.

As we consider the sounding of the seventh trumpet, let us first set the scene, then look at the sounds of heaven and the singing of the saints.

Setting the Scene

Revelation 11:19 is crucial for understanding this passage. Some commentators think this verse belongs to Revelation 12, but I believe it belongs with chapter 11, because it provides the setting for what is to follow. It offers a quick look at what this trumpet introduces. Verse 19 says, "And the temple of God was opened in heaven, and there was seen in his temple the ark of his testament: and there were lightnings, and voices, and thunderings, and an earthquake, and great hail."

That is a kind of "open house" look at what will follow. Perhaps you have gone to your children's school for an open house. The walls of the school's classrooms and hallways were bright with samples of the work that the children had done during the year. You could also talk to the teachers and find out how your child had been doing. Many institutions and organizations have such open houses.

Verse 19 tells us that when the last trumpet sounds and Jesus Christ returns to earth on the clouds, God will hold an open house for the universe. He will display to the entire cosmos what He has been doing in this world since the dawn of time. He will open up His temple for inspection. He has been building this temple, not with bricks and stones, but with living stones, that is, living people (1 Peter 2:5). That is already happening now. Whenever someone is converted and becomes a Christian, he becomes a living stone in God's temple. One day, the very last person for whom Christ died upon the cross will be saved. The last stone will be placed, and the temple will be complete. On that day, God will open the temple and show forth His works on earth.

The tabernacle and temple in the Old Testament were just architectural models, built on a human scale. Their rituals and ceremonies were mere scaffolding. In the New Testament days, the scale models were laid aside, and the scaffolding discarded as God built His church. When the trumpet sounds, the church will be complete.

Verse 19 refers to the ark of the covenant of the Old Testament. It was the preeminent sign of God's presence among His people and of the covenant of grace. Inside that ark were the two tablets of the law. The lid of the ark was the mercy seat, on which the priest would sprinkle blood to atone for sin, thereby obtaining pardon for God's people. The ark of the covenant was a wonderful symbol of the Lord Jesus Christ, who is both God and man. It was made of gold and wood, representative of Christ, who is the gold of deity and the wood of humanity.

The tablets of the law are also fulfilled in Jesus Christ. He came from heaven to earth to keep God's law perfectly, which is something we cannot do. He not only fulfilled God's commandments on our behalf, but went to the cross to shed His blood to atone for our sins and to reconcile unworthy sinners with the holy God. As the ark of the covenant was the sign, so Christ is the substance of God dwelling among us to reconcile us to Himself and to commune with us at the mercy seat. God's unchangeable promises are fulfilled and His kingdom established forever in Christ.

On the last day, when the trumpet sounds, everybody will see all this and much more. William Hendriksen writes, "Hence, when this ark is now seen, that is, fully revealed, the covenant of grace in all its sweetness is realized in the hearts and lives of God's children."[1] That will be the most rewarding day in a believer's life, for God will throw open His temple and allow believers to see, in a way they never have before, what He has been doing all along.

However, it will be a terrible day for those who are not Christians. Hendriksen says: "But for the wicked that same ark, which is God's throne, is a symbol of wrath. Also this wrath will now be fully revealed. Because of this there follow flashes of lightning, and rumbling and peals of thunder, and quaking, and a great hail-storm."[2]

Sometimes people declare that death will bring them no regrets. But if you are an unbeliever when the trumpet sounds, you *will* have regrets. When God shows what He has been doing, and you see you have no part in it, then you will realize how much you have missed out on. Your regrets will be so severe that you will feel as if you are in hell because of your stubborn refusal to participate in Christ's kingdom.

---

1. Hendriksen, *More than Conquerors*, 133.
2. Hendriksen, *More than Conquerors*, 133.

The Sounds of Heaven

Revelation 11:15 says that when the seventh trumpet sounds, it is accompanied by "great voices in heaven." Revelation is a very noisy book; it is full of sounds. In chapter 1, the Lord introduces Himself to us with a great voice like the sound of a trumpet (v. 10). In chapter 4, John is summoned by a great trumpet-like voice to receive the vision of the seals (v. 1).

If you go through Revelation to see how the sounds are distributed, you soon discover the cyclical nature of the book. You are constantly brought from the first coming of Christ to His second coming. As you get closer to the sounding of this seventh trumpet, the noise gets louder. At first, some voices occasionally shout out, but as you approach eternity, many voices resound with singing and shouting. This is one way the vision builds a sense of excitement.

It is sad that some people will not share in that excitement, for they have nothing to shout about. But while they burn with regret for their sins, true believers will shout and sing, for this is the day that heaven has been waiting for. The angels will also clap their hands and shout for joy. Paul says in Romans 8:19 that all of creation is standing on tiptoe, craning its neck to see Jesus return.

Verse 15 says that the sounding of the seventh angel is accompanied by great voices in heaven. We are not told whose voices these are. All we know is that they are "great," that is, *loud*. Verse 15 says: "There were great voices in heaven, saying, The kingdoms of this world are become the kingdoms of our Lord, and of his Christ; and he shall reign for ever and ever." This verse does not predict that political organizations will be won over to Christ, or that the saints will seize all the positions of power such as the offices of the prime minister of Britain and the president of the United States so they can govern the world according to principles of Scripture. Some postmillennial evangelicals believe that all the nations and kingdoms of this world will ultimately be taken over by the saints and Christianized, but that cannot be true because verse 15 does not refer to the present age; it refers to eternity. Echoing the song of Moses by the Red Sea (Ex. 15:18), Revelation anticipates the ultimate victory of God's people over their wicked enemies when the kingdom of Christ comes to earth (Dan. 2:34–35, 44).

It is significant to note that most Greek manuscripts use the word *kingdom* in verse 15 rather than *kingdoms*. If the singular sense is correct, this implies that verse 15 probably does not refer to the various political, geographic, and ideological kingdoms of this world, but to the kingdom that surpasses all of them—that of Satan, the usurper, who has set up his kingdom in opposition to God.

Satan is described as "the prince of this world" (John 12:31). He has challenged God's sovereignty and made a bid for power. He came to the wilderness to tempt Jesus to sin. One of the temptations was for Christ to accept the devil's offer to receive all the kingdoms of this world. Luke 4:5–7 says: "And the devil, taking him up into an high mountain, shewed unto him all the kingdoms of the world in a moment of time. And the devil said unto him, All this power will I give thee, and the glory of them: for that is delivered unto me; and to whomsoever I will I give it. If thou therefore wilt worship me, all shall be thine."

You might ask: "Who does Satan think he is? What an extravagant claim—to have power to give all the kingdoms of the world to the Son of God." But the devil's temptation was far more sinister than that. This wasn't just a silly boast or an empty claim on his part. There was enough truth in Satan's words to make the situation most serious. In this temptation, he was challenging the absolute sovereignty of God. He was making another bid for power. He was trying to launch a coup in heaven to overthrow God.

This challenge was also sinister because Satan had already made the human race an accomplice in this act of rebellion. That is what the fall was all about. The deadliness of Adam's sin was not that he ate a piece of forbidden fruit; it was that he assisted Satan in defying God as sovereign of the universe.

The devil came to Adam and Eve in the garden, questioning what God had said to them. He asked Eve in Genesis 3:1, "Yea, hath God said, Ye shall not eat of every tree of the garden?" Surely not, he implied; God couldn't be that unreasonable and childish.

Then Eve affirmed that God had given them permission to eat of every tree in the garden but one, the tree of life, of which, she added, "God hath said, Ye shall not eat of it, neither shall ye touch it, lest ye die" (v. 3). At that point, Satan resorted to a blatant lie, saying, "Ye shall not surely die!" (v. 4). These assaults on the truth and trustworthiness of God's Word were not idle questions, for they challenged the very sovereignty of God. They were direct attacks on the authority of God. And you and I were involved in that sin, whether we like it or not. By nature, we are accomplices in this crime. When we sin, we aid and abet the devil in his attack on God's sovereignty and glory.

Do not misunderstand this shouting in heaven as if there were any doubt about the outcome of Satan's attempt to dethrone God. These are shouts of victory, not shouts of surprise or relief. There is no doubt that God will win against the devil. God's sovereignty has always been absolute. But as far as time is concerned, this authority is disputed by the devil and the people under his control. When the last trumpet sounds, however, the rebellion will be quashed, and Satan's kingdom of this world will be no more. Only the kingdom of God and of His Christ will stand forever.

God is sovereign between the fall of the first Adam and the final triumph of the last Adam, and nothing can stand in His way. That is the point here. The heathen may rage, and the kings of the earth set themselves against the Lord and against His Anointed (Ps. 2:1–2). But the greatest battle of history is the one that Satan and the powers of darkness have waged and continue to wage against God and His saints.

For example, in Psalm 2, the kingdoms or nations of the earth are said to be battling against the Lord and against His Anointed. This messianic psalm is the background of Revelation 11:14–19. In Acts 4:25–26, the apostles quote this psalm because they are aware of the powers of darkness around them. They look back to this psalm and what it says about the Lord Jesus Christ. The psalm not only looks forward to the birth of the Messiah, Jesus Christ, but to His final triumph in the second coming. Psalm 2:1 asks, "Why do the heathen rage, and the people imagine a vain thing?" To imagine that human beings in whatever numbers or combinations can overthrow the rule of God's Anointed One is truly vain, an exercise in group self-delusion. That is true personally, corporately, and nationally.

Verses 2–4 of the psalm go on to say: "The kings of the earth set themselves, and the rulers take counsel together, against the LORD, and against his anointed, saying, Let us break their bands asunder, and cast away their cords from us. He that sitteth in the heavens shall laugh: the Lord shall have them in derision."

God does not mock as humans do. The Lord in heaven responds to the efforts of men to unseat Him with a righteous and holy laughter. He scoffs at those who attempt to rebel against Him. This divine mockery expresses how incredibly foolish it is for men and nations to set themselves against the Lord.

Many individuals throughout history have challenged God. That is utterly pointless, because the Lord will have not only the last laugh, but also the last word. As Psalm 2:4-7a says: "Then shall he speak unto them in his wrath, and vex them in his sore displeasure. Yet have I set my king upon my holy hill of Zion. I will declare the decree." God is saying that even though earthly kings war against Him, He will win the battle because He has enthroned His Son as King of kings.

The Lord addresses His Anointed One (that is, His Christ) in the middle of Psalm 2:7, saying: "The LORD hath said unto me, Thou art my Son: this day have I begotten thee." He continues in verses 8–9: "Ask of me, and I shall give thee the heathen for thine inheritance, and the uttermost parts of the earth for thy possession. Thou shalt break them with a rod of iron; thou shalt dash them in pieces like a potter's vessel."

It is extraordinary that the Lord Jesus Christ is invited to pray to the Father in order to receive His inheritance. "Ask of me," says God the Father to His Son, the Anointed One. The Lord Jesus Christ receives His inheritance to rule the nations and to possess all of the earth because He asks. Throughout His life here on earth, Christ asked much of His Father and He received much.

Then, in verses 10–12a, God says to the kings of the earth: "Be wise now therefore, O ye kings: be instructed, ye judges of the earth. Serve the LORD with fear, and rejoice with trembling. Kiss the Son, lest he be angry." He is pleading with the kings of the earth: "Don't be foolish; come down from your proud pedestal of rebellion and humble yourself at the feet of the Son of God. Kiss the Son, lest He be angry. Be reconciled to God through the Son." The gospel is clearly evident in this psalm.

Revelation 11:17–18 goes on to describe how we should rightly respond to God's gospel message: "We give thee thanks, O Lord God Almighty, which art, and wast, and art to come; because thou hast taken to thee thy great power, and hast reigned. And the nations were angry, and thy wrath is come, and the time of the dead, that they should be judged, and that thou shouldest give reward unto thy servants the prophets and to the saints, and them that fear thy name, small and great." These words parallel what is said in Psalm 2, only John sees in his vision that the day that the psalmist saw from afar is now at hand.

Which kingdom do you belong to: the devil's kingdom or that of our Lord Jesus Christ? Are you working for the kingdom of darkness or for the kingdom of God's Son? If you are serving the world and its ruler, the prince of darkness, you can, by God's grace, leave this kingdom to walk in the kingdom of light.

Mark 1:14 tells us, "Now after that John was put in prison, Jesus came into Galilee, preaching the gospel of the kingdom of God." The gospel is good news. It offers an alternative to Satan's dark domain, where people live in slavery to their lusts. The good news is that when Jesus Christ came into this world and died for sinners, God's kingdom drew near. It is close to us today. Jesus tells us that the way to enter His kingdom is by repenting of sin and believing the gospel.

The kingdom of God is at hand if you are not a Christian. And the way into that kingdom is to repent right where you are. By the grace of the Holy Spirit, you must turn your back on sin and face the Lord Jesus Christ, God's Son. You must put your trust in Him, believing what He has taught and relying on what He has done. Repent and believe, by God's free grace. That is the gospel.

In Colossians 1:12–14, Paul reminds his readers how they became Christians. He urges them to give thanks "unto the Father, which hath made us meet to be partakers of the inheritance of the saints in light: who hath delivered us from the power of darkness, and hath translated us into the kingdom of his dear Son: in whom we have redemption through his blood, even the forgiveness of sins." You can come out of Satan's domain and enter God's kingdom. The record of your guilt can be removed through the blood of Jesus Christ, and you can enter the everlasting kingdom of God's dear Son.

The Singing of the Saints

When the last trumpet sounds, Revelation 11:16–17 tells us, the twenty-four elders fall down on their faces and worship God. These elders represent the church of the Old Testament and the New. Notice what they say: "We give thee thanks, O Lord God Almighty, which art, and wast, and art to come; *because*...." The word *because* teaches us something crucial about worship. Many people think that in order to worship God, you have to slip your brain into neutral and let your emotions run wild. That is not true biblical worship. We are told that the twenty-four elders worship God in heaven by giving thanks. They remind themselves that they worship the God who is, who was, and who is to come, and they worship *because* what He says and does is worthy of praise. We need to remind ourselves of that.

I might praise my wife often, but it would get a bit annoying if my praise had no content. But if I say, "That was a great meal, sweetheart; thank you so much for cooking it," or, even better, "That was a great act of kindness you just showed; thank you," that is praise plus content.

If you think that in heaven you will be shouting "Hallelujah, praise the Lord" all the time, you are mistaken. Repeating clichés is not praise. We must use our minds in worshiping God. We should say, "We thank Thee *because*...." We praise Him not just to ventilate nice feelings bubbling up inside us, but because God has done wondrous things, and He is faithful and true to His promises. That is why we worship Him and give Him thanks.

According to verses 17–18, the elders' worship, amid outbursts of praise and singing, is focused on judgment day: "We give thee thanks, O Lord God Almighty...because thou hast taken to thee thy great power, and hast reigned. And the nations were angry, and thy wrath is come, and the time of the dead, that they should be judged, and that thou shouldest give reward unto thy servants the prophets and to the saints, and them that fear thy name, small and great; and shouldest destroy them which destroy the earth."

We have heard the song of creation (Rev. 4:8–11) and the song of redemption (Rev. 5:9–10). Now we hear the song of judgment day. Judgment is a system of reward and punishment; it is not just assessment and comment. Some people view the day of judgment as the time when God assesses everything that has gone on in the world and makes His comments. But there is really not much to shout or sing about if this is what judgment day is about. Scripture teaches us that a great day is coming when evil will be punished and righteousness rewarded. On that day, all the wrongs suffered by persecuted believers will be righted and God's justice will be vindicated. That is something to sing and shout about.

Revelation was written to comfort Christians suffering under the persecution of the Roman Empire. The emphasis in verse 18 is that on judgment day, the dead will be raised, the nations will be judged, and God will reward His servants, many of whom have suffered so much—*all* the saints, small and great. He says, in effect, to the humble Christians suffering under Rome: "Caesar will eventually come to nothing. But you, dear Christians, will be rewarded and given thrones in My kingdom, from which you will reign with Christ for all eternity." That too is something worth singing and shouting about.

How wonderful that day will be for believers! We can look forward to it with rejoicing and singing, just as the twenty-four elders do. The saints believed that what God had promised would surely come to pass, and they rejoiced when those promises were fulfilled. But the reality will far surpass any of our expectations. When the last trumpet sounds and God sits upon His judgment throne with the nations gathered before Him, that will be glorious! Will you be there?

Revelation 11 gives us a glimpse of what heaven will be like. But like most pictures of stunningly beautiful places, this picture also falls far short of reality. Some time ago, my wife and daughter went to a beautiful island off the coast of Greece. When they met me later in Amsterdam, my daughter showed me pictures of the place. But the pictures could not capture the majesty and beauty of what she had seen. Likewise, heaven will so exceed our expectations that we will cry out in shouting and singing as we praise God.

D-Day was the day the Allies invaded Normandy, France. It was the decisive day of World War II, when power began shifting away from Adolf Hitler and his forces. But while D-Day was decisive, the war didn't actually end until VE Day, nearly a year later. This was when victory was declared, and people across the world began to sing and shout about the end of the war in Europe. Likewise, when the trumpet sounds, believers will celebrate something like the ultimate VE Day, for God will have the final victory over Satan. Believers will continue to enjoy that celebration for all eternity.

Do you belong to the winning side of this war? Do you know what Jesus Christ, the Captain of our salvation, accomplished on the cross? At Calvary, Jesus crushed the head of the serpent and took away the sting of death. Are you with Him or against Him? If you are on Satan's side, you are on your way to hell. For you, the ark will only signify, as verse 19 says, "lightnings, and voices, and thunderings, and an earthquake, and great hail." It will be like God's shaking of Mount Sinai, warning people not to come closer lest they be destroyed (Exodus 19). God's final judgment is imminent; no one can stand before Him outside of His Son.

The seventh trumpet will soon sound. Meanwhile, the battle is still going on, and Christians must continue to face hardship, persecution, and suffering. But Calvary and the empty tomb assure believers that there is no doubt about who will win the war between God and Satan.

Our tendency in the midst of perplexity, pain, tribulation, and trials is to fixate on ourselves. We do that not only physically but metaphorically. We look into ourselves, and we go over and over the sadness of our condition. Scripture tells us to examine ourselves and to mortify sin, but we are to run the race of life primarily by looking to Jesus (Heb. 12:1–2). John is saying the same thing: keep your eyes on glory.

Let us be of good cheer, for Christ has overcome the world. He protects His people against satanic opposition and comforts us in suffering. His saints will proclaim the gospel until the kingdom comes in all its glory. Believers will be vindicated and raised from the dead. They will join Christ in His heavenly kingdom, which will triumph forever. So let us join the heavenly choir in praising and glorifying God the Father, Son, and Holy Spirit until the trumpet sounds!

21

The Man-Child and Woman Versus the Dragon

REVELATION 12:1–17

And there appeared a great wonder in heaven; a woman... and she being with child cried, travailing in birth, and pained to be delivered. And there appeared another wonder in heaven; and behold a great red dragon...stood before the woman which was ready to be delivered, for to devour her child as soon as it was born. And she brought forth a man child, who was to rule all nations with a rod of iron: and her child was caught up unto God, and to his throne. And the woman fled into the wilderness, where she hath a place prepared of God, that they should feed her there a thousand two hundred and threescore days. And there was war in heaven: Michael and his angels fought against the dragon; and the dragon fought and his angels, and prevailed not; neither was their place found any more in heaven. And the great dragon was cast out, that old serpent, called the Devil, and Satan, which deceiveth the whole world: he was cast out into the earth, and his angels were cast out with him. And I heard a loud voice saying in heaven, Now is come salvation, and strength, and the kingdom of our God, and the power of his Christ: for the accuser of our brethren is cast down, which accused them before our God day and night. And they overcame him by the blood of the Lamb, and by the word of their testimony; and they loved not their lives unto the death.... And the dragon was wroth with the woman, and went to make war with the remnant of her seed, which keep the commandments of God, and have the testimony of Jesus Christ.

The Christian in this life is always at war, for he belongs to the militant church on earth. He is engaged in holy war not only against the world's temptations and his own old nature, but he is also involved in a necessary, serious, spiritual, and holy war against Satan. This is a fierce battle. Thank God that Satan is only a fallen angel and does not have the power of God. On the other hand, however, he *is* a fallen angel, and therefore is much more powerful than we are and more powerful than the church is in her own strength. The believing church can only get the victory over Satan by faith in and through the Lord Jesus Christ.

So how does the living, militant church go about engaging, ejecting, enraging, and overcoming Satan? That is what Revelation 12 is all about.

Revelation 12–14 offers a fourth cycle of visions that falls between that of the seven trumpets (chs. 8–11) and that of the seven vials (chs. 15–16). These other cycles each begin with the first advent of Christ and end with His second coming. Likewise, this cycle begins in Revelation 12 with the birth and ascension of the Lord Jesus Christ and ends in chapter 14 with judgment day, with one "like unto the Son of man, having on his head a golden crown, and in his hand a sharp sickle" (v. 14).

The end of chapter 11 marks the halfway point in the book of Revelation—not only numerically, but also in terms of the message of Revelation. Chapter 12 is the very heart of the message of this book. Revelation 1–11 gives us a surface picture of the church persecuted by the world. Its trials and tribulations are depicted by the seven seals and the seven trumpets. But chapters 12–22 tell us what is going on behind the scenes of this conflict, nothing less than war in heaven.

The three main characters in the vision of Revelation 12 are the woman, the dragon, and the man-child. We must understand who these characters represent before we delve into the unfolding development of the vision.

Three Principal Characters

The Woman

Revelation 12:1–2 describes "a woman clothed with the sun, and the moon under her feet, and upon her head a crown of twelve stars: and she being with child...." Contrary to what some Roman Catholics say, and what much medieval art portrays, Scripture does not teach that this woman is the Virgin Mary. In fact, she is not any particular woman in history.

According to verse 1, this woman appears as a "great wonder" or a great sign in the heavens. She is a symbolic figure. The sun, moon, and stars around her remind us of Joseph's dream in Genesis 37:9–10: "And he dreamed yet another dream, and told it his brethren, and said, Behold, I have dreamed a dream more; and, behold, the sun and the moon and the eleven stars made obeisance to me. And he told it to his father, and to his brethren: and his father rebuked him, and said unto him, What is this dream that thou hast dreamed? Shall I and thy mother and thy brethren indeed come to bow down ourselves to thee to the earth?"

Clearly, Jacob understood the implication of Joseph's dream. Jacob surmised that the sun and the moon were symbols for him and his wife. The eleven stars were his eleven other children. So the woman of Revelation, who is "clothed with the sun, and the moon under her feet, and upon her head a crown of twelve stars," represents, first of all, the people of God under the old covenant, the twelve tribes of Israel. As such, she is the church in confinement, the church under the law, waiting for the birth of the Messiah from her body. Even then, she has a glory about her, for she is the beloved of the Lord (Song 6:10). She is clothed with the sun, which indicates her beauty. She has the moon under her feet, which represents her authority. And she is surrounded by twelve stars, which represent her royal status.[1]

---

1. Philip E. Hughes, *The Book of Revelation: A Commentary* (Grand Rapids: Eerdmans, 1990), 135.

Soon after the woman brings forth her child, Revelation 12:5 says that "her child was caught up unto God, and to his throne." He is snatched away from the jaws of the enormous red dragon and taken up to heaven. The woman flees into the wilderness, where God nourishes her, feeds her, and looks after her for three and a half years (v. 6), which is symbolic of the gospel age.

The woman represents not only the church of the Old Testament, but also the New Testament church. The number twelve represents not only the twelve tribes of Israel, but also the twelve apostles of the Lord (cf. Rev. 21:12, 14). She is not only the church of the Old Testament waiting to give birth to the Messiah, for after the child is born, the woman flees into the wilderness in an effort to escape the devil. But Satan, having been frustrated in his efforts to devour the child, persecutes her; in other words, he refocuses on the destruction of the New Testament church (vv. 13, 17). John is speaking here to first-century Christians who are suffering in "the wilderness," enduring one conflict after another. John assures them that though the dragon is pursuing them, God will provide for them and care for them (v. 14).

Thus, the woman represents the people of God in all ages. She is the embodiment of God's covenant promise to Abraham and his seed, that out of his line would come a Messiah who would bring saving blessing to all nations.

The Dragon

If the woman is the church, then the dragon is the devil. Revelation 12:9 says, "And the great dragon was cast out, that old serpent, called the Devil, and Satan, which deceiveth the whole world." The dragon is not an apocalyptic monster who will come to earth at a future date. He is the same serpent who deceived Adam and Eve in the Garden of Eden, who now persecutes God's church, and who one day will work powerfully through the antichrist.

Today, many people—even some who call themselves Christians—joke about the devil. Satan no doubt rejoices in such foolishness, but he is no laughing matter. He wants us to forget that he is the wily one who is the sworn enemy of Christ and all who belong to Him. Verse 10 says this "accuser of our brethren" is constantly accusing us of sin or trying to persuade us to sin. He tries to convince us that we are not Christians, thus robbing us of assurance of faith. He is the dragon with seven crowns and ten horns (v. 3), who dominates the whole earth. He is at work around us everywhere—in our homes and churches, in our unconverted relatives and friends, in our schools, offices, and worksites, and in governments throughout the nations. We need to see what a massive foe Satan really is. He is the dragon, the serpent, the devil, and the accuser of the brethren. Paul warns us in 2 Corinthians 2:11 to be wary of this dangerous enemy, "lest Satan should get an advantage of us: for we are not ignorant of his devices."

The Man-Child

We are told in Revelation 12:5 that the woman, here representing the Old Testament church, labors until she delivers "a man child, who was to rule all nations with a rod of iron." That is a quote from Psalm 2, a messianic psalm that refers to the Lord Jesus Christ. Next, the child is "caught up unto God, and to his throne." This refers to Christ's life, death, and resurrection, which are summed up in His ascension. This vision focuses on the ascension because John's purpose is to show first-century Christians that they are living in the wilderness in the post-ascension era, when Christ is no longer bodily present. This is to prepare them for heaven, where they will be with Jesus Christ forever.

With Revelation 12:5 in mind, consider verse 10: "And I heard a loud voice saying in heaven, Now is come salvation, and strength, and the kingdom of our God, and the power of his Christ: for the accuser of our brethren is cast down, which accused them before our God day and night." As the man child who brings salvation and strength to believers is taken up into heaven, the dragon is cast down. That is a great theme of Scripture.

These, then, are the three principle characters in Revelation 12. The woman, the dragon, and the man-child are the church, the devil, and Christ Jesus. Now let us look at the four main points of John's vision in this chapter: the dragon engaged (vv. 1–6); the dragon ejected (vv. 7–12a); the dragon enraged (vv. 12b–17); and the dragon overcome (v. 11).

The Dragon Engaged

Verse 3 describes the devil as a "great red dragon, having seven heads and ten horns, and seven crowns upon his heads." John is speaking symbolically here, not literally. He is painting word pictures to make an immediate impression on us, not defining things for us in a minute, technical way. Thus, we are not to think of a literal beast that will arise at some point in the future. Neither will we see a creature with seven heads and ten horns. The numbers here are symbols of royalty, so the beast with seven heads and seven crowns represents the one who is crowned king by this ungodly world (2 Cor. 4:4). His ten horns represent his power, showing us this enemy is mighty indeed.

By saying that the devil is a seven-headed monster, John is stressing that Satan has authority and influence all through the world. The apostle says in his First Epistle that the whole world lies in the power of this monster (1 John 5:19). Likewise, Jesus in the Gospels speaks of the devil as "the prince of this world" (John 12:31).

Satan's power is also emphasized in Revelation 12:4, which says that "his tail drew the third part of the stars of heaven." The stars pulled down from heaven represent the angels who joined Satan in his rebellion against God at some point after creation and before the fall of man. Notice that only a third part fell, indicating that though a large number of angels sided with Satan, the majority remained pure and obedient to God.[2]

The books of Isaiah and Ezekiel also mention the fall of Satan. They say that Satan was once a glorious angel, perhaps even one of

---

2. Another interpretation of Revelation 12:4 is that the sweeping of the stars from heaven by the dragon represents Satan's persecution of the saints (Dan. 8:10, 24; cf. Gen. 15:5).

the few archangels, who led the hosts of angels. There was a rebellion in heaven, in which Satan persuaded a third of the angels to rise up with him against God and make a bid for power. The fall of Satan is the backdrop of the fall of Adam. The tragedy of the human situation is that Satan and his accomplices, having been thrown out of heaven and cast down to earth, are presently granted by God a limited opportunity to instigate rebellion among mankind.

People are often mystified about the scope of original sin. What, they ask, was so terrible about Adam's eating a piece of fruit that it has affected the entire human race ever since? The answer is that the sin of Adam and Eve made them—and us—accomplices of Satan. We are guilty of aiding and abetting the devil in his attempt to dethrone God. That is the enormity of sin.

I am told that according to human law, an accomplice can be as guilty as the one who perpetrates a crime. We are in such a predicament. As fallen creatures, we are accomplices in Satan's bid for power and in his rebellion against the sovereignty of God. Remember how Satan whispered to Adam and Eve: "Has God said that you should not eat of that tree? Surely not! God wouldn't be so petty or so trifling as to say something like this" (see Gen. 3:1). Satan's motive was to undermine the authority of God. He also assured our first parents: "You won't die. God only told you that because He didn't want you to become like Him" (see Gen. 3:4–5). With his lies, Satan involved the entire human race in his attempt to overthrow God.

I suppose God could have stamped out the rebellion straightaway. I suppose God could have ignored it. But God doesn't work like that; He personally took on the enemy. That is what redemption through the Lord Jesus Christ is all about.

Genesis 3:15, the first announcement of the gospel, is the foundation of Revelation 12. Have you ever noticed who that gospel was first preached to? The first time the gospel was preached in this world was not to Adam and to Eve. Rather, God was talking to the serpent. Genesis 3:14–15 says: "And the LORD God said unto the serpent...I will put enmity between thee and the woman, and between thy seed

and her seed; it shall bruise thy head, and thou shalt bruise his heel."
Clearly God was speaking to the devil here. He was proclaiming
the gospel to the serpent, and Adam and Eve overheard it. That
was God's intention. They were saved by truly believing what they
overheard. There are many indications in Genesis 3 and 4 that our
first parents believed the gospel and were saved by it.

The gospel was God's answer to Satan's challenge. It was a savor
of life unto life to Adam, as it is to all who believe, but it is a savor of
death to that old serpent Satan. Every time the gospel is preached,
either in the shadowy types and ceremonies of the Old Testament
or in the full light of its fulfillment in the New Testament era, Satan
hears his death sentence. The history of redemption is based on the
conflict between Satan and Jesus Christ. In this war, God is engaging the enemy. The dragon, ever wary, stands ready to devour the
seed of the woman, but he knows that his days are numbered.

In the fullness of time, the Messiah came. Out of the stream
of humanity and out of the midst of the church came a man-child
who would crush the head of Satan and destroy his evil works. So
here in Revelation 12, which opens with the coming of Christ,
Satan is wary. Verse 4 says, "The dragon stood before the woman
which was ready to be delivered, for to devour her child as soon as
it was born." Time after time, Satan tries to devour the seed of the
woman. This is inherent in the conflicts of all ages, beginning with
the Old Testament accounts of Cain versus Abel, Ishmael versus
Isaac, and Esau versus Jacob. It is evident in Pharaoh's order that
his people destroy all of Israel's male children; the Egyptian army's
attack on the Israelites at the Red Sea; Haman's plot to destroy
the Jews in Esther's time; and Herod's slaughter of the infants
of Bethlehem.

But eventually the New Testament era dawns, and with it comes
the fulfillment of the messianic promises. As verse 5 says, "She
brought forth a man child, who was to rule all nations with a rod of
iron: and her child was caught up unto God, and to his throne." That
is a beautiful summary of our Lord's incarnation, life, death, resurrection, post-resurrection appearances, and ascension to the right hand

of God in heaven. The rebellious devil was waiting to attack Christ and His people. But as soon as the Savior came, He was snatched away from the devil. He died, rose again, and ascended to heaven. Satan failed to conquer Jesus by temptation in Judea's desert. He failed to induce Jesus to sin in Gethsemane, at the trial before the Sanhedrin, and at Golgotha. The only possibility Satan had of taking over the universe was to destroy the man child. But that child was snatched from the evil one at a place called Calvary.

The war of the ages has been fought and won, for Christ has decisively defeated the devil by His atoning death. The cross was not an unforeseen tragedy; it was the battlefield God prepared, before the foundation of the world, where His Son, Jesus Christ, would decisively defeat the dragon. Hebrews 2:14 says that in His death, Jesus destroyed Satan, who had the power of death. And Colossians 2:15 says that upon the cross, Christ openly triumphed over all principalities and powers of darkness. He came to this earth to destroy the power of the devil, and He has done that. He did it at Calvary. He also did it at the empty tomb. He does so now as He sits in heavenly places "to rule all nations with a rod of iron." And He will do it finally and forever in His final judgment.

The Dragon Ejected

Revelation 12:7–12a should not be seen as describing events that will happen in the future. Neither should this passage be seen as a chronological addendum to the verses that precede it. Rather, it should be viewed as a kind of replay of Christ's victory over Satan. When a sporting event is broadcast, the scoring of a goal is often shown again and again from different perspectives. Likewise, the effect of the historical events of Christ's life, death, and resurrection on earth and in heaven, which has already been pictured for us in verses 1–6, is depicted here in a new way.

Verses 7–8 tell us: "There was war in heaven: Michael and his angels fought against the dragon; and the dragon fought and his angels, and prevailed not." While Jesus hung on the cross just outside of Jerusalem, He could be seen by soldiers and passersby.

But at the same time, an invisible conflict was taking place in the heavenly realms. There was war in heaven between Michael and his angels against the dragon and his devils. All the time that Christ was living, dying, and being raised from the dead, a cosmic battle was going on.

In John 12:31–32, Jesus says of His death: "Now is the judgment of this world: now shall the prince of this world be cast out. And I, if I be lifted up from the earth, will draw all men unto me." The world might view Calvary as the lowest point in Jesus' life, for after His humiliation and sham judgment, He was sentenced to die as a criminal on a cross. But Jesus sees Calvary as the high point of His work on earth. He says that He is glorified in death. Being lifted up on the cross, He defeated the prince of this world, Satan, who was then hurled down.

The accuser of the brethren no longer has the power to destroy us. Because of the death of Christ on the cross, Satan has lost his place and his power over us. Soon he will be damned to hell forever. So Paul in Romans 8:33 argues: "Who shall lay any thing to the charge of God's elect?" Paul is, in effect, saying, "The devil has no argument and no case to bring against us because Christ has died and has been raised from the dead. Our sin has been paid for once and for all; thus, Satan can no longer accuse us or terrify us by showing us our sin. Christ has been raised for our justification. It is just as if we have never sinned."

The war of the worlds has been won. The devil is fighting for survival, but he has already been defeated and continues to be thrown down. No wonder, then, that heaven resounds with a shout of triumph. Revelation 12:10 says: "And I heard a loud voice saying in heaven, Now is come salvation, and strength, and the kingdom of our God, and the power of his Christ: for the accuser of our brethren is cast down, which accused them before our God day and night." The sovereign power of God the Father, the unassailable victory of the Son, and the guarantee of Spirit-worked salvation have been conclusively demonstrated at Golgotha. It is little wonder, then, that the devil is enraged.

The Dragon Enraged

Although Satan has been defeated and is on the run, he is still a force to be reckoned with. That is the main thrust of Revelation 12. It is the message John wants to share with Christians who are being persecuted by the Roman Empire. The apostle wants these believers to see the enemy and to understand what is going on. Satan is frustrated and angry because he has been defeated at Calvary, so he has turned his attention to the church and is trying to trap her with a stream of lies and delusions. When that is unsuccessful, Satan turns his attention to individual believers. Verse 17 says, "And the dragon was wroth with the woman, and went to make war with the remnant of her seed [Christians], which keep the commandments of God, and have the testimony of Jesus Christ." As individual believers, we all belong to the same family. We are that remnant.

Hebrews 2:10–12 says of the incarnation: "For it became him, for whom are all things, and by whom are all things, in bringing many sons unto glory, to make the captain of their salvation perfect through sufferings. For both he that sanctifieth and they who are sanctified are all of one: for which cause he is not ashamed to call them brethren, saying, I will declare thy name unto my brethren, in the midst of the church will I sing praise unto thee." God's purpose is to bring believers to glory. He does that by providing a Captain to fight the devil, who has the power of death. Christ is the Captain of our salvation. But this Captain had to be perfectly suited to the task. He had to be born of the Virgin Mary and become a man so that in His humanity, He might learn obedience through suffering and death as the punishment for our rebellion against God. This Captain is one of us.

Meantime, the devil, having been defeated by the Captain of our salvation, turns on us, the brethren of Christ. He turns in all his fury upon individual believers. One sure sign that you are related to Christ is that Satan attacks you personally. Samuel Rutherford, a Scottish Puritan, writes: "The devil's war is better than the devil's peace.... Suspect dumb holiness: when the dog is kept out of doors he howls to be let in again."[3]

Notice that Satan is given several titles in this chapter. He is the devil (v. 9), the slanderer, and the accuser of the brethren (v. 10). As the accuser, the devil can influence our memory of past sins. Dirty jokes we heard years before we were converted still stick in our minds. Sinful relationships we entered before we were converted still haunt us. Filthy images that we saw years ago still pollute our minds. Yet we can't remember last week's sermon! That is because the devil likes to dredge up our past and then blackmail us with the record of our sin. He is constantly accusing us before God.

Christians must be fortified against such attacks by learning the basic truths of the gospel. They must continually remember that in Jesus Christ and through His blood, both their sin and their remaining infirmity have been covered, buried in the deepest sea. God does not look at their sin anymore; He has forgotten it. But we are reminded of it often because the devil is on our backs. He accuses us, slanders us, and blackmails us.

Satan is also our adversary. The word *Satan* literally means "adversary." Peter tells us the devil prowls around like a roaring lion, seeking to devour whom he will (1 Peter 5:8). Sometimes he comes on tiptoe; sometimes he appears as an angel of light (2 Cor. 11:14). The devil plays so many games! For example, when you sit down to listen to the news in the evening, you can easily absorb what it says. But if you turn from the news and pick up your Bible, suddenly your concentration is gone. Likewise, you can surf the Internet for hours, but when you try to pray, you suddenly begin to get sleepy. That is how Satan works.

Joseph Hall says, "Satan lulls us to sleep, as he doth always rock the cradle when we sleep at our devotions."[4] We must be wary of Satan's devices. He tiptoes into our private devotions and begins to

---

3. Samuel Rutherford, *The Trial and Triumph of Faith* (Edinburgh: The Assembly's Committee, 1845), 403.

4. Joseph Hall, *Contemplations on the Historical Passages of the Old and New Testament* (London: Society for Promoting Christian Knowledge, 1846), 3:284.

rock us in the cradle, and before we know it, we are fast asleep. We need to recognize that Satan is our adversary. He has countless ways of getting at us.

Then, too, Satan is the tempter, the old serpent who wound his way into the Garden of Eden. He also winds his way into our lives. Think of King David, for example. When he was just a shepherd boy, he took on a bear and a lion to protect his sheep. When he was a little older, he took down a blasphemous giant named Goliath. As a young adult, he escaped the deadly machinations of King Saul. With an army of misfits, he established a kingdom. Yet a woman bathing on the roof next door brought him down. That sort of fall is also the work of the tempter, for he knows our weak points. He knows where to slither in to push us into sin. We must be on guard against Satan by watching and praying. We must be equipped to face the fury of an enraged enemy and, by grace, overcome him.

The Dragon Overcome

The highlight of Revelation 12 is verse 11: "And they overcame him by the blood of the Lamb, and by the word of their testimony; and they loved not their lives unto the death." This verse makes the following points about the church's victory over Satan through Jesus Christ.

First, *we are safe in Christ*. If you belong to the true church of Christ, Revelation 12 assures you that God has put you in a safe place. Verse 11 tells us that we will overcome Satan even unto death. Verse 6 says, "The woman fled into the wilderness, where she hath a place prepared of God, that they should feed her there a thousand two hundred and threescore days." And verse 14 says the woman is "given two wings of a great eagle, that she might fly into the wilderness, into her place, where she is nourished for a time, and times, and half a time, from the face of the serpent." These numerical references, which equate to 1,260 days, 42 months, or 3.5 years, correspond to the period of time during which the prophet Elijah called down a famine upon Israel and hid from the anger of wicked Ahab and Jezebel in the wilderness. During this time, the prophet was miraculously fed by ravens in the wilderness, and then stayed with a widow, where again God miraculously provided food for them (1 Kings 16). Just as God cared for, protected, and vindicated Elijah, so too He will protect and care for us against the enraged enemy. When Satan is furious, God bears us out of harm's way. When the enemy tries to drown us, God raises us up. When Satan distracts, attacks, accuses, and slanders us, God is by our side, ready to nourish, protect, and feed us.

Second, *we are more than conquerors in Christ.* Revelation 12:11 says, "And they overcame him by the blood of the Lamb, and by the word of their testimony; and they loved not their lives unto the death." We can overcome the dragon, resist the wiles of the serpent, and stand up to Satan—but only by the blood of Christ. We cannot resist him in ourselves, of course, for that would be a mismatch. Indeed, the greatest mismatch of all time is a pregnant woman versus a dragon. The woman gives birth in the wilderness, where a dragon with seven heads stands ready to devour the child. But the child is snatched up to heaven, and the woman goes to a safe house God has prepared for her. In ourselves, we are no match for the devil, but by the blood of Jesus, we can overcome.

I once read of someone who was in the middle of a wheat field when it caught on fire. With flames threatening to overcome him, he suddenly remembered a friend telling him that in such a situation, he should light a fire at his feet and let the wind blow upon it until there was a significant area where the wheat had been burned. Then, if he stood in the middle of that burnt ground, he would be all right. The fire would rage around him, but as long as he stood on the burnt ground, he would be safe.[5]

However true that may be physically, it is certainly true spiritually. It is what John means when he speaks of believers overcoming the devil by the blood of the Lamb. The only way to stand firm against the dragon and to keep your testimony to the end is to trust

---

5. Michael Green, *I Believe in Satan's Downfall* (Grand Rapids: Eerdmans, 1981), 223.

in the blood of Christ. God's wrath has already fallen upon Christ and His justice has been satisfied. The fires of divine judgment will never touch Him again. If you are in Christ, you are on safe ground. So flee to the burnt ground of Calvary, where the wrath of God has already burned against sin. Rest upon that ground and trust your Savior. As John Newton says:

> Be thou my shield and hiding place!
> That, sheltered near thy side,
> I may my fierce accuser face,
> And tell him, "thou hast died."[6]

We are no match for this fearsome dragon who threatens to destroy us. But we can face our accuser when we stand on burnt ground and trust in the blood of Jesus Christ as a propitiation for our sin. We are justified before God. We are more than conquerors. We are not working and waiting for victory, but working because victory has already been won. We are standing at Calvary, where Satan was decisively defeated. And we are on the side that will ultimately triumph, no matter how much persecution we must endure in this life.

We can also overcome Satan and sin by moving forward in the sanctifying power of the Holy Spirit. According to verse 17, the first key to this overcoming life is *a thorough grounding in God's Word and commandments*. This must be joined with our testimony, which is grounded in God's Word. We can say with John that we, by grace, are empowered to "keep the commandments of God, and have the testimony of Jesus." By God's grace, we stand firm in our faith in Scripture and walk accordingly. We can say with David, "Thy word [that is, God's commandments, law, and gospel] have I hid in mine heart, that I might not sin against thee" (Ps. 119:11). We are learning to view life through lenses that have been ground for us in the Scriptures. If we do that, we will be able to recognize Satan when he comes after us. We will unmask him and overcome him through

---

6. John Newton, "Approach, My Soul, the Mercy-seat" (1779).

the power of the Word of Christ, which dwells in us richly as we walk in the way of God's commandments.

The second key to overcoming is *perseverance*. Revelation 12:17 says the dragon is so furious that he will continue to wage war with believers, but verse 11 says that the overcomers "loved not their lives unto the death." We must be willing to suffer, even to die, for our Lord who died for us. We must persist in our faith, obedience, and testimony to the gospel. We might prefer an easier way than taking up our cross and denying ourselves, but Christ has told us that this is the only way to follow Him (Luke 9:23).

God will give us grace to press on, no matter how much we are persecuted. He will give us grace to follow God fully, as faithful Caleb did after investigating the Promised Land (Num. 14:24). In the end, the mighty cause of our perseverance with God is His perseverance with us (Jer. 32:39–40). He will not forsake us, but will guard us by faith through all our trials (1 Peter 1:5). We overcome because Christ has overcome.

As Sinclair Ferguson says: "You need to persist in your testimony. You need Spirit-given courage to overcome Satan by the blood of the Lamb—He has died for your sins—and the word of your testimony as one who does not love his or her life to death." Ferguson admits that he would prefer an easier way to overcome the dragon than to give all of himself to Christ. We are prone to think, "If I can give only 95 percent of my life to Jesus Christ, I can be sure I can overcome the dragon." But Ferguson goes on to warn us that the devil has grown from a serpent to a dragon because of people who have been only 95 percent committed. "No; the only way to overcome the dragon is when Christ has all of you and you have all of Christ," Ferguson says. "You are only safe when He has *all* of you. But oh the glory when He has all of you, because then you know that you have all of Him."[7]

---

7. Sinclair B. Ferguson, Sermon on Revelation 12.

Believers may rest gloriously in the victory and love of Jesus Christ, for He has overcome! As the songwriter Stuart Townend confessed:

> In Christ alone my hope is found;
> He is my light, my strength, my song.
> This cornerstone, this solid ground,
> Firm through the fiercest drought and storm.
>
> What heights of love, what depths of peace
> What fears are stilled when strivings cease;
> My comforter, my All in all
> Here in the love of Christ I stand.[8]

---

8. "In Christ Alone" (2001).

22

The Dragons Helpers: The Two Beasts

REVELATION 13:1–18

And I stood upon the sand of the sea, and saw a beast rise up out of the sea, having seven heads and ten horns, and upon his horns ten crowns, and upon his heads the name of blasphemy.... And they worshipped the dragon which gave power unto the beast: and they worshipped the beast, saying, Who is like unto the beast? Who is able to make war with him? And there was given unto him a mouth speaking great things and blasphemies; and power was given unto him to continue forty and two months. And he opened his mouth in blasphemy against God, to blaspheme his name, and his tabernacle, and them that dwell in heaven. And it was given unto him to make war with the saints, and to overcome them: and power was given him over all kindreds, and tongues, and nations. And all that dwell upon the earth shall worship him, whose names are not written in the book of life of the Lamb slain from the foundation of the world.... And I beheld another beast coming up out of the earth; and he had two horns like a lamb, and he spake as a dragon. And he exerciseth all the power of the first beast before him, and causeth the earth and them which dwell therein to worship the first beast, whose deadly wound was healed.... And he causeth all, both small and great, rich and poor, free and bond, to receive a mark in their right hand, or in their foreheads: and that no man might buy or sell, save he that had the mark, or the name of the beast, or the number of his name. Here is wisdom. Let him that hath understanding count the number of the beast: for it is the number of a man; and his number is Six hundred threescore and six.

The Bible is clear and plain about the way of salvation and about the way we should live in this world. If you are serious about living for the purpose for which you are created, namely, to live to God's glory, there is no clearer book on earth to guide you than the Holy Bible. Do you read, know, search, love, and strive to live out the clear directions of the Holy Scriptures? If you do, you know the blessings of such a life, which are better felt and experienced than explained and defended.

Some details of the Bible, however, can be challenging and difficult to understand. Peter states that this is true of some of Paul's profound theological writing in his epistles (2 Peter 3:15–16). It is also true of certain genres used in Scripture, particularly apocalyptic literature such as we find in the books of Daniel and Revelation.

Chapter 13 is one of the most difficult chapters in Revelation. The main teaching of this chapter is quite plain, but some of the details seem mysterious and obscure. Therefore, let us examine the chapter as a whole; with that understanding, the significance of the details will become more evident.

Chapter 13 continues the theme of the previous chapter by describing the dragon's war on the church. Jesus, the man child of chapter 12, has been caught up to heaven. Throughout the history of the Old Testament, the devil attempted to destroy God's people and prevent the coming of Christ. Each time, his attacks failed. So, having been utterly thwarted and defeated by the birth of the man child, the devil has turned his attention to the woman in the wilderness, who represents the church in the New Testament age. With the fury of frustration, Satan is waging war against the saints of God. In this context, John sees two beasts rise, one from the sea (13:1) and the other from the earth (13:11). The whole chapter can be summarized under four headings: the distinction between the beasts, the identity of the beasts, the mark and number of the beasts, and the Sovereign in control over the beasts.

The Distinction between the Beasts

The two beasts in Revelation 13 are both allies of Satan in his war on the church. As his agents, they are invested with his power, throne, and authority. Verse 1 says, "I stood upon the sand of the sea, and saw a beast rise up out of the sea, having seven heads and ten horns, and upon his horns ten crowns, and upon his heads the name of blasphemy." Then verse 2 says, "The dragon gave him his power, and his seat [throne], and great authority," and verse 7 adds, "It was given unto him to make war with the saints, and to overcome them: and power was given him over all kindreds, and tongues, and nations." Next, verse 11 says, "I beheld another beast coming up out of the earth; and he had two horns like a lamb, and he spake as a dragon." Then verse 12a adds, "And he exerciseth all the power of the first beast before him." These two beasts, closely resembling their lord and prince, fight alongside Satan against the saints.

Therefore, the two beasts represent earthly powers which the devil employs to accomplish his purposes. In some respects, we have a demonic reflection of the Trinity here, for the dragon empowers the first beast to rule (like the Father has appointed His Son to reign), and the second beast glorifies the first beast among men (like the Spirit glorifies the Son). Revelation 16:13 says of the unholy trinity of the dragon and the two beasts, "And I saw three unclean spirits like frogs come out of the mouth of the dragon, and out of the mouth of the beast, and out of the mouth of the false prophet." These three figures also suffer the same fate: punishment in the "lake of fire" (Rev. 19:20; 20:10).

Though these beasts belong together and work together to serve the interests of Satan, the seven-headed beast from the sea and the beast that looks like a lamb from the land are quite different.

First, *the beasts differ in appearance.* The first beast has seven heads, ten crowned horns, feet like a bear, a body like a leopard, and a mouth like a lion (vv. 1–2). This beast has the same characteristics of the four beasts Daniel saw in a vision (Daniel 7). Philip Hughes explains,

It was like a leopard (as also was Daniel's third beast); its feet were like those of a bear (Daniel's second beast was like a bear); its mouth was like the mouth of a lion (Daniel's first beast was like a lion); and (like Daniel's "terrible and dreadful and exceedingly strong" fourth beast) it had ten horns. These features emphasize its fearsome aspect and also the concentration of the savage ungodliness of the successive empires of this fallen world.[1]

By contrast, the second beast seems quite docile. It looks like a child's pet lamb, but its appearance is deceptive because it speaks like a dragon. Hughes writes, "Like a lamb with two horns, it parades as a saviour similar to, but in reality quite other than, the Lamb that was slain for our redemption (verse 8). But it is a false saviour with a false message of salvation: it spoke like a dragon since its voice is no different from the voice of the dragon (verse 3) and its lying words are the lying words of the dragon."[2] Like the first beast, this beast is Satan's helper in his efforts to destroy the true worship of God throughout human history.

Second, *the beasts differ in their domains.* The first beast is Satan's secular friend. The first half of chapter 13 describes the power of the first beast as political. His glory lies in his military power, such that the wicked marvel, "Who is able to make war with him?" (Rev. 13:4). By comparison, the second beast's power is religious, leading the world to worship the first beast by signs and wonders. The first beast, then, is Satan's political friend, while the second is Satan's religious ally. F. F. Bruce says, "The second beast is not the Antichrist in person; he is rather his public relations officer, or minister of propaganda, the 'false prophet of a false god.'"[3]

The two beasts seek to usurp the position of Christ, and therefore are rightly called antichrist, although in different ways. The first

---

1. Hughes, *The Book of Revelation*, 146.
2. Hughes, *The Book of Revelation*, 151.
3. F. F. Bruce, "Antichrist in the Early Church," in *A Mind for What Matters: Collected Essays of F. F. Bruce* (Grand Rapids: Eerdmans, 1990), 188.

beast would take the position of Christ the King. Beale notes the following parallels between the first beast and the royal Messiah:

- Both were slain and rise to new life (5:6 and 13:3).
- Both have followers with their names written on their foreheads (13:16 and 14:1).
- Both have horns (5:6 and 13:1).
- Both have authority over every "tribe, tongue, people, and nation" (5:9; 7:9 and 13:7; 17:12, 15).
- Both receive worldwide worship (5:8–14 and 13:4, 8).
- Both have a final coming or manifestation, though one is to destruction and the other to eternal victory (17:7–18).[4]

The second beast would take the position of Christ the Prophet and Priest. Like the Lord Jesus, this beast is described as a lamb with horns. The beast directs the worship of the people. He works miracles like the prophet Elijah (1 Kings 18:36–38; 2 Kings 1:10, 12), and is later called "the false prophet" (Rev. 16:13; 19:20; 20:10). The Lord Jesus warned, "For there shall arise false Christs, and false prophets, and shall shew great signs and wonders; insomuch that, if it were possible, they shall deceive the very elect" (Matt. 24:24). John wrote that even in his day there were "many antichrists" who disrupted the church and taught false doctrine (1 John 2:18–19, 22).

The two beasts, which look so different, warn us not to be ignorant of Satan's devices. The devil can be perfectly beastly at times, but he can also be positively charming. It is easy to recognize an attack of the devil when he comes at you as a beast with seven heads and ten horns or as a roaring lion. But it is not so easy to recognize Satan in the guise of a lamb. Some of us are woefully ignorant when it comes to discerning truth from error. If something looks like a lamb, we pat it on the head. If a church calls itself Christian, evangelical, or Reformed, we are prone to embrace it. We must

---

4. Beale, *Revelation: A Shorter Commentary*, 271.

remember that though the devil comes like a roaring lion, he can
also appear as an angel of light (2 Cor. 11:14)—or as a wooly lamb.

In the Sermon on the Mount, Jesus warns us, "Beware of false
prophets, which come to you in sheep's clothing, but inwardly they
are ravening wolves" (Matt. 7:15). People in the media who broadcast Christian messages seem nice and sincere, but often what
comes out of their mouths is unbiblical. We must exercise discernment in regard to what we hear or read. We must be on our guard
against Satan's devices. John Calvin describes the devil as "God's
ape," meaning that what he does on earth only imitates the work
of God.[5]

The Identity of the Beasts

Many have tried to identify who these beasts represent. Some interpretations are sincere and some are sensational; some are serious
and some are silly; some are intelligent and some are inane. But the
Christians of John's day would have had no trouble identifying the
two beasts. These first readers of Revelation were being persecuted
by officials of the imperial government. Whether the persecution
was instigated by Nero, Domitian, or some local ruler, it came upon
believers with brutal savagery. In such wicked rulers, early Christians
saw the first beast: the deified military and political power of man.

As to the second beast, the Roman imperial powers did not
oppose the worship of various gods, so long as those worshipers
honored the Emperor. In fact, in Asia Minor there were priests
and temples devoted specifically to the worship of the genius of
the Emperor. One such temple in Ephesus housed a large statue of
Domitian. Christians in Asia Minor felt increasing pressure to publicly offer worship to the Emperor, and refusal to participate could
result in economic exclusion from commerce, and worse yet, capital
punishment from the civil authorities.[6]

5. Calvin, *Commentaries*, on Acts 21:10–11.
6. Beale, *The Book of Revelation*, 712–16.

Therefore, although John wrote in cloaked language, it would have been clear to the first recipients of this book that he referred to the idolatrous political and religious systems by which Satan attacked the church through the civic and cultural institutions of the world.

One of the heads of the first beast seems to have a fatal wound, but the wound heals (Rev. 13:3). That is a good description of the power of Rome, which was unrelenting in its persecution of Christians. Who could fight against this empire and its rulers? No doubt Christians in John's day hoped that when Nero was killed, persecution would cease and Rome would be finished. But no sooner is one head mortally wounded than another Caesar comes to the throne and renews the attacks against the church.

Written on each of the seven heads of the first beast is a blasphemous name (v. 1). This name is an encoded reference to the cult of emperor worship. People in the Roman Empire couldn't buy and sell anything unless they had coins engraved with an image of the emperor's head and inscribed with the title "divine," honoring his claim to be God. They couldn't conduct ordinary business or even go into a shop and buy something unless they had this mark of the beast. Satan worked in the Roman Empire through its emperors, just as he works through today's world leaders.

The Caesars sought to unify their empire through religion. Think of all the nations and religions that were under Rome's rule. To unify people of such diverse cultures, the emperors ordered everyone under their jurisdiction to acknowledge them as Lord and God. Priests were appointed to implement the worship of Caesar. One such priest was in Asia, where John had established churches. This priest had total control of religion in his region, and his whole purpose, despite appearing to be religious, was to unify the empire by bringing the people of Asia into compliance with Caesar's demands. People could keep their religions if they wanted to, but, to create a semblance of unity and loyalty, they all had to acknowledge that the emperor was God.

John is referring to Rome in chapter 13, but he speaks in symbolic language. He writes this way to protect himself, his readers, and the book of Revelation itself. If he were to specifically name Caesar or the priest in Asia, Revelation would not be distributed. Any person found reading the book would be sentenced to death. So John writes in code about a dreadful reality in history. He writes about Rome as a secular and religious power that is raining destruction upon the followers of Christ.

But we should not confine the interpretation of Revelation's beasts to first-century Rome. We have seen throughout Revelation that symbols refer both to historic events and to what is going on today. These two beasts have appeared together in human history in many places and times as nation after nation has arisen to fight against God and His Christ. Very often, the state has enlisted the help of religion in waging war against Christ and His people.

For example, during the Reformation, true believers were persecuted by both state and church under the influence of the Bishop of Rome. That explains why the Reformers and Puritans found very good reasons to view the pope as the antichrist. When one reads their list of Scripture proofs and reasons for identifying the papacy as antichrist, their case seems irrefutable.

The same beasts are also at work today, as politics and religion unite against the people of God. The World Council of Churches tolerates any kind of religion, except those that believe that the Bible is true.

Revelation 13 teaches us that these two beasts have labored to destroy the church throughout history. They represent what the Bible describes elsewhere as the "spirit of antichrist" (1 John 4:3). John comforts the early Christians by noting that these antichrists are a sign we are living in the last times (1 John 2:18). The last times stretch from the first coming of Christ to His second coming, during which time there have already been many antichrists. But Scripture also tells us that at the end of time *the* antichrist will come, who is the epitome of rebellion against God. This may be a person or an institution, but John's point is that the spirit of antichrist is evident throughout history.

Paul also warns believers in 2 Thessalonians 2:1–7:

Now we beseech you, brethren, by the coming of our Lord Jesus Christ, and by our gathering together unto him, that ye be not soon shaken in mind, or be troubled, neither by spirit, nor by word, nor by letter as from us, as that the day of Christ is at hand. Let no man deceive you by any means: for that day shall not come, except there come a falling away first, and that man of sin be revealed, the son of perdition; who opposeth and exalteth himself above all that is called God, or that is worshipped; so that he as God sitteth in the temple of God, shewing himself that he is God. Remember ye not, that, when I was yet with you, I told you these things? And now ye know what withholdeth that he might be revealed in his time. For the mystery of iniquity doth already work: only he who now letteth will let, until he be taken out of the way.

Paul is saying here that the man of sin is both a person and a principle. He will certainly come, though he is "let" or restrained at the present time. However, his spirit is already at work. That is why Paul says, "The mystery of iniquity doth already work."

John has something far greater than Nero in his sights here. John's contemporaries undoubtedly thought that the beast that came up out of the sea stood for the power of Rome. But the greater devastation the beast wreaks is bringing all human wickedness and godlessness together into one great alliance of evil. That is what John is warning us about. He says in Revelation 13:4, "They worshipped the dragon which gave power unto the beast: and they worshipped the beast, saying, Who is like unto the beast? Who is able to make war with him?"

John initially says that it seems that no one can defeat the beast. The antichrist is so clever that he fools the masses, evoking worldwide admiration. That is true not only of the secular beast of humanism, but also of the man-centered religious power of the papacy throughout the ages. No wonder, then, that John says that the whole world is under the power of the evil one (1 John 5:19).

Actually, the situation is even worse—the world *worships* the beast and makes the dragon "the god of this world" (2 Cor. 4:4).

Fallen mankind substitutes Satan-worship for God-worship. That is evident all around us today, as people do what they think is right in their own eyes. All the while godly people are judged as intolerant when they refuse to bow down to the forces of humanism that degrade the Bible, mock Christians, promote unbridled sex, kill unborn babies, promote homosexuality, and desecrate the Lord's day. Similarly, millions of people exalt the papacy as Christ's infallible spokesman on earth, all the while blind to the fact that the papacy—as the Reformers and Puritans show so poignantly in their writings—manifests every quality about the antichrist that the scriptures set forth. Then too, many false religions can live quite happily with a wicked and tyrannical government, and many pastors and priests, including some claiming to be Christians, willingly become the tools of an intolerant state and culture.

How can we stand against such beasts? How can we be true to God when the powerful secular world around us argues, "Everybody is doing it; so why shouldn't you?" or "Nobody believes the Bible is infallible anymore"? How can we stand against the religious world that promotes self-worship, sacrifices Christ afresh in every Mass, or teaches that the Koran is more trustworthy than Holy Scripture? In a world that does not worship, know, trust, or love the Lamb of God, finding its salvation in Him alone, how can we boldly and unashamedly put all our trust in Him?

Paul tells us how to stand firm against the beasts. He says in Ephesians 6:10–12: "Finally, my brethren, be strong in the Lord, and in the power of his might. Put on the whole armour of God, that ye may be able to stand against the wiles of the devil. For we wrestle not against flesh and blood, but against principalities, against powers, against the rulers of the darkness of this world, against spiritual wickedness in high places." Revelation 13 confirms Paul's statement that we do not wrestle against flesh and blood, but against principalities and powers of darkness. Behind the visible manifestations of the beasts stands the devil, the ancient serpent. A network of evil lurks behind this world. The world is in the grip of institutions and ideologies that transcend the individual and condition his lifestyle.

We live in a consumer society that is rife with hidden persuaders, multinational companies, ideologies, and -isms that wage war against Christ and His church. We should look behind these things to see the beasts of Revelation, the mystery of iniquity, the power of antichrist, and the devil's schemes against the church.

Revelation 13 tells us not to be swept along or intimidated by such evil. Rather, we are to watch and pray. We are to put on the whole armor of God: the belt of truth, the breastplate of righteousness, the sandals of peace, and the helmet of salvation, and to take up the shield of faith, the sword of the Spirit, and the sword of all prayer. So armed, we may go forth and fight the beasts of Satan in the Lord's strength.

The Mark and Number of the Beast

Verses 16 and 17 tell us how to identify the beasts. They say, "And he causeth all, both small and great, rich and poor, free and bond, to receive a mark in their right hand, or in their foreheads: And that no man might buy or sell, save he that had the mark, or the name of the beast, or the number of his name."

The mark of the beast, like so many things in Revelation, should not be taken literally but symbolically. We are not to look for a barcode, a brand mark, or a credit card number that is to be embedded on the forehead or the right hand. Myriad suggestions have been made by those who view the entire book of Revelation as literal. Their interpretations and predictions may be entertaining and sell books, but they mishandle Revelation and its symbols.

The mark of the beast is not a literal mark any more than is the mark of God's elect, which seals them as His own (Rev. 7:3–4). The mark of the beast is simply a sign of ownership. In the days of Roman rule, slaves were marked with their owner's seal, which meant they had to serve that person. Receiving the mark of the beast, then, means that you belong to Satan, serve him, and worship him. The mark is pressed upon the forehead, which symbolizes the mind or philosophy of a person; or on the right hand, symbolizing a person's actions, deeds, trade, and industry. In other words, when people's thinking and actions are controlled by someone who hates Christ, they bear the mark of the beast.

Has the beast left his mark upon you? You may profess with your mouth that you are Christian. But what do you think about the Lamb, and how do you act? Do your thoughts and actions tell others that you belong to Christ? Or do you appear more like a slave of the great red dragon and his world?

It is possible to profess that you belong to the Lamb while thinking and acting like a dragon. When you habitually behave like dragon people, speak like dragon people, or think like dragon followers, your profession is false. May God help those who delude themselves and those around them that they are sealed by the blood of the Lamb.

Some of you say you are Christians, but what you do in business is contrary to what is taught in the Bible. You say, "We are in the world; so we must use the methods of the world." Yes, we are in this world, but it is pervaded by the spirit of antichrist. To what extent has this left its mark on our heads and hands?

The beast out of the earth also has a number. Verse 18 says, "Here is wisdom." Notice that it doesn't say, "Here is a riddle for you to solve if you're clever enough." Many people have attempted to interpret the number of the beast, and their theories range from the pope's phone number, to a special number on a computer, to the name of a particular man reduced to a number by a code. These ideas are simply ludicrous. John's advice is clear. In speaking of wisdom, he says, "Let him that hath understanding count the number of the beast: for it is the number of a man; and his number is Six hundred threescore and six"—that is, 666. In Scripture, the number *six* is often a symbol of fallen man, with all his sins and shortcomings. Hendriksen explains this succinctly: "Six is not seven, and never reaches seven. It always fails to attain to perfection; that is, it never becomes seven. Six means missing the mark, or failure. Seven means perfection or victory. Rejoice, O Church of God! The victory is on your side. The number of the beast is 666, that is, failure upon failure upon failure. It is the number of man, for the beast glories in man; and must fail."[7]

The number of the beast, then, is the number identifying those who do not fear God. The sixes of the beast fall far short of the sevens of the Holy Trinity. So those with the mark of the beast are ungodly. They refuse to worship God, preferring lies about Him rather than the truth, and going their own way into increasing ungodliness.

Do you have any spiritual insight, wisdom, or understanding about what is going on in this world and behind it? Have you seen what this world and its ideologies, institutions, and personalities add up to? They are marked with 666, the number of human failure. John wants us to be wise about the world in which we live, which is pervaded by the spirit of antichrist. This world can be so impressive and intimidating that we are afraid to call it what it is. But John says the world is doomed to fail.

The Sovereign over the Beasts

All is not lost, however strong the dragon and his beasts appear, for we know that the ultimate victory belongs to our Lord Jesus Christ and His chosen ones, not to the dragon and his beastly followers. That is true for two reasons. First, the dragon and his beasts will be defeated because their authority is limited in duration. Their power will last only forty-two months, John says, and then will come to an end. In Revelation 12:12, John says the devil himself knows "he hath but a short time."

Also, Satan and his beasts will be defeated because their authority is not supreme. At times they may appear to conquer the saints as they make war against them, as Revelation 13:7 states. Many saints in this world are arrested, imprisoned, and killed. Yet the victory of Satan and his helpers is only temporary. This is not only because they are creatures and not the almighty Creator, but also because, as John says in Revelation 12:11, believers who are persecuted shall

7. Hendriksen, *More than Conquerors*, 151.

overcome the evil one by the blood of the Lamb. Christ, who is God, will have the final word over Satan.

The great composer Johann Sebastian Bach had a rather unusual way of getting up in the morning. His children would go to the piano and play a few lines of music, leaving off the last note. Bach would awaken, get out of bed, and strike the last chord. That is much like what John is saying here about the number of the beast. Everything that is created by man and the world is incomplete. John wants believers to yearn for the perfection found only in Christ. He wants to wake us from the sleep of death so we may hear the last trumpet sound. The whole creation groans and travails for the time when Jesus Christ will return and create a new heaven and earth. Like Bach, it waits for the last chord to sound. As Christians, we are not to be satisfied by a mere 666. We are to strive for perfection and completeness in Christ.

If you have any wisdom, says John, calculate the number of the beast. Understand that ultimate victory belongs to the Lamb and His followers. Revelation 10 offers a marvelous picture of Christ as the great angel of God with a book in His hand. Verses 1 and 2 say: "And I saw another mighty angel come down from heaven, clothed with a cloud: and a rainbow was upon his head, and his face was as it were the sun, and his feet as pillars of fire: and he had in his hand a little book open: and he set his right foot upon the sea, and his left foot on the earth." That should give us the correct perspective on the battle between the dragon and the Lamb.

The great red dragon is frightening until you look up to Christ, who stands with one foot in the sea and one foot on the land. Christ towers over all the movements and institutions of men. He dwarfs every human civilization that has ever been. He crushes sinful human endeavors with feet that were hammered to a cross for our salvation. He rules the earth. We are told that God has put all things under His feet. That includes the beasts, the dragon, and, yes, us as well. Paul tells us that by His death Christ openly triumphed over all principalities and powers of darkness. By Christ's blood, we shall also overcome! We can say with Paul, "Thanks be to God, which giveth us the victory through our Lord Jesus Christ" (1 Cor. 15:57). As he says elsewhere, "We are more than conquerors through him that loved us" (Rom. 8:37).

We must realize that if we are not in Christ, we are on the side of the great red dragon and will fail with him. In Revelation 13:8, John tells us that all of us by nature worship Satan and his helpers. Our only hope is that our name is "written in the book of life of the Lamb slain from the foundation of the world."

Here are some ways for you to personally respond to chapter 13:

First, *pray for grace to recognize the beasts of Satan.* You know their character. You know what they are and how they operate. You know that they not only persecute Christians around the globe in violent ways, but also in seductive, subtle, and even religious ways that are not biblical. Do not be ignorant of Satan's devices.

Second, *repent of all the ways you think, speak, and act that flow out of your selfish and beastly heart.* Repent of your tendencies to cater to the lusts of the flesh, the lusts of the eye, and the pride of life (1 John 2:16). Ask for the Spirit's grace to show you who you truly are, to cause you to abhor your sin, and to help you repent in dust and ashes before Almighty God and this glorious Lamb.

Third, *trust in the Lamb.* Recognize that Jesus is Lord over all. Trust in His perfect work of redemption on behalf of sinners. Do not rest until you can say, "He is my Lord and my God." Continue until you are assured that your name is written in the Lamb's Book of Life and you are forever safe in Him. Only the triune God, Father, Son, and Holy Spirit, can meet your every need and lift you out of failure into increasing perfection as you follow the Lamb.

23

The Lamb on Mount Zion

REVELATION 14:1–5

And I looked, and, lo, a Lamb stood on the mount Sion, and with him an hundred forty and four thousand, having his Father's name written in their foreheads. And I heard a voice from heaven, as the voice of many waters, and as the voice of a great thunder: and I heard the voice of harpers harping with their harps: and they sung as it were a new song before the throne, and before the four beasts, and the elders: and no man could learn that song but the hundred and forty and four thousand, which were redeemed from the earth. These are they which were not defiled with women; for they are virgins. These are they which follow the Lamb whithersoever he goeth. These were redeemed from among men, being the firstfruits unto God and to the Lamb. And in their mouth was found no guile: for they are without fault before the throne of God.

Have you ever noticed that life often feels like a series of contrasts? There are contrasts between the rich and the poor, the educated and the uneducated, Western and Eastern civilization. There are theological contrasts between God's sovereignty and man's responsibility, the objective and subjective truths of Christianity, righteousness and unrighteousness, the believer and the unbeliever.

The Bible too is often packed with contrasts. Particularly Revelation is a book of contrasts. It repeatedly focuses on God's throne, mentioned thirty-two times. The throne of God is unsurpassed in majesty and sovereignty. But it is not unchallenged. Revelation also shows us that Satan is continually waging war against God's throne.

When we compare the vision of the two beasts in Revelation 13 with the vision of the Lamb on Mount Zion in Revelation 14:1–5, a staggering contrast is apparent. By looking closer at these visions, we may appreciate and draw comfort from this contrast.

Keep in mind that Revelation 14 is not history; that is, the vision of the Lamb on Mount Zion does not follow chronologically from the vision of the two beasts in the last chapter. Rather, the two chapters are counterparts; chapter 13 describes the kingdom of antichrist, while chapter 14 describes the kingdom of the Lamb.

Let me illustrate from the experience of the prophet Elisha at Dothan, when he and his servant were surrounded by the Syrians. Second Kings 6:15–17 says:

> And when the servant of the man of God was risen early, and gone forth, behold, an host compassed the city both with horses and chariots. And his servant said unto him, Alas, my master! how shall we do? And he answered, Fear not: for they that be with us are more than they that be with them. And Elisha prayed, and said, LORD, I pray thee, open his eyes, that he may see. And the LORD opened the eyes of the young man; and he saw: and, behold, the mountain was full of horses and chariots of fire round about Elisha.

When chapter 13 ends, it appears that the kingdom of Christ is a lost cause. When you read about the kingdom of antichrist, the strategy of the dragon and his accomplices, the two beasts, and how Satan holds sway over the whole earth, the future seems grim for the people of God in this world. But then John looks again, and what he sees astonishes him. He says: "I looked again, and this time I saw things from a different vantage point. I saw things from the perspective of heaven. I saw things spiritually. I saw the Lamb standing in majesty on Mount Zion with all His people, safe under His protection." What a comfort this vision must have been for the people of John's time!

We, too, need this comfort. We can face trials, temptations, tests, and trouble only by opening our eyes, trusting Christ, and believing what 1 John 4:4 says: "Greater is he that is in you, than he that is in the world." Therefore, let us now take a closer look at the vision of the Lamb under the following headings: Who is the Lamb? Where does He stand? Who stands with Him? How should we respond to Him?

Who Is the Lamb?

The Lamb is John's code image for Christ. Revelation is written in symbols because the people of God to whom John writes are being persecuted by the Roman Empire. If John's book gets into the hands of the Roman authorities, the Christians already under attack will suffer even more. So John writes this vision in coded, symbolic language. When Christ is described as a lamb, none of us takes that literally. Rather, we think of John the Baptist, who introduced Christ to his disciples by saying, "Behold the Lamb of God, which taketh away the sin of the world" (John 1:29). The Lamb of God is Christ Jesus, the God-man.

John's use of the word *lamb* here and throughout the book of Revelation is striking, for a lamb is an apparently weak, vulnerable animal. John says, "Behold, I looked, and I saw a weak, vulnerable lamb standing on Mount Zion surrounded by 144,000." John's emphasis on the vulnerability of the Lamb is a stark contrast to the fearful might of the wild beasts of chapter 13, a seven-headed, ten-horned monster from the sea with feet like a bear, a body like a leopard, and a mouth like a lion (vv. 1–2), and the monster from the earth, which speaks as a dragon (v. 11).

The way God tackles the problems of sin and evil is summed up by "I saw a lamb." In 2 Corinthians 13:4, Paul says: "For though he was crucified through weakness, yet he liveth by the power of God. For we also are weak in him, but we shall live with him by the power of God toward you." God chose not to solve the problem of sin by sheer power alone. He might have done that. He could have blasted Satan and all his accomplices out of existence. He could have destroyed the entire world the moment Adam sinned. God could have put down Satan's rebellion by sheer force. But God did not choose to deal with evil that way. He says in 2 Corinthians 12:9, "My strength is made perfect in weakness." Thus, believers, like Paul, learn, by the Spirit's grace, to confess in the midst of suffering and pain, "When I am weak, then am I strong" (v. 10).

The principle of strength in weakness is also how God saves sinners. Who would ever have imagined that Satan could be defeated by a lamb? Yet that is God's way. It is also His way to turn the world's supposed wisdom on its head when it comes to the sacrifice of that lamb. In 1 Corinthians 1:23–25, Paul says: "But we preach Christ crucified, unto the Jews a stumblingblock, and unto the Greeks foolishness; but unto them which are called, both Jews and Greeks, Christ the power of God, and the wisdom of God. Because the foolishness of God is wiser than men; and the weakness of God is stronger than men." What could have been more foolish than a Savior who was condemned by His own people and died as a criminal? That sounds like nonsense to the world. It was a stumbling block to the Jews, who looked for a powerful Messiah to free them from tyranny; and it was foolishness to the Greek philosophers, who trusted in human wisdom to lead us to a better world. But for those of us who are being saved, it is "the power of God, and the wisdom of God."

This must surely be one of the greatest evidences for the truth of the gospel. If you wanted to create a religion that would attract great crowds, you wouldn't begin with a crucified Savior, would you? Yet this mystery is so unlikely that it must be true. Nowhere does Satan appear to have as much power as in the book of Revelation. Yet in that book, the devil is overcome by a lamb. That is the mystery of God—that by weakness, by yielding, by God becoming man, by the helplessness of infancy, and by suffering and death, the awful powers of evil personified in the beasts of Revelation are overcome forever. That is God's way of salvation.

Do you believe that? Does all your trust, hope, and confidence rest in the God of all creation, who took on frail human flesh and subjected himself to death at the hands of His creatures? Are you convinced that you are saved by a crucified Savior, who is a lamb?

Stand in awe at the weakness of Calvary, for it is a sign of the power and wisdom of God. It is the only way sinners are saved.

Where Does He stand?

Revelation 14:1 says the Lamb stands on Mount Zion. Some Christians interpret these words literally. They say, "At the end of time, when the Lord comes back, He will physically return to Mount Zion in Jerusalem, and there, with 144,000 hand-picked troops, He will take on the antichrist and his hosts at the end of the world." We do not accept that interpretation of the book of Revelation. The whole book is written in code, so we are not to understand Mount Zion literally any more than we are to understand the Lamb literally, or any other symbol.

Mount Zion is God's code term for heaven, of which the earthly Zion is only a type. Psalm 2 is a beautiful summary of Revelation 13 and 14. At the beginning of the psalm we read: "Why do the heathen rage, and the people imagine a vain thing? The kings of the earth set themselves, and the rulers take counsel together, against the LORD, and against his anointed, saying, Let us break their bands asunder, and cast away their cords from us" (vv. 1–3). Likewise, Revelation 13 speaks of the antichrist, who seeks dominion over the whole earth. Through a confederacy of evil, he conspires against the Lord and His Anointed.

When we view the battle between good and evil with our natural eyes, it seems as if the whole world is worshiping the first beast, political and military antichrist. The second beast, who is the false prophet, is succeeding in deceiving people into following the first beast. But Psalm 2 says: "He that sitteth in the heavens shall laugh: the LORD shall have them in derision. Then shall he speak unto them in his wrath, and vex them in his sore displeasure. Yet have I set my king upon my holy hill of Zion" (vv. 4–6).

While the heathen are raging and the kings of this earth are taking counsel together against the Lord and His Anointed, Christ is standing on Mount Zion. God has set His King there. In other words, Christ is reigning from heaven. That is the spiritual reality.

The only other place in the New Testament where Mount Zion is mentioned is Hebrews 12, where God tells us precisely what and where that heavenly mountain is: "But ye are come unto mount Sion, and unto the city of the living God, the heavenly Jerusalem, and to an innumerable company of angels, to the general assembly and church of the firstborn, which are written in heaven, and to God the Judge of all, and to the spirits of just men made perfect, and to Jesus the mediator of the new covenant, and to the blood of sprinkling, that speaketh better things than that of Abel" (vv. 22–24). "You are come to Mount Zion," he says, "which is where you truly belong even while you are here in this world and being intimidated by the powers of antichrist."

The Lord wants us to understand that human institutions, ideologies, and rulers are in the grip of antichrist today. Yet the Lamb stands with His people on Mount Zion in the position of triumph. God has set His King upon the holy mountain and has given Him the heathen for His inheritance.

So do not think of Mount Zion as a real place in the world, a mountain in Jerusalem where a lamb will appear with 144,000 troops. The comfort of Revelation is that even now the Lamb is standing on Mount Zion in the Jerusalem that is from above. The King of kings reigns from God's holy hill, and no powers of antichrist can thwart the purposes of God's grace. The heathen will be His. How those poor persecuted Christians must have been comforted as they looked by faith to the Lamb standing on Mount Zion, knowing that despite all appearances to the contrary, the victory was theirs.

The Lamb on Mount Zion is what heaven is all about. As one divine writes, "Heaven and Christ are the same things; to be with Christ is to be in heaven, and to be in heaven is to be with Christ."[1] What a comfort it is to know that the essence of heaven is Christ, the Lamb who stands victorious!

1. Samuel Rutherford, cited in Spurgeon, *Metropolitan Tabernacle Pulpit*, 3:26.

Who Stands with Him?

In 1970, Hal Lindsey published a book, *The Late, Great Planet Earth*, which sold more than ten million copies. *The New York Times* called it the number one non-fiction bestseller of the decade. In the book, Lindsey argues that the 144,000 mentioned in Revelation 14:1 are 144,000 "Billy Grahams," or evangelists. Through the preaching of these men, a great multitude, which no one can number, will be saved.[2] To Lindsey, then, the 144,000 are a select group of premillennial preachers. They are Christ's bodyguard, a special elite force who will stand on the earth at the last day.

However, such an interpretation does not arise from Revelation 14. The text says nothing about this group of people having a special, evangelistic mission. Rather, we are told at the end of Revelation 14:3 that the 144,000 are they "which were redeemed from the earth." They are followers of the Lamb. In other words, they are Christians. But will only 144,000 people be saved? Of course not. This number, like all others in the book of Revelation, is symbolic.

Our problem is that we don't think about numbers the way people did in Jesus' day. For example, when Peter asks Jesus how many times he should forgive someone who wrongs him, he asks, "Till seven times?" Jesus answers, "I say…Until seventy times seven" (Matt. 18:21–22). Is Jesus telling Peter to forgive only up to 490 times? Of course not. In Scripture, seven is a symbol of completeness or perfection. It is God's number. So Jesus is saying, "You keep on forgiving until you are forgiving completely and perfectly." In other words, we are to understand seventy times seven in a spiritual sense, not in terms of math.

Likewise, the numbers in Revelation are to be understood spiritually. Twelve is the number of the church. There are the twelve patriarchs of Israel in the Old Testament. The twelve apostles in the New Testament are the foundation of the church. And 144,000, or 12 times 12 times 1,000, represents the complete church. It is

---

2. Hal Lindsey, with C. C. Carlson, *The Late Great Planet Earth* (Grand Rapids: Zondervan, 1970), 111.

the symbolic number of the elect, for whom Christ has died. The
144,000 represent the great multitude of the redeemed, which no
one can number.

Revelation 14:1 says they have the "Father's name written in
their foreheads." This reminds us of the 144,000 of chapter 7, who
have God's seal on their foreheads and are a multitude that no man
can number.

The number 144,000 should remind us that God knows each of
His redeemed by name. The multitude He will save, though specific
in number, is beyond our comprehension. He will save all the millions of people whom He has chosen and appointed to eternal life
from before the foundation of the world.

The followers of the Lamb have five characteristics, some of
which are surprising:

First, *they are pure*. Verse 4a says, "These are they which were
not defiled with women; for they are virgins" (v. 4a). Again, we must
think symbolically here. We are not to think of 144,000 celibates,
as though celibacy were a mark of spirituality. Roman Catholicism
teaches that celibacy is spiritually superior to the married state.
Rather, we are to accept the image in verse 4a as a symbol of the
spiritual purity of the church of Christ. This image directly contrasts
the image of the world as a prostitute (Revelation 17). There is a
virgin-like quality to this body of Christ in her undivided devotion
to her Lord.

The Bible uses the metaphor of marriage to describe the relationship between the covenant people of the Old Testament and
God. They are often referred to collectively as the bride of God, who
are in covenant relationship with Him. Conversely, spiritual unfaithfulness is described as adultery. Time and again, God is angered by
His people, who have "gone a whoring" (Lev. 17:7) after other gods.

Likewise, Paul is angry with people who stray from God. He
says in 2 Corinthians 11:2: "For I am jealous over you with godly
jealousy: for I have espoused you to one husband, that I may present you as a chaste virgin to Christ." Paul sees himself as a friend
of the Bridegroom, and his mission is to commend his Lord to

unfaithful people. He is rightly jealous when the church, a chaste virgin engaged to Christ, prefers to listen to other gods.

Have you forsaken all others to be joined with Christ? Do you cleave to Him, or are you spiritually unfaithful? Do you place your faith, hope, and trust in things of this world? If so, you are unfaithful to Christ. How much better it would be if you said with the hymn writer—and lived it out:

> The dearest idol I have known
> Whate'er that idol be
> Help me to tear it from thy throne
> And worship only Thee.[3]

Those who stand with the Lamb strive to be spiritually pure and faithful to Christ. They are engaged to Him, so they heed John's admonition: "Little children, keep yourselves from idols" (1 John 5:21).

Now look at that relationship in the context of Revelation 13 and 14. The whole world is flirting with antichrist. The whole world is whoring with the beasts. Only those who are espoused to Christ and remain faithful to Him are pure.

Second, *they are committed followers of Christ.* Verse 4b says these people "follow the Lamb whithersoever he goeth." "A follower of the Lamb" is a good name for a child of God. We often talk about people who have been converted or who have been born again, and appropriately so, but in some parts of Scotland until recent years, when someone was saved, God's people would say, "So and so has begun to follow the Lamb." That, too, is scriptural, for it is the Lamb who makes sinners into believers by His Spirit so that they follow Him and keep following Him. A Christian is someone who has begun to follow the Lamb and is committed to do so through all eternity.

We should not hesitate to use the word *commitment* here. It is often misused. For example, the phrase "committed Christian" is a misnomer because it suggests that it is possible to be a Christian

---

3. William Cowper, "O For a Closer Walk with God" (1772).

without being committed. The idea that commitment or consecration is a second step, a second experience, or a second blessing in the Christian life is simply not scriptural. But that does not mean that we should throw out the word *commitment*, as though it had no biblical value whatsoever. Commitment is an integral part of conversion. It is bound up with what it means to become a Christian. Those who follow the Lamb wherever He goes are committed to Him. Jesus says in John 10:27, "My sheep hear my voice, and I know them, and they follow me." He is saying that *all* of His sheep, not *some* of them, hear His voice and follow Him.

Christ's sheep are marked on the ear and the foot. Because of that, these sheep hear His voice and follow Him. You may say that you belong to Christ, but do you have His mark on your ear and your foot? Do you listen to Him in His Word? Are you following Him wherever He goes? Are you committed to the words and ways of Christ, or do you follow Him only when it is convenient for you and doesn't interfere too much with your lifestyle?

Third, *they are guileless.* Revelation 14:5a says that no guile is found in the mouth of God's chosen. Guile is deceit; in this case, saying things you do not mean, in an attempt to deceive others. God's people speak truth from the heart. That characteristic is probably singled out here because of its contrast with the antichrist. The antichrist is a liar. Likewise, anyone who denies that Christ has come in the flesh is a liar (1 John 2:22; 4:2). Sometimes I wonder if we stress this enough. We believe in the sanctity of life, and rightly so. We are against abortion, euthanasia, and genocide. But shouldn't we be just as active in supporting the sanctity of truth? God is truth, just as He is life. Let us be advocates for the truth.

Those who are with the Lamb on Mount Zion are transparent and honest. They are like their Lord, in whose mouth there was no deceit (Isa. 53:9). The devil is a liar (John 8:44). It is because of the devil's lies that the world is as it is. And when we play around with the truth, twisting, bending, or exaggerating it, we are siding with the devil and with antichrist. That should never be. Those who follow the Lamb have no guile in their mouths.

Fourth, *they are faultless*. Revelation 14:5b says the 144,000 are "without fault before the throne of God." John sees these believers in heaven, where they are without fault. "The spirits of just men made perfect" (Heb. 12:23)—what a glorious sight! In this present world, no one is more conscious of his imperfection than a true Christian, who examines himself in the light of Scripture. He grieves over his sins, but trusts nonetheless that they are forgiven him only for the sake of Christ, who died for them on the cross. He strives to cease from sin and to live according to all the commandments of God. But in this life, even the holiest Christian has only a small beginning of the perfection that all true believers will have in heaven (see Heidelberg Catechism, Q. 114), where sin itself will be banished, our weakness turned to strength, and our works no longer stained with imperfection or mixed with sin.

Sin-free forever—it seems almost too good to be true! But one day we will experience that in actuality. Sin will be no more, and those inconsistencies that we bemoan and the secret sins that cause us the greatest sorrow will be no more. No more will we have to say with Paul, "Evil is present with me" (Rom. 7:21). We will truly be without fault before the throne of God. Not a speck of sin will mar our souls or bodies. We will be Christ's spotless, faultless, sin-free bride. Oh, what glory that will be, when everything good will be walled in and all evil walled out! Thomas Binney writes about that time:

> Eternal light! Eternal light!
> How pure the soul must be,
> When, placed within Thy searching sight,
> It shrinks not, but with calm delight
> Can live, and look on Thee.
>
> The spirits that surround Thy throne
> May bear the burning bliss;
> But that is surely theirs alone,
> For they have never, never known
> A fallen world like this.

O how shall I, whose naked sphere
Is dark, whose mind is dim,
Before the Ineffable appear,
And on my naked spirit bear
The uncreated beam?

There is a way for man to rise
To that sublime abode:
An offering and a sacrifice,
A Holy Spirit's energies,
An Advocate with God.[4]

Do you know the way to that sublime abode? Do you know how to stand before the holy God without fault on the great day of judgment? The gospel tells us how: we are to follow the Lamb, who went to Calvary and took upon Himself the sins of His people.

Fifth, *they are singing*. Revelation 14:3 says, "And they sung as it were a new song before the throne." There are four things worth noting about this singing.

- The only people who are able to sing this song are those who are "redeemed from the earth." Have you been redeemed by the blood of the Lamb? It is sheer folly to hope that you will go to heaven and sing this song unless you have been saved on earth. Even if you were permitted to go to Mount Zion as an unsaved sinner, you would find no joy in listening to the singing of God's redeemed people.

- They sing, "as it were, a new song." The singing of a "new song" is associated in the book of Psalms with the mighty works of God in fulfilling the promises of His covenant and accomplishing the redemption of His people (Psalm 98). This is not a new song altogether. The redeemed have

---

4. Thomas Bilney (1798–1874), "Eternal Light!," accessed http://www.bartle by.com/294/482.html

already begun to sing this song on earth. But it *sounds* new because it is being sung with millions of other believers in heaven's choir, those who have been safely gathered home. They sing now as the church triumphant, with no more battles to be fought. They sing knowing that the song will never end.

- They sing beautifully. Noise in itself is not music, but here we read that John "heard the voice of harpers harping with their harps" (Rev. 14:2b). The harp is one of the most ethereal instruments, so the sound of many "harpers harping" blends beautifully with the heavenly choir as they sing before the throne.

- They sing with a loud voice. John says the voices of the 144,000 are "as the voice of many waters" (v. 2a). The sound is like ocean waves crashing on shore as millions of voices offer a loud, victorious cry of praise to the Lamb. May God teach us to sing the following words:

> When oceans vast their depths reveal
> And moons have ceased to wane,
> The Lamb, who died and rose again,
> On Zion's hill shall reign.[5]

How Should We Respond to Him?

Knowing that Christ is standing on Mount Zion as a lamb ought to encourage us to come before Him in prayer. Charles H. Spurgeon writes: "To a lion-Christ we need fear to come; but the Lamb-Christ!—oh, little children, were you ever afraid of lambs? Oh, children of the living God, should you ever fail to tell your griefs and sorrows into the breast of one who is a Lamb? Ah, let us come boldly to the throne of the heavenly grace, seeing a Lamb sits upon it."[6]

---

5. Morgan Rhys (1716–1779), "When Oceans Vast Their Depths Reveal," trans. Edward M. Powell (1852–1928).

6. Spurgeon, *Metropolitan Tabernacle Pulpit*, 3:27.

But are you truly a follower of the Lamb? Recently, a wife of a theology student told me: "The Lord has made me willing to follow my husband unconditionally, no matter where the Lord is pleased to lead him." Is that how you feel about Christ Jesus? Have you followed the Lamb to the Father's right hand, in dependence on His constant intercession? Are you following the Lamb right now by denying yourself, taking up His cross, walking in His footsteps, and running in the way of His commandments? Are you willing to follow Him wherever He leads you?

Are you following the Lamb so that you may be more like Him? Is He your pattern to follow hour by hour? Consider what Spurgeon says: "Try to put your feet down in the footprints that he has left you. Do aim at complete conformity to Christ; and wherein you fail to reach it, mark that you come so far short of what you ought to be. To be like Christ is that which God intends for you."[7]

Conform us increasingly, Lord Jesus, to be like Thyself.

---

7. Spurgeon, *Metropolitan Tabernacle Pulpit*, 39:423.

24

The Vision of the
Three Angels

REVELATION 14:6–13

And I saw another angel fly in the midst of heaven, having the everlasting gospel to preach unto them that dwell on the earth, and to every nation, and kindred, and tongue, and people, saying with a loud voice, Fear God, and give glory to him; for the hour of his judgment is come: and worship him that made heaven, and earth, and the sea, and the fountains of waters. And there followed another angel, saying, Babylon is fallen, is fallen, that great city, because she made all nations drink of the wine of the wrath of her fornication. And the third angel followed them, saying with a loud voice, If any man worship the beast and his image, and receive his mark in his forehead, or in his hand, the same shall drink of the wine of the wrath of God, which is poured out without mixture into the cup of his indignation; and he shall be tormented with fire and brimstone in the presence of the holy angels, and in the presence of the Lamb: and the smoke of their torment ascendeth up for ever and ever: and they have no rest day nor night, who worship the beast and his image, and whosoever receiveth the mark of his name. Here is the patience of the saints: here are they that keep the commandments of God, and the faith of Jesus. And I heard a voice from heaven saying unto me, write, Blessed are the dead which die in the Lord from henceforth: yea, saith the Spirit, that they may rest from their labours; and their works do follow them.

Revelation 14 contains three visions: the vision of the Lamb on Mount Zion (vv. 1–5), the vision of the three angels (vv. 6–13), and the vision of the end-time harvesting of the earth (vv. 14–20). These three visions convey a sobering message to us.

In any church, there is an invisible dividing line; some people are followers of the Lamb, and others are followers of Satan and the beasts. Revelation 14 clearly contrasts those who are on either side of this line. On one side are the followers of the Lamb, the 144,000, representing the church made up of the total sum of the elect. On the other side are those who worship the beast. The gospel is the dividing line between these two groups. Revelation 14 also says that this division will continue until the final harvest of the earth and the final judgment.

Painful as it is to admit, some of us are not following the Lamb, which means that we are actually allies of the beast. Which side of the great divide do we belong to? Are we followers of the Lamb or worshipers of the beast? The followers of the Lamb will stand with Him on Mount Zion, singing a new song. The worshipers of the beast will have no peace, but will live in endless torment and punishment. Now is the time for us to identify with the Lamb and His followers. How do we leave the kingdom of antichrist and identify with the Lamb and His kingdom? The answer is given in the vision of the three angels.

This vision is the testimony of God to a rebellious world. The three angels belong together, for they have one purpose, namely, to warn mankind of the coming judgment. They warn everyone in the grip of antichrist to flee from the wrath that is to come. They have good news to preach to the world. What is called "the everlasting gospel" in verse 6 is the testimony of God, which is symbolically given to three angels or messengers to deliver.

Each angel delivers a somewhat different message. The first angel exhorts all the inhabitants of the earth, every nation, tribe, tongue, and kindred, to fear God, glorify Him, and worship Him as Maker of heaven and earth, because the hour of His judgment is approaching. The second angel announces to the world that "Babylon is fallen, is fallen." The third angel warns those who worship the beast of the wrath of God to come.

The vision of the three angels reminds us of the forbearance and patience of God. God does not take delight in the death of the wicked. It is not His will that sinners should perish, but that they should come to repentance. His concern is that the gospel be preached to the ends of a rebellious world. During this age of the gospel, God sends out His messengers to warn of judgment to come and to plead with sinners to be reconciled to Him before it is forever too late.

Let us consider, then, from Revelation 14:6–13, the messages of the three angels and then the future of the saints. At first, there seems to be little connection between those four messages. But as we make our way through these verses, we may soon realize that they all coalesce into one: the testimony of God to a rebellious world.

The First Message: Fear, Glorify, and Worship God

Revelation 14:6–7 tells us that the first angel appears flying "in the midst of heaven," that is, in the sky between heaven and earth, so as to be clearly visible to all. He is sent to proclaim the "everlasting gospel," John says (v. 6). That has created difficulties for some commentators, who find no gospel at all in the first angel's message, for there appears to be no mention of sin or atonement.

Some premillennial, dispensational commentators distinguish between the gospel of the kingdom and the gospel of grace, and say this is neither of these gospels, but a third kind of gospel preached in the tribulation period.[1] But that can hardly be true since the Bible clearly tells us there is only one gospel. Paul says in Galatians that even if an angel comes from heaven and preaches to us any gospel other than the true gospel, as preached by Christ and His apostles, "let him be accursed" (Gal. 1:8). The gospel of Jesus Christ is the everlasting gospel, the same gospel we are to preach to the end of the age (Matt. 24:14). Christ is described in Revelation as

---

1. *The Scofield Reference Bible*, ed. C. I. Scofield (Oxford: Oxford University Press, 1909), 1343; John F. Walvoord, *The Revelation of Jesus Christ: A Commentary* (Chicago: Moody Press, 1966), 217.

"the Lamb slain before the foundation of the world" (Rev. 13:8). In the mind and purpose of God, there has always been one way of salvation through faith in Christ, and that is the gospel preached by the first angel.

Part of the problem here may be that we like to have the gospel preached in a way to which we are accustomed. If the gospel is not preached the way we expect, we are unhappy. We assume that the gospel can be reduced to a few simple propositions, and we expect preachers to present them to us over and over again. If they don't, we conclude that they are not preaching the gospel! Yet in Scripture, the same gospel is preached in many different ways. We too often forget that the gospel is also preached when the minister proclaims the dire consequences of rejecting it (e.g., Paul in Rom. 1:16–18; 2 Cor. 2:14–16; Acts 17:28–32)!

The gospel, while sharply focused on Calvary, is as big as the Bible. It is woven into everything that God has revealed to us. You won't understand the Bible unless you realize that the focal point of Scripture is Christ crucified. Everything the Bible has to say leads us to Christ, and from there directs us into the way we are to live as His followers. So we are to understand this message of the first angel as the gospel of Jesus Christ. It is good news.

This first angel preaches the gospel in terms of fearing, glorifying, and worshiping God. This declaration should be read in light of Romans 1, which indicts the human race for refusing to acknowledge and glorify the God who made heaven and earth, but turning away from Him and taking up the worship of idols, exchanging the truth of God for a lie. The angel then speaks of the judgment of God that is fast approaching. The apostle Paul would certainly recognize the angel's message as part and parcel of the gospel he himself preached as "the power of God unto salvation" (Rom. 1:16), which contains the need to glorify and worship God (Rev. 14:7). That is also a legitimate way to preach the gospel. You might ask, "How can that be when there is no mention of sin here?" In reply, I would ask, what is sin? When we sin, we do not fear God, but despise Him, His Word, and His commandments. The problem with our world today is that people do not fear God. They do what seems to be right in their own eyes. In doing so, they despise the God who made them. Therefore, this is a gospel call to repentance. Sometimes the gospel is summarized by its command for sinners to repent (Matt. 4:17), with the implied promise that if they do, God will mercifully forgive them.

At the heart of repentance is turning back to God with a recognition that we failed to fear and glorify Him. In Psalm 51, David confesses his sin before God. He has committed adultery with Bathsheba and ordered the murder of her husband, Uriah. He is guilty of hypocrisy, lying, and all manner of sin. Yet he sees that his wickedness is primarily an offense against God. He says: "Against thee, thee only, have I sinned, and done this evil in thy sight" (v. 4).

Didn't David also sin against Uriah by taking his life, and against Bathsheba by sleeping with her? He also sinned against his own people, who had made him king, by betraying their confidence and trust in him. Visibly, his sin was against individuals, country, and society, yet David says: "Against *thee, thee only*, have I sinned." In order to sin at all, David had to despise God. That is what his sin was: pushing aside the commandment "Thou shalt not commit adultery" (Ex. 20:14) by saying, in effect: "I don't care what God says. I want to commit adultery, so I will." In doing so, David despised God and His law. He did not fear God.

The awfulness of sin is that it is committed *against God*. We talk about big sins and little sins. But it doesn't matter how you weigh your sins, or whether you see them as whoppers or the equivalent of "little white lies." In order to sin at all, you have to despise God and His law. And that law is written upon your heart, in your conscience, so that every time you sin, you despise the God who made you. So the gospel is wonderfully evident here in the first angel's words: "Fear God" (Rev. 14:7).

Ecclesiastes is a difficult book for many people to accept because it seems to be so negative. Some people suggest the book shouldn't be in the Bible because it is so devoid of hope. The message of Ecclesiastes at first sight seems to be that everything in this life is a waste of time: "Vanity of vanities...all is vanity" (1:2). The Preacher seems to have no gospel to preach. Yet if you read this book with different eyes, it becomes the most marvelous evangelistic book, especially for people today. Go to Ecclesiastes 12:13–14, where the Preacher says: "Let us hear the conclusion of the whole matter: Fear God, and keep his commandments: for this is the whole duty of man. For God shall bring every work into judgment, with every secret thing, whether it be good, or whether it be evil."

The key to understanding Ecclesiastes is to remember that the Preacher is examining life and the world from two very different viewpoints. First, he looks at the world from the view of the unconverted man. From that perspective, he can only conclude that life is futile. But when he looks at life from the perspective of a believer who knows and loves God, life appears very different. The Preacher moves back and forth between these opposing viewpoints throughout the book. So, in essence, the message of the book is that for those who do not fear, glorify, and worship God, life truly is a waste of time. Only when we see that can we understand why Jesus Christ came into the world.

Jesus came to save us from eternal damnation for our sin. He came to save us from habits that have enslaved us. But Jesus also came to make us God-fearing worshipers. He wants to bring us back to the purpose for which we were created—that we might worship and glorify God. That is the message of this angel as he flies over a world held in the grip of antichrist and evil. He sees all the potential, capacity, and skill with which man is endowed as a creature made in the image of God, but he also sees how those gifts are being wasted. So the angel says, "Fear God, and give glory to him,...and worship him."

That message presents us with three marks of grace, by which you may know whether you belong to the Lamb or to antichrist. Ask yourself three questions:

By the Spirit's grace, *do you fear God?* According to John Brown, to fear God means "the fear of offending God," and for those who fear the Lord, "it matters little to them that the world frowns on them, if he smiles; and it matters little to them that the world smiles, if he frowns."[2] Such fear is rooted in the conviction that God is, and that He is a rewarder of those who diligently seek Him (Heb. 11:6). Fearing God means submitting to Him through Jesus Christ, and to His will for your life in all things. Is this both your desire and your drive in life? Whom do you fear—the Lamb on Mount Zion or the beastly Satan in hell?

With the Spirit's help, *are you giving glory to God?* The Hebrew word for glory, *kabod*, is derived from a root word meaning "weight." For example, the value of a gold coin is determined by its weight. To have weight, therefore, is to have value or worth. The Greek word for glory, *doxa*, means "opinion." This word refers to the worth or value which we, in our opinion, assign to someone or something. The Hebrew word speaks of what is inherent in God—His intrinsic value or worth— while the Greek word speaks of the response of intelligent and moral beings in acknowledging the value or worth of God, His Word, and His works.

In both Testaments of the Bible, the word *glory* refers to the display of God's excellence and praiseworthiness (glory *shown*), as well as our response of honor and adoration to this display (glory *given*). God's glory is manifested inwardly in His beautiful, manifold perfections, as well as outwardly in the radiant splendor that breaks forth from those perfections. His excellence of character shines forth in His works of creation, providence, and redemption (Isa. 44:23; John 12:28; 13:31–32). Saints and angels give God glory by praising, thanking, and obeying Him (John 17:4; 21:19; Rom. 4:20; 15:6, 9; 1 Peter 4:12–16).

---

2. John Brown of Edinburgh, *Expository Discourses on the First Epistle of the Apostle Peter* (New York: Robert Carter and Brothers, 1855), 103.

God's goal in this world is to manifest His glory in all that He does, most remarkably in displaying His holiness or moral excellence to His creatures and evoking their praise for its beauty and for the benefits it brings them (cf. Eph. 1:3). God's glory makes Him gloriously magnificent in the sight of angels and men.

Our primary purpose in this world is to glorify God. In all that we do, by word and by deed, we must seek to bring glory to our Creator, Redeemer, and Sanctifier. In doing this, we find happiness, for glorifying God is the highest, most rewarding human occupation. The Westminster Shorter Catechism (Q. 1) says it most succinctly: "Man's chief end is to glorify God, and to enjoy him forever."[3]

Do you glorify God? Do you live for Him? Do you yearn to use every gift that God has given you to glorify Him? You can do that by confessing your sins to God and fleeing to Christ for forgiveness. You can do it by praising, worshiping, and delighting in the triune God as Creator, Provider, and Redeemer. You can do it by trusting God and surrendering all things into His hands. You can do it by walking humbly, thankfully, and cheerfully before God as you become increasingly conformed to the image of His Son. In short, you glorify Him by trusting in Him and doing His will with a ready mind and heart.

Finally, in the Spirit's power, *are you worshiping God?* Worship is the heartfelt response of a creature in the presence of the Creator. The most fundamental act of worship is to acknowledge God as Maker of heaven and earth. The creation around us declares His glory and shows itself to be His handiwork (Ps. 19:1). When our eyes and ears are opened and our hearts are renewed by the Spirit, we feel compelled to bow down before God, confessing His greatness and our comparative nothingness. As the redeemed of the Lord, we delight in the duty of offering the sacrifice (Heb. 13:15). Filled with the Spirit, we sing and make melody in our hearts to the Lord (Eph. 5:18–19). Those who are dead in trespasses and sins find worship to

---

3. *Reformed Confessions of the Sixteenth and Seventeenth Centuries*, 4:353.

be a tedious burden of empty ceremony and unintelligible words. Those who are alive to God through Jesus Christ desire above all else to dwell in the Lord's house, to behold His beauty as it shines in all His ordinances (Ps. 27:4).

The Second Message: The Fall of Babylon

In Revelation 14:8, the second angel announces the fall of Babylon: "And there followed another angel, saying, Babylon is fallen, is fallen, that great city, because she made all nations drink of the wine of the wrath of her fornication." Initially, this doesn't seem to connect with what we have just been discussing. But when we understand what Babylon represents, we see the connection.

The story of Babylon's fall is recorded in Revelation 17–19, which we will examine in succeeding chapters. But first we must understand what Babylon represents and what its fall signifies. The message of the second angel is a proleptic or anticipatory announcement of the fall of Babylon, drawn from Isaiah 21:9, where the prophet delivers the same message: "Babylon is fallen, is fallen."

It is incorrect to identify Babylon as signifying one institution or a particular place or time in history. Babylon does not represent *only* the Roman Catholic Church here, though this church certainly appears to be a powerful representation of Babylon. The Bible makes it clear that Babylon is a constant factor in human history. It is a symbol not of just one city, institution, person, or movement, but of severe opposition to God. Babylon is the capital of antichrist's kingdom, just as the heavenly Jerusalem is the capital of God's kingdom.

The first mention of Babylon in Scripture is found in the account of the Tower of Babel. After the flood, God commanded the survivors to "Be fruitful and multiply, and replenish the earth" (Gen. 9:1), but instead they huddled together. They discussed what to do and decided that instead of spreading out over the earth, they would unite and make a name for themselves. So they built a city and began raising a tower that would reach up to heaven. God confused the language of the people to stop this building project, for the tower represented the ongoing defiance and rebellion of man against Him, but figuratively and spiritually, that scene is repeated throughout Scripture. Babylon is man setting himself against the decrees and counsels of God. Babylon is the world, the kingdom of antichrist, which is opposed to God and His people.

God's people were once captives in the land of Babylon. Psalm 137:1–4 recalls how difficult that time was: "By the rivers of Babylon, there we sat down, yea, we wept, when we remembered Zion. We hanged our harps upon the willows in the midst thereof. For there they that carried us away captive required of us a song; and they that wasted us required of us mirth, saying, Sing us one of the songs of Zion. How shall we sing the LORD's song in a strange land?"

We are still being seduced by Babylon. If you watch or listen to ads on various forms of media, you are being tempted by Babylon, for Babylon is the world, with all its suggestive and seductive powers. As the angel tells us here, Babylon makes all the nations of the earth "drink the wine of the wrath of her fornication." We read all through Scripture of the seductive, intoxicating power of the world.

For instance, James warns against this power: "Ye adulterers and adulteresses, know ye not that the friendship of the world is enmity with God? Whosoever therefore will be a friend of the world is the enemy of God" (James 4:4). James is not speaking specifically about adultery here, but about the sin of worldliness. He is saying that worldliness is *spiritual* adultery, for it compromises our fidelity to Christ.

Some of us can't sing the songs of Zion because our ears are ringing with the songs of Babylon. Some of us can't truly worship with God's people because we don't feel like we belong. That is often because we have been in the world too much. How can we sing the songs of Zion if our minds and our desires have been marinated and steeped in the world? Some of us love the attractions of this world so much that it is no wonder we find it hard to concentrate on worshiping God in His house. The message of this angel is a warning for those who are being seduced by the world, for Babylon, however great she may be now, will soon fall into ruins and be destroyed forever.

In Hebrew, repetition underscores certainty. For example, in Genesis 41, Pharaoh has a dream that Joseph interprets, saying, "And for that the dream was doubled unto Pharaoh twice; it is because the thing is established by God, and God will shortly bring it to pass" (v. 32). So the angel's repetition of "is fallen" means that the end of worldly Babylon is absolutely certain. What a warning this is to us in our Babylonian world, with our proneness to embrace its worldly ways! We need to repent of our worldliness before our worldliness destroys us.

Are you living as if Babylon's fall is certain? What excites you most—searching the Scriptures or surfing the Internet? What conversations do you most enjoy, those that focus on worldly trivia or those that focus on Jesus Christ? Who are your best friends, those who sincerely love the Lord Jesus Christ or those who flirt with worldliness even while they continue to attend church?

There is far too much of the world in all of us. Let us flee from Babylon, lest we share her eternal destruction. The second angel warns us that if our hearts are with the world, we are on the side of the beast, and when the hour of God's judgment comes, we will share in the doom and destruction of the world. "Babylon is fallen, is fallen." If we believe that Babylon will fall but continue to live in worldly ways, we toy with pleasures that God has condemned. We are playing with eternal hellfire.

The Third Message: The Overthrow of Antichrist's Followers

The third angel proclaims the dreadful fate of those who worship the beast. Verses 9–11 say: "And the third angel followed them, saying with a loud voice, If any man worship the beast and his image, and receive his mark in his forehead, or in his hand, the same shall drink of the wine of the wrath of God, which is poured out without mixture into the cup of his indignation; and he shall be tormented with fire and brimstone in the presence of the holy angels, and in the presence of the Lamb: and the smoke of their torment ascendeth up for ever and ever: and they have no rest day nor night, who worship the beast and his image, and whosoever receiveth the mark of his name." What a horrifying picture! How can a God of love inflict such cruel punishment on people who follow the beast? Here are some things to consider:

First, *worshiping the false trinity of this world will end in disaster on judgment day.* Worshiping the beast of man's power may keep Satan from persecuting you for a short time, but you will eventually pay the terrible price of having the wrath of God poured out upon you. There are temporary rewards for following the world's ways and receiving its propaganda, but in the end all who have identified with the system of Satan will fall under the full wrath of God. Sinclair Ferguson says:

> The third angel announces the terrible judgment of God that will come on those who have received the false sacrament of the false trinity. The people of God received the mark, the sacrament, as it were, the identity marker of the Father and the Son and the Holy Spirit. We are named for Him in our baptism. The ungodly are named for the dragon and the sea beast and the earth beast. They have received the false sacrament and they are proud of it. They don't realize that this is the very thing that will identify them for the judgment of the great day of Babylon. And that is described as drinking the wine of God's wrath poured full strength into the cup of His indignation.[4]

Second, *hell is a dreadful place.* The wrath of God against human ungodliness and unrighteousness has been revealed from heaven through all history (Rom. 1:18). So these followers of the beast are without excuse. It is just and right that God should pour out His unmitigated wrath on those who worship the beast. As Revelation 14:10 says, they "shall drink of the wine of the wrath of God, which is poured out without mixture into the cup of his indignation." There will be no mercy or grace in hell for those who worship the beast. The wine of God's wrath will be undiluted; His fury will neither soften nor slow nor diminish.

---

4. Sinclair B. Ferguson, preached sermon on Rev. 14.

Hell is internal and external torment. Simon Kistemaker writes of those who worship the beast, "By drinking the cup of God's wrath, they burn inwardly as it affects their soul day and night, and outwardly as they experience burning fire and smell the stench of sulfur forever."[5] William Still warns, "The eternal fire of God's wrath is described in extreme physical terms, not merely to shock and horrify, but also to indicate that the spiritual reality will be far worse than any earthly fire."[6] It would be dreadful to fall unprepared into the hands of the living God (Heb. 10:31).

Third, *hell is everlasting.* The sins of the world are sins against the infinite and eternal majesty of God, so they deserve infinite, eternal punishment. Revelation 14:11 says of the ungodly, "the smoke of their torment ascendeth up for ever and ever: and they have no rest day nor night." The wicked will have no relief or intermission from God's fury. They will be ever dying, yet never dead. The wrath of God will never be exhausted, because He is infinitely angry against sin that is committed against Him. James Hamilton writes, "Hell lasts forever because God is infinitely important. Hell is about the worth and majesty of God. If you understand what it means for God to be God, you will understand why hell lasts forever."[7] Moreover, those in hell will keep on sinning, adding to the eternal day of wrath forever and ever. Thomas Watson says, "Oh eternity! Eternity! Who can fathom it?"[8]

The only way to escape such damnation is through the Lamb who endured the agonies of hell for those who worship Him in Spirit and truth. Note the end of verse 10, which says that the torments of hell will be inflicted on the followers of the beast not only in the presence of the holy angels, but also "in the presence of the Lamb." How fitting it is that the Lamb should preside over the

5. Simon J. Kistemaker, *Exposition of the Book of Revelation*, New Testament Commentary (Grand Rapids: Baker Academic, 2001), 411.
6. Cited in Richard Brooks, *The Lamb Is All the Glory: The Book of Revelation*, Welwyn Commentary Series (Darlington, England: Evangelical Press, 1986), 136.
7. Hamilton, *Revelation*, 287.
8. Thomas Watson, *A Body of Divinity* (Edinburgh: Banner of Truth, 1983), 63.

condemnation and punishment of the wicked, for He also drank the cup into which all of God's wrath was poured.

In the garden of Gethsemane, Jesus cried out to His Father: "If it be possible, let this cup pass from me" (Matt. 26:39). He recognized that all of the distilled wrath and anger of a holy God against sin had been poured into the cup He had to drink. On Calvary, Jesus downed that bitter brew to its last dregs for sinners like us who trust Him for salvation.

Are you ready for eternity? If not, know that unless you repent, you will suffer eternal consequences for worshiping the beast. You cannot live apart from Christ and get away with it. He is indispensable as Savior, and He is inescapable as Judge.

The Future of the Saints

Happily, this solemn text closes on a positive note. After the three angels speak, John says in verses 12–13: "Here is the patience of the saints: here are they that keep the commandments of God, and the faith of Jesus. And I heard a voice from heaven saying unto me, Write, Blessed are the dead which die in the Lord from henceforth: Yea, saith the Spirit, that they may rest from their labours; and their works do follow them."

If you are ready for eternity, then you will persevere in faith, serving God, for God's grace will grant you "the patience of the saints." These verses summarize the affirmation of chapter 14 concerning Lamb worshipers, who live by God's grace. Here are three clear differences between those who worship the Lamb and those who worship the beast:

First, *the saints patiently persevere in righteousness while the ungodly persevere in unrighteousness.* "Here is the patience of the saints," says verse 12. Even in the midst of persecution, by the Spirit's grace, believers bear up patiently. They are in Christ, so they do not panic. This has always been true of Christian martyrs. In the 1680s, moments before his death on a scaffold, Archibald Alison, a Scottish Covenanter, said to onlookers: "What think ye of Heaven and Glory that is at the back of the cross? The hope of this makes me look upon pale death as a lovely messenger to me. I bless the Lord for my lot this day.... Friends, give our Lord credit; he is aye good, but O! He is good in a day of trials, and he will be sweet company through the ages of eternity."[9] As dreadful as it is to face persecution in this life, when Christ comes, the future will be worse for those who worship the beast.

Second, *the saints keep God's commandments.* Those commandments are summarized in the Decalogue and are enlarged upon throughout the Bible. As those who worship the beast increasingly turn away from the Scriptures, those who worship the Lamb increasingly rely upon Scripture and "run the way of [God's] commandments" (Ps. 119:32). Believers want to obey Jesus, no matter what it costs them. They know by experience that there is great reward in keeping God's commandments (Ps. 19:11).

Do you strive to obey God's commandments out of gratitude to God for your salvation in Christ Jesus? Do you believe that "God's law endures throughout the ages, need not be amended, is relevant in all cultures, and will never be repealed"?[10] Does your life show that you believe this?

Third, *the saints abide in "the faith of Jesus."* He increasingly becomes their all-in-all throughout their lives. Their lives show their constant faithfulness to Him. How different that is from those who worship the beast! They have no God-glorifying worldview, no object of saving faith that encompasses their entire lives, and no constant and faithful lifestyle. Without God and without hope in the world, they live for themselves, doing as they please, following their lusts, and walking in the broad way that leads to destruction.

Fourth, *the saints will enter God's blessed rest.* What a hopeful pronouncement about the future of the saints! Despite their trouble, trials, and testing, the Lamb worshipers will find eternal rest

---

9. Cited in Douglas F. Kelly, *Revelation*, Mentor Expository Commentary (Ross-shire, Scotland: Christian Focus, 2012), 269.

10. Kistemaker, *Revelation*, 413.

in Christ. They must labor in this world, but in glory, believers will be at rest.

The sweet pronouncement of the Spirit does not say that the deeds of Christians will precede them. As they enter into the presence of the heavenly King, the redeemed will not say, "I am coming here on the basis of my deeds." There is no entry for those who come on that basis, for weighed in the balance of God, their deeds will be found wanting, broken into a thousand useless pieces. Rather, they will come on the basis of faith in the Lord Jesus Christ, trusting in His glorious sacrifice on the cross and in His marvelous resurrection. But when they look behind them, to their astonishment, they will see that their deeds are following them, one by one. All that they did out of faith in God, for His glory, and according to His commandments will follow them, and they will bow their heads and be amazed that He should have done so much through their short lives.

Those who die are said to "die in the Lord"; that is, believers who look to Jesus (Heb. 9:28) as the Author and Finisher of faith (Heb. 12:2) need not fear death, for they will be eternally safe in Christ. That is a sharp contrast with unbelievers, who are filled with fear in anticipation of eternal destruction (Rev. 6:15–17). Lamb worshipers are blessed. Their death in Christ will be gain for them. That was true not only in John's day, but "from henceforth," till the end of time!

The Spirit is saying that believers will rest from their works. God does not forget the works of His saints, but graciously rewards them far more than they deserve. He crowns the saints' efforts with abundant rewards of grace (Rev. 6:11; Heb. 6:10; 1 Cor. 9:25; 2 Tim. 4:8). God will judge you when you "give allegiance to antichristian forces, but will give an eternal reward to the faithful who persevere through oppression."[11]

In conclusion, I urge Lamb-worshipers to go on believing that grace will be rewarded and to let a blessed future (in contrast to the cursed future of beast worshipers) motivate you to go on believing

---

11. Beale, *The Book of Revelation*, 747.

in Christ and keeping God's commandments. As Hamilton writes: "Brand your brain with images of the redemption of the faithful and the punishment of the wicked in 14:1–11."[12] Do you need help fighting the temptations of the world? Ask God to help you remember the fall of Babylon and the wine of God's wrath that beast worshipers will drink. When Babylon tempts you, think of how she will fare on the day of judgment. When the beast demands your worship, think of the torment his worshipers will experience in the presence of the Lamb. They will never rest, day or night. The smoke of their torment will rise forever. Oh, keep on keeping on, obeying the commands of God and believing in Jesus by reminding yourself of the outcome of those who would tempt you to disobedience and unbelief!

Note that the gospel proclaimed by the three angels is in the form of a warning of judgment to come, while the Holy Spirit proclaims the gospel of comfort. The gospel is true from eternity to eternity, and this good news is proclaimed to every sinner, "unto them that dwell on the earth, and to every nation, and kindred, and tongue, and people" (Rev. 14:6). That expression is repeatedly used in Revelation (cf. 11:9; 13:7; 17:15), implying two things: first, that every sinner on the face of the earth needs to repent from sin and turn back to God before the day of judgment (and that includes all of you who are not yet in Christ), and second, that everyone in the world desperately needs to hear the gospel contained in the angelic pronouncements.

If you love the gospel, you should feel a tremendous sense of responsibility to do whatever you can—be it through prayer, evangelizing others, or giving sacrificially to your church—so that the gospel may be spread around the globe and that all the nations of this world will hear about Christ.

---

12. Hamilton, *Revelation*, 288.

25

Earth's Final Harvest

REVELATION 14:14–20

And I looked, and behold a white cloud, and upon the cloud one sat like unto the Son of man, having on his head a golden crown, and in his hand a sharp sickle. And another angel came out of the temple, crying with a loud voice to him that sat on the cloud, Thrust in thy sickle, and reap: for the time is come for thee to reap; for the harvest of the earth is ripe. And he that sat on the cloud thrust in his sickle on the earth; and the earth was reaped. And another angel came out of the temple which is in heaven, he also having a sharp sickle. And another angel came out from the altar, which had power over fire; and cried with a loud cry to him that had the sharp sickle, saying, Thrust in thy sharp sickle, and gather the clusters of the vine of the earth; for her grapes are fully ripe. And the angel thrust in his sickle into the earth, and gathered the vine of the earth, and cast it into the great winepress of the wrath of God. And the winepress was trodden without the city, and blood came out of the winepress, even unto the horse bridles, by the space of a thousand and six hundred furlongs.

Harvest can be a happy but also a stressful time—happy because a farmer sees that all his efforts are paying off; stressful because that same farmer works very long hours, together with his helpers, to complete the harvesting of his fields; and sad because it is possible that the harvest must be destroyed.

There is no harvest so critical, so far-reaching, so all-decisive as the earth's final harvest. For that harvest you and I must be prepared. That may cause us great stress at times, but it may also bring us great joy in the final harvest to ascend on high and forever be with the Lord. Sadly, however, it may cause us much grief if we prove to be the chaff and not the wheat to be harvested on the final judgment day. The middle section of Revelation 14 makes all of this and more abundantly plain as it symbolically unfolds the earth's final harvest for us. In that harvest each of us is intimately involved. What subject could be more important than this one?

Revelation is a symbolic book, and we are looking at it in terms of seven parallel cycles rather than one linear narrative. Each visionary cycle takes in the entire gospel age. First, chapters 1–3 present John's vision of Christ in the midst of the seven golden candlesticks, addressing the seven churches. Second, chapters 4–7 describe the opening of the book or scroll with the seven seals. Third, chapters 8–11 record the sounding of the seven trumpets of judgment. Chapters 12–14 are about war between the dragon and his helpers against the angels and saints of God. Chapters 15–16 present the outpourings of the seven vials of wrath. Chapters 17–19 tell about the fall of the great harlot and the beasts. The book concludes with chapters 20–22, a vision of the new Jerusalem.

Revelation 14:14–20 is the final scene in the fourth cycle of visions. It is a close-up description of what will happen at the end of time, when Christ comes again from heaven to judge the living and the dead. This final judgment, which will be the culmination of world history and the consummation of God's kingdom, has been announced repeatedly in earlier visions. But here it is actually described for us in increasingly graphic detail.

Under the theme of earth's final harvest, we will examine: (1) the harvester himself, or, the One who does the harvesting; (2) his helpers and the actual process of harvesting; and (3) the harvest itself, particularly what kind of a harvest it is.

The Harvester

Verse 14 says, "And I looked, and behold a white cloud, and upon the cloud one sat like unto the Son of man, having on his head a golden crown, and in his hand a sharp sickle." Can there be any doubt at all who the harvester is when we read this description? It is surprising that some commentators say it is an angel, but clearly it is the Lord Jesus Christ. Each detail of the portrait John gives us confirms this conclusion.

The White Cloud

There is, first of all, the white cloud, serving as a chariot to convey its distinguished occupant to His appointed destination. We are not to understand this cloud as a meteorological phenomenon. John is not describing a dark rain cloud or a woolly, fleecy, cumulus cloud such as you might see in the sky on a bright summer's day. This cloud has nothing to do with the weather. Rather, it has theological and spiritual significance.

This cloud is the same cloud that filled the temple in the days of Solomon (1 Kings 8:10). It is the same cloud that people saw leaving the temple when the glory departed from Israel (Ezek. 10:18). It is the cloud that enveloped Christ on the Mount of Transfiguration when His garments became glistening white and His face shone like the sun (Matt. 17:5). It is the cloud into which He was received when He ascended from the Mount of Olives to His Father (Acts 1:9). It is the *shekinah* cloud—the cloud of God's glory. Isn't this how Jesus Himself puts it in the Gospels, answering His disciples' questions about the signs of His return and the end of the world? Christ's answers conclude on this high note: "And they shall see the Son of man coming in the clouds of heaven with power and great glory" (Matt. 24:30).

This cloud, then, is His royal chariot. Christ is coming again, and He is coming with all the power and glory of God. He is not coming as the humble carpenter, despised and rejected of men, but seated on a cloud of glory, vested with all the power and insignia of His high office as the One "ordained of God to be the Judge of quick and dead" (Acts 10:42). That is what John sees here.

The Son of Man

John sees that the white cloud is occupied by One "like unto the Son of man." That is how John saw Christ in the midst of the seven candlesticks (Rev. 1:13). And the four Gospels identify the Lord Jesus as "the Son of man" eighty times. In seventy-nine of those times, the phrase proceeds from His own lips. It was His characteristic way of referring to Himself.

Some have objected that John here is saying that he didn't really see the Son of man, but only "one…like unto" the Son of man. John does say that, but remember that John intimately knew the Lord on earth. This is the disciple who rested his head on Christ's bosom in the Upper Room. This is the disciple whom Jesus especially loved. As John looks into heaven, he sees this same Christ, but not as he remembers Him. He looks like the Son of man as John knew Him on earth, but now He is exalted and coming on the clouds of heaven. There is continuity but also contrast in John's description: it is the same Jesus of Nazareth, but now wondrously exalted. The words "like unto the Son of man" do not express uncertainty, but rather express wonder and amazement—John recognizes the One seated upon that cloud, but now he sees Him glorified. Furthermore, the language here reflects Daniel 7:13, where Daniel reports that he saw that "one like the Son of man came with the clouds of heaven."

The Golden Crown

John tells us that the Son of man comes back to earth with something on His head, "a golden crown." There are two words for *crown* in Greek, *diadema* and *stephanos*. The word *diadema*, from which we get the word *diadem*, is the crown worn by kings and rulers of the earth. It symbolizes God-given power to rule among men. The word used here in Revelation 14:14 is *stephanos*, the victor's crown, such as the one given to the victors in the Olympic games. The man who outperformed his competitors in all the events was given a wreath of laurel branches to wear upon his head and was invited to sit next to the emperor in the stadium. When John sees the Son of man coming on the clouds of glory, he sees Christ wearing not a diadem, but a victor's wreath. Now, don't misunderstand me. The diadem belongs to Him as well. But that is not what John sees Him wearing here. He sees Christ with a wreath of victory upon His head, made of imperishable gold, not laurel branches. He is coming as the One who has conquered sin, death, and Satan. He is coming as the One who has been successful in all that He strove to attain for us. He is coming as the One who has finished the work that He came to do. He is coming as the One who has triumphed on the cross over all principalities and powers. Christ is the Victor. That is how we should see Him here.

> Look, ye saints, the sight is glorious.
> See the man of sorrows now,
> From the fight returned victorious
> Every knee to Him shall bow:
> Crown Him, crown Him, crown Him, crown Him
> Crowns becomes the victor's brow.[1]

It should be a matter of tremendous comfort for us to know that it is Christ our Savior who comes to judge the living and the dead. It means that we can face the prospect of judgment day with confidence if we belong to Christ.

> Bold shall I stand in thy great day;
> For who ought to my charge shall lay?
> Fully absolved through these I am,
> From sin and fear, from guilt and shame.[2]

Believer, on that great and dreadful day of judgment, when heaven and earth shall pass away, Christ shall come on the clouds of glory and with a crown of victory upon His head. And you, believer, as His faithful servant, will receive "a crown of glory that fadeth not away" (1 Peter 5:4). The apostle Paul says, "But thanks be to

---

1. Thomas Kelly, "Look, Ye Saints, the Sight Is Glorious" (1809).
2. Nicolaus von Zinzendorf, "Jesus, Thy Blood and Righteousness," trans. John Wesley (1739).

God, which giveth us the victory through our Lord Jesus Christ" (1 Cor. 15:57). We will appear before Him without shame on that day because our Savior has triumphed over sin, death, and the grave, and His victory is our victory. He is coming with the Victor's crown on His brow to judge the living and the dead.

The Sharp Sickle

John sees the One "like unto the Son of man" holding "a sharp sickle." Perhaps nothing surprised John so much as to see his Lord carrying a farm implement. Jesus of Nazareth was a carpenter, not a farmer (although it is quite possible that, as a young man, Jesus went into the fields of His neighbors wielding a sickle to help gather in their crops at harvest time). John could not have missed the significance of this tool in his Master's hand. The Son of man is on a mission once more; He has work to do and the power to accomplish it. If John has any doubt, it is quickly dispelled by the voice of an angel sent out of the temple to proclaim the divine commission: "Thrust in thy sickle, and reap: for the time is come for thee to reap; for the harvest of the earth is ripe" (Rev. 14:15).

The meaning of this part of the vision is so clear that it scarcely needs any further explanation. Jesus Christ, the eternal Son of God who became flesh and dwelt among us in deep humiliation, has been raised and exalted by His Father, and appointed to be our Judge. He will come again to judge the living and the dead. The harvest of the earth is ripening fast, and the time to reap cannot be far off. From Christ's parables, we know what that will mean: the wheat will be separated from the tares, and the chaff from the wheat (Matt. 13:40–43). The wheat will be garnered in, the tares will be burnt in the fire, and the chaff will be driven away. In other words, the mixed multitude of humanity will be sorted out once and for all—the wicked will perish and the righteous will gaze in rapture on the face of the One whom they trusted and served faithfully through all their trials and toils on earth.

What an awesome thought! The One who is going to judge us and the world is the One in whose breast beats the heart of true love for mankind. The One who is going to judge you, unbeliever, is the One who loves sinners.

However, that makes the prospect of judgment frightful. If it were someone else, if He didn't care, or if it were a mere stranger, it wouldn't matter so much. But precisely because Christ is so gentle, tender, and loving, His anger is even more fierce. Sometimes the most sensitive people can be the most indignant when it comes to injustice. So there is no more frightful verse for the unsaved in the Bible than this one, speaking of the wrath of the Lamb.

That is what many are going to face. To be judged by a Savior is an awful, frightful prospect. This is One who is gentle, yet terrible. He is absolutely fair and yet full of righteous indignation and wrath. That is how He is coming; that is how John sees Him here, seated upon a cloud of glory with the crown of victory upon His head, but also with a sickle of judgment in His hand.

The Helpers and the Harvesting

John sees that as the Lord of the harvest, Christ has helpers. He is not alone in this work of harvesting. Indeed, we almost get the impression that He merely supervises the work, but it is not quite like that. The harvesting is done mostly (but not entirely) by His helpers, the angels. At least three angels are mentioned in verses 15–19:

> And another angel came out of the temple, crying with a loud voice to him that sat on the cloud, Thrust in thy sickle, and reap: for the time is come for thee to reap; for the harvest of the earth is ripe. And he that sat on the cloud thrust in his sickle on the earth; and the earth was reaped. And another angel came out of the temple which is in heaven, he also having a sharp sickle. And another angel came out from the altar, which had power over fire; and cried with a loud cry to him that had the sharp sickle, saying, Thrust in thy sharp sickle, and gather the clusters of the vine of the earth; for her grapes are fully ripe. And the angel thrust in his sickle into the earth, and gathered the vine of the earth, and cast it into the great winepress of the wrath of God.

These angels, then, are His helpers—His laborers in the field, as it were. They are the reapers of whom Jesus speaks in the parable of the wheat and the tares.

However, there is a slight theological problem here with regard to the involvement of the angels. One of these helpers seems to overstep the mark and forget his place. We read that an angel comes out of the temple and cries to Christ, "Thrust in thy sickle, and reap" (v. 15), whereupon He who "sat on the cloud thrust in his sickle on the earth; and the earth was reaped" (v. 16). Since when did the Lord Jesus Christ take orders from angels? How can it possibly be right for angels to give orders to the Son of man?

That is how it appears on the surface. But we must remember that we are in the realm of symbolism, and there is no suggestion here at all that this angel has authority over Christ. This passage is merely a reminder to us of a very important theological truth: Christ is still the Mediator between God and man. Even in His glorified state, He is the Man Christ Jesus, and, as such, He does nothing of Himself. He takes orders and commands from God the Father. This angel, in other words, is simply the Father's messenger. That puts the angel's directive in its proper perspective. From the Father to the Son, it is time for harvest.

When our Lord was questioned by His disciples regarding the time of judgment, Christ insisted that as the Mediator, He does not know the hour and time of judgment. Nor do the angels in heaven know. These times and seasons are known only to the Father (Mark 13:32). But in John's vision, the time to reap and the season of harvest have arrived, and the Father sends a messenger out of the temple to the Son, declaring: "The harvest is ripe; the time is come; put in Thy sickle." It is a signal that judgment day has arrived; the earth's final harvest is at hand. So there is an important truth here. The Son does nothing but what the Father commands. He does not come to judge until the Father gives the order, which He does here by sending an angel to carry His message.

But I want you to notice a little more about the involvement of these angels and the part they play in this harvest. When Jesus comes to judge the world, the Bible tells us, He will have all His holy angels with Him (Matt. 25:31), and it won't just be for show. These angels are coming as workers, as reapers, as laborers in the field. They are not coming merely as bodyguards in ceremonial dress to heighten the impressiveness of the occasion. Our Lord doesn't need the glory of angels to exalt His glory. They are coming to work. They are coming to be involved in the harvesting.

There is a lot of coming and going. Verses 17–18: "Another angel came out of the temple which is in heaven, he also having a sharp sickle. And another angel came out from the altar, which had power over fire; and cried with a loud cry to him that had the sharp sickle, saying, Thrust in thy sharp sickle." The symbolism here is very important. It shows us the principle upon which these angels oper- ate, when it says, "another angel came out from the altar, which had power over fire." It tells us something about the guidelines within which they carry out their work of harvesting the earth. It all has to do with the temple, the altar, and the fire.

In the Old Testament symbolism, the altar of sacrifice bore the lamb to be sacrificed. It also bore the fire that was to consume the lamb. The message here is this: the judgment fire over which these angels have charge and which is to rain upon the earth is the same fire that fell at Calvary upon the altar and upon the sacrificial Lamb. And the simple message is that if you will not have the Lamb, you must bear the fire. If, rejecting the Spirit's willingly offered grace, you will not come confessing your sins and laying your hands upon the head of the Lamb at Calvary, trusting in the crucified Savior to be your substitute to bear the wrath that your sin deserves—if you won't have the Lamb of God, Jesus Christ, as your Savior—then you must bear the wrath of God yourself. That is the message. There are two places where God can deal with the problem of your sin—at Calvary, in the person of a substitute Savior, or in hell. If you will not come to Calvary and receive Jesus Christ as your Savior, then you must bear the consequences of your sin forever in hell.

Now, there is nothing unjust or unfair about that. God has provided a Lamb for a burnt offering. He has provided a Savior for sinners. Dear friend, there is no reason why you should perish under the wrath of God. God has made provision for the salvation of sinners. But if you, in your stubborn, rebellious sinfulness, will not receive that provision, then you must bear the consequences forever in your own body and spirit. You must either have the Lamb or the fire.

That is the principle on which these angels operate. That is how they distinguish between people as they gather the nations in from the four corners of the world. These angels are simply executing God's will, issued at Calvary by the Judge of all the earth. They are acting in complete harmony with the righteousness and holiness of God that was revealed there. That explains something of their eagerness for the work. We feel that when we read these verses. They keep crying out to one another, "Put in the sickle." The harvest is ripe (v. 15), yes, fully ripe (v. 18).

These angels are not involved in Calvary's salvation in the same way that we are because they are not sinners. They do not need to be saved as we do. Nevertheless, at Calvary, these angels saw the righteousness and holiness of God in a way that they had never seen before. At Calvary, when Jesus bore our sins and endured punishment for them, these angels saw just how holy and righteous God really is. And then they look at the world, long overdue for punishment. It is crying out for punishment. They are jealous for what they saw at Calvary. They are jealous for what they saw on the altar. They are jealous for the holiness and righteousness of God. So these angels, with all their pent-up emotions in heaven, cry out, "The harvest is due!" They do not cry this out in a spirit of vindictiveness, but with a holy jealousy and regard for the One who sits upon the throne.

Today, like no other day in history, we must say that the world has been the breeding place for sin and rebellion for so long that the harvest seems overdue. We marvel that Jesus Christ still has not come for the final reaping. The signs of the last days are upon us. We don't know if the Son of man will come this week, this year, or this decade. No man knows the day or the hour, but we may certainly say that the time for the earth's final harvest seems to be ripe.

Will Christ come in our lifetime? I don't know. I do know that the message of this harvest vision must be, "Be always ready, for you know not when the Son of man will come."

The Harvest

This is the final harvest. There is a sense in which history repeats itself, so that there have been many harvests. The principle stated in Galatians 6:7, "Be not deceived; God is not mocked: for whatsoever a man soweth, that shall he also reap," has been confirmed throughout world history. It applies not only to individuals, but to nations and civilizations. There is a sense in which harvesting is always going on in the earth. But what is before us in Revelation 14 is the culmination of all this—the final judgment, here called *the final harvest*. It is called "the winepress of the wrath of God," drawing upon the imagery of Isaiah 63:1–6, where the Lord appears with red-stained clothing because, "I have trodden the winepress alone; and of the people there was none with me: for I will tread them in mine anger, and trample them in my fury; and their blood shall be sprinkled upon my garments, and I will stain all my raiment. For the day of vengeance is in mine heart, and the year of my redeemed is come" (vv. 3–4).

Not only does the language throughout Revelation 14 imply this, but the arithmetic in verse 20 also requires it. This verse says, "And the winepress was trodden without the city, and blood came out of the winepress, even unto the horse bridles, by the space of a thousand and six hundred furlongs."

Again, numbers in Revelation are to be understood spiritually, not literally. We are to understand this distance spiritually. We are told, in essence, that the area that is affected by the judgment of God is 1,600 furlongs—184 miles and deep enough for a horse to swim in. In other words, verse 20 presents a picture of the vast extent of the judgment.

The number 1,600 is the square of 40. No matter how you arrive at this number—whether four times four multiplied by ten times ten, or another way—the numbers that are involved are *four* and *ten*. Now, *four* is the number of the earth in Scripture. We even acknowledge this in our own day when we speak of the four points of the compass or the four corners of the earth. The number *four* in Scripture invariably applies to the created sphere. *Ten* is the number of completion. So what we have here is a picture not of a bloody battle in Palestine or Armageddon as many premillennialists understand it; rather, this is a symbolic representation of a judgment encircling the whole earth—a full, final, and complete judgment of the world. These 1,600 furlongs contain the lifeblood of the whole world. That is the picture.

A day is coming when the very lifeblood will be squeezed out of this world in the winepress of God's wrath. That is the message of this vision—and, ultimately, the message of the entire Bible. It is the picture you get when you read of multitudes in "the valley of decision" (Joel 3:14). Is that an evangelistic crusade? That is how it is often taken. The evangelist supposedly stands up before thousands at the football stadium. But that is not what Joel is talking about. The decision is God's final verdict on mankind. Joel is giving a description of what is going to happen at the last day. The Lord is going to summon all the nations of the earth to the valley of Jehoshaphat—to the valley of decision—for judgment and for His final verdict.

So Revelation 14:20 is a picture of the final judgment. The question is, what is that going to mean for you and for me personally? Are you ready for the final judgment? Are you washed in the blood of the Lamb?

There is something else we need to notice about this final harvest. It is actually a twofold harvest, or, we might almost say, two harvests back to back. There is a wheat harvest and then a grape harvest; or, to speak technically, there is a harvest and a vintage. That is very clear if you read the passage carefully. It is certainly strongly implied in the Greek. In verse 15, we are told that "the harvest of the earth is ripe," and in verse 18, we are told that "her grapes are fully ripe." In verse 15, the word translated as "ripe" means "dry." In verse 18, the word translated as "ripe" literally means "overripe." You can see how these varying translations apply. Wheat is not ready for harvest as long as it is green. It is only when the wheat becomes dry that the harvest is ready. Grapes become tender when they are ready to be picked. So that is the picture of two harvests—of a gathering in of wheat and a treading down of grapes. And the two things are quite distinct and separate. The wheat is gathered in first before the grapes are trodden.

The gathering in of the wheat in verses 14–16 is symbolic of believers being acquitted of all sin in Christ and being brought into the presence of God in heaven. The treading of the grapes in verses 17–20 is symbolic of unbelievers being judged, condemned, and cast into hell. This double harvest evokes two very contrasting responses—a response of great comfort for the believer and a response of great terror for the unbeliever.

First, *there is great comfort for believers in the final judgment.* It is a very comforting truth for true Christians to know that before God tramples the lifeblood out of this world, He will first gather in all of His wheat. Paul speaks about the second coming and says, "For the Lord himself shall descend from heaven with a shout, with the voice of the archangel, and with the trump of God: and the dead in Christ shall rise first: then we which are alive and remain shall be caught up together with them in the clouds, to meet the Lord in the air: and so shall we ever be with the Lord" (1 Thess. 4:16–17). If there is any doctrine of the rapture in Scripture, that's it, but it is not what the premillennialists mean by the rapture. Paul is clear that it all happens at once, instantaneously. There is no period of a thousand years between the rapture of the church and the judgment of God. The Lord descends from heaven with a shout. And even as He is coming upon the clouds of glory, those who are His are caught up to meet Him. That is the picture here. It is not the angels but the One who sits upon the cloud (v. 16) who stoops down and, with a sweep of His powerful arm, gathers up His wheat. That is what Jesus' return will mean for you if you are a Christian. You will be caught up to meet Him in the air.

Remember how the Lord puts it in Matthew 24:36–37: "Of that day and hour knoweth no man, no, not the angels of heaven, but my Father only. But as the days of Noe [Noah] were, so shall also the coming of the Son of man be." A few verses later we read: "Then shall two be in the field; the one shall be taken, and the other left. Two women shall be grinding at the mill; the one shall be taken, and the other left. Watch therefore: for ye know not what hour your Lord doth come" (vv. 40–42).

How was it in "the days of Noe" (Noah)? The whole earth suffered the judgment of God—but not until Noah and his family were safely shut up in the ark. Every type and every foreshadowing that you find in Scripture follows that pattern. How was it in the plains of Sodom and Gomorrah, when the fire and brimstone fell upon those cities and consumed them? First of all, Lot and his family were warned and led out of the city. And this is how it will be on the last day. When the Lord comes upon the clouds of glory, He will first gather to Himself His elect. That is what Matthew 24:22 means: "for the elect's sake" the day shall be shortened. They will not be left to witness the awful scene that is to follow. They have no place there and no part in that. There will be no final judgment for them in the sense of facing God's wrath and condemnation on the last day.

Second, *there is great terror for unbelievers in the final judgment.* On the day of final judgment, what is comforting for believers will be terrifying for unbelievers. Hendriksen summarizes the sobering vision:

> The vine of the earth symbolizes the entire multitude of evil men; its grapes are the individual unbelievers. Just as grapes are trodden, pressed, crushed, so the wicked are going to be destroyed and punished everlastingly. The grapes are cast into the great winepress of the wrath of God and crushed. In the picture which John sees, a lake of blood results. It is so deep that horses can swim in it. It spreads out in all directions.... This is the thoroughly complete judgment of the wicked.[3]

---

3. Hendriksen, *More than Conquerors*, 155–56.

So I ask again, as I close this chapter, where do you stand in relation to this last day? There are many ways in which the Bible speaks about the final judgment, but it is very significant that the symbolism here is that of a harvest. It is a reminder to us that this day is not far off. And it is not unrelated to today, for what a man sows, that will he reap. If your addiction to sin causes you to sow to the flesh nothing but sin from day by day, and if you refuse to repent of those sins and to flee to Christ for forgiveness, then you will reap a harvest of destruction and restlessness. What is going to happen to you on the day of judgment is integrally bound up with what you are now. I ask you: have you been washed in the blood of the Lamb and become His follower? Are you trusting in Jesus Christ alone for salvation? Is your life hid with Christ in God? Or are you treasuring up, day after day, more wrath against the day of wrath?

26

Celebrating on the
Sea of Glass

REVELATION 15:1–4

And I saw another sign in heaven, great and marvellous, seven angels having the seven last plagues; for in them is filled up the wrath of God. And I saw as it were a sea of glass mingled with fire: and them that had gotten the victory over the beast, and over his image, and over his mark, and over the number of his name, stand on the sea of glass, having the harps of God. And they sing the song of Moses the servant of God, and the song of the Lamb, saying, Great and marvellous are thy works, Lord God Almighty; just and true are thy ways, thou King of saints. Who shall not fear thee, O Lord, and glorify thy name? for thou only art holy: for all nations shall come and worship before thee; for thy judgments are made manifest.

In the 1800s, an African-American slave secretly picked melons from his master's field, then distributed some to slaves who had been denied food that day. The next day, when the footprints were matched to the melon-picker's feet, he was brutally beaten. Then he was sent to the field to pick his quota of cotton in the sweltering sun. Because of his late start and weakened physical condition, the slave realized that he could not meet his quota, meaning he would be beaten again that evening. At that point, he decided to run away. He crawled through the cotton, slipped into a nearby forest, and began to run north. After he had run about fifteen miles, the sun set and the slave collapsed in a field of tall grass.

The next morning, he woke with the sun beating on his face. He bathed his wounded body in a nearby stream and found some apples to eat. He walked all morning, and by midafternoon he began to feel the exhilaration of freedom. He had never felt so alive, so he began to sing about his safe arrival in Canada. But his song was interrupted by the distant barking of bloodhounds. Terror-stricken, he ran like a rabbit, saying, "I just knew it was too good to be true!"

Sometimes sinners set free by salvation in Christ feel that the good news of the gospel is too good to be true. Satan, our old master, persistently refuses to give up his ownership rights to us. He sends the black dogs of temptation and persecution to drag his former property back home. In those hours of trial, we sometimes think that we are not fully delivered from all the devil's power after all.

Revelation 15:1–4 is a kind of respite that can comfort us when we are distressed by the cares of this life. Trumpets are sounding, foundations are crumbling, nations are in commotion, false prophets are misleading thousands, iniquity is rampant, and persecutions assail us. In such circumstances, drawing near to God and catching even a momentary glimpse of His goodness and greatness, and of the might of His kingdom, is just what we need to reassure us, to strengthen our faith, and to deepen our hold on the hope of glory. Let us examine this amazingly comforting passage under these headings: experiencing heavenly tranquility; finding freedom in exodus; understanding with clarity; and enjoying worshipful festivity.

Experiencing Heavenly Tranquility

In Revelation 15–16, John sees a new vision. This time, the vision is about seven vials of God's wrath that will be poured out on the earth. It is the fifth cycle of visions in the book of Revelation, each of which sweeps through church history from Christ's first advent to His second coming.

Note how John begins: "And I saw another sign in heaven." The last time that phrase appeared was in 12:1, when an enormous red dragon launched his campaign of persecution against the woman and her child. Revelation 12:1 says, "And there appeared a great wonder [or sign] in heaven." That verse marked the beginning of the fourth cycle of visions of Revelation.

Revelation is a very intense book, occasionally punctuated with breathing points, welcome respites, and comforting prospects of heaven's tranquility. God knows that His people need such tension-relieving interludes. Spiritual battle fatigue can settle in our minds, causing us to confess, "The book of Revelation keeps sending me back into intense conflicts." The Holy Spirit knew that when He inspired this book; thus, at periodic places in this book, He provides us with Sabbath days or furloughs, during which we can leave the battlefield and find relief in a heavenly retreat. That is what happens in Revelation 15:1.

That happens often in Revelation. After running the circuit of the seven churches in chapters 2 and 3, the Lord says in Revelation 4:1, "Come up hither." We are given a glimpse of heaven. On earth, there is danger, turmoil, and destruction; in heaven, there is glory, order, and peace. The sea of glass that surrounds the heavenly throne is smooth and tranquil (4:6).

Then we go back to the battlefield to view the turbulent opening of the seven seals. But after all of the seals are opened, Revelation 8:1 says, "When he had opened the seventh seal, there was silence in heaven about the space of half an hour." Away from the noise and commotion of the earth, heaven is silent as its occupants stand in awe at God's judgments.

Again, after the saints are hunted down by the dragon and stalked by the beast trying to brand his number 666 on their fore-heads, and the Judge sweeps across the world with His mighty sickle, Revelation 15:2 offers another glimpse of the tranquility of heaven. It says: "And I saw as it were a sea of glass mingled with fire: and them that had gotten the victory over the beast, and over his image, and over his mark, and over the number of his name, stand on the sea of glass, having the harps of God." We can catch our breath again. We still have to confront the outpouring of God's wrath in the seven vials, but first we can linger in this scene of joy and tranquility.

The Lord's Supper is a foretaste of that heavenly tranquility for believers. It is an oasis in the hectic wilderness of this world, where the tyranny of the urgent too often dominates our lives. Our compassionate heavenly Father knows we are frail. He is mindful that we are but dust (Ps. 103:14). Thus, He provides His embattled children with a preview of the victory celebration that we will enjoy once the war is won by His grace.

On this earth, we sometimes feel besieged by sickness, sorrow, and strife. Enemy bullets seem to be striking all around us. We might be tempted to ask, "Is this battle against Satan, the world, and our flesh really worth the price?" Then Christ calls us to sit at His table, there to remember what He has done for us and what that will mean for eternity. He says, as it were, "Come to Me and sit for a moment in heavenly places. When your earthly sorrows are over, heaven awaits you. And, yes, it will be worth the price."

I recently heard of a marathon runner who was asked about the challenges of the race. "How do you keep going?" someone inquired. He said, "As I am running, especially uphill, I think about hugging my wife and my kids once I cross the finish line." That was the image he imprinted on his mind.

Likewise, God gives us something to imprint on our minds as we struggle toward the finish line. As Philippians 3 says, we are to forget those things that are behind and reach forth "unto those things which are before" (v. 13), namely, the promise of entering into God's rest (Heb. 4:1). So Brooks writes of the assembly of saints John now sees in heaven, "As for the great company of people who were victorious over the beast, this victorious, praising and God-glorifying gathering...is descriptive of all the saints of God, all the church of Christ. Which means that in this vision, John saw you and me, dear fellow believer."[1]

Seven plagues will afflict our world until the promise of Revelation 15:2 is fulfilled, but, by God's grace, we will make it! We will then join the saints in heaven in the victorious celebration of God

1. Brooks, *The Lamb Is All the Glory*, 143.

and His Son, our Savior, Jesus Christ. We will extol His victory over the beast and the dragon.

Finding Freedom in Exodus

Furthermore, Revelation 15:3a tells us that we will sing the Song of Moses, the servant of God, and the Song of the Lamb. The Song of Moses is a reference to what happened many hundreds of years ago. John is drawing a parallel between the victory of God's people on the last day and the exodus, the going up of Israel out of Egypt, celebrated as the salvation of God in the Song of Moses, recorded in Exodus 15.

For many years, the people of Israel had been harshly treated as slaves in Egypt. Then Moses came to Pharaoh, ruler of Egypt, and said, "The Lord says, 'Let My people go.'" Pharaoh asked, "Who is the Lord that I should hearken unto Him?" (see Ex. 5:1–2).

With a series of ten plagues, the Lord broke the tyrant's power over Israel. The final plague was death to all the firstborn in Egypt. The Pharaoh who had sneered, "Who is the Lord?" now begged Moses to "rise up, and get you forth from among my people…go, serve the LORD as ye have said" (Ex. 12:31). Israel was finally set free to travel into the wilderness, where they would be led by a pillar of fire by night and a pillar of cloud by day. They had never felt so alive, for now they were breathing the air of freedom!

But when the Israelites reached Baal-zephon, God said to Moses, "Speak unto the children of Israel, that they turn and encamp before Pihahiroth, between Migdol and the sea, over against Baal-zephon: before it shall ye encamp by the sea" (Ex. 14:2). So the people encamped on the shore of the Red Sea.

Meantime, Pharaoh had a change of heart. He and his army, with six hundred chariots and horses, raced off to capture the runaway nation. The Israelites were trapped between Pharaoh and the Red Sea. "I knew it was too good to be true!" some might have said. "We are still Pharaoh's slaves, and he will take us back to Egypt in chains." As Pharaoh approached, "the children of Israel lifted up their eyes, and, behold, the Egyptians marched after them; and they were sore afraid: and the children of Israel cried out unto the LORD. And they said unto Moses, Because there were no graves in Egypt, hast thou taken us away to die in the wilderness? wherefore hast thou dealt thus with us, to carry us forth out of Egypt? Is not this the word that we did tell thee in Egypt, saying, Let us alone, that we may serve the Egyptians? For it had been better for us to serve the Egyptians, than that we should die in the wilderness" (Ex. 14:10–12). In short, they were saying that freedom is too good to be true.

Do you sometimes feel that way? Dear believer, once we were enslaved to sin and Satan, but Jesus set us free. By grace, we repented and believed on Him. By grace, we brushed His blood on the doorposts of our souls; He liberated us from our sins. Our lives changed in many ways. But then the spiritual struggles intensified and became more difficult. The bloodhounds began to bay, and we feared that we would no longer be free.

In Revelation 12–14, the great dragon pursues God's saints and tries to destroy their souls. When you sense the talons of the dragon nipping at your heels, are you tempted to give up? Do you say, "I'm afraid that I am on the failing end"? I know that if I am to join the saints in heaven, I must have no lie in my mouth and I must not be defiled; I must live a life of obedience to God. I become very concerned when I think of that, and I confess: "I am prone to wander—Lord, I feel it! I am prone to leave the God I love. How often I fall short of God's commands."

Spurgeon writes for such a time: "'Surely,' you say, 'I cannot hold on my way with such a host seeking to drive me back; I must again become the slave of my iniquities.' And thus dreading apostasy, and feeling that you would rather die than become what you were; you this morning are filled with trepidation and fear.... You have tasted for a moment the joys of holiness and the sweets of liberty; and now again to go back to endure the bondage of a spiritual Egypt, would be worse than before."[2]

---

2. Charles H. Spurgeon, *The New Park Street Pulpit* (Pasadena, Tex.: Pilgrim, 1975), 3:234.

God did not abandon His children who had placed lambs' blood on their doorposts to be saved when the tenth plague passed through the land of Egypt. God was with them on the shore of the Red Sea. He put His angel and a pillar of cloud between Israel and Pharaoh's troops. At His command, the east wind blew upon the Red Sea, parting the waters so that they stood up like walls, protecting the children of Israel while they walked on dry ground to the other side of the sea. When Pharaoh and his chariots attempted to follow Israel through the sea, the wind fell and the walls of water came crashing down, drowning all of the mighty men of Egypt.

Exodus 15:1 says, "Then sang Moses and the children of Israel this song unto the LORD, and spake, saying, I will sing unto the LORD, for he hath triumphed gloriously: the horse and his rider hath he thrown into the sea." Israel was exhilarated! The people had seen the great power of the Lord. They were safe. Freedom now seemed too good *not* to be true!

What those Israelites experienced at the Red Sea thousands of years ago is what the church of God will enjoy when Jesus returns. Then we will sing both the Song of Moses and the Song of the Lamb. The Passover and the exodus point ahead to the redemption of sinners accomplished by the Messiah, our Passover Lamb, who came to earth to shed His blood once and for all, that through His death we as believers might be forever redeemed and freed from all the tyranny of Satan. Those whom the Lamb's blood covers cannot be destroyed by the dragon.

What a comfort it is to know that the Lord is with us as we travel through the wilderness of this world. When we think we're all alone, the Lord is with us like a pillar of cloud and a pillar of fire, guarding and protecting us. As we walk through the wilderness toward the Promised Land, Satan is pursuing us, yes, but the Lord is protecting us with walls on the right and the left, before and behind. Before we know it, God will swallow up the dragon and the two beasts, and those who are trying to brand us with the mark of the beast.

Revelation 20:10 reassures us, saying, "And the devil that deceived them was cast into the lake of fire and brimstone, where the beast and the false prophet are, and shall be tormented day and night for ever and ever." All of those demonic powers will be drowned in the sea of God's wrath. And we will be amazed at what God has done.

Harry Buis writes, "When the Egyptians were drowned in the Red Sea, Moses sang a song of praise to God who had delivered the Israelites from their enemies. In like manner, God's redeemed people have a victory song to sing."[3] So, on the last day, we, along with Moses and all the 144,000, will sing, "He hath triumphed gloriously: the horse and his rider hath he thrown into the sea" (Ex. 15:1).

As we enjoy this interlude, consider the place where we will stand. Revelation 15:2 says, "And I saw as it were a sea of glass mingled with fire: and them that had gotten the victory...stand on the sea of glass, having the harps of God." The saints are not just standing on the beach, but on a sea of glass. Yet the surface of the sea is so sturdy that it supports the multitude of saints who stand on it.

Christians who agonize about whether their remaining sins will yet disqualify them from entering the Promised Land of heaven should remember that the Lord drowned Pharaoh and all his chariots in the sea. They should also remember that at the right time, the trumpet will sound and Christ will return to earth for the day of judgment. All of our concerns are assuaged by God's saving work on our behalf.

A late nineteenth-century traveler wrote on his return home from an overseas trip:

It was stormy from shore to shore without a single fair day, but the place to which we were going was my home. There was my family; there was my church; there were my friends, who were as dear to me as my own life. And I lay perfectly happy in the midst of sickness and nausea. All that the boat could do to me could not keep down the exultation and the joy which rose up in me. For every single hour it was carrying me nearer

---

3. Harry Buis, *The Book of Revelation: A Simplified Commentary* (Philadelphia: Presbyterian and Reformed, 1960), 84.

and nearer where was all that I loved in the world. It was deep, dark midnight when we came to Halifax. I could see nothing. Yet, the moment we came into still water, I rose from my berth and got up on deck.[4]

That is what is suggested by the sea of glass in Revelation 15:2. Saints are weather-beaten, storm-tossed, weary, and sick to their stomachs because of affliction and persecution. But soon they will be going home to everyone they love to enjoy the rest and peace of heaven forever; they shall stand on a sea of glass, and there shall be no wind of trouble to roil the waters under their feet.

That is possible only in Christ Jesus. So with your eyes fixed on your Savior, sing the Song of Moses and the Song of the Lamb until the day you will sing with all the saints in heaven.

Understanding with Clarity

This sea of glass is also clear. You can see through it. Elsewhere, Revelation emphasizes the transparency of glass. For example, Revelation 21:18 describes the New Jerusalem, saying, "And the building of the wall of it was of jasper: and the city was pure gold, like unto clear glass." Notice that it says "*clear* glass." Furthermore, verse 21 says, "And the twelve gates were twelve pearls; every several gate was of one pearl: and the street of the city was pure gold, as it were transparent glass." This glass is transparent. You can see through it. The still, peaceful clarity of this sea is in marked contrast to the normal churning of the sea's waters (Isa. 57:20–21).

So think about what it will be like in heaven to have clear understanding. Dennis Johnson writes, "Heaven's floor will be the earth's ceiling."[5] When you get to heaven, everything will become clear to you as you look back at the history of the earth. You will look down and see all the difficulties, hardships, struggles, and battles that believers are enduring. Within the tranquility of our heavenly

---

4. "Earth-sickness," in *The Christian Pioneer* 28 (1874): 68.

5. Dennis Johnson, *Triumph of the Lamb: A Commentary on Revelation* (Phillipsburg, N.J.: P&R Publishing, 2001), 215.

home, we will see how sin roiled and befouled the waters of the sea, so that what was happening was unclear to us. But when we see from heaven how God has been working in this world all along, our understanding will be complete. As Revelation 15:3 says, we will sing, "Great and marvellous are thy works, Lord God Almighty; just and true are thy ways, thou King of saints."

Notice also that the sea of glass is mixed with fire, giving it a reddish hue (v. 2). Some commentators say this refers to the persecution of God's people on earth; others say the color reflects the unleashing of God's wrath in the winepress of His anger. Either way, rage, wrath, and persecution have plagued believers throughout history.

At times, God's saints have questioned why they must suffer. Beleaguered Job asked, "Why, Lord, am I being assaulted?" God's purpose was murky and unclear to Job. In the New Testament, the disciples of John the Baptist must have asked why their leader was beheaded. Today we might ask why Jim Elliot and Nate Saint had to be killed by people they were trying to lead to the Lord. Personally, we might ask: "Why didst Thou snatch my loved one away so early and so young, Lord? Why dost Thou allow people to be gassed to death or buried alive or murdered while still in their mothers' wombs? And, why, oh, why can't I conquer the sin that continues to plague me? So much is unclear to me; why?"

Psalm 36 directs us to God's unfathomable wisdom, saying, "Thy judgments are a great deep" (v. 6). In John 13:7, Jesus explains, "What I do thou knowest not now; but thou shalt know hereafter." And Romans 11:33 says: "O the depth of the riches both of the wisdom and knowledge of God! how unsearchable are his judgments, and his ways past finding out!" We can't fathom what God is doing while we are here on earth. He is too deep. Things are murky now, but when we finally stand on the tranquil sea of glass in heaven, all things will become clear.

Revelation 15:4b says, "For thy judgments are made manifest." The word *manifest* means God's judgments will be disclosed and uncovered for us in heaven. As 1 Corinthians 13:12 says, "For now we see through a glass, darkly; but then face to face: now I know in part; but then shall I know even as also I am known."

My wife and daughter once toured Europe. Their tour guide said to them: "I am an atheist, because my wife, whom I dearly loved, died of cancer at a young age. I cannot believe in a God who would ever do something like that. And if there is such a God who would take my wife like that, then I want nothing to do with Him."

We weep for this young man's loss, but we also realize that he doesn't understand that here on earth we look at a half-finished work. Brooks puts it this way: "You and I are still in this world. There are many things we do not understand, many things that perplex us, many things that we can so easily misinterpret." We experience that at every level—internationally, nationally, in the church, in family life, and in personal life. Brooks concludes, "We need a larger perspective on history than we can obtain merely by viewing our own limited life-span."[6]

That larger perspective will be ours on the last day, for then we will understand what God was doing in our lives, our countries, our churches, and in all the great movements of world history. Then we will see clearly, and God's judgments will be all the more marvelous in our eyes. Then we stop asking why the man at Lester during England's civil war in the seventeenth century was shot in the head by a musket ball while he was standing guard at night. John Bunyan was supposed to take the watch that night, but someone else volunteered for the job. Bunyan, who was an unbeliever at that time, was very moved by the man's death and eventually was converted. God then used Bunyan to write *The Pilgrim's Progress* so that people through the centuries, and still today, may read it and be saved. Marvelous are Thy works, O Lord!

People must have questioned God's wisdom in taking the parents of John Brown of Haddington when he was a child. But he later wrote, "My father dying about the eleventh year of my age, and my mother soon after, I was left a poor orphan, and had nothing

---

6. Brooks, *The Lamb Is All the Glory*, 144.

to depend on but the providence of God—and I must say that the Lord hath been 'the father of the fatherless, and the orphans stay.'"[7] Through such terrible trials, God raised up a man of remarkable godliness, humility, and learning, whose writings continue to bless the world today.

Perhaps you have a loved one who is fighting cancer right now, and it seems as if your prayers for healing are not being answered. You should remember that disease is a part of life in this fallen world. Believers and unbelievers alike get sick. Perhaps your loved one won't be healed, but will suffer and die. Pain is a part of life in this world. It affects us all. Everything contained in the seven vials in Revelation 15 and 16 affects us all. We must all pass through the Red Sea. The difference is that the Israelites *go through* and *out of* the water, while the Egyptians *go under*.

Our comfort as believers is that when we face sickness, bereavement, disappointments, and losses, we will be led through it all by God. As Paul says in 1 Corinthians 10:13, "There hath no temptation taken you but such as is common to man: but God is faithful, who will not suffer you to be tempted above that ye are able; but will with the temptation also make a way to escape, that ye may be able to bear it." No trial that besets you is unique to you. We often think nobody has ever suffered as we have. But Paul says that is nonsense. The trials you are facing now are common to all people. That is because this fallen world is under the wrath of God.

But note how Paul promises that God will "with the temptation also make a way to escape." Literally in the Greek, the word for "a way to escape" means "a way up out of." With every Red Sea that seems to hem you in, God provides a way up out of it—an exodus and a triumphant walk through trouble—that one day you may join all the saints of God singing the Song of Moses and the Song of the Lamb.

---

7. *Select Remains of the Rev. John Brown, Late Minister of the Gospel at Haddington* (Pittsburgh: Cramer, Spear, and Eichbaum, 1810), 10.

God's Word to us today is the same as it was to His people trapped at the Red Sea. It is the same Word that has been true throughout the generations of the church. So stand firm and see the salvation of the Lord. As William Cowper writes,

> Ye fearful saints, fresh courage take
> The clouds ye so much dread
> Are big with mercy, and shall break
> In blessing on your head.[8]

God's works of providence are somewhat like the Hebrew language, which is read backward for us—from right to left. John Flavel explains, "Sometimes providences, like Hebrew letters, must be read backward."[9] In heaven at the end of time, we will see all the way back to the beginning and say, "Lord, it is marvelous what Thou hast done; truly Thou dost wipe away every tear."

Enjoying Worshipful Festivity
In heaven one day, we will sing: "Great and marvellous are thy works, Lord God Almighty; just and true are thy ways, thou King of saints. Who shall not fear thee, O Lord, and glorify thy name? For thou only art holy: for all nations shall come and worship before thee; for thy judgments are made manifest" (Rev. 15:3–4).

Just as the Israelites who had passed through the Red Sea said in exhilaration, "Sing unto the LORD, for…the horse and his rider hath he thrown into the sea" (Ex. 15:1), so we also will overflow with worship and praise one day, singing to God about His marvelous deeds. Reading about the winepress of God's wrath may make us recoil now, but once the dragon, beast, and false prophet have been thrown into the sea of God's wrath, we will no longer question God's ways.

When we get to heaven, we will discover that no one who is covered by the blood of the Lamb will have the mark of the beast

---

8. William Cowper, "God Moves in a Mysterious Way" (1774).

9. John Flavel, *Navigation Spiritualized: Or, a New Compass for Seamen*, in *The Works of John Flavel* (1820; repr., Edinburgh: Banner of Truth, 1968), 5:284.

on his forehead. Not one of Satan's hounds will have damaged any of God's sheep. All will be free at last in the Promised Land. If our true home is heaven, we can have a foretaste of its wonder by singing, "Great and marvellous are thy works, O Lord!"

I don't have time or space in this book to describe all that believers will enjoy in worshipful festivity as they sing the Song of Moses. The most important part of this festivity, which we celebrate in part in the Lord's Supper, is *God Himself.* Throughout the Song of Moses, God is praised, not Moses. Everything is about God in Christ Jesus.

Ultimately, all our worshipful festivity is focused on Christ. The Song of Moses and the Song of the Lamb are not two songs but one, illustrating once again the unity of the Old and New Testaments, and the oneness of all believers in every age in Christ Jesus. From beginning to end, the song in essence says, "Unto him that loved us, and washed us from our sins in his own blood…to him be glory and dominion for ever and ever" (Rev. 1:5–6). William Perkins thus writes to preachers, "Preach one Christ by Christ to the praise of Christ."[10]

In Christ, we celebrate the triune God and His attributes, which include His omnipotence ("Lord God Almighty"); His justice and faithfulness ("just and true are thy ways"); and His holiness ("for thou only art holy"). We also celebrate His works, for they also are just and true, and His judgments when they are made manifest. We celebrate His names, too, such as *Lord God Almighty* and *King of saints,* for "Who shall not fear thee, O Lord, and glorify thy name?" At the last day, we will celebrate the universal worship offered to God: "for all nations shall come and worship before thee." Thus, Spurgeon writes to saints in the heat of oppression, "O Christian, fear not the foe, and remember now that the harder his blows, so the sweeter thy song."[11]

---

10. William Perkins, *The Arte of Prophecying: Or, A Treatise Concerning the Sacred and Onely True Manner and Methode of Preaching,* trans. Thomas Tuke (London: by Felix Kyngston for E.E., 1607), 148.

11. Spurgeon, *New Park Street Pulpit,* 3:238.

During the English Civil War, after Oliver Cromwell inflicted a crushing defeat upon royalist forces at Naseby, he reported, "This is none other than the hand of God, and to Him alone give glory."[12] The heartbeat of the Reformed faith is to give all the glory to God. Stephen Rees writes, "This is the distinctive note of Reformed Christianity. We are obsessed with God himself. We are overwhelmed by his majesty, his beauty, his holiness, his grace."[13]

We may sing the Song of Moses and the Song of the Lamb now, for it is the song of the redeemed. We sing it by faith, though, and not by sight, all the while "looking forward to that glorious day when, delivered from sin and oppression, delivered from the enemy who is always on our tail, and set free in heaven truly to glorify the God of our salvation, we shall be able to sing this song together as we have never sung it before!"[14]

Does the Song of the Lamb ring in your heart? Do you yearn to go to heaven, where you can join all the saints in this song? If you have little interest in heaven, then heaven is not your homeland. So ask yourself, "Who shall not fear thee, O Lord, and glorify thy name?" Do you fear God? Have you ever glorified God with all your heart? Every knee will bow and every tongue will confess—whether from below the surface of the sea of glass or above it, in the lake of fire or in heaven—that Jesus Christ is Lord.

As we noted earlier, Revelation 15:2 says that the sea of glass is mingled with fire. This strange mix of glass and fire symbolizes the combination on judgment day of God's transparent righteousness in Christ for believers (the sea of glass) and His judgments upon the wicked (mingled with fire). As Hamilton writes: "That fire swirling in the sea of glass appears to be a depiction of the cosmic disturbance resulting from the wrath of God. The fire is about to

---

12. Barry Coward, *Oliver Cromwell*, Profiles in Power (London: Routledge, 1991), 40.

13. Stephen Rees, "The Heart of the Reformed Faith," *Banner of Truth* (August 1, 2000), https://banneroftruth.org/us/resources/articles/2000/the-heart-of-the-reformed-faith/, accessed June 14, 2016.

14. Brooks, *The Lamb Is All the Glory*, 145.

fall. Judgment is about to be visited on all the rebels who refused to give God the honor and gratitude rightly due him."[15]

Do not let that fire fall on you on judgment day. Don't be like Pharaoh, whose heart was hard as flint when he said, "Who is the Lord that I should hearken unto Him?" If you do not repent of your sin and embrace the gospel by Spirit-worked faith, God's fiery wrath will descend upon you. So ask God to soften your heart. Ask the Spirit for grace to receive the Lamb of God as your greatest treasure and your greatest joy. Be like the boy who looked at the martyr burning at the stake and said, "I am going to take up my cross and follow Him."

---

15. Hamilton, *Revelation*, 304.

27

The Seven Vials
of Wrath

REVELATION 15:5–16:21

And after that I looked, and, behold, the temple of the tabernacle of the testimony in heaven was opened: and the seven angels came out of the temple.... And one of the four beasts gave unto the seven angels seven golden vials full of the wrath of God.... And the first went, and poured out his vial upon the earth; and there fell a noisome and grievous sore upon the men which had the mark of the beast, and upon them which worshipped his image. And the second angel poured out his vial upon the sea; and it became as the blood of a dead man: and every living soul died in the sea. And the third angel poured out his vial upon the rivers and fountains of waters; and they became blood.... And the fourth angel poured out his vial upon the sun; and power was given unto him to scorch men with fire.... And the fifth angel poured out his vial upon the seat of the beast; and his kingdom was full of darkness; and they gnawed their tongues for pain, and blasphemed the God of heaven because of their pains and their sores, and repented not of their deeds. And the sixth angel poured out his vial upon the great river Euphrates; and the water thereof was dried up, that the way of the kings of the east might be prepared.... And the seventh angel poured out his vial into the air; and there came a great voice out of the temple of heaven, from the throne, saying, It is done. And there were voices, and thunders, and lightnings; and there was a great earthquake, such as was not since men were upon the earth, so mighty an earthquake, and so great.... And every island fled away, and the mountains were not found. And there fell upon men a great hail out of heaven, every stone about the weight of a talent: and men blasphemed God because of the plague of the hail; for the plague thereof was exceeding great.

Revelation is a cyclical book. Heaven opens repeatedly, first to admit John into the heavenly vision of the divine throne-room (Rev. 4:1). Later in the book we find heaven opening in the final cataclysm of Christ's return (Rev. 11:19; 19:11). So too here, in the fifth cycle of visions which consists of the seven vials of wrath, we find that "the temple of the tabernacle of the testimony in heaven was opened," and the glory of God is manifested in His judgments upon a wicked world (Rev. 15:5).

God speaks from the altar of His temple, and one by one the angels emerge from the temple in priestly garments. Each of these angels has one of "the seven plagues" (v. 6), and they are given golden vials or bowls, "full of the wrath of God" (v. 7). The angels are then sent to pour out the contents of these vials upon the earth. As these messengers of wrath are commissioned, "smoke from the glory of God" fills the temple (v. 8).

The seven vials parallel the order of the seven trumpets that sound in chapters 8–11. The first trumpet announces something that will happen to the earth; likewise, the first vial is poured upon the earth. The second trumpet and the second vial both affect the sea; the third, the rivers; the fourth, the sun; the fifth, the abode of the beast or the realm of the wicked; and the sixth, the River Euphrates. The seventh trumpet and seventh vial both have to do with the final judgment.

Although the trumpets and the vials follow the same pattern, the vials of judgment are more intense than the former patterns of seven. For example, as the seven seals are opened, 25 percent of things is destroyed. When the trumpets sound, the destruction increases to 33 percent. By Revelation 16, everything is under the judgment and wrath of God.

This parallel structure stresses the Christian view of history over against the secular view that history simply goes round and round without purpose. The biblical view of history is that God marches on through the centuries, moving forward to a glorious final end. What a comfort that truth must have been to John and the persecuted church of his day, and what a comfort it still is to believers today. It reminds us that the day will come when God's sovereign justice will be gloriously manifested to a world that is rapidly moving toward destruction.

Let us examine the seven vials of God's wrath under these three headings: the character of God's judgments; the recipients of God's judgments; and the cup of God's judgments.

The Character of God's Judgments

The vast display of angels and vials in Revelation 15 and 16 teaches us much about the essential character of God's judgments. As you read these verses, you hear echoes of God's judgments on Egypt in the Old Testament. These vials of wrath are reminiscent of what God did in judging the Egyptians and bringing salvation to His people.

From that point, the exodus from Egypt becomes the paradigm for understanding how God saves His people. Many psalms cite the exodus as a symbol of God's way of delivering His people from their enemies and bringing them to a place of safety, blessing, and rest.

As part of the deliverance of His people, God judges the nation that oppresses them. He sends plague after plague upon the land of Egypt, culminating in the plague of death in the dark of night, slaying all the firstborn of men and beasts. Each plague is a visitation of wrath, a particular judgment sent down from the throne of God in heaven. The Bible always connects God's wrath with His justice; His wrath and justice are made manifest as judgments imposed on sinful man from on high. One judgment follows upon another, because God in His goodness and longsuffering gives sinners space to repent. But the day comes when goodness and longsuffering must give way to wrath and justice, and a final judgment is imposed.

Revelation 15 and 16 are the final consummation of that pattern. John sees that all of these judgments are accompanied by a sense of the holiness, righteousness, and integrity of God as Judge (Rev. 15:5; 16:1, 5, 7). The character of God's judgments is absolutely moral and righteous.

Revelation 15:4 says, "Thy judgments are made manifest." His righteousness is revealed in the way the angels are clothed as the instruments of judgment. They wear pure, bright linen robes with golden belts around their chests. The entire picture speaks about the purity, beauty, and imperishable worth of God's absolute righteousness. Revelation 16:5 confirms that explicitly: "Thou art righteous, O Lord…because thou hast judged thus." Verse 7 moves from the specific judgment in view to a general statement about all God's judgments: "True and righteous are thy judgments."

We are inclined to ask, "What sin could possibly be so great as to make these severe judgments righteous?" Scripture turns the question around: "Since these judgments are absolutely righteous and are sent from the throne of a perfectly just and thrice holy God, how great is the sin of men and women in His eyes?" We must be blind if we fail to see how immeasurably far we have fallen short of God's glory in our lives.

God's judgments are absolutely true. Revelation 15:3 says, "Just and true are thy ways." The word *just* means that God's judgments are consistent with His righteous character. The word *true* means that these judgments accord with the ways we have sinned against Him. Revelation 16:6 offers a great illustration of this concept: "For they have shed the blood of saints and prophets, and thou hast given them blood to drink." God's judgments are perfectly matched to our sins.

Jesus Christ is the supremely fair, true, and righteous Judge. We will be judged by Him, not by a jury of our peers, on judgment day. We could never stand before the judgment seat of God and say, "Righteous God, I demand that a verdict be rendered by a jury of my peers," because our peerless Peer is standing beside His throne. At this, our mouths will be shut, as Paul says in Romans 3:19. Christ understands our temptations far better than we do because He has faced them all, yet without sin (Heb. 4:15). You and I have often given in to the lust of the flesh, the lust of the eyes, and the pride of life (1 John 2:16), but Jesus never gave in, even when confronted by the devil himself. So He is capable of perfectly assessing you and me. His judgment is absolutely just and absolutely true—and therefore absolutely and irreversibly final.

Nebuchadnezzar and Paul agree in warning us not to question God's judgments: "None can stay his hand, or say unto him, What doest thou?" (Dan. 4:35) and "O man, who art thou that repliest against God?" (Rom. 9:20). God is supremely just. No one will end up in hell who doesn't fully deserve to be there.

The Recipients of God's Judgments

The recipients of God's judgment include the following:

First, *those who bear the mark of the beast and worship his image.* According to Revelation 16:2, the first vial of wrath is poured on these people because of their idolatry. The effects of this first vial are similar to what followed the sixth Egyptian plague. It produces painful boils and sores (Ex. 9:9–11). The second and third vials (Rev. 16:3–4) produce death in a watery grave, including every living thing in the sea, which parallels turning the Nile into blood, resulting in the death of fish (Ex. 7:17–21). And the fourth vial scorches the ungodly with fire so that they are seared by the intense heat (Rev. 16:8). Notice that verse 9 says God Himself does this, for He has power over all plagues. Notice, too, that this judgment does not produce repentance, but escalates the very blasphemy that provoked the judgment. God is warning us here that if we live an ungodly lifestyle, the vials of His wrath will be justly poured out against us on the final day (v. 5).

Second, *the trinity of evil, which includes the dragon (Satan—Rev. 12:3, 9), the beast (the antichrist—Rev. 13:1), and the false prophet (the second beast—Rev. 13:11).* Satan opposes the Father, the antichrist opposes Christ, and the second beast opposes the Holy Spirit. Revelation 16:10 says the fifth vial is poured on the throne of the beast, thereby challenging the very seat of Satan's government. When this vial is poured out, it plunges Satan's kingdom into darkness, much like the plague of darkness in Egypt that obliterated everything and caused mass confusion and disorder (Ex. 10:22–23). That plague was also a direct attack on Pharaoh himself, who claimed to be an incarnation of the sun god, Ra. The fifth vial boldly asserts Jehovah's sovereignty over Satan and his forces. But once again, Revelation 16:11 says this judgment does not lead to repentance.

The sixth vial introduces us to the battle of Armageddon (v. 16). The word *Armageddon* occurs only once in the Bible, with little explanation, so scholars have long speculated on its meaning. The word is also challenging to translate from the Hebrew. A transliteration of the term produces either *har-mageddon*, which means "mount (*har*) of Megiddo," or *h'ar-mageddon*, which means "the city (*ar*) of Megiddo." Either way, Megiddo was on a plateau overlooking the plain of Esdraelon, where many ancient battles were fought. Israel's armies defeated Sisera and his armies there in the days of Deborah (Judg. 5:19). Here, too, the Six Day War of 1967 was fought.[1]

Throughout church history, some have thought that Armageddon should be interpreted literally.[2] Some modern theologians say the battle will happen after seven years of tribulation and prior to the wedding of the Lamb. Wicked nations will besiege Jerusalem until Christ and His saints return to deliver the Jews.

Others view Armageddon literally as a battle between two nations, such as Russia and the United States; but there is not even a hint in Scripture that this is so. Revelation speaks of a worldwide battle and revolt against God, not a war between two particular countries.

Others theorize that Armageddon is the struggle between the gospel, as represented by the sword in Christ's mouth (Rev. 1:16; 2:16; 19:15, 21), and paganism. They teach that Christianity will ultimately gain victory by evangelizing the heathen, but, in Revelation 2:16, the word *sword* indicates destruction, not evangelism and conversion of the pagans.

One helpful clue is the battle at Megiddo described in Judges 5. During the time of Deborah, the Canaanite King Jabin and his general, Sisera, had nine hundred iron chariots poised to destroy

---

1. Kistemaker, *Revelation*, 452.
2. On the following views of Armageddon, see Hendriksen, *More than Conquerors*, 162n1.

God's people. The Israelites were vastly outnumbered and led by a seemingly powerless woman, Deborah. But God wonderfully rescued His children. Judges 5:19–20 says: "The kings came and fought, then fought the kings of Canaan in Taanach by the waters of Megiddo; they took no gain of money. They fought from heaven; the stars in their courses fought against Sisera."

The point is that God often wondrously rescues His people against seemingly unbeatable odds. Judges 4:14–15 says: "And Deborah said unto Barak, Up; for this is the day in which the LORD hath delivered Sisera into thine hand: Is not the LORD gone out before thee? So Barak went down from mount Tabor, and ten thousand men after him. And the LORD discomfited Sisera, and all his chariots, and all his host, with the edge of the sword before Barak; so that Sisera lighted down off his chariot, and fled away on his feet." The very heavens above fought for the people of God. Against all odds, Israel gained victory at the first recorded battle at Megiddo at the plain of Esdraelon.

Hendriksen writes, "Armageddon then is a symbol of every battle in which, when a need is greatest and believers are oppressed, the Lord suddenly reveals His power in the interest of the distressed people and strikingly defeats His enemies."[3] That is what Armageddon seems to be about. It is not a literal place, but a battle against spiritual forces of wickedness in heavenly places. There will be an Armageddon in the end, but it will be fought not literally in Megiddo, but under circumstances in which God gives His saints victory against all the raging hordes of evil.

Third, *the Babylonians or those who try to make a name for themselves.* The earliest Babylonians tried to build the tower of Babel to make a name for themselves (Gen. 11:4). Ever since, Babylon has been used in Scripture as a symbol of antithesis to Jerusalem. Jerusalem symbolizes God's religion, while Babylon symbolizes man's religion. Babylon is the kingdom of this world, while Jerusalem is the kingdom of God—and the two cannot be merged, for no

---

3. Hendriksen, *More than Conquerors*, 163.

one can serve God and mammon. In Revelation 16, the hostility between Babylon and Jerusalem reaches its apex. In verse 19, Babylon is given a cup filled with the wine of the fury of God's wrath, which leads to judgment day. But notice again that Babylon does not repent.

These judgments upon an unbelieving, impenitent world teach us that the day is coming when God's patience will come to an end and the vials of His undiluted wrath will be poured out on those who refuse to bow before the Christ. When God's patience is exhausted, His judgment is inevitable. The solemn truth is that either we repent or perish.[4]

We've already noted that this vision of the seven vials covers the same ground as the vision of the seven trumpets. They are parallel, and yet there is progress. The trumpets warn of what is to come, while the vials depict wrath actually poured out.

In the vision of the trumpets, only a third of the earth, sea, and sky are affected. But Revelation 15:1 says the last seven plagues have a specific purpose: they "fill up" or complete the wrath of God. They also affect the whole earth rather than only a third. So the message of the seven vials is that God's Spirit will not strive with man forever (Gen. 6:3). There is an invisible boundary line between God's patience and wrath. And whoever refuses to be warned by the sounding of the trumpets will inevitably be destroyed by the outpouring of the vials.

Many people in this world may have already crossed the line between the trumpet and the vial, or between the patience of God and the final wrath of God. God's Spirit will not always strive with man.

Scripture constantly tells us that we ignore God's warning cries to our peril. God sent ten plagues to Egypt; these were warning trumpets, but Pharaoh did not heed the blasts. He kept saying he would let God's people go, then changing his mind. He resisted until God hardened his heart. God's gracious patience with Pharaoh was

---

4. Cf. Hendriksen, *More than Conquerors*, 163–65.

Pharaoh's last chance, but because of the impenitence of his heart, Pharaoh was brought to judgment.

God's wrath is still being poured out today. As Romans 1:18 says, "For the wrath of God is revealed from heaven against all ungodliness and unrighteousness of men, who hold the truth in unrighteousness." The verb is in the present tense, meaning that Paul is saying: "Even now the wrath of God is being revealed against ungodliness and unrighteousness. It is happening right now." It was happening in Paul's day, and it was happening in John's day as Christians were persecuted by the Roman emperor. It is also happening today. The vials of God's wrath are being poured out on mankind because of persistent, impenitent ungodliness and unrighteousness. Three times in Romans 1 Paul says that God gave ungodly people up to themselves because they suppressed the truth, did not believe in God, and did not live responsibly before Him. They preferred to worship the creature rather than the Creator. They snuffed out the light of their consciences. They deliberately suppressed the truth. So God eventually gave them up to their reprobate minds. God does not allow hardness of heart to go unpunished. The Bible tells us that He is angry with the wicked every day (Ps. 7:11).

We must not understand God's anger in terms of human anger, however. God's wrath is not irritability, maliciousness, or spitefulness. It is *righteous anger*. Revelation 16 says that the outpouring of God's anger is approved by all of creation. It is entirely justified by the circumstances. Verses 5–6 say: "And I heard the angel of the waters say, Thou art righteous, O Lord, which art, and wast, and shalt be, because thou hast judged thus. For they have shed the blood of saints and prophets, and thou hast given them blood to drink; for they are worthy." God's anger is not capricious; it is not spiteful or malicious, but it is holy, righteous, and just. And that anger is being poured out even now.

God's anger is like a dam. Behind the dam is a tremendous reservoir of water. Every now and then, when it has been raining heavily and the reservoir is getting dangerously full, the sluice gates are opened and some water is let out so that too much pressure is

not put on the dam. The wrath of God is like that; it isn't entirely
pent up, but is drawn down and poured out from time to time.
However, on the day of judgment, the dam will break and the wrath
of God will be poured on this world without restraint. The wrath
that is going to break upon this world on judgment day is even now
being revealed, says Paul. God is allowing some of that wrath to
overflow into this world, into the lives of individuals.

The wrath of God is being revealed against the ungodliness and
unrighteousness of men. God uses all the horrible contents of the
seven vials to bring the impenitent to judgment. He works upon the
land and the sea, and in the air. But on judgment day, He will move
heaven and earth to hurl the wicked into hell.

The vials represent God's judgment. It may be inoperable cancer, a sudden heart attack, an exploding plane, famine brought by
drought, wars and rumors of war, a tsunami, a hurricane, or civil
upheaval. God uses such disasters to reveal His wrath against the
impenitent. All the things described in chapter 16 are really a day of
judgment for the impenitent who refuse to repent of sin and cling
to Christ. The Word of God softens the hearts of some people, but
it hardens the hearts of others. It is like the sun shining on the tarmac of a road. It softens the tarmac, but the mud on the side of the
road just gets harder.

Today, when you hear God's voice, do not harden your hearts
against it, because sooner or later you will cross the boundary line,
and God will have no more dealings with you (Ps. 95:7b–11). Your
conscience will be seared and heaven will be closed to you. That is
the picture here. Revelation 15:8 says that as the angels prepare to
pour out their vials of wrath, the temple of God is shut; "no man
was able to enter into the temple, till the seven plagues of the seven
angels were fulfilled." God refuses to listen to the cries and prayers
of the impenitent once they have crossed this line.

The trumpets are sounded and the vials of God's wrath are
poured out at the same time. And what for one person is a trumpet
of warning may be for another a vial of wrath. In Acts 12, King
Herod blasphemes the name of God. We are told in verses 21–24:

"And upon a set day Herod, arrayed in royal apparel, sat upon his throne, and made an oration unto them. And the people gave a shout, saying, It is the voice of a god, and not of a man. And immediately the angel of the Lord smote him, because he gave not God the glory: and he was eaten of worms, and gave up the ghost. But the word of God grew and multiplied." What for Herod was a vial of wrath served as a trumpet of warning to many of his subjects.

The dividing line between the trumpets and vials is often difficult to discern. No one knows when a sounding trumpet will give way to the outpouring of a vial of wrath. So we must keep watch and pray lest the day of judgment come suddenly upon us. Jesus says in Revelation 16:15: "Behold, I come as a thief. Blessed is he that watcheth, and keepeth his garments, lest he walk naked, and they see his shame."

Imagine a family that comes back from vacation and finds that their house had been burglarized. They agonize about what they could have done to prevent the break-in, saying, "If only we had done this or that, we might have been protected." In a far more profound way, Jesus says He will come as a thief in the night, unexpected and unannounced. The person who agonizes about this shows that his heart is not sealed shut; thus, he is still open to the gospel. But those who have truly given up don't know they have given up. Their impenitence and hardness of heart has turned them away from God.

Why did Christ reveal these disturbing visions to John, the disciple whom He most loved? He did so, first, in order that His friend John would know that the world will not keep on going forever without justice ultimately being done. Second, these visions assured the apostle in exile. Christ says: "John, do you see now how much I love you? I have loved you so much that I have borne this for you also." Once you have grasped that God's judgments are just, that His justice is true, and that His judgment will be absolutely final in the midst of all the misunderstandings, false accusations, and puzzling circumstances of your life, then you will be supremely grateful to say, "My exalted and coming Savior will be my Judge."

We can then heap coals of fire—that is, acts of kindness—upon the heads of those who have abused us, persecuted us, and mocked us, knowing that Jesus Christ will judge them (Rom. 12:20).

The Cup of God's Judgments

God's wrath is poured out on all idolatry and immorality. Revelation 16:2 says: "And the first went, and poured out his vial upon the earth; and there fell a noisome and grievous sore upon the men which had the mark of the beast, and upon them which worshipped his image." And in Revelation 16:19, God's wrath is poured out on Babylon and all its sexual immorality. All through Scripture, idolatry and immorality walk hand in hand. Many in the United States are so morally bankrupt that Muslims are appalled at our immorality. In Ezekiel, idolatry began within Jerusalem itself and spread outward. God's judgment on idolatry and immorality is thus right and just.

When people repent of their sin, the Lord is gracious to them. But when they do not, they feel the heat of God's wrath. Revelation 16:9 says, "Men were scorched with great heat, and blasphemed the name of God, which hath power over these plagues: and they repented not to give him glory." Verse 11 says that they "blasphemed the God of heaven because of their pains…and repented not of their deeds."

Let no one even so much as imply that God's judgments are false. The unrighteousness of the impenitent is evident in their willful alienation from God and in their hatred, opposition, and rebellion against Him.

The fact that these vials of wrath are poured out on unbelievers (v. 1), for they are said to come upon those who have the mark of the beast (v. 2), are guilty of killing the saints (v. 5), and are part of the beast's kingdom (v. 10), does not mean that God's people are immune from suffering, pain, accidents, or harm. We live in a world under judgment and we face the same trials and difficulties as unbelievers, but with a difference: our trials and tribulations are not God's punishments. All of our sin—past, present, and future— has been punished in the death of Jesus Christ upon the cross.

God's wrath has been poured out upon His sinless, spotless Son. He bore the anger due to your sin, dear child of God, exhaustively, completely, finally, and forever. When you experience bereavement, sickness, disappointment, and loss, remember that God is with you. He is correcting and disciplining you. It is the discipline of the home and not that of a court of law. It is loving discipline, and it will not destroy you.

In Romans 8, Paul says that all things work together for good. The first verse plainly says, "There is therefore now no condemnation to them which are in Christ Jesus." There is no condemnation for us because our condemnation has fallen on Christ. Thus, Paul later says that nothing "shall be able to separate us from the love of God, which is in Christ Jesus our Lord" (v. 39). In tribulation, distress, persecution, famine, nakedness, peril, or sword—in all these, we are more than conquerors. These trials do not usher believers into judgment. They are not vials of wrath poured out on us. By the end of Romans 8, Paul confidently says, "For I am persuaded, that neither death, nor life, nor angels, nor principalities, nor powers, nor things present, nor things to come, nor height, nor depth, nor any other creature, shall be able to separate us from the love of God, which is in Christ Jesus our Lord" (vv. 38–39). Nothing on the land, in the sea, in the air, from the pit, or anywhere in creation can separate us from the love of God in Christ.

Revelation 16 offers the basic gospel message of the Bible. God has two cups in His hands. The Old Testament prophets say the first cup will be drunk by the nations unless they turn to the Lord in repentance (Ps. 75:8). Revelation 16:19 calls this "the cup of the wine of the fierceness of his wrath." It is the cup of God's curse. But God has another cup in His hand, the cup of blessing (1 Cor. 10:16).

On the night when He was betrayed, Jesus took the cup of God's curse from God's hand and drank it for the sake of those who would trust in Him so that they might never have to drink it. He offers the cup of blessing to those who believe. But if we refuse the cup of blessing in Jesus Christ, we will have to take the cup of God's wrath. We will be like those who *do not* repent and *will not* repent—who therefore *cannot* repent. Christ says to them: "The day will come when you will take the cup of My judgment against you, and I will say to you, 'Drink from it, all of you.'" What a contrast that is to the cup of blessing in Holy Communion: "This cup is the new testament in my blood; this do ye, as oft as ye drink it, in remembrance of me" (1 Cor. 11:25).

Which cup will you receive? One sign of being a true believer is that when you have sat at the Lord's Table and have taken the bread and have drunk from the cup, you instinctively say, "I want to be with Thee forever." Do you really want to be with Christ forever, where He is glorified, loved, and magnified? Then, by His Spirit's grace, drink the cup signifying that He has shed His blood for the forgiveness of your sins. Be assured that He will never fail to protect you and will one day bring you home to the marriage supper of the Lamb.

The Puritan Thomas Adams writes about the need for repentance, particularly in the midst of great trials. He says: "There is no other fortification against the judgments of God but repentance. His forces be invisible, invincible; not repelled with sword or target [shield]; neither portcullis nor fortress can keep them out; there is nothing in the world that can encounter [oppose] them but repentance."[5] If we are harboring sin in our lives, like Sheba, son of Bichri (2 Samuel 20), we need to pull it into the open, behead it, repent of it, cast our rebellion over the wall, and make peace with God. Then God will withdraw His anger.

If you resist surrendering to God, God is battering you, dear unbeliever, as you hold out against conversion. Likewise, if believers resist sanctification, God may choose to chasten them for a while, saying: "Render to Me Sheba; you are holding your sin, you are loving it, you are cuddling it. Behead it and throw it over the wall!" (see 2 Sam. 20:21–22).

---

5. Thomas Adams, *The Sinner's Mourning-Habit*, in *The Works of Thomas Adams* (1861–1866; repr., Eureka, Ca.: Tanski, 1998), 1:55.

Revelation 16:9 warns: "They repented *not* to give *him* glory." You say that you have repented, but let me ask: "Is your repentance sincere or counterfeit?" In the book of Joshua, Achan was outwardly living a righteous life. But secretly he had taken booty from the city of Ai, in disregard of God's command, and hidden it under his tent. No one knew about the hidden treasure, not Joshua, not Achan's neighbors, nor even his wife, but *Achan* knew about it. So Joshua said to Achan, once the booty was exposed: "Give…glory to the LORD God of Israel" (Josh. 7:19). He was saying: "Don't take God's name in vain. He knows what is under your tent."

Spurgeon describes genuine evangelical repentance that gives glory to God:

1. Repentance "reverences and adores God's omniscience." The penitent recognizes that he cannot hide from God's all-knowing eye.

2. "The truly penitent gives glory to the righteousness of God in his law." One who is truly repentant confesses that the law is good, even though it condemns the sinner.

3. A true believer "adores and glorifies the justice of God in His punishment of transgression." He knows he deserves nothing more than death and hell.

4. "True repentance glorifies the sovereignty of God in his mercy." The guilty penitent realizes he has no claim on God's sovereign mercy. If he finds mercy, it is only because God wills to be merciful out of His amazing grace and love.

5. True repentance trusts "that there is a way by which God can be just and yet the justifier of the ungodly." A true believer looks to Christ alone as the way of salvation.

6. Having found mercy in Jesus Christ, true repentance "ever afterwards craves after holiness."[6]

6. Spurgeon, *Metropolitan Tabernacle Pulpit*, 34:642–44.

Spurgeon goes on to speak of a *carnal* repentance, in which the sinner becomes, like King Saul, "another man but not a new man." There is also the *temporary* repentance of King Ahab, which continues only as long as God is putting him through trials. Spurgeon says of that kind of repentance:

> Some shake because of their sins but are not shaken out of their sins. Mariners far out at sea, when the labouring barque [ship] threatens to go down to the bottom, will repent; but such repentance is only a few qualms of conscience, because they are in dread of death, and judgment, and hell. So that men lie on a bed of sickness, when their bones ache, and their hearts melt, and the grave yawns beneath their couch, will often repent; and yet, if they could be raised up, they would return to their sins as a dog returns to his vomit.[7]

Is God calling you today to repentance? Is He prompting you to deal with ongoing sin by means of genuine, evangelical repentance?

Sometimes we are like children. We burn our hands on the stove and back away. Then we reach out for the hot surface again, and we get another burn. But we keep coming to God. And we must not despair if our sins seem insurmountable. Don't despair like Judas; be like the thief on the cross, who cried out in the final hour of his life, "Lord, remember me when thou comest into thy kingdom" (Luke 23:42).

Many old divines used to say, "One thief was saved on the cross that none might despair. But only one, that none might presume." Do not presume you can put off repentance and turning from sin. Now is the time! Open your heart to God.

If you are an unbeliever, God may not yet have taken away your precious earthly things. Yet you have held out like a fortress city against God. So listen to the trumpets of warning, repent of your sins, and believe in the Lord Jesus, the Lamb of glory, before God's vials of wrath are poured out on you—*forever!*

---

7. Spurgeon, *Metropolitan Tabernacle Pulpit*, 34:639–40.

28

The Mystery Woman and Babylon's Fall

REVELATION 17:1–18:24

And there came one of the seven angels which had the seven vials, and talked with me, saying unto me, Come hither; I will shew unto thee the judgment of the great whore that sitteth upon many waters: with whom the kings of the earth have committed fornication, and the inhabitants of the earth have been made drunk with the wine of her fornication. So he carried me away in the spirit into the wilderness: and I saw a woman sit upon a scarlet coloured beast, full of names of blasphemy, having seven heads and ten horns. And the woman was arrayed in purple and scarlet colour, and decked with gold and precious stones and pearls, having a golden cup in her hand full of abominations and filthiness of her fornication: and upon her forehead was a name written, MYSTERY, BABYLON THE GREAT, THE MOTHER OF HARLOTS AND ABOMINATIONS OF THE EARTH.... And after these things I saw another angel come down from heaven, having great power; and the earth was lightened with his glory. And he cried mightily with a strong voice, saying, Babylon the great is fallen, is fallen, and is become the habitation of devils, and the hold of every foul spirit, and a cage of every unclean and hateful bird. For all nations have drunk of the wine of the wrath of her fornication, and the kings of the earth have committed fornication with her, and the merchants of the earth are waxed rich through the abundance of her delicacies. And I heard another voice from heaven, saying, Come out of her, my people, that ye be not partakers of her sins, and that ye receive not of her plagues. For her sins have reached unto heaven, and God hath remembered her iniquities.... And a mighty angel took up a stone like a great millstone, and cast it into the sea, saying, Thus with violence shall that great city Babylon be thrown down, and shall be found no more at all.... For by thy sorceries were all nations deceived. And in her was found the blood of prophets, and of saints, and of all that were slain upon the earth.

In his great classic, *The City of God*, Augustine powerfully sets before us the two cities on the earth, the city of God and the city of man. The two cities stand in marked contrast to each other. You and I are citizens of one of these two cities. To which city do we belong?

As we have seen, Revelation is a series of visions, each of which portrays the conflict between the evil trinity (the dragon, the beast from the sea, and the beast from the land) against the Holy Trinity of God the Father, Son, and Holy Spirit. Each of these unequal but opposing trinities is building a city. The evil trinity is building the city of Babylon, while the Holy Trinity is building the city of Jerusalem. Satan is seducing mankind through the great harlot, and God is calling sinners to Himself to make a holy bride. Chapters 17 and 18 tell us how the city of Babylon will be defeated, while Christ and His New Jerusalem will reign victorious.

Revelation 17:5 says about Babylon: "And upon her forehead was a name written, MYSTERY, BABYLON THE GREAT, THE MOTHER OF HARLOTS AND ABOMINATIONS OF THE EARTH." Revelation 18:2 adds, "Babylon the great is fallen, is fallen."

Let us consider these chapters under the following headings: first, the vision of the mystery woman, and second, the vision of Babylon's fall.

The Vision of the Mystery Woman

The sixth cycle of visions of John has been rightly called the vision of the mystery woman. Chapter 17 describes the mystery woman, and chapter 18 tells about her downfall. The name of this mystery woman is recorded in Revelation 17:5: "Upon her forehead was a name written, MYSTERY, BABYLON THE GREAT, THE MOTHER OF HARLOTS AND ABOMINATIONS OF THE EARTH."

Immediately the word *mystery* warns us against being too clever or glib in interpreting this vision. There is something mysterious about this woman. And yet, we must not be too shy about examining the text, because *mystery* does not mean an unsolvable riddle or puzzle. The word *mystery* in Scripture is a technical word. The gospel is described as a mystery hidden from all ages that is now made known (Rom. 16:25–26). So the word *mystery* really means "an open secret." A biblical mystery is something that we would not know unless God told us.

John is mystified, filled with wonder, and moved to admiration by what he sees (v. 6b), but he is mildly rebuked by one of the seven angels who poured out the vials of God's wrath in Revelation 16. He says to John: "Wherefore didst thou marvel? I will tell thee the mystery of the woman, and of the beast that carrieth her" (Rev. 17:7). So we don't need to guess the identity of this woman, for the angel goes on to explain much about her. Consider four things about the woman: her identity, strategy, support, and frailty.

The Identity of the Woman

The woman is called "the mother of harlots." She is "the great whore" (v. 1). The woman's titles, her expensive clothing, her gold and jewels, and her self-indulgent lifestyle all confirm that she is a prostitute. But she is not just an ordinary prostitute; she is *the mother* of prostitutes. She is the queen bee in the hive of prostitutes. This description of this woman immediately helps us to identify her as evil. The woman is not the church. She is not the woman in Revelation 12, who is chased into the wilderness by the dragon after giving birth to a man child who is now being persecuted by the dragon.

This woman is a *prostitute*, not an adulteress. The word in Greek is *porne*, from which we get our word *pornography*. It is not the word *moichalis*, meaning "adulteress." This woman has never been married to Christ. This woman is not an adulteress; she is a temptress, a harlot. Her titles identify her as an immoral woman and a wicked city. She is seen as "the mother of harlots" and as "Babylon the Great."

REVELATION

Babylon reminds us of King Nebuchadnezzar. Daniel 4:30 says the king became so puffed up with pride as he gazed upon the city of Babylon, one of the great wonders of the world, that he said, "Is not this great Babylon, that I have built for the house of the kingdom by the might of my power, and for the honour of my majesty?" Immediately God took everything away: all of Nebuchadnezzar's power, splendor, and glory. The king went insane and lived like a beast of the field. Babylon almost ruined Nebuchadnezzar by enticing and seducing him. She is the mother of harlots. She is the world.

In his first epistle, John describes the world: "For all that is in the world, the lust of the flesh, and the lust of the eyes, and the pride of life, is not of the Father, but is of the world" (1 John 2:16). Babylon symbolizes the world—not the creation, but the world as a spiritual, moral entity created by men in opposition to God. Babylon is first mentioned in Genesis 10 and 11. "Babel" was the beginning of Nimrod's kingdom (Gen. 10:10). At Babel, Nimrod and his people tried to build a tower to reach up to heaven, until God confused their language and thwarted their plans; the name Babel means "confusion" (Gen. 11:9). Throughout Scripture, Babylon represents the world of sinners opposed to God. This means Babylon is always with us. It is not confined to a particular place, time, or culture. Babylon is a continuing presence and power in human history.

Much in Revelation 17 is difficult to understand. But one truth that emerges is that Babylon is viewed as past, present, and future. Babylon was, is, and is to come. Her essence is the same despite any changes in her outward appearance. John would have recognized the essence of Babylon in Rome, the imperial city, set in the midst of seven hills (v. 9). But in his vision, the mountains give way to ten horns and then to ten kings (v. 12), meaning that Babylon is constantly changing. Babylon's particular form may change, but her essence is always the same in this world.

Babylon, then, is the world as the center of industry, commerce, culture, and power. This woman stands for everything that tempts, seduces, and draws people away from God, all that stirs the lust of the flesh, the lust of the eyes, and the pride of life. This mystery woman is the harlot city.

The Strategy of the Woman

This woman is powerful and influential. Revelation 17:2 describes her celebrity clientele: "With [her] the kings of the earth have committed fornication, and the inhabitants of the earth have been made drunk with the wine of her fornication." In verse 18, we are told she "reigneth over the kings of the earth."

Worldliness is not unique to our Western society; it is universal. However, there is no place or time that exists without the mystery woman. Verse 1 says she sits upon many waters. Verse 15 explains: "The waters which thou sawest, where the whore sitteth, are peoples, and multitudes, and nations, and tongues." In other words, no nation, no class, and no generation is safe from the clutches of this mystery woman. Her clientele includes capitalists and communists, dictators and presidents, as well as both rich and poor. Worldliness is a problem for the poor as well as the rich. All the inhabitants of the earth have been enticed by this woman and have drunk of her fornications. There is no system of government, no political ideology, and no human philosophy untainted by this woman. She is everywhere. Not even the church is safe from her.

We tend to think of the world as being "out there" or remote from us. We also tend to identify worldliness in terms of outward appearance or conduct. But that is far too simplistic. Worldliness is so much more than smoking, drinking too much, listening to ungodly music, and watching sinful movies. Worldliness is an attitude of the heart toward God and our fellow human beings. It includes lovelessness and pride. It includes self-centeredness, bitterness, and indulgence. It is thinking too highly of yourself while ignoring the pain of others. Worldliness is admiring people instead of worshiping God. It is making God small and people big.

Worldliness can get into a church and spoil a Christian. Horatius Bonar says, "I looked for the church and I found it in the world.

I looked for the world and I found it in the church."[1] A. W. Tozer speaks about the effect of worldliness on church attendance: "It is scarcely possible in most places to get anyone to attend a meeting where the only attraction is God."[2] Something else must be offered to entice people to come to church today, whether music, celebrity guests, movies, special programs for young people, and the like.

The lust of the flesh, the lust of the eyes, and the pride of life are not out there, but are alive and at work inside each one of us. We may have persuaded ourselves that we don't have anything to do with this woman. We may be scandalized by her behavior and how people run after her. And yet, all the while, we may be flirting with her in our own way.

Revelation 17:6 describes both the bloodthirsty nature of this woman and her power over all mankind: "And I saw the woman drunken with the blood of the saints, and with the blood of the martyrs of Jesus: and when I saw her, I wondered with great admiration." The world has always persecuted the church. She not only strives to kill the church through worldliness, but also through persecution. As bad as persecution is, it is eclipsed by the woman's strategy of worldliness. Far more Christians have been slain spiritually by the seduction of this woman than by her opposition. Her beauty and charms can still impact them at any age, causing them to look at her too long with eyes of admiration even as they detest her bloodthirsty nature.

The Support of the Woman

Revelation 17:3 says John is carried behind the scenes by the angel: "So he carried me away in the spirit into the wilderness: and I saw a woman sit upon a scarlet coloured beast, full of names of blasphemy, having seven heads and ten horns."

The flashy clothes and painted face of the woman are only a façade; she dwells in a *wilderness*. Behind the dazzling lights of this

---

1. Cited in John Blanchard, *The Complete Gathered Gold* (Darlington, England: Evangelical Press, 2006), 680.

2. A. W. Tozer, "Religious Boredom," in *Man: The Dwelling Place of God* (Harrisburg, Pa.: Christian Publications, 1966), 136.

world is desolation. That is the real truth about the world. Has God, by the Spirit, shown you the wilderness where this woman lives? She promises you so much pleasure and satisfaction, but in the end, you will be doomed to live with her in a barren, hostile wilderness, "a dry and thirsty land, where no water is" (Ps. 63:1). Can you say,

> I tried the broken cisterns, Lord,
> But ah, the waters failed;
> Even as I stooped to drink they fled,
> And mocked me as I wailed.[3]

Verse 4 tells us the woman holds "a golden cup in her hand full of abominations and filthiness of her fornication." She offers us something that looks precious and promising, but is really abominable.

Robert Pollok described the worldly life of Lord Byron as follows:

> Drank every cup of joy, heard every trump
> Of fame; drank early, deeply drank, drank draughts
> That common millions might have quenched—then died
> Of thirst, because there was no more to drink.[4]

Sadly, Byron was the victim of this great whore, whom he followed to the bitter end.

That is the truth about Babylon. The woman lives in a wilderness where everything is desolate, where you can never be filled. You only hunger and thirst for more, but nothing satisfies.

John sees the woman sitting upon "a scarlet colored beast, full of names of blasphemy, having seven heads and ten horns" (v. 3). She depends upon her mount to convey her where she wants to go in order to ply her wicked trade. In other words, the woman is

---

3. Emma Frances Shuttleworth Bevan, "O Christ, in Thee My Soul Hath Found."

4. Robert Pollok, "The Course of Time," in *Select Works of the British Poets... from Southey to Croly* (Philadelphia: Thomas Wardie, 1845), 705.

financed, protected, and supported by the devil himself, who uses her for his own ends.

In Matthew 4:8–10, Jesus is led by the Spirit into the wilderness to be tested or tempted by the devil, who offers Him all the world has to offer: "Again, the devil taketh him up into an exceeding high mountain, and sheweth him all the kingdoms of the world, and the glory of them; and saith unto him, All these things will I give thee, if thou wilt fall down and worship me. Then saith Jesus unto him, Get thee hence, Satan: for it is written, Thou shalt worship the Lord thy God, and him only shalt thou serve." In other words, the devil presents Christ with Babylon the great, in all her glorious apparel; he says, "If Thou wilt worship me, I will give Thee the world." He holds up the world in all its glitter and glamour to Jesus, the Son of God; but Satan's purpose is to entice Christ away from doing the will of His Father in heaven.

That is the devil's strategy. The woman rides this beast. Beneath this world is a plotting, scheming devil whose only interest is to thwart the purposes of God and ruin the cause of Christ. If you side with the world, you are siding with the devil. If you flirt with this woman, you are putting yourself into the hands of Satan. You are offering yourself to him instead of to Christ.

James calls worldliness spiritual adultery: "Ye adulterers and adulteresses, know ye not that the friendship of the world is enmity with God? whosoever therefore will be a friend of the world is the enemy of God" (James 4:4). James is not talking about an occasional brush with the world. None of us can avoid that. But whoever intentionally and deliberately chooses to be a friend of the world is an enemy of God. He is saying, as it were: "As a believer, you are promised to another; you are engaged to Christ to be His bride. When you live for the luxuries and vanities of this world rather than for Christ, you are guilty of adultery."

The Frailty of the Woman

The closing verses of Revelation 17 tell us that the worldwide sway of the mystery woman will one day be overthrown. Her lovers, suitors, and slaves will rise up and destroy her. Verses 15 and 16 say: "The waters which thou sawest, where the whore sitteth, are peoples, and multitudes, and nations, and tongues. And the ten horns which thou sawest upon the beast, these shall hate the whore, and shall make her desolate and naked, and shall eat her flesh, and burn her with fire." This passage is not describing a future revolution or global conflict in which the world turns against the church and the political world legislates against the ecclesiastical world. This is the lesson of the harlot, who is never loved but only *used*. So what begins as infatuation and animal attraction to her eventually turns into revulsion and disgust (cf. 2 Sam. 13:15).

An example of this is Judas Iscariot, outwardly a disciple of Christ, but inwardly a man who worshiped at the shrine of mammon; his real interest was money, and how much money could be made in the name of religion. He betrayed his Lord for a mere thirty pieces of silver. Matthew 27:3–5 records the end of this man: "Then Judas, which had betrayed him, when he saw that [Jesus] was condemned, repented himself, and brought again the thirty pieces of silver to the chief priests and elders, saying, I have sinned in that I have betrayed the innocent blood. And they said, What is that to us? see thou to that. And he cast down the pieces of silver in the temple, and departed, and went and hanged himself."

Judas was a worldly, covetous, and greedy man, and the devil used those traits to destroy him. Those thirty pieces of silver that were so attractive to him bought him nothing but regret, revulsion, self-hatred, and suicide.

Thus, do not be lured by the glittering, glamorous promises of the world, for they are false and lead to destruction. If you live for the world, you will feel nothing but remorse when you approach death, like Judas. The pleasures of this world last only for a season. How tragic it would be if this season ended and eternity stretched ahead of you with no pleasures left because you had spent them all! The treasure of this world is in Babylon, and Babylon is a place of slavery to the lusts of the flesh—not a place of freedom.

So will you live for the world or, by grace, choose to live for Christ? Think of how Moses turned from a life of privilege to be used as God's servant. Hebrews 11:24 says, "By faith Moses, when he was come to years, refused to be called the son of Pharaoh's daughter." Most commentators say that Moses was being groomed for the throne of Egypt. As the son of Pharoah's daughter, he was heir to Pharoah's throne. Hebrews 11 says Moses weighed these things in his mind and decided to refuse the offer, "Choosing rather to suffer affliction with the people of God, than to enjoy the pleasures of sin for a season; esteeming the reproach of Christ greater riches than the treasures in Egypt: for he had respect unto the recompense of the reward" (vv. 25–26).

We are confronted with the same choice: to follow God or mammon, to suffer with Christ or luxuriate in Egypt. A worldly Christian is a contradiction in terms, like a heavenly devil, as a Puritan once said. You cannot have it both ways! This world with all its attractions is passing away, but eternity is forever.

The only way for us to be safe from this world is to side with the Lamb of God. Revelation 17:14 says, "These shall make war with the Lamb, and the Lamb shall overcome them: for he is Lord of lords, and King of kings: and they that are with him are called, and chosen, and faithful." If you believe in Christ and follow Him, then you will overcome the world, as 1 John 5:4–5 says: "For whatsoever is born of God overcometh the world: and this is the victory that overcometh the world, even our faith. Who is he that overcometh the world, but he that believeth that Jesus is the Son of God?"

By nature, we are weak. We cannot stand up to the advances of this woman of the world apart from Christ. Only by exercising faith in Jesus Christ, the Son of God, can we hope to escape the clutches of the world. He who believes that Jesus is the Son of God is born of God and will overcome the world.

The Vision of Babylon's Fall

Augustine began writing *The City of God* when he was in his late 50s, and labored on this great apologetic work for over a decade. The basic premise of the book is that there are two cities—the heavenly city, *Jerusalem*, and the worldly city, *Babylon*. The entire human race belongs to one or the other of those two cities. We are citizens of Babylon or of the heavenly Jerusalem. All of human history can be reduced to a tale of these two cities. The most important question that confronts all of us is this: "Which city do I belong to? Am I a citizen of Babylon or of Jerusalem?"

Revelation 18 presents us with solemn truths about the end of the world, the collapse of civilization, and the fall of Babylon. In doing so, it presents us with a great certainty, a powerful warning, a final retribution, and a solemn disillusionment. Let me consider each of these with you.

The Great Certainty

The fall of Babylon is certain. As Revelation 18:2 says, "Babylon the great is fallen, is fallen, and is become the habitation of devils, and the hold of every foul spirit, and a cage of every unclean and hateful bird."

John uses the prophetic past tense proleptically to describe the fall of Babylon, which is still to happen, as if it has already happened. He can do so because it is so certain to happen. John repeats the words "is fallen," thereby emphasizing the certainty of this fall (cf. Isa. 21:9).

The words that follow speak of utter desolation and ruin. Verse 2 says Babylon "is become the habitation of devils, and the hold of every foul spirit, and a cage of every unclean and hateful bird." The symbolism here is taken from the Old Testament prophets (Isa. 13:19–22; Jer. 50:39–40). This sophisticated, modern world of ours will become a wasteland haunted by evil spirits and wild animals, a place where people will be afraid to go at night.

Verse 3 tells us that Babylon comes to this tragic end because of her fornication, or, as one translation has it, because of "the maddening wine of her adulteries." Prior to her destruction, Babylon is a crazy, besotted, infatuated world—a godless society rooted in the here and now. Its atheistic, materialistic kings and merchants are obsessed with success in government, trade, industry, business, and the arts, as a credit to themselves.

Any society that forsakes God and roots itself in the here and now will end in collapse, ruin, and despair. That was true of Greece, Egypt, and Rome. We fear that it will happen to our decadent society, too, as we ignore God, moving Him out of our schools, public places, and even churches as we continue to be intoxicated by the harlot Babylon. The inevitable consequence will be fall, ruin, and disaster if we continue to refuse to repent.

Civilization is fragile; it does not take very much for it to collapse, even today. We pride ourselves on being modern, sophisticated, civilized people, but the words of Revelation 18 are also written for us. Written across this entire world is "DESTRUCTION." Centuries ago, Samuel Rutherford advised Christians to "build your nest in no tree here; for ye see God hath sold the forest to death."[5] The days of this world are numbered. "Babylon the great is fallen, is fallen."

A Powerful Warning

Revelation 18:4–5 issues a warning specifically addressed to God's people: "And I heard another voice from heaven, saying, Come out of her, my people, that ye be not partakers of her sins, and that ye receive not of her plagues. For her sins have reached unto heaven, and God hath remembered her iniquities" (see Isa. 48:20; 52:10–12).

It is not possible for us literally or physically to come out of the world. We can lock ourselves away in a convent or monastery, but that doesn't get us away from the world if the world is in our hearts. That's why Jesus did not pray that His Father would take Christians out of the world, but that He would take the world out of Christians (John 17:11–18).

Lot's wife is an example of someone whose heart was dominated by the world. Physically, she left Sodom, which was doomed to destruction; but she looked back at the city, and that backward

---

5. *Letters of Samuel Rutherford*, 41.

glance indicated that in her heart she was still in the world and the world was still in her heart. Because she was not spiritually separated from Sodom, she perished with the inhabitants of Sodom.

What God requires of us is *spiritual separation from this world*. The warning is, "Come out of her, my people, that ye be not partakers of her sins, and that ye receive not of her plagues."

It is a possible to distance ourselves a bit from the world by refraining from some of her more notorious sins. We can resort to legalism, making up rules and regulations that go beyond Scripture, and deceive ourselves with our apparent virtue and sanctity (Col. 2:18–23). But the only way we can truly and spiritually come out of the world and still live in it is through the cross of Christ.

Paul reminds us in Galatians 1:4 that Christ "gave himself for our sins, that he might deliver us from this present evil world, according to the will of God and our Father." Paul is saying that you need a Savior in order to be spiritually separate from the world and to escape the destruction that is coming upon it. You need someone stronger than yourself to lead you out of this wilderness. Jesus has given Himself to us for this very purpose. He has gone to Calvary for us and borne the wrath of God against sin. He has done this so that you and I might be delivered from this present evil world and its ultimate destruction.

In Galatians 6:14, Paul makes this tremendous statement: "God forbid that I should glory, save in the cross of our Lord Jesus Christ, by whom the world is crucified unto me, and I unto the world." If you come to the cross and have Jesus Christ as your Savior, then you are crucified to the world, and the world is crucified to you. Now that you have a living Savior, you will view the world as but a rotting corpse.

Whenever you feel the lure of worldliness, go back to Calvary, look at the cross, and ask yourself: "If He did this for me, how can I possibly have anything to do with the world that crucified Him?" The only way to be separated from the world is through the cross. So, by the blood that bought you, "come out...that ye be not partakers of her sins."

A Final Retribution

The world, which ignores the warnings and predictions of doom, finally gets what's coming to her. Revelation 18:5–8 says: "For her sins have reached unto heaven, and God hath remembered her iniquities. Reward her even as she rewarded you, and double unto her double according to her works: in the cup which she hath filled fill to her double. How much she hath glorified herself, and lived deliciously, so much torment and sorrow give her: for she saith in her heart, I sit a queen, and am no widow, and shall see no sorrow. Therefore shall her plagues come in one day, death, and mourning, and famine; and she shall be utterly burned with fire: for strong is the Lord God who judgeth her."

Yet for the present, the world does not concede. She boasts in verse 7, "I sit a queen, and am no widow, and shall see no sorrow" (cf. Isa. 47:5–11). She is like the rich fool, who lived for worldly pleasures, such as expanding his business and gathering his riches into barns, eating and drinking all the while to toast his good fortune (Luke 12:13–21). The world says, "I am a queen; I am no widow; I shall know nothing of sorrow."

The psalmist Asaph was rattled by the good fortune of worldly people. In Psalm 73:3, he says, "I was envious at the foolish, when I saw the prosperity of the wicked." When you look at this pleasure-seeking, carefree world with all its toys, haven't there been times when you have envied it? What does the world know about pangs of conscience or conviction of sin? The psalmist puts his thoughts into words in verses 13–14: "Verily I have cleansed my heart in vain, and washed my hands in innocency. For all the day long have I been plagued, and chastened every morning."

As you move about in this world, you can't help but notice how the wicked prosper. Sometimes you might be tempted to envy them. But Asaph's attitude changed when he went to God's house. Verse 17 says, "Until I went into the sanctuary of God; then understood I their end." He realized that there was something about the wicked and the world that he had failed to consider. Stuck in the here and now, he had forgotten there will be a day of reckoning, when all iniquities and injustices will be judged before God. On that day, Babylon will receive double for all her sins. That doesn't mean she will be punished twice as much as she deserves, because that would not be just. It simply means that the punishment that Babylon will suffer will be the exact counterpart to her sin. That is the meaning of Revelation 18:5–8. There is a day coming when God will exact full and just punishment from Babylon for her sins. There is a day coming when the scales will be balanced.

Sin is usually measured in terms of its object. If you were to kill someone's pet dog, you would probably be fined or even arrested. But if you were to plunge a knife into the owner of that pet dog, that would be a far more serious crime, and your punishment would be far more serious.

No matter what type it is, all sin is ultimately directed against God. He is infinitely and immeasurably greater than man. Though murdering a human being is a greater crime than killing an animal or stealing someone's car, any sin is committed against the eternal, infinite God. And that sin must be punished. So when you are tempted to envy the wicked who prosper here and now, remember that a day is coming when wicked, worldly, happy people will receive double for their sins. They will receive from God the exact payment for sin.

The story is told of an American farmer who wrote to the editor of his local newspaper, who was a Christian: "In defiance of your God I plowed my fields this year on Sunday, I disked and fertilized them on Sunday, I planted them on a Sunday, I cultivated them on Sunday, and I reaped them on Sunday. This October I had the biggest crop I have ever had. How do you explain that?" The man was defiant, arrogant, and godless. The editor published the letter, but with this footnote: "God does not always settle all His accounts in October."[6]

When we see wicked people living it up and getting away with it, remember that they will not get away with it forever. God will

---

6. http://www.family-times.net/illustration/Judgment/200140/ (accessed June 21, 2016).

settle all accounts exactly and justly. This world of sin and evil will be destroyed.

A Solemn Disillusionment

Things are not always as they appear in this world. We see people living it up, apparently happy as can be; but if you look deeper, you soon discover they are as miserable as sin. Revelation 18:9 and following (almost to the end of the chapter) show us what's really going on in people who cohabit with the world. In a word, they soon become disillusioned. Kings, merchants, travelers, importers, exporters, businesspeople, and politicians are also powerless as Babylon collapses. They weep and mourn over her, but they are terrified.

During the collapse of Wall Street several decades ago, people suddenly and unexpectedly went bankrupt. Fortunes were lost, families were ruined, and some people committed suicide. That is the picture presented in these verses. Kings and merchants, businessmen, freight haulers, tradesmen, jet setters, and the whole busy world are suddenly horrified as, in just one hour, it all collapses. Everything they have banked their lives on; everything they have worked for; and everything they have sold their souls for is suddenly gone. The message here is this: "What shall it profit a man, if he shall gain the whole world, and lose his own soul?" (Mark 8:36).

I was struck by what Dr. Martyn Lloyd-Jones said some months before he died: "Our greatest danger is to live upon our activity." Rather than grieving over the fact that he could no longer preach, he spoke to Iain Murray of how our joy must be in the Lord, and so we can face death without fear.[7] Even preaching can become a worldly enterprise if it's what we live for. The church can become worldly if we live for our church. The same is true of our families, our grandchildren, and our spouses. They can be idols if they are more important than your relationship with God. The Bible clearly says

---

7. Iain H. Murray, *D. Martyn Lloyd-Jones: The Fight of Faith, 1939–1981* (Edinburgh: Banner of Truth, 1990), 738.

that whatever you are living for, if it is not Christ, you are a loser, because this world and everything in it will pass away.

Heavenly treasures are a far better investment. Jesus said, "Lay not up for yourselves treasures upon earth, where moth and rust doth corrupt, and where thieves break through and steal: but lay up for yourselves treasures in heaven, where neither moth nor rust doth corrupt, and where thieves do not break through nor steal: for where your treasure is, there will your heart be also" (Matt. 6:19–21). So invest your heart, soul, and mind in Christ.

This present evil world is going to finally, irretrievably, and irrecoverably disappear. The images of this destruction are taken from Isaiah and Jeremiah. In the closing verses of Revelation 18, an angel takes up "a stone like a great millstone" and casts it into the sea. As great as it is, taking up and casting down this great stone is but the work of a moment. He hurls it into the depths of the sea, so that it disappears from view forever. "Thus with violence shall that great city Babylon be thrown down, and shall be found no more at all" (Rev. 18:21; cf. Jer. 51:63–64). Only the mighty power of God can accomplish such an overthrow. Time is running out both for the mystery woman and the beast she rides upon—and for you, too, if you are an unbeliever.

But for God-fearers, this sudden end is something to rejoice in, for in Babylon's place will appear a new heaven and a new earth (2 Peter 3:13)—a world governed by righteousness. It will be a sin-free world where Jesus Christ will be the all-in-all.

29

Hallelujah: The Coming Lord Prepares His Bride

REVELATION 19:1–10

And after these things I heard a great voice of much people in heaven, saying, Alleluia; Salvation, and glory, and honour, and power, unto the Lord our God: for true and righteous are his judgments: for he hath judged the great whore, which did corrupt the earth with her fornication, and hath avenged the blood of his servants at her hand. And again they said, Alleluia. And her smoke rose up for ever and ever. And the four and twenty elders and the four beasts fell down and worshipped God that sat on the throne, saying, Amen; Alleluia. And a voice came out of the throne, saying, Praise our God, all ye his servants, and ye that fear him, both small and great. And I heard as it were the voice of a great multitude, and as the voice of many waters, and as the voice of mighty thunderings, saying, Alleluia: for the Lord God omnipotent reigneth. Let us be glad and rejoice, and give honour to him: for the marriage of the Lamb is come, and his wife hath made herself ready. And to her was granted that she should be arrayed in fine linen, clean and white: for the fine linen is the righteousness of saints. And he saith unto me, write, Blessed are they which are called unto the marriage supper of the Lamb. And he saith unto me, These are the true sayings of God. And I fell at his feet to worship him. And he said unto me, See thou do it not: I am thy fellowservant, and of thy brethren that have the testimony of Jesus: worship God: for the testimony of Jesus is the spirit of prophecy.

In George Frideric Handel's *Messiah*, the most recognizable piece is the "Hallelujah Chorus." The inspiration for this chorus came from the hallelujahs sung by the heavenly host in Revelation 19. The

Hebrew word *hallelujah* appears many times in the Old Testament Psalms. It literally means "Praise the Lord!" It was taken over into Greek as *allelouïa* and into Latin as *alleluia*, which in turn became the English word that appears in our translation of Revelation 19, the only place in the New Testament where the word appears. It is mentioned four times in our passage.

The chapter begins with a chorus of hallelujahs. The word *alleluia* in verse 1 is not just a catchphrase or a mindless word to be chanted. Rather, it is a heartfelt expression of worship and therefore includes significant content. Let's consider some of the content of the hallelujahs in this chapter by surveying three headings: first, hallelujah, the Lord's judgments are true and righteous; second, hallelujah, the Lord receives His bride; and third, hallelujah, the Lord calls guests to the marriage supper.

Hallelujah, the Lord's Judgments Are True and Righteous

Notice that this passage includes two things: a funeral and a wedding. If you can imagine the setting of Revelation 19, you can almost see the smoke of Babylon on the horizon—not the smoke of industry and life, but the smoke of destruction and ruin. "Babylon the great is fallen, is fallen" (18:2). The great world city is no more. All that remains is a smoldering ruin. But in the foreground of this setting, a wedding is going on. Festivity, rejoicing, and singing accompany this event, for it is the marriage of the Lamb. That is what all the singing and shouting is about. The hallelujah choruses of the heavenly host celebrate the funeral of this world and the wedding of the Lamb.

Matthew Henry writes, "The church will survive the world and be in bliss when it [the world] is in ruins."[1] Take comfort and courage from that as we examine this chapter. The world can be so intimidating. It cons us into believing that the "here and now" is forever. We must remind ourselves that history is progressing not

---

1. Matthew Henry, *Matthew Henry's Commentary on the Whole Bible: Complete and Unabridged in One Volume* (Peabody: Hendrickson, 1994), 809, on Ps. 46:1–5.

toward the building of a great world empire, but toward the destruction of Babylon and the marriage of the Lamb. The great question that should concern us is this: "Am I heading to the funeral of this world, where I will be personally condemned to hell forever, or am I heading to an eternity of bliss in union with Christ?"

Revelation 19:1–5 speaks briefly about the joy of the holy angels and the redeemed over the destruction of Babylon, which represents all worldliness that opposes God. The saints and angels sing with unbounded joy: "Hallelujah, the Lord redeems through judgment!" The message of verses 1–5 is this:

First, *God redeems His people from their enemies—hallelujah!* Verse 1 says, "And after these things I heard a great voice of much people in heaven, saying, Alleluia; Salvation, and glory, and honour, and power, unto the Lord our God."

Second, *God dispenses truth and righteousness for His own glory— hallelujah!* Verse 2 says, "For true and righteous are his judgments: for he hath judged the great whore, which did corrupt the earth with her fornication, and hath avenged the blood of his servants at her hand."

Third, *God permanently destroys Babylon and crushes man's rebellion—hallelujah!* Verse 3 says, "And again they said, Alleluia. And her smoke rose up for ever and ever."

The saints and angels praise the Lord and ascribe all glory to Him because His judgments are true and righteous. He said He would punish Babylon according to the measure of her sins, and He has done so. He promised to avenge the blood of His servants, and He has done so. There is perfect justice and unchanging truth (faithfulness) in these acts of God. All that is left of Babylon is smoke. That calls forth praise from everyone around the throne of God: "And the four and twenty elders and the four beasts fell down and worshipped God that sat on the throne, saying, Amen; Alleluia. And a voice came out of the throne, saying, Praise our God, all ye his servants, and ye that fear him, both small and great" (vv. 4–5).

Believers will rejoice at the funeral of Babylon on judgment day. They will rejoice when Babylon's unholy mix of religion, sexual permissiveness, idolatry, and injustice turns to smoke in the fire of God's wrath. Here on earth, God's saints suffer much because of the world around them. They struggle with injustice in the world, with the sufferings of the righteous and the prosperity of the wicked. They are tempted by evil, enticed by idolatry, and lured by immorality. But God will graciously bring them through all these trials and preserve them through the Vanity Fair of this world. One day, their struggles will be over, for Babylon will be destroyed—hallelujah!

Every time we are tempted by idolatry, immorality, and evil, we should remember the end of the harlot Babylon. Let us never forget, as James Hamilton writes, that "evil, injustice, immorality, and idolatry will only result in regret. If you do not repent and trust in Christ, your regret will last forever. We want these images of God's justice to be sealed to our hearts so that when sin tempts us we see smoke rising from the ruins of Babylon."[2]

Hallelujah, the Lord Receives His Bride

Revelation 19:7 tells us to praise the Lord, "for the marriage of the Lamb is come." Then John talks about the wedding, the Bridegroom, the bride, and the guests. Let's consider each of these in turn.

The Wedding

The kind of wedding described here is a Jewish wedding, which is very different from a Western wedding. The arrangements are different, the protocol is different, and the festivities and ceremony are different.

For one thing, there is a great difference between what we mean by engagement and what the Bible means when it speaks about betrothal or espousal. Matthew 1:18–20 says: "Now the birth of Jesus Christ was on this wise: When as his mother Mary was espoused to Joseph, before they came together, she was found with

---

2. Hamilton, *Revelation*, 349–50.

child of the Holy Ghost. Then Joseph her husband, being a just man, and not willing to make her a publick example, was minded to put her away privily. But while he thought on these things, behold, the angel of the Lord appeared unto him in a dream, saying, Joseph, thou son of David, fear not to take unto thee Mary thy wife: for that which is conceived in her is of the Holy Ghost."

Notice that the text refers to Joseph as Mary's husband and Mary as Joseph's wife, even though the two have not yet begun to live together. Understandably, then, Joseph is greatly troubled when he discovers that Mary is pregnant. Betrothal was much stronger and more binding than our engagements (Deut. 22:23–27). A couple would be betrothed before witnesses. Under their watching eyes, the terms of the marriage covenant would be accepted and a blessing would be pronounced on the union. From that day on, the couple would be regarded as husband and wife, but they wouldn't live together (cf. Deut. 20:7). There would be an interval of time in which the bride would stay in her own house while the husband would go off to earn money to pay the dowry.[3] When he had enough, he would give it to the bride's father to purchase his wife. At the end of that interval, he would dress in his best clothes and come with his best friends down the lane to his wife's house to collect his bride and take her to their new home. He would lead her to his father's home or to their own new home. Then the festivities would begin. During that weeklong time of festivity and celebration, the marriage supper would take place (cf. Matt. 25:1–13).

All Christians are betrothed to Christ. Paul was thus jealously protective of believers who were being troubled by false apostles who preached another gospel. He says in 2 Corinthians 11:2–4: "I am jealous over you with godly jealousy: for I have espoused you to one husband, that I may present you as a chaste virgin to Christ. But I fear, lest by any means, as the serpent beguiled Eve through his subtilty, so your minds should be corrupted from the simplicity that is

---

3. On the dowry or bride-price (KJV "dowry"), see Gen. 34:12; Ex. 22:16–17; 1 Sam. 18:25; cf. Deut. 22:28–29.

in Christ. For if he that cometh preacheth another Jesus, whom we have not preached, or if ye receive another spirit, which ye have not received, or another gospel, which ye have not accepted, ye might well bear with him." Paul casts himself in the role of the marriage broker or matchmaker. In his love for Christ, he desires to present Him with a chaste virgin bride; in his concern for the Corinthians, he resents anyone who wants to lead them astray into spiritual fornication or infidelity.

Paul is not just preaching a set of abstract truths. He is not just presenting people with some philosophy. He is proclaiming the person of Christ, and through his preaching, he is presenting that person to the congregation. "I have betrothed you to Christ," he says. "You are engaged to be His."

Samuel Stone says so beautifully about the church:

> From heaven He came and sought her
> To be His holy bride;
> With His own blood He bought her
> And for her life He died.[4]

Christ has paid the bride-price dowry for all the elect. Therefore, we who are true believers are legally and inseparably His. He is coming again for His bride, the church, to lead us home to His Father's house, where He will present us spotless before His Father in heaven. There will be a wedding procession and festivities that will last not for a week or two, but for all eternity. We will be with Christ and behold His glory. The story of salvation is a love story. The covenant of grace is not like a legal document from a solicitor's office; it is a marriage contract. Before the worlds were made, God the Father chose a bride for His Son and drew up a marriage contract between them. This wedding involves choice, not mutual attraction. It is a one-sided choice, for God chose us in eternity. Christ bought us at Calvary and took us to be His own through the preaching of the

---

4. Samuel Stone, "The Church's One Foundation" (1866).

gospel. Soon He will come back for us. When He comes back, we will enjoy intimacy and fellowship with Him forever.

The whole Trinity is involved in this marriage. The Father gives us His Son as our Bridegroom and gives us as a bride to the Son. As Ephesians 5:25–27 says, Christ purchased His bride with His blood and death. Ephesians 1:13–14 says the Holy Spirit is given to us as an *earnest* or guarantee. That guarantee, in ancient times, was shown by a down payment. Today, this is commonly symbolized by an engagement ring. When Christ betroths us to Himself, He gives us the Spirit as a kind of engagement ring that guarantees we will arrive at the last day for the actual wedding.

The marriage of Jesus Christ and His bride involves the greatest wedding ever. James Hamilton puts it so well when he writes, "We can scarcely imagine the glory of that wedding day," noting that:

- Never has there been a worthier bridegroom.
- Never has a man gone to greater lengths, humbled himself more, endured more, or accomplished more in the great task of winning his bride.
- Never has a wealthier Father planned a bigger feast.
- Never has a more powerful pledge been given than the pledge of the Holy Spirit given to this bride.
- Never has a more glorious residence been prepared as a dwelling place once the bridegroom finally takes his bride.
- Great will be the rejoicing. Great will be the exultation. There will be no limit to the glory given to the Father through the Son on that great day.[5]

At the great wedding, the holy angels will act as witnesses. They will joyfully testify to this marriage as being legally binding when God the Father declares believers to be married to His Son. So Revelation 19:6b–7 says: "Alleluia: for the Lord God omnipotent

---

5. James M. Hamilton, Jr., *Revelation: The Spirit Speaks to the Churches*, Preaching the Word, ed. R. Kent Hughes (Wheaton, Ill.: Crossway, 2012), 351. Select statements from his paragraphs are taken and put in bullet point form.

reigneth. Let us be glad and rejoice, and give honour to him: for the marriage of the Lamb is come."

The Bridegroom

The term *marriage of the Lamb* is strange because lambs don't get married. But Jesus Christ is presented here in His capacity as Savior. The Lamb of this marriage shows us His love by living for us and dying for us. This love is a very one-sided affair, at least to begin with. "We love him," says John, "because he first loved us" (1 John 4:19).

When we think of the ideal marriage, we think about two lovers gazing at one another, starry-eyed with love. That is a Western view of marriage. It is different in other parts of the world. There, the parents of a bride decide when she is to marry. She may have no say in the matter. She may not even know who her husband will be. She often does not meet him until the day they are married. She learns to love him as her husband, and he learns to love her as his wife. We see this pattern, for example, in the marriage of Isaac and Rebekah (cf. Gen. 24).

In some ways, that is the kind of marriage we have with Christ. We love Christ. But we love Him only because He loved us first. He loved us while we were yet sinners and were utterly unattractive and undeserving. He loved us while our carnal minds were still at enmity with Him. Our hearts were against Him, yet He loved us.

The prophet Hosea provides us with a powerful example of this love. God said to Hosea, "Go and take Gomer; marry her and love her, and go on loving her even when she runs off with another man, which she will. And there will be other men as well. But keep on loving her." That is what happened. Gomer ran off and had a succession of affairs, and when her youth and attractiveness were spent, she ended up in the slave market. But Hosea followed Gomer to the slave market and bought her back—not to exact revenge on her for the rest of her life, but out of sheer love (Hos. 3:2). He proved himself to be a faithful husband despite her unfaithfulness to him.

That is how God loves you, dear believer in Jesus Christ! You bring nothing to Christ but sin. However, the triune God has set

His love upon us in and through Christ. When we were still sinners—unclean, unfaithful, adulterous, and promiscuous—He loved us. The apostle John says, "Having loved his own which were in the world, [Christ] loved them unto the end" (John 13:1). He loved them to the farthest limits of love.

We can't measure the length, breadth, height, and depth of the love of God; it surpasses knowledge. Jesus Christ loves us beyond our wildest imagination. He loved us all the way to the cross of Calvary. And there on that cross, He paid the dowry to free us from the penalty of sin. Oh, the out-flowing, ever-flowing, overflowing love of God! He sought for the best He could find—even His own Son, to give Him for the worst He could find—even hellworthy sinners like you and me.

Sometimes, when two people marry, one has a substantial bank account, while the other is in debt. But before they marry, they merge their accounts, for "one flesh" (Gen. 2:24) means one bank account. That is precisely what Christ has done for us. When we were up to our necks in debt to a holy God because we had broken His law thousands of times, Christ took our liabilities (our sins) and paid them all. He was made sin for us. He identified with us as sinners to such an extent that He could talk about sin as if He were a sinner though He never sinned: "For innumerable evils have compassed me about: mine iniquities have taken hold upon me, so that I am not able to look up; they are more than the hairs of mine head: therefore my heart faileth me" (Ps. 40:12). Christ became one flesh with His church. Her sins became His sins, and His perfect righteousness becomes hers through faith.

What happened on Calvary is the most brutal thing this world has ever seen, because there on that cross the Head of the body of His elect took the deathblow. The Head suffered for what the feet and hands had done. It was the hand that pulled the trigger; it was the feet that brought that criminal to the scene of the crime. But the Head received the punishment. Our Lord Jesus Christ came to Calvary to take the deathblow that belonged to us, His body, for the crimes that we had committed, dear children of God. He paid the price upon that cross for us. In His capacity as the Lamb of God, as the Savior of sinners, as the Husband of His church, as the Head of the body, He now effects salvation in us by His Word and Spirit.

Today, some people talk about Jesus Christ as Master, Example, or Lord, but seldom as Savior. He is all of these, of course, and all are important, but unless you know Jesus Christ as Savior, you don't know Him at all. As someone has written, "When you call Him Savior, you call Him by His real name."

In his book, *The Best Match*, Edward Pearse seeks to woo sinners to come to Christ as their spiritual Husband. Like a good matchmaker, Pearse extols the virtues of this Bridegroom who calls us to become His, and His alone. Do you want a match who has honor and greatness? He is God and man, the brightness of His Father's glory, the King of kings and Lord of lords. Do you want riches and treasures? Christ's riches are the best, for they last forever, are infinitely great, and will satisfy all your desires. Are you looking for a generous heart in a spouse? Jesus Christ is willing to lay out His riches for His spouse so that her joy may be full. Do you want wisdom and knowledge? The infinite wisdom of God shines in Him; He is Wisdom itself, and knows perfectly how to glorify Himself and do good to those who love Him. Are you looking for beauty? He is altogether lovely, more than all the beauty of human beings and angels combined. Are you seeking someone who will truly love you? Christ is love itself, love that is higher than the heavens and deeper than the seas. Do you want a husband who is honored and esteemed? This Husband is adored by the saints and angels. Everyone whose opinion really matters treasures Him, and God the Father delights in Him. Do you seek a match who will never die and leave you a widow? Christ is the King immortal and eternal; He is the resurrection and the life.[6]

Behold the Lamb of God! Do you know Christ as the Lamb? Have you received Him as your heavenly Husband? Have you come

---

6. Edward Pearse, *The Best Match: The Soul's Espousal to Christ*, ed. Don Kistler (Grand Rapids: Soli Deo Gloria, 1994), 56–70.

to Him, repenting of your sin and throwing yourself on His mercy? Will you have Jesus Christ, the Son of God, to be your Savior, to love, honor, and obey, from this day forth and forever more? Will you have the Lamb of God to be your Husband—the Sin-bearer to be your Bridegroom? If you will have Him like that, you are invited to the marriage supper of the Lamb, but if you won't, you will not have Him at all. Dreadful will it be on the judgment day to fall into the hands of the living God unprepared.

Have you ever seen that you are a vile, helpless, hopeless, hell-worthy sinner, whose only hope is a substitute Lamb, a Savior? At the wedding feast of the Lamb, Jesus Christ reigns over His bride. That is reason enough to raise hallelujahs. Happily, our text speaks not only of a wedding and a Bridgroom, but also of His bride.

The Bride

The Bible is clear about who the bride is. Paul tells us in Ephesians 5:25 that Christ loved the church and gave Himself for her, that He might make her holy. Revelation 19:7–8 says about the church: "Let us be glad and rejoice, and give honour to him: for the marriage of the lamb is come, and his wife hath made herself ready. And to her was granted that she should be arrayed in fine linen, clean and white: for the fine linen is the righteousness of saints."

When a bride purchases her wedding dress, she often tries it on again after she comes home. She can't wait for the wedding. As the days go by, she checks them off her calendar, counting how many are left before the big day. This is the picture we have here of the bride of Christ. She has made herself ready for the Bridegroom long before the wedding.

Paul speaks of this anticipation in 2 Timothy 4:6–8. He says: "For I am now ready to be offered, and the time of my departure is at hand. I have fought a good fight, I have finished my course, I have kept the faith: henceforth there is laid up for me a crown of righteousness, which the Lord, the righteous judge, shall give me at that day: and not to me only"—and then he widens it out to encompass the whole church, every believer—"but unto all them also that love his appearing."

Charles H. Spurgeon says, "It ought to be a daily disappointment when our Lord does not come; instead of being, as I fear it is, a kind of foregone conclusion that he will not come just yet."[7] So are you longing for Christ's return? Here, through listening to the preaching of the gospel, partaking of the Lord's Supper, and participating in prayer meetings, we see Christ, but through a glass darkly. We prize the means of grace, but how much more will we prize the day when we shall see Christ face to face!

What is most amazing is that Christ loves us and desires to be with us. As a pastor, I counsel young couples who can hardly wait to be married. One young man wondered aloud why he and his fiancée had set their wedding date so far in the future. Likewise, the Lord Jesus Christ yearns for His eternal marriage with His beloved bride. Psalm 45:11 says: "So shall the king greatly desire thy beauty." Dear believer, in His great love, Jesus Christ will beautify you now with His own image and holiness because He is looking forward to embracing you one day as His bride.

The Bridegroom is also eager for the wedding. Psalm 45:11 says of the anticipated marriage between Christ and His bride, "So shall the king greatly desire thy beauty." In His great love, Jesus will beautify believers here because He is looking forward to seeing them as His beautiful bride one day. Jesus is the King of heaven, and we will be beautiful in His sight. The King of kings rules over the whole universe, and He will make us the queen of heaven. The angels will be our servants, and the King will take us into His garden. He will take us by the hand and lead us to Paradise forever.

We know both from the Bible and experience that marriage is the closest human relationship. The intimacy between a loving husband and a loving wife is beyond words, for the two indeed become one flesh (Eph. 5:31). But Paul speaks of an even greater mystery "concerning Christ and his church" (v. 32). In glory, dear believer,

7. Spurgeon, *Metropolitan Tabernacle Pulpit*, 37:155.

our closeness to Christ will far surpass even the intimacy between a husband and wife.

Due to being saved by grace alone from the enormity of our sin, our intimacy with the Lord Jesus Christ will be greater than what He experiences with the holy angels who have been with Him in perfect holiness for thousands of years. We will have a direct, personal, intimate, mystical union with the Lord Jesus Christ, which will allow no distance between us.

> When I in righteousness at last
> Thy glorious face shall see,
> When all the weary night is past,
> And I awake with Thee
> To view the glories that abide,
> Then, then I shall be satisfied.[8]

Ephesians 5:25 says that Christ purchased His bride with His death. The bride will also be beautifully adorned for her Husband (Rev. 21:2). In most weddings a bride wears a special gown, which she has chosen and paid for. But in heaven we do not have to purchase a wedding dress, for that dress is the gift of God's grace. Isaiah 61:10 says, "I will greatly rejoice in the Lord, my soul shall be joyful in my God; for he hath clothed me with the garments of salvation, he hath covered me with the robe of righteousness, as a bridegroom decketh himself with ornaments, and as a bride adorneth herself with her jewels."

The robe of righteousness that we wear on our glorious wedding day is the realization of our imputed blamelessness and holiness through Christ (Eph. 5:27), for He has redeemed us from sin's guilt and purifies us to be zealous for Him (Titus 2:14). So, this gown is the robe of Christ's perfect righteousness imputed to us in justification (2 Cor. 5:21). Christ takes off the filthy garments of our guilt and clothes us with the clean and beautiful clothing of His merit (Zech. 3:1–5). His obedience is credited to us. We read in Revelation

---

8. *The Psalter,* no. 31:7 [Ps. 17:15].

7:14 of countless people from every nation who "have washed their robes, and made them white in the blood of the Lamb." How did they wash their robes and make them white? By trusting in Christ alone for justification from the guilt of all sin. You can receive this cleansing only through faith—the self-abandonment of trusting Christ alone to make you acceptable to God.

Next, Christ continues to cleanse us from impurity in our sanctification. One day that sanctification process will be perfected and perfect holiness will be the gown that is given to us. Revelation 19:8 says, "And to her was granted that she should be arrayed in fine linen, clean and white: for the fine linen is the righteousness of saints." Literally, the Greek text says "the righteous deeds [δικαιώματά] of the saints." Thus getting ready for the day that Christ comes for you does involve effort on your part. We are told in verse 7 that "his wife has made *herself* ready." The man who says he belongs to Christ and yet never lifts a finger to purify himself is deceived. The Christian life means getting ready. It means putting off the old way of living and putting on the new.

As Paul says in Colossians 3:8–9: "But now ye also put off all these; anger, wrath, malice, blasphemy, filthy communication out of your mouth. Lie not one to another, seeing that ye have put off the old man with his deeds." Then verse 12 says, "Put on therefore, as the elect of God, holy and beloved, bowels of mercies, kindness, humbleness of mind, meekness, longsuffering." It is serious business to make ourselves ready for the return of Christ. There are no short cuts, no secrets, and no easy escape routes. We have to *make ourselves ready!*

At the same time, this preparation is entirely a matter of grace. Notice here that "fine linen, clean and white…the righteousness of saints" (v. 8) is *given* to the bride to wear. You and I ought to be totally involved in the business of sanctification; yet, at the same time, sanctification is entirely a matter of grace. In short, the Lord reigns over His prepared bride, making her willing by His power! Verse 6 puts it this way, "Alleluia: for the Lord God omnipotent reigneth."

Christ reigns over every part of our salvation—even our sanctification. As Paul says in Ephesians 5:25–27: "Christ also loved the church, and gave himself for it; that he might sanctify and cleanse it with the washing of water by the word, that he might present it to himself a glorious church, not having spot, or wrinkle, or any such thing; but that it should be holy and without blemish."

A wrinkle or spot is a sign of age or disease. People spend a fortune to get rid of spots and wrinkles. We are told here that Christ is going to present His church without a single spot or wrinkle to His Father in heaven. He will come with all His holy angels and will take the church by the hand. He will lead her before God and the assembled hosts of the universe. In eternity He chose us, motivated only by perfect love. There is nothing in us to merit His choice. What is more, He bought us with His own blood at Calvary. And now He is beautifying us by the gospel and by His Holy Spirit. We remember that Christ Jesus accomplished complete salvation for us when we partake of the Lord's Supper.

As all the hosts of heaven look at the bride on her wedding day, they will give God all the glory. Verses 6–7 tell us: "And I heard as it were the voice of a great multitude, and as the voice of many waters, and as the voice of mighty thunderings, saying, Alleluia: for the Lord God omnipotent reigneth. Let us be glad and rejoice, and give honour to him: for the marriage of the Lamb is come, and his wife hath made herself ready." Salvation, then, is all of grace—it is grace alone, by Christ alone, based on Scripture alone, through faith alone, to the glory of God alone—for the *guests* of the marriage supper!

Hallelujah, the Lord Calls Guests to the Marriage Supper

Vers 9 says, "Blessed are they which are called unto the marriage supper of the Lamb." If the church is the bride, then who are the guests? Some have said the bride is the church and the guests are the Old Testament saints and tribulation saints.[9] You get the impression

---

9. Walvoord, *The Revelation of Jesus Christ*, 273.

that some saints will be married to the Lamb, while other saints will simply be onlookers or guests at the wedding.

We can dispense with such incorrect views by remembering that the language of Revelation is symbolic. This is the marriage of the Lamb, but, of course, lambs don't get married. Likewise, when Jesus says in John 10, "I am the door of the sheep" (v. 7), and then says, "I am the good shepherd" (v. 10), you wonder how He can be both. But He is really more than that; indeed, He is more than all the descriptions and designations in Scripture put together. Of course He is both the Good Shepherd and the door to the sheepfold. And in the same kind of way, the church is both the bride of Christ as well as the guests at the wedding. Marriage speaks of union with Christ. That is the essence of heaven. It is not gold-paved streets and heavenly mansions, but everlasting, sacred, intimate, sin-free union and fellowship with Christ. Heaven is a place where the believer's marital relationship will be consummated.

But heaven is also a place of festivity. Yes, you will be thoroughly and profoundly happy in heaven, for it is a place of everlasting bliss, happiness, celebration, and festivity. In heaven, we will feast upon Christ.

In biblical times, sharing supper with someone was a sign of fellowship and closeness. That's why the Pharisees were so upset with Jesus for eating with publicans and sinners. But what Jesus did makes the gospel accessible to us. "Hallelujah—this man receives sinners!" we cry out.

When Jesus invites needy sinners to the marriage supper, He offers us an experience of fellowship that is beyond words. The Bible says that when a couple gets married, they are to leave their parents to enter into a new relationship. While they were children, the closest relationship the bride and groom had was with their parents. But now the closest relationship they have is as husband and wife. That is the ideal metaphor to describe Christ and the church. As we feast with Christ in heaven, we will have an intimacy that can be described only as that between a husband and wife—yet it far surpasses even that. We will have an intimacy with the Lord Jesus that will be greater than that of the angels, who have been holy for thousands of years.

Some medieval writers called this union of supreme joy "the beatific vision." Just as in human marriage, when the two become one, Paul says we become one spirit with the Lord Jesus. We retain our individual identities, but we are so woven together that we can't think about one without thinking about the other. But in heaven, we will experience far greater closeness with Christ. God will reveal certain things to us that He will not reveal to the angels. Christ will be our best friend, and we will enjoy being with Him for eternity.

Unlike in human marriage, there will be no sexual relations in heaven (Matt. 22:30). However, we will have an intimacy that is even greater. We will have an eternal "romance" with the Lord Jesus Christ far beyond anything here on earth. We will enjoy embraces of love and expressions of our love for Him. There will be heavenly ecstasy without any sin or hindrance. It will be the purest, deepest emotion of love possible between the perfect Husband and the purified wife. When we are married to Jesus Christ, we will obtain our greatest delight in Him, and He will be delighted with us. Then 1 Peter 1:8 will be truly fulfilled: "Whom having not seen, ye love; in whom, though now ye see him not, yet believing, ye rejoice with joy unspeakable and full of glory."

In his book *Heaven Help Us*, Steven Lawson tells about a young aristocrat, William Montague, who was stricken with blindness at the age of ten. The boy was very intelligent and went on to the university despite his handicap. While he was in graduate school, he met the beautiful daughter of a British admiral. The courtship soon flamed into romance. Though he had never seen this woman, William fell in love with the beauty of her soul. The two became engaged.

Shortly before the wedding, at the insistence of the bride's father, William agreed to have eye surgery that might or might not restore his sight. The doctors operated on William and bandaged his eyes. He was then confined to bed with his eyes covered with bandages until the wedding.

William requested that the bandages be removed from his eyes during the ceremony, just when the bride made her way down the center aisle. As the organ signaled for the bride to enter, every heart waited to see what would happen. As she approached, William's father began to unwrap the gauze over his son's eyes. When the last bandage was removed, light flooded into William's eyes. Slowly, William focused on the radiant face of his precious bride. Overcome with emotion, William whispered, "You are more beautiful than I ever imagined."[10]

Something like that will happen to us, friends, when the bandages are taken away from our eyes and we see Jesus. Then we will worship our heavenly Husband forever. He will gaze upon us as His bride and see only beauty—only His work in us. He will see no sin. We shall be like Him and see Him as He is. We will be as perfect in soul and in body as He is.

Truly, "Blessed are they which are called unto the marriage supper of the Lamb!" (Rev. 19:9). John is so overwhelmed that he begins to worship the angel who brought him the invitation. The angel has to rebuke him, saying, as it were: "John, you've got it wrong; worship God. Worship only the One who has invited you to the marriage of the Lamb!" (cf. vv. 9–10). The angel is right, of course, for God alone is worthy to be praised.

Though the word *hallelujah* is not used in verse 10, the essence of hallelujah fills the entire verse. It is as if the four hallelujahs in the preceding verses roll over into John's heart so that he cannot help but respond with a quiet, worshipful hallelujah. If you have had such hallelujah moments in this life because the Lord has saved you and invites you to the marriage supper of the Lamb, what must it be like to actually dine with the Lamb in that land of never-ending hallelujahs? As 1 Corinthians 2:9 says, "Eye hath not seen, nor ear heard, neither have entered into the heart of man, the things which God hath prepared for them that love him." Hallelujah!

---

10. Steven J. Lawson, *Heaven Help Us!* (Colorado Springs: Navpress, 1995), 168–69.

If your only hope for salvation is in Christ, and you long to be with Him forever, then He invites you to the marriage supper of the Lamb. And, as Revelation 19:9 says, "Blessed are they which are called unto the marriage supper of the Lamb."

This Babylonian world will one day be a smoldering ruin. This great world that thinks it is going places is going nowhere at all. But Christ is coming back for His church, His bride—yes, for you, dear believer! Hallelujah! Praise be to His name!

A Glorious Invitation

The Lord Jesus offers His hand in marriage to you. Do you receive it by faith and repentance?

There is a sense in which everyone is called to this wedding. The gospel is to be preached to all creatures. God freely and lovingly invites *all*. The invitations are out. Everyone is welcome to come to Christ.

But to come to this wedding, you must be born again. You must know something of the marks of the Spirit's saving grace in your soul. You must know what it means to respond to God's overtures of salvation with true repentance and saving faith. You must learn of your need of the Bridegroom, who is your only hope of salvation. You must know something of your depravity and something of Christ's marvelous deliverance. And you must want to live for Him in gratitude if you are going to sit at His table with His wedding garment. You must be prepared for this table by being stripped of your righteousness. You must long for the day of eternal marriage with Christ.

If you are unsaved, you don't have these marks of grace. You are indeed invited to come to Christ for salvation, but you do not yet share in the hope of His wedding banquet. If you're unsaved now, your greatest need is to be born again. You must come as a sinner just as you are, responding to Christ's invitation. Fall at His feet, casting yourself on mercy alone for salvation.

You can get to heaven without money, without education, without beauty, or without friends. But you cannot get there without

Christ. Only those now engaged to Christ will be married to Him in heaven one day.

I can't tell you how this world is going to end. But I can tell you that there will be a wedding, the wedding of all time, and you're invited! And the gospel demands a response from you—your R.S.V.P. As Paul says in Ephesians 5: "For this cause shall a man leave his father and mother, and shall be joined unto his wife, and they two shall be one flesh. This is a great mystery: but I speak concerning Christ and the church" (vv. 31–32). The gospel demands that you repent of your sin and cleave to this only Savior by true saving faith.

Those who do repent and trust in Christ can sincerely confess that their greatest hope is the hope of being with Christ and beholding His glory. David sings of this hope in Psalms 16:11 and 17:15: "Thou wilt shew me the path of life: in thy presence is fullness of joy; at thy right hand are pleasures for evermore.... As for me, I will behold thy face in righteousness: I shall be satisfied, when I awake, with thy likeness." All who share this faith and cherish this hope can sing:

> O Christ, He is the fountain,
> The deep, sweet well of love!
> The streams on earth I've tasted
> More deep I'll drink above:
> There to an ocean fullness
> His mercy doth expand,
> And glory, glory dwelleth
> In Immanuel's land.
>
> The King there in His beauty,
> Without a veil is seen:
> It were a well-spent journey,
> Though seven deaths lay between:
> The Lamb with His fair army,
> Doth on Mount Zion stand,

And glory, glory dwelleth
In Immanuel's land.[11]

Dear believer, I conclude with three practical lessons we can apply from this truth of Christ, the centerpiece of heaven, to whom we may one day be married in the greatest wedding of all time.

1. Since Christ is the jewel in heaven's crown—for He is what makes heaven, heaven—strive to make Him the center of your life here on earth. You can get to heaven without money, education, beauty, or friends. But you cannot get there without Christ. Only those who are now engaged to Christ will one day be married to Him in heaven. So put all your energy into focusing on Christ in His person, names, natures, states, offices, and benefits.

2. As a bride prepares herself for her wedding, we must do likewise. The more we yearn for our marriage with Christ, the more we shall seek for that holiness without which no man shall see Lord. But the less we think of it, the less we will follow the Lord Jesus in this life. During an engagement, those who are betrothed to each other are not allowed to court other people. We must not flirt with sin but push it far from us and say, "I will keep myself pure for the Lord Jesus Christ."

The story is told of a young woman who became a Christian when she was a child. As she grew older, she continued to follow Jesus. But she never married. She was into her forties and fifties, still living at home and caring for her father. Then she became very sick with tuberculosis, and it looked as if she would die.

One day, the woman was talking with her father and said, "Dad, I've got some good news for you."

The father asked, "What is it?"

She said, "I'm going to be married at last."

---

11. Anne R. Cousin, "The Sands of Time Are Sinking," poeticizing Samuel Rutherford, in *The Christian Treasury* (1857), stanzas 2, 5. http://cyberhymnal.org/htm/s/a/sandtime.htm (accessed June 24, 2016).

The father thought his daughter was delirious and tried to change the subject, but she was persistent. He said, "My dear daughter, the doctor said that you will be dying soon."

She said: "Dad, I know that, but don't you see that I am going to be married to Jesus real soon? I will soon be with my real Husband."

3. Remember that death will soon usher you into glory to be forever with your heavenly Husband. In John 14:2–3 Jesus says, "In my Father's house are many mansions: if it were not so, I would have told you. I go to prepare a place for you. And if I go and prepare a place for you, I will come again, and receive you unto myself; that where I am, there ye may be also." Death for believers is our gateway into His throne room, to see the beautiful face of our Lord and Savior and Bridegroom, Jesus Christ, in a truly utopian marriage. Thus through all our lives and on our deathbeds we can sing:

> Whom have I, Lord, in heaven but Thee,
> To Whom my thoughts aspire?
> And, having Thee, on earth is nought
> That I can yet desire.
>
> Though flesh and heart should faint and fail,
> The Lord will ever be
> The strength and portion of my heart,
> My God eternally![12]

Recently, one of our older Nigerian seminary students introduced me to one of our new Nigerian students. As he did so, the new student only gave me momentary, furtive glances, and he would then quickly look away. The older student noticed right away, and said, "No, no; you are in America now; in Nigeria it would be an insult to look your teacher fully in the face, but in America it is an insult not to do so." The new student then tried to look at me a bit longer. The glances were now about half a second long before he

---

12. *The Psalter*, no. 203 (Ps. 73).

looked away. He just could not bring himself to look fully at me for any length of time.

That is how it is too often with us as Christians in this life. Too often we have only momentary glimpses of Christ. We see Him only through a glass darkly, Paul says in 1 Corinthians 13. But oh, blessed be God, the day is soon coming, dear believer, when you will never look away from Christ. You will gaze upon Immanuel, your Beloved, forever, without any shame, for you will be as holy as He is holy. Oh, blessed beatific vision!

Truly, "Let us be glad and rejoice, and give honour to him: for the marriage of the Lamb is come, and his wife hath made herself ready" (v. 7).

30

The King's Victorious Return

REVELATION 19:11–21

And I saw heaven opened, and behold a white horse; and he that sat upon him was called Faithful and True, and in righteousness he doth judge and make war. His eyes were as a flame of fire, and on his head were many crowns; and he had a name written, that no man knew, but he himself. And he was clothed with a vesture dipped in blood: and his name is called The Word of God. And the armies which were in heaven followed him upon white horses, clothed in fine linen, white and clean. And out of his mouth goeth a sharp sword, that with it he should smite the nations: and he shall rule them with a rod of iron: and he treadeth the winepress of the fierceness and wrath of Almighty God. And he hath on his vesture and on his thigh a name written, KING OF KINGS, AND LORD OF LORDS.... And I saw the beast, and the kings of the earth, and their armies, gathered together to make war against him that sat on the horse, and against his army. And the beast was taken, and with him the false prophet that wrought miracles before him, with which he deceived them that had received the mark of the beast, and them that worshipped his image. These both were cast alive into a lake of fire burning with brimstone. And the remnant were slain with the sword of him that sat upon the horse, which sword proceeded out of his mouth: and all the fowls were filled with their flesh.

The book of Revelation is the tale of two cities: earthly Babylon and heavenly Jerusalem. Revelation 19 is the tale of two feasts. We have discussed the marriage supper of the Lamb. Now, verse 17 tells us about "the supper of the great God." There couldn't be a greater contrast. At the wedding supper of the Lamb, all is happiness, festivity, and blessing. In contrast, the supper of the great God is more like a nightmare. The Lord Jesus Christ is in the midst of both of these feasts. He is central to the wedding supper, where He is the Bridegroom and the Lamb. But He is also the King riding the white horse at the supper of the great God.

Revelation 17–19 is the sixth of seven parallel visionary cycles in Revelation. The last half of Revelation 19 divides naturally into three parts as John tells us what he sees. In verse 11, he sees a magnificent King mounted on a white horse. In verse 17, he sees an angel standing in the sun, inviting carnivorous birds to devour men slain in battle. And in verse 19, he sees a beast, kings, and armies gathered for a final battle against the King and His army. Let us examine this chapter under these headings: the King mounted on a white horse (vv. 11–16); the King hosting a dreadful supper (vv. 17–18); and the King conquering in the final battle (vv. 19–21).

The King Mounted on a White Horse

There is no doubt who the rider on the white horse is. If you just glance at the names He is given and the titles He bears, this is surely the Lord Jesus Christ. He is described in verse 11 as "Faithful and True." He is called "The Word of God" in verse 13. As John explained in his Gospel, this title means that Christ bears the very nature of God and is the living agent of His will (John 1:1–3). And He is named in verse 16 as "KING OF KINGS, AND LORD OF LORDS."

We are told in verse 12 that Christ has another name that no one but He Himself knows. This reminds us that whenever we talk about the Lord Jesus, we are talking about God. He may be Jesus of Nazareth, but He is also the unfathomable God. We cannot know everything there is to know about the Lord Jesus Christ. He is too great and too glorious for that. As much as we know about Him, there is still more that we don't know. In that sense, no one knows His name but He Himself.

One of His names is "Faithful and True." As Simon Kistemaker says, "Christ is faithful because he fulfills everything the Scriptures reveal of and about him, and he is true because he personifies truth (John 14:6)."[1] Hasn't your Savior always been faithful and true to you? Has He ever deceived you? When has He failed you or forgotten to be gracious to you? Hasn't He been to you the very truth of God incarnate? Has He not kept every promise He has ever made to you and fulfilled every word He has spoken? How sweet and rich is every name of God and of Christ!

God's titles often match their context in remarkable ways. For example, the apostle Paul prays for the Thessalonian believers, saying: "And the very God of peace sanctify you wholly" (1 Thess. 5:23). Paul wants the church to have peace, so he addresses his prayer to the God of peace. In the High Priestly Prayer of John 17, when Jesus prays for the sanctification of His church, He says throughout, "Holy Father, sanctify them; make them holy." Repeatedly we find that the titles of God are not just used at random. They fit their context.

The context of Revelation is the day of Christ's victorious return to earth as Judge. Nations and kings who have defied Him and His Word will be punished. He has the right to judge the nations because He is "King of kings and Lord of lords." He is coming to a world that ignores Him and instead worships an unknown God. There is no excuse for that, because God has not left Himself unknown. He has revealed Himself richly in Jesus Christ. So Christ is coming to a world that thinks it has the measure of Him. He is coming to churches, theologians, thinkers, and philosophers who have written books about Him and made pronouncements about Him. But the One who is coming is the One who has a name that no one fully knows (Rev. 19:13). All the theologians, philosophers, and thinkers of the world together know only a small fraction of who Christ is.

He is coming to judge a world that long ago gave up any idea of judgment. He is coming to people who scorn the very idea of His

---

1. Kistemaker, *Revelation*, 519.

return. Some say He is waiting too long to come. But because He is Faithful and True, we can be sure that all the promises He has given in His Word will be fulfilled. All the names and titles of Christ can bolster our faith and give us peace as we face the prospect of our Lord's return, the climax of history, and the final judgment.

An old Scottish saint was near death. She was full of glory, assurance, joy, and peace. Her minister came to see her and asked some probing questions to make sure that her faith was resting on a solid foundation. When he asked where her soul was resting, she responded that she was resting on Christ's "good name." She said, "If I should awake in eternity to find myself among the lost, the Lord would lose more than I would, for all that I would lose would be my immortal soul, but He would have lost His good name." Her faith was grounded in the names and titles of Christ Jesus. She took refuge in them.

Proverbs 18:10 says, "The name of the LORD is a strong tower: the righteous runneth into it, and is safe." I fear that some of you are running away from Christ's names and titles—even from Christ Himself. But you must not run away from God. God is holy and we are sinners. The only way we will be saved is to turn around and run to God as He has revealed Himself in Christ. We are to run to His name, the psalmist says. His name is a strong tower, and all who run into that tower are safe for eternity, even when Christ returns to judge the nations.

Notice also Christ's *appearance* in this passage. He is mounted on a white horse. Revelation 19:12–15a says that "His eyes were as a flame of fire, and on his head were many crowns.... And he was clothed with a vesture dipped in blood.... And out of his mouth goeth a sharp sword." We are told that He comes to judge and to make war. We need to remind ourselves not only of the kindness of God, but also of His severity. There is more to Jesus than His meekness and mildness. He also exemplifies severity, holiness, justice, firmness, and strength.

The rider on the white horse is symbolic not only of what Christ will do on the last day, but also of what He always is. Just as a horse is a symbol of power, victory, and speed, so Christ, the rider, symbolizes a powerful, victorious King. The color white is associated with victory in Revelation. So Jesus Christ is a victorious conqueror. Verse 16 says in striking capital letters that He is "KING OF KINGS, AND LORD OF LORDS," meaning that He is the greatest ever. He is the most exalted Sovereign of all time and all eternity. He reigns with all authority, power, and dominion.

Sometimes, after preaching the gospel, an evangelist invites people to accept Christ. "It is up to you now; you must decide," he says. But the Christ of Scripture rides on a white horse, meaning that He has won the battle. In ancient times, an emperor would come back from battle on a white charger, symbolizing that he had won the victory. Likewise, the Christ of the gospel rides on a white horse, for He is always the conqueror and always the Captain of the armies of heaven. On the last day, everybody will know it. But it is also true now. And it was true at Calvary. When He seemed to be His weakest and it seemed the devil had triumphed, Christ conquered sin, death, and Satan on the cross. Hebrews 2:14 says that in death, He destroyed the devil, who has the power of death. As William Williams writes:

> Bruised was the dragon by the Son,
> Though two had wounds, there conquered One
> And Jesus was His name.[2]

This is a picture not just of the last day, but of all times when Christ rides out among the nations of this world, conquering and to conquer. It is the picture of Christ with His gospel sword, riding around this world and conquering His subjects.

Revelation 19:14 goes on to describe the armies that accompany Christ: "The armies which were in heaven followed him upon white horses, clothed in fine linen, white and clean." Some say these armies in heaven must be made up of angels. That is a possibility, as

---

2. William Williams, "In Eden—Sad Indeed that Day," trans. Robert Maynard Jones (eighteenth century).

angels are sometimes pictured as being clothed with the whiteness of purity, and angels minister to the church on earth more than she is aware. But I am convinced that this heavenly army has two components: the saints as well as the angels.

When we compare verse 14 with verse 8, it seems clear that these armies are the saints of God. In the first part of the chapter, we are told that the bride is "granted that she should be arrayed in fine linen, clean and white: for the fine linen is the righteousness of saints" (v. 8). So the bride represents the saints of God, the church of Christ. Now, in this parallel vision, Christ is riding on His white horse, accompanied by armies dressed in the same fine white linen that is the righteousness of the saints.

The armies are composed of soldiers of Jesus Christ. They are all mounted on horses. They follow their King, who leads His church— the church militant. And the gospel triumphs in the world. As David cries out: "Gird thy sword upon thy thigh, O most mighty, with thy glory and thy majesty. And in thy majesty ride prosperously because of truth and meekness and righteousness; and thy right hand shall teach thee terrible things. Thine arrows are sharp in the heart of the king's enemies; whereby the people fall under thee" (Ps. 45:3–5).

Christ said that before He returns, the gospel must first be preached in every nation (Matt. 24:14). Don't think that our Lord means that a missionary will simply spend a few weeks visiting a nation and slip a few tracts into people's pockets. Neither does He mean that every nation will merely have an intellectual acquaintance with the gospel. Surely what He means is that a numberless multitude in many nations will fall to the gospel. Kingdoms and civilizations, yes, every strata of society and every area of life—many will come under the sovereign sway of King Jesus. That is what we look forward to.

Even now, far more people are bending the knee to King Jesus than we know—especially in Africa and throughout the vast nation of China. On Christ's head are many crowns, Revelation 19:12 says. These are diadems, the crowns of rule, multiplied many times, too many to count, indicating the fullness of Christ's kingship, the

plenitude of His royal power, and the many nations He has conquered. The crowns of South Korea, Ethiopia, Brazil, and all other
nations are on His head. The whole world belongs to Him. Oh, He
is a mighty Conqueror. The greatest force in human history is the
gospel of the Lord Jesus Christ.

Let us take comfort from this. Let it also spur us on in evangelism, motivating us to train men for the ministry and send them
around the globe. We should not rest until every city and every rural
area on the planet has at least one biblical preacher proclaiming the
riches of sovereign grace to poor sinners. What the world needs
most is faithful ministers who preach the gospel, combined with the
Holy Spirit's blessing on that gospel.

Oh, Lord Jesus, ride on swiftly with the gospel and with the
armies of Thy saints behind Thee, proclaiming Thy great and glorious name. Bring sinners all around the globe to their knees before
Thee. Make us willing subjects of Thy powerful, sovereign grace, so
that we may say with the poet:

> Oh, sovereign grace my heart subdue;
> I will be led in triumph, too,
> A willing captive to my Lord,
> To sing the triumphs of his Word.[3]

But how do we dare hope for victory in our own lives, the lives
of our families, and the lives of those in our churches and nations if
things are going to get worse before the Lord returns, to the point
where He can find hardly a believer anywhere on the earth? It is
true that as the gospel is preached and nations bend the knee to
King Jesus, there will be opposition. You see that in the world today.
While many people are coming to Christ across the globe, they are
also encountering fierce opposition. And as the gospel makes progress, the persecution gets worse. Yet I cannot believe that when our
Lord returns, He will find only a handful of people. He rides forth
with many crowns and with the armies of heaven.

---

3. Cited in Spurgeon, *New Park Street Pulpit*, 5:454.

Scripture seems to be saying that two things will happen simultaneously in the end times: the ungodly will become more ungodly and will increase their opposition to Christianity, and the godly will become godlier and will love Christ more.

If you are not a Christian, I tell you on the authority of God's Word that you are in deep trouble. You are living a life that will end in defeat, confusion, and damnation. The gospel is preached and the claims of Christ are presented to you, and you think, "Now that is very interesting; shall I receive it or shall I not?" Perhaps you say: "I don't think I'm very interested in Christianity at the moment. I have other things that fill my mind. Perhaps some other time I might be interested." I urge you not to do that. Christ is a Conqueror and a King. He comes on His own terms. You must either submit to Him unconditionally or you will be destroyed by Him. There is a sharp sword in His mouth. Unless you fall beneath that sword in repentance and faith, by the Holy Spirit's grace, it will fall on you in judgment.

Paul says, "The gospel is at the same time a savor of life unto life to those who believe, and a savor of death unto death to those who won't believe" (see 2 Cor. 2:15–16). The gospel will either save you or damn you.

The King Hosting a Dreadful Supper

On the nearly barren island of Patmos, gazing out across the water and hearing nothing but the sound of the sea and the seagulls, John has another vision. This time it is of an angel standing in the sun.

The mammoth angel blots out the sun. But the appearance of the angel is not as crucial as his message. He stands in the sun to draw John's attention, for he has an important announcement to make. Revelation 19:17–18 tells us: "And I saw an angel standing in the sun; and he cried with a loud voice, saying to all the fowls that fly in the midst of heaven, Come and gather yourselves together unto the supper of the great God; that ye may eat the flesh of kings, and the flesh of captains, and the flesh of mighty men, and the flesh of horses, and of them that sit on them, and the flesh of all men, both free and bond, both small and great."

The key to this symbolism is in the Bible itself. In the Old Testament, to give someone's flesh to the birds expressed the idea of total defeat and shameful subjection to the enemy. There was no one left to give the bodies of the slain a decent burial.

Think, for example, of the account of David and Goliath in 1 Samuel 17. Goliath, the champion of the Philistines, arrogantly defied the armies of God. David volunteered to go against the giant, armed with only a little sling and a few stones. King Saul tried to make the shepherd boy wear armor, but the suit was too heavy for him. So David took his sling and five stones from the brook, and went out to meet this giant. He said to Goliath, "This day will the LORD deliver thee into mine hand; and I will smite thee, and take thine head from thee; and I will give the carcases of the host of the Philistines this day unto the fowls of the air, and to the wild beasts of the earth; that all the earth may know that there is a God in Israel" (1 Sam. 17:46). That is the message of the angel John sees standing in the sun.

The story of David and Goliath must have comforted first-century Christians, who likely felt like David before the giant Rome, which defied and persecuted the church. Yet this little band of believers would turn the world upside down by preaching a simple message about a crucified Messiah. And through that seemingly foolish message, Rome also would come tumbling down.

Paul explains this phenomenon in 1 Corinthians 1:18–21: "For the preaching of the cross is to them that perish foolishness; but unto us which are saved it is the power of God. For it is written, I will destroy the wisdom of the wise, and will bring to nothing the understanding of the prudent. Where is the wise? where is the scribe? where is the disputer of this world? hath not God made foolish the wisdom of this world? For after that in the wisdom of God the world by wisdom knew not God, it pleased God by the foolishness of preaching to save them that believe."

A little stone from the brook, rightly aimed by the Spirit of God, will bring down a giant. We want to see people saved, but we must avoid the temptation to adopt the slick techniques and methods of the world to win the world. There is only one way this mighty giant can be won for Christ. You and I must take the gospel and aim it, by the power of the Spirit, at sinners, and the Spirit must graciously bless it so that God's Word, just as He promised, does not return to Him void.

The second thing John sees is much like what the prophet Ezekiel saw when God called birds and animals to consume the flesh of mighty men, princes, soldiers, riders, and horses. As Kistemaker notes in commenting on Revelation 19: "The birds of prey who have been created to consume carcasses and thus remove unsightly scenes and dreadful smells have been called to be present at the aftermath of Christ's battle against the antichrist and his followers. This, then, is the exact fulfillment of Ezekiel's prophecy against Gog in the land of Magog (Ezek. 38–39)."[4]

Woe be to us if we depend on the Goliaths and other mighty men of this world, but not the King of kings. On the Great Day, we will be food for vultures.

The King Conquering in the Final Battle

As the sixth cycle of visions draws to a close, John sees the King of kings, Jesus Christ, with His garments dipped in blood and His head crowned with many crowns, galloping across the field of human history with the armies of the church. The King has His saints by His side to share in His victory. Paul says, "Thanks be to God, which giveth us the victory through our Lord Jesus Christ" (1 Cor. 15:57).

Then John hears a remarkable announcement made by the angel standing in the sun. The outcome of the battle is certain, the angel announces. This world will be destroyed for all its arrogance and defiance, and its flesh will be given to the fowls of the air. It will

---

4. Kistemaker, *Revelation*, 525.

suffer the most crushing, humiliating, and unexpected defeat at the hands of the crucified Savior-King.

Revelation 19:19 describes the final battle—the final conflict of all time. The battle lines are drawn up as opposing armies face one another at the place called Armageddon. We saw when considering Revelation 16:16 that the word *Armageddon* may be derived either from *har-mageddon*, which means "mount (*har*) of Megiddo," or *h'ar-mageddon*, which means "the city (*ar*) of Megiddo." The city was on a plateau that overlooked the plain of Esdraelon, where many ancient battles were fought. Here Israel's armies defeated Sisera and his armies in the days of Deborah (Judg. 5:19).

That was an unexpected victory. King Jabin and his general, Sisera, had chariots of iron. Israel could not possibly win against such a foe. When the Israelites asked, "Who is going to fight for us?" Deborah responded, "The Lord will fight for us." That day on the plain of Esdraelon, Sisera's chariots bogged down in mud and his army was totally defeated. Armageddon is symbolic of every battle in which believers are oppressed and powerless, and the Lord uses His power to defeat the enemy.

Yet the battle at the end of Revelation 19 looks beyond all these conflicts to the final, climactic confrontation between the powers of Satan and God. God takes Satan and his minions down and throws them into the lake of fire. There will be an Armageddon in the end, but not at the literal place of Megiddo. It will take place when God extraordinarily intervenes for His people and gives them victory over all their enemies. Armageddon is symbolic of the triumph of the Lamb. Armageddon can be traced throughout the history of the gospel, but its ultimate manifestation will be at the very end, when Christ comes again.

Armageddon is described in 2 Thessalonians 1:7–10, where Paul writes: "The Lord Jesus shall be revealed from heaven with his mighty angels, in flaming fire taking vengeance on them that know not God, and that obey not the gospel of our Lord Jesus Christ: who shall be punished with everlasting destruction from the presence of the Lord, and from the glory of his power; when he shall come to be glorified in his saints, and to be admired in all them that believe (because our testimony among you was believed) in that day."

Will you survive Armageddon? The determining factor will be whether or not you have obeyed the gospel. Jesus Christ is coming again, and He will come in flaming fire to take vengeance on all who do not know God and do not obey the gospel of salvation. Revelation 19:15 says that He will strike unbelievers down with the sword of His mouth, rule them with a rod of iron, and tread them underfoot as He treads "the winepress of the fierceness and wrath of Almighty God."

The final battle is over very quickly. We are told that "with the spirit [breath] of his mouth," Christ defeats all His enemies upon His glorious return (2 Thess. 2:3–12). The sword going out of His mouth and His breath are symbols for His Word and Spirit; He will conquer with such spiritual weapons. His very presence vanquishes His enemies (2 Thess. 2:8). The results of the battle are final and forever. Revelation 19:19–20 says that the beast from the sea and the false prophet (antichristian persecution and religion) are thrown into the lake of fire, and their followers are slain and thrown in after them. John tells us later that the devil and all of Christ's opponents will remain eternally in that lake of fire (20:10, 14–15; 21:8). Kistemaker writes: "This lake is a vast area of fire that burns ceaselessly with the nauseating smell of sulfur. The impossibility of ever leaving this burning pool is self-evident, and everlasting pain and horror are the lot of those consigned to hell."[5]

Christ's triumph, together with His followers, is glorious and complete, while Satan's defeat, together with his followers, is horrific and complete. Have you obeyed the gospel, which calls you to repentance and faith, or are you obeying the world, which calls you to the lusts of the flesh, the lusts of the eyes, and the pride of life (1 John 2:16)? By the Spirit's grace, have you repented of your sins and put your trust in Jesus Christ alone as your Savior, whom God has "exalted with his right hand to be a Prince and a Saviour, for to

5. Kistemaker, *Revelation*, 527.

give repentance to Israel, and forgiveness of sins" (Acts 5:31)? Or are you still rejecting the overtures of the Lamb of God and the King of kings? If so, remember that, outside of Christ, "it is a fearful thing to fall into the hands of the living God" (Heb. 10:31).

What will your future be? How will life end with you? Will you be one of the blessed ones who are seated as guests at the marriage supper of the Lamb, or will you—God forbid—be served up as food for the vultures in the great supper of God?

31

The Millennium

REVELATION 20:1–10

And I saw an angel come down from heaven, having the key of the bottomless pit and a great chain in his hand. And he laid hold on the dragon, that old serpent, which is the Devil, and Satan, and bound him a thousand years, and cast him into the bottomless pit, and shut him up, and set a seal upon him, that he should deceive the nations no more, till the thousand years should be fulfilled: and after that he must be loosed a little season. And I saw thrones, and they sat upon them, and judgment was given unto them: and I saw the souls of them that were beheaded for the witness of Jesus, and for the word of God, and which had not worshipped the beast, neither his image, neither had received his mark upon their foreheads, or in their hands; and they lived and reigned with Christ a thousand years. But the rest of the dead lived not again until the thousand years were finished. This is the first resurrection. Blessed and holy is he that hath part in the first resurrection: on such the second death hath no power, but they shall be priests of God and of Christ, and shall reign with him a thousand years. And when the thousand years are expired, Satan shall be loosed out of his prison, and shall go out to deceive the nations which are in the four quarters of the earth, Gog and Magog, to gather them together to battle: the number of whom is as the sand of the sea. And they went up on the breadth of the earth, and compassed the camp of the saints about, and the beloved city: and fire came down from God out of heaven, and devoured them. And the devil that deceived them was cast into the lake of fire and brimstone, where the beast and the false prophet are, and shall be tormented day and night for ever and ever.

A great classical score has certain themes. Sometimes a theme is only vaguely suggested at the start, but as the piece progresses, the theme keeps recurring until eventually all the themes in the work come together in a final movement and the grand finale. The book of Revelation is like that. It progresses like a symphony. It is not a linear history, but a series of parallel visions. Certain themes keep recurring as the book unfolds.

Chapters 20 through 22 take up the themes from previous chapters in Revelation and bring them to a marvelous conclusion. In chapter 20, the theme of the *millennium*, which means, "one thousand years," summarizes prior themes and thereby serves as the beginning of the final movement of this book.

Major Millennial Views

Before I explain chapter 20, let us consider simply and succinctly the major views that Christians have on the millennium.

Premillennialism

This view teaches that Christ will come again, establish His kingdom on earth, and reign for a literal thousand years. This will be a golden age of peace, lasting until a final rebellion and judgment day. But several problems with this position emerge when we compare Scripture with Scripture:

First, premillennialism tends to view God's kingdom as primarily physical and national. In contrast, Scripture views the kingdom primarily as spiritual and universal, much as the New Testament views other Old Testament prophetical terms, such as "Abraham's seed" (John 8:37); the "tabernacle of David" (Acts 15:14–17); and "Jerusalem" (Rev. 21:10).

Second, premillennialism tends to view Christ's kingdom as still to come rather than as a present reality. However, Scripture testifies that the kingdom is already present in New Testament times (Matt. 12:28; John 18:36).

Third, premillennialism tends to separate the major events of eschatology by many years, while Scripture sees all the major events of the last times as transpiring in rapid succession (Matt. 13:39–50; 24:29–31; 25:31–34).

Fourth, premillennialism says that Christ will physically return to earth a thousand years before the end of the world, but Scripture teaches that Christ will be in heaven until the end of time (Acts 3:20–21; Heb. 10:12–13).

Postmillennialism

This view says that before Christ comes again, the entire world will be won for Christ through conversion to the gospel. During this time, sin and conflict will gradually be defeated, and righteousness and peace will increasingly reign throughout the world. This present time will culminate in a golden age of success in missions and the transformation of society. It is called *post*millennialism because the golden age comes first, before Christ's return. But there are problems with this view as well:

First, like the premillennial view, postmillennialism errs in picturing God's kingdom as primarily temporal or physical rather than spiritual, and as something that will begin in the future rather than something that has already been inaugurated.

Second, postmillennialism views the last years of this world with extreme optimism. However, Scripture says that though there may be some encouraging times of revival near the end of the world, the last days will largely be times of unbelief (Luke 18:8); self-centeredness (2 Tim. 3:2); worldliness (Matt. 24:38–39); worship of the antichrist (2 Thess. 2:3–4, 8–9); and great tribulation and persecution (Matt. 24:7–10, 21–22).

Third, postmillennialism tends to view the present age as smoothly transitioning into the coming age. However, Scripture testifies to a great catastrophe, a tremendous intervention of God, and a passing away of the old heavens and earth and the establishment of a new heaven and earth (Matt. 24:29–31; 2 Peter 3:10–13).

Amillennialism or Inaugurated Millennialism

This view is held by most Reformed Christians. It teaches that the millennium is not a future earthly kingdom. Rather, the millennium is a symbolic description of the spiritual kingdom of God that is now present every since Pentecost in the church's missionary advance and heavenly reign, even as the church suffers persecution and waits for Christ's return and judgment day. The term *amillennialism* is not an accurate description of this view, because the prefix *a-* means "no," as in, "no millennium." Amillennialists *do* believe in a millennium. This position might better be called *inaugurated millennialism*, because we believe that the millennium has already been inaugurated. Thus, inaugurated millennialism believes that the millennium is not an exact period of a thousand years, but is really a symbolic description of the entire gospel age until Christ returns on the clouds.

With due respect to Christians who hold differing views, we believe that the book of Revelation, including the most highly debated section of chapter 20, favors an *amillennial* interpretation.[1] Here are some reasons why:

First, the New Testament teaches that God's promises to Israel have already found partial fulfillment in the church as a spiritual, international kingdom; and yet, they will be fulfilled in ultimate glory rather than in a nationalistic, earthly reign of Christ (Matt. 12:28; Luke 17:20–21; John 18:36–37; Acts 15:13–18; Rom. 2:28–29; 4:16; 14:17; Gal. 3:28–29; 4:26; Heb. 12:22–24, 28).

Second, Scripture indicates that Christ's coming in glory, the resurrection of both the righteous and the wicked, judgment day, and the end of this age will all take place together in rapid succession, as opposed to being dispersed over a thousand-year period (Dan. 12:2; Matt. 13:39–43; 16:27; 24:29–31; 25:31–46; John 5:28–29; Acts 24:15; 1 Thess. 4:13–5:11).

Third, Revelation is a book of symbolic visions. Therefore, one must interpret the numbers (such as *one thousand*) and images (such as *binding with a chain* and *sealing in a pit*) in chapter 20 as symbols. This is not inconsistent with a literal interpretation of God's Word,

---

1. Portions of this chapter are adapted from *The Reformation Heritage KJV Study Bible*, 1864.

but only the recognition that parts of Scripture communicate via metaphors and symbols.

Fourth, Revelation follows a cyclical structure, repeatedly bringing the reader to the return of Christ at the end of each cycle. Chapter 19 ends the cycle of the conquest of Babylon and culminates in the destruction of the wicked. Chapter 20, like chapter 12, steps back to consider the era between Christ's first and second comings before moving ahead to judgment day and eternity.

In Revelation 20:1–10, we discover three truths about the millennium. In verses 1–3, we are told that Satan is bound for a thousand years. In verses 4–6, we are told that the saints reign for a thousand years. In verses 7–10, we are told that at the end of the thousand years, Satan is let loose for a short time. Let us examine the millennium under these three headings: the binding of Satan; the reign of the saints; and the loosing of Satan.

The Binding of Satan

Revelation 20:2 describes Satan as "the dragon, that old serpent, which is the Devil." John uses these titles to remind his readers that the opposition they face from the forces and powers arrayed against them is as old as the world itself (Gen. 3:1).

We are *all* tempted by Satan during times of opposition and persecution. When we are most weak, the devil attacks us, insinuating that we are just hypocrites and even that we are not Christians at all. When we are facing such opposition, we may be tempted to think that what we are going through is unique to ourselves. We need to remind ourselves that the devil is an *ancient* serpent.

If you are being harassed by the devil, that is nothing new. There is no trial that can come upon you that is not common to all men (1 Cor. 10:13). Get things into proper perspective. We are participants in an age-old conflict. The devil is an old enemy.

Some find this truth difficult to accept. For example, you may have tried to defend the Bible in a college science class, only to have the teacher come down hard on you and say: "Surely you don't believe that nonsense! No one believes in the biblical account of creation anymore!" We need to remind ourselves that there is nothing new about unbelief. Unbelief is positively antiquarian. It goes all the way back to the Garden of Eden. It is as old as the serpent himself.

Yet, we are told in Revelation 20:1–3 that Satan is bound and thrown into the pit, where he is locked away for a thousand years. How are we to understand this? Allow me to illustrate. Whenever you go to a zoo, you are very glad the animals are in cages or enclosures. It is very comforting to see the bars. That is the picture we are given in verses 1–3.

In this gospel age, Satan is bound. He is behind bars. He is on a chain and confined to a pit. Still, a lion in a cage is dangerous, even though he is caged. Similarly, in these gospel days, God has seized Satan and thrown him into the abyss, where he remains under lock and key to this very day. Yet, he remains dangerous.

But you might say: "When we read the newspapers and walk the streets, Satan doesn't appear to be bound. He seems to be very active." The question we must ask is this: In what sense is Satan bound? It is possible to tie up a dog in the backyard and yet still allow him a certain amount of activity—a certain scope in which he can be active. He can't go *beyond* the lead. He can wreak havoc only *within* the radius of the lead.

That is how we are to understand the binding of Satan. His binding is a result of Christ's death and resurrection. His power over the nations is now broken and his influence curtailed. He cannot deceive the nations anymore. This is what we are told in verses 2–3. God has bound Satan and cast him into a bottomless pit, where he is to remain until the thousand years are fulfilled. But he is still active. He is bound, but not in every way. There is still much that he can do. We must thus regard him as dangerous still. He is to be feared, even though he is bound as far as the nations are concerned.

If you go to someone's house, ring the doorbell, and are greeted by a person holding a ferocious-looking dog on a leash, you hardly dare to enter the house. But when the person says, "It's all right; I've got him," that gives you enough confidence to enter. In the same way, the Lord Jesus says to us: "It's all right; I've got Satan. In the future, I will let him loose for a little season, but right now, I've got him. Now is the time to evangelize the world. Now is the time to convert the Gentiles. Now is the time to preach the gospel to every living creature. The devil is a frightening sight, but I've got him; so off you go."

Before our Lord's coming, the devil held sway over the nations. Before Jesus came, the Gentiles were in utter darkness. But now that Christ has died and risen again, and poured out His Spirit, Satan's power over the world is curtailed and defeated.

Some say John's account of the binding of Satan cannot refer to the present time because the devil remains active in the world today. However, other Scripture passages affirm that the devil was conquered by Christ's death on the cross. Speaking of the approaching hour of that death, Christ declared, "Now is the judgment of this world: now shall the prince of this world be cast out" (John 12:31). The devil is "judged" (John 16:11); Christ came to "bind" him (Matt. 12:29) and has "spoiled" him (Col. 2:15); and Christ partook of our flesh and blood "that through death he might destroy him that had the power of death, that is, the devil" (Heb. 2:14). Such absolute language does not mean that Satan no longer has any influence in the world, but the devil cannot stop the Lord Jesus from saving lost sinners among the nations.

To summarize the first three verses of Revelation 20, the seventh and final cycle of Revelation begins with a symbolic overview of God's kingdom in this present age. "A thousand years" symbolizes fullness (ten times ten times ten; cf. Rev. 5:11; 7:4; 14:1; 21:16), and the phrase, "the dragon, that old serpent, which is the Devil, and Satan," links John's vision to the defeat of Satan at Christ's exaltation to heaven (Rev. 12:9). The Lord Jesus bound Satan at His first coming (Matt. 12:28–29; cf. Isa. 24:21–23). Now, as the resurrected Christ, He has authority ("the keys") over the forces of death and hell (Rev. 1:18). He now has control over Satan's forces (2 Peter 2:4; Jude 6) according to God's holy purposes (Rev. 9:1–11). His victory over Satan is as decisive and complete as if the devil were already dead and buried.

Many Scripture passages testify to Christ's absolute conquest (Luke 10:18; John 12:31; 16:11; Col. 2:15; Heb. 2:14; Rev. 5:5). That does not mean that demonic influence has utterly ceased on earth, however (Rev. 13:14). But Satan cannot overcome those redeemed by the Lamb (Rev. 13:8; 17:14). In the context of Revelation 20:1–3, Satan's binding implies two things. First, the devil can no longer keep the Gentiles in spiritual darkness outside of Israel, because Christ is gathering His redeemed people from among all nations through the gospel (Rev. 5:9; cf. John 12:31–33). Second, the devil cannot destroy the church (Rev. 12:15–16), though he will be permitted one last, brief attack at the end of the age (20:7–10).

Consider also Jesus' words to the Pharisees in Matthew 12:28–29. Responding to their attacks against his ministry, Jesus says: "If I cast out devils by the Spirit of God, then the kingdom of God is come unto you. Or else how can one enter into a strong man's house, and spoil his goods, except he first bind the strong man? And then he will spoil his house." Here we find the same word, *bind*, that is used in Revelation 20. Up until Christ's first coming, Satan reigned over the nations. But then One greater than Satan came to bind him and release his captives. The binding of Satan is a sign and necessary condition for the coming of Christ's kingdom upon earth.

Consider also Jesus' words in John 12:31–33: "Now is the judgment of this world: now shall the prince of this world be cast out. And I, if I be lifted up from the earth, will draw all men unto me. This he said, signifying what death he should die." The word translated as "be cast out" is basically the same word that we find in Revelation 20:3, 10, and 14. Christ's death by crucifixion meant two things. First, it meant the casting out of Satan from his seat of power. Second, it meant the drawing in of the nations, with all sorts and conditions of men.

Colossians 2:15 says the crucified Christ has spoiled principalities and powers, and has made an open show of them, triumphing over them in the cross. Hebrews 2:14 tells us that Christ has destroyed "him that had the power of death," who kept people in bondage through the fear of death. In Galatians 3:13–14, Paul says, "Christ hath redeemed us from the curse of the law, being made a curse for us: for it is written, Cursed is every one that hangeth on a tree: that the blessing of Abraham might come on the Gentiles through Jesus Christ; that we might receive the promise of the Spirit through faith." So if we are believers, Christ has redeemed us from the curse of the law. And the consequence of our Lord's taking the curse from us on Calvary's cross is that the blessing of salvation is extended to the Gentiles. From Calvary onward, Satan is bound. His power over the nations is broken. He can no longer deceive the nations.

We should understand the millennium not as a future golden age, but as the whole gospel era, in which we are now living. "A thousand years" is no more to be taken literally than any other number in Revelation. It symbolizes a significant period of time in which the gospel is preached throughout the earth; the Gentiles are gathered in; and unbelieving Israel is restored to faith through the conversion of the Jews to Christ (Rom. 11:1–32). It is therefore critical that we get on with the work of preaching the gospel while Satan is bound.

Revelation 7 offers us a marvelous picture of the end of time. After Babylon has gone up in smoke, what is left is the church of Jesus Christ. It is the *universal* church, made up of believers from all cultures, languages, tribes, and nationalities. This is the goal for which we should pray. And as we evangelize in this multicultural, multinational society in which we live, we should expect people to come to Christ, because the devil is bound. His power to deceive must yield to the greater power of the gospel of Jesus Christ (Rom. 1:16).

The Reign of the Saints

During the time in which Satan is bound, the saints reign. Revelation 20:4–6 says: "And I saw thrones, and they sat upon them, and judgment was given unto them: and I saw the souls of them that were beheaded for the witness of Jesus, and for the word of God, and which had not worshipped the beast, neither his image, neither had received his mark upon their foreheads, or in their hands; and they lived and reigned with Christ a thousand years. But the rest of the dead lived not again until the thousand years were finished. This is the first resurrection. Blessed and holy is he that hath part in the first resurrection: on such the second death hath no power, but they shall be priests of God and of Christ, and shall reign with him a thousand years."

This vision parallels the previous one; thus, the binding of Satan and the reigning of the saints happen at the same time. But in what sense can we speak about the saints reigning in this gospel age? This is a difficult passage to understand properly. The key to interpreting it is verse 5, which refers to the "first resurrection."

The reign of the saints seems to be synonymous with the first resurrection. This first resurrection is not the resurrection of the body, because John says that he sees only the "souls" of the martyrs (v. 4). So this first resurrection is a resurrection of the soul, not of the body. It is a *spiritual* and *heavenly* resurrection.

There are two ways of understanding what the reign of the saints means, both of which have merit:

First, this could be a reference to the *intermediate state* between death and the return of Christ. What happens to our loved ones, our Christian relatives and friends, who die? Their bodies are in the grave, but their souls are with Christ. John could be describing this intermediate state of the faithful departed.

John might speak to his readers about the intermediate state because he is a pastor, and he is writing to people who need pastoral comfort. Believers are being persecuted. Many have lost loved ones under Rome's cruel regime. Some of them will have to face martyrdom. Some will be beheaded for the sake of Christ because they refuse to bow and worship Caesar. These suffering saints might be asking, "Is following Christ worth it?"

John is saying, in effect: "Let me show you the state of the faithful departed, those brothers and sisters of yours who have been beheaded because they refused to compromise. They are seated on thrones in glory with Christ. They have never been as alive as they are now, reigning with Christ in glory and waiting for His coming and the resurrection of the body."

If this is John's purpose, it would certainly tie in with what Paul tells us in two of his epistles. He says of persecution and suffering in 2 Corinthians 4:16–17: "For which cause we faint not; but though our outward man perish, yet the inward man is renewed day by day. For our light affliction, which is but for a moment, worketh for us a far more exceeding and eternal weight of glory." Paul wants suffering Christians to keep things in proper perspective. He is saying to them: "What you will suffer under imperial Rome is only a moment of affliction. But what awaits you is to reign eternally with Christ in glory."

He also says in Romans 8:16–18: "The Spirit itself beareth witness with our spirit, that we are the children of God: and if children, then heirs; heirs of God, and joint-heirs with Christ; if so be that we suffer with him, that we may be also glorified together. For I reckon that the sufferings of this present time are not worthy to be compared with the glory which shall be revealed in us." Like Paul in these passages, John in our passage may be comforting hurting Christians by reminding them that their deceased brothers and sisters are in an intermediate state between suffering and the glory that awaits them.

Second, the reign of the saints could refer to a *present reality*. It is possible to understand the first resurrection not in terms of death, but in terms of Jesus' resurrection and our resurrection to new spiritual life through regeneration. Paul says in Ephesians 2:4–7: "But God, who is rich in mercy, for his great love wherewith he loved us, even when we were dead in sins, hath quickened us together with Christ (by grace ye are saved;) and hath raised us up together, and made us sit together in heavenly places in Christ Jesus: that in the ages to come he might shew the exceeding riches of his grace in his kindness toward us through Christ Jesus."

Paul is saying to ordinary Christians that we were once dead in sin, but God has quickened us. Through Christ's death and resurrection, God has raised us from the dead and made us alive in Christ. Likewise, just as God raised Christ up to heaven to be seated at

His right hand, so we also are raised up with Christ and seated in heavenly places with Him.

So it is possible to understand the first resurrection in terms of the new birth, or regeneration. John says, in effect, "Those who have known the second birth will never know the second death." If you are born again, then nothing in this world can harm you in an ultimate sense. "Fear not them which kill the body…but rather fear him which is able to destroy both soul and body in hell" (Matt. 10:28). The saints were not to be afraid or intimidated by Nero or Rome, but to fear God. Like them, you must remember that you have been resurrected from the dead. You have been born again by the Holy Spirit. You are thus more than conquerors through Christ who loved you.

The reign of the saints is not just about the intermediate state. I believe that Christian loved ones who have gone on ahead of us are reigning with Christ now, and that gives me great comfort. But I also believe that the reign of the saints is a present biblical reality. God has made us kings and priests through Jesus Christ here on this earth.

The context of 1 Corinthians 6 is interesting. It seems that some Christians were suing each other in court. Paul tells them that Christians shouldn't be dealing with one another like that. He uses a powerful argument in verses 2–3: "Do ye not know that the saints shall judge the world? And if the world shall be judged by you, are ye unworthy to judge the smallest matters? Know ye not that we shall judge angels? How much more things that pertain to this life?" What a message for beleaguered saints today!

The Reformers understood the significance of our death, resurrection, ascension and heavenly session with Christ. The Heidelberg Catechism poses a most important question: "Why art thou called a Christian?" The answer is stated in terms of Christ's threefold office as Prophet, Priest, and King, and how believers share in it now and in the life to come: "Because I am a member of Christ by faith, and thus am partaker of His anointing; so that I may confess His name [as a prophet], and present myself a living sacrifice of thankfulness to Him [as a priest]; and also that with a free and good conscience I may fight against sin and Satan in this life, and afterwards reign with Him eternally over all creatures [as a king]" (Q. 32).[2] The Christian's combat against sin and Satan is invested with royal strength and dignity; he fights as a king should fight for the honor and glory of his kingdom. He is as truly a king now as he will be in the life to come.

Many of us were taught in geography class that it is impossible for a river to rise higher than its source. But Christians *can* rise higher than their source. Our achievements can rise above our organizational skills, our strength, our personality, or our weakness. Our achievements in this life can rise to the level of its real source, which is hid with Christ in God. We can reign with Him. We can sit on a throne. John says that he saw thrones, and those who refused to bow the knee to the beast were sitting on them. That is you, dear believer, as a follower of the Lamb.

To summarize verses 4–6, God's mediatorial kingdom has already come in its spiritual power and reality to His people (John 18:36–37; Rom. 14:17; Eph. 1:19–21; Col. 1:12–13), and those who possess the kingdom are already blessed by God (Matt. 5:3; cf. Rev. 1:3; 14:13; 16:15; 19:9; 22:7, 14). Even now, God's people, symbolized in an earlier vision by the twenty-four elders, are crowned and enthroned in God's heavenly presence (Rev. 4:4, cf. Eph. 2:6). In this world, they suffer and die at the hands of wicked rulers for their refusal to participate in its idolatry. Yet those who are faithful unto death still live (Rev. 2:10) as priests (Isa. 61:6) and kings because of Christ's death for them (Rev. 1:6; 5:10) and the Spirit's work in them (cf. the spiritual resurrection in Ezek. 37:1–14). In Revelation 20, just as the second death is the ultimate punishment of hellfire (v. 14) after the first death of the body, so the first resurrection is a gift of spiritual life before the second resurrection of the body (vv. 12–13). A spiritual resurrection precedes the physical resurrection, as Christ taught (John 5:24–29), for believers are united

---

2. "The Heidelberg Catechism," *The Three Forms of Unity*, 78.

to Him who is the resurrection and the life—even after they die
(John 11:25–26; Col. 3:1–4; cf. Matt. 22:21–32).

The Loosing of Satan

Verses 7–10 describe the loosing of Satan: "And when the thousand
years are expired, Satan shall be loosed out of his prison, and shall
go out to deceive the nations which are in the four quarters of the
earth, Gog and Magog, to gather them together to battle: the number of whom is as the sand of the sea. And they went up on the
breadth of the earth, and compassed the camp of the saints about,
and the beloved city: and fire came down from God out of heaven,
and devoured them. And the devil that deceived them was cast
into the lake of fire and brimstone, where the beast and the false
prophet are, and shall be tormented day and night for ever and ever."

This vision fills out what we were told in verse 3 regarding
Satan's little season. He is to be bound captive for a thousand years
and then released for "a little season." This also agrees with what
the rest of Scripture teaches. In 2 Thessalonians 2, for example, we
are told that a principle of lawlessness ("mystery of iniquity," v. 7)
is already at work, but the man of lawlessness ("that man of sin,"
v. 3), the final embodiment of evil, appears to have not yet arrived.
Something is restraining him. Lawlessness is on a chain. Satan is
bound. Some believers in Thessalonica were so disturbed by reports
of the return of Christ that Paul had to say to them: "No, Christ
is not coming yet. The gospel must be preached first." The Gentiles
need to be gathered in. But when that which restrains and curtails
the power of Satan is removed, then the man of lawlessness will
come and there will be a falling away—an apostasy. Then Christ
will come.

To summarize, Revelation 20:7–10 says that at the end of this
age, when the church has completed its mission, the Lord will grant
the devil a short time (v. 3) to rally the wicked for a final assault on
God's people (2 Thess. 2:1–11; Rev. 11:7–10; 16:12–16). The sequence
of chapters 20–21 corresponds to Ezekiel's visions of the spiritual
resurrection of Israel and its reunification under the Davidic king

in the new covenant (Rev. 20:4–6; Ezekiel 36–37); the attack of an international enemy against God's peaceful people (*Gog*, Rev. 20:7–9; Ezekiel 38–39); and the return of God's glory to a new temple (Revelation 21; Ezekiel 40–48). That attack is summarized here, as it also is in previous cycles of Revelation (16:17–21; 19:17–21).

Scripture is not referring to an actual military battle, but is using warfare as an image for persecution (12:17) against the church, symbolized as Israel in the wilderness of testing (Ex. 14:19–20; Deut. 23:14; cf. Rev. 12:6, 14) and as Jerusalem (Ps. 87:2–3; Isa. 66:10) surrounded by enemies from all nations. The church may be overwhelmed by the number of her enemies (Josh. 11:4; Judg. 7:12; 1 Sam. 13:5) and their threat to extinguish God's promises to the patriarchs (Gen. 22:17; 32:12; 1 Kings 4:20). But when Christ returns, supernatural intervention in judgment will deliver the church and destroy her enemies, to the glory of God (2 Kings 1:10–14; Ezek. 38:22–23; 39:6; 2 Thess. 1:6–10; 2:8). Just as wicked rulers and false teachers will be damned to hell (Rev. 19:20), so Satan (v. 2) will be condemned to everlasting torment (14:11; 19:3).

Summary

First, this last vision of Revelation is a picture of the church at the end of the age. It is a beautiful picture. Verse 9 says the church is both "the camp of the saints…and the beloved city." We need to hold on to this truth. We will see more of the beloved city in the last few chapters. But we must remember this vision for now, for there is room for neither defeatism nor triumphalism in our attitude. In this world, we have no continuing city. In this world, we are pilgrims and strangers, encamped for a time as we journey to another country. There is something fragile and vulnerable about a camp. That is what the church is like in the world. This is also how the church will appear at the end of the age. Yet this same church is also an indestructible city with foundations, whose builder and maker is God.

Second, there is a great disparity between the thousand years of gospel advance and the short season of Satan's activity. That is one reason why we are told that the time of gospel advance is a "thousand years." We are not to be pessimistic about the future. We are not to say, "Things are only going to get worse and worse, and when Christ comes He will find hardly any Christians left on earth." For a thousand years, the gospel will advance; a significant remnant from nation after nation will fall to the good news. Myriads of people from all nations will be gathered into the church. Satan is bound at the present time for this very purpose. And his release will be brief.

Third, in the process of Satan's release, there will be a marvelous interruption. In John's vision, as Gog and Magog gathered to battle against the saints, "fire came down from God out of heaven, and devoured them. And the devil that deceived them was cast into the lake of fire and brimstone, where the beast and the false prophet are, and shall be tormented day and night for ever and ever" (vv. 9b–10). We can thank God for this great assurance that all the forces marshaled against the church will one day be destroyed. Satan, the beast, the false prophet, and all who have worshiped them will be overthrown and tossed into the lake of fire. The gates of hell shall not prevail against the church.

Three Conclusions

First, though the church suffers on earth, Christ's kingdom is already here. Satan was defeated once and for all at the cross and empty tomb. Still, Christians today live with the paradox that they are conquering Satan spiritually even as he seems to conquer them physically. The outward man perishes, while the inward man is renewed day by day (2 Cor. 4:16). Yet the worst thing that this world can inflict upon us—death—can only usher us into the heavenly company of the saints who reign on high with Christ. Therefore, let us not fear for the church or for ourselves, since we belong to Christ in life and in death.

Second, though Christians should not expect all the nations to get better and better until the coming of Christ, we should pray and labor to bring the lives of people and nations under the power of the gospel so that they may walk in the light of God's Word and be prepared for Christ's return. Let us pray and labor incessantly for reformation and revival, even as we remember that Christ's return will be a cataclysmic reversal of all this world has known. The book of Revelation warns us that at the end of the age, the godly will become more godly even as lawlessness and rebellion against God will spiral out of control. Christians must prepare themselves with a hope that is realistic, idealistic, and optimistic.

Third, judgment day will demonstrate the truth of Jesus' statement, "By their fruits ye shall know them" (Matt. 7:20). What do your fruits and works say about who you are? Do they certify that you are a genuine believer in Christ, saved by His blood?

32

The Great White Throne

REVELATION 20:11–15

And I saw a great white throne, and him that sat on it, from whose face the earth and the heaven fled away; and there was found no place for them. And I saw the dead, small and great, stand before God; and the books were opened: and another book was opened, which is the book of life: and the dead were judged out of those things which were written in the books, according to their works. And the sea gave up the dead which were in it; and death and hell delivered up the dead which were in them: and they were judged every man according to their works. And death and hell were cast into the lake of fire. This is the second death. And whosoever was not found written in the book of life was cast into the lake of fire.

In the Gospels, Jesus uses a variety of images to describe the final judgment. In Matthew 13, He speaks about sifting wheat from weeds. In the same chapter, He speaks about sorting good fish from bad. In Matthew 25, He speaks about separating sheep from goats. But here in Revelation 20, the imagery is taken from a court of law.

Revelation 20:13 includes the stupendous declaration of the resurrection of the dead. In verse 11, John sees "the earth and the heaven," or the sky above the earth, flee from the face of the One seated on the great white throne. The world that seemed so substantial and important fades into irrelevance. All that matters now are the great white throne and the verdict about to be rendered by the One who occupies that throne. The day of resurrection is the day of judgment. For some, it is a resurrection to eternal life, through Jesus Christ. Robed in the perfect righteousness of Christ, these blessed ones appear before His judgment seat without terror. For others, it is the resurrection of damnation (John 5:29). For them, there is no blessing in being summoned to appear before this throne, for it is the embodiment of all their worst fears. They have gone all their days in the way of sin, unbelieving and impenitent, and now it is too late to turn back. There is nothing to hide them from the wrath of the Lamb. This is the grand picture presented in Revelation 20:11–15.

Let us look at the final judgment before the great white throne under three headings: the judge on this throne, the judged before this throne, and the judgment from this throne.

The Judge on the Great White Throne

John says in verse 11, "And I saw a great white throne, and him that sat on it, from whose face the earth and the heaven fled away; and there was found no place for them." The portion of Scripture before us is unspeakably solemn. Though cloaked in symbolic language, it speaks of the final day, when we all must appear before God's great white throne. The bodies of all who have died will be raised from death and reunited with their souls for this great event. As the Westminster Confession (33.1) says, "All persons who have lived upon earth shall appear before the tribunal of Christ, to give an account of their thoughts, words, and deeds, and to receive according to what they have done in the body, whether good or evil."[1]

The Judge on the throne is Christ Jesus (Acts 17:31). Jesus Himself confirms that in many other places. For example, in Matthew 25:31–32, He says, "When the Son of man shall come in his glory, and all the holy angels with him, then shall he sit upon the throne of his glory: and before him shall be gathered all nations: and he shall separate them one from another, as a shepherd divideth his sheep from the goats." There can be no doubt that Jesus is speaking about Himself here.

1. *Reformed Confessions of the Sixteenth and Seventeenth Centuries*, 4:271.

Notice that the One who sits on the great white throne is a *man*. This means the judgment is to be *humane*. No one will be able to say on that day, "He doesn't know what it is like to be human; the Judge is out of touch." No one will say that because Christ Jesus, who became man for us, is the One who will judge us. He took our nature on Himself, was touched by our infirmities, and was tempted in every point as we are, "yet without sin" (Heb. 4:15). The fact that He will judge us should comfort God's people. As Calvin says, "It is no inconsiderable security that we shall stand before no other tribunal that that of our Redeemer."[2]

John sees this Judge seated upon a throne that is both great and white. Let us look at what each of these symbols represents:

First, in Scripture, a throne speaks of *great judgment*. Psalm 9:7b says, "He hath prepared His throne for judgment." In a court of law, places are prepared for the judge and for the accused. Though you and I may not be ready, God's throne will be fully prepared for judgment. We must all appear before that throne, according to God's appointment.

Second, a throne speaks of *great authority*. The Second Person of the divine Trinity, clothed with our nature, will be visible to all of us. John says, "I saw...him that sat on it" (Rev. 10:11a). Christ has been appointed and anointed, and is thereby qualified to sit on this throne by the command of His Father: "Yet have I set my king upon my holy hill of Zion" (Ps. 2:6).

If you have not yet bowed before the authority of the King of kings, consider that Jesus Christ will judge you from this throne. John 5:22 says, "For the Father judgeth no man, but hath committed all judgment unto the Son." The day is coming when the very Christ whom you have spurned will sit on His great white throne as the Judge appointed by almighty Jehovah. If you by grace do not

---

2. Calvin, *Institutes*, 2.16.18. See John Calvin, *Institutes of the Christian Religion*, trans. John Allen (New-Haven: Hezekiah Howe; Philadelphia: Philip H. Nicklin, 1816), 1:564.

turn to Christ and repent before that great day, you will have nothing to look forward to but a fearful judgment.

Third, a throne speaks of *great royalty*. A throne is for a king, and Christ judges as part of His kingly office. Isaiah unites Christ's royalty with His judgment, saying, "The LORD is our judge, the LORD is our lawgiver, the LORD is our king" (Isa. 33:22).

This is important because when a person appears before a lower-court judge, he can appeal his ruling to a higher court. In the United States, this appeal process can proceed up to the Supreme Court, where nine justices determine the case with finality. Christ is a one-man Supreme Court. There is no court above His own, for He judges as King of kings. He tells us that at the final judgment, "Then shall *the King* say…" (Matt. 25:34).

This King still goes forth in the chariot of the gospel to conquer unruly sinners. As He rides in majesty and splendor, He subdues His people, causing them to submit to Him and cast themselves upon His mercy. In the same kingly office, on the last day, He will cast away all the enemies of the believer.

Fourth, a throne implies a *great summons*. You and I will be royally summoned on the last day to the royal throne of judgment. This summons will be unavoidable. It will go to every person who has ever lived, including you and your children. Verse 11 says that the heavens and earth will flee away from this great white throne and Him that sits on it, but not one of us will be able to flee from it. "It is appointed unto men once to die, but after this the judgment" (Heb. 9:27).

Fifth, a throne speaks of *great condemnation*. If you are not in Christ, the day of judgment will be a day of condemnation. You will be consigned to everlasting fire and torment, together with the devil and his angels.

You may try to ignore this warning, but you will not be able to put it out of your mind on that day. If you are not in Christ, you will cry out to the mountains and rocks: "Fall on us, and hide us from the face of him that sitteth on the throne, and from the wrath of the Lamb" (Rev. 6:16).

When the great day of His wrath comes, His face, which has turned to you hundreds and thousands of times in the gospel, declaring on God's behalf, "I have no pleasure in your death, but that you should repent and live" (cf. Ezek. 33:11), will turn away from you.

Sixth, a throne speaks of *great glory*. Christ says in Matthew 25:31, "When the Son of man shall come in *his glory*, and all the holy angels with him, then shall he sit upon the throne of *his glory*."

While on this earth, Christ was in the state of His humiliation. His glory was largely veiled in the manger; in life, when He had no place to lay His head; in His passion, when He hung upon the cursed tree; and in death, when His body was laid in a tomb. Some, by faith, beheld His glory, "the glory as of the only begotten of the Father,) full of grace and truth" (John 1:14). But when Christ sits on His throne as Judge, His glory will shine forth for all to see.

In this world, Christ was despised and rejected of men, but that is no longer true, and it will not be true on the day of His glory. He who hung on the cross as a criminal will sit on the throne of glory. Then, every knee shall bow before His throne and every tongue confess that He is Lord. "Behold, he cometh with clouds; and every eye shall see him" (Rev. 1:7).

Seventh, the throne is *greatly personal*. John says, "I saw a great white throne, and him that sat on it." The throne belongs to Christ. He will judge all people on the basis of their relationship to Him. He will judge them on the basis of His laws, His gospel, His role as Mediator, and His work as Prophet, Priest, and King.

On the last day, Christ will tell you personally what He thinks of you, and this will be directly related to what you think of Him. When your thoughts of Christ are put on the scales of heaven on the great day of days, will they be worthy of Christ?

Pilate said to the Jews, "Behold your king!" (John 19:14) as He presented Jesus to be crucified, but you will one day behold this King in glory. Do not put off bending the knee to Him, saying, "I will pledge allegiance to Thee, but not yet." If you die without making that choice by Spirit-worked grace and appear before the King of kings, He will cast you into hell.

Eighth, this throne is still a *throne of grace*. During the days of the gospel, the Lord invites us to come to His throne, where He dispenses grace instead of judgment. As Acts 5:31 says, at this throne of grace, Christ offers repentance and forgiveness of sins. Here, He opens blind eyes and unstops deaf ears. Here, He calls out, "Come unto me, all ye that labour and are heavy laden, and I will give you rest" (Matt. 11:28).

O sinner, flee to the throne of grace. Come to Christ, leaning upon the merits of Christ. As Hebrews 4:16 says, "Let us therefore come boldly unto the throne of grace, that we may obtain mercy, and find grace to help in time of need."

Ask the Spirit of God to draw you to the throne of grace, so that you simply *must* come. Ask Him to convict you of sin, to show you your need of grace, and to draw you into the welcoming arms of Christ. Come to the throne of grace before you are dragged to the throne of judgment.

Those Judged before the Great White Throne

In Revelation 20:11, John says he sees a *great* throne. The throne is great not only because of the greatness of the Lord Jesus Christ as the Judge who sits upon it, but also because of the greatness of the scope of His authority to judge. *Everyone* will appear before this throne on the day of judgment.

We are told in verses 12–13: "And I saw the dead, small and great, stand before God; and the books were opened: and another book was opened, which is the book of life: and the dead were judged out of those things which were written in the books, according to their works. And the sea gave up the dead which were in it; and death and hell delivered up the dead which were in them: and they were judged every man according to their works."

When the Son of man comes again, everyone will hear His voice. Those who are in the grave will be raised, some to life and others to condemnation. Everyone will be present before the great white throne. Verse 12 says we shall "stand before God" and see Him with our own eyes. Each person will be raised, not with someone else's body, but with the body he or she had or has now. It will be transformed for eternity, but it will be the same body. In your flesh, you will see the Judge on that last day. We will all be there in our bodies before the judgment throne of Christ, to give an account of what we have done with our lives.

Christians will not escape the scrutiny of God. The Bible says that we will all be called to account at the great white throne. If the sins of believers will be recalled in that day, however, it will only be done in the context of God's amazing grace to His own glory. We will not be condemned, because Christ is our Savior; nevertheless, we will be there. That ought to wake us up as Christians. We can't sit back comfortably and say, "Well, I'm a Christian; this coming day of judgment has nothing to do with me." That's not true; we will all be there.

Understanding this great throne of judgment should motivate us also to bring the gospel to the lost. Knowing that our friends and relatives, as well as our neighbors and the people we work with, will have to appear before the great tribunal of Christ should make us eager to invite them to come to Christ now. The certainty of judgment and the terror of the Lord ought to make us urgently persuasive.

The Judgment from the Great White Throne

The throne John sees is also great because of what will happen on what Peter calls "that great and notable day of the Lord" (Acts 2:20). Revelation 6:17 speaks of "the great day of his wrath [that] is come."

Some people speak about great days they have experienced. "We had such a good time when we went to that place," they say. "It was a great day." But what do they think about *the* great day? This great day will make every other great day seem insignificant.

First, there will be *great surprises* on that day. The Lord Jesus will come as a thief in the night, when people are eating and drinking, marrying and giving one another in marriage. As in the days of Noah, when the flood came, and in the days of Lot, when Sodom and Gomorrah were destroyed by fire and brimstone, people will be surprised when the Son of Man returns to earth. Like death—which is always a surprise, even when it is expected—so will this last great day be.

Second, there will be *great sounds*: a great noise, a great shout, and the sound of the great, last trumpet. The heavens and earth will add to this noise as they are consumed with fire.

Third, Christ will come with *a great host of attendants* and with *great glory*. He will come with thousands upon thousands of holy angels and with the souls of just men made perfect.

Fourth, when Christ comes, as verse 11 tells us, there will be a *great renewal*. "The earth and the heaven" will flee from His face. In the new creation, the universe will be renewed, but not replaced. Simon Kistemaker writes: "Scripture teaches a meltdown of the elements but not their elimination.... Not creation itself but the defects of the old order are removed to make place for the new."[3] When Christ comes in the clouds, there will be, as Hendriksen writes, "a dissolution of the elements with great heat (2 Peter 3:10); regeneration (Matt. 19:28); restoration of all things (Acts 3:21); and deliverance from the corruption of bondage (Rom. 8:21)."[4]

Fifth, a *great gathering* shall take place around the great throne. All the generations of people, from Adam to the last person on earth, will be present. No one will be excused.

Sixth, the judged will be brought before the *greatest judgment*. Man's judgments and God's judgments in this world will pale in comparison to this final judgment. It will be the *judgment of all judgments*.

Seventh, this judgment will have *great jurisdiction*. In this world, a court has a limited jurisdiction. United States courts cannot preside over foreign countries and their courts. But the great throne presides over all the inhabitants of the earth. All men and all devils must appear before this throne to have their deeds exposed before the living Judge.

---

3. Kistemaker, *Revelation*, 546.
4. Hendriksen, *More than Conquerors*, 196.

Eighth, God will summon *great witnesses* in this judgment. God Himself will be a witness against us if we are outside of Christ. He says to the ungodly in Malachi 3:5, "And I will come near to you to judgment; and I will be a swift witness against…[those who] fear not me."

If you, in your self-righteousness, say, "Well, I'm not as bad as others; I will just do my best and hope that God won't condemn me," you will be lost. Weighed in the balances of God's law, no one will stand before Him. Our own consciences will accuse us, Romans 1 says. Christ and the gospel will also testify against us. The very blood of Calvary will witness against us if we do not surrender to Christ in repentance and faith.

Ninth, Christ's throne is also called great because a *great separation* shall be made before it: the sheep will be placed on the right hand of Christ and the goats on the left. From this great throne, a great gulf will be fixed between those in glory and those in hell. Those in glory shall never leave glory. Those in hell shall never escape hell.

The sheep will be assessed on that day, but they will not enter into condemnation. Rather, the great Judge shall proclaim: "Come, ye blessed of my Father, inherit the kingdom prepared for you from the foundation of the world" (Matt. 25:34). His sheep will enjoy perfect blessedness for all eternity.

The goats will hear of their great condemnation. The great Judge will proclaim: "Depart from me, ye cursed, into everlasting fire, prepared for the devil and his angels" (Matt. 25:41). They shall experience condemnation in hell for all eternity because of their wickedness. Instead of perfect blessedness, they will know unmitigated misery for all the ungodly deeds that they have committed against God.

Revelation 20:12–13 says we will be judged on the basis of what we have done in life: "And I saw the dead, small and great, stand before God; and the books were opened: and another book was opened, which is the book of life: and the dead were judged out of those things which were written in the books, according to their works. And the sea gave up the dead which were in it; and death and hell delivered up the dead which were in them: and they were judged every man according to their works."

These books are symbols of God's divine memory. That means that all you and I have ever thought, said, or done is on record. We tend to forget things over time, so we find it hard to believe that God does not forget. But it is nothing for the infinite God to remember all the thoughts, words, and events of your life. On that day, the books of God's memory of your life will be opened.

Jesus said in Luke 12:2–3: "For there is nothing covered, that shall not be revealed; neither hid, that shall not be known. Therefore whatsoever ye have spoken in darkness shall be heard in the light; and that which ye have spoken in the ear in closets shall be proclaimed upon the housetops." On judgment day, every thought, word, and deed will flash past us when the books are opened.

It is wrong to tell people that they will be judged only according to whether or not they have received Jesus Christ. When Christ comes to judge the living and the dead, He will also open the books of believers' lives and judge them according to what they have done. Revelation 20:12–13 indicates that God applies one standard to all, rendering to every man according to his works (Rom. 2:6), and that one standard is His moral law, written upon the human heart at creation, engraved so deeply that sin has never entirely effaced it (Rom. 2:13–15). The law can be obeyed only by a regenerated believer who does his works according to the spirit of the law (love for God and neighbor), by true faith, and for God's glory. Such good works provide evidence of God's sanctifying grace in the believer as a fruit of the believer's justification in Christ.

The Lord will judge all people *according to their works*, not because salvation is by works (Eph. 2:8–9), but because salvation produces works (Eph. 2:10). Therefore, works demonstrate whether or not a person is chosen and redeemed by God (Rev. 3:5; 13:8; 17:8; 20:12, 15; 21:27; cf. Eph. 1:4; 1 Thess. 1:2–10; 2 Thess. 2:13). Our sanctification visualizes our election. That's why Jesus said, "By their fruits ye shall know them" (Matt. 7:20).

Happily, however, these good works give evidence that believers have been truly justified by free and sovereign grace through Christ's blood alone. So our eternal destiny does not depend upon the perfection or number of our good works, but only upon God's grace to us in Christ Jesus.

The other book mentioned in Revelation 20 is the Book of Life. We are told in verse 15 that "whosoever was not found written in the book of life was cast into the lake of fire." In other words, the question of your destiny, from God's perspective, depends on whether or not your name is written in the Book of Life. There are two books: the book of your life, which has smudges, blots, and cross-outs on every page; and the Book of Life, in which you are presented in Christ as perfect and spotless. Are you listed in the Book of Life?

What a comfort it is to know that if you have truly repented and believed in Christ alone for salvation, you may stand without dread when God opens the book of your life, for He will read only "Christ" on its pages. In Psalm 32:1–2, David celebrates the blessedness of being justified in Christ: "Blessed is he whose transgression is forgiven," that is, for the sake of Christ alone; "whose sin is covered," that is, by the atonement provided in the death of Christ for sinners; and "blessed is the man unto whom the LORD imputeth not iniquity," that is, because He imputes to us the perfect righteousness of Christ, His Son, our Redeemer (cf. Rom. 4:6–8).

Tenth, from this throne shall flow *great salvation*. The Christ who sits on this great throne as the great Judge is a great Savior, a great God, and a great Redeemer. His salvation is so great that He is able to save the greatest of sinners. Cry to Almighty God to give this great salvation to you, though you are a great sinner. Pray with David, "For thy name's sake, O LORD, pardon mine iniquity; for it is great" (Ps. 25:11).

Eleventh and finally, this throne has *great whiteness*. The Bible often refers to whiteness, especially regarding Christ's second coming. Christ will come on a white cloud, we are told. He will ride a white horse. White is a symbol of four attributes, the first three being attributes of God.

1. White is symbolic of *righteousness*. "Shall not the Judge of all the earth do right?" Scripture asks (Gen. 18:25). When Christ sits down on this white throne, He will do what is right. Thus, the whiteness of this throne is an indication to us of the *righteous character of the Judge.*

The Lord's judgments will also be clear, with no mixture of bias or vanity, and no "respect of persons" (Rom. 2:11). David confesses in Psalm 51:4, "Against thee, thee only, have I sinned, and done this evil in thy sight: that thou mightest be justified when thou speakest, and be clear when thou judgest." The Lord's judgment will be so clear that no one will be able to say that it is unfair. Every conscience will agree with His judgment. "The judgments of the LORD are true and righteous altogether" (Ps. 19:9).

2. White is symbolic of *holiness*. Christ's judgment will be holy: "God sitteth upon the throne of his holiness" (Ps. 47:8). He will be holy in consigning the goats to condemnation. He will also be holy in granting acquittal to His sheep. But are not the elect just as guilty of sin as the others? Are they not just as fallen in Adam? Have they not done, spoken, and thought the same sinful things? Yes, they have. How, then, can Christ be perfectly righteous and holy in admitting them into heaven? They will be accepted only because all their sins have been blotted out through Christ's atoning blood.

3. White is symbolic of *justice*. Revelation 20:12 says there is another book: the Lamb's Book of Life. Those whose names are written in this book will be dressed in white and gathered to Christ's right hand as His sheep on judgment day. They will have received grace to wash their garments in Christ's blood. As Revelation 7:13–15 says: "And one of the elders answered, saying unto me, What are these which are arrayed in white robes? and whence came they? And I said unto him, Sir, thou knowest. And he said to me, These are they which came out of great tribulation, and have washed their robes, and made them white in the blood of the Lamb. Therefore are they before the throne of God."

The Judge, who is also the Lamb, has provided all they needed to cleanse their garments. Christ can now smile upon them, for justice itself can find no fault with sinners who have washed their robes in the blood of the Lamb. Indeed, justice would be at fault in condemning them, for the price of their sins has already been paid.

4. White is a color of *conspicuousness*. A white throne is conspicuous in its brightness and majesty. On the last great day, when there will be much confusion as heaven and earth pass away, God's great white throne will be the object of every eye. John says in Revelation 1 that when the Lord Jesus Christ comes again in judgment, no one will miss seeing the great King-Lamb upon the throne (v. 7).

If you would see Jesus Christ vindicate you from His great white throne one day, do not rest until you are moved by the Spirit to believe in Him alone for salvation. Let this be your prayer: "How solemn Thy Word is, O God! Prepare us for Him who shall sit upon the great white throne on the great last day, judging with white righteousness. Oh, wash us in the blood of the Redeemer! Make our robes white in the redeeming blood of Christ's righteousness."

33

Utopia: Life in the World to Come

REVELATION 21:1–8

And I saw a new heaven and a new earth: for the first heaven and the first earth were passed away; and there was no more sea. And I John saw the holy city, new Jerusalem, coming down from God out of heaven, prepared as a bride adorned for her husband. And I heard a great voice out of heaven saying, Behold, the tabernacle of God is with men, and he will dwell with them, and they shall be his people, and God himself shall be with them, and be their God. And God shall wipe away all tears from their eyes; and there shall be no more death, neither sorrow, nor crying, neither shall there be any more pain: for the former things are passed away. And he that sat upon the throne said, Behold, I make all things new. And he said unto me, Write: for these words are true and faithful. And he said unto me, It is done. I am Alpha and Omega, the beginning and the end. I will give unto him that is athirst of the fountain of the water of life freely. He that overcometh shall inherit all things; and I will be his God, and he shall be my son. But the fearful, and unbelieving, and the abominable, and murderers, and whoremongers, and sorcerers, and idolaters, and all liars, shall have their part in the lake which burneth with fire and brimstone: which is the second death.

The Last Battle is the last book in C. S. Lewis's *Chronicles of Narnia*. The final chapter, titled "Farewell to Shadow Land," includes these words:

> The things that began to happen after that were so great and beautiful that I cannot write them. And for us this is the end of all the stories, and we can most truly say that they all lived

happily ever after. But for them it was only the beginning of the real story. All their life in this world and all their adventures in Narnia had only been the cover and the title page: now at last they were beginning Chapter One of the Great Story which no one on earth has read, which goes on forever: in which every chapter is better than the one before.[1]

That sums up the message of the closing chapters in the book of Revelation. We have now moved out of the shadow land. Satan, the beast, the false prophet, and all who have worshiped and followed them are no longer threatening enemies. They have been thrown into the lake of fire. This is the beginning of a new age for the seed of the woman. As Lewis writes: "It is the dawning of a new day. The dream has ended: this is the morning."[2]

In 1513, Sir Thomas More introduced a new word into the English language: *utopia*. He used the word to describe an imaginary island with a perfect society and political system. People have always dreamed about a perfect society. Only a century ago, people dared to believe that such a golden age was just around the corner, only to have their hopes dashed by two world wars and the threat of a third.

Yet, for true believers, utopia is not an idle dream. The message of the Bible is that God is already working to bring us into the new age of His perfect society, known as the kingdom of God. We have had some foretastes of it already in this life. Hebrews 6 speaks of our tasting "the powers of the world to come" (v. 5). The author of Hebrews is not talking only about Christians. He is also talking about nominal Christians, who are deceived about their Christianity. But they too sit under the preaching of the gospel and mingle with true Christians. So they also have tasted "the powers of the world to come." Whenever the gospel is preached in the power of the Spirit, it foretokens the age to come.

---

1. C. S. Lewis, *The Last Battle*, The Chronicles of Narnia, Book 7 (New York: HarperCollins, 2000), 210–11.

2. Lewis, *The Last Battle*, 210.

In expounding Revelation 21:1–8, our focus will be on verse 5a: "And he that sat upon the throne said, Behold, I make all things new." We will consider the theme "Utopia: Life in the World to Come" under three questions: "Whose utopia is it?"; "What is going to happen?"; and "Who is going to be there?"

Whose Utopia Is It?

We are talking about *God's utopia* here, not man's, because only God can make all things new. People imagine that with better education, a better environment, better legislation, or a more equitable distribution of wealth, they can usher in a new era—a golden age. But God is saying to us in Revelation 21, "I make all things new. You can't do it. With all your institutions, political parties, think tanks, pressure groups, international councils, and other resources, you cannot make this world new." Only God can renew and restore people, as well as society and the universe in which we live.

In a sense, God is already bringing in His new creation. In 2 Corinthians 5:17, Paul says, "Therefore if any man be in Christ, he is a new creature [literally, a new creation]: old things are passed away; behold, all things are become new." When a person is converted—born again by the Spirit of God and brought to saving faith in the Lord Jesus Christ—he becomes a new creation.

This rebirth is as amazing as what happened at the very beginning of time, when God spoke the world into existence. Whenever people are saved, God makes things new. That is the only hope for our world. We should never despise the miracle of the new birth as though it were only the beginning—as if there were much greater things for us to experience or possess. There is nothing greater than what happened to you when you became a Christian. Don't dare ever despise that! Don't dare to forget what happened to you. When you turned from your sins to Jesus Christ, there was a new creation. Indeed, we need to remind ourselves that, in fact, this is the only hope for our world. Society can be truly and permanently changed only when individuals are changed by the power of the gospel.

Some historians say times of great revival, such as the Reformation or the Great Awakening, did a great deal to save countries from many terrors. England, for example, experienced the Evangelical Awakening in the middle of the eighteenth century. This revival spared the country from the bloody revolution that took place in France at the end of that century. The Awakening was a revival of true religion. During this time, God empowered the preaching of the Word to convict multitudes of sinners of their need for salvation, and the whole society was changed.

The gospel makes things new; it rectifies the evils of the world. I suppose one of the greatest evils in New Testament times was slavery. Yet nowhere in the New Testament does Paul directly address this issue. He was not in favor of slavery (1 Cor. 7:22), but he viewed the gospel as the preeminent answer to slavery. In Paul's letter to Philemon regarding the slave Onesimus, Paul expressed his confidence in the power of the gospel to change the relationship between masters and their slaves.

Today, one of the greatest moral issues is abortion. The legalized killing of unborn babies in our country and around the world is an abomination. We can react to this by staging demonstrations or drawing up petitions—and it is right to do so. But the only real hope to rid our society of that kind of evil is through the preaching of the gospel in the Spirit's power. You can't stop abortions merely by legislation or even by overturning the Supreme Court's Roe v. Wade decision—as great as that would be. People's hearts need to be changed, and God alone can do that. So we ought to be praying for reformation and revival from the Spirit of God.

But all this is only a small beginning of what John is describing. He is not speaking of the regeneration of a few individuals. He is talking about the renewal of the entire universe. On the last day, when Christ comes again to judge the living and the dead, the old will pass away and the new creation will come.

What Is Going to Happen?

In Revelation 21:1, John says, "I saw a new heaven and a new earth: for the first heaven and the first earth were passed away; and there was no more sea." This transformation will take place in an instant. In the previous chapter, we are told that when the Lord comes in judgment, earth and sky, here called "the first heaven and the first earth," will flee from His presence. Peter tells us in his epistle that "the heavens shall pass away with a great noise, and the elements shall melt with fervent heat, the earth also and the works that are therein shall be burned up" (2 Peter 3:10). This world will be consumed by fire on that last day. Yet the moment heaven and earth are destroyed, they will be replaced by a new heaven and a new earth.

Jesus tells us in Matthew 19:28, "Verily I say unto you, That ye which have followed me, in the regeneration when the Son of man shall sit in the throne of his glory, ye also shall sit upon twelve thrones, judging the twelve tribes of Israel." Jesus is talking about the future age, about His return. He is saying: "When all things are made new, when the Son of man will sit on the throne of His glory, then you who have followed Me in regeneration shall sit upon twelve thrones. The whole earth will be changed, and I will reign; and you will be with Me."

When someone is born again, he becomes a new person, but he does not become another person. You say, "That person is new; there is something different about him." Yet he is the same person. His basic personality and temperament have not changed. Jesus says that when He returns to earth, all things will be regenerated; they will be made new, but not altogether different. It will be a transformed world, but we Christians won't find ourselves in an alien order of being on that day. We won't find ourselves in a world that is totally and absolutely different from the world in which we now live. We will find ourselves in a recognizable environment. It will be a physical world, because we are and still will be physical creatures. We believe in the bodily resurrection. The graves will be opened and these bodies will be raised and reconstituted. We will be physically alive in a physical world when Jesus comes. And that world will bear resemblance to the world in which we now live.

Peter describes this transformation in Acts 3:19–21: "Repent ye therefore, and be converted, that your sins may be blotted out, when the times of refreshing shall come from the presence of the Lord; and he shall send Jesus Christ, which before was preached unto you: whom the heaven must receive until the times of restitution of all things, which God hath spoken by the mouth of all his holy prophets since the world began." Do you see what Peter is saying? He says, "If you read your Old Testament, you will clearly see that the prophets have been saying since the world began that there is going to be a consummation and restoration of all things." Peter's message is that at the end of time, when Jesus comes again, God is going to restore this world to what He intended it to be. This world is not going to be obliterated or destroyed altogether, but it will be regenerated. It will be renewed. Since the world began, prophets have been predicting that a day will come when everything that has been marred by sin will be restored to what God intended it to be. God will burn "this old world with fire and flame to cleanse it" (Belgic Confession, Art. 37).

Romans 8:18–21 says something similar: "For I reckon that the sufferings of this present time are not worthy to be compared with the glory which shall be revealed in us. For the earnest expectation of the creature waiteth for the manifestation of the sons of God. For the creature was made subject to vanity, not willingly, but by reason of him who hath subjected the same in hope, because the creature itself also shall be delivered from the bondage of corruption into the glorious liberty of the children of God." Though now the creation suffers from the effects of the fall, Paul is saying that a time is coming when the creation will be liberated from the curse of sin and radically restored. As believers, we will live in our transformed bodies in a transformed universe full of beauty, complexity, and unspeakable joy.

John says God will be everywhere present in this new world. He writes: "I John saw the holy city, new Jerusalem, coming down from God out of heaven, prepared as a bride adorned for her husband. And I heard a great voice out of heaven saying, Behold, the tabernacle of God is with men, and he will dwell with them, and they shall be his people, and God himself shall be with them, and be their God" (Rev. 21:2–3). In addition to a new heaven and a new earth, John sees a new Jerusalem, the bride of Christ. And God will be everywhere in this restored universe; as John says, "the tabernacle of God is with men." The tabernacle is no longer out in a wilderness in the backside of a desert. The tabernacle is no longer in Shiloh or Jerusalem. Now the dwelling place of God, the Holy Place and the Holy of Holies, fills the earth. And there is no land, no place, and no time in this new age where God is not.

Sometimes at work, you forget about God, and that grieves you. But there will be no activity in the new age in which God will not be manifestly present to you. There will not be a moment without the presence of God. Our darkest moments as Christians are when we feel like the heavens are as brass (Deut. 28:23). The Puritans used to talk about the "dark night of the soul," when God withdraws Himself from the consciousness of His people. There will be no times like that in the new age, for the Lord will dwell with His people all the time.

John adds something very personal and human: "And there was no more sea" (Rev. 21:1b). As a prisoner on an island, John constantly heard the sound of crashing waves, the cry of wild birds in the sky, and the roar of thunder. The sea formed the walls of his prison. It separated him from everyone he loved in Christ. In the distance, he could see mountains on the mainland. He knew that the people he loved in the seven churches of Asia were there. But the sea prevented him from leaving the island. Now God says to him: "John, in the new age, there will be no more sea for you. There will be no more goodbyes, no more separations, and no more broken fellowship. You will no longer suffer isolation, persecution, pain, or suffering for the sake of Christ. It will be a world where there will be none of this, where you will dwell with Me." Or, as John saw it, "there [will be] no more sea."

The description of the new age is given largely in negative terms. In fact, there are seven negative statements in these two chapters. Verse 4 includes four negative statements, the first of which is that there will be no more tears, for "God shall wipe away all tears from their eyes." John goes on to say, "And there shall be no more death, neither sorrow, nor crying, neither shall there be any more pain: for the former things are passed away."

We might go to the doctor, perhaps in pain, only to hear him say: "I'm sorry, there is nothing we can do. You will have to live with this for the rest of your life." Some of you have lost loved ones, and although time does heal, you never get over it completely. You have to live with the loss of your loved one for the rest of your life. But John is saying that a day is coming when you will live without these pains and sorrows. A day is coming when there will be no more death, no more sorrow, no more crying, and no more pain. A day is coming when all of these things will be eradicated, purged from the earth. A day is coming when we no longer will suffer the aching void of loss, the debilitating pain of arthritis, or the humiliation of diseases such as dementia and Alzheimer's. These things shall be no more. As Lewis writes, "Farewell to shadowlands."[3]

This description of the new age, God's utopia, is largely negative because so much of heaven is beyond our understanding. It is easier to say what will not be there than what will be. As 1 Corinthians 2:9 says, "Eye hath not seen, nor ear heard, neither have entered into the heart of man, the things which God hath prepared for them that love him." Notice the phrase "for them that love him." I wonder how many readers of this book that shuts out. Heaven is for those who love God. Do you love Him? I am not asking if you pay Him the respect of coming to church on Sunday. I am asking something much more profound and important. Do you *love* Him? God has prepared this new age for those who love Him. It is illogical for someone to expect to have everything to do with God in the

---

3. Lewis, *The Last Battle*, 198 (title to chapter 16).

next world after having nothing to do with Him in this world. *Do you love Him?*

Who Is Going to Be There?

That brings me to the last point I want to make—*Who is going to be there?* "And he that sat upon the throne said, Behold, I make all things new. And he said unto me, Write: for these words are true and faithful. And he said unto me, It is done. I am Alpha and Omega, the beginning and the end. I will give unto him that is athirst of the fountain of the water of life freely. He that overcometh shall inherit all things; and I will be his God, and he shall be my son. But the fearful, and unbelieving, and the abominable, and murderers, and whoremongers, and sorcerers, and idolaters, and all liars, shall have their part in the lake which burneth with fire and brimstone: which is the second death" (Rev. 21:5–8).

The only people who will live in this new world are those who are joined to Jesus Christ by true faith. God gives them victory over sin and death (1 Cor. 15:57). You are either an *overcomer* (Rev. 21:7) who will inherit all of these things we have been talking about, or else you are one who is *overcome* by sin and by Satan (v. 8), and you will have no part in God's utopia. You will burn in the lake of fire. Some of you know this is true, but you are not prepared to pay the cost of surrendering to Christ. You don't want your comfortable life to be disturbed. You want to do as you see fit. But if you continue to drag your feet, resisting God's will, you will have no place in God's new creation.

You are either an overcomer or you are overcome. All of us by nature are somewhere in verse 8, aren't we? The list includes "the fearful and unbelieving," and this was particularly relevant in John's day, a time of persecution. Fear and unbelief are a deadly combination. People do not yield themselves to God in faith because they are afraid of the consequences. Unbelief is put on a par with the most abominable things, including murder, fornication, sorcery, idolatry, and lying. For example, consider sorcery. Apparently, the Greek word translated as "sorcerer" literally means "dispenser of drugs." I suppose one of the lowest of the low in our society is a drug pusher. You can't get much lower than that. God puts your fearful unbelief on a par with drug dealing!

Perhaps you haven't murdered anyone. Yet Jesus says in His Sermon on the Mount that if you hate your brother or are angry with him without cause, God considers you a murderer (Matt. 5:22). You may not be involved with prostitutes, either. Yet Jesus says that if you so much as look at a woman with lust, you have committed adultery with her in your heart (Matt. 5:28).

The question to ask yourself is: Am I overcome by these things, or have I overcome these things? As long as I am overcome by these things, I will have no place in God's new world. Only "he that overcometh" will inherit glory.

Paul tells how we can overcome these sins in 1 Corinthians 6:9–11: "Know ye not that the unrighteous shall not inherit the kingdom of God? Be not deceived: neither fornicators, nor idolaters, nor adulterers, nor effeminate, nor abusers of themselves with mankind, nor thieves, nor covetous, nor drunkards, nor revilers, nor extortioners, shall inherit the kingdom of God. And such were some of you: but ye are washed, but ye are sanctified, but ye are justified in the name of the Lord Jesus, and by the Spirit of our God." In other words, some of you were overcome by these things, but not anymore. You are no longer overcome, you are overcomers. You have been washed and sanctified by the Spirit. You are justified in Christ. Evil no longer has its grip on you. It did before, but no longer. By the power of God, you have been delivered from the sins that used to dominate your life. You may have been charged with murder; you may have been a drug pusher or a fornicator; you may be guilty of the vilest of sins. But now, justified by faith, you are "righteous in Christ, before God, and an heir of eternal life" (Heidelberg Catechism, Q. 59).[4]

Not only are you pardoned, being justified by faith, but a title is gifted to you as well. Revelation 21:7 says, "He that overcometh

---

4. *The Three Forms of Unity*, 86.

shall inherit all things." God owns you as His child, and all things will be yours. That is no pipe dream, for verse 5 says, "These words are true and faithful." They are trustworthy. You can rest your future on these words, because they are not John's words. They come from the One who sits upon the great white throne. He is the Alpha and Omega, the Beginning and the End of all things.

He is also the Alpha and Omega of our spiritual lives, and what a blessing that is! That truth can give you comfort all the way to the valley of the shadow of death and for all eternity. A few weeks before my God-fearing mother died at age 92, I read Revelation 21 to her. When I came to verse 6, I asked her if she knew what "Alpha and Omega" meant. As soon as I asked the question, I berated myself, thinking: "That was foolish to ask considering that Mother has dementia. Of course she won't know." But she looked at me and said, "Honey"—that was everyone's name, because she couldn't remember anyone's name—"are those the names of Jesus that mean that Jesus is our *A* and our *Z* and everything in between?" "Yes, Mother," I replied, "that's exactly right!" Is Jesus your *A* and *Z* and everything in between, in terms of your salvation? Is He your all in all?

In ancient mythology, the pillars of Hercules at the Straits of Gibraltar bore the warning, *Ne Plus Ultra*, meaning, "nothing more beyond," for across the Atlantic was a great unknown. However, after Christopher Columbus discovered the New World, Emperor Charles V adopted as his motto *Plus Ultra*, meaning "more beyond," which with the pillars of Hercules became the national emblem of Spain. That is the message of the book of Revelation: there is more beyond for all who, by God's grace, confess their sins and come to Jesus Christ for salvation. Death for them will not be what Sir Walter Scott called "the long halt" which closes all.[5] It will rather be like

---

5. David Douglas, ed., *The Journal of Sir Walter Scott, 1825–32*, new ed. (Edinburgh: David Douglas, 1891), 1:325.

what Lewis said: "Chapter One of the Great Story...which goes on forever: in which every chapter is better than the one before."[6]

If you are scurrying about as if this world is the only world there is, listen to the gospel of Jesus Christ and respond to it. Are you clinging to this world, as though this life is the only life that you will ever have? Have you discovered that there is a new world ahead, a new heaven and a new earth? Have your horizons been enlarged by the gospel of Jesus Christ? Fix your eyes on the world that lies just beyond this one, "looking for and hasting unto the coming of the day of God" and looking "for new heavens and a new earth, wherein dwelleth righteousness" (2 Peter 3:12–13).

---

6. Lewis, *The Last Battle*, 211.

34

New Jerusalem

REVELATION 21:9–27

And there came unto me one of the seven angels which had the seven vials full of the seven last plagues, and talked with me, saying, Come hither, I will shew thee the bride, the Lamb's wife. And he carried me away in the spirit to a great and high mountain, and shewed me that great city, the holy Jerusalem, descending out of heaven from God, having the glory of God: and her light was like unto a stone most precious, even like a jasper stone, clear as crystal; and had a wall great and high, and had twelve gates, and at the gates twelve angels, and names written thereon, which are the names of the twelve tribes of the children of Israel.... And the twelve gates were twelve pearls; every several gate was of one pearl: and the street of the city was pure gold, as it were transparent glass. And I saw no temple therein: for the Lord God Almighty and the Lamb are the temple of it. And the city had no need of the sun, neither of the moon, to shine in it: for the glory of God did lighten it, and the Lamb is the light thereof. And the nations of them which are saved shall walk in the light of it: and the kings of the earth do bring their glory and honour into it. And the gates of it shall not be shut at all by day: for there shall be no night there. And they shall bring the glory and honour of the nations into it. And there shall in no wise enter into it any thing that defileth, neither whatsoever worketh abomination, or maketh a lie: but they which are written in the Lamb's book of life.

New Jerusalem is the capital city of the new heaven and earth because it is where God the King dwells. But in an ultimate sense, it is the *only* city. It descends from God and fills the new heaven and earth. It is a vast, cosmopolitan city. Its inhabitants are countless; they are from every tribe, nation, and tongue.

Revelation 21:9–10 says: "And there came unto me one of the seven angels which had the seven vials full of the seven last plagues, and talked with me, saying, Come hither, I will shew thee the bride, the Lamb's wife. And he carried me away in the spirit to a great and high mountain, and shewed me that great city, the holy Jerusalem, descending out of heaven from God." Let us take a walk with the apostle John and explore the New Jerusalem under six headings: the church's origin (vv. 9–10); the church's beauty (vv. 11, 18–21); the church's invulnerability (vv. 12a, 17, 25); the church's universality (vv. 12b–13); the church's foundations (v. 14); and the church's glory (vv. 22–24).

Since this passage is symbolic, we should rid ourselves of any idea of a literal city. Some interpret Revelation literally, but it is wrong to think that this city literally falls from the skies. For one thing, it is too big. If you look at the measurements of the city in verse 16, you see it is twelve thousand furlongs wide, long, and high, which means that it extends fourteen hundred miles in every direction. This city would be half the size of the United States. The city is a symbol, for the angel says to John: "I will shew thee the bride, the Lamb's wife. And he...shewed me that great city, the holy Jerusalem, descending out of heaven from God" (vv. 9–10).

This isn't a picture of a millennial city on earth. This is not even a picture of heaven. This city is the bride, the wife of the Lamb. She is the church triumphant, the perfected, glorified church of Jesus Christ. In this passage, we are not so much looking through a window into the world to come but into a kind of mirror. As members of Christ's body, the church, we see ourselves as we are now in principle and as we shall be hereafter in perfection. We are not only spectators of this vision, but we are also the spectacle itself. We are not merely going to the Celestial City, we *are* the Celestial City. We who believe, together with all the redeemed of the Lord, are represented here. Let us examine this city now, beginning with its origin.

The Church's Origin

Verses 2 and 10 tell us that New Jerusalem comes down from heaven, that is, from God. The Christian church is not a man-made institution. It is not the consequence of the interplay of sociological, economic or other human factors. We can't explain the church in those terms. The church comes from God; it comes down out of heaven.

Every Christian is from heaven in the sense of the supernatural origin of our salvation. Early in His ministry, Christ had a nighttime encounter with Nicodemus, a Pharisee (John 3). Nicodemus had religion, but he did not have Christ. So Jesus said to him, in essence, "Nicodemus, you must be born again. Your religion is all very well and good, but it won't save you. You need something other than religion. You need to be born from above." As the sons of God, Christians are "born, not of blood, nor of the will of the flesh, nor of the will of man, but of God" (John 1:13). As "lively stones" (1 Peter 2:5), we are "builded together for an habitation of God through the Spirit" (Eph. 2:22). Revelation 21 shows us that "habitation of God" coming down from heaven.

In Galatians 1, Paul relates how he became a Christian. He says in verses 15–16a: "It pleased God, who separated me from my mother's womb, and called me by his grace, to reveal his Son in me." Surely there is a great need for us today to stress in our evangelism that Christians can come only from God. They are not the fruit or result of any methods that we might use to reach out with the gospel. Christ is the One who builds His church (Matt. 16:18), and without His work from heaven, we toil in vain to build it on earth (Ps. 127:1).

Today's great need is for ministers, church planters, evangelists, and laypeople to evangelize with the realization that the church is built from above through the means of the gospel. We need God to work the new birth from above in the souls of men, women, teenagers, and children by means of evangelistic efforts that are grounded in His Word and blessed by His Spirit.

The Church's Beauty

The most striking thing about the city is its beauty. Revelation 21:10–11 says, "And he carried me away in the spirit to a great and high mountain, and shewed me that great city, the holy Jerusalem, descending out of heaven from God, having the glory of God: and her light was like unto a stone most precious, even like a jasper stone, clear as crystal." As he looked at the heavenly Jerusalem, John saw her as a city of light, a sparkling jewel, clear as crystal in the distant skies. The light that gave this jewel its extraordinary brilliance was nothing less than the glory of God within her. What a glorious sight that must have been.

Later, verses 18–21 tell us about the many precious stones and metals that adorn this city. The walls are encrusted with them. Every gate is a massive pearl. The buildings, the streets, and even the spaces between are overlaid with the purest gold. Think of all the colors: the deep orange red of sardius, the white jasper, the green emerald, and the blue sapphire. All these precious stones sparkle in the walls and the gates of the city, while the very foundations shimmer with the light of the glory of God.

The colors of the city appear like a rainbow. Earlier in Revelation, after John had seen the vision of the seven churches, he saw a throne set in heaven and the Lamb in the midst of the throne. The throne and the One seated on it were encircled by a rainbow (Rev. 4:3). The rainbow is the sign of God's covenant. And as John sees this city coming out of heaven from God, it is sparkling and shimmering in all the colors of the rainbow. Surely that reminds him of God's grace and God's covenant. You can't have a rainbow unless storm clouds cluster on one side of the sky and sunshine breaks forth out of the other. At Calvary, the storm clouds and sunshine met in the person of Jesus Christ. There, hanging on that Roman gallows, He bore in His body the wrath of the holy God. The storm of God's anger broke around His head and raged in His soul. Yet the sunshine of God's love and mercy was the result of that sacrificial act, for now that love and mercy is promised to those who turn from their sins and trust in the Lord Jesus Christ. So this beautiful rainbow city is full of color and light, full of the glory of God, and full of reminders of the covenant mercy and love of God in Jesus Christ.

That glory is not always so clear to us. When we try to see the church as God sees it and as it will one day be, we mainly see the dark side of the church as it is now, with its shoddy turf wars, theological confusion, power struggles, sinful inconsistencies, and pitifully weak efforts at Christian discipleship.

Then we must remember what Paul says in 1 Corinthians 3:

> I have laid the foundation...let every man take heed how he buildeth thereupon. For other foundation can no man lay than that is laid, which is Jesus Christ. Now if any man build upon this foundation gold, silver, precious stones, wood, hay, stubble; every man's work shall be made manifest: for the day shall declare it, because it shall be revealed by fire; and the fire shall try every man's work of what sort it is. If any man's work abide which he hath built thereupon, he shall receive a reward. If any man's work shall be burned, he shall suffer loss: but he himself shall be saved; yet so as by fire. (vv. 10b–15)

Paul says we must be careful how we build upon the foundation, which is the Christ of Scripture and apostolic testimony. You and I must build upon that foundation by preaching Christ. We are to present the message of the Bible to people all around us. But we must be careful how we do it. We must build up the church with gold, silver, and precious stones, not wood, hay, and stubble.

The most serious objection I have to some types of mass evangelism is "easy believism." Christ's church is built of precious stones, gold, and silver. We must take care that we don't settle for anything less than genuine biblical conversions. The idea that a man can just put up his hand, go to the front of a church, or sign his name on a decision card, then return to his daily life virtually the same as he was before, amounts to building with wood, hay, and stubble.

This also applies to our Christian work and life. So much of our Christian service is giving God second best. We take pains at what we do for ourselves and for others, but in church, anything will do!

REVELATION

That is contrary to what God intends His church to be. His goal is a beautiful church, built with precious stones and shimmering with gold. That is how we should view the church. We should be working to enhance the beauty of Christ's bride. We need to examine everything we say and do by this criteria: is this beautifying God's church?

The Church's Invulnerability

Revelation 21:12a says the New Jerusalem has "a wall great and high" around her, which measured 144 cubits or 216 feet (v. 17). This city has magnificent defenses. Of course, the church in glory doesn't need a wall around it because it doesn't need defending. In verse 25, we are told that all the gates of this city are left open. Perhaps when you were a child, your parents did not lock the doors of your house when they left it or went to bed at night. The area around the house was safe enough to do that. The gates of the heavenly Jerusalem are likewise always open. There is no need to shut them because there is no longer any danger. All the enemies of this city have been cast into the lake of fire. They have been destroyed. There is no night in this city. There is nothing to be afraid of anymore.

So why does the new city have this massive wall? It represents the city's invulnerability. It reminds us of the difference between Paradise lost and Paradise regained. It contrasts the first creation and the new creation.

When Jesus Christ, the second Adam, came to rescue sinners, He didn't come only to return us to "square one." There is more to the gospel. The Bible tells us that where sin abounded, grace abounded much more (Rom. 5:20). Isaac Watts said in his hymn:

> In Him the tribes of Adam boast
> More blessings than their father lost.[1]

---

1. Isaac Watts, "Jesus Shall Reign Where'er the Sun" (1719).

Adam was on probation. There was always the possibility that he would fall. If you and I are in Christ, there is no possibility whatsoever that we will ever be separated from Him.

That ancient serpent somehow insinuated himself into the Garden of Eden, God's earthly Paradise. There were no walls to keep him out. But around the heavenly Jerusalem and the church of Christ, there is a great, high, thick wall. The point is surely this: there is no possibility whatsoever of Satan or any other enemy invading the new creation. No one uninvited will get into New Jerusalem. The walls of God's truth and justice will keep them out. "Walk about Zion, and go round about her: tell the towers thereof. Mark ye well her bulwarks, consider her palaces; that ye may tell it to the generation following. For this God is our God for ever and ever" (Ps. 48:12–14a).

We are better off than Adam if we are in Christ. We are safer than he was, thanks to the work of our second Adam. We are surrounded by a great, high, impenetrable wall, and no serpent will come slithering into the new heaven and earth.

The Church's Universality

Revelation 21:12b–13 says New Jerusalem is a cosmopolitan city: "And [the city] had a wall great and high, and had twelve gates, and at the gates twelve angels [messengers], and names written thereon, which are the names of the twelve tribes of the children of Israel: on the east three gates; on the north three gates; on the south three gates; and on the west three gates."

Written on each gate are the names of three of the twelve tribes of Israel, and these gates are on every side of the city—on the north side, the south side, the east side, and the west side. Messengers stand at the mouth of each gate. This is perfectly in line with the covenant of grace God made with Abraham: "In thy seed shall all the nations of the earth be blessed" (Gen. 22:18). Until Jesus came, the Jewish nation was the guardian and trustee of the gospel. That is why Israel was kept under the Mosaic law, as Paul argues in Galatians 3. And that is why the names of the twelve tribes of Israel are written on the doors of this city. To Israel belong "the adoption, and the glory, and the covenants, and the giving of the law, and the service of God, and the promises," as Paul notes in Romans 9:4. The gospel is a Jewish gospel. Its roots are in the Old Testament, in God's covenant with Abraham and his seed, and yet the blessing of Abraham included reaching out to believers of all nations, to the north, south, east, and west. The gates of the city face every direction and are open to all types of people.

Revelation 21 presents us with the church as God sees it. It has gates on every side. We need to ask ourselves: Does our local church have an open door on the north, south, east, and west? Do we truly welcome people in these doors, no matter what their language, their race, their socioeconomic status, their background, or their history of sin? Are we open to all, seeking to win all sinners to the Savior?

The gospel is to be preached indiscriminately to human beings of all kinds, in all walks and conditions, without any restriction or distinction. It is a free gospel. Sinners are welcome, no matter how bad their sins may be. However hopeless you think you are, there is a way for you to come into the Celestial City. Jesus said, "I am the door: by me if any man enter in, he shall be saved" (John 10:9). You don't need any key but the key of faith in Christ. Enter by this door; enter by this gate. Jesus said that if any man enters in by Him, he shall be saved. You don't need a road map or a GPS device to find the Savior. In preaching, He finds His way to you. The gate is open.

The Church's Foundations

John also observes the foundations of New Jerusalem as he watches the city descend from heaven. Revelation 21:14 says, "And the wall of the city had twelve foundations, and in them the names of the twelve apostles of the Lamb." John is standing on a high mountain. The city is coming down, and as it gets nearer, he sees the foundations, which are garnished with precious stones (v. 19). Each is inscribed with the names of the twelve apostles of Christ. John sees his own name there, because he is one of the twelve; in fact, he is the only surviving apostle. All the others have gone to be with the Lord.

John must have been very lonely on the island of Patmos. All his fellow apostles had gone on ahead, and he alone was left to defend the gospel. In his loneliness, God gives him this marvelous vision. As John looks, he sees his name on one of the foundation stones. God is saying, in effect: "These are not wasted days on Patmos. The suffering you are going through is worthwhile. John, in your life and ministry, you are helping to lay the foundation for this city of light." How encouraging that must that have been for the old apostle.

But note something else about the foundations. The psalmist asks, "If the foundations be destroyed, what can the righteous do?" (Ps. 11:3). We are living in days when the foundations of the church are being undermined. Though there is no other foundation than Christ Jesus, some liberals embrace a Christ who has little or nothing to do with the Bible. We need to remember from John's vision that the foundation of the church is the Christ of Scripture, as attested by His chosen apostles. The true church is apostolic in doctrine, worship, order, and life.

Before His death, Jesus said to Peter, "Upon this rock I will build my church; and the gates of hell shall not prevail against it" (Matt. 16:18). Was Peter the rock? How could a church built on impulsive, mouthy Peter survive? Christ did not say He would build the church on Peter's personality; rather, He would build it upon the confession Peter had just made: "Thou art the Christ, the Son of the living God" (v. 16). Jesus was saying, "On the rock of this confession you have just made, on the rock of apostolic testimony, I will build My church, and the gates of hell will not prevail against her." We need to appreciate that the foundation of the church is the person and work of Christ, and the testimony of the apostles and prophets (Eph. 2:20).

Historically, the most difficult task for a church is to hold to its God-given foundation. By God's grace, we trust we have the apostolic doctrine, but do we have the ethos of an apostolic church? Are we truly striving to fulfill our mission to disciple believers in Christ and evangelize unbelievers for God's glory? One theme of the Reformation church was *Ecclesia reformata sed semper reformanda*—"The church reformed, but always being reformed."[2] That ought to be our motto, too, always striving according to the Word of God to attain our Reformed ideals.

The Bible is the foundation of the church. The only guarantee that a church will stay on course, survive, and continue to grow is that we keep coming back to this Book. We keep reforming our church life, our own lives, and everything else in the light of what we read in the Book.

The Church's Glory

Our text also speaks about the church's glory as the dwelling place of God. John says in Revelation 21:22, "And I saw no temple therein: for the Lord God Almighty and the Lamb are the temple of it." Go back to earlier verses in the chapter that tell about the measurements of this city. Verse 16 says, "The length and the breadth and the height of it are equal." In other words, the city is a perfect cube, just as was the Holy Place in the Jerusalem temple and the Holy Place in the wilderness tabernacle. This symbolizes perfect communion with the triune God in genuine worship. Oh, how perfect, rich, complete, and free the worship of the saints will be as they glorify the Father, Son, and Spirit forever and ever in glory. Truly, then, they will be able to say with Samuel Rutherford more than they ever could on earth, "I know not which divine Person I love the most, but this I know, I love each of them and I need them all."

God told Moses that he was to follow exactly the measurements and instructions given to him for the building of the tabernacle, "after their pattern, which was shewed thee in the mount" (Ex. 25:40). The same was true for Solomon when he was tasked with building the temple (1 Chron. 28:19). The Holy of Holies, God's throne room, was off limits to anyone but the high priest, who could enter it only once a year on the Day of Atonement. There he would

---

2. See Michael Bush, "Calvin and the Reformanda Sayings," in *Calvinus Sacrarum Literarum Interpres: Papers of the International Congress on Calvin Research*, ed. Herman J. Selderhuis (Gottingen: Vandenhoeck and Ruprecht, 2008), 285–99.

see the ark of the covenant, the mercy seat, cherubim, and then the Shekinah cloud, the manifestation of God's glory. In Revelation 21, New Jerusalem *is* the Holy of Holies, the place where God's glory dwells, the most holy place where glorified believers will be "made perfectly blessed in the full enjoying of God to all eternity" (Westminster Shorter Catechism, Q. 38).[3] They will know Him, enjoy Him, live in Him, and delight in Him forever as they bask in His smile, feast in His presence, and breathe in His glory! Truly, as Jonathan Edwards writes, "Heaven is a world of love!"

John saw no temple in the new city because the city itself is God's temple. No matter how far you might travel in the city, in whatever direction, you cannot leave the loving, worshipful presence of God and the Lamb. You cannot lose a moment of God's presence in this city because it is all temple. There is no place in the city where God's Shekinah glory does not shine forth. He dominates the east, west, north, and south. There will be no Sabbaths, no Lord's Days, no stated times of worship, no ministers to preach the gospel, and no means of grace, because we will live forever in the immediate presence of the God of love, and we will never lose a moment of His sacred, loving, joyful, overwhelming presence.

Dr. R. C. Sproul had a sickly father. As a young man, he often had to help his father walk to the dinner table. After his father died, Dr. Sproul told me that he often dreamed of his father in his needy condition. But one night, he dreamed that he and his father were in heaven. His father had no more infirmities, but was fully energized. In his dream, Dr. Sproul said to his father, "Dad, take me to where I can see the glory." And his father said to him: "Son, it is all glory! It is all glory!" That is why there is no temple—because *all* is temple!

In the Bible, God always had a temple, that is, a sacred place where He met with His people. In the beginning, the temple was the Garden of Eden, where God came down to meet with Adam and Eve. Then, when Israel was wandering in the wilderness, God gave them a tent or tabernacle so they could gather round it for

---

3. *Reformed Confessions of the Sixteenth and Seventeenth Centuries*, 4:358.

worship and instruction, then fold it away and carry it with them when it was time to move on. And when they became city dwellers, He gave them a temple in which His glory was revealed. Then, in the climax of His glorious revelation, He gave His Son to be the new temple. Now, in the world to come, all is temple! At last, our worship will be unhindered. Our worship will be whole-souled and whole-bodied! Our worship will be eternally perfect, as we believers serve as everlasting priests and kings unto God.

Where Will You Dwell?

Will you dwell in the Celestial City? Paul says in Philippians 3:20, "For our conversation is in heaven; from whence also we look for the Saviour, the Lord Jesus Christ." Dear believer, our names, by God's grace, are enrolled in the church membership book of New Jerusalem, the heavenly city. Our citizenship is already in heaven, even while we wait for the Savior to come again in glory.

You need to know the Lamb of God to get to that city. Look at Revelation 21:27: "And there shall in no wise enter into it any thing that defileth, neither whatsoever worketh abomination, or maketh a lie: but they which are written in the Lamb's book of life." Unrepentant sinners will not get into the city. As long as you remain in your sin, whatever it is and however respectable it may be in your eyes, you will not enter New Jerusalem. You must abandon your sin or else abandon all hope of entering this city. Only those who are registered in the Lamb's Book of Life, that is, only those who belong to Him body and soul, in life and in death, will be admitted.

What a tragedy it will be to have sat under the gospel all your life, only to be excluded from New Jerusalem on the great judgment day—all because you refused to abandon your defiling, abominable, lying sins. You refused to lay all your sins at the feet of the Lamb of God, who alone can take them away.

The name of the Lord Jesus is not mentioned once in Revelation 21, but He is mentioned repeatedly in terms of His identity as "The Lamb...the Lamb...the Lamb." Is your Savior the Lamb who takes away the sin of the world?

In the old tax books of France, it is noted that the village of Domremy, France, did not pay taxes for years, because of a simple notation, "La Pucelle" ("the Maid"), written in red ink across the page of an official record book. The idea was the village's taxes were remitted for the maid's sake!" The maid was Joan of Arc, remembered in France as the "Maid of Orleans." Domremy was her birthplace. The French were so grateful to Joan of Arc, the "Maid of Orleans," for defeating the English that they honored her birthplace and remitted all the taxes that were due from that village for her sake.[4]

Likewise, in the Lamb's Book of Life, next to your name, with all your liabilities and all your obligations to the holy God and His holy law, this is written: "Sins remitted for the Lamb's sake!" That is what Paul means in Colossians when he writes that the Lord Jesus Christ, the Lamb of God, has blotted out the handwriting of ordinances that was against us (Col. 2:14). He has taken our sins out of the way and nailed them to His cross. He has redeemed us from the curse and penalty of the law due to us for our sins. He has satisfied for all our sins with His precious blood. The gates of the Celestial City are now open, and we may freely enter in.

Whatever your spiritual condition may be, the only way for you to know that your name is written in the membership book of New Jerusalem, the Lamb's Book of Life, is to repent of your sin and take refuge in Him as your Savior and Lord, trusting in what He has done upon the cross all your life long. Then you too will be able to say with James Renwick, a well-known Scottish Covenanter martyr, as he waited to climb the ladder to die on the gallows: "I shall soon be above these clouds; then I shall enjoy Thee and glorify Thee without interruption or intermission for ever."[5]

---

4. Louis de Conte, *Personal Recollections of Joan of Arc*, trans. Jean F. Alden (Hartford, Conn.: American Publishing Co., 1901), 2:60–61.

5. Jock Purves, *Fair Sunshine: Character Studies of the Scottish Covenanters* (London: Banner of Truth, 1968), 120.

35

New Jerusalem's City Center

REVELATION 22:1–5

And he shewed me a pure river of water of life, clear as crystal, proceeding out of the throne of God and of the Lamb. In the midst of the street of it, and on either side of the river, was there the tree of life, which bare twelve manner of fruits, and yielded her fruit every month: and the leaves of the tree were for the healing of the nations. And there shall be no more curse: but the throne of God and of the Lamb shall be in it; and his servants shall serve him: and they shall see his face; and his name shall be in their foreheads. And there shall be no night there; and they need no candle, neither light of the sun; for the Lord God giveth them light: and they shall reign for ever and ever.

In the previous chapter on Revelation 21, we toured the heavenly Jerusalem. We walked around the city, looking at its walls, gates, and foundations. We admired its beauty, its transcendence, and its shape as a perfect cube, like the Holy of Holies—the city that is one great temple. We saw that this city is designed for perfect and uninterrupted communion with God.

Let us now visit the city center of New Jerusalem. Often, we try to avoid the centers of large, congested cities. We are grateful for highways that bypass them. But this city center is not to be avoided, for God's throne is at the heart of this city (Rev. 22:3). Down the high streets of New Jerusalem flows the pure river of the water of life. And on either side of that river is a beautiful boulevard of trees. The lights and sights of the cities of earth cannot compare with the lights and sights of New Jerusalem, for we are told that there will be no night in heaven (v. 5). There is no need for candles or sunlight, for God Himself is all the light that is needed.

Let us examine New Jerusalem's city center under these headings: a garden city, a cosmopolitan city, a capital city, and an illuminated city.

A Garden City

When you step inside New Jerusalem, you will see a beautiful garden, a forest of trees, and a pure flowing river (vv. 1–2). You won't see office buildings, skyscrapers, and housing developments. New Jerusalem is a garden city.

Revelation tells us in no uncertain terms that this city is *the church of Christ*: "One of the seven angels...talked with me, saying, Come hither, and I will shew thee the bride, the Lamb's wife. And he...shewed me that great city, the holy Jerusalem, descending out of heaven from God" (21:9–10).

If we are true believers, you and I belong to this city. We are not just going to the city, we *are* this city. Everything about the city—its foundations, walls, gates, the pure flowing river, and the tree of life—applies to us. John sees the Christian church as it shall be in perfection, but also as it is now in principle.

Bearing that in mind, let's try to interpret the symbolism here. Much of the imagery suggests the Garden of Eden. That garden, too, had a river, a tree of life, and, most importantly, the presence of God (Gen. 2). God walked in the garden in the cool of the day and spoke with Adam. But there is more than just an allusion to Eden here.

It is interesting that the Bible ends where it began. The opening chapters of Genesis give the account of the first creation. The closing chapters of Revelation describe God's creation of the new heaven and the new earth. Genesis tells about Paradise lost. Revelation tells about Paradise regained. But the most encouraging part of Revelation 22 is not simply a *return to* Genesis 2, but an *advance on* Genesis 2. New Jerusalem is the "city which hath foundations, whose builder and maker is God" and the "better country, that is, an heavenly," that was the object of Abraham's spiritual quest (Heb. 11:10, 16). In Christ we gain more than Adam lost.

This is what Paul means in 1 Corinthians 15:45–49 when he says: "And so it is written, The first man Adam was made a living soul; the last Adam was made a quickening spirit. Howbeit that was not first which is spiritual, but that which is natural; and afterward that which is spiritual. The first man is of the earth, earthy: the second man is the Lord from heaven. As is the earthy, such are they also that are earthy: and as is the heavenly, such are they also that are heavenly. And as we have borne the image of the earthy, we shall also bear the image of the heavenly." That means that you and I are not simply going back to the Garden of Eden. Eden was an *earthly* paradise. We are going beyond that earthly Eden to its *heavenly* counterpart.

Eden was only a shadow of the heavenly garden, much as the earthly tabernacle and temple were shadows of the heavenly sanctuary where God dwells. The kingdom of glory is far greater than the kingdoms of this world. Where sin did abound, says Paul, grace did much more abound (Rom. 5:20).

Genesis 2 tells about the creation of the first man and his wife, and they were beautiful. But Revelation 22 tells about the second Adam, the Lord Jesus Christ, and His bride, the church. There is only a faint comparison between that first couple and the last, for there is a definite advance here from what we see in Genesis. Sin, death, and the curse entered the Garden of Eden, but here we are told there will be no more curse (v. 3). In Eden, the trees yielded their fruit in season, but in the New Jerusalem, the one tree will be fruitful all year round (v. 2). The leaves of this tree will be used to heal the nations (v. 2). There will be no sin, no illness, no decay, and no death in this city. The leaves of the tree will prevent that.

But the main point of this passage is that the city is coming down from heaven, from God. It has not yet arrived in its fullness, but it is coming even now. This is the tension we find in the New Testament between the *now* and the *not yet*. Now is the kingdom come among you, says Jesus (Luke 11:20), and yet, the kingdom is still to come. This tension is true also regarding the heavenly Jerusalem. By the power of God's Spirit and through the preaching of His Word, the church is coming down out of heaven. The true church is not a mere human institution or organization. It comes from God. Likewise, a Christian is one who has been born from above by the Spirit of God. The salvation that we now enjoy as Christians is not just a return to our original state before the fall, but an advance on it.

Do you believe that you are better off now under the gospel than our father Adam was? Are you rejoicing in that today? You should be. Adam was innocent, you say. You have something better than that. You have the righteousness of Christ, which is much more than innocence. By God's regenerating work in your heart, you have been made a partaker of the divine nature in a sense that Adam was not.

Adam lived in an earthly paradise. He was lord of Eden. However, we are joint heirs with Christ. We sit in heavenly places in Him. Adam was on probation. He was forbidden to eat of the tree of the knowledge of good and evil. That tree is not mentioned in Revelation 22, for you and I are eternally secure in our Lord Jesus Christ. There is no probation in glory. We can say with Paul, "Nothing can separate me from the love of God which is in Christ Jesus" (see Rom. 8:38–39). This is an advance on the Garden of Eden.

The symbolism in this chapter attests to the superabundant character of our salvation, but there is more to it than that. Notice that the garden will be in the *city*. The tragedy of the fall and of subsequent human history is that the garden and the city became separate (Gen. 4:16–17). Man, because of his sin, was driven out of the garden. And since he had to live outside of Eden, the human race has lived in estrangement from both the garden of God and the city of God. Yet the city has been crying out for the garden, and the garden for the city.

Now, in Christ's church, the garden is the city. People are no longer cut off from the presence of God and denied access to the tree of life, with its abundant fruit and healing leaves. As Christians, you and I are no longer cut off from the source of supply for our deepest needs. That is the picture. Although this is ideally and perfectly true of the future state for us, it is powerfully true now for genuine Christians. John says: "You are now come to Mount Zion. You have come now to this heavenly city, this New Jerusalem. You have come through the Mediator and through the blood of the covenant. But you have now come to this city" (see Heb. 12:22).

Jesus says in the Gospels, "He that believeth on me hath everlasting life" (John 6:47). He doesn't say you have to wait for it; He says you *have* it. If you are a believer, you are in the garden of God. You have access to the tree of life.

In John 4, Jesus talks to a Samaritan woman at a well, and He says to her, "Whosoever drinketh of the water that I shall give him shall never thirst; but the water that I shall give him shall be in him a well of water springing up into everlasting life" (v. 14). That is the picture of the river that flows *out* of the throne of God. So Jesus says to the woman at the well, "If you come to Me out of your sin and if you trust in Me as your Savior, I will give you living water that will well up from within you, springing up unto everlasting life." That water comes only from Christ. It springs up in us and flows out of us due to the sovereign grace of God.

In John 7:37–39, we are told: "In the last day, that great day of the feast, Jesus stood and cried, saying, If any man thirst, let him come unto me, and drink. He that believeth on me, as the scripture hath said, out of his belly shall flow rivers of living water. (But this spake he of the Spirit, which they that believe on him should receive: for the Holy Ghost was not yet given; because that Jesus was not yet glorified.)" You don't have to wait until heaven to enjoy the significance of Revelation 22. If you are a Christian today, the river of the water of life already flows from the throne of God—the sovereign grace of God working in you and through you.

Psalm 46:4–5 offers a beautiful description of the church in this world: "There is a river, the streams whereof shall make glad the city of God, the holy place of the tabernacles of the most High. God is in the midst of her; she shall not be moved: God shall help her, and that right early." The great commandment of this psalm is also interesting. "Be still, and know that I am God" (v. 10a) doesn't only mean that we should be quiet and submit to God's ways. These are ultimately God's words to His church assailed by the raging nations: "Be still!"

Psalm 46 appears to address the siege of Jerusalem such as by Sennacherib, king of Assyria (2 Kings 19). The city was surrounded by the Assyrians. The situation looked hopeless for Judah. But God said, "Be still, and know that I am God." He delivered the city from her enemies. It is a picture of the church in the world, not yet glorified, not yet triumphant, but militant. She is surrounded by her enemies and besieged by the world.

When an enemy besieges a city, he first cuts off or pollutes the water supply. In the heavenly Jerusalem, the water supply will not come from outside the city, but will spring up from beneath the throne of God. The river won't flow *into* the city, but *out of* the city. Jerusalem will be a garden city. No matter how it is besieged, it will never be destroyed because all its resources will be found within the walls.

What a comforting picture of God's church that is. Her life does not depend on what comes to her from the world around. Rather, as the psalmist says, all our springs are in God (Ps. 87:7). Are you complete in Christ in this world? "There is a river, the streams whereof shall make glad the city of God" (Ps. 46:4).

So New Jerusalem will be a garden city. It will have the horticultural beauty of a garden and the metropolitan order of a city. That is Christ's church. There will be no crime in New Jerusalem because the tree of life and the throne of God will be there. The tree of life represents irrevocable eternal life (Gen. 3:22), satisfying happiness (Prov. 3:18; 13:12), and complete restoration from all damage to body and soul (Ps. 103:3; Isa. 53:5; 57:19). Noticeably absent from the new garden are the tree of the knowledge of good and evil and the serpent (Gen. 2:17; 3:1), for testing, temptation, and sin will be abolished for all time, together with the curse that came on us all because of Adam's sin (Gen. 3:17; 4:11). God's reigning presence on His throne will constantly overflow to His people as a pure river of the water of life (Rev. 7:17; 21:6; 22:17; Ezek. 47:1–12; Zech. 14:8–9). This is a symbol of delighting in God (Pss. 1:2–3; 36:8; 46:4–5) through the graces of the Holy Spirit (Isa. 32:2, 15; 35:6; 43:19–21; 44:3–5), imparted to us by our Savior, Jesus Christ.[1]

A Cosmopolitan City

At the end of Revelation 22:2, we are told that the leaves of the tree in New Jerusalem are meant for the healing of the nations. In Revelation 21:22–26, John tells us that he "saw no temple therein: for the Lord God Almighty and the Lamb are the temple of it. And the city had no need of the sun, neither of the moon, to shine in it: for the glory of God did lighten it, and the Lamb is the light thereof. And the nations of them which are saved shall walk in the light of it: and the kings of the earth do bring their glory and honour into it. And the gates of it shall not be shut at all by day: for there shall be no night there. And they shall bring the glory and honour of the nations into it."

New Jerusalem will be a cosmopolitan city, that is, a city free of any one ethnic or national character. Its inhabitants will be drawn from every tribe and nation. The best from all the cultures and nations of this earth will have a place in the city. Nothing good will be lost (Phil. 4:8). Surely that is what we are told at the end of chapter 21, when John says that "the nations of them which are saved...shall bring the glory and the honour of the nations into it," and "the kings of the earth do bring their glory and honour into it."

The inhabitants of this city will retain their national identity, but not in a political or nationalistic sense, or even a patriotic sense. There will be no flag-waving in New Jerusalem. There will be no cultural superiority, no national rivalry, no one-upmanship, and no triumphalism. All separations and divides between or among people will be done away with, because the nations will be healed, or

---

1. Portions of this chapter are adapted from my notes in *The Reformation Heritage KJV Study Bible*, 1897–98.

made whole. Everything that separates us one from another will be removed. Evil will be walled out and good will be kept within.

Everyone will not look alike in heaven. God loves diversity; that is why He created the world with so many textures, varieties, and colors. Surely the new heaven and new earth will not be less glorious than that. Whatever is best, glorious, and God-honoring from all the cultures and nations of this earth will be purified, enhanced, and glorified in the heavenly Jerusalem.

That is a lesson for us in our evangelism and church life. We belong to a multiracial society—an international, cosmopolitan city. It is possible for us to grieve God's Holy Spirit by not taking that properly and biblically into account. We may make the mistakes that some of our forefathers made. I hesitate to criticize missionaries of a previous generation who sacrificed a great deal for the Lord and who were far greater and better men than any of us. But the Great Commission does not say we are to go into the world and make every creature Americans, Englishmen, or Dutchmen. When we welcome converted people into the church, we should not demand that they conform to our cultural ethos. We must simply bid them to follow Christ according to Scripture.

Revelation 21:23 offers a marvelous description of a missionary church. Like a city set upon a hill, a city that cannot be hidden, it is ablaze with light, reminding us that we must let our light shine before men. Jesus is surely saying here: "My church in this world is not to be a little hamlet hidden away in the hills. It is to be a city blazing with light."

When you are driving on the highway at night, sometimes you can see light in the distant skies. You know you are about to drive past a good-sized city. When our Lord talks about the heavenly Jerusalem, He is saying that the church is not to take a low profile in the world. We must shine with the light of the gospel blazing out of every window. We must be light in this dark world so that the nations around us can walk by the light that we cast.

Are we illuminating our city with gospel light? There is no nightlife in the heavenly Jerusalem. There are no neon lights; in fact, there is no artificial lighting of any kind. The Lamb is the light by which the nations must walk. Our task as the church in the world is to reflect the light of our Savior. By doing that, we can be a light to those who do not yet believe.

Everything that is good will be provided in the heavenly Jerusalem: a garden city, people we love, safe streets, unending supplies of food and water, and the stupendous relationship and harmony of the Holy Trinity. That is also true now, albeit imperfectly realized today in the church. We ought to be a testimony to a divided society that people of all nations can live in harmony in the church. Though getting along is challenging in some ways now, the glorious truth is that in the future, people from all the nations—every tribe, kindred, and tongue—will come together as one to worship the Lamb.

A Capital City

The "throne of God and of the Lamb" will be in the center of this city. It will be the seat of universal government. It will be the home of divine royalty. This is a wonderful picture of the grandeur and gentleness of God.

The term "Lamb" reminds us of the meekness of Jesus Christ. The grandeur of God and the gentleness of the Savior will mingle together at the center of city life.

Earlier in Revelation, John spoke about the Lamb being "in the midst of the throne" (Rev. 5:6). The Greek word translated as "midst" refers more to a position of centrality than to being in the middle of the throne. The Lamb not only *sits on* the throne; He stands *in front of* the throne, a position that presents Him as both central and accessible. The government of God is not a totalitarian, oppressive regime. His throne is not protected by secret police who keep the people under control. God is an absolute sovereign, yet that power is made accessible to us through the Lamb. When we come to the city center, we will see the throne of God. But we won't see that throne without seeing the Lamb. The Lamb is in the midst of the throne.

There is no hint in these verses of any rebellion against God. We are told in verse 3 that we shall see God and serve Him, and we will reign with Christ forever and ever. The great unifying factor in this city will be the Lamb. The powerful effects of the atonement will hold the whole city together. Satan asked Adam in Eden: "Isn't God unreasonable? Isn't God being petty, putting these restrictions on you and telling you not to eat of that fruit? He knows that if you eat it, you will be equal to Him" (see Gen. 3:1–5). That was Satan's lie, and Adam believed it. But none of us who look at the Lamb can think that God is petty or trivial, can we? None of us want to rebel and say, "It's not fair." Surely our hearts will melt when we consider the salvation God has accomplished for us in sending His Son to die on Calvary for sinners.

John sees New Jerusalem coming down from heaven, with the throne of God and the Lamb at the center of it. Is the throne of God and the Lamb at the center of our churches and of our lives? Is it the center of our worship? Does the throne of God and the Lamb constrain us, keep us going, and motivate us? Does the power of the atonement, our view of a crucified Savior, and our gratitude to Him for saving us move us to love, worship, and service? Are we under the sovereignty and authority of God's throne? Or do we just do what seems right in our own eyes, come what may? To what extent can we see our churches even now coming down out of heaven from God?

An Illuminated City

Finally, John speaks of the church as an illuminated city. He says in Revelation 22:4–5: "And they shall see his face; and his name shall be in their foreheads. And there shall be no night there; and they need no candle, neither light of the sun; for the Lord God giveth them light: and they shall reign for ever and ever." That theme is repeated from what John said just verses earlier, in Revelation 21:23–24a. There we read that the Lamb is the church's light, and the nations of the saved walk in that light.

Spurgeon says this light can be understood in three ways.[2] First, light is the cause of joy. This is a joyous city, for light in Scripture is symbolic of joy, just as darkness is symbolic of sorrow. Christ is heaven's joy. Believers in heaven rejoice in their golden harps, palm branches, and white robes, because these are Christ's love gifts. However, the essence of their joy is Jesus Himself and seeing His face, as John says in Revelation 22:4. Their joy is the beatific vision come true, that now they bask in Jesus' smile and feast in His presence. Their joy consists of this, says Spurgeon: "Jesus chose us, Jesus loved us, Jesus bought us, Jesus washed us, Jesus robed us, Jesus kept us, Jesus glorified us; here we are, entirely through the Lord Jesus—through him alone."[3]

Second, this light imparts *beauty* to this city. The Lamb is the light of heaven. All that is beautiful about heaven—including the saints themselves—flows from the Lamb. Their beautiful excellence, their beautiful triumph, and their beautiful glory are all due to the Lamb, who is the light of heaven.

Third, this light is *knowledge*. There is no need for light in heaven because Christ is the source of all that believers must know. Christ manifests Himself to His saints here on earth, "for God, who commanded the light to shine out of darkness, hath shined in our hearts, to give the light of the knowledge of the glory of God in the face of Jesus Christ" (2 Cor. 4:6). "In thy light shall we see light" (Ps. 36:9).

In glory, this light will be far brighter, so the knowledge will be much greater. When the wife of one of my best friends passed on to glory, I said to him, "In the first five minutes that she entered into glory, she became a better theologian of Christ than you or I have ever been." Because Christ is the light of heaven, Spurgeon says, "We shall know more of Christ in five minutes...when we get to heaven, than we shall know in all our years on earth."[4] And in knowing Christ far better, we will be able to solve other mysteries

---

2. Spurgeon, *Metropolitan Tabernacle Pulpit*, 10:443–46.

3. Spurgeon, *Metropolitan Tabernacle Pulpit*, 10:443.

4. Spurgeon, *Metropolitan Tabernacle Pulpit*, 10:444–45.

as well. All our riddles will be resolved in glory, for then we shall see Him face to face.

Revelation 22:4 says, "And they shall see his face; and his name shall be in their foreheads." Facing Christ without any shame or hesitation is the height, depth, and breadth of the authentic beatific vision of the heaven of heavens! Oh, what glory it will be to stand before the face of God in Jesus Christ with a perfect soul and in a perfect body, in perfect freedom and full assurance, to commune with Him. Job, David, and the saints of all ages will also see that their Redeemer lives. With their own eyes they will behold their Lord's face in righteousness. They will be satisfied when they awake with His likeness (Job 19:25–27; Ps. 17:15).

Our faith will be turned into sight. We will see our King in all His beauty (Isa. 33:17), no longer "through a glass, darkly" (1 Cor. 13:12), just His back parts (Ex. 33:23), or the hem of His garment, but face to face. Bunyan writes of Mr. Stand-fast in *Pilgrim's Progress*. When this man is called to cross the River of Death into the Celestial City, he bares his heart with these words: "The thoughts of what I am going to…doth lie like a glowing coal at my heart." He has these parting words for his friends: "I am going now to see that head that was crowned with thorns and that face that was spit upon for me. I have formerly lived by hearsay and faith, but now I go where I shall live by sight and shall be with him in whose company I delight myself."[5]

Drawing on the writings of Rutherford, Anne Ross Cousin beautifully expressed this thought in a poem titled "The Sands of Time Are Sinking":

> The bride eyes not her garment,
> But her dear Bridegroom's face;
> I will not gaze at glory
> But on my King of grace.
> Not at the crown he gifteth,

---

5. Bunyan, *Pilgrim's Progress*, in *Works*, 3:243.

> But on his pierced hand;
> The Lamb is all the glory
> Of Emmanuel's land.[6]

Do you long to see Jesus face to face, always and forever in all His glory, so that He is never out of your sight?

All of this is confirmed by the promise at the end of Revelation 22:4: "his name shall be in their foreheads." Philip Hughes comments, "This signifies not only their preciousness to him, to whom they gladly belong (cf. 1 Cor. 6:19f.) but also that in the multitude of the redeemed who populate the holy city there will be none who are unknown and unloved, none whose identity is lost in the crowd, and none who miss seeing him face to face."[7] That includes you, too, dear beginner in grace!

Finally, light is the radiance of love. God Himself is "the cause and fountain of love," and heaven is His special dwelling place, Jonathan Edwards says. He goes on to say: "God is the fountain of love, as the sun is the fountain of light. And therefore the glorious presence of God in heaven, fills heaven with love, as the sun placed in the midst of the hemisphere [sky] in a clear day, fills the world with light. The Apostle tells us that 'God is love' (1 John 4:8). And therefore seeing he is an infinite Being, it follows that he is an infinite fountain of love. Seeing he is an all-sufficient Being, it follows that he is a full and over-flowing and inexhaustible fountain of love. Seeing he is an unchangeable and eternal Being, he is an unchangeable and eternal source of love."[8] Those in heaven are continually irradiated, illuminated, and warmed by God's love.

Yes, the new heaven and earth will be illuminated by Christ, and the redeemed will reflect God's glory as clear gems sparkling in the light of the Lamb. Heaven will know no darkness, no ignorance,

---

6. Anne R. Cousin, "The Sands of Time Are Sinking" (1857).

7. Hughes, *The Book of Revelation*, 233.

8. Jonathan Edwards, *Charity and Its Fruits*, Sermon 15, "Heaven Is a World of Love," in *The Works of Jonathan Edwards, Volume 8, Ethical Writings*, ed. Paul Ramsey (New Haven: Yale University Press, 1989), 369.

no sorrow, and "no more curse," as verse 3 says—all because "Christ hath redeemed us from the curse of the law, being made a curse for us: for it is written, Cursed is every one that hangeth on a tree" (Gal. 3:13)." And, as Revelation 22:3 says, Christ's "servants shall serve him" forever. They will rejoice, walking in His light, and serving Him for all eternity in ways we now cannot imagine.

This may be hard for you to believe. You may ask, "Can I be a perfect reflector of Christ's light and be sinless, never to fall again?" The comfort here is that because the glory of Christ cannot be dimmed or put out, the glory of the individual believer cannot be dimmed or extinguished. The moon has no light of its own, but reflects the light of the sun. You will reflect the light of God's Son, Christ Jesus. As long as the sun is shining, all is well. Nothing can come between Christ and His people. He will shine in glory forever, and they shall reflect His glory forever. A fall into sin is impossible because of Christ!

Yes, but what about now? What about the times when we still sin? Start with these words from Scripture, addressed to the Colossians: "Christ [is] in you, the hope of glory" (1:27). The converted are joined to Christ, not just outwardly, but inwardly. His glorious light already shines in your soul. That is why you love Him. That is why the thought of sinning grieves you. The evidence of God's grace in you is evidence that Christ's light is in you. This is a foretaste of eternal light. The Heidelberg Catechism asks in Question 58, "What comfort takest thou from the article 'of life everlasting'?" The answer: "That since I now feel in my heart the beginning of eternal joy, after this life, I shall inherit perfect salvation, which 'eye hath not seen, nor ear heard, neither hath it entered into the heart of man' to conceive, and that to praise God therein for ever."[9]

The Puritans used to speak of grace as "young glory."[10] Grace, they said, is glory in the bud. Think of a tulip bulb. It does not look like much to the eye, but inside it is a beautiful tulip on the

---

9. *The Three Forms of Unity*, 86.
10. Manton, *Works*, 13:331.

way. God's gracious light in the heart now is His glorious light begun below.

Because Christ's glory will always shine undimmed in the city of light, His praises will never grow old. Through an endless eternity, dear believer, you will never run out of reasons to sing His praises.

The Way into This City

How do we get to this wonderful city of light? Christians already know something of the reality of this city in their lives and experience. We can testify to others about how this city, even now, is coming down out of heaven from God into our lives. But how can people come into the city? After Adam and Eve rebelled against God in the Garden of Eden, God "drove out the man; and he placed at the east of the garden of Eden Cherubims, and a flaming sword which turned every way, to keep the way of the tree of life" (Gen. 3:24). There was no way back into the garden. Adam could not find his way back into the presence of God.

The only place in the Bible where Jesus Christ used the word *paradise* is when He was on the cross. He said to the dying thief, "To day shalt thou be with me in paradise" (Luke 23:43). The only way to the paradise of heaven is *through Christ's death*. At Calvary, God's Son in human flesh, in the place of sinners, allowed that sword of justice and God's anger against sin to fall on Him. Now, for all who come through Him, the crucified Savior is the way into God's Paradise.

Spurgeon tells the story of Andrew Fuller, who had to cross a deep river to reach the church where he was to preach. Not knowing the current of the river, he hesitated, but an old farmer, who happened to see him, called out, "Mr. Fuller, you will get through all right, sir." But when Fuller got nearly halfway across the river, he was in so deep he scarcely dared to take another step. Then the old farmer called out again, "Go on, Mr. Fuller, go on; I know it will be all right." Fuller replied, "Well, then, I will go on; I will go on by faith," and he made it safely across.[11] Spurgeon goes on to say,

> Now, sinner, it is very like that with you. You think that your sins are so deep that Christ will never be able to carry you over them; but I say to you—It is all right, sinner; trust Jesus, and He will carry you through hell itself, if that is needful. If you had all the sins of all the men that have ever lived, and they were all yours, if you could trust Him, Jesus Christ would carry you through the current of all that sin. It is all right, man! Only trust Christ. The river may be deep but Christ's love is deeper still.[12]

When, by Spirit-given grace, you trust Christ alone for salvation, then you have eternal life. Then you are, in one sense and in principle, already in the garden, by the river, and in the New Jerusalem; and you will never have to leave. Richard Baxter, a Puritan pastor, writes, "Our first and earthly Paradise in Eden, had a way out, but none that we could find, in again: But this eternal paradise hath a way in (a milky way to us, but a bloody way to Christ), but no way out again."[13]

Thank God for the blood atonement and righteousness of the second Adam. Thank Him for the security of New Jerusalem's city center, where the second Adam sits on the throne as the Lamb of God. Hallelujah!

---

11. Spurgeon, *Metropolitan Tabernacle Pulpit*, 57:247.

12. Spurgeon, *Metropolitan Tabernacle Pulpit*, 57:247.

13. Richard Baxter, *The Saints Everlasting Rest* (London: by Rob. White, for Thomas Underhil and Francis Tyton, 1650), 131 (1.7.19).

36

"I Come Quickly"

REVELATION 22:6–21

And he said unto me, These sayings are faithful and true: and the Lord God of the holy prophets sent his angel to shew unto his servants the things which must shortly be done. Behold, I come quickly: blessed is he that keepeth the sayings of the prophecy of this book.... And, behold, I come quickly; and my reward is with me, to give every man according as his work shall be. I am Alpha and Omega, the beginning and the end, the first and the last. Blessed are they that do his commandments, that they may have right to the tree of life, and may enter in through the gates into the city.... And the Spirit and the bride say, Come. And let him that heareth say, Come. And let him that is athirst come. And whosoever will, let him take the water of life freely. For I testify unto every man that heareth the words of the prophecy of this book, If any man shall add unto these things, God shall add unto him the plagues that are written in this book: and if any man shall take away from the words of the book of this prophecy, God shall take away his part out of the book of life, and out of the holy city, and from the things which are written in this book. He which testifieth these things saith, Surely I come quickly. Amen. Even so, come, Lord Jesus. The grace of our Lord Jesus Christ be with you all. Amen.

The book of Revelation is a triumphant finale to the Bible. It gathers up the themes of the symphony of Scripture in a closing burst of glorious music. In addressing several of those themes, we will focus on the dominant note that runs throughout Jesus' last message in the Bible, which is stated in Revelation 22:7 and then repeated in verses 12 and 20: "Behold, I come quickly." Let us look at this theme under these headings: its triple assertion, its triple confirmation, its triple warning, and its triple invitation.

Its Triple Assertion

Three times in Revelation 22, Jesus promises, "Behold, I come quickly" (vv. 7, 12, 20). There is no reason to doubt that this triple assertion refers to Jesus. Verse 16 says: "I Jesus have sent mine angel to testify unto you these things in the churches. I am the root and the offspring of David, and the bright and morning star." And verse 13 asserts, "I am Alpha and Omega, the beginning and the end, the first and the last." Jesus is saying through the last page of the Bible, "I am coming."

Note that Jesus speaks of His second coming in the present progressive tense. He says, "Behold, I am coming." He doesn't say that He *will* come; He deliberately uses the present tense. He says, in essence, "I am already on the way." He is on the way in the events described in this book: in the lampstands, in the seals, in the trumpets, in the vials, and in all they symbolize.

Even more remarkably, Jesus says, "Behold, I am coming *quickly*." It may not have seemed like that to most people. When you don't feel well and can't sleep, the night seems to go on forever. You lie awake in your bed for hours, watching the clock move. Waiting for Jesus' return must have seemed like that for Christians who were persecuted by Caesar and his forces. To these people in particular, Jesus says, "I am on my way; I am coming quickly."

But He also says the same to us, for the book of Revelation was written for the church of all ages. We often think that our Lord is a long time in coming. Two thousand years is too long by our standards. And yet, He says in His Word that He is coming *quickly*. How should we understand that?

Peter warns about people who scoff at the promise of Christ's coming, saying, "There shall come in the last days scoffers, walking after their own lusts, and saying, Where is the promise of his coming?" (2 Peter 3:3–4a). These people disparage the very idea of Christ's return, saying, "Since the fathers fell asleep, all things continue as they were from the beginning of the creation" (v. 4b). They argue that the promise of the coming of the Lord has been proclaimed for a long time, but nothing has ever come of it: "If in all this time, the Lord hasn't come back, He just isn't coming. Get used to it!"

How should we answer such people? In what sense has Jesus been coming quickly ever since the days of the New Testament? Let me answer this question with an illustration.

Today there are wars and rumors of wars all around the world. Often, when the United States plays a role in these wars, we tell our allies that we are coming. But so much is involved before we actually arrive. When you consider the preparation that is needed—soldiers to be trained, proper supplies to be gathered and shipped, and weapons and all sorts of other things to be prepared—it is easy to see why it may be some time before our soldiers set their boots down on foreign soil. Often our allies who wait for us fear we will not come in time or, worse yet, will never come.

Though Christ is on His way, His coming also involves a great deal of preparation. He says in Matthew 24:14, "And this gospel of the kingdom shall be preached in all the world for a witness unto all nations; and then shall the end come." All of Christ's elect church from every nation—everyone whom the Father has given to the Son to save and everyone for whom Christ died on Calvary's cross—must be gathered in before He can return. That cannot be done overnight. Likewise, the mystery of iniquity and the power of evil have to run their course. Jesus may not be coming as soon as we'd like, but He is on His way. Meantime, He is completing the massive preparations necessary to fulfill His Father's eternal decrees.

Christ's second coming involves more than just the possibility that He may return at any time. The message of Revelation 22 is that Jesus not only may return at any time, but that He is even now on the way. In other words, the second coming of Christ is not just an event that will happen at the end of time; it is also a process, a work in progress, that has long since begun and is well under way.

He is even now on the way. Suddenly and gloriously, He will appear. But we need to understand, even as we look for His appearance, that He is on the way now: "Behold, I come quickly." The book of Revelation helps us to see that Christ is on His way, something that is evident in events that are happening around us and in the things that are happening to us individually.

That is a tremendous, comforting truth, for the world thinks we are foolish for believing this. But you need to understand this truth, says John, because in all these things that are happening to you, Christ's foot is on the stairs of your personal life, as well as of all history. He is coming. We are prone to think that with all the chaos and war going on in so many nations today, this world is out of control. But He is coming. That ought to reassure us. When we are despairing or panicking, we need to remember that He is coming and soon will appear. "Behold, I come quickly," says Jesus. He makes this promise three times.

Its Triple Confirmation

Jesus confirms His second coming in a variety of ways in the Bible's last chapter. Three of these ways stand out to us.

First, our attention is drawn to the *authenticity* of the doctrine of Christ's second advent. Jesus Himself vouches for the truth of it. In Revelation 22:6 and following, the apostle John hears the voice of an angel. This is the same voice he has been hearing throughout his visions. But here the voice says: "I am coming soon.... You must not worship me; I am a fellow servant with you.... I am coming soon.... I Jesus" (see vv. 7, 9, 12, 16). If you read those verses carefully, you will see that John is hearing one message from two voices, but it is difficult to distinguish who is speaking sometimes. Is it the angel or Christ? Does the angel refuse John's worship, while the divine Christ expects John's worship? Perhaps the light is so bright that it is difficult for John to distinguish who is speaking at any one moment. It is all too easy for John to mistake the messenger for the Author of the message. The angel is not Christ; they are distinct. Yet their message is one. John is looking into heaven, and what he sees and hears is so glorious that he can scarcely distinguish the audible from the visible. Is it the angel or is it Christ? Both seem to come together in the sheer light and power of this vision, and their message is indistinguishable. That is the point.

This book has the divine imprimatur, or signature, of Jesus on it. Revelation is not the product of the fevered imagination of an old man on a rocky island. Neither is it the wishful thinking of a persecuted church. The visions John sees are inspired by God Himself. The words he hears are the very words of Christ, delivered by the angel to the apostle for the church. Verse 6 makes this explicit: "And he said unto me, These sayings are faithful and true: and the Lord God of the holy prophets [literally: the Lord God of the spirits of the prophets] sent his angel to shew unto his servants the things which must shortly be done." The word *servants* here covers not only John, but also the angelic messengers that he hears from and the prophets from the Old Testament that he quotes. Verse 6 is saying that just as the Old Testament prophets "spake as they were moved by the Holy Ghost" (2 Peter 1:21), so, too, the message delivered to John by the angel is the word of the living God. As such, "these sayings are faithful and true." That is a clear statement of the authenticity, infallibility, and inerrancy of this divinely inspired book that John wrote and delivered to the church.

So the first reason why we believe that Jesus is coming back is because this is God's Word. That needs to be said today, because many so-called evangelical Christians put more stock in how they feel about things than in what Scripture says. That is totally erroneous and dangerous. You and I are to believe that Jesus is coming back simply because God says so. The second coming is, as Francis Schaeffer would say, "true truth." It is not a myth; it is what God has revealed by His Spirit, speaking by the angel to John, just as He spoke to the prophets of the Old Testament whom John quotes.

We are living in days when people attempt to downgrade the written Word in favor of the living Word. This is what the modernists do. They say that what matters is Jesus; never mind about the Bible. The Bible might be helpful, but it is the living Word we want—Jesus. Yet in these verses I have just quoted, you find the living Word magnifying the written Word. Take note of that. John is the recipient of objective truth, not the victim of some religious experience, which is nothing more than psychological subjectivism. John was moved by the Spirit to write down exactly what God wanted him to write—*God's truth*. We need to understand all of Revelation like that.

Often John reports that the Spirit or the angel says to him, "Write these things down." So what we have here is God's written Word. Some people have never believed that Jesus rose from the dead. Thus, they are not expecting Him to return. There will be no returning Jesus if there is no risen Jesus. Jesus' rising from the dead might be totally contrary to everything that we know or can understand. His second coming might be contrary to everything we understand about this world. But we are not to argue about it or reason it away; we are simply to accept what God has revealed in Scripture. This is God's truth, and we are to believe it simply because it is written in His Word.

Second, notice that Christ's second advent is *imminent*. Revelation 22:10 says, "And he saith unto me, Seal not the sayings of the prophecy of this book: for the time is at hand." This is the opposite of what Daniel was told in the Old Testament. When Daniel was in exile in Babylon, he received a vision very similar to the one John received on Patmos. There are many close parallels, and John obviously quotes a great deal from Daniel. But Daniel was told to seal up the prophecy because the time was *not* yet: "Wherefore shut thou up the vision; for it shall be for many days.... Shut up the words, and seal the book, even to the time of the end" (Dan. 8:26; 12:4a). But John is told, "Seal not the sayings of the prophecy of this book: for the time is at hand."

People often ask me if we are living in the last times. My answer is, "Yes, we are living in the last times, but we have been living in the last times ever since New Testament days." The apostle Paul, writing to the Corinthians, says, "All these things...are written for our admonition, upon whom the ends of the world are come" (1 Cor.

10:11). The gospel age is "the last days." We are living in the end times. And that ought to have an effect upon us. John has not been writing and talking about something that will happen in the future, but something that is already happening now. It is taking place all around us. Paul says to the Romans, "Now it is high time to awake out of sleep: for now is our salvation nearer than when we believed" (Rom. 13:11).

The mother who is getting her children off to school says, "It's nearly time to catch the bus; it is high time for you to get up." That is what Paul is saying to the Christians in Rome: "It is no good stretching in your bed and saying, 'I have lots of time!' The time is now! These are the last days. Christ is on His way; He is nearly here. You Roman Christians are relaxing in your beds, sleeping away the day of grace and losing all sorts of opportunities. It is high time for you to wake up and get on with putting Christ and His righteousness first. The time is at hand."

Third, notice that the Lord's return is *final*. Revelation 22:11–13 says: "He that is unjust, let him be unjust still: and he which is filthy, let him be filthy still: and he that is righteous, let him be righteous still: and he that is holy, let him be holy still. And, behold, I come quickly; and my reward is with me, to give every man according as his work shall be. I am Alpha and Omega, the beginning and the end, the first and the last."

Verse 11 is a summary of human destiny. The words indicate the fixed state in which both the righteous and the wicked find themselves at Christ's return: "He that is unjust, let him be unjust still…he that is holy, let him be holy still." The truth is that when our Lord returns, there will be no second chance. There will be no further opportunities for repentance. When He comes, everything will be fixed. So says Hebrews 9:27–28: "And as it is appointed unto men once to die, but after this the judgment: so Christ was once offered to bear the sins of many; and unto them that look for him shall he appear the second time without sin unto salvation."

John is making the point that when a person dies, his eternal destiny is fixed. As Solomon put it, "In the place where the tree falleth, there it shall be" (Eccl. 11:3). John appeals to the orthodoxy of his readers by asking: "You don't believe in reincarnation, do you? You don't believe that when a man dies he comes back and has another opportunity to repent and believe the gospel, do you? No, of course not. When a man dies, that's it; the judgment comes, and everything is settled and fixed."

Hebrews 9 says our Lord is coming back, but not to offer a second chance to those who lived all their lives with no repentance from sin or faith in Him. He is not coming back to initiate some kind of salvage operation to improve on what He did during His first advent. That work is finished and complete. He is coming back, according to Revelation 22:12, not to *redeem* but to *reward*! When He comes back, there will be no further opportunity to repent and be saved.

The "wait and see" game that people play is so dangerous. They too often say: "If what you say is true, if this Jesus is really coming back, we'll just wait and see. We'll know then, won't we?" John says it will be too late then. Jesus is not coming back to give you another chance. Now is the day of salvation. And your reward, whatever it will be, will depend on whether you know Jesus Christ as your Savior and Lord when He returns.

But how do we know that we know Him? John tells us repeatedly in his first epistle that we can know that we know Him by the fruits of our lives, for those who know Him love Him and do His commandments. Sanctification gives evidence of our justification. The King James Version translates Revelation 22:14 as, "Blessed are they that do his commandments, that they may have right to the tree of life, and may enter in through the gates into the city."

Some ancient manuscripts translate verse 14 as, "Blessed are those who wash their robes," referring to those who have the right to the tree of life and access to God's city. Every one of us wears a robe. All our thoughts, words, and deeds go into the making of this robe. This robe is splattered, dirty, and full of holes, the Bible tells us. Even our righteousness is as filthy rags in God's sight. The only hope we have of entering the New Jerusalem is somehow to clean and mend our robes. Nothing on planet earth can cleanse a sinner's filthy rags except the blood of Jesus Christ. Blessed are they who wash their robes in that blood. All who plunge beneath that stream lose their guilty stains.

So if you have recourse to the only Savior, and out of that recourse you begin to live according to His commandments, then you will be blessed when Jesus returns. Justification through His blood and sanctification by His blood—these are the two hallmarks by which we must examine ourselves to prepare not only for the Lord's Supper on earth, but also for the eternal Lord's Supper in heavenly glory. In this way, both translations can be merged together, though the emphasis here is on the obedience of faith that flows out of justification.

According to verse 15, if we lack these marks of grace, we will be excluded from heaven: "For without are dogs, and sorcerers, and whoremongers, and murderers, and idolaters, and whosoever loveth and maketh a lie." By nature, we are all sinners. None of us has a right to enter the presence of God. Only if we are cleansed, forgiven, and purified by the saving work of Jesus Christ do we have any hope of entering heaven and New Jerusalem, where we have access to the tree of life and fellowship with God forevermore.

So whatever state you are in when Christ appears, you will continue in that state forever. That is the finality of our Lord's return. We need to impress that upon ourselves and others.

The triple confirmation of Jesus' second advent, then, is the authenticity of His Word, the imminence of His return, and the finality of His return.

Its Triple Warning

The Bible's last chapter includes a triple warning about Christ's return and our response to the book of Revelation. By implication, the warning applies to all of Scripture.

First, Revelation 22:7–9 warns us *against disobeying the Word of God*. In verse 7, a blessing is pronounced on those who obey the words in Revelation. There are seven beatitudes in Revelation, and this is the final one: "Blessed is he that keepeth the sayings of the prophecy of this book." It is important for us to understand that the purpose of prophecy, here and throughout Scripture, is not to fire the imagination or to intrigue the intellect. It is to challenge the conscience and feed our faith so as to produce obedience to God rather than conformity to the pressing claims of the world. The foremost purpose of studying the book of Revelation is not to understand mysteries we have never understood before, but to encourage our obedience to God, to His law and gospel, so as to make progress in sanctification.

That is the effect all Scripture should have upon us. But this is especially true for the book of Revelation, for it helps to deepen our sense of worship. Verses 8–9 say: "And I John saw these things, and heard them. And when I had heard and seen, I fell down to worship before the feet of the angel which shewed me these things. Then saith he unto me, See thou do it not: for I am thy fellowservant, and of thy brethren the prophets, and of them which keep the sayings of this book: worship God." The great concern of the book of Revelation is that the glory of the worship of heaven might somehow be reflected in the church of Jesus Christ on earth.

Notice that John is diverted in his worship from the worship of God. He has a spontaneous emotional reaction to the shining angel, and therefore worships him. But the angel is jealous for the glory of God and says, "See thou do it not: for I am thy fellowservant, and of thy brethren." One error creeping into the ancient church was the "worshipping of angels" (Col. 2:18). John makes this mistake more than once (see Rev. 19:10), and the rebuke he receives is one that he intends his readers to take to heart.

The focus of our worship must be God alone, the angel is saying. God is jealous of His glory and will not give it to another. The angels apparently share that jealousy. It is dangerous to divert your worship from the eternal God to any lesser figure, especially to any of His servants. At some stage in life, you will be disappointed in God's servants, but you will never be disappointed in God or in Christ (Ps. 34:5).

Second, Revelation 22:10–17 warns us *against sealing up the Word of God*. Verse 10–11 tell us: "Seal not the sayings of the prophecy of this book: for the time is at hand. He that is unjust, let him be unjust still: and he which is filthy, let him be filthy still: and he that is righteous, let him be righteous still: and he that is holy, let him be holy still."

The point of this warning is that the message of Revelation must not be ignored or silenced, but rather published and proclaimed. There is an urgency about not sealing up the message of this book because the day of grace will soon end and the day of judgment will be upon us. When that day comes, change will be impossible, for it will be too late to think about repentance. In the parable of the ten virgins, Jesus says that people who have been lazy and careless will discover too late that the door to the marriage supper is closed to them. There will be no second opportunity to return with refueled lamps. The day of grace will have ended. The wise virgins will be secure within, while the foolish will be eternally outside (Matt. 25:1–13).

Third, Revelation 22:18–19 warns us *against tampering with the Word of God*. These verses say, "I testify unto every man that heareth the words of the prophecy of this book, if any man shall add unto these things, God shall add unto him the plagues that are written in this book: and if any man shall take away from the words of the book of this prophecy, God shall take away his part out of the book of life, and out of the holy city, and from the things which are written in this book." This solemn warning against altering the Word of God applies particularly to the book of Revelation, but by implication, it applies to all of the Word of God. God is saying here what Paul says in 2 Corinthians 4:2, where he renounces "handling the Word of God deceitfully." Do not tamper with the Word of God!

This last warning of the Bible is set in the context of the last gospel invitation for people to come to Christ (Rev. 22:17). The whole gospel must be proclaimed. We must not add to the Word of God as we may see fit or take away anything that grieves us or mystifies us. We must not manipulate it so that it becomes more acceptable to sinful men. This is a warning to preachers and teachers, but also a warning to all of us in our use of Holy Scripture.

When we talk to others about certain things in Scripture, some people say, "Yes, I know the Bible says that, but...." That is a very serious attitude to take regarding Scripture. You might be like the liberals, who pick and choose what to accept while cutting out supernatural events such as the virgin birth. Or perhaps you are like the traditionalists, who add the decrees and determinations of church councils or synods to the Bible. You can take away the truth of Scripture by your attitude toward it. You can add to Scripture, too, by attaching little riders to the truth, saying, "Yes, I believe the Bible speaks about election, but I would like to explain it this way...." God says, "Don't do that."

We must swallow the Word whole. We must know the Word, believe the Word, and live by the Word. That is a solemn responsibility for us all. What difference would it make in your life if whole chunks of the Bible were removed? And what difference do you think it would make if the church truly lived by every word that proceeded out of the mouth of God?

The Puritan Thomas Goodwin once went to Dedham to hear a famous preacher named John Rogers. As Rogers preached, he spoke earnestly about people's failure to take in the Word of God. Speaking on behalf of God, Rogers said, "You shall have my Bible no longer." He closed the big Bible on the pulpit, tucked it under his arm, and made as if he was going to take it out of the church. Then he turned and began to play the part of the people, saying, "Lord, whatsoever thou dost to us, take not thy Bible from us."

Then Rogers, again speaking on God's behalf said, "Well, I will try you a while longer; and here is my Bible for you, I will see how you will use it, whether you will love it more." Goodwin was overwhelmed. At the end of the service, he went out to his horse to go back to Cambridge, and hung on the neck of his horse and for fifteen minutes he wept and wept, that he might be such a man to be fed on the whole counsel of God.[1]

God's Word is all we need. Yet it seems that we will do almost anything but immerse ourselves in the Word of God. Are you gripped, fed, and transformed by the Word of God? A. W. Tozer says, "Only a whole Bible will make a whole Christian."[2]

Remember, Jesus is coming. Be warned, therefore, against disobeying the Word of God, against sealing up the Word of God, and against tampering with the Word of God.

Its Triple Invitation

Finally, the concluding verses of the Bible issue a glorious triple invitation to witness Christ's return. Revelation 22:16–17 tells us how to respond to the gospel: "I Jesus have sent mine angel to testify unto you these things in the churches. I am the root and the offspring of David, and the bright and morning star. And the Spirit and the bride say, Come. And let him that heareth say, Come. And let him that is athirst come. And whosoever will, let him take the water of life freely." These verses represent a warm invitation to embrace the gospel. Charles Spurgeon says about these verses: "It is placed at the very end of the Bible, and placed there because it is the sum and substance, the aim and object of the whole Bible. It is like the point of the arrow, and all the rest of the Bible is like the shaft and the feathers on either side of it."[3]

The triple invitation in verse 17 contains more than just a straightforward invitation. It includes the following elements. It is:

---

1. *The Works of the Rev. John Howe* (New York: John P. Haven, 1835), 2:1084–85.
2. A. W. Tozer, *Of God and Men* (Harrisburg, Pa.: Christian Publications, 1960), 67.
3. Spurgeon, *Metropolitan Tabernacle Pulpit*, 46:350.

A Welcome Invitation

When the Spirit and the bride say, "Come," they are not talking to unbelievers, but to Christ. The church, animated by the indwelling Spirit, is expressing her longing to be with Christ now and forever.

Are you yearning for the Lord to come? Is your church praying for it? Verse 17 says that we should do so: "Let him that heareth say, Come." So the first aspect of this invitation is a command to welcome Christ.

In verse 20, Jesus reminds us that He is the author of Revelation and repeats His promise: "He which testifieth these things saith, Surely I come quickly." And John confirms that fact, turning the Lord's great promise into a prayer: "Amen. Even so, come, Lord Jesus."

The old man who has been laboring for Christ for sixty years and who now lives in lonely exile on the barren island of Patmos can still lift up his head and look for Christ to come as Judge from heaven, to cast all His enemies into everlasting condemnation and to bring all His chosen ones to Himself, into heavenly joys and glory. "Even so, come, Lord Jesus," he says. He wants Christ to come because he wants to be with Christ forever for His sake. The love of Christ constrains him.

A Warning Invitation

There is also a warning in verse 17. Paul makes this clear in 2 Thessalonians 1:7–10: "The Lord Jesus shall be revealed from heaven with his mighty angels, in flaming fire taking vengeance on them that know not God, and that obey not the gospel of our Lord Jesus Christ: who shall be punished with everlasting destruction from the presence of the Lord, and from the glory of his power; when he shall come to be glorified in his saints, and to be admired in all them that believe (because our testimony among you was believed) in that day." Christ is coming. Some people are looking forward to it, but others should dread it because they do not know God and have not obeyed the gospel.

But even in this warning, there is still an invitation. How many times do you have to hear the gospel preached before you obey it? What are you waiting for? Are you waiting for some special experience to make it easier for you?

The requirements of the gospel are simple: *repent and believe.* If you will not respond to those demands, then you will perish in your sins when you die and be condemned when Christ comes again. You will be cast into the lake of fire, where your burning tongue will not receive one drop of water. Hell offers no intermission or respite from the gnawing worm of conscience. Pray for grace to respond to God's overtures of mercy now with repentance from sin and faith toward Christ.

A Wide Invitation

"Whosoever will" (Rev. 22:17)—how can an invitation get any wider than this? In whatever person that the Holy Spirit stirs a desire to have Christ and be reconciled to God, that person may come and find salvation. Spurgeon says,

> "Whosoever will, let him take of the water of life freely." "Oh, but he is a very poor man!" What does that matter? "Whosoever will." "But he is a very ignorant man, he does not even know his letters." What has that to do with the text? "Whosoever will." "Ah, but he has been a very bad man!" Well, what about that? It is "whosoever will." Does he will to trust Christ? Is he willing to take the water of life? Then, "let him come and take the water of life freely."[4]

There is nothing about this word to support the erroneous theories of universal salvation. We know that those who do come have been ordained to eternal life in the secret counsel of God (Acts 13:48). Even so, no one who has heard the gospel can say that the invitation is not addressed to him.

---

4. Spurgeon, *Metropolitan Tabernacle Pulpit*, 46:356.

A Wooing Invitation

Revelation 22:17 is one of the most compelling gospel invitations: "The Spirit and the bride say, Come. And let him that heareth say, Come. And let him that is athirst come. And whosoever will, let him take the water of life freely."

All the commands in this verse for people to come are related, because the welcome the church offers to the returning Christ and the invitation of the gospel to lost sinners go together. They haven't always gone together in the history of the church. Many Christians have become so taken up with prophecy and its interpretation that they have forgotten about evangelizing the lost. On the other hand, some have become so obsessed with evangelism that they have never bothered to come to grips with what the Bible actually teaches about Christ's return. Both of those positions are flawed: "The Spirit and the bride say, Come.… Even so, come, Lord Jesus" (vv. 17, 20).

The church longs for and welcomes the coming Christ, saying, in effect: "Come, Lord, in the way that Thou hast revealed in this book through the lampstands, through the seals, through the trumpets, and through the vials. With everything that means for us and with the sacrifice and suffering that is involved for us, if this is the way Thou art coming, Lord, come; we welcome Thee." But as you are crying for Jesus to come with one hand, hold out the other hand to sinners, saying: "Come, everyone who is thirsty. Come while there is still time and while it is still the day of grace—while it is still the day of salvation. Come to the welcoming Savior. Come now. Come and welcome."

Think of how many people need to hear the Bible's last invitation. Christ Himself is speaking here. The context makes that plain. And He identifies with the Spirit and the bride, and with everyone who says: "Sinners everywhere, come. Whoever you are, come and take the water of life freely." That is a pressing invitation because the day of salvation is running out.

But it is pressing in another sense as well. If you are invited to an event or function, someone might phone to see if you are coming. Then the person might come to your door to make sure you are coming. Still later, if you bump into the person on the street, he might say, "Are you coming next week?" That is a pressing invitation. It is also the way Christ invites you to come to Himself. Christ says, "Come." The Spirit says, "Come." The bride says, "Come." The Trinity and the church in every age and in every generation unite in urging you to come to the Lord Jesus Christ and take freely of the waters of life.

Likewise, everyone who hears says, "Come." Think of the day of Pentecost, when a handful of people stood up with Peter when he first began inviting sinners to come to the Lord Jesus Christ. Before he finished preaching, three thousand people were shouting, "Come." A few days later, another five thousand joined in. I don't know how many Christians are in the world today, but every one of them is personally commissioned by Christ to cry out to an unconverted world, "Come, everyone, and take the water of life freely!" It is a very pressing invitation.

A Relevant Invitation

Some of the invitations you receive may not be appropriate. Some you can safely ignore. Some you may decline, sending your regrets. But the invitation in Revelation 22:17 cannot be ignored: "Let him that is athirst come. And whosoever will, let him take the water of life freely." A person can live without food for weeks or even months. But you can't live without water very long. Water is absolutely essential. What God promises to you in the gospel is as indispensable as water. You need Christ. You need Him to save you as much as you need water to quench your thirst. You need Christ to satisfy your deepest needs and longings. You were made for Christ. Augustine says, "Thou hast formed us for Thyself, and our hearts are restless until they find rest in Thee."[5]

---

5. Augustine, *Confessions*, 1.1, in *A Select Library of the Nicene and Post-Nicene Fathers*, Series 1, ed. Philip Schaff (Buffalo: The Christian Literature Co., 1886), 1:45.

Every human being, whether he admits it or not, thirsts for fulfilment, and that can only be found in Christ. To live forever, you must ask Christ to wash you from your sins. Just as a man who is filthy needs water to wash him from the filth he has accumulated, so you need Christ and His atoning blood to wash you from your sins. You need the water of life. You need Christ to put out the fires that rage within you.

What would you think of a man going on vacation to the Sahara Desert stocked with everything except water? You would think he had lost his mind. Yet some of you are rushing to eternity without the one thing you *really* need. If you are going to live forever, you need Christ. That is why Christ cries out to sinners, "Come, and take the water of life freely!" It is a relevant and reasonable invitation.

In speaking about gospel invitations, Martin Luther said he was glad that they were not addressed to him personally. If someone had said, "Martin Luther, you can come," he said, "I would always be looking over my shoulder to see whether there was another Martin Luther in the world." This invitation says, "Whosoever will, let him come."

An enemy of George Whitefield once said that whenever he didn't know what to say next to his congregation, he would just cry out, "Come to Jesus!" That was true to a certain extent; Whitefield seldom ended a sermon without urging sinners to come to Christ. At the end of nearly every sermon, his hands would rise and tears would stream down his face as he pleaded with sinners to come. And, by the Spirit's grace, *they did come.* They came by the hundreds and thousands: ordinary working-class people, miners from Bristol, housewives, and shop girls.

Some of you, I fear, have never responded to this pressing invitation. You attend church regularly, you listen to the preaching of the gospel, and you read the Bible, but you *have not come to the Lord Jesus Christ.* That is the whole point of Scripture. All the books of the Bible, all the prophets of the Bible, all the apostles of the Bible, all the warnings of the Bible, and all the promises of the Bible merge into this one point—that you should come and take of the waters of life freely.

Let me urge you, then, to come to Christ with all your sins. How terrible it would have been if this book finished at verse 11, and I had to say, "He that is unjust, let him be unjust still: and he which is filthy, let him be filthy still: and he that is righteous, let him be righteous still: and he that is holy, let him be holy still." But God closes His Word with an invitation for you to come to His Son and be transformed by His grace, that you should not perish, but have life everlasting.

The New Testament ends with this glorious free invitation to all who are thirsty. It takes God's grace to change a man's will. Nevertheless, the invitation goes out to all. Whoever you are, you are invited to come. Take hold of the promise, crying:

> Thou art my God, O God of grace,
> And earnestly I seek Thy face,
> My heart cries out for Thee;
> My spirit thirsts Thy grace to taste,
> An exile in this desert waste
> In which no waters be.[6]

It is remarkable that a book so filled with images of cursing, wrath, judgment, and punishment—as Revelation is—nonetheless ends with a blessing: "The grace of our Lord Jesus Christ be with you all." To that, every true believer can respond with heart, mind, and strength: "Amen. Even so, come, Lord Jesus." Amen.

---

6. *The Psalter*, #164:1 (Ps. 63:1).